MOVING TOWARDS SUSTAINABLE BUSINESSES AND DEVELOPING MORE RESILIENT ECONOMIES

This book presents the official proceedings of the International Conference on Business, Management, Economics, and Information Systems (ICBMEIS 2025), held at York College, City University of New York (CUNY). It brings together high-quality research, practical insights, and scholarly debate to advance sustainable business practices and build resilient economic systems in a rapidly changing global environment.

The volume compiles peer-reviewed papers, keynote insights, and thematic discussions that reflect the multidisciplinary nature of modern business research. It covers key areas such as business management, economics, supply chain and operations management, marketing, information systems, entrepreneurship, sustainability, human resource management, and business analytics. The chapters explore the contemporary challenges faced by organizations worldwide, including digital transformation, ESG expectations, global supply chain disruptions, and emerging economic risks, while offering innovative models, empirical evidence, and actionable strategies. The contributions underscore the importance of sustainable decision-making, technology-driven business solutions, and collaborative approaches among stakeholders. Collectively, the proceedings outline new research pathways and offer conceptual and practical frameworks to foster resilient enterprises and adaptive economic environments.

This book is designed for academics, researchers, graduate students, business practitioners, policymakers, and industry leaders seeking evidence-based insights and emerging perspectives across business and economic disciplines. It serves as a valuable resource for those seeking to strengthen strategic decision-making, enhance organizational resilience, and stay current with global trends in sustainable business practices.

Taylor & Francis Proceedings in Business, Management and Economics

This series is a compilation of peer-reviewed conference proceedings in business, management and economics. An interdisciplinary series for researchers, professionals and leaders, elaborating on the important principles for effective handling of finances and enterprises.

Moving Towards Sustainable Businesses and Developing More Resilient Economies
Edited by Aamir Rashid and Fenio Annansingh-Jamieson

For more information about this series, please visit: https://www.routledge.com/Taylor-and-Francis-Proceedings-in-Business-Management-and-Economics/book-series/TFPBME

PROCEEDINGS OF THE INTERNATIONAL CONFERENCE ON BUSINESS, MANAGEMENT, ECONOMICS, AND INFORMATION SYSTEMS (ICBMEIS 2025), NEW YORK, USA, OCTOBER 25TH—26TH, 2025

Moving Towards Sustainable Businesses and Developing More Resilient Economies

Edited by

Aamir Rashid and Fenio Annansingh-Jamieson
City University of New York (CUNY), U.S.A

CRC Press
Taylor & Francis Group
Boca Raton London New York Leiden

CRC Press is an imprint of the
Taylor & Francis Group, an **informa** business

First edition published 2026
by CRC Press
4 Park Square, Milton Park, Abingdon, Oxon, OX14 4RN

and by CRC Press
2385 NW Executive Center Drive, Suite 320, Boca Raton FL 33431

CRC Press is an imprint of Informa UK Limited

British Library Cataloguing-in-Publication Data
A catalogue record for this book is available from the British Library

ISBN: 978-1-041-08875-2 (hbk)
ISBN: 978-1-041-08876-9 (pbk)
ISBN: 978-1-003-64730-0 (ebk)

DOI: 10.1201/9781003647300

Typeset in Times New Roman
by MPS Limited, Chennai, India

Table of contents

Preface ix
Acknowledgements xi
Editor biographies xiii
Committees xv

Stock market and green bond issuance: Evidence from emerging markets 1
Tabassum Riaz

What is to be sustained? Value or satisfaction: The homestay tourism overview 8
B.R. Olaleye, T.J. Sekhampu, and N. Khumalo

Online buyers' dynamic click strategies 15
R. Vragov and D. Shang

Prompt engineering: Unlocking better responses from large language models 30
A. Kamruzzaman, N. Samdrup, and D. Nurse

Fiscal policy and economic transformation for sustainable growth in KSA 38
Mohd Naved Khan

Leadership development and succession planning: Ensuring sustainable organizational growth 46
Jayanthi Rajendran

Intrinsic and extrinsic life aspiration satisfaction: A study on generation Z workers 54
Dwivedula

Preventing runway incursions using artificial intelligence: A review of aviation practices 61
Vasilios (Billy) Constantine Metallinos

Urban public transportation demand, pricing, and smart mobility 68
Clifford N. Opurum

An investigation into the relationship between workplace bullying and employee turnover intentions in Carib Trust Bank Limited Trinidad and Tobago: The mediating role of emotional exhaustion 88
TW Williams, DE Esdelle, IH Hosein, MS Singh, SA Abraham, and JR Ramdhan

AI analysis of psychological biases in German stock market investments 97
O. Idrizi and M. Kazo

Secure precision agriculture throughout the agribusiness value chain leveraging 5G RedCap IoT and blockchain protocols 104
E.U. Ogbodo, A. Kamruzzaman, and L.L. Mendes

Cohesion in remote teams 112
N. Belušić and M. Vidović

The impact of fraudulent SMS notifications on marketplace adoption of digital payment systems in developing countries 121
Abdulmumini Yinka Ajia

Neo Banking in India – A paradigm shift 126
B K Suresh, P Paramashivaiah, Y Muniraju, and M Venkateshwarlu

A study of implications of goods and services tax in India 136
P Paramashivaiah

Perceived workplace bullying, job satisfaction, and work engagement in selected South African banks: The moderated-mediation role of psychological empowerment 144
N. Khumalo, A. Mapuko, and B.R. Olaleye

Managing the crisis facing health professionals in the health sector 152
A.G. Alshareef

Net neutrality for the Indian marginalized community to transact on e-commerce platforms 161
Y. Muniraju and B K. Suresh

Breaking barriers: Diversity, equity, and inclusion initiatives for employees with disabilities 169
Ume Sumayya, Sajjad Nawaz, and Ume Amen

Innovation in firm enterprise and female ownership effects: Evidence from selected sub-Saharan African countries 175
O.A. Adediran

Leveraging artificial intelligence in business decision-making: A study on predictive analytics in retail management 181
Md Sharfuddin, Nazmul Islam, and Omor Fahad

A conceptual investigation into graduates' employability attitudes: The significant role of protean career attitudes 189
Muhammad Latif Khan, Tasawar Kamran, Suad Al Kindi, and Zakia AL Abri

Innovation management in practice: Framework analysis of Walmart and Microsoft 202
Akhmadbek Bakhtiyorov

Ethical AI lending practices: Ensuring fairness and resilience in USA mortgage approvals 209
M.A. Hasan, M.T.R. Mazumder, M.S.H. Shourov, and S. Nashid

Integrating artificial intelligence in IT project management: A review of tools, techniques, and use cases 218
Kh Maksudul Hasan, Md Sazzad Hossen, Ariful Islam, and Al Akhir

Generative AI: Ethical governance and strategic innovation 227
Shokhrukh Komilov

Design and deployment of a fuel logistics information system 234
Mohamed Loutis and Esma Aïmeur

Navigating interconnected risks in the creative industry: A case study on the relationship between operational risks and cyber, financial, human, strategic, and reputational risks 242
A.A.P. Jaquias, G.E. Ceballos, B.T. Melchor, J.A.A. Santiago, E.T. Untalan, J.M. Abad, and J.T. Tenerife

Leadership perceptions and strategic readiness: A multivariate and qualitative study on AI figintegration in industry 251
P. Hernandez, J. Tenerife, J. Flores, J.A. Padullon, M.T. Landicho, R.A. Dela Cruz, M.L. Belen, J.C. Candaza, N.L. Tabasa, and M. Navarro

Risk governance assessment: Analyzing the sustainable management strategies of a steel fabrication company 266
C.N.F. Dee, J.L.B. Dela Paz, F.N.R.A. Dimaano, S.M.L. Galit, D.A.S. Maquilan, and J.T. Tenerife

Effect of tariff on the correlation between the dollar and international investment assets 273
Joseph Cheng and Victor Shahnazarian

Analyzing the effects of weather on stock prices for investment management 278
John Goodermote, Jola Pham, Tracy Phan, and Loyal Goodermote

An orthogonal approach to simple linear regression model 286
Raja R. Vatti

Sustainability controlling and the limits of ESG monetization 289
Julius Winterhalter and Ronny Gebhardt

Analyzing the impact of adopting IFRS S1 and S2 sustainability standards on strategic managerial accounting practices 297
Ghazi Maan Faisal and Saba Kareem Abbood

Relationship between organizational intelligent and digital transformation readiness 307
S. Ebrahimi Mehrabani and M. Shajari

AI for automating financial consolidation and reporting 315
Srinivas R. Gottimukkala and Shiva Kumar Bhuram

AI-driven fraud detection in accounts payable 323
Srinivas R. Gottimukkala and Shiva Kumar Bhuram

Using cognitive load theory as a facilitator for teaching and learning accounting 331
E.S. QUAYE

Developing and framing the influence of AAI environment on consumer buying behaviour: Consumer buying is controlled or influenced? 338
Md Uzir Hossain Uzir, Siti Norida Wahab, Ishraq Jerin, Sharmini A.P. Gopinathan, and Pek Chuen Khee Pek

Author index 347

Moving Towards Sustainable Businesses and Developing More Resilient Economies –
Rashid and Annansingh-Jamieson (Eds)
 ISBN: 978-1-041-08875-2

Preface

It is our great pleasure to present the Proceedings of the International Conference on Business, Management, Economics, and Information Systems (ICBMEIS-2025), held on October 25–26, 2025, at York College, City University of New York (CUNY). The theme of this year's conference, "Moving Towards Sustainable Businesses and Developing More Resilient Economies," reflects the urgent need for innovative thinking, evidence-based research, and interdisciplinary collaboration in a rapidly transforming global environment. These proceedings capture the scholarly contributions of researchers, practitioners, and graduate students from multiple countries who participated in our hybrid conference. The collection showcases empirical studies, conceptual advancements, and practical insights that address contemporary challenges across business, economics, information systems, supply chain management, sustainability, human resource management, and related fields. We hope this volume serves as a valuable resource for academics and practitioners committed to enhancing organizational resilience and fostering sustainable economic systems. We extend our sincere appreciation to all authors, reviewers, keynote speakers, panelists, and participants whose efforts have enriched the intellectual quality of the conference. Their contributions and engagement have helped shape a productive academic platform that fosters global dialogue, learning, and innovation.

Acknowledgements

The preparation of these proceedings would not have been possible without the valuable contributions of many individuals. We extend our heartfelt gratitude to all the authors who submitted their work, the reviewers who provided rigorous and constructive feedback, the volunteers, MUJO Learning (sponsor), Al-Falah Foundation New York (sponsor), and the keynote speakers who enriched the conference with their expert insights. We also extend our gratitude to the faculty, staff, and administrators of the Department of Business and Economics and the School of Business and Information Systems at York College – CUNY for their unwavering support. Special appreciation goes to the York College - CUNY Office staff for their operational and logistical assistance throughout the planning and execution of the conference. Finally, we acknowledge the efforts of the entire organizing committee for their dedication, professionalism, and commitment to ensuring the success of ICBMEIS-2025. Their teamwork has helped create a meaningful academic platform that will continue to inspire future scholarship.

 ISBN: 978-1-041-08875-2

Editor biographies

Aamir Rashid is Assistant Professor of Supply Chain Management in the Department of Business and Economics at York College, City University of New York (CUNY). He earned his Ph.D. in Supply Chain Management and holds postgraduate qualifications in Supply Chain and Human Resource Management. With over 25 years of industrial experience and extensive academic service, Dr. Rashid's research focuses on AI-enabled supply chain resilience, circular and sustainable supply chains, digital transformation, and organizational learning. He has published over seventy peer-reviewed papers in top-tier journals, including Supply Chain Management, Supply Chain Forum, Journal of Manufacturing Technology Management, Cleaner Logistics and Supply Chain, Journal of Enterprise Information Management, and Journal of Science and Technology Policy Management. He serves on multiple editorial boards, including Discover Sustainability, the International Journal of Public Administration, and Cleaner Logistics and Supply Chain. He also serves as a reviewer for over ninety leading journals and has presented widely at international conferences. Dr. Rashid has organized and chaired several international conferences, most recently the International Conference on Business, Management, Economics and Information Systems (ICBMEIS 2025). His current projects integrate AI, sustainability, and human-centric design to enhance supply-chain agility and policy impact in underserved U.S. states.

Fenio Annansingh-Jamieson is Dean of the School of Business and Information Systems at York College, City University of New York (CUNY). She earned her Ph.D. in Information Studies and M.S. in Information Systems from the University of Sheffield, UK. Her teaching and research span information systems, knowledge management, cybersecurity, data analytics, and smart-city innovation. With over two decades of experience in higher education in the U.S. and U.K., Dr. Jamieson has served as faculty at the University of Plymouth (UK) and York College (CUNY), where she leads initiatives that integrate technology and business education. She has secured major grants from the National Science Foundation (NSF), the National Security Agency (NSA), and the New York State Education Department, with a focus on STEM and cybersecurity teacher training. Her recent books include Data Analytics for Business: Foundations and Industry Applications (Routledge, 2022) and Examining the Socio-Technical Impact of Smart Cities (IGI Global, 2021). She also serves as a reviewer for several leading journals and has presented widely at international conferences. Her current research explores AI-driven knowledge management, digital transformation, and cyber resilience in education and business systems.

Moving Towards Sustainable Businesses and Developing More Resilient Economies – Rashid and Annansingh-Jamieson (Eds)
© 2026 The Editor(s), ISBN: 978-1-041-08875-2

Committees

CONFERENCE SECRETARIATE

Conference Chair
Dr. Fenio Annansingh-Jamieson (Dean)
Department of Business and Economics, School of Business and Information Systems, York College – CUNY
Conference Organizing Chair
Dr. Aamir Rashid
Department of Business and Economics, School of Business and Information Systems, York College – CUNY

ORGANIZING COMMITTEE

Dr. Lloyd Amaghionyeodiwe (Chair)
Department of Business and Economics, School of Business and Information Systems, York College – CUNY
Dr. Phoebe Massimino
Department of Business and Economics, School of Business and Information Systems, York College – CUNY
Prof. Wayne Forrester
Department of Business and Economics, School of Business and Information Systems, York College – CUNY
Dr. Yong Kyu Lee
Department of Business and Economics, School of Business and Information Systems, York College – CUNY
Dr. Aghajan Mohammadi
Department of Business and Economics, School of Business and Information Systems, York College – CUNY
Dr. John Kolmos
Department of Business and Economics, School of Business and Information Systems, York College – CUNY
Dr. Efstathia Korkou
Department of Business and Economics, School of Business and Information Systems, York College – CUNY
Dr. Joseph Sesay
Department of Business and Economics, School of Business and Information Systems, York College – CUNY
Dr. Billy Metallinos
Department of Business and Economics, School of Business and Information Systems, York College – CUNY
Dr. Abu Kamruzzaman
Department of Business and Economics, School of Business and Information Systems, York College – CUNY

Dr. Adedeji Olugboja
Department of Business and Economics, School of Business and Information Systems, York College – CUNY
Prof. Jasper Ojongtambia
Department of Business and Economics, School of Business and Information Systems, York College – CUNY
Dr. Rizwana Rasheed
Department of Management, The Lucille and Jay Chazanoff School of Business, College of Staten Island – CUNY, and Department of Business Administration, Iqra University, Karachi, Pakistan

SESSION MODERATORS

Dr. Lloyd Amaghionyeodiwe
Department of Business and Economics, School of Business and Information Systems, York College – CUNY
Prof. Wayne Forrester
Department of Business and Economics, School of Business and Information Systems, York College – CUNY
Dr. Efstathia Korkou
Department of Business and Economics, School of Business and Information Systems, York College – CUNY
Dr. Joseph Sesay
Department of Business and Economics, School of Business and Information Systems, York College – CUNY
Dr. Abu Kamruzzaman
Department of Business and Economics, School of Business and Information Systems, York College – CUNY
Dr. Adedeji Olugboja
Department of Business and Economics, School of Business and Information Systems, York College – CUNY
Prof. Jasper Ojongtambia
Department of Business and Economics, School of Business and Information Systems, York College – CUNY
Dr. Rizwana Rasheed
Department of Management, The Lucille and Jay Chazanoff School of Business, College of Staten Island – CUNY, and Department of Business Administration, Iqra University, Karachi, Pakistan

Moving Towards Sustainable Businesses and Developing More Resilient Economies –
Rashid and Annansingh-Jamieson (Eds)

Stock market and green bond issuance: Evidence from emerging markets

Tabassum Riaz
Assistant Professor / Incharge Department, Department of Business Administration, University of the Punjab Jhelum Campus, Jhelum-Pakistan

ABSTRACT: This paper explores stock market reaction to green bond issuance in emerging markets, where the use of green bonds as a financial instrument to finance environmental projects is expanding. It seeks to determine whether such announcements affect investors' attitudes toward and valuation of a firm. The study examines 65 green bond issuers from 2015 to 2023 and utilizes an Event Study methodology to test the behaviour of the market around the announcement dates. The findings suggest that there were no strong stock market reactions, which imply that the confidence of investors was low. This could be due to greenwashing, especially in less regulated markets, with green bond proceeds not truly serving a sustainable purpose.

1 INTRODUCTION

Green finance has become essential in the global fight against climate change and environmental degradation. The disastrous consequences of climate change for the planet and its inhabitants necessitate immediate action. Over a million species may face extinction as a result of the rapid decline in biodiversity. Numerous households and their means of subsistence are at risk due to rising sea levels. In light of the severity of the issue, it is essential to concentrate research and attention on green finance to fully realize its potential (Fu *et al.* 2024). Consequently, green bonds have emerged as a favored financial instrument. Green bonds finance environmentally beneficial projects, such as pollution prevention, energy conservation through renewable sources, and energy efficiency initiatives. Green bonds have integrated into sustainable finance, which seeks to fund projects that positively impact the environment (Zhao *et al.* 2022).

Mostly, the idea of "green bonds" came from developed economies. However, these securities are now being bought in developing economies where industrialization and growth have hurt the environment. So, they have also been popular in emerging countries. The dynamics of developing markets provide a compelling framework for examining the impacts of green bonds due to the substantial differences between these markets and developed markets regarding economies, legal systems, and evolving investors (Fatica and Panzica 2021). These markets often exhibit strong growth rates, with increasing foreign investments and a heightened importance placed on ESG considerations (Liu *et al.* 2021). Thus, the issuance of green bonds in these markets functions as a mechanism for financing environmentally sustainable initiatives and as a communication tool to investors on the company's commitment to sustainability and future wealth generation (García *et al.* 2023).

The existing research demonstrates a relationship between the use of green bonds and investor sentiments, which eventually influences the securities market. The signaling theory posits that the issuance of green bonds can position a company as environmentally

DOI: 10.1201/9781003647300-1

responsible, so improving its reputation and attracting investors who emphasize sustainability (Flammer 2021). Consequently, when investors perceive the issuance of green bonds as a credible signal of a company's ESG standing and prospective success, stock prices may demonstrate positive abnormal returns (Naeem *et al.* 2021). The adoption of green bonds may differ among countries, especially in emerging regions experiencing regulatory changes and an increasing awareness of green financing.

Few studies have examined how emerging markets' markets respond to green bond issuance, in contrast to the abundance of literature on established markets. Tang and Zhang (2020) found that investors generally reward companies with good returns for their green initiatives, as the examination of relevant literature shows that introducing green bonds is often associated by positive abnormal returns. However, this trend can look different in developing markets where market efficiency is lower, regulations are less advanced, and there is a wider range of ESG awareness.

This paper aims to address the existing research gap by examining the stock market's reaction to the issuance of green bonds in emerging markets. Event study methodology is used to determine whether green bonds are regarded as a form of value-enhancing tool by assessing the impact of the green bond announcement on stock performance around the day of the announcement. This study revealed an insignificant stock market reaction to green bond issuance in emerging markets. The research results will thus be valuable in enhancing understanding of the impact of green bonds on the value of firms in emerging economies and expanding knowledge on sustainable financing in developing countries.

The paper enhances understanding in the following manners: Firstly, it provides empirical evidence on the perception of green bond offerings by the stock market in emerging market companies, which has been a subject of little previous study. Furthermore, this study offers valuable information on the potential of green bonds to enhance the value of firms in these specific domains. This information is relevant for policymakers, investors, and business management aiming to integrate their financial strategy with sustainability goals through green bonds. At last, the research concludes that it is essential for developing nations to improve the suitable legislative framework and increase investors' knowledge of green finance.

2 LITERATURE REVIEW

This literature review analyzes research on the stock market and its participants, concentrating on studies that investigate the reaction to green bond issuance in emerging and global economies. The emergence of green bonds has garnered positive reception from investors, hence enhancing the notion that environmental sustainability elevates a bond's value. A recent study by Tang and Zhang (2020) indicates that green bond issuances near the announcement date are associated with a significant positive abnormal return. The issuing of green bonds enhances the company's attractiveness to ESG-oriented investors, therefore elevating stock prices.

According to Flammer (2021), stock returns are higher for corporations that issue "green" bonds. Green bonds not only instill confidence in investors, but they also serve as an indicator of improved sustainability performance and corporate valuation, according to the study. Investor awareness, issuer trustworthiness, and the efficacy of third-party or partner verification all play a role in how severely the stock market reacts. Green bonds that have been verified by independent organizations are more likely to be purchased. Certification, on the other hand, reassures consumers even further that their funds are going toward long-term initiatives (Bachelet *et al.* 2019).

Camacci (2022) noted that stock prices rise when European corporations declare green bonds. On average, prices increase by 0.41% following the announcement. In a similar vein, the issuance of green bonds in India correlates with positive performance in the stock market. It indicates that investors recognize the value of sustainable financing (Verma and Bansal 2021). Strong correlations between green bonds and emerging stock markets indicate long-term connections that influence returns and market volatility (Acikgoz 2024). Laborda and Sánchez-Guerra (2021) assert that green bond issuances enhance companies' share values, indicating a positive response from the European stock market to green bonds.

Sreelakshmi and Greeshma (2023) assert that the stock market initially reacts adversely to the issuing of green bonds, particularly in developing countries, before exhibiting a positive response in subsequent days. The research by Cioli *et al.* (2021) showed that when green bonds are issued for the first time, investors respond positively by seeing big jumps in stock prices. However, this response becomes less strong for subsequent issues, showing that the marginal benefits eventually decline.

Moreover, the Ehlers and Packer (2017) indicate that the stock market reaction to green bond issuances is typically more pronounced in developed markets compared to emerging markets. The announcement of green bonds generally results in positive abnormal returns near the announcement date. This effect is especially significant for green bonds issued by companies from developed markets, characterized by greater market efficiency, heightened investor awareness of ESG issues, and more supportive regulatory frameworks. Green bonds have emerged as a crucial element of high-quality financial systems in developed nations, including Europe and North America, where strong regulatory frameworks ensure transparency concerning sustainability ratings that are increasingly important for investors. Ehlers and Packer (2017) further analyze the effect of green bond issuances on prices in economies with a strong regulatory framework for green financing, exemplified by the EU.

On the other hand, investors may not regularly react positively to green bonds in emerging markets due to the unpredictable nature of stock market responses. Wang *et al.* (2020) illustrate that, over the long term, green bond issuances generate positive abnormal returns, but to a lesser degree than those seen in developed markets. The capacity of green bonds to generate positive stock returns is constrained in countries with insufficient investor awareness of environmental, social, and governance (ESG) considerations and illiquid markets.

The literature indicates that green bond issuances enhance stock markets in developed markets; however, the efficacy of similar dynamics in emerging markets remains under investigation. The literature predominantly investigates the effects of green bonds on firm value, rather than their influence on stock market behavior in atypical contexts, such as emerging economies. The efficiency of emerging markets, regulatory support, quality, and investor perception of ESG factors may influence the financial markets' reaction to green bond issuance. This study proposes the following hypothesis derived from the literature evaluation and identified research gap.

Hypothesis: Stock market responds positively to green bond issuance in emerging markets

3 DATA COLLECTION AND METHODOLOGY

This study is based on a sample of green bonds issued by companies in emerging countries from 2015 to 2023. We got information about when green bonds were issued and about the issuer from the International Capital Market Association (ICMA) and business reports. A total number of 65 green bond issuers data were collected for this study based on its availability. A total of 65 green bond issuing companies were analyzed in this study subject to the availability and completeness of data. Criteria for selection were that issuers were listed in emerging markets and had issued green bonds between 2015 and 2023. Also, only issuers for which public data are available on the stock price, the dates of bond issuances, and the market index corresponding to the stock were included in the analysis. The 65 is the total number of issuers that met all of these criteria over the period, not a predetermined number for sampling. The stock prices and stock market index data were gathered from the data stream. Based on the literature, different event windows around the date of the green bond issuance announcement (day 0) are considered. The estimation time, which starts 200 days before each event window and ends a week before it, determines the normal returns for this window.

This work uses the event study method to examine how the market reacts to announcements about green bonds in emerging markets. This method is often used for this kind of research because it helps researchers see how stock prices change in response to certain events and how the market perceives them. This study's abnormal return (AR) is calculated by taking the difference between the real and expected returns. The market model is used to calculate the expected returns:

$$R_{it} = \alpha_i + \beta_i R_{mt} + \epsilon_{it}$$

Where R_{it} is the return on stock i at time t, R_{mt} is the market return at time t, and ε_{it} is the error term.

The cumulative abnormal return (CAR) is calculated by summing the abnormal returns over the event window for each stock.

$$CAR_i(t_1, t_2) = \sum_{t=t_1}^{t_2} AR_{it}$$

Where

t_1 and t_2 represent the start and end date of the event window, respectively.

Cumulative average abnormal return (CAAR) is calculated by taking the average of the CARs across all the stocks in the sample.

$$CAAR = \frac{1}{N}\sum_{i=1}^{N} CAR_i$$

Where

N is the total number of stocks in the sample.

4 RESULTS AND DISCUSSIONS

Table 1 reports the stock market response to emerging markets' green bond issuance results. Specifically, this study focused on the cumulative average abnormal return (CAAR) computed for various event windows for emerging markets. Results indicate that the CAARs for

Table 1. Green bond issuance and stock market reaction in emerging markets.

Event window	CAAR	T-statistics	No. of observations
−2+5	0.0510	0.1492	65
−2+10	0.1204	0.6912	65
−1+1	0.0180	0.5714	65
−1+100	0.321998	−0.1551	65
0+1	0.0137	0.5485	65
−2+20	0.2071	1.2097	65
−2+40	0.3264	1.3071	65
−2+60	0.275274	0.629405	65
−2+100	0.328579	0.772192	65
−5+10	0.1174	0.6914	65
−10+10	0.1457	0.8512	65
−10+20	0.24187	0.319227	65
−10+40	0.313252	0.350973	65
−10+100	0.379686	0.49376	65

green bond issuers from emerging markets are statistically insignificant for all analyzed event windows. The insignificant CAAR highlights that the stock market does not respond to green bond issuance in emerging markets, suggesting that investors do not bother with green bond issuance in emerging markets. Insignificant cumulative average abnormal returns (CAAR) following green bond issuances in emerging markets indicate a lack of strong or persistent market response to these events.

Furthermore, in Figure 1, this study presents the CAAR around the announcement day to visually represent the stock market's response.

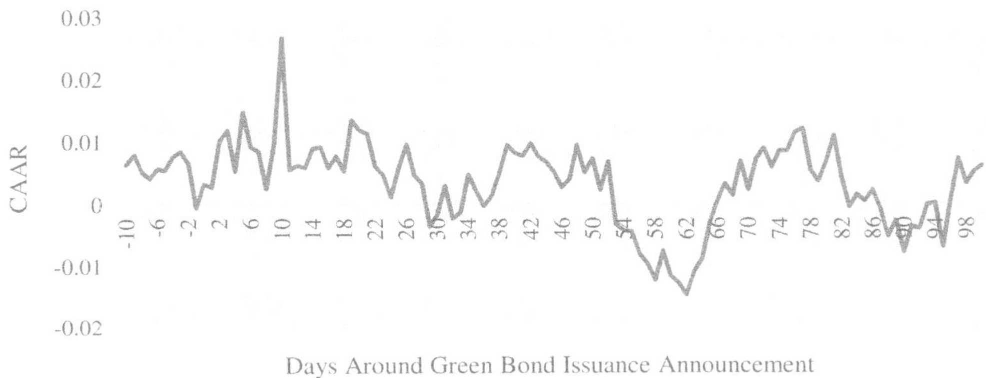

Figure 1. CAAR around green bonds issuance announcements.

The insignificant result may be ascribed to several variables highlighting the unique features of developing economies and the essence of green bonds. For example, investors in emerging markets may not fully understand the importance and financial implications of green bonds compared to conventional bonds. As the broader financial community typically fails to differentiate green bonds from conventional debt products, this lack of awareness can lead to insignificant market reactions. Green bonds are commonly perceived as ordinary financial instruments within many emerging markets, free of any distinctive impact on a firm's value. This perspective leads to negligible price fluctuations, as investors may not perceive any immediate financial benefits from the issuance of green bonds.

Moreover, the growth and maturity of the green finance market in many emerging markets is ongoing. Reduced investor interest and a lack of substantial market reactions can be attributed to insufficient market depth, low liquidity, and fewer green bond issuances. Similarly, emerging markets lack robust institutional support, such as specialized green bond indices or actively involved ESG-focused investors, which are essential for generating significant fluctuations in stock prices.

In markets with less stringent regulatory supervision, investors may have concerns about greenwashing, which refers to misappropriating funds from green bonds for sustainable initiatives. Such doubt can result in subdued or insignificant stock market responses. One more potential explanation for the less significant performance of most stocks in emerging nations could be the high level of volatility risk in these markets. Given that this risk entails the potential for adverse returns, these negative returns can aggregate with the impacts of positive abnormal returns and produce insignificant results.

5 CONCLUSION

This study aims to find out whether market players see the issuance of a green bond in emerging markets as good news by creating abnormal returns around the date of their issuance announcement. This study applied the event study method with a market model and event windows. The results show that the stock market has an insignificant raction to the announcements of a Green Bond issuance. The possible explanation for these results would be that investors in emerging markets may not fully understand the importance and financial implications of green bonds compared to conventional bonds. As the broader financial community typically fails to differentiate green bonds from conventional debt products, this lack of awareness can lead to insignificant market reactions.

Considering there was no significant reaction from the stock market to the issuance of green bonds in emerging economies, this study proposes a few concrete actions to improve the impact and effectiveness of green finance in such regions. For policymakers, it is critical to improve the policies and rules related to the issuance of green bonds. There should also be uniform rules, stringent reporting requirements regarding the use of proceeds, and independent verification systems that must be complied with to guarantee trust and trustworthiness. such actions would alleviate concerns on greenwashing and improve investor trust. Furthermore, policy makers should look at the possibility of using tax rebates, subsidies or risk sharing benefits to foster green investments and draw in a wider pool of issuers and investors. Broader exposure and investment communities can be more informed, as well as understand the importance of green finance in national development agendas, through more public awareness campaigns and policy dialogues.

Further, Investors must incorporate environmental, social, and governance (ESG) factors into their investment decision-making processes. In addition to their financial returns, investors can evaluate the environmental impact of their portfolios in order to more actively engage in the promotion of sustainable finance. Institutional investors, in particular, should engage with issuers to guarantee that proceeds from green bonds are allocated appropriately and to enhance transparency in the reporting of results. Additionally, investors are encouraged to participate in initiatives that promote green market infrastructure, such as sustainable investment platforms and green bond indices, and to diversify their portfolios with green financial products.

To go further in green bond research, future research might be to find out how the stock market of emerging markets responds to green bonds differently from other ESG financial instruments, such as social bonds or sustainability-linked bonds. That would make it possible to find the green or sustainable finance tools that have worked best. Further, future research may be conducted on how regulatory settings may play a role in shaping market behaviour. It might be useful to know how policy incentives (or lack of them) affect the success or failure of green bonds.

REFERENCES

Acikgoz, T. (2024). An econophysics perspective on green bonds and stock market nexus: Can green finance be an investment option for emerging stock markets?. *Fluctuation and Noise Letters*, 23(04), 2450038. https://doi.org/10.1142/S021947752450038X.

Bachelet, M.J., Becchetti, L., and Manfredonia, S. (2019). The green bonds premium puzzle: The role of issuer characteristics and third-party verification. *Sustainability*, *11*(4), 1098. https://doi.org/10.3390/su11041098.

Camacci, R. (2022). Corporate green bond: Issuance and equity market reaction. In *Climate Change Adaptation, Governance and New Issues of Value: Measuring the Impact of ESG Scores on CoE and Firm Performance* (pp. 227–249). Cham: Springer International Publishing.

Cioli, V., Andrea Colonna, L., Giannozzi, A., and Roggi, O. (2021). Corporate green bond and stock price reaction. *International Journal of Business and Management*, *16*(4), 75. https://doi.org/10.5539/ijbm.v16n4p75.

Ehlers, T., and Packer, F. (2017). Green bond finance and certification. *BIS Quarterly Review*, *July*, 89–104.

Fatica, S., and Panzica, R. (2021). Green bonds as a tool against climate change? *Business Strategy and the Environment*, *30*(5), 2688–2701. https://doi.org/10.1002/bse.2771.

Flammer, C. (2021). Corporate green bonds. *Journal of Financial Economics*, 142(2), 499–516. https://doi.org/10.1016/j.jfineco.2021.01.010.

Fu, C., Lu, L., and Pirabi, M. (2024). Advancing green finance: A review of climate change and decarbonization. *Digital Economy and Sustainable Development*, *2*(1), 1.

García, C.J., Herrero, B., Miralles-Quirós, J.L., and del Mar Mirallles-Quirós, M. (2023). Exploring the determinants of corporate green bond issuance and its environmental implication: The role of corporate board. *Technological Forecasting and Social Change*, *189*, 122379.

Laborda, J., and Sánchez-Guerra, Á. (2021). Green bond finance in europe and the stock market reaction. *Estudios de Economia Aplicada*, *39*(3). https://doi.org/10.25115/eea.v39i3.4125.

Liu, N., Liu, C., Da, B., Zhang, T., and Guan, F. (2021). Dependence and risk spillovers between green bonds and clean energy markets. *Journal of Cleaner Production*, *279*, 123595. https://doi.org/10.1016/j.jclepro.2020.123595.

Naeem, M.A., Nguyen, T.T.H., Nepal, R., Ngo, Q.T., and Taghizadeh–Hesary, F. (2021). Asymmetric relationship between green bonds and commodities: Evidence from extreme quantile approach. *Finance Research Letters*, 43, 101983. https://doi.org/10.1016/j.frl.2021.101983.

Sreelakshmi, P., and Greeshma, R.J. (2023). Green bonds: A propitious financial instrument of climate finance. *Vision,* 09722629221138679.

Tang, D.Y., and Zhang, Y. (2020). Do shareholders benefit from green bonds?. *Journal of Corporate Finance*, *61*, 101427.. https://doi.org/10.1016/j.jcorpfin.2018.12.001.

Verma, R.K., and Bansal, R. (2021). Stock market reaction on green-bond issue: Evidence from Indian green-bond issuers. *Vision*, *27*(02). https://doi.org/10.1177/09722629211022523.

Wang, J., Chen, X., Li, X., Yu, J., and Zhong, R. (2020). The market reaction to green bond issuance: Evidence from China. *Pacific-Basin Finance Journal*, *60*, 101294. https://doi.org/10.1016/j.pacfin.2020.101294.

Zhao, L., Chau, K.Y., Tran, T.K., Sadiq, M., Xuyen, N.T.M., and Phan, T.T.H. (2022). Enhancing green economic recovery through green bonds financing and energy efficiency investments. *Economic Analysis and Policy*, *76*, 488–501.

Moving Towards Sustainable Businesses and Developing More Resilient Economies –
Rashid and Annansingh-Jamieson (Eds)
 ISBN: 978-1-041-08875-2

What is to be sustained? Value or satisfaction: The homestay tourism overview

B.R. Olaleye, T.J. Sekhampu, and N. Khumalo
North-West University Business School, Potchefstroom, South Africa

ABSTRACT: Sustainability in tourism, focusing on value creation and tourist satisfaction, is increasingly important for governments, businesses, and tourists, considering social, environmental, and economic impacts. This study consolidates research by highlighting homestay tourism's role in sustainable development goals. It examines the interaction between knowledge of homestays and benefits to tourists, recreational centers, and sustainability, especially in boosting environmental awareness. Data from 223 tourists, analyzed with descriptive, inferential statistics, and PLS-SEM, show that local community attitude and perceived value are crucial for homestay sustainability and tourist satisfaction. However, perceived value does not significantly influence satisfaction, nor does community attitude strongly moderate the nexus. The study notes research gaps in promoting homestay tourism, urging stakeholders to make it more economically, socially, and environmentally sustainable.

Keywords: Attitude, Homestay perceived value, homestay tourism, Tourist satisfaction

1 INTRODUCTION

Sustainable tourism development has become a global imperative as destinations seek to balance economic gains with environmental protection, community welfare, and visitor experience. Among alternative tourism models, homestay tourism has gained prominence due to its capacity to promote cultural immersion, local empowerment, and responsible travel (Rakpathum *et al.* 2025). Homestays offer tourists an intimate experience within host communities while fostering direct socio-economic benefits for local residents. However, achieving long-term viability in homestay tourism requires understanding what exactly needs to be sustained: the perceived value tourists derive from their experience or the satisfaction that ensures repeat visitation and positive word-of-mouth. Although both constructs are integral to tourism success, their interaction—and the role of environmental sustainability—remains an evolving area in tourism scholarship.

Homestay tourism also aligns with SDGs on decent work, inequality reduction, and responsible consumption, stimulating local economies through jobs, cultural exchange, and environmental care. Value in tourism is co-created by hosts and guests, fostering authentic interactions, cultural learning, and emotional bonds. Tourists seek meaningful engagement with local cultures, enriching experiences, and fostering mutual respect (Streimikiene N. Khumalo Ahmed 2021).

In recent years, environmental sustainability has become a critical determinant of how tourists evaluate their stay in community-based accommodations. Likewise, the perceived value tourists derive from cultural authenticity, eco-friendly practices, and community engagement shapes their overall satisfaction (Chen N. Khumalo Chen 2010). Yet, the influence of local community attitude, which reflects residents' support, hospitality, and pro-tourism behaviours, may alter

DOI: 10.1201/9781003647300-2

these relationships. Furthermore, the moderating role of local community attitude remains underexplored. Community residents are integral to homestay operations, yet few studies assess how their attitudes influence tourists' post-experience evaluations. This omission limits understanding of the socio-cultural dimension of sustainability in homestays. This raises an important question: *To what extent do sustainability practices and community attitudes influence what should be sustained in homestay tourism—value or satisfaction?*

The inconsistency in empirical findings leaves uncertainty about whether perceived value or tourist satisfaction should be prioritized for the long-term sustainability of homestay ventures. Additionally, the moderating role of the local community's attitude—an important component of sustainable tourism—has not been sufficiently theorized within the homestay context. Many studies focus on tourists' perspectives on homestays (Dey *et al.* 2020), often neglecting the crucial insights of the local community for sustainable tourism (Artal-Tur *et al.* 2019). Nigeria faces challenges in the tourism sector, particularly in the north, which threaten its sustainability. Therefore, this study addresses these gaps by examining the direct effects of environmental sustainability on perceived value and satisfaction, the mediating role of perceived value in satisfaction, and the moderating effect of community attitude on these outcomes.

2 LITERATURE REVIEW AND HYPOTHESES DEVELOPMENT

2.1 *Theoretical framework*

This research examines how attitudes, norms, and perceived control influence homestay tourists' decisions using Ajzen's (1991) Theory of Planned Behavior. The theory states that community involvement and sustainability shape value, with tourists choosing homestays for authentic experiences and local support. In Nigeria's sustainable context, social dynamics and awareness impact standards and decisions. Perceived control affects confidence; barriers like accessibility or lack of information can hinder actions, while increased control encourages them. The study explores how intentions affect satisfaction and value, and how operators can influence attitudes, norms, and control. It offers insights for researchers, students, and tourism professionals on decision-making and improving tourist experiences.

2.2 *Environmental sustainability practices, perceived value, and tourist satisfaction in Nigerian homestays*

Developed countries lead in environmental and technical progress (Satrovic *et al.* 2025). In Nigeria, sustainable practices like energy conservation, waste reduction, water management, and eco-friendly materials improve tourists' emotional and cognitive evaluations. Tourist satisfaction often aligns with environmental responsibility (Han *et al.* 2019; Nwosu N. Khumalo Adeyemi 2024). Travelers prefer eco-friendly lodging. Sustainability enhances the quality, competitiveness, and guest satisfaction of Nigerian homestays, fostering industry growth. Operators recognize this, but barriers like poor infrastructure and knowledge hinder progress, especially in rural areas (Okeke, Nwankwo, N. Khumalo Eze 2022; Olaleye *et al.* 2021).

In homestays, these practices reinforce authenticity and ethics, improving experience quality (Su *et al.* 2023). Perceived value encompasses tourists' assessments of benefits relative to costs, including monetary, experiential, social, and environmental value (Zeithaml 1988). Eco-friendly initiatives contribute meaningfully to these value dimensions by offering responsible travel options and environmental reassurance (Streimikiene N. Khumalo Ahmed 2021). Homestays practicing sustainability, therefore, provide enhanced perceived value. Continued research on these initiatives' impact on tourist satisfaction is vital for progressing Nigerian tourism and sustainability. Therefore, our stance is:

H1: Environmental sustainability enhances homestay tourist satisfaction.
H2: Environmental sustainability positively influences the homestay perceived value

2.3 *Perceived value and tourist satisfaction*

Tourist satisfaction, which is essential for the homestay industry, influences travel decisions and service utilization, thereby shaping post-purchase sentiments (Cetinkaya N. Khumalo Öter 2016). Perceived value is contingent upon factors such as cost, quality, and emotional responses (Chen N. Khumalo Chen 2010; Olaleye *et al.* 2024), and it impacts satisfaction levels, intentions for repeat visits, recommendations, and overall sustainability. Tourist satisfaction is strongly driven by the value they feel they received from an experience.

Empirical evidence shows that higher perceived value—functional, emotional, or social—significantly increases overall satisfaction in tourism contexts (Chen N. Khumalo Chen 2010). Homestay visitors who derive meaningful cultural and experiential value are more likely to be satisfied. Therefore, the proposed relationship between these two constructs is delineated as follows.

H3: The perceived value derived from the homestay tourism experience has a positive effect on tourist satisfaction.

2.4 *Moderating role of local community attitude*

In sustainable homestay tourism, local communities are central, running, owning, or overseeing accommodations. Rai *et al.* (2021) describe homestays as modest establishments that promote cultural exchange and regional ties, making them a genuine option for rural tourism. Sustainable tourism reduces resource overuse and encourages sustainable development addressing environmental, social, and economic impacts.

Local support is crucial for tourism growth because residents influence satisfaction and word-of-mouth (Chin *et al.* 2022). Sustainable development needs community involvement, as residents affect tourist retention and destination sustainability (Pekerşen N. Khumalo Kaplan 2023). Oluwafemi *et al.* (2023) found community-based tourism in Osun State boosts local economy and social cohesion. Community-owned homestays support economic and environmental empowerment, but limited promotion restricts growth, as Bello and Onifade (2024) note.

Local community attitude shapes the hospitality climate and sociocultural environment of homestays. Positive resident attitudes—warmth, support, openness, and cultural sharing—amplify tourists' perceived value and enhance satisfaction (Wang and Xu 2015). Conversely, unfriendly or reluctant attitudes may weaken the value–satisfaction link. Understanding community views is essential for developing sustainable tourism policies. Consequently, we infer:

H4: *The local community's attitude positively moderates the relationship between perceived value and homestay tourists' satisfaction.*

Following the discussion above, this study proposes the conceptual model in Figure 1 below:

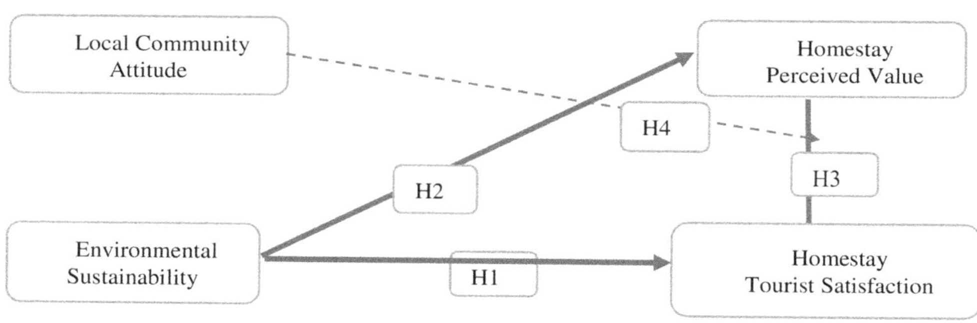

Figure 1. Research model. Source: Authors' research compilation.

3 METHODOLOGY

The study employed a descriptive cross-sectional survey to examine how local community attitudes, tourists' perceived value, satisfaction, and environmental sustainability are related. It used a quantitative approach targeting homestay tourists in southwestern Nigeria, including sites like Badagry, Lekki Conservation Centre, Olumo Rock, Osun Osogbo Sacred Grove, Erin-Ijesa Waterfall, and Ikogosi Warm Springs across four states. Questionnaires were self-administered via drop-off and collection by researchers, involving multi-stage sampling: selecting the region, four states, and distributing 400 surveys, with 223 valid responses out of 241 returned. The sample size exceeded the minimum 200 estimated by the Taro Yamane formula, ensuring good population representation. The questionnaire, reviewed for clarity, measured variables using established scales, with analysis via PLS-SEM for measurement and structural models.

4 RESULTS

4.1 *Assessing the model using PLS*

Evaluating a model with PLS involves analyzing both measurement and structural models. The measurement model assesses validity and reliability between latent variables (LVs) and observable variables, while the structural model focuses on the relationships among constructs. In this study, the measurement model was evaluated through discriminant and convergent validity tests and scale reliability, with results shown in Table 1. Both composite reliability (CR) and Cronbach's Alpha values surpassed 0.7, indicating reliable scales. The variance inflation factor (VIF) was used to identify multicollinearity, with scores ranging from 1.047 to 2.664—well below the threshold of 3.0—indicating minimal bias. Convergent validity was confirmed with loadings between 0.741 and 0.941 and AVE values above 0.5. Discriminant validity, assessed using Fornell and Larcker's criteria, showed that the square root of AVE was higher than inter-variable correlations (see Table 2).

Table 1. Factor loading, AVE, and reliability of variables.

Latent Variables	Loadings (λ)	CA	rho_A	CR	AVE
Environmental Sustainability	**EVS**	0.817	0.823	0.891	0.731
EVS1	0.838***				
EVS2	0.884***				
EVS3	0.842***				
Homestay Perceived Value	**HPV**	0.928	0.942	0.945	0.775
HPV1	0.844***				
HPV2	0.839***				
HPV3	0.941***				
HPV4	0.918***				
HPV5	0.857***				
Homestay Tourist Satisfaction	**HTS**	0.758	0.768	0.862	0.676
HTS1	0.836***				
HTS2	0.741***				
HTS3	0.883***				
Local Community Attitude	**LCA**	0.899	0.902	0.937	0.833
LCA1	0.937***				
LCA2	0.904***				
LCA3	0.897***				

Note: $\chi 2$ = 489.976, NFI = 0.796, d_ULS = 0.597, d_G = 0.344, and SRMR = 0.075.

Table 2. Discriminant validity of variables (Fornell-Larcker Criterion).

Constructs	1	2	3	4
1. Environmental Sustainability (EVS)	**0.855**			
2. Homestay Perceived Value (HPV)	0.255	**0.880**		
3. Homestay Tourist Satisfaction (HTS)	0.421	0.251	**0.822**	
4. Local Community Attitude (LCA)	0.213	0.745	0.276	**0.913**

4.2 *Structural model evaluation*

Figure 2 presents the Partial Least Squares Structural Equation Modeling (PLS-SEM) bootstrapping results. Table 3 summarizes these results, evaluating hypotheses within the structural framework. The research hypothesis is confirmed. Hypothesis 1 (H1) confirms a positive relationship between Environmental Value System (EVS) and Homestay Tourist Satisfaction (HTS) (β=0.371, t=4.001, p<0.001). Hypothesis 2 (H2) indicates that environmental sustainability positively influences perceived homestay value (β = 0.101, t = 2.039). However, Hypothesis 3 (H3) shows that perceived value, while positive, does not significantly affect tourist satisfaction (β=0.114, t=0.953), while the fourth hypothesis revealed a weak and moderating role of local community attitude toward homestay tourism to the effect of perceived value on satisfaction.

Table 3. Hypotheses testing.

	Parameters	β	SE	t-value	*p*-value	R^2	F^2	Decision
	Direct effects							
H1	EVS → HTS	0.371	0.093	4.001	0.000	0.237	0.169	S
H2	EVS → HPV	0.101	0.050	2.039	0.041	0.565	0.023	S
H3	HPV → HTS	0.114	0.119	0.953	0.341	0.237	0.006	NS
	Indirect effect							
H4	LCA* MOD_HPV → HTS	0.101	0.053	1.923	0.055	0.031		NS

Key: SE – standard error, NS – Not significant; S – Significant

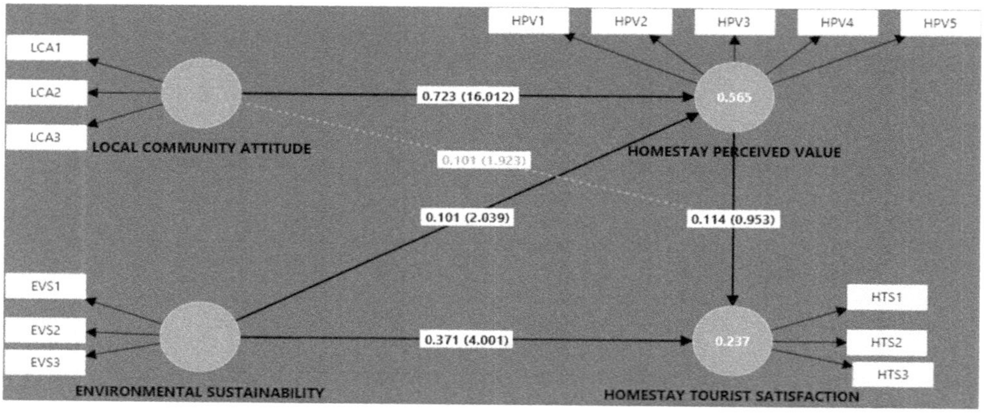

Figure 2. Path analysis.

5 DISCUSSION AND CONCLUSION

5.1 *Discussion of findings*

Homestay programs boost local tourism and community growth by increasing income. This study looked at perceived value, satisfaction, and community attitudes. Results show environmental sustainability improves tourist satisfaction and perceived value by protecting natural and cultural assets, supporting Hypotheses 1 and 2. Tourists are satisfied when environmental benefits outweigh costs; dissatisfaction occurs if perceived as unsustainable. However, Hypotheses 3 and 4 were unsupported; perceived value did not significantly influence satisfaction, conflicting with past studies. Despite some non-significant links, the study highlights sustainability's importance in community development.

Hypothesis H3 results show perceived value has a positive but insignificant effect on homestay tourist satisfaction, aligning with expectation–confirmation theory. While important, other factors like emotional connection and safety likely have a greater impact. Reasonable pricing is standard across many homestays, and the subjective nature of perceived value and diminishing returns limit its effect. Thus, perceived value supports but doesn't drive satisfaction; focusing on experiential quality and service is crucial. The local community's attitude has a positive but insignificant moderating effect, indicating community support is less influential than core service elements such as cleanliness, amenities, and hospitality. Limited community interaction further reduces this influence. Although the effect is not statistically significant, the observed positive trend aligns with social exchange theory, which suggests that positive local interactions can augment perceived value. Nonetheless, satisfaction primarily depends on direct service attributes, as posited by expectation–confirmation theory, with community attitude functioning as a supplementary factor. The focus should therefore be maintained on service quality and engagement efforts to enhance overall satisfaction.

5.2 *Implications, limitations and future research*

Homestay program directors must ensure customer satisfaction to attract tourists, emphasizing perceived value. Assessing impressions is complex, as feedback may not fully reflect travelers' true views. Homestays in Nigeria's multicultural, emerging economy offer eco- and cultural tourism benefits, with friendly locals and rich culture creating unforgettable experiences. This industry boosts the economy, enhances local living standards, and promotes sustainable tourism. Homestay tourism improves rural livelihoods by increasing income, creating jobs, reducing migration, and preserving culture. For sustainable growth, locals should share their culture with visitors, enriching their experience. Success depends on providing unique, functional, and relevant accommodations that are clean, accessible, peaceful, and welcoming. Our Nigeria-based research highlights community-based tourism's potential and the importance of positive host-guest relationships. Better service encourages repeat visits and recommendations. The study allows comparison and further research but overlooks factors like host–guest interactions, cultural authenticity, or service customization, which may affect satisfaction.

5.3 *Conclusion*

Tourism, especially homestays, plays a vital role in Nigeria's economy and is supported by government efforts. However, community and eco-tourism approaches focused on sustainability lack clear definitions. The research recommends co-management involving government, NGOs, academia, tour operators, and locals to improve governance and fairness. Nigerian Tourism Authorities should engage youth and promote digital literacy to enhance management. Incorporating community participation, governance, digital skills, and ecological planning can boost sustainability and growth. While maintaining homestay value and visitor satisfaction is important, community attitudes are less influential. Effective management and evaluation are essential for guest satisfaction and tourism success.

REFERENCES

Ajzen, I. (1991). The theory of planned behavior. *Organizational Behavior and Human Decision Processes, 50*(2), 179–211. https://doi.org/10.1016/0749-5978(91)90020-T

Artal-Tur, A., Briones-Peñalver, A.J., Bernal-Conesa, J.A., and Martínez-Salgado, O. (2019). Rural community tourism and sustainable advantages in Nicaragua. *International Journal of Contemporary Hospitality Management*, *31*(6), 2232–2252.

Bello, R.A., and Onifade, A.O. (2024). Eco-tourism and community development: A sustainability perspective in Nigeria. *Nigerian Journal of Environmental Research, 10*(1), 34–48.

Çetinkaya, M.Y., and Öter, Z. (2016). Role of tour guides on tourist satisfaction level in guided tours and impact on re-visiting Intention: a research in Istanbul. *European Journal of Tourism, Hospitality and Recreation*, *7*(1), 40–54.

Chen, C.F., and Chen, F.S. (2010). Experience quality, perceived value, satisfaction and behavioral intentions for heritage tourists. *Tourism management, 31*(1), 29–35.

Chin, C.H., Wong, W.P.M., Ngian, E.T., and Langet, C. (2022). Do Environmental Stimuli Matter to Tourists ' Satisfaction and Revisit Intention: A Study On Rural Tourism Destinations in Sarawak, Malaysia. *Geo Journal of Tourism and Geosites*, *42*, 683–692.

Dey, B., Mathew, J., and Chee-Hua, C. (2020). Influence of destination attractiveness factors and travel motivations on rural homestay choice: the moderating role of need for uniqueness. *International Journal of Culture, Tourism and Hospitality Research*, *14*(4), 639–666.

Nwosu, I.K., and Adeyemi, S.A. (2024). Assessing the perceived value of eco-tourism in Nigeria's hospitality sector. *African Journal of Tourism Studies, 14*(2), 95–110.

Okeke, C., Nwankwo, J., and Eze, B. (2022). Tourist satisfaction in rural tourism: An assessment of homestay services in Southeast Nigeria. *International Journal of Hospitality and Tourism Management, 8*(1), 15–29.

Olaleye, B.R., Adeyeye, O., Efuntade, A.O., Arije, B., and Anifowose, O.N. (2021). E-quality services: A paradigm shift for consumer satisfaction and e-loyalty; Evidence from postgraduate students in Nigeria. *Management Science Letters*, *11*(3), 849–860.

Olaleye, B.R., Lekunze, J.N., and Olorunsola, F.F. (2024). Exploring the Link Between Customer Satisfaction, Service Quality, and Perceived Organizational Support: The Mediating Role of Relational Psychological Contract. *Studia Universitatis Vasile Goldiş Arad, Seria Ştiinţe Economice*, *34*(3), 60–78.

Oluwafemi, A., Adebisi, K., and Salawu, T. (2023). Rural tourism and environmental sustainability: A study of homestay adoption in Southwest Nigeria. *Nigerian Journal of Tourism and Ecological Studies, 5*(1), 68–82.

Pekerşen, Y., and Kaplan, M. (2023). The perceptions of a local community on tourism development: The case of Akyaka as a Cittaslow. *Community Development*, *54*(2), 292–311.

Rai, S.S., Ansari, I.A., Ganguly, K., Giri, S., and Rai, S. (2021). Lean practices in homestay operations: a case study. *Journal of Quality Assurance in Hospitality & Tourism*, *22*(4), 395–424.

Rakpathum, N., Wang, H., and Lee, Y. (2025). Community-based tourism and sustainable homestay development: The case of Mae Kampong Village, Thailand. *Asia Pacific Journal of Tourism Research, 30*(1), 1–18.

Satrovic, E., O.A. Somoye, Olaleye, B.R. and J.N. Lekunze (2025). Reconciling the nexus between fiscal decentralization and environmental sustainability in European Union: Moderating role of environmental policy stringency. *Frontiers in Environmental Science, 13.* doi: 10.3389/fenvs.2025.1600303

Streimikiene, D., and Ahmed, R.R. (2021). The integration of corporate social responsibility and marketing concepts as a business strategy: evidence from SEM-based multivariate and Toda-Yamamoto causality models. *Oeconomia Copernicana*, *12*(1), 125–157.

Su, L., Yang, X., and Swanson, S.R. (2023). The influence of motive attributions for destination social responsibility on residents' empowerment and quality of life. *Journal of Travel Research*, *62*(8), 1737–1754.

Wang, S., and Xu, H. (2015). Influence of place-based senses of distinctiveness, continuity, self-esteem and self-efficacy on residents' attitudes toward tourism. *Tourism Management*, *47*, 241–250.

Zeithaml, V.A. (1988). Consumer perceptions of price, quality, and value: a means-end model and synthesis of evidence. *Journal of marketing*, *52*(3), 2–22.

Moving Towards Sustainable Businesses and Developing More Resilient Economies –
Rashid and Annansingh-Jamieson (Eds)
© 2026 The Author(s), ISBN: 978-1-041-08875-2

Online buyers' dynamic click strategies

R. Vragov
Queensborough Community College & CUNY Graduate Center, New York, USA

D. Shang
University of North Florida, Jacksonville, Florida, USA

ABSTRACT: Digital sales platforms allow buyers to search for product information online and click through multiple product pages before making a final purchase decision. These sequential click-and-buy behaviors can be observed directly and recorded by the platform. However, little is known about the buyer's actual search strategies and motivation behind this observed behavior because each buyer's expected gain from a click and its associated click (or search) cost is private and unobservable. This article uses data from a laboratory search experiment, in which subjects' values and click costs are induced, to investigate the extent to which a forward-looking expected utility model can predict buyers' sequential click behavior.

1 INTRODUCTION

E-commerce volume reached $5.8 trillion in 2023 and is expected to surpass $8 trillion by 2027 (Chevalier 2024). The number of buyers using various digital sales platforms to purchase a product or a service was 2.64 billion in 2024 (Mosby 2024). E-commerce businesses use different digital sales platforms (search engines, online and mobile retailers, social media sites) to attract buyers and drive sales up (Purmono 2023). As soon as a potential buyer opens a browser window or many a mobile app, she is served commercial messages that try to attract her to one of these digital sales platforms. Once a buyer chooses a platform, then the platform itself shows commercial information about products or services in a certain sequence determined by the platform, and the buyer has to sift through all this information, make the appropriate clicks, and hope to successfully conclude the search with the appropriate purchase.

Buyers' click behavior has normally been analyzed through two different lenses that identify different groups of factors that influence it. Information processing theory has identified two groups of factors: structural factors that are related to how the product/service/ad information is displayed and semantic factors that are related to the meaning of the information being provided (Whitley *et al.* 2025, also see literature review and exposition in Mattke 2019). Decision theory has identified a group of strategic factors that influence click behavior which are related to click cost, price, expected value from the eventual purchase decision, ranking and payment policies of the digital platform, etc. (Vragov *et al.* 2019, Choi *et al.* 2018, Armstrong 2017, Agarwal and Mukhopadhyay 2016, Chan and Park 2015, Ye *et al.* 2014).

The influence of the structural factors on buyer click behavior can easily be ascertained through observation because these factors are directly observable and in most cases there is not much subjectivity (Bruce *et al.* 2017). When subjectivity exists, machine learning approaches can be used to some extent (Gong *et al.* 2018) to assess the significance of these

DOI: 10.1201/9781003647300-3

factors. The semantic factors are a little bit harder to investigate because of possible subjective interpretations but this can usually be handled well either with surveys (Zhang and Mao 2016) or psychology experiments (Wang and Chou 2018). The influence of the strategic factors is hard to evaluate because some of them (expected values and click costs) are subjective, not directly observable, and hard to estimate reliably through surveys (Vragov *et al.* 2019, Gupta *et al.* 2018). The best approach for analyzing the importance of these factors has been through theoretical modeling. So far strategic models of buyer click behavior online assume that buyers behave rationally, they are forward-looking expected utility maximizers and their sequential decision process can be modeled as a dynamic programming problem (Ursu *et al.* 2023, Choi *et al.* 2018, Armstrong 2017, Chan and Park 2015, Agarwal and Mukhopadhyay 2016). Although these models provide good explanations for some readily observed features of online or mobile commercial search, none of these models have been empirically tested even though a recent paper is providing comprehensive guidance on how this might be accomplished in a natural setting (see Honka *et al.* 2024) and a few other studies have attempted a limited analysis of online retail data based on quite restrictive assumptions (see Yao and Mela 2011, Kim *et al.* 2010). In this study we would like to investigate the extent to which a current theoretical model of dynamic buyer click behavior that focuses on strategic factors reflects actual human dynamic decision-making in sequential search.

The best way to achieve our goal is by using the research methodology of experimental economics (Smith 2002, Gupta *et al.* 2018, Roth 1995) because variables, which are normally unknown in practice, can be easily induced and manipulated in the laboratory (Smith 1976). An experimental laboratory environment that eliminates the influence of the first two groups of factors discussed above and many context-specific variables while focusing only on the strategic factors has already been created and described in Vragov *et al.* (2019). That study focuses on teasing out the effect of different ranking and pricing policies on the ad revenues of an online platform as well as on buyer surplus and advertiser profits and only offers a static model of buyer behavior. However, since subjects in that study have to make decisions in a sequence, we argue that the experimental data generated by the buyers' sequential decisions in that environment can be used to test the extent to which a current dynamic click model of strategic buyer behavior that incorporate the assumptions of forward-looking expected utility maximization and the use of dynamic programming can explain strategic dynamic decision-making in the laboratory. The experimental methodology could also help us detect the presence of any known behavioral decision-making biases (Baik 2015). We use the above-mentioned theoretical sources to generate hypotheses about dynamic buyer click behavior and we test the hypotheses using experimental data provided by Vragov *et al.* (2019).

Our model predicts the first click with very good accuracy, the second click with fairly good accuracy, and subsequent clicks with lower accuracy but overall the accuracy is better than extant models of buyer click behavior. The experimental results provide strong support for several hypotheses regarding buyer click behavior. High proportions of first clicks on the top link across both relevance and CTR treatments, and second-click patterns aligned with the predicted product category behavior. Significantly higher rankings of category B products under the relevance treatment. However, click frequency did not significantly change over time.

The article is organized in the following way: the next section provides a literature review, then follows the theoretical discussion and hypothesis, a short description of the experimental design and data, the results from the test we perform, discussion of the results, the conclusion, limitations, and future research.

2 LITERATURE REVIEW

Consumer online search behavior has been an important subject of investigation in the business literature since a large portion of consumers started using computers, smart phones, and other devices to search for product information and purchase products directly online or through a mobile app. The basic theoretical framework that has been most frequently used to analyze consumer online search behavior based on the strategic factors is described in Weitzman (1979). That model assumes that each buyer's utility from purchasing a product has two components: the first component is known prior to search and the second component is uncertain but with a known distribution. The second component's value is discovered after the buyer incurs some search cost and receives more information about the product. The second component can reflect product characteristics such as price (Honka 2014) or combinations of other characteristics (Yao *et al.* 2017, Compiani *et al.* 2024). Buyers search products sequentially until they decide to stop searching and buy one or more of the products or leave the platform without a purchase. The model calculates the reservation value for each product which depends on the known component of utility, the search cost, and the distribution of the unknown component. The reservation value defines the point at which the buyer is indifferent between searching and not searching for the product. The buyer then performs the optimal search starting from the highest reservation value and then the second highest, etc. until the maximum utility among the searched products exceeds the maximum reservation value of the products that have not been searched. After the search has stopped, the buyer purchases the products with the highest realized utility.

Vragov *et al.* (2019) construct a decision-making situation for the buyer that is very similar to Weitzman's theoretical model, however, in order to consider both the buyers' and the sellers' perspectives, they develop a static game-theoretic model of the matching process in which the buyers and the sellers make their decisions simultaneously and with perfect information. The model requires that sellers know what values buyers place on their products and the buyers' click costs. The authors show that if buyers' click costs are positive, the buyers should only click on the products they end up buying. The model also predicts no difference in click behavior if ad ranking is done by relevance or by click-through rate. The authors test the predictions of their model with a laboratory experiment, and they find that buyers' click behavior does not match well with their static model. A dynamic model of buyers' search behavior is not considered because the main purpose that research project is to find how differences in payment and ranking policies affect the economic performance of an online platform. Their experimental environment models explicitly several important aspects of digital sales platforms: 1) buyers have (induced) values for the products being sold on the platform, 2) the platform sets the product (ad) ranking rules and also the seller participation rules and informs both the buyers and the sellers about these rules, 3) sellers have (induced) costs for the products that they sell and they decide their product's prices, 4) Buyers make click and purchase decisions in a sequence as illustrated on Figure 1 in Agarwal and Mukhopahyay (2016) while incurring (induced) click costs, 5) Buyers face uncertainty in payoffs since the price of a product is not revealed until the buyer clicks on a product.

3 SUMMARY OF EXPERIMENTAL DESIGN

We are providing a summary of the experiment described in Vragov *et al.* (2019) but we encourage interested readers to refer to that article for more details. The experimental environment consists of a virtual sales platform with six buyers, six sellers, and six products for sale, where each seller can produce up to 6 units of his/her product at a constant marginal cost of production. Products differ in terms of their cost of production. Products are also divided into two mutually exclusive categories, A & B, with three products within each category. If a buyer buys one product from each category, then the buyer receives a bonus, which makes a product from category B a complement to a product from category A. Buyers' values for each product from category A differ but are the same for products in category B. Buyers also differ in terms of their search cost, which is incurred at every click.

Next, we describe the sequence of decisions within the experiment. In every round sellers are first asked to submit a price for their product and a bid. The bids are used by the platform to decide which products and in what order the products will be shown to each buyer. They are also used to determine how much a seller will have to pay to participate in the market platform. Sellers of products in category A can submit up to three different bids to be matched with buyers preferring each of the three different products in category A. Once the prices and bids are submitted, the platform decides which four out of the six products to show to each buyer. Buyers can see their values for each of the four products available for sale (and two products not available for sale in the current round) but not the price. Each buyer can then click consecutively on one, two, three, or four of the available products to reveal their prices that the corresponding sellers submitted earlier and then decide which products to buy. If a buyer buys more than one product from category A, the buyer only receives the value of the highest-valued product among the ones the buyer bought. The same applies to buying more than one product from category B.

Figure 1 shows an example of a buyer screen in the experiment before the prices are revealed. Notice that the buyer is shown two products from category A: A1 & A3, and two products from category B (B1 & B2) along with their values. The products are ordered from top to bottom according to their value to the buyer. In order to check the price of a product, the buyer must click on the "Click price (Cost: 5)" button and incur a click cost of 5 experimental dollars. This screen is taken from the treatment in which products are ranked by their value to the buyer (i.e. ranked by relevance). Figure 2 shows an example of a buyer screen after a buyer has clicked three times to reveal the prices of three products: A1, A3, and B1. The software displays to the buyer the potential profit from each purchase. To buy a product, the buyer has to click the "Buy" button. Notice that the "Buy" button for product

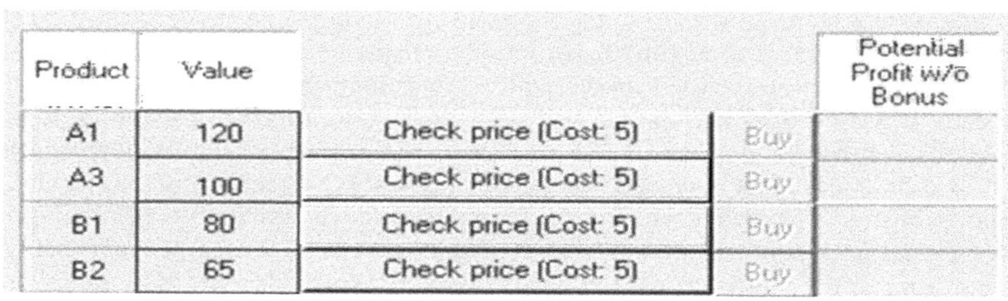

Figure 1. An example buyer screen before the buyer has clicked on any products. As you can see in the figure, the buyer is shown two products from category A: A1 & A3, and two products from category B (B1 & B2) along with their values. The products are ordered from top to bottom according to their value to the buyer. In order to check the price of a product the buyer must click on the "Click price (Cost: 5)" button and incur a click cost of 5 experimental dollars.

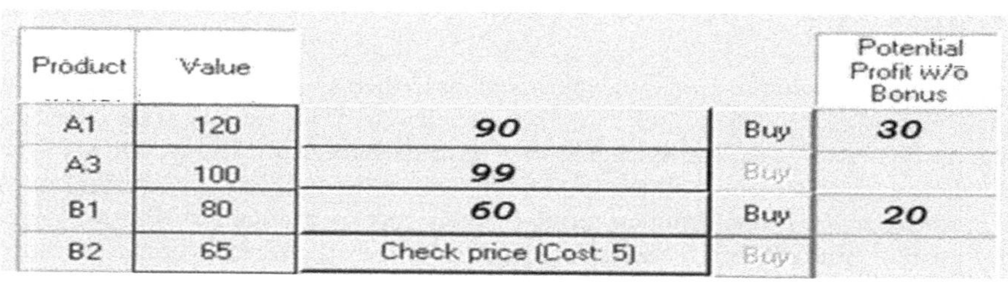

Figure 2. An example buyer screen after the buyer has clicked on three products (A1, A3, and B1) and has revealed their prices. The software displays to the buyer the potential profit from each purchase. To buy a product, the buyer has to click the "Buy" button. Notice that the "Buy" button for product A3 is disabled so that the buyer is prevented from choosing a product from the same category that will bring the buyer a lower profit.

A3 is disabled so that the buyer is prevented from choosing a product from the same category that will bring the buyer a lower profit.

4 DYNAMIC MODEL OF BUYER CLICK BEHAVIOR

4.1 *Dynamic model for a single product variety*

Suppose that a buyer is interested in buying a variety of product A from a digital sales platform. Product A has *k* varieties sold on the platform. The buyer's value for each product variety is unique; the buyer knows this value and understands that other buyers have different preferences over the product varieties available on the platform. The buyer has no information about the production costs of the various product varieties. The buyer faces all varieties of product A on the digital sales platform sorted in some order. Suppose further that, in order to find out the exact price of a product, the buyer has to click on the product and read all the product details (shipping, tax, discounts, etc.), which incurs a cost of *e*. Since we are trying to model the buyer's dynamic choice we assume that the buyer makes decisions in a sequence. In period 1 the buyer decides on which product variety to click, then after clicking and discovering the price, the buyer moves to the second period where the buyer decides where to click second, and so on. Let us designate by v^i the ith highest value from all product varieties' values and p^i the price of the product variety with the ith highest value. Also let v_j be the value of the product whose price p_j is discovered by the buyer during period j. The buyer can also decide to stop the clicking and complete a transaction given the price information the buyer has uncovered. At that point the buyer exits the platform and the buyer's profit can be calculated. Let Cj be the set of all potential (gross) profits from separately buying one of each of the product varieties whose price the buyer has discovered up to and including the last possible period. For example, $C_1=\{v_1-p_1\}$, $C_2=\{v_1-p_1, v_2-p_2\}$, etc. So, if the buyer exits the platform in period j, then the buyer's net profit is $W_j=\max\{Cj\}-j \times e$.

4.1.1 *Making the choice in the first period*

Since product varieties with a lower value for a buyer are likely high-value varieties for other buyers, it is reasonable to infer that when the buyer is making the first choice, the buyer expects that the prices of all product varieties are drawn from the same distribution centered around some mean m_1 . This is also because sellers on the platform cannot offer different prices to different buyers. If the buyer decides to buy and exit the platform in period j, the buyer expects that $EC_j=\{v_1-m_1, v_2-m_1, v_3-m_1, \dots , v_j-m_1\}$. Then the expected net profit is $EW_j=\max\{v_j\}-m_1-j*e$. To maximize the expected net profit the buyer has to choose to click on the product variety with the highest value in the first period and then buy the product and exit the platform without further clicking, which will lead to an expected net profit of $EW=v^1-m_1-e$. Any other choice will lead to a lower expected net profit.

4.1.2 *Making the choice in period 2 and further periods*

Once the buyer makes the choice to click on the highest-value product variety, the buyer can see its price p^1. The buyer can then buy the product and exit the platform, which will result in a net profit of $W_1= v^1-p^1-e$ or the buyer can continue the search and move on to period 2 by clicking on and revealing the price of more product varieties. Now $C_j=\{v^1-p^1, v_2-m_2, v_3-m_2, \dots , v_j-m_2\}$ where m_2 is the updated expected value for the price of the remaining product varieties given p^1. Then $EW_j=\max\{v^1-p^1, \max\{v_j\}-m_2\}$ $-j*e$. To maximize expected net profit the buyer should choose to click on the product variety with the second-highest value in period 2, which will lead to an expected net profit of $EW_2=\max\{v^1-p^1, v^2-m_2\}$ $-2*e$. Using the same logic, we can determine that the optimal policy for the buyer given the information that the buyer has is to click on product varieties in the order of their value starting from the highest-valued product variety to the lowest-valued product variety. The decision of when to stop is determined by the actual prices that the buyer reveals during the click process.

4.2 *Adding a complementary product*

Suppose that, in addition to showing the buyer varieties of product A, the digital sales platform also shows the buyer varieties of a complementary product B. The buyer's value for each product B variety is unique; the buyer knows this value and understands that other buyers have different preferences over the complementary product varieties available on the platform. Let z^i be the ith highest value to the buyer among all values of product B varieties to the buyer. Let r be the value of complementarity that is added to the buyer's net profit if the buyer buys one variety of product A and one variety of product B. Suppose further that a buyer places higher value overall on Product A varieties and lower value overall on Product B varieties.

Let j still represent the number of times the buyer clicks on a product A variety and n represent the number of times the buyer clicks on a product B variety. The current period is then given by j+n. Let s_n be the price of the product B variety revealed on the nth click. Let D_n be the set of all potential (gross) profits from separately buying one of each of the product B varieties whose price the buyer has discovered up to and including the last click on that variety n or $D_1=\{z_1\text{-}s_1\}$, $D_2=\{z_1\text{-}s_1, z_2\text{-}s_2\}$, etc. If the buyer exits the platform in period j+n where $j > 0$ and $n > 0$ then the buyer's net profit is $W_{j+n}=\max\{C_j\} + \max\{D_n\}+r\text{-}(j+n)e$. (Consider j=0, n=0, or $z < s$).

4.2.1 *Making the click decision in the first two periods*

Assume that the buyer expects the mean price of a Product B variety to be q_1. Then the buyer expects that $ED_1=\{z_1\text{-}q_1\}$, $ED_2=\{z_1\text{-}q_1, z_2\text{-}q_1\}$, etc. If the buyer considers buying one of each product varieties and exiting the platform in period j+n then the expected net profit is $EW_{j+n}= \max\{v_j\}\text{-}m_1+ \max\{z_n\}\text{-}q_1+c\text{-}(j+n)e$. Clearly exiting in the first period by clicking and buying only a product A variety leads to an expected net profit of $v_1\text{-}m_1\text{-}e$ and by clicking and buying only a product B variety is $z_1\text{-}q_1\text{-}e$. Unless the click costs e is too high, or the expected prices are higher than the maximum values of either of the two product varieties, both of these expected outcomes are dominated by the expected outcome of clicking on the highest-valued product B variety and product A variety in the first two periods and then exiting the platform.

We find it reasonable to assume that the buyer makes click decisions based on the expected profit from a purchase that can eventually result from a click unless the buyer is influenced by some behavioral bias.

4.2.2 *Making the click decision in further periods*

If the buyer has already checked the prices of the two highest-valued products from each category, then continuing the search at this point only makes sense if the buyer finds the price of either of the products to be too high above the expected price. If the buyer thinks that the p1 is too high the buyer will click on the product variety A with the next highest value and if the buyer thinks that s1 is too high the buyer will click on the product variety B with the next highest value. If the buyer keeps following the highest expected profit the buyer will continue clicking in the order of the product variety's values from highest to lowest and the decision to exit will be determined by the specific prices that the buyer discovers.

4.3 *The effect of ranking*

According to the discussion above dynamic buyer click behavior is determined by the values of the various products to the buyer, his or her expectations about prices, and the prices that s/he reveals during the click process. We next investigate how the ad ranking policy of the digital platform can affect buyer click behavior.

4.3.1 *Ranking by relevance*

Even though buyer values are unknown, digital platforms can calculate a relevance score based on past behavior or other known buyer characteristics and then present the collection of available products to the buyer in order of their relevance. For the analysis here let us suppose that relevance is perfect – so products are always ordered in terms of their value to the buyer. In such a situation we should observe buyers clicking first on the highest-value product from the A category which will always be ranked first or on the highest value product from category B, which will be in some position after 1 since, overall, products from category B have lower values. If we assume an order bias on the part of the buyer, then the buyer will always click first on the product listed first – the highest valued product from category A. Unless the revealed price of the product is too high, the buyer will click on the highest-value product from category B the second. The buyer can stop here or continue checking the remaining products with a decreasing probability in order of their values – which means in this case – in order of their ranks.

4.3.2 *Ranking by click-through rate (popularity)*

If the collection of displayed items is ordered in terms of past click-through rate, the buyer expects that products will not necessarily be ranked by value, i.e. It is no longer the case that the highest -valued product is ranked first. The dynamic click strategy then entirely depends on the prices that the buyer expects in each position and the decision becomes cognitively a little more difficult than under ranking by relevance. We should expect that the buyer will click first on the highest-valued product from category A or B.

4.3.3 *Raking by bid*

If the collection of displayed items are ranked in order of the bid solicited from the seller by the digital sales platform, then it is possible that higher bids might require higher prices, and so the buyer might expect that the price of an item is related to its ranking, i.e. product varieties ranked higher are more expensive and those ranked lower are less expensive on average. In that case the buyer will click first on the product from category A and the product from category B which are bringing the highest expected surplus and those products might not necessarily be the ones with the highest values to the buyer.

4.4 *The role of prior knowledge*

A new buyer does not have *apriori* information about the expected prices of different products. When a new buyer makes click decisions, the buyer might not be considering the conclusions we reached above but can use the shopping experience as an opportunity to learn more about the prices through clicking and so the buyer will decide to check as many prices as possible so that the buyer can make more informed choices later. There is some value to price information itself.

4.5 *The effect of click costs*

Obviously, the click costs should affect the probability of checking another product of the same category. If click costs are higher, the probability that the buyer will click on two products from the same category is lower.

5 HYPOTHESES

The discussion above allows us to propose several hypotheses about the buyers' dynamic click behavior that can be easily tested in a laboratory experiment with human subjects whose value information is simulated by the experimenter. We divide our hypotheses in 5 groups. The first three groups are specifically related to the click order, the fourth is related to click costs, and the fifth group is a combination of other more general hypotheses that can be derived from our model.

5.1 *Hypotheses related to the first click*

H1: If products are listed by relevance, the first click will be on the product listed on top of the list which also has the highest buyer value for a product from category A. (from section 4.3.1)

H2: The probability of the buyer clicking on the first spot first when products are listed by CTR is lower than when products are listed by Relevance. (from section 4.3.2)

H3: If products are listed by CTR, the first click should be either on the highest-valued product from category A or the highest-valued product from category B. (from section 4.3.2)

5.2 *Hypothesis related to the second click*

H4: The second click will be on the highest-value product from a different category with higher probability than on another product from the same category in both treatments. For the relevance treatment the second click will be on a category B product residing in a spot higher than 2nd.

5.3 *Hypothesis related to the 3rd click*

H5: The third click and any subsequent clicks will happen only if the revealed prices in previous clicks are deemed too high by the buyer.

5.4 *Hypothesis related to click costs*

H6: Buyers with higher click costs will click less and will click on a different product from the same category with a lower probability.

5.5 *Other general hypotheses*

H7: Category B products will be ranked higher in ctr versus relevance.

H8: A buyer that has more price information will click on less products in both treatments

H9: If products are listed by relevance and the buyer checks the prices of more then one product from the same category, the rank of the second choice will be higher than the rank of the first choice. Overall buyers will not reverse ranking during the dynamic click process under ranking by relevance.

6 EXPERIMENTAL RESULTS

Overall subjects used 17 different dynamic click strategies both in the Relevance & CTR treatments with the total number of clicks from all 5 sessions being 838 and 861 respectively. We next proceed by testing our hypotheses and explaining how they are operationalized within the context of Vragov *et al.*'s experimental design.

6.1 *Results related to the first click*

We choose to test H1 by calculating the proportion of first clicks on the top link that contains the highest-valued product from category A in the relevance treatment in each of the five sessions. H1 predicts a value of 100%. The actual results are 98.15%, 93.06%, 95.9%, 90.11%, and 93.95%. If we assume a reasonable error rate on the part of the subjects in the experiment, we can determine that H1 is well supported.

We proceed with H2 and count the proportion of first clicks on the top link in the CTR treatment. The corresponding values in each session are listed in Table 1. Based on the Mann-Whitney U test ($p = 0.016$), we conclude that H2 is also well supported.

Table 1. Proportion of first clicks on the top product.

Session	Relevance treatment	CTR treatment
1	98.15%	82.58%
2	93.06%	90.86%
3	95.90%	82.95%
4	90.11%	73.00%
5	93.95%	84.62%

We list below in Table 2 the proportion of first clicks on the highest-value product from category A or category B in each session of the CTR treatment. The prediction is 100% but we consider the error here too large, so H3 does not receive enough support from the data.

Table 2. Proportion of first clicks on the highest-value product from category A or B in the CTR treatment.

Session	Proportion
1	75.28%
2	95.43%
3	67.05%
4	84.05%
5	81.07%

6.2 *Results related to the second click*

To test H4 we can calculate the average rank of the product clicked second and see if the result is significantly higher than 2. The session averages are reported in Table 3 and they confirm one part of our hypothesis.

Table 3. Average rank of second click.

Session	Rank
1	2.84
2	2.68
3	2.60
4	3.26
5	2.66

We can also check the proportion of second clicks that are on the highest-value product from a different category. The session averages for both treatments are listed in Table 4. H4 predicts that the proportion should be higher than 50% in both treatments. The prediction is confirmed.

Table 4. Proportion of second clicks on the highest-value product from a different category.

Session	Relevance treatment	CTR treatment
1	93.57%	70.18%
2	64.63%	87.43%
3	74.28%	81.40%
4	90.06%	85.35%
5	60.33%	88.02%

6.3 *Results related to the third and fourth click*

To test H5 we first calculate the average prices of category A products and category B products for the first 20 rounds of the experiment. We can use these numbers as proxies for the mean price that the buyers might expect for the different products. We then count the proportion of times during the last 10 rounds that the buyer clicked a third time because the price of a product from the same category that has already been clicked is higher than the average price from the previous rounds. The results are displayed in Table 5. We can see that H5 is relatively well supported for category A products in both treatments but not for category B products.

Table 5. Proportion and number of third-time clicks.

Relevance treatment			CTR treatment		
Category	Proportion	Observations	Category	Proportion	Observations
A	95.45%	22	A	92.86%	56
B	35.37%	82	B	73.58%	83

Regarding the fourth click we should keep in mind that the experiment is set up to allow a maximum of four clicks, so in addition to the situation described in the hypothesis a buyer might click on a fourth product because the first three products the buyer clicked on are from the same category. This is simply an end-game artifact of the specific experimental design and is reported separately in the Table 6 below. Overall, we do not think that H9 is getting enough support from the data and so is rejected.

Table 6. Fourth click proportions and number of observations.

Relevance treatment			CTR treatment		
Proportion	End-game effect	Observations	Proportion	End-game effect	Observations
23.63%	12.73%	55	65.52%	13.79%	58

6.4 *Results related to click costs*

The experimental design provides two levels of click cost. The low level is about 4% of the highest value for a product in category A and the high level is about 12% of the highest value for a product in category A. We can test the first part of H6 by comparing the number of clicks of low-click -cost versus high-click-cost buyers. Table 7 below displays the average number of clicks per round in each session for both treatments.

Table 7. Number of clicks for buyers with low click costs versus buyer with high click costs.

Relevance treatment Session			CTR treatment	
	Low click cost	High click cost	Low click cost	High click cost
1	2.49	2.32	3.22	1.60
2	2.84	2.48	3.07	1.27
3	3.11	2.43	2.02	2.46
4	2.33	1.95	2.67	1.19
5	2.42	1.60	2.58	1.37

The second part of the hypothesis is harder to test. We create a subset of the data taking only occasions when buyer decide to click three times. Then we calculate the proportion of times that the buyers click on the same product category on the first and the second click and we look for differences depending on the click cost. The hypothesis states that buyers with high click costs are less likely to click the second time on a product from the same category. We post the results in Table 8 and we see that there is not enough support for the hypothesis. The problem is that we have as few as 2 or 5 observations in some of these cells, so more data is necessary to reliably test the second part of H6.

Table 8. Number of clicks for buyers with low click costs versus buyer with high click costs.

Relevance treatment Session			CTR treatment	
	Low click cost	High click cost	Low click cost	High click cost
1	10.20%	30.33%	47.62%	40.00%
2	39.50%	37.50%	18.45%	50.00%
3	00.00%	27.27%	17.62%	31.03%
4	22.23%	37.50%	20.00%	00.00%
5	37.14%	14.29%	17.86%	10.00%

6.5 *Other general results*

Table 9 shows a comparison of the average rankings of category B products in the two treatments. H7 predicts that the rankings will be higher under Relevance and we can easily reject the hypothesis of no difference with high significance. H7 is supported (Mann-Whitney U test, p=value = 0.008).

Table 9. Average ranking of products from category B.

Session	Relevance treatment	CTR treatment
1	3.18	3.00
2	3.36	2.96
3	3.24	2.46
4	3.50	2.23
5	3.39	2.44

We next test hypothesis H8. In the experiment subjects have no price information before the first round. Once they start participating in the experiment, they start collecting price information based on the products they have clicked. We can test this hypothesis by testing whether the number of clicks in the first 10 rounds of the experiment differs significantly from the number of click during the last 10 rounds. The session averages are reported in Table 10. Based on Wilcoxon signed-rank test for the paired values, we cannot reject equality for both treatments (p-value = 0.063 and 0.125 respectively). So, H8 is not supported.

Table 10. Number of clicks.

Relevance treatment			CTR treatment	
Session	First 10 rounds	Last 10 rounds	First 10 rounds	Last 10 rounds
1	153	143	187	163
2	161	150	174	152
3	176	165	165	138
4	134	133	152	135
5	177	65	145	149

To test H9 we list the proportion of dynamic strategies with reversals. The prediction is 0% and given the data reported in Table 11, the hypothesis is supported.

Table 11. Proportion of dynamic strategies with reversals.

Session	Proportion
1	0.00%
2	0.00%
3	0.00%
4	0.60%
5	0.00%

7 DISCUSSION

Our dynamic model has received strong support from the experimental data that we use. Six of our hypotheses are well supported and two of our hypotheses are partly supported. The result from testing the first three hypotheses strongly supports our model's assumption that, before buyers engage with the experimental market, they assume that prices for different products are drawn from the same distribution. Clearly this assumption might be violated in naturally occurring online markets so when a model is constructed and applied to data from such markets this assumption has to be reconsidered. It is also interesting to note that the result persisted throughout the experiment, which means that the buyers' expectation that prices will not dramatically differ actually materialized in the laboratory. This result also demonstrates that if ranking is done by click-through rate, one can use the ranking to predict the first click just as accurately as it one is using the relevance score.

The results from testing the hypotheses related to the second click demonstrate that once the buyers find some price information about the top value product, they proceed with searching for price information regarding the complementary product rather than finding more price information about the first product. We also find that buyers devote their second click on the highest-valued complementary product. This means that in markets with complementary products predicting the second click is easier if it is based on relevance rather than ranking.

The hypotheses related to the third and fourth click are the ones that have not received enough support. It seems like subjects continue to click on products even if they have discovered the best possible combination of one product from category A and one product from category B and they know that it is highly unlikely to find a product with a lower price. We posit that this might be due to another behavioral bias that we do not explicitly model here – removal of buyer remorse. This means that even though the buyer has discovered the optimal choice the buyer has to verify for himself/herself that this in fact is the case by clicking on more products than necessary or even on all remaining products. Another possible explanation is that buyers simply put value on being informed about prices. The price information they discover might be unnecessary for the moment but might prove useful in a future market or a future situation. Another way to explain this is just to say that buyers put value of learning about markets and how prices are formed within them.

The results related to click costs offer mixed evidence. While buyers with higher click costs do click less overall—as predicted—there is insufficient data to support the prediction that they are more selective in sticking with one category. The limited sample size in some sessions constrains the power of this test, and future studies with larger samples are needed to draw more reliable inferences. Product rankings in the relevance treatment align more closely with value-based sorting. The lack of support for H8 indicates that participants did not significantly adjust their click behavior between early and later rounds. The unexplained persistence in exploratory clicking and some inconsistencies in cost-sensitive strategies suggest the presence of unmodeled cognitive or emotional factors—such as regret aversion, curiosity, or risk preferences—that may warrant incorporation in future extensions of the model.

8 CONCLUSION, LIMITATIONS, AND FUTURE RESEARCH

We have proposed and successfully tested a dynamic model of buyer click behavior. The model is able to predict a higher percentage of buyer click behavior than existing static search models. Unlike static search models our model predicts a non-zero percentage of clicks on more than two products and provides some guidance on the factors that can lead buyers to make that decision. This study contributes to the theory of shopping on digital platforms because it is a model of sequential search that incorporates rational decision-making as well as known human behavioral biases to explain how buyers shop in sequence given the information they discover. As far as we know this is also the first dynamic model that incorporates product complementarities as part of the decision-making environment. Our ability to use experimental data to show the relationship between values that are unobservable in practice and buyer actions is also practically valuable. Mainly, there are four important implications for practice: 1) if a platform is ranking results by relevance and buyers are not clicking first on the top product and second on a complementary product, the platform's measure of relevance is not precise and needs to be revised, 2) one can use either relevance or rank to predict the probability that a buyer will click on a certain product first, 3) in markets with complementary products, the second click can be predicted better by relevance rather than by the ranking of the complementary product, 4) once a buyer has clicked on the first product, a buyer could be guided to a list of possible complementary products rather than list of primary product substitutes

The next step is to test the model using data from naturally occurring click behavior. Hypothesis 2, 4, 5, 7, and 9 with some modifications and calibration can be tested without knowing the buyers' private values. This model can be extended to incorporate dynamic behavior for sellers as well which can provide us with further guidance as related to profitability and efficiency of digital sales platforms.

Our study has many limitations. Our model makes some assumptions that might not be true in practice. For example we assume that the platform's relevance ranking is perfect. We also assume that buyers know the values of the products to them *apriori* and so the ranking itself does not provide information about value. We also assume that buyers are able to form rational expectations about product prices by observing the transactions on a platform and we also assume that buyers do not update these expectations when they click on several products and observe their prices. We have also failed to incorporate all known behavioral biases in decision-making but we hope that we can extend our model in the future to address some of these limitations.

There also some limitations in the way we test our model's hypothesis since we have to operationalize them in order to use the data generated by a prior experimental design. The process of operationalization is not free of errors but fortunately future experimental designs can test different operationalizations of the same hypotheses. Also, since the experiment we use is not specifically designed to test our model, there is not enough data to robustly test some of our hypotheses. A new experimental design can be executed whose purpose can be specifically to test our model or some of its future extensions. Our testing process also suffers from all limitations related to using data generated from laboratory experiments – limitations which have been described in detail in Vragov *et al.* (2019).

REFERENCES

Agarwal, A., and Mukhopadhyay, T. (2016). the impact of competing ads on click performance in sponsored search. *Information Systems Research*, *27*(3), 538–557. https://doi.org/10.1287/isre.2016.0637

Armstrong, M. (2017). Ordered consumer SEARCH. *Journal of the European Economic Association*, *15*(5), 989–1024. https://doi.org/10.1093/jeea/jvx017

Baik, S. (2015). *The Wiley-Blackwell handbook of judgment and decision making* (G. Keren and G. Wu, Eds.; 1st ed.). Wiley Blackwell.

Bruce, N.I., Murthi, B.P.S., and Rao, R.C. (2017). A dynamic model for digital advertising: the effects of creative format, message content, and targeting on engagement, *Journal of Marketing Research* (54:2), pp. 202–218.

Chevalier, St. (2024). Global retail E-commerce sales 2014–2027 *Statista*, May, 22, 2024 accessed on Dec., 28, 2024 at https://www.statista.com/statistics/379046/worldwide-retail-e-commerce-sales/#:~:text=In%202023%2C%20global%20retail%20e%2Dcommerce%20sales%20reached,to%20surpass%20eight%20trillion%20dollars%20by%202027.

Choi, M., Dai, A.Y., and Kim, K. (2018). Consumer search and Price competition *Econometrica*, *86*(4), 1257–1281. https://doi.org/10.3982/ECTA14837

Compiani, G., Lewis, G., Peng, S., and Wang, P. (2024). Online search and optimal product rankings: An empirical framework. *Marketing Science*, *43*(3), 615–636.

Gong, J., Abhisek, V., and Li, B. (2018). "Examining the Impact of Keyword Ambiguity on Search Advertising Performance: A Topic Model Approach," *MIS Quarterly* (42:3), pp. 805–829.

Gupta, A., Kannan, K., and Sanyal, P. (2018). Economic experiments in information systems. *MIS Quarterly*, *42*(2), 595–606. https://doi.org/10.25300/MISQ/2018/13049

Honka, E. (2014). Quantifying search and switching costs in the u.s. auto insurance industry *RAND J. Econ.*, 45 (4) (2014), pp. 847–884

Honka, E., Seiler, S., and Ursu, R. (2024). Consumer search: What can we learn from pre-purchase data? *Journal of Retailing*, *100*(1), 114–129. https://doi.org/10.1016/j.jretai.2024.02.003

Kim, J.B., Albuquerque, P., and Bronnenberg, B.J. (2010). Online demand under limited consumer search. *Marketing Science (Providence, R.I.)*, *29*(6), 1001–1023. https://doi.org/10.1287/mksc.1100.0574

Mattke, J. (2019) "Advertising-funded IS: A literature review on factors influencing user's clicking behavior for In-App Ads", *Proceedings of the 25th Americas Conference on Information Systems*, Cancun, Mexico, 2019

Mosby, A. (2024) 100 Online Shopping Statistics 2024 (Trends Data) Yaguara.co, Sept. 22, 2024 accessed on Dec. 28, 2024 at https://www.yaguara.co/online-shopping-statistics/

Purnomo, Y.J. (2023) Digital marketing strategy to increase sales conversion on E-commerce platforms. *Journal of Contemporary Administration and Management (ADMAN)*, vol. 1, no. 2, Aug. 2023, pp. 54–62, doi:10.61100/adman.v1i2.23.

Roth, A.E. (1995). Introduction to experimental economics. *The handbook of experimental economics*, *1*, 3–109.

Smith, V.L. (2002). Experimental economics. In *Behavioural and Experimental Economics* (pp. 75–98). London: Palgrave Macmillan UK.
Smith, V.L. (1976). Experimental economics: Induced value theory. *The American Economic Review*, *66*(2), 274–279. http://www.jstor.org/stable/1817233
Ursu, R., Seiler, S., and Honka, E. (2023). The sequential search model: a framework for empirical research. Working Paper.
Vragov, R., Shang, R.D., Smith, V., and Porter, D. (2019). Let's play the search game: Strategic and behavioral properties of sponsored search auction mechanisms. *Electronic Commerce Research and Applications*, *33*, 100809. https://doi.org/10.1016/j.elerap.2018.10.001
Wang, S.S., and Chou, H.-Y. (2019). "Effects of game-product congruity on in-app interstitial advertising and the moderation of media-context factors," *Psychology & Marketing* (36:3), pp. 229–246.
Whitley, S.C., Chakravarty, A., and Wang, P. (2025). Positive Emotions During Search Engine Use: How You Feel Impacts What You Search for and Click On. *Journal of Marketing*, *89*(1), 77–93. https://doi.org/10.1177/00222429241263012
Yao, S., and Mela, C.F. (2011). A Dynamic Model of Sponsored Search Advertising. *Marketing Science (Providence, R.I.)*, *30*(3), 447–468. https://doi.org/10.1287/mksc.1100.0626
Yao, S., W. Wang, Y. Chen (2017) Tv channel search and commercial breaks *J. Mark. Res.*, 54 (5), pp. 671–686
Ye, S., Aydin, G., Hu, S. (2014) Sponsored search marketing: dynamic pricing and advertising for an online retailer, *Management Science*, v61 n6, June 2015, pg. 1255–1274
Zhang, J., and Mao, E. (2016). From Online Motivations to Ad Clicks and to Behavioral Intentions: An Empirical Study of Consumer Response to Social Media Advertising, *Psychology & Marketing* (33:3), pp. 155–164.

*Moving Towards Sustainable Businesses and Developing More Resilient Economies –
Rashid and Annansingh-Jamieson (Eds)*
 ISBN: 978-1-041-08875-2

Prompt engineering: Unlocking better responses from large language models

A. Kamruzzaman and N. Samdrup
Department of Business and Economics, School of Business and IS, York College, the City University of NY, Queens, New York, USA

D. Nurse
Department of Mathematics and Computer Science, School of Arts & Sciences, York College, the City University of NY, Queens, New York, USA

ABSTRACT: The research explores how different prompt engineering strategies affect the performance of Large Language Models, using York GPT and ChatGPT as the primary test systems. Both models were used to evaluate three prompt engineering strategies: zero-shot, few-shot, and chain-of-thought. Research highlights the importance of prompt design and addresses the challenges in establishing a consistent strategy that generates well-defined output. By implementing a well-crafted prompt, the research demonstrates it can significantly improve the quality of a model response.

1 INTRODUCTION

Large Language Models (LLMs) have greatly improved in mimicking human language, answering queries, and completing tasks. Prompt engineering—developing structured and purposeful input—is vital for generating high-quality responses. As LLMs grow more sophisticated, trained on extensive data to perform tasks like summarization or question answering (Cao *et al.* 2023), the design of prompts becomes increasingly important. Studies show that using examples within prompts (few-shot learning) can significantly enhance response accuracy (Zhou *et al.*2022). Research also indicates that refining prompt strategies helps maintain performance across diverse tasks (Sahoo *et al.* 2024). To address the gap, this research explores experiments with three prompting strategies: zero-shot, few-shot, and chain-of-thought methods and evaluates their influence on LLM responses. The study uses two models: OpenAI's ChatGPT-4 Mini and YorkGPT, a model trained on York College content.

2 GENERAL BACKGROUND

Prompt engineering refers to the practice of formulating clear instructions for LLMs, like ChatGPT, to generate meaningful results. Researchers found that carefully written prompts, which provide context and specify the task, improve model performance (Patel & Parmar 2024). This is further illustrated in Figure 1, where the user prompt is refined through prompt engineering with instructions and context, leading to an improved response. Over time, this field has expanded to include multiple strategies for improving prompt interpretation. More recent methods, like chain-of-thought prompting, guide models to explain their reasoning, helping them tackle complex tasks more effectively (Jin *et al.* 2025).

DOI: 10.1201/9781003647300-4

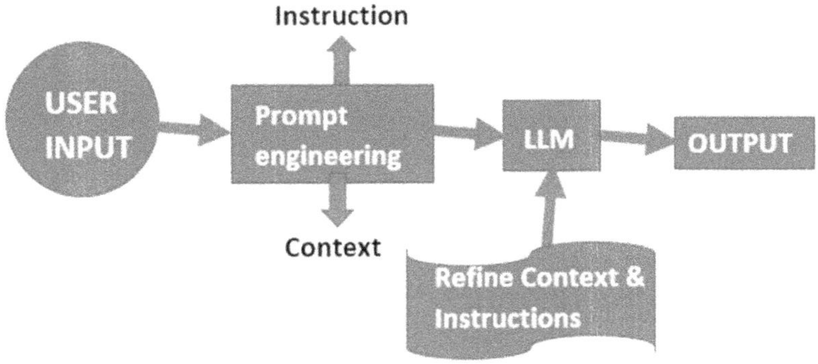

Figure 1. User input refined through prompt engineering before LLM output.

3 LITERATURE REVIEW

Prompt engineering plays an essential role in enhancing how well large LLMs, such as ChatGPT, perform. Research indicates that the way a prompt is phrased can strongly influence the relevance, clarity, and precision of AI-generated responses. (Shin *et al.* 2023) examine several strategies, like zero-shot and few-shot prompting. These methods help LLMs perform tasks with minimal or no prior examples, making them particularly effective in settings where limited training data is available. Chain-of-thought (CoT) prompting has attracted interest due to its ability to support advanced reasoning. This approach guides models to solve problems step by step, resulting in more coherent and logically structured responses. Techniques like Auto-CoT and LogiCoT seek to improve this by automating prompt design and minimizing reasoning errors in outputs (Hsieh *et al.* 2023). Another method, known as Retrieval-Augmented Generation (RAG), incorporates external data into prompts, allowing models to pull in relevant facts when generating answers. This improves both the factual correctness and reliability of their responses. Although these methods have advanced prompt engineering, some challenges remain. There is currently no universal guideline for writing prompts, and the success of each technique can vary depending on the model and the task. As research in this area progresses, developing effective prompting techniques will be key to unlocking the full capabilities of LLMs.

4 RESEARCH DESIGN & METHODOLOGY

This study analyzes how effective three prompting strategies—zero-shot, few-shot, and chain-of-thought (CoT)—are in improving the performance of LLMs. Two models were tested: YorkGPT, which was fine-tuned for York College tasks, and OpenAI's Chat GPT-4o-mini, accessed through the OpenAI API. The goal was to assess how these prompting techniques influenced response quality in terms of relevance, clarity, completeness, and reasoning across both specific and general task domains. The test focused on prompts related to accessing York email and IT services and ChatGPT-4-mini photosynthesis experiment used the following prompt styles:

(I) *Zero-Shot Prompting:* YorkGPT: A simple query, such as "How do I activate my York email and get help using it?" was used to evaluate the model's ability to generate brief and relevant responses without added context. ChatGPT-4-mini: The model was asked, "What is photosynthesis?" to test its ability to provide a brief definition.

(II) *Few-Shot Prompting:* YorkGPT: Before posing the main question, examples like "How do I create an email account?" were introduced, followed by "Now explain how to activate a York email account and where to find help." This approach examined how well the model could use examples to give structured replies. ChatGPT-4-mini: Before asking the main question, two examples were shared—one explaining water absorption and the other discussing sunlight capture. These examples created a context, allowing the model to deliver a more thorough explanation.

(III) *Chain-of-Thought Prompting:* YorkGPT: The prompt guided the model step by step, requiring it to describe the steps for accessing and activating a York email account, as well as how to find support services. ChatGPT-4-mini: A detailed prompt asked the model to explain the roles of sunlight, water, and carbon dioxide in photosynthesis and describe how glucose and oxygen are produced.

The two models were tested on separate tasks aligned with their training data. YorkGPT, trained specifically in York College content, was evaluated using a campus -related task (email activation). In contrast, ChatGPT-4 mini was assessed on a general topic (photosynthesis). This comparison was designed to explore how a domain-specific model like YorkGPT performs against a general-purpose model, based on the nature of the task. To maintain fairness, the ChatGPT-4-mini experiment applied token limits: 100 tokens for zero-shot, 250 for few-shot, and 300 for CoT prompting (Zhou *et al.*, 2022). YorkGPT had no token restrictions due to its narrower scope. Figure 2 (flowchart) illustrates the methodology used to conduct the ChatGPT -4-mini experiment, detailing each step from prompt creation to output analysis.

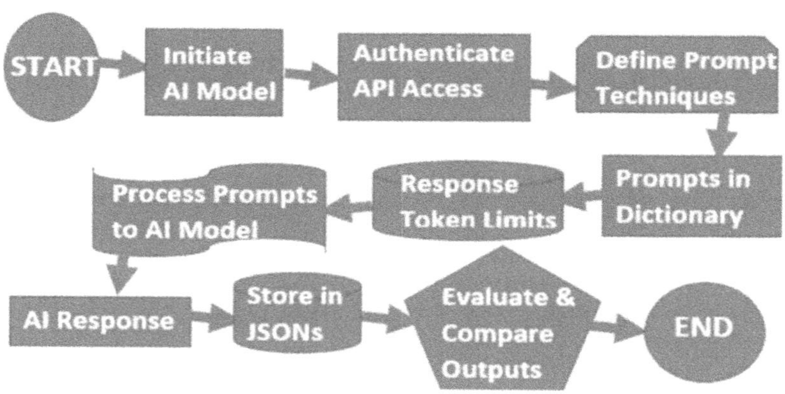

Figure 2. Flowchart showing the step-by-step process of the experiment.

In both cases, responses were evaluated based on predefined metrics: relevance to the task, clarity of instructions, completeness of details, and reasoning quality (Patel & Parmar 2024).

As highlighted by Patel & Parmar (2024) in their research proposal, Prompt Engineering for LLMs, their study explores how different prompting techniques influence AI model performance and effectiveness. This study followed a structured approach to compare the output of two language models—YorkGPT and ChatGPT-4-mini. Both were evaluated using the same three prompting formats: zero-shot, few-shot, and chain-of-thought. Each type of prompt was carefully created to ensure consistency in the tasks given to both models. The evaluation focused on four criteria—relevance, clarity, completeness, and reasoning (Patel & Parmar 2024)—and was applied to all prompt types to ensure a fair comparison. This structure helped guide the data collection process and ensured consistency across test conditions. To assess the quality of model outputs across different prompting strategies, a rubric-based evaluation method was implemented. Each response was evaluated using four key criteria. Relevance measured how well the response addressed the prompt; clarity focused on the coherence and ease of understanding; completeness evaluated whether all required components of the answer were present; and reasoning & quality assessed the depth and quality of explanation provided. This scoring rubric was applied uniformly to all responses generated by both ChatGPT-4-mini and YorkGPT across the zero-shot, few-shot, and chain-of-thought prompting strategies. Each criterion was rated on a scale from 1 to 10, where a score of 10 indicated the highest quality performance. The resulting scores provided the raw data necessary for calculating mean scores and statistical analysis.

A total of three prompts were used for each model. Each model's response was evaluated using a structured scoring rubric across four key criteria. These four evaluation criteria served as the basis for statistical analysis. To determine whether the differences in performance between prompt strategies were statistically significant, a series of paired t-tests were conducted. The analysis focused on three strategy comparisons: (1) Zero-shot vs. Few-shot, (2) Few-shot vs. Chain-of-thought, and (3) Zero-shot vs. Chain-of-thought. For each comparison, the rubric scores across the four evaluation criteria were treated as matched pairs, resulting in a sample size of $n = 4$ per test.

The statistical analysis followed these steps:

(1) Score differences were calculated by subtracting each criterion score of one prompt strategy from the corresponding score of the other.
(2) The Mean Difference of the paired scores was computed to observe the average performance gap between the strategies.
(3) The T-statistic (t) was obtained using the formula: t = (mean difference) / (standard error)
(4) The P-value was then determined using two methods:
   - Manually, via a t-distribution table using degrees of freedom ($df = n - 1 = 3$)
   - Programmatically, using Python for greater precision.

A p-value less than 0.05 was interpreted as statistically significant, indicating a meaningful difference in performance between the prompt strategies. P-values greater than 0.05 suggested that any observed differences may not be statistically meaningful. In summary, the experiment offered a reliable method to assess how different prompting strategies affect the performance and response quality of LLMs.

5 PROJECT REQUIREMENTS AND DATASET IMPLEMENTATION RESULTS

The study compared ChatGPT-4-mini and YorkGPT to evaluate their effectiveness in handling both general scientific questions and task-specific queries. The objective was to assess how each prompting technique affects clarity, accuracy, and completeness in responses. To achieve this, various tools and procedures were used to evaluate the impact of different prompting methods on both the model's performance.

To evaluate model performance, a custom scoring rubric was applied. Each model response was scored from 1 to 10 on four evaluation criteria, across all three prompt types, with higher scores reflecting better performance. This produced a total of 12 scores per model for each prompt strategy (3 prompts $\times$ 4 criteria).

Scores were assigned using a standardized scoring rubric designed to ensure consistency across different prompt types and model responses. YorkGPT's Zero-shot responses performed the weakest, especially in reasoning and completeness, indicating that minimal guidance reduced quality. Few-shot prompting (York GPT) improved scores across relevance, clarity, completeness, and reasoning. Chain-of-Thought prompting (York GPT) consistently delivered the strongest results in reasoning and completeness. A similar pattern emerged with ChatGPT-4-mini, where Few-shot and Chain-of-Thought prompts generally outperformed Zero-shot. These observed trends in the raw scores provide preliminary evidence of performance variation across prompting techniques. To determine whether these differences were statistically significant, paired t-tests were conducted using the mean scores for each prompting strategy along with their corresponding p-values. The Zero-shot strategy for ChatGPT produced a mean score of 5, while Few-shot and Chain-of-Thought (Cot) both achieved a mean score of 8, indicating that additional context or examples enhanced response quality. In contrast, YorkGPT demonstrated more variation. The Zero-shot approach scored 4.25, the lowest among all configurations, while Few-shot improved to 7.625, and Chain-of-Thought (Cot) further increased to 8.875, the highest mean observed in the study. These results suggest that both models benefited from more structured prompt strategies.

To ensure consistency, prompts were implemented programmatically. Python code used to define the ChatGPT-4-mini prompts and demonstrates how the dataset was structured for evaluation. The YorkGPT prompts followed a similar structure, tailored to a domain-specific task

Each prompt type was given a specific token limit to balance response length and clarity in the ChatGPT-4-mini experiment. The script used to assign token limits, which were set as follows:

- 100 tokens for zero-shot prompts to ensure concise responses.
- 250 tokens for few-shot prompts to allow for examples and details.
- 300 tokens for CoT prompts to accommodate logical reasoning.

The dataset for ChatGPT-4-mini experiments focused on general knowledge queries, such as explaining photosynthesis. In contrast, YorkGPT's dataset included York-specific queries, like email activation processes. For example, few-shot prompts in YorkGPT experiments featured examples of account creation to guide users through email activation steps. Similarly, ChatGPT-4-mini's experiments used examples of water absorption and sunlight capture to contextualize the explanation of photosynthesis processes. These tailored datasets enabled both models to deliver responses relevant to their respective domains (Hsieh *et al.* 2023). Token constraints were applied in the ChatGPT-4-mini experiments to ensure consistent outputs. This approach, influenced by (Zhou *et al.* 2022), helped control verbosity while maintaining clarity in the responses. The experiments demonstrated that adapting prompt strategies to the task and dataset significantly enhances model performance, reaffirming findings in prior studies on the impact of tailored prompting (Cao *et al.* 2023).

6 DISCUSSION

This research explored how effective three prompting methods—zero-shot, few-shot, and chain-of-thought (CoT)—were when applied to Chat GPT-4-mini and YorkGPT, which is tailored for York College use cases. The purpose was to analyze how each technique influenced clarity, completeness, relevance, and reasoning quality across both general and York-specific tasks. The findings showed that each strategy produced different outcomes. Zero-shot prompts often led to brief responses that missed important steps, such as troubleshooting in YorkGPT or photosynthesis stages in Chat GPT-4-mini 's responses. This aligns with prior research suggesting that zero-shot is suitable for straightforward tasks but less effective for complex, multi-step questions (Cao *et al.* 2023). Few-shot prompting, by contrast, incorporated guiding examples that made responses complete and more organized, especially when including IT-related context for YorkGPT or deeper science content for Chat GPT-4-mini. This supports previous findings on the strengths of few-shot methods in improving clarity and adaptability (Sahoo *et al.* 2024). CoT prompting worked particularly well in tasks that demanded logical thinking. It generated logically structured responses, but they were lengthy —an issue also mentioned by (Jin *et al.* 22025). Overall, the study emphasizes the importance of choosing an appropriate prompting technique to enhance the

LLM's performance. Few-shot prompting balanced clarity and detail, CoT excelled in logical structure, and zero-shot was most effective for simple queries.

Results from zero-shot prompts produced fast but shallow replies, often missing important details like email setup steps in YorkGPT or the full explanation of photosynthesis stages in ChatGPT-4-mini. These responses were short and efficient but lacked the depth needed for more complex or multi-step tasks. Few-shot prompting generated more well-rounded and thorough responses by including examples that helped the model better grasp the task. This approach was especially useful in YorkGPT, where example-based prompts led to clearer instructions, and in ChatGPT 4-mini, where scientific explanations became more detailed and structured (Sahoo *et al.* 2024). CoT prompts gave the most logical and in-depth answers by walking through tasks step by step, which helped in tasks requiring reasoning or multiple stages of explanation. However, this strategy occasionally resulted in longer responses than necessary, which may not always be ideal for users looking for quick answers. To further support these observations, a series of paired t-tests was conducted to determine whether the observed differences in performance across prompt strategies were statistically significant.

For both ChatGPT-4-mini and YorkGPT, zero-shot vs. few-shot comparisons yielded p-values well below the $\alpha = 0.05$ significance threshold (0.024 and 0.0057, respectively), indicating that few-shot prompting significantly outperformed zero-shot in both models. These findings statistically validate the earlier observation that zero-shot responses were consistently weaker in depth and clarity. However, when comparing zero-shot vs. chain-of-thought, the p-values (0.0663 for ChatGPT-4-mini and 0.0085 for YorkGPT) revealed mixed outcomes. While YorkGPT showed a statistically significant improvement with chain-of-thought prompting, ChatGPT's result narrowly missed the significance threshold. This suggests that although chain-of-thought was descriptively better, the evidence was not strong enough to claim a statistically meaningful difference for ChatGPT at the $\alpha = 0.05$ level. In the few-shot vs. chain-of-thought comparison, both models returned p-values above 0.05 (1.0 for ChatGPT-4-mini, 0.0632 for YorkGPT), suggesting no statistically significant difference between these two strategies. This implies that while CoT may appear more logical or structured, it is not consistently superior to few-shot prompting from a statistical standpoint. These findings are visualized in Figure 3, a bar chart that displays the p-values for each pairwise comparison between prompt strategies.

Together, the statistical results and observational findings support the conclusion that few-shot prompting is consistently effective. Zero-shot approaches tend to underperform, especially on complex tasks. Chain-of-thought prompting shows strength in logical reasoning but yields mixed statistical significance. These differences highlight that each prompt strategy has its strengths depending on the task at hand. Selecting the right strategy based on task complexity is essential for improving performance across contexts (Sahoo *et al.* 2024).

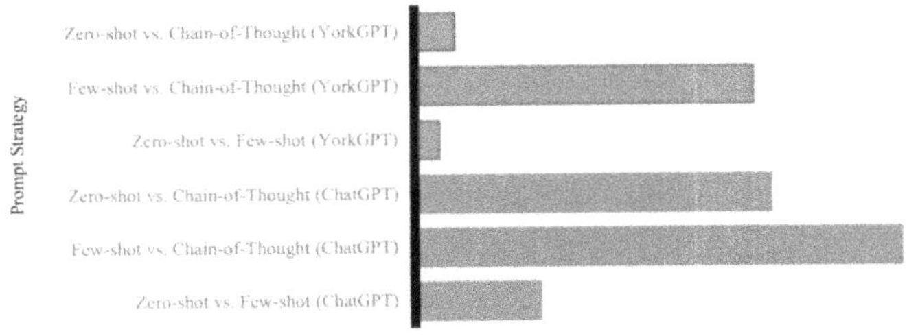

Figure 3. P-values for prompt strategy comparisons.

7 LIMITATIONS AND FUTURE WORK

This study showed that prompt engineering can strongly influence the performance of LLMs, but several limitations were identified. A major challenge involved the inconsistency in responses, which stemmed from the inherent randomness in how LLMs produce text. This aligns with (Liu *et al.* 2024), who observed that the unpredictable output of models like ChatGPT is largely due to their design architecture. In this study, for example, ChatGPT-4-mini occasionally produced different outputs for the same prompt, especially in zero-shot and few-shot conditions. This suggests that even well-designed prompts can yield unstable results depending on how the model samples text. This highlights the need for more refined prompt strategies that help produce consistent outputs (Liu *et al.* 2024). Another limitation involved token truncation during the ChatGPT-4-mini experiment. In chain-of-thought (CoT) prompts, some responses were cut off when they exceeded the token limit, resulting in incomplete answers. (Cao *et al.* 2023) also observed that strict token constraints can limit a model's ability to generate complete, detailed, or multi-step responses. This issue was especially noticeable in longer CoT responses, where key parts of reasoning were sometimes omitted. To mitigate this, future work could explore dynamic token allocation or truncation warnings during response generation to alert users. A further limitation relates to the task-specific performance differences observed between ChatGPT-4-mini and YorkGPT. While YorkGPT performed well on institution-specific tasks—such as answering questions related to York College—its performance declined in more general scientific or open-domain prompts. In contrast, ChatGPT-4-mini was more robust across general domains but lacked depth on York-specific content. This difference underscores the tradeoff between specialization and generalizability in LLMs.The use of a domain-specific dataset for YorkGPT also presented both strengths and weaknesses. While YorkGPT performed well in tasks related to York College, its smaller and narrower dataset limited its ability to handle general topics. (Liu *et al.* 2024) emphasized that diverse and large-scale datasets are important for building models that perform well across different subjects. The YorkGPT training dataset, sourced from the publicly available York College website, is valuable for building contextual responses in a campus-specific setting. However, its limited scope restricts the model's adaptability outside of that niche.To address these limitations, future work should explore ways to reduce response variability and improve the model's ability to carry context over longer outputs. Incorporating methods such as temperature tuning or response re-ranking could help reduce randomness in generated answers. Adding a system that allows the model to adjust its responses based on previous user input—like a feedback loop—could also help the model generate more accurate and personalized answers (Cao *et al.* 2023). Broadening the YorkGPT dataset to cover more diverse topics could enhance its ability to generalize while maintaining its effectiveness in specialized tasks (Liu *et al.* 2024). Additionally, (Liu *et al.* 2024) highlighted ethical concerns related to how prompts are designed. As prompt engineering becomes more powerful, future research should include clear safeguards to prevent harmful use and ensure that these technologies are applied responsibly for public benefit.

8 CONCLUSIONS

This research demonstrates how a prompt is framed directly influences the clarity and effectiveness of responses produced by LLMs. Through the evaluation of three prompting strategies—zero-shot, few-shot, and chain-of-thought—on Chat GPT-4-mini and YorkGPT, the results showed that few-shot and chain-of-thought methods led to responses that were more thorough, coherent, and logically structured. These findings support the original hypothesis that well-designed prompts improve LLM output quality. The results are in line with existing studies by (Sahoo *et al.* 2024) and (Jin *et al.* 2025), which emphasize that example-based and step-by-step prompting improve the reasoning and clarity of language model responses. This outcome is particularly important as LLMs are increasingly used in education, customer support, and workplace tools where accuracy and completeness are essential. In these practical applications, few-shot prompting can support student learning by offering structured examples that clarify expectations and guide understanding. Similarly, chain-of-thought prompting enhances multi-step reasoning in customer service by helping the model produce clearer, step-by-step responses that improve user comprehension and satisfaction. By aligning prompt strategies with specific use cases, developers and practitioners can significantly enhance the quality and reliability of AI-generated outputs. Overall, this study reinforces the importance of selecting the right prompting technique based on task complexity. Effective prompt engineering allows users to optimize LLM performance, ensuring AI-generated responses are more accurate, reliable, and useful across different applications.

REFERENCES

Cao, D. *et al.* (2023) TEMPO: Prompt-based Generative Pre-trained Transformer for time series forecasting, *arXiv [cs.LG]*. Available at: http://arxiv.org/abs/2310.04948.

Cao, J. *et al.* (2025) A study on prompt design, advantages and limitations of ChatGPT for deep learning program repair, *Automated software engineering*, 32(1). Available at: https://doi.org/10.1007/s10515-025-00492-x.

Hewing, M. and Leinhos, V. (2024) The Prompt Canvas: A literature-based practitioner guide for creating effective prompts in Large Language Models, *arXiv [cs.AI]*. Available at: http://arxiv.org/abs/2412.05127.

Hsieh, C.-J. *et al.* (2023) Automatic engineering of long prompts, *arXiv [cs.AI]*. Available at: http://arxiv.org/abs/2311.10117.

Jin, C. *et al.* (2025) APEER : Automatic prompt engineering enhances large language model reranking, in *Companion Proceedings of the ACM on Web Conference 2025*. New York, NY, USA: ACM, pp. 2494–2502.

Knoth, N. *et al.* (2024) AI literacy and its implications for prompt engineering strategies, *Computers and Education: Artificial Intelligence*, 6(100225), p. 100225. Available at: https://doi.org/10.1016/j.caeai.2024.100225.

Li, H., Leung, J. and Shen, Z. (2024) Towards goal-oriented prompt engineering for large Language Models: A survey, *arXiv [cs.CL]*. Available at: http://arxiv.org/abs/2401.14043.

Lin, Z. (2024) How to write effective prompts for large language models, *Nature human behaviour*, 8(4), pp. 611–615. Available at: https://doi.org/10.1038/s41562-024-01847-2.

Liu, Yi *et al.* (2023) Jailbreaking ChatGPT via Prompt Engineering: An Empirical Study, *arXiv [cs.SE]*. Available at: http://arxiv.org/abs/2305.13860.

Pornprasit, C. and Tantithamthavorn, C. (2024) Fine-tuning and prompt engineering for large language models-based code review automation, *Information and software technology*, 175(107523), p. 107523. Available at: https://doi.org/10.1016/j.infsof.2024.107523.

Patel, H. & Parmar, S. (2024) Prompt engineering for large language model,ResearchGate. Available at: https://www.researchgate.net

Sahoo, P. *et al.* (2024) A systematic survey of prompt engineering in large language models: Techniques and applications, *arXiv [cs.AI]*. Available at: https://rotmandigital.ca/wp-content/uploads/2024/09/A-Systematic-Survey-of-Prompt-Engineering-in-Large-Language-Models.pdf (Accessed: June 6, 2025).

Shin, J. *et al.* (2023) Prompt engineering or fine-tuning: An empirical assessment of LLMs for code, *arXiv [cs.SE]*. Available at: http://arxiv.org/abs/2310.10508.

Vaswani, A. *et al.* (2017) *Attention is all you need, Neurips.cc*. Available at: https://proceedings.neurips.cc/paper_files/paper/2017/file/3f5ee243547dee91fbd053c1c4a845aa-Paper.pdf (Accessed: June 6, 2025).

Zhou, Y. *et al.* (2022) Large language models are human-level prompt engineers, *arXiv [cs.LG]*. Available at: https://openreview.net/pdf?id=92gvk82DE- (Accessed: June 6, 2025).

Moving Towards Sustainable Businesses and Developing More Resilient Economies – Rashid and Annansingh-Jamieson (Eds)

Fiscal policy and economic transformation for sustainable growth in KSA

Mohd Naved Khan
College of Administration and Financial Sciences, Saudi Electronic University, Riyadh, KSA

ABSTRACT: This article examines the effect of fiscal policy on economic growth in KSA, a country undergoing significant economic transition. Recognizing the Kingdom's efforts to diversify its revenue streams away from oil, the study uses econometric analysis and descriptive data to examine the connection between government spending, revenue, and economic growth. The data show that government spending has a positive and statistically significant impact on GDP growth, and revenue also has a positive but less evident effect. The article also looks at the impact of the Fiscal Sustainability Program in establishing a balanced budget and developing fiscal discipline. The study also investigates how specific fiscal policy measures, such as renewable energy and tourism expenditures, affect overall economic performance. This report, which emphasizes the efficacy of smart fiscal policy in driving economic development and diversification, offers valuable advice to policymakers navigating Saudi Arabia's changing economic landscape.

Keywords: Fiscal Policy, Economic Growth, Government Expenditure, Government Revenue, Vision 2030

1 INTRODUCTION

Fiscal policy, which includes government taxing and spending (Leibfritz *et al.* 1994), greatly influences a country's economic environment. Knowing how fiscal policy affects economic expansion is essential in KSA, a nation undergoing a major economic transition (Moshashai *et al.* 2020). Oil earnings have historically played a significant role in Saudi Arabia's economy (Al-Moneef 2024). Nonetheless, the nation is working to diversify the country's economy and minimize its dependency on oil through Vision 2030. Significant fiscal reforms, such as adjustments to taxation, spending, and public investment strategies, are part of this ambitious agend. These reforms aim to boost employment, promote economic expansion, and improve the nation's general economic stability. This is likely an intriguing study examining how fiscal policy affects economic development in the KSA.

According to traditional Keynesian models, the fiscal multiplier will be higher than the unit and positive. Fiscal policy influences the hours they have worked through two channels in neoclassical models: intertemporal substitution behavior and the negative wealth effect. However, according to neoclassical models, fiscal multipliers can have positive or negative values based on the type of state expenditure, how it is funded, and the country's overall health. In addition to predicting considerably smaller multipliers equal to or less than the unit, Nominal constraints and limitations on credit are also introduced by modern Keynesian models (AlMarzoqi *et al.* 2023).

DOI: 10.1201/9781003647300-5

1.1 *Government expenditure and revenue diversification*

One essential weapon the government uses to control economic activity is fiscal policy (Junior *et al.* 2022). Governmental expenditure is a crucial component of fiscal policy that has a direct bearing on economic expansion. Saudi Arabia is making large investments in healthcare, education, and infrastructure – critical for sustained economic growth (Singh *et al.* 2022). In addition, by raising non-oil revenues through several reforms and initiatives, the government is working to broaden its revenue streams. Economic resilience and stability depend on this diversity, particularly when dealing with volatile oil prices. By improving economic resilience, effective fiscal policy can help the economy with weather shocks like oil price changes or downturns in the world economy (Mohaddes *et al.* 2022). For example, prompt budgetary actions helped lessen adverse effects on the Saudi economy during the COVID-19 pandemic.

1.2 *Research questions*

(a) How do government spending and revenue affect Saudi economic growth? This subject focuses on the fundamental link between fiscal policy and economic performance.
(b) How effective has Saudi Arabia's Fiscal Sustainability Program been in promoting fiscal discipline and economic stability? This question involves analyzing specific policy interventions.
(c) How much have fiscal policy initiatives contributed to Saudi Arabia's economic diversification and growth?

2 LITERATURE REVIEW

The purpose of this literature review is to investigate how different fiscal policies have impacted the recent economic growth trajectory of Saudi Arabia.

A study, by Alshahrani and Alsadiq 2014, shows that various forms of government spending affect Saudi Arabia's economic growth. This study revealed that healthcare spending, as well as government and private investment, significantly and positively impacted Saudi Arabia's long-term economic growth. Interestingly, the study also found that increasing housing spending and trade openness can temporarily increase economic output.

A related study by Mann and Sephton (2015) looks at the relationship between Saudi Arabia's economic development and private investment concerning various categories of government spending. According to the research, trade openness benefits Saudi Arabia's non-oil industry, and FDP aims to raise the caliber of government services and the business environment. However, spending on defense may limit private investment, which could impede economic expansion in general. Al-Abri *et al.*, (2018) and Sturm *et al.*, (2009) find that, as in other GCC nations, defense expenditures and public sector salaries and wages account for more than 80% of Saudi Arabia's current government spending.

Using a model that considers economic fluctuations (such as booms and recessions), Eid and Awad (2017) investigate the connection between Saudi Arabia's non-oil private sector and government spending. The study discovered that, only during recessions, higher government spending—investment and consumption—had a detrimental influence on the growth of GDP in the non-oil private sector. This point shows a crowding-out effect, in which government expenditure drives out private sector activity during recessions.

Using annual data from 1980 to 2016, Gurdal *et al.* (2020) analysis found a bidirectional association between government expenditure and economic development for G7 countries but a unidirectional causal relationship between tax receipts and spending. Moreover, there was no correlation between tax revenue and economic expansion. Hasanov *et al.*, (2022) looked at the connection between economic growth in Saudi Arabia's non-oil sector and government spending. The results show that the non-oil economy tends to grow as government spending rises, with capital and current spending appearing to contribute to the growth of the non-oil GDP.

A recent study looked at how Saudi Arabia's sustainable economic growth is affected by military spending, tourism, and exports (Aziz *et al.* 2021). The research analyzed short- and long-term effects using an ARDL technique. The findings demonstrated that while oil prices have an adverse effect on economic development, capital, tourism, and non-oil exports had a favorable effect (Aziz *et al.* 2021). The literature emphasizes how crucial it is for Saudi Arabia to diversify its economy by reducing its reliance on oil earnings and increasing its investments in non-oil industries like exports and tourism.

Research evidence indicates that fiscal policy plays a major role in improving Saudi Arabia's economy. Diversified policies promote stability and complement Vision 2030. Future research should further elaborate on the changing relationship between fiscal policy and growth considering changing global conditions.

3 RESEARCH METHODOLOGY

This paper examines the impact of Saudi Arabia's fiscal policy on economic growth, utilizing data from 2015 to 2023 analyzing revenues, expenditures, and GDP. The GDP growth rate is the dependent variable, while the independent variables are government spending, tax revenue, and other fiscal measures. Data from the World Bank, IMF, SAMA, and Vision 2030 (Table 1) support the analysis. Regression techniques will estimate the magnitude and direction of the fiscal effects on GDP. By combining both descriptive and inferential methods, the study provides a clear overview of how Saudi Arabia's budget strategy molds overall economic trends. The relationship between several predictor variables and a criterion variable is modelled by regression analysis:

$$Y = \beta_0 + \beta_1 X_1 + \beta_2 X_2 + \cdots + \beta_k X_k + \epsilon$$

where:
Y = dependent variable (e.g., economic growth measured by GDP growth rate);
X_1, X_2, X_k = independent variables (e.g., government expenditure or tax revenue);
β_0 = intercept; β_1, β_2, β_k = independent variables' coefficients; and ϵ = error term.

In this analysis, the dependent and independent variables are assumed to have a linear relationship. The error components have a normal distribution and constant variance (homoscedasticity), and the observations are unrelated.

The Ordinary Least Squares approach, which minimizes the sum of the squared differences between the observed and predicted values of the dependent variable (Y), is used to estimate the coefficients (β).

The following formula is used to determine the OLS estimates:

$$\beta = (X'X)^{-1} X'Y$$

where X = independent variables' matrix; Y = dependent variables' vector; X′ = X transpose; and $(X'X)^{-1}$ = (X′X) inverse.

Once the coefficients are estimated, the predicted values Y can be calculated as:

$$\hat{Y} = X\hat{\beta}$$

R^2 is computed independently for every dependent variable (GDP) and independent variable (revenue and expenditure) in order to investigate their relationship at a deeper level.

First, the correlation coefficient (Pearson's r) – which quantifies the strength and direction of the linear relationship between GDP and revenue/expenditure – is computed individually for each year with the following formula:

$$r = \frac{n(\sum xy) - (\sum x)(\sum y)}{\sqrt{\left[n\sum x^2 - \left(\sum x\right)^2\right]\left[n\sum y^2 - \left(\sum y\right)^2\right]}}$$

Where n = number of data points (years); $\sum xy$ = sum of the product of GDP and revenue/expenditure for each year; $\sum x$ = sum of GDP values; $\sum y$ = sum of revenue/expenditure values; $\sum x^2$ = sum of squared GDP values; and $\sum y^2$ = sum of squared revenue/expenditure values

After that, the R^2 value can be obtained by square-rooting the correlation coefficient. Following the completion of the calculation of the correlation coefficient r, the R^2 value can be obtained by simply quadrupling the correlation coefficient:

$$R^2 = r^2$$

R^2 shows how much of the variation in GDP is explained by the independent variable, revenue/expenditure, as presented in Table 4. A t-test then checks whether the coefficients are statistically significant, with the null hypothesis that each coefficient equals zero (H_0). The data is organized and analyzed, after which a summary, conclusion, and recommendations are made.

4 RESULTS AND DISCUSSION

According to the regression study, the country's expenditure and economic development in the Kingdom are positively and statistically significantly correlated (Joharji and Starr 2010). This implies that greater government spending on healthcare, education, and infrastructure can support KSA's economic development.

Nevertheless, the data given in Table 1 also demonstrate that the makeup of national expenditures affects economic expansion. In particular, the findings show that capital spending, which includes investments in long-term assets and physical infrastructure—has a bigger effect on economic expansion than current expenditures, which include social services and public sector salaries. (Alshahrani and Alsadiq 2014)

Table 1. Revenue and expenditure.

FY	Revenue	Revenue growth	Expenditure	Expenditure growth	Balance	GDP	GDP growth
2015	612	–	978	–	−366	2510	−12.67
2016	519	−15.20	830	−15.13	−311	2497	−0.52
2017	691	33.14	930	12.05	−239	2681	7.36
2018	906	31.11	1079	16.02	−173	3174	18.40
2019	927	2.32	1059	−1.85	−132	3144	−0.95
2020	782	−15.64	1076	1.61	−294	2753	−12.44
2021	965	23.40	1039	−3.44	−74	3278	19.05
2022	1268	31.40	1164	12.03	104	4157	26.82
2023	1212	−4.42	1293	11.08	−81	4003	−3.70

Source: World Bank, Ministry of Finance, KSA.

Table 1 shows a notable increase in income during 2017 (33.14%), 2018 (31.11%), 2021 (23.40%), and 2022 (31.40%). Revenue dropped noticeably in 2016 (−15.20%), 2020 (−15.64%), and 2023 (−4.42%). With significant increases in 2017 (12.05%), 2018 (16.02%), and 2022 (12.03%), expenditure exhibited an overall increasing tendency. Spending dropped in 2016 (−15.13%), 2019 (−1.85%), and 2021 (−3.44%). From 2015 to 2021, the balance was always in deficit, save for a surplus in 2022. The deficit dropped during 2015 (−366), which was the biggest deficit whereas 2021 shows the smallest (−74) deficit. With a remarkable increase in 2018 (18.40%), 2021 (19.05%), and 2022 (26.82%), GDP displayed marked swings. During 2015 (−12.67%), 2016 (−0.52%), 2019 (−0.95%), 2020 (−12.44%), and 2023 (−3.70%) GDP fell.

This shows Saudi Arabia's economic flexibility and fortitude in responding to both internal and international situations. The notable increase in GDP and income in some years emphasizes the success of policy changes meant to stabilize the economy and promote economic diversification.

Regarding income, the analysis indicates that initiatives to diversify the government's sources of income, such as enacting a VAT and other non-oil taxes, benefit economic expansion. This research emphasizes how crucial it is to lessen the nation's dependency on oil earnings to maintain resilience and long-term economic stability. (Ouassaf *et al.*, 2023)

4.1 *Descriptive statistics*

The descriptive statistics used in this investigation are specified in Table 2. These statistics show variables' variability, central tendency, and distribution. The study includes government spending or tax income as well as economic growth as indicated by the growth rate in GDP.

Table 2. Descriptive statistics.

	Mean	SD	Kurtosis	Skewness	Range	Min	Max
GDP	3133	609.265	-0.587	0.774	1660	2497	4157
Revenue	875.778	254.506	-0.817	0.276	749	519	1268
Expenditure	1049.778	133.111	0.750	0.219	463	830	1293

Source. Authors' calculation.

Table 2 demonstrates that the standard deviation, 609.265, indicates the dispersion around the mean level of GDP. High figures signify higher variability around the average. The kurtosis, at -0.587, is negative, which follows the platykurtic distribution described by Romeo (2020) as lighter-tailed. The positive skewness exhibited at 0.774 indicates a right tail where GDP and, consequently, revenue are longer, hence indicating that in certain periods, there has been growth above the average, translating to high revenue realized. Revenue variability, SD 254.506, is tied to the varying prices of oil, especially the 2015 fiscal restructuring characterized by subsidy cuts as observed by Alsweilem K., *et al.* (2024).

Average revenue is 875.778 units, with the sound standard deviation of 254.506 indicating much fluctuation. Negative kurtosis (-0.817) once more reflects lighter tails, while the positive skewness (0.276) indicates occasionally higher values. Lower kurtosis in GDP than in the expenditure suggests even symmetrical dispersion of GDP. Saudi Arabia, too, started imposing VAT in 2018 at 5% along with further subsidy adjustments.

The average expenditure is 1049.78 units, and the SD (133.111) reflects moderate dispersion, especially over the COVID-19 stimulus and healthcare expansion periods (Alsweilem K. *et al.*, 2024). With positive kurtosis (0.750), the tails are heavier, while the skewness is 0.219, with a right tail longer than the left. Expenditure is greater than revenue every year, suggesting deficits in budgets. The variability in expenditure is less than the variability in revenues, indicating more stable spending.

Table 3. Regression results.

	Coefficients	Standard error	t Stat	P-value	Lower 95%	Upper 95%	Lower 95.0%	Upper 95.0%
Intercept	1478.726	500.012	2.957	0.025	255.240	2702.212	255.240	2702.212
Revenue	2.653	0.390	6.799	0.0005	1.698	3.608	1.698	3.608
Expenditure	−0.638	0.746	−0.855	0.426	−2.463	1.188	−2.463	1.188

Source: Authors' calculation.

The intercept in Table 3 shows that GDP growth is expected to be 1478.726 units when revenue and expenditure are zero. Its p-value, 0.025, shows the statistical significance of the intercept at the 5% level. The government expenditure coefficient is positive and statistically significant: holding other factors constant, a one-unit rise in expenditure is associated with a 2.08-unit rise in GDP. In 2021, fiscal reforms focused on reducing the fiscal deficit, debt management, and diversification of non-oil revenues (Alsweilem K., *et al.* 2024). Revenue has a strong positive effect, where each one-unit increase raises GDP growth by 2.653 units; the very low p-value (0.0005) and the 95% CI [1.699, 3.608] confirm significance. However, the effect of expenditure was −0.638, and its p-value (0.426) and CI [-2.463, 1.188] denote no significance of effect. The revenue strongly drives GDP growth. Figure 1 depicts an increasing trend of GDP over time with a slope of 195.42 and an intercept of -391413, with R^2 of 0.772.

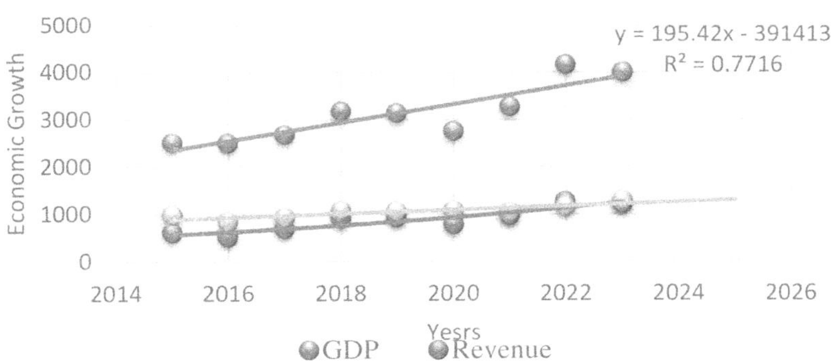

Figure 1. Effect of revenue and expenditure on GDP. Source: Author's calculation.

The exponential trend line suggests that revenue has been increasing at an accelerating rate over time. The Ministry of Finance announced proactive fiscal and structural adjustments in 2023 to support the objectives of Vision 2030 and improve economic resilience (Ministry of Finance, 2024). This type of growth is typical for variables that compound over time, such as revenue from oil exports in an expanding economy. The rapid increase in revenue could be due to rising oil prices, increased production, or successful economic policies aimed at boosting revenue.

The linear trend line for expenditure suggests a consistent increase over time. This indicates that government spending has been growing steadily (Alshahrani and Alsadiq, 2014). The steady increase in expenditure could be due to ongoing investments in infrastructure, social services, and other government initiatives to support economic growth and development.

The expenditure is increasingly related to the rise in GDP, which goes to say that government spending supports growth, though weaker than its impact on revenue, according to regression analysis. The falling and rising tendency of revenue and spending jointly points toward the balanced budget for fiscal stability or sustainable growth. Shaddady A. (2022) emphasizes that aligning income with expenditure will generate steady growth economically.

Figure 1 illustrates the positive effect of fiscal policy measures (revenue and expenditure) on the Kingdom's GDP. The robust linear correlation between revenue and GDP, as shown by the high R^2 value, underscores the importance of revenue generation for economic growth. The steady increase in expenditure further supports this growth, although its impact may be less pronounced.

4.1.1 *Non-significant cost coefficient*

There is no statistically significant relationship between government spending and GDP growth, as indicted by i) a high p-value of 0.426, which is greater than the 0.05 level of significance, indicating that the observed relationship is due to chance; ii) a 95% confidence interval of spending (-2.463 to 1.188) including zero; and iii) the effect is rather weak, in that spending does not appear to strongly or significantly impact GDP growth compared to the other variables.

5 CONCLUSION AND POLICY RECOMMENDATION

Descriptive statistics and econometric analysis showed the government expenditure was positively and significantly related to GDP growth, although with a smaller magnitude of revenue. Further, the targeted investments in green energy and tourism were noted to contribute to long-term sustainable development due to their alignment with Vision 2030.

In this regard, the study concludes by advocating the targeting of high-growth sectors such as renewable energy, technology, and tourism; investing in human capital through education, healthcare, and skills development; the maintenance of fiscal stability through the continuity of the Sustainability Program; expansion of the tax base and improvement in tax collection; promoting R&D and innovation to build a knowledge-based economy; and preparing annual budgets that reflect current fiscal conditions to enhance transparency and strengthen non-oil revenue growth.

6 LIMITATIONS AND RECOMMENDATIONS FOR FURTHER RESEARCH

This study offers valuable insights into the linkage between Saudi Arabia's fiscal strategy and economic growth; however, several limitations do exist. The use of aggregate macroeconomic data might obscure sector-specific or income-group effects, and thus the need for micro-level analysis cannot be ruled out. The restricted timeframe may not show long-term fiscal impacts, and there is a need for studies related to an extended period. Reliance on quantitative methods leaves out qualitative insights that interviews with policy thinkers or industry leaders can provide. Such comparisons with other oil-exporting countries can also clearly spell out the type of fiscal measures that best support diversification and sustainable growth. Addressing these deficiencies would yield a more comprehensive understanding of the role of fiscal policy in shaping the economic future of Saudi Arabia.

REFERENCES

Al-Abri, A., Genc, I.H., and Naufal, G. (2018). The impact of government spending on GDP in a remitting country. *The IZA Institute of Labor Economics,* https://docs.iza.org/dp11676.pdf

AlMarzoqi, R., Ben Slimane, S., and Altamimi, S. (2023). Nonlinear fiscal multipliers in Saudi Arabia. *Economies,* 11(1). https://10.3390/economies11010011

Al-Moneef, M. (2002). The role of oil and gas in the saudi economy: The interaction between economic development and oil and gas strategies. *The Journal of Energy and Development,* 28(1), 95–106. http://www.jstor.org/stable/24808867

Alshahrani, S.A., and Al-Sadiq, A. (2014). Economic growth and government spending in Saudi Arabia: An empirical investigation. *International Monetary Fund.* https://10.5089/9781484348796.001

Alsweilem, K., Lepech, M., Monk, A., and Rietveld, M. (2024). Saudi Arabia: From the big push to the long push building resilience beyond vision 2030. *Center for Sustainable Development and Global Competitiveness at Stanford University and the Stanford Research Initiative,* https://sdgc.stanford.edu/sites/g/files/sbiybj18741/files/media/file/saudi-resilience_big-to-long-push_1_aug_24.pdf

Aziz, G., Alsaggaf, M.I., and Khan, M.S. (2021). The significance of military expenditure, tourism, and exports for sustainable economic growth. *Frontiers in Environmental Science*, 9. https://www.frontiersin.org/journals/environmental-science/articles/10.3389/fenvs.2021.800878

Eid, A.G., and Awad, I.L. (2017). Government expenditure and private sector growth in Saudi Arabia: A markov switching model analysis. *Economic Issues, 22*(2), 83–104. https://www.economicissues.org.uk/Files/2017/217Eid_web.pdf

Gurdal, T., Aydin, M., and Inal, V. (2021). The relationship between tax revenue, government expenditure, and economic growth in G7 countries: new evidence from time and frequency domain approaches. *Economic Change and Restructuring,* 54(2), 305–337. https://10.1007/s10644-020-09280-x

Hasanov, F.J., Alkathiri, N., Alshahrani, S.A., and Alyamani, R. (2022). The impact of fiscal policy on non-oil GDP in Saudi Arabia. *Applied Economics,* 54(7), 793–806. https://10.1080/00036846.2021.1966370

IMF Middle East and Central Asia Dept. (2024). *Saudi Arabia: 2024 Article IV Consultation-Press Release; and Staff Report.* International Monetary Fund. https://10.5089/9798400288043.002

Joharji, G., and Starr, M. (2010). Fiscal policy and growth in Saudi Arabia. *American University, Department of Economics, Working Papers,* 6. https://10.2202/1475-3693.1305

Junior, C.J.C., Garcia-Cintado, A.C., and Junior, K.M. (2022). A modern approach to monetary and fiscal policy. *International Review of Economics Education,* 39, 100232. https://10.1016/j.iree.2021.100232

Leibfritz, W., D. Roseveare and P. Van Den Noord. (1994). Fiscal Policy, Government Debt and Economic Performance. *OECD Economics Department Working Paper*, No.144. https://dx.doi.org/10.1787/038702083230

Mann, J., and Sephton, P. (2015). Revising fiscal policy and growth in Saudi Arabia. *Journal of Reviews on Global Economics*, 4(0), 139–146. https://10.6000/1929-7092.2015.04.13

Ministry of Finance. (2024). *Saudi Ministry of Finance Announces Pre-Budget Statement for Fiscal Year 2024.* Retrieved November 6, 2024, from https://mof.gov.sa/en/MediaCenter/news/Pages/News_30092023.aspx

Mohaddes, K., Raissi, M., and Sarangi, N. (2022). Macroeconomic effects of global shocks in the GCC: evidence from Saudi Arabia. *Middle East Development Journal,* 14(2), 219–239. https://10.1080/17938120.2022.2144022

Moshashai, D., Leber, A.M., and Savage, J.D. (2020). Saudi Arabia plans for its economic future: Vision 2030, the National Transformation Plan, and Saudi fiscal reform. *British Journal of Middle Eastern Studies,* 47(3), 381–401. https://10.1080/13530194.2018.1500269

Ouassaf, S., Guendouz, A., and Khababa, N. (2023). The export-economic growth nexus: The case of Saudi Arabia. *Problems and Perspectives in Management,* 12(2), 796–808. https://http://dx.doi.org/10.21511/ppm.21(2).2023.70

Romeo, G. (2020). Data analysis for business and economics. In G. Romeo (Ed.), *Elements of Numerical Mathematical Economics with Excel* (pp. 695–761). Academic Press. https://10.1016/B978-0-12-817648-1.00013-X

SaudiVision2030. (2024). *Saudi Arabia's Vision for the Future.* https://www.vision2030.gov.sa/en. Retrieved 15 October 2024, from

Shaddady, A. (2022). Is government spending an important factor in economic growth? Nonlinear Cubic Quantile Nexus from Eastern Europe and Central Asia (EECA). *Economies,* 10(11). https://10.3390/economies10110286

Singh, H., Singh, A., Alam, M., and Agrawal, V. (2022). Impact of sustainable development goals on economic growth in Saudi Arabia: Role of education and training. *Sustainability,* 14, 1–26. https://10.3390/su142114119

Sturm, M., Gurtner, F., and Alegre, J.G. (2009). Fiscal policy challenges in oil-exporting countries: A review of key issues. https://www.ecb.europa.eu/pub/pdf/scpops/ecbocp104.pdf

Moving Towards Sustainable Businesses and Developing More Resilient Economies –
Rashid and Annansingh-Jamieson (Eds)

Leadership development and succession planning: Ensuring sustainable organizational growth

Jayanthi Rajendran
Associate Professor & Head, Department of English, SRM Easwari Engineering College, Chennai, Tamil Nadu, India

ABSTRACT: In an era of globalisation that transcends borders and entrepreneurial business domains, leadership development and succession planning have emerged as essential strategies for ensuring organisational stability and sustainability. Effective leadership development cultivates a pipeline of capable leaders, while strategic succession planning mitigates risks associated with leadership transitions. This paper explores the interconnection between these two domains and their significance in fostering resilient organizations. The discussion will focus on four key areas: *Building a leadership pipeline*: Organisations must invest in identifying and nurturing talent through structured mentorship programs, leadership training, and experiential learning. Developing a robust leadership pipeline ensures that emerging leaders are equipped with the skills and competencies necessary to address evolving business challenges. *Strategic succession planning models*: A well-defined succession plan integrates competency mapping, leadership assessment tools, and performance tracking. This segment examines contemporary models of succession planning, such as the Nine-Box Grid and talent review processes, to facilitate effective continuity in leadership responsibilities. *Bridging leadership gaps in a digital era*: The rise of digital transformation has reshaped leadership expectations. Organisations must adapt by fostering digital leadership competencies, emotional intelligence, and agile decision-making to navigate complexities in a technology-driven world. *Diversity and inclusion in leadership succession*: Embedding diversity, equity, and inclusion (DEI) into leadership development and succession planning fosters innovation and ensures diverse voices are represented in leadership decisions. This paper underscores the necessity of aligning leadership development with long-term organisational goals to create a sustainable and adaptable leadership framework.

Keywords: leadership development, succession planning, organisational growth, talent management, sustainability, digital transformation, generational leadership

1 INTRODUCTION

In the contemporary business environment, leadership development and succession planning are integral to achieving long-term organisational sustainability and competitive advantage. This work highlights how integrated leadership and succession initiatives contribute to sustainable organisational strength. By synthesising insights from existing literature, examining case studies from various industries, and integrating emerging trends, the paper identifies best practices and strategies for implementing effective leadership pipelines. The research also highlights the implications of digital transformation, generational shifts, and global challenges on leadership strategies. The study concludes with a comprehensive framework and recommendations for aligning leadership initiatives with organisational goals to ensure sustainable growth.

Today's organizations navigate a rapidly shifting landscape marked by volatility, uncertainty, complexity, and ambiguity (VUCA). Globalisation, digital disruption, and shifting

 DOI: 10.1201/9781003647300-6

workforce dynamics are transforming how businesses operate. This paper explores how these processes not only prepare leaders but also foster organisational resilience, adaptability, and innovation.

2 LITERATURE REVIEW

2.1 *Leadership development*

Leadership development literature emphasizes the importance of structured, strategic approaches to cultivating leadership capabilities across organisational levels. Day *et al.* (2014) outlines that effective leadership development involves integrating formal training, experiential learning, and mentoring to build cognitive, emotional, and behavioural competencies. Transformational leadership, as defined by Bass and Avolio (1994), remains a cornerstone of leadership theory, highlighting the importance of vision, inspiration, and individualised consideration in leadership behavior. More recent research underscores the shift from leader-centric models to collective leadership approaches. Yukl (2013) suggests that adaptive and distributed leadership practices are vital in the face of dynamic global challenges. Leadership development programs are now expected to be agile, personalised, and aligned with broader organisational change initiatives (Groves 2007). Research indicates that leadership development significantly enhances employee engagement, drives innovation, and positively shapes organisational culture (Ready and Conger 2007).

2.2 *Succession planning*

Succession planning literature focuses on the identification, preparation, and placement of high-potential individuals into key organisational roles. Rothwell (2015) argues that succession planning must be continuous, inclusive, and data informed to maintain leadership continuity and minimise disruption. Garman and Glawe (2004) further contend that succession planning must be future-focused, incorporating scenario analysis and competency-based assessments. A key trend in recent literature is the movement toward democratized succession planning moving beyond C-suite roles to include mission-critical positions at various organisational levels (Charan *et al.* 2011). Additionally, diversity, equity, and inclusion (DEI) are now essential components of modern succession strategies, ensuring that leadership pathways are accessible to underrepresented groups (Conger and Fulmer 2003).

2.3 *Integration of leadership development and succession planning*

The integration of leadership development and succession planning is well documented in the literature as a best practice for creating sustainable leadership pipelines. Groves (2007) demonstrates that aligning leadership development initiatives with succession planning yields superior organisational outcomes by fostering internal talent mobility, improving retention, and accelerating readiness. The use of competency models, talent matrices, and leadership scorecards is widely recommended for achieving this integration. Research also highlights the importance of organisational culture and leadership commitment in embedding these practices effectively. Without top-level endorsement, leadership development and succession planning often remain isolated initiatives with limited strategic impact (Ready and Conger 2007).

3 THEORETICAL FRAMEWORK

The foundation of effective succession planning lies in human capital theory, which posits those investments in employee development yield long-term organisational benefits

(Becker 1993). Transformational leadership theory underpins leadership development by encouraging organisations to cultivate visionary leaders who inspire and empower teams (Bass and Avolio 1994). Additionally, systems theory and strategic talent management perspectives highlight the need for an integrated approach that aligns individual capabilities with organisational objectives. These frameworks collectively provide a comprehensive exploration of the role leadership development and succession planning play in shaping effective leadership pipelines. Three major theories provide a comprehensive understanding of leadership development and succession planning are given below.

3.1 *Human capital theory (Becker 1993)*

This theory views individuals' knowledge, skills, and competencies as assets that organisations invest in to achieve long-term returns. By developing internal talent, organisations increase productivity, foster innovation, and ensure continuity in leadership. This perspective underscores the value of structured leadership development and its alignment with long-term organisational goals.

3.2 *Transformational leadership theory (Bass and Avolio 1994)*

This theory emphasizes the role of visionary leadership in inspiring and motivating followers to exceed expectations. Transformational leaders serve as role models, foster trust, and drive cultural change. This theory supports leadership development practices that cultivate emotionally intelligent, adaptive, and future-oriented leaders.

4 METHODOLOGY

This research paper utilises a qualitative research methodology centred on a systematic review and thematic analysis of secondary data. Data sources include peer-reviewed journal articles, books, industry whitepapers, and case studies from reputable organisational and academic databases. The approach involves the following steps:

4.1 *Data collection*

Literature was gathered from scholarly databases such as JSTOR, ScienceDirect, and Google Scholar, as well as reports from consulting firms like McKinsey & Company, Deloitte, and PwC. Keywords used in the search included "leadership development," "succession planning," "talent pipeline," and "organizational sustainability."

4.1.1 *Initial records retrieved*

About 500 to 600 records were found by searching many databases at the same time. This is in line with what has been found in similar systematic reviews, such as 590 initial articles from Scopus and Web of Science in research on leadership development and succession planning.

4.1.2 *De-duplication*

About 550 unique records were left after removing the usual duplicate rates (about 5–10%).

4.2 *Inclusion criteria*

Studies and reports selected were published within the past 20 years, with emphasis on relevance, empirical rigour, and applicability to leadership strategy and planning. Priority was given to literature that examined integrated approaches, emerging trends, and cross-industry case applications.

4.2.1 *Exclusion criteria*

Publications that were published as conference abstracts, editorials, commentaries, or critical reviews were not included since they usually lacked methodological rigor and peer-reviewed empirical data. In order to ensure consistency and relevance, publications that did not provide empirical evidence—such as theoretical or narrative pieces—as well as works written in languages other than English or released prior to 2005 were also disqualified.

Articles discussing general leadership topics that had nothing to do with talent pipelines, succession planning, development, or organizational sustainability were excluded since they weren't relevant to this review's objectives. Studies with inadequate or weak methods were recognized during quality assessment and either excluded or handled carefully in sensitivity analyses.

4.3 *Thematic analysis: Coding process*

4.3.1 *Phase 1 – Data familiarization*

Researchers study a lot of peer-reviewed research, white papers, and case studies over and over again to get a better understanding of the background and subtleties. Memoing in a reflexivity diary helped with interpretative transparency and guided later coding by recording first impressions and new thoughts that came up.

4.3.2 *Phase 2 – Generating initial codes*

A combination of inductive codes that developed naturally from the data and deductive codes that were taken from the body of literature already available on succession planning and leadership development was employed. Phrases and paragraphs were examples of coding units. Code definitions were refined through cycles of extension, merging, splitting, or renaming using CAQDAS tools (e.g., NVivo, ATLAS.ti) or hand annotation.

4.3.3 *Phase 3 – Searching for themes*

The codes were methodically arranged into higher-order theme candidates, including generational dynamics, technology integration, leadership abilities, strategy alignment, and implementation hurdles. The clustering of linked codes into logical topic groupings was facilitated by visual tools such as code hierarchies and thematic maps.

4.3.4 *Phase 4 – Reviewing and refining themes*

For consistency and uniqueness, themes were evaluated against the complete dataset and the coded data extracts. Themes that overlapped or lacked support were combined, reinterpreted, or eliminated. Every theme was guaranteed to express a significant pattern pertinent to the research subject through this recursive method.

4.3.5 *Phase 5 – Defining and naming themes*

A precise, evocative title and scope statement were assigned to each final theme. The codebook contained illustrative data extraction, constituent codes, and theme definitions. Definitions encapsulated each theme's essential significance in connection to ideas of succession and leadership.

4.3.6 *Phase 6 – Producing the analytical narrative*

Themes were written up as a cohesive narrative and integrated into the larger theoretical framework. This involved incorporating thematic discoveries with leadership theory and practice and providing reputable quotes or extracts to back up each theme. Reflective memos recorded the evolution of coding choices over time.

4.4 *Case study selection rationale*

Purposive sampling was used to carefully select case studies in order to optimise theoretical relevance and information richness. Cases were chosen to show significant variance and illustrative complexity in leadership development and succession processes, as opposed to choosing typical or random organisations. Selected cases include are as follows.

4.4.1 Extreme or aberrant examples:

Organisations where succession planning succeeded or failed catastrophically, revealing fundamental mechanisms

4.4.2 *Maximum variation examples:*

Firms from varied sectors (e.g., corporate, nonprofit, government) varying in size, leadership pipeline maturity, and usage of technology to demonstrate contrast and support cross-case comparison.

5 DISCUSSION AND ANALYSIS

5.1 *Leadership development*

Leadership development encompasses structured training programs, mentoring, coaching, and experiential learning opportunities. It involves identifying leadership competencies, conducting 360-degree assessments, and fostering emotional intelligence. Programs such as action learning, rotational assignments, and leadership simulations enhance decision-making, strategic thinking, and interpersonal effectiveness. Organisations that invest in leadership development not only enhance individual capabilities but also build a culture of continuous learning and innovation (Day *et al.* 2014). Leadership development should be embedded within the organisational fabric, supported by top management, and aligned with future leadership demands.

5.2 *Succession planning*

Succession planning is the process of identifying and preparing internal candidates to assume key roles when current leaders leave. It ensures business continuity, reduces risks associated with leadership vacuums, and supports organisational memory retention (Garman and Glawe 2004). Effective succession planning involves talent mapping, readiness assessments, and leadership transition strategies. It should be proactive, inclusive, and forward-looking, considering future organisational needs and environmental changes. Organisations must develop comprehensive succession plans that address critical roles across all levels, not just executive leadership.

5.3 *Integration of leadership development and succession planning*

Successful organizations integrate leadership development with succession planning to create robust leadership pipelines. This integration involves assessing leadership potential, mapping career paths, and providing targeted development interventions (Charan *et al.* 2011). The use of talent matrices, leadership competency frameworks, and individual development plans (IDPs) ensures alignment between leadership readiness and strategic objectives. Integrated systems allow organisations to identify gaps, monitor progress, and ensure continuity. This approach also promotes diversity and inclusion by providing equitable opportunities for underrepresented groups to ascend into leadership positions.

6 CASE STUDIES

6.1 *ITC limited*

ITC places a strong emphasis on identifying high-potential leaders early on, followed by cycles of performance reviews and organised cross-functional rotations. By integrating succession planning into routine HR procedures, this integrated approach supports long-term alignment with strategic corporate aims.

6.2 *Tata motors*

Tata Motors runs flagship initiatives like the Management Career Acceleration Track (MCAT) and the Fast Track Selection Scheme (FTSS), which rigorously develop leadership talent through high-profile projects, professional evaluations, and accelerated promotion pathways—ensuring internal and strategic alignment.

6.3 *Tata group (TMTC)*

The Pune-based Tata Management Training Centre (TMTC) offers more than 250 leadership-focused courses, such as executive, strategic, and emerging leaders' seminars. Every year, about 4,000 Tata managers take part, and the centre collaborates closely with international academic institutions to strengthen succession planning throughout the organization.

7 CHALLENGES AND CONSIDERATIONS

Despite its importance, many organisations struggle with succession planning due to a lack of clarity, insufficient data, and resistance to change. Organisational silos, limited leadership commitment, and inadequate tracking systems further hinder success. Overcoming these challenges requires a strategic mindset, cross-functional collaboration, and cultural alignment. Common pitfalls include focusing only on executive roles, neglecting diversity, and failing to communicate succession plans transparently. Addressing these issues involves continuous communication, stakeholder engagement, and alignment with business goals.

7.1 *Lack of strategic integration & data visibility*

Succession planning, talent development, and performance management are often separated in siloed operations. Because of this fragmentation, it is challenging to identify high potential personnel or gauge the success of programs since it restricts visibility of bench strength and preparedness within the organisation.

7.2 *Weak leadership commitment and resistance to change*

In the absence of senior leadership support, succession planning frequently fails. Managers may be unwilling or reluctant to take part in evaluations or mentoring procedures, and resistance may arise from discomfort with turnover or a fear of losing power.

7.3 *Oversimplified criteria and narrow talent pools*

The lack of precise, impartial succession criteria is still another difficulty. When choosing successors, organisations frequently rely on instinct or familiarity, which results in skewed choices and underutilisation of up-and-coming talent. The problem is made worse by an overemphasis on executive positions.

7.4 *Poor communication and low transparency*

Employee engagement and trust are undermined by opaque succession talks that are restricted to boardrooms. Employee annoyance and retention are weakened when leadership standards and pathways are opaque, particularly when workers feel ignored or sidelined.

7.5 *Implementation-specific challenges*

- For succession tracking, a lot of businesses use spreadsheets or outdated HR systems. These solutions produce out-of-date or insufficient insights because they are not scalable, have no real-time updates, and are not integrated with performance or development data.
- *Adoption of new technologies frequently encounters cultural inertia*: unless backed by strong stakeholder involvement and training, staff may perceive succession tech as intrusive or superfluous, limiting uptake.

7.6 *Implementation considerations*

Organizations should take a strategic, systems-based approach to addressing these issues, concentrating on:

- *Cross-functional alignment*: To increase visibility and coherence, integrate talent development, performance, and succession planning systems.
- *Engagement of leadership*: Obtain executive support and directly involve managers through mentoring accountability and formal succession review boards.

7.7 *Industry-specific differences in leadership strategies*

7.7.1 *Manufacturing & physical goods*

The principles of agile manufacturing place a strong emphasis on cross-functional teams and ongoing learning cycles. Self-managing teams and promoting knowledge sharing across operational silos are the main goals of leadership development.

- *Mentoring & Leadership Rotations*: Move high-potential individuals between strategic, R&D, and shop floor positions. To expose leaders to a variety of fields and roles, use stretch assignments and shadowing.
- *Culture Focused on Values*: Give ethical leadership and a solid set of values a priority. Organizations such as TAFE concentrate on integrating ethics and values into leadership transitions.

7.7.2 *Technology & digital services*

In Technology and Digital Services, the style of leadership fosters independence, quick decision-making, and ongoing feedback, making it ideal for volatile, fast-paced settings.

- *Data-Driven Succession*: Proactively uncover and nurture leadership talent by utilising performance indicators and AI-powered evaluations (such as prediction models).
- *Dynamic Pipeline Management*: To stay up to date with new technological requirements and strategy shifts, update leadership development plans every three months.

8 CONCLUSION

Leadership development and succession planning form the bedrock of sustainable organisational growth in today's volatile, uncertain, complex, and ambiguous (VUCA) environment. The convergence of these two strategic initiatives enables organisations to build leadership capacity that is not only aligned with current business objectives but also agile enough to respond to future challenges. By investing in leadership capabilities and establishing robust succession pipelines, companies ensure continuity, foster innovation, and maintain competitive advantage.

The findings of this paper underscore the critical need for organisations to adopt an integrated, system- based approach to talent development. The theoretical frameworks employed—Human Capital Theory, Transformational Leadership Theory, and Systems Theory—collectively illustrate the multifaceted nature of leadership strategy and the importance of embedding these initiatives within the broader organisational structure. When leadership development is viewed as an investment in human capital, guided by transformational principles and supported by interconnected systems, it becomes a catalyst for long-term success.

Leadership development and succession planning are vital to building resilient organisations capable of sustaining long-term growth. By strategically integrating these functions, businesses can mitigate leadership gaps, foster innovation, and enhance adaptability. As organisations face rapid technological, social, and environmental changes, cultivating a robust leadership pipeline is not just a competitive advantage but a strategic necessity. A proactive, inclusive, and data-informed approach to leadership development and succession planning will empower organisations to thrive in a dynamic global landscape.

9 RECOMMENDATIONS

Leadership resilience that strikes a balance between present performance requirements and future preparation is created when succession planning and leadership development come together. Theoretical frameworks like as Systems Theory, Transformational Leadership Theory, and Human Capital Theory emphasise the need for institutional integration of leadership strategy as a systemic investment in organisational capacity. The results validate that the cornerstones of successful implementation in many situations are cultural support, strategic alignment, and ongoing evaluation.

REFERENCES

Bass, B.M. and Avolio, B.J. (1994). Improving organisational effectiveness through transformational leadership. *Sage Journal.*

Becker, G.S. (1993). *Human capital: a theoretical and empirical analysis, with special reference to education* (3rd ed.). Chicago: University of Chicago Press.

Charan, R., Drotter, S. and Noel, J. (2011). *The leadership pipeline: how to build the leadership-powered company* (2nd ed.). San Francisco: Jossey-Bass.

Conger, J.A. and Fulmer, R.M. (2003). Developing your leadership pipeline. *Harvard Business Review* 81(12): 76– 84.

Day, D.V., Fleenor, J.W., Atwater, L.E., Sturm, R.E. and McKee, R.A. (2014). Advances in leader and leadership development: a review of 25 years of research and theory. *The Leadership Quarterly* 25(1): 63–82.

Garman, A.N. and Glawe, J. (2004). Succession planning. *Consulting Psychology Journal: Practice and Research* 56(2): 119–128.

Groves, K.S. (2007). Integrating leadership development and succession planning best practices. *Journal of Management Development* 26(3): 239–263.

Ready, D.A. and Conger, J.A. (2007). Make your company a talent factory. *Harvard Business Review* 85(6): 68–77.

Rothwell, W.J. (2015). *Effective succession planning: ensuring leadership continuity and building talent from within* (5th ed.). New York: AMACOM.

Yukl, G. (2013). *Leadership in organisations* (8th ed.). Upper Saddle River, NJ: Pearson.

Moving Towards Sustainable Businesses and Developing More Resilient Economies – Rashid and Annansingh-Jamieson (Eds)
© 2026 The Author(s), ISBN: 978-1-041-08875-2

Intrinsic and extrinsic life aspiration satisfaction: A study on generation Z workers

Dwivedula
Brandon University, Manitoba, Canada

ABSTRACT: The study examined life aspiration satisfaction among 426 Generation Z workers using a mixed-methods approach. Principal component analysis identified two distinct aspiration satisfaction factors-intrinsic and extrinsic, explaining 63.5% of variance (KMO = 0.77; $p \leq .00$). Confirmatory factor analysis supported a second-order factor model (CFI=.936; SRMR = .047; RMSEA = .099). Sentiment analysis indicated intrinsic aspiration satisfaction stems from personal growth and aligning work with passion, while extrinsic aspiration reflects financial stability, professional growth and material goals. Theoretical and managerial implications of findings are presented.

Keywords: intrinsic life aspirations, extrinsic life aspirations, Generation Z, empirical research

1 INTRODUCTION

The modern work environment, shaped by knowledge-based roles, flexibility, and automation, emphasizes continuous learning, adaptability, and well-being. Broader societal expectations-corporate social responsibility, diversity and inclusion, and sustainability -further redefine work. As Generation Z enters the workforce, understanding their values, aspirations, and satisfaction at work is crucial (Plakhotnik *et al.* 2024). This study examines Generation Z's fulfillment of life aspirations at work using a cross-sectional, mixed-method design across industries and regions.

2 LITERATURE REVIEW

2.1 *Defining life aspirations*

The satisfaction of life's aspirations is intertwined with personal and work goals, though prioritizing one domain may limit others. Viñas-Bardolet *et al.* (2020) identify two perspectives: the "top-down" view, where life satisfaction stems from stable socio-economic and personal traits (Rostovskaya 2023) and the "bottom-up" view, where satisfaction arises from domains such as health, work, and family (Recksiedler *et al.* 2019). However, research on life aspirations research in case of Generation Z workers is sporadic. The aspiration index, grounded in self-determination theory (Deci and Ryan 2000; Ryan and Deci 2017) offers a framework to assess this construct (Nishimura and Komura 2023).

2.2 *Aspiration index scale*

This study builds on extensive prior research on the Aspiration Index (Kasser and Ryan 1993; Schmuk *et al.* 2000; Ryan *et al.* 1999; Utvaer *et al.* 2014; Ewa; Sonmez 2023) to classify Generation Z employees' life goals into intrinsic and extrinsic aspirations.

DOI: 10.1201/9781003647300-7

3 METHODOLOGY

3.1 *Method*

A mixed-method approach was employed using an online survey (Google Forms; approved by author's university research ethics committee) comprising seven structured and one open-ended question, with informed consent and data management details was shared with 500 responses.

3.2 *Sample*

Using snowball sampling, 426 valid responses were obtained, consistent with prior Generation Z studies (Shen *et al.* 2020; Fratrièová and Kirchmayer 2018). Sampling adequacy was satisfactory (KMO =.65; Pallant 2013).

3.3 *Items*

Table 1 presents seven items based on the Aspiration Index Scale (Kasser 2019), assessing the extent to which work satisfies life aspirations. Each item was explained and one open-ended question was included.

Table 1. Items (description).

GET-Community (example: work for betterment of society, make the world a better place, improve others' lives)
GET-Personal growth (example: to learn new things, doing something meaningful in life, to do what you like doing)
GET-Relationships (example: to have good friends, to share life with someone you love, to feel that there are people who love you and whom you love, long-committed relationships)
GET-Health (example: physically healthy, physically healthy lifestyle)
GET-Fame (example: admired and known by many people, being famous))
GET-Image (example: to have people comment on how attractive you look, to keep up with fashions in hair and clothing, to have an image that others find appealing)
GET-Wealth (example: to be rich, to buy everything you want, financial success, own expensive items)

3.4 *Data analysis*

Table 2 presents the descriptive statistics, inter-item correlations (Get-Intrinsic aspiration satisfaction, and Get-Extrinsic aspiration satisfaction) and residuals for the Aspiration index dimensions among 426 respondents.

Table 2. Summary of aspiration index descriptive statistics, correlations, and residuals.

Variable	N (Valid)	Missing	Mean	SD	Min	Max	Correlations (Intrinsic & Extrinsic)	Residuals
GET-wealth	426	0	4.751	1.684	1.000	7.000	Wealth–Fame (.503), Wealth–Image (.457), Wealth–Extrinsic (.771)	Residuals with Fame (.013), Image (.029)
GET-fame	426	0	3.230	1.918	1.000	7.000	Fame–Image (.616), Fame–Extrinsic (.859)	Residual with Image (.008)

(continued)

Table 2. Continued

Variable	N (Valid)	Missing	Mean	SD	Min	Max	Correlations (Intrinsic & Extrinsic)	Residuals
GET-image	426	0	3.887	1.821	1.000	7.000	Image–Extrinsic (.814)	
GET-personal growth	426	0	5.878	1.255	1.000	7.000	Growth–Relationships (.423), Growth–Community (.514), Growth–Health (.363), Growth–Intrinsic (.706)	Residuals with Relationships (−.010), Community (−.025), Health (.034), Wealth (.010), Fame (.065), Image (.023)
GET-relationships	426	0	5.268	1.521	1.000	7.000	Relationships–Community (.435), Relationships–Health (.538), Relationships–Intrinsic (.770)	
GET-community	426	0	5.207	1.544	1.000	7.000	Community–Health (.418), Community–Intrinsic (.749)	
GET-health	426	0	4.803	1.796	1.000	7.000	Health–Intrinsic (.755)	

Sample sphericity was tested via Barlett's test and factorability via KMO (>.80). Internal consistency used Cronbach's $\alpha \geq 0.70$. PCA with varimax rotation preceded CFA (MLM) following Hu and Bentler's criteria (RMSEA $\leq$ .05; TLI, CFI > .95). Sentiment analysis was performed on the responses obtained for open-ended question.

4 FINDINGS

4.1 *Principal component analysis*

The results of the principal component analysis (with varimax rotation) reveal a two-factor structure that cumulatively explain 63.5 % of variance (Overall KMO=0.77; X2=877; df=21; p<=.001). Components 1 and 2 explain 32.8%, and 30.7% of the variance respectively. Component 1 includes four items- GET-Community, GET-Personal growth, GET-Relationships, and GET-Health. The item loadings are significantly correlated with Component 1, which is labelled 'GET-Intrinsic Aspiration'. On the other hand, Component 2 includes three items- GET-Fame, GET-Image, and GET-Wealth. The item loadings are significantly correlated with Component 2, which is labelled 'GET-Extrinsic Aspiration'. Uniqueness measures the proportion of variance in each original item that is not explained by the principal components. The low uniqueness values suggest that the component explains more of the variance in the original data.

Table 3. Principal component analysis and reliability of get-intrinsic aspiration satisfaction and get-extrinsic aspiration satisfaction items.

Variable / Component	PCA Component 1	PCA Component 2	Mean	SD	Cronbach's α	McDonald's ω
GET-community	.791					
GET-personal growth	.779					
GET-relationships	.748					
GET-health	.656					
GET-fame		.858				
GET-image		.830				
GET-wealth		.723				
GET-intrinsic aspiration			5.29	1.17	.759	.765
GET-extrinsic aspiration			3.96	1.50	.079	.774

4.2 *Confirmatory factor analysis*

Correlations for GET-Intrinsic Aspiration (r=.70-.77; inter-item r=.35-.53; p<=.01) and GET-Extrinsic Aspiration (r=.77-.85; inter-item r=.45-.61; p<=.01) were significant. CFA fit indices (CFI=.93; TLI=.89; RMSEA=.099 [.77-.12], SRMR=.047) indicate acceptable fit (Hu and Bentler 1999; Chen *et al.*.2008). All item loadings were strong (GET Intrinsic Aspiration : λ=.60-.70 ; GET-Extrinsic Aspiration λ=.62-.78; p<=.01; Tabachnick and Fidell 2007)

Table 4. Confirmatory factor analysis-fit measures.

			RMSEA 90% CI				
CFI	TLI	SRMR	RMSEA	Lower	Upper	AIC	BIC
.936	.897	.047	.009	.077	.124	10612	10701

Average Variance Extracted (AVE), Cronbach's Alpha, and Composite Reliability were considered to establish the construct reliability and validity.

Table 5. Construct reliability and validity.

	Cronbach's α (standardized)	Composite reliability	Average variance extracted
GET-extrinsic aspiration	.76	.77	.53
GET-intrinsic aspiration	.76	.76	.44

The discriminant validity was established using Heterotrait-monotrait ratio (HTMT) which is .51 (GET-Intrinsic Aspiration ->GET-Extrinsic Aspiration)

Table 6. Confirmatory factor analysis-loadings.*

Factor	Indicator	Estimate	SE	Z	Standard estimate
GET-intrinsic aspiration	GET-Personal Growth	.759	.0641	11.8	.605
	GET-Relationships	1.084	.0735	14.7	.714
	GET-Community	.995	.077	12.8	.645
	GET-Health	1.267	.088	14.3	.706
GET-extrinsic aspiration	GET-Wealth	1.052	.082	12.7	.625
	GET-Fame	1.501	.091	16.5	.784
	GET-Image	1.411	.086	16.3	.776

*p<=.001.

4.3 *Path analysis*

Path analysis (Figure 1) shows all predictors significantly contribute to their factors. Fit indices (RMSEA=.045; SRMR=.005) indicate excellent fit. Intrnsic aspirations are positively predicted by Get-Health (β=.34), Get-community (β=.32), Get-Relationships (β=.33) and Get-Personal growth (β=.28), while extrinsic aspiration satisfaction are driven by Get-Image (β-.37), Get-Fame (β=.44) and Get-Wealth (β=.38). The correlation between intrinsic and extrinsic aspirations is negligible ($r = -.01$).

4.4 *Sentiment analysis*

Using the Auto Code Wizard function of NVivo 14 software, the study analyzed the statements of the respondents to identify sentiment nodes present in the document. In total, "very positive" sentiments account for 18% , "moderately positive" accounts for 35%, "moderately negative" accounts for 9%, and "very negative" accounts for 9% of the total sentiment references.

5 DISCUSSION

5.1 *A two-factor model of intrinsic and extrinsic aspiration satisfaction among generation Z workers*

Findings indicate that Generation Z prioritizes fulfilling intrinsic psychological needs for growth, autonomy, and relatedness at work (Utvaer *et al.* 2014) while intrinsic aspirations contribute to well-being reflecting early career priorities. Confirmatory factor analysis supports the two-factor Aspiration Index model (Sonmez 2023) with intrinsic and extrinsic aspirations emerging as distinct constructs (r=-.01; $p \leq .01$). Intrinsic aspirations arise from personal interest, competence, and meaningful work (Fratričová and Kirchmayer 2018), while extrinsic aspirations align with financial stability, fame, and positive image-values reinforced by self-concept (Rahayu and Marka 2024). Meaningful work, autonomy, and value alignment enhance engagement and growth (Goh and Lee 2018). Societal value shifts and economic instability further heighten Generation Z's focus on financial security (Terrell 2024).

5.2 *Sentiment analysis of satisfaction of life's aspirations through job*

Respondents' intrinsic aspirations are driven by personal growth, passion and alignment of work with long-term goals, eliciting predominantly positive or very positive sentiments. Positive intrinsic experiences reflect skill development and meaningful work, while negative sentiments arise from misalignment (between work and personal values), lack of growth opportunities, and poor interpersonal relationships, which reduce engagement and satisfaction

(Fratričová and Kirchmayer 2018). Extrinsic aspiration satisfaction is influenced by financial stability, career advancement and material goal attainment. Very positive sentiments emphasize work's instrumental role in achieving long-term material objectives, whereas negative sentiments stem from unmet pay expectations and limited advancement opportunities (Fratričová and Kirchmayer 2018). Overall, Generation Z pursues both intrinsic and extrinsic aspirations, with optimism tied to alignment of personal and professional goals.

6 IMPLICATIONS

6.1 *For practice*

Managerial practices should address both intrinsic and extrinsic aspirations of Generation Z by promoting personal growth, financial stability, and job satisfaction (Venida 2022). Training programs enhancing skills, leadership and career advancement (Paulo and Gochangco 2024), along with transparent promotion systems (Barhate and Dirani 2021) foster motivation. Meaningful work aligned with personal values and CSR engagement enhances intrinsic fulfillment (Chomatowska *et al.* 2021). Integrating both aspiration types effectivel engages early career professionals (Greco and Kraimer 2020).

6.2 *For theory*

The findings confirm that the proposed parsimonious instrument reliability and validly measures intrinsic and extrinsic aspiration satisfaction among Generation Z workers. The two-factor model aligns with prior studies (Kasset 2002; Kasser and Ryan 1993). Integrating quantitative and sentiment analysis (Sonmez 2023) provides novel cross-cultural and affective insights into the emotional and motivational dimensions of life aspiration satisfaction through work.

7 FUTURE RESEARCH

The current paper is a part of the larger research study that investigates the relationship between job characteristics and work motivation, with satisfaction of life aspirations as moderating variables. The study considers Self Determination Theory as a lens to conduct this investigation. The findings of the current paper indicate the relationship between motivating job characteristics and forms of extrinsic and intrinsic motivation. Thus, subsequent research will understand this relationship using structural equation modeling.

8 CONCLUSION

The study examines how work fulfills Generation Z's intrinsic and extrinsic life aspirations, revealing their complementary nature. Aligning passion, growth, and financial stability fosters positive job sentiments, while misalignment and poor pay evoke negativity. The findings guide managerial practices and HR systems to integrate intrinsic and extrinsic motivators (Nieżurawska *et al.* 2022) promoting holistic engagement and well-being.

REFERENCES

Fratričová, J., and Kirchmayer, Z. (2018). Barriers to work motivation of Generation Z. *Journal of Human Resource Management, 21*(2), 28–39. https://doi.org/RePEc:cub:journl:v:21:y:2018:i:2:p:28-39

Gabrielova, K., and Buchko, A. (2021). Here comes Generation Z: Millennials as managers. *Business Horizons, 64*(4), 489–499. https://doi.org/10.1016/j.bushor.2021.03.004https://doi.org/10.1521/jscp.2009.28.9.1100

Gochangco, J. 2024. Exploring the work motivational factors of Generation Z workforce in selected BPO companies: Basis for job satisfaction. *International Journal for Multidisciplinary Research, 6*(3), 1–8. https://doi.org/10.36948/ijfmr.2024.v06i03.20912

Goh, E., and Lee, C. 2018. A workforce to be reckoned with: The emerging pivotal Generation Z hospitality workforce. *International Journal of Hospitality Management, 73*, 20–28. https://doi.org/10.1016/j.ijhm.2018.01.016

Greco, L.M., and Kraimer, M.L. (2020). Goal-setting in the career management process: An identity theory perspective. *Journal of Applied Psychology*, 105(1), 40–57. https://doi.org/10.1037/apl0000424

Hu, L.-t., and Bentler, P.M. (1999). Cutoff criteria for fit indexes in covariance structure analysis: Conventional criteria versus new alternatives. *Structural Equation Modeling: A Multidisciplinary Journal, 6*(1), 1–55. https://doi.org/10.1080/10705519909540118

Kasser, T., and Ryan, R.M. (1993). A dark side of the American dream: Correlates of financial success as a central life aspiration. *Journal of Personality and Social Psychology, 65*(2), 410–422. https://doi.org/10.1037/0022-3514.65.2.410

Kirchmayer, Z., and Fratričová, J. (2018). Barriers to work motivation of Generation Z. *Journal of Human Resource Management, 21*(2), 28–39.

Nieżurawska, J., Kycia, R.A., Ludviga, I., and Niemczynowicz, A. (2022). Model of work motivation based on happiness: Pandemic related study (arXiv:2210.14655). *arXiv.* https://doi.org/10.48550/arXiv.2210.14655

Núñez-Rodriguez, S., de Souza, A.P.L., and Koller, S.H. (2016). Cross-cultural adaptation and psychometric properties of the Portuguese version of the Aspiration Index (AI). *Temas em Psicologia, 24*(3), 1169–1180. https://doi.org/10.9788/TP2016.3-20

Plakhotnik, M.S., Volkova, N.V., and Shahzad, M.B. (2025). Investigating job characteristics of generations Y and Z: A latent profile analysis. *Global Business and Organizational Excellence, 44*, 24–37. https://doi.org/10.1002/joe.22270

Rahayu, T., Marka, M.M., Septanti, A.L., and Nijwah, I.S. (2024). The role of personal branding in increasing Generation Z career success. *Jurnal Ilmiah Manajemen Kesatuan, 12*(3), 673–682. https://doi.org/10.37641/jimkes.v12i3.2530

Recksiedler, C., Settersten, R.A., Jr., Geldhof, G.J., and Hooker, K. (2019). Stable goals despite economic strain: Young adults' goal appraisals across the Great Recession. *International Journal of Behavioral Development, 43*(2), 147–156. https://doi.org/10.1177/0165025418798494

Rostovskaya, T. (2024). Demographic processes in the context of demographic well-being. *Changing Societies* and *Personalities, 8*(2), 261–266. https://doi.org/10.15826/csp.2024.8.2.273

Ryan, R.M. (2017). *Self-determination Theory: Basic Psychological Needs in Motivation, Development, and Wellness.* Guilford Press.

Ryan, R.M., and Deci, E.L. (2000). Intrinsic and extrinsic motivations: Classic definitions and new directions. *Contemporary Educational Psychology, 25*(1), 54–67. https://doi.org/10.1006/ceps.1999.1020

Ryan, R.M., Chirkov, V.I., Little, T.D., Sheldon, K.M., Timoshina, E., and Deci, E.L. (1999). The American dream in Russia: Extrinsic aspirations and well-being in two cultures. *Personality and Social Psychology Bulletin, 25*(12), 1509–1524. https://doi.org/10.1177/01461672992510007

Sonmez, F. (2023). Psychometric properties of the Turkish version of the Aspiration Index and the relationship between aspirations and subjective well-being. *International Journal of Happiness and Development, 8*(1), 28–43. https://doi.org/10.1504/IJHD.2023.10055261

Tabachnick, B.G., and Fidell, L.S. (2007). *Experimental designs using ANOVA.* Thomson/Brooks/Cole.

Terrell, J.D. (2024). Recruiting and retaining millennials and Gen Zs in the workplace. *University of Phoenix Research Center.* https://www.phoenix.edu/content/dam/edu/research/doc/white-papers/educational-instructional-technology/2024/062024-recruiting-retaining-millennials-genz-jterrell.pdf

Venida, A.C. (2022). Exploring Generation Z teachers' work values: Implications to educational leadership and management. *International Journal of Education, 15*(1), 1–9. https://doi.org/10.17509/ije.v15i1.46153

Viñas-Bardolet, C., Guillen-Royo, M., and Torrent-Sellens, J. (2020). Job characteristics and life satisfaction in the EU: A domains-of-life approach. *Applied Research in Quality of Life, 15*, 1069–1098. https://doi.org/10.1007/s11482-019-09720-5

Moving Towards Sustainable Businesses and Developing More Resilient Economies –
Rashid and Annansingh-Jamieson (Eds)

Preventing runway incursions using artificial intelligence: A review of aviation practices

Vasilios (Billy) Constantine Metallinos
York College, City University of New York, Jamaica, United States

ABSTRACT: The focus of this review is the application of artificial intelligence in promoting runway incursion prevention. Runway incursions are threats to aviation safety, which can be mitigated by applying best practices. Best practices are often founded on technological innovation, such as artificial intelligence. The application of artificial intelligence in aviation, specifically to mitigate runway incursions, has been supported by the increasing complexity of airport operations and human error. The need for advanced solutions is underpinned by the essence of promoting situational awareness and providing aviation personnel with proactive alerts to address runway incursions. The review of current literature on the topic resulted in identifying that artificial intelligence can be applied in advanced surveillance systems, predictive analytics, and enhanced alerting systems. Advanced surveillance systems are associated with the application of computer vision and machine learning in promoting the real-time detection and tracking of aircraft and vehicles on the airport surface. Predictive analytics involves the application of artificial intelligence in analyzing historical data and identifying patterns that could result in incursions, fostering preemptive intervention. The application of enhanced alerting systems refers to implementing artificial intelligence-powered systems that provide warnings to pilots and air traffic controllers, promoting situational awareness and reducing response time. In essence, artificial intelligence can promote aviation safety by supporting the prevention of runway incursions. Artificial intelligence needs to be leveraged as a strategy for advancing proactive approaches for mitigating runway incursions. The future of runway incursion mitigation is founded on AI, which supports the need to balance innovation with reliability.

Keywords: Runway incursions, artificial intelligence, aviation safety, pilots, air traffic control

1 INTRODUCTION

Runway incursions are any occurrence at an aerodrome involving the incorrect presence of an aircraft, person, or vehicle on the protected area of a surface intended for aircraft landing and taking off (Federal Aviation Administration [FAA] 2022). There are four categories of runway incursions: Category A, B, C, and D. Category A is assigned to serious incidents, where incidents were narrowly avoided. Category B is an incident where separation is reduced and there is a significant possibility of a collision occurring, which could result in a time-critical corrective/evasive response to avoid a collision. Category C is an incident that can be attributed to ample time and/or distance to mitigate a collision. Category D incidents are runway incursions such as the incorrect presence of a vehicle, aircraft, or person in the protected area, which is designated for landing and take-off of aircraft, but does not have any immediate safety consequences (FAA 2022).

Runway incursions can be grouped into three: Operational incidents, pilot deviations, and vehicle/pedestrian deviations (U.S. Department of Transportation Office of Inspector

DOI: 10.1201/9781003647300-8

General 2025). Operational incidents occur because of an air traffic control (ATC) action or inaction. For instance, when an ATC leaves less than the minimum separation between two or more aircraft, vehicles, and obstacles, or when an aircraft lands or departs on a closed runway. Pilot deviations happen when a pilot's action violates the FAA's regulations, such as failing to comply with ATC clearance or instruction. Pedestrian or vehicular deviation is an event that is caused by the driver of a vehicle, a non-pilot operating an aircraft, or a pedestrian being in any portion of the airport's movement area without the ATC's consent (U.S. Department of Transportation Office of Inspector General 2025).

In the 2024 financial year, there were a total of 1,758 runway incursions in the United States, which was an approximately 12% increase from 2021, but essentially the same as those that happened in 2019 (see Table 1, FAA, 2025a). In 2025, there have been some near misses, which supports the need for continued initiatives to mitigate aviation safety issues. For instance, on February 25, 2025, at Chicago Midway Airport, the crew of Southwest Airlines Flight 2540 initiated a go-around maneuver when Flexjet, a business jet, entered the runway without authorization (FAA 2025b).

Table 1. Total runway incursions financial years 2019-2024.

Financial year	Runway incursions
2019	1,753
2020	1,261
2021	1,574
2022	1,730
2023	1,760
2024	1,758

When runway incursions occur, they result in confusion, incidents, and delays in airport operations (Chen and Juang 2019; Koc and Cınar 2025). As such, it is essential to integrate technological innovation as a strategy for promoting safety and efficiency. Technology-based initiatives such as advanced surveillance, alerting systems, and infrastructure improvements have been implemented to promote runway safety (Pang *et al.* 2025). For instance, Runway Status Lights (RWSL) uses real-time surveillance data to alert aircrews and vehicle operators about any hazardous runway conditions. Surface surveillance systems such as Airport Surface Detection Equipment (ASDE-X) or Airport Surface Surveillance Capability (ASSC) offer air traffic controllers accurate and integrated displays of surface movement. Advancements such as Taxiway Arrival Prediction alert controllers when aircraft deviate from their assigned paths, which decreases misalignment perils (Pang *et al.* 2025). Conversely, the ASDE-X and ASSC do not consider input from ATC radio communication signals, which makes it challenging to check for pilot-ATC communication-induced risks. According to Omosebi *et al.* (2023), the use of ASDE-X and RWSL can decrease the occurrence of runway incursions by 70%.

Advancements in AI provide opportunities to understand and extract information from voice communications using machine learning (ML) (Pang *et al.* 2025). The purpose of this literature review is to explain how AI has been or can be applied to prevent runway incursions. The research questions answered are: (a) What AI has been applied to prevent runway incursions, and (b) How can AI be applied to prevent runway incursions?

2 ARTIFICIAL INTELLIGENCE APPLICABLE IN PREVENTING RUNWAY INCURSIONS

A comprehensive literature search was conducted on Science Direct, Wiley, Sage, and Springer. A search on Google Scholar was conducted to ensure that the literature review was exhaustive. The keywords used in the search are runway incursions, AI, aviation safety, pilots, and air traffic control. Boolean operators AND and OR were used to create search phrases. The search phrases are runway incursions AND AI, runway incursions AND aviation safety, runway incursions AND pilots OR air traffic control AND AI. Studies were considered eligible for inclusion in the review if they were (a) written in English, (b) published between 2018 and 2025, (c) available in full-text, and (d) peer-reviewed or from credible government-funded organizations.

The advancement of technologies such as AI, ML, and deep learning (DL) has provided new approaches for promoting aviation safety (Demir *et al.* 2024). Technology can be used to assess big data, recognize patterns, and identify potential safety risks, promoting proactive action. The technologies that have been implemented to prevent runway incursion include the Surface Awareness Initiative (SAI), AI-enhanced ASSC, and Approach Runway Verification (ARV) (FAA 2024; U.S. Department of Transportation Office of Inspector General 2025). The proposed technologies are creating an AI sensor using a convolutional neural network (CNN), NLP, and AI-powered taxi assist solutions (Chen and Juang 2019; Pang *et al.* 2025; Universal Avionics 2024). Table 2 contains a summary of the AI that has been or can be applied to prevent runway incursions.

Table 2. Summary of AI technologies.

AI implemented	Proposed AI to be implemented
SAI	CNN
AI-enhanced ASSC	NLP
ARV	AI-powered taxi assist solutions

2.1 *Advanced surveillance systems*

Advanced surveillance systems involve the use of computer vision and machine learning in promoting the real-time detection and tracking of aircraft and vehicles on the airport surface (Chen and Juang 2019). The advanced surveillance systems that can be used in preventing runway incursions are SAI, AI-enhanced ASSC, and an AI sensor CNN model. Machine learning can be used to detect and identify airport signs and markings to enhance operational safety, particularly in low-visibility scenarios (Chen and Juang 2019). The outcome is achieved using an AI sensor for detecting the pixels created and modeled using a CNN. Trained deep learning models can be applied to identify and mark runway designation sign pictures within an aircraft's motions at airports. In the study, it was identified that the use of the AI sensor model system can assist pilots by enabling them to identify runway numbers and their relative locations (Chen and Juang 2019).

Notably, ASSC can be expanded with AI-based voice communication to enhance an understanding of surface movement collision risk assessment (Pang *et al.* 2025). The proposed framework contains ASR and surface collision risk modeling. The purpose of the ASR is to process choice communication transcripts, generating information tables that are used as references for creating potential taxi plans and formulating the peril of surface movement collisions (Pang *et al.* 2025). Additional research is needed on the advanced surveillance systems that can be applied in mitigating runway incursions because there is limited evidence and understanding of the subject.

2.2 *Predictive analytics*

Predictive analytics comprises applying artificial intelligence to assess historical data and identify patterns that could result in incursions, fostering preemptive intervention

(Song *et al.* 2018). Predictive analytics involves applying real-time software to assess large amounts of flight data to detect emerging hazards (Bartulovic and Steiner 2023). The adoption of predictive AI can support decision-making that could help mitigate safety risks. For instance, AI models using ML can be implemented to detect unusual patterns such as a vehicle crossing an active runway without clearance or a plane lining up on the wrong landing strip. Predictive analytics can offer real-time warnings to ATCs, vehicle operators, or pilots. There is limited research on the concept, which supports the need for additional research on predictive analytics that can be applied to mitigate runway incursions. The limited research can be attributed to the limited adoption of AI in preventing runway incursions.

2.3 *Enhanced alerting systems*

Runway verification is a major procedure for ensuring that aircraft land on the designated runway during approach (FAA 2024). Reducing the peril of an aircraft landing on the wrong runway is important in mitigating the occurrence of runway incursions. The use of enhanced alerting systems refers to implementing artificial intelligence-powered systems that offer warnings to pilots and ATCs, promoting situational awareness and decreasing response time. The ARV system offers ATCs alerts and notifications if an aircraft is on the wrong taxiway and runway (U.S. Department of Transportation Office of Inspector General 2025). The ARV has been installed at ATC towers across the nation (FAA 2024). The purpose of ARV is to improve ATC's situational awareness of the airport surface, which is essential in promoting safety. The use of ARV provides controllers with audible and visible alerts in the instance where an incoming aircraft is aligned to land on the wrong airport surface. When an aircraft is approaching the airport, the ATC issues a landing clearance. The pilot may believe that they are aligned with the right runway, but they could be lined up with the adjacent one, or even the taxiway. In such instances, the ARV alerts the controller in instances where the aircraft is not aligned with the runway they are authorized to land (FAA 2024).

The ARV is one of the three surface situational awareness incidents that constitute the FAA's surface safety protocol (FAA 2024). The other two are the SAI and Runway Incursion Device (RID). Although RID is not AI-based, the technologies are essential in improving situational awareness. The SAI is a system that uses Automatic Dependent Surveillance-Broadcast (ADS-B) data to show surface traffic to ATCs at airports that lack surface surveillance tools. Aircraft and vehicles that have ADS-B installed appear as icons in the airport map that shows hold ramps, runways, taxiways, and other areas (U.S. Department of Transportation Office of Inspector General 2025). As of October 2024, SAI systems had been installed at Austin-Bergstrom, Indianapolis, Nashville, and Dallas Love Field ATC towers. The FAA plans to install SAI in an additional 55 towers by 2026 (U.S. Department of Transportation Office of Inspector General 2025).

At the Aircraft Electronics Association 2025, Universal Avionics introduced an AI-powered taxi assist solution for mitigating safety issues by decreasing runway incursions (Universal Avionics 2024). Innovation can mitigate errors by leveraging speech-to-text technology developed for noisy environments. The technology functions by assessing verbal ATC instructions and processing them, turning them into visual directions that are displayed on the flight deck. The solution intelligently fuses real-time video analysis from numerous cameras and AI-powered insights, integrated with ADS-B information, to offer a comprehensive image containing visual instructions that are projected to the cockpit and head-up displays. The features that include visual positioning, obstacle identification, traffic awareness, and taxi guidance empower ATCs and pilots to make proactive decisions using real-time data, enhancing safety in the air and on the ground (Universal Avionics 2024).

The system allows pilots to focus on the assigned tasks and decrease distractions because instructions are identified specifically to an aircraft's registration number and call sign (Universal Avionics 2024). The main features of the technology include verification of pilot readback against ATC confirmation, graphical displays containing runway indicators and warnings on navigation maps, and logged clearance instructions offering status updates to pilots at each stage of the taxi process. The suitability of the technology is that it provides complex directions in real-time, decreasing pilots' reliance on memory or handwritten notes (Universal Avionics 2024).

3 CHALLENGES AND FUTURE DIRECTIONS

The runway serves as the start and end of aircraft operations, which makes the facilities' safety essential (Chen and Pan 2021). The emerging AI technologies have the potential to improve aviation safety by assisting airport tower paths in planning to decrease human workload, identify the runway number, determine runway out-of-control areas, and offer judgment to decrease the occurrence of errors. The FAA and its partners need to continue assessing the application of AI in reducing runway incursions. An additional understanding of how AI can be implemented in aviation contexts, specifically in preventing runway incursions, is needed. Although the RID is a memory aid for ATCs and underpins situational awareness of occupied or closed runways, it is not AI-based. Additional initiatives are needed to explore how AI can be integrated into RID to improve ATC's situational awareness using visual and auditory alerts.

Advancements in AI, specifically Natural Language Processing (NLP), can promote understanding and assessing the contextual meaning of the language spoken by humans (Pang *et al.* 2025). The use of NLP helps understand voice communication transcripts, which are also referred to as Automatic Speech Recognition (ASR). Information retrieval involves extracting keywords and useful contexts from ASR-converted texts using contextual or token-based language models through Named Entity Recognition. While NLP has demonstrated accuracy in other domains, the use of the technology in ATC is significantly regulated by communication rules and standards to achieve clarity, safety, and consistency in all interactions, which limits the incorporation of the innovation. There is a gap in understanding how the regulated ATC rules can be incorporated into a data-driven NPL framework (Pang *et al.* 2025).

The FAA should collaborate with industry professionals to develop an AI roadmap for creating a framework for adopting emerging technologies to mitigate runway incursions. Collaboration would ensure that the roadmap addresses practical challenges, such as integrating AI into legacy systems. The roadmap should contain clear timelines and budgets related to the adoption of AI in managing runway incursions. Specific milestones should be outlined in the roadmap, for example, allocating a budget to AI trials, algorithm development, stakeholder workshops, and simulation/testing annually. The primary objective of the roadmap is to create a framework that can seamlessly integrate AI into runway safety systems. A framework would be essential to ensure that the implemented AI technologies complement ATCs and the pilot's role, because all it would take is one missed prediction or inaccurate classification for safety to be compromised. Although the FAA has adopted risk management standards to promote the national airspace, new adaptations are needed based on technological advancements. There is a need to adopt AI risk management methodologies and best practices to promote the sustainability of the technologies. Additional research is needed to explore how AI can be leveraged to enhance the currently implemented runway incursion technologies, such as ASDE-X, RWSL, and ASSC.

4 LIMITATIONS OF THE STUDY

The conducted review is impacted by some limitations. The review was performed to offer an overview of the approaches for preventing runway incursions using AI. For this reason, the researcher did not collect primary data. Rather, the researcher retrieved secondary information published in peer-reviewed articles and credible sources to inform the review. The secondary sources of information could be subject to publication bias, which has a negative impact on the study findings. Another limitation is that the application of AI in aviation is still an emerging concept. For this reason, there is limited literature on how AI has been implemented or could be adopted to mitigate runway incursions. The limitation creates a need to acknowledge that the AI-based initiatives for preventing runway incursions that have been discussed in this paper might not be all the available ones. There is a possibility that there are AI-based solutions for mitigating runway incursions that the researchers did not discuss, especially if the concepts have been discussed in publications that are not freely available.

Another limitation is that some of the discussed AI-based approaches for preventing runway incursions are not FAA-approved. For instance, the AI sensor using CNN and AI-powered taxi assist solutions are mainly theoretical and practical approaches to runway incursions, which have not received FAA approval for use in ATC towers, aircraft, or airports. The other limitation is that, in addition to the limited availability of research on the topic, information on the concepts was retrieved from heterogeneous sources. The heterogeneity of the studies reviewed could have hindered information reliability. The limited availability of literature hindered the development of a synthesis on the effectiveness of AI. The limited evidence hindered in retrieval and synthesis of quantitative evidence on runway incursion reduction rates. The literature gap is also limited in synthesizing literature on the cost estimates associated with the adoption of AI in reducing runway incursions, which creates a need for additional research on the topic. Despite the limitations, the researcher in the review provided an overview of the AI applications that can be implemented to mitigate the occurrence of runway incursions, which contributes to existing literature.

5 CONCLUSIONS

Runway incursions are issues in modern aviation, with data supporting their recurrence, including the near-miss that happened in 2025 at Chicago Midway. The potential for runway incursion occurring makes it essential to integrate technology that can be used to promote civil aviation safety. The integration of AI is one of the transformative tools that can proactively mitigate runway incursions through advanced surveillance, predictive analytics, and enhanced alerting systems. Advanced surveillance systems such as SAI, AI-enhanced ASSC, and CNN-based sensors leverage AI to enhance awareness and decrease the peril of runway incursions. Enhanced alerting systems, specifically ARV and Universal Avionics' Taxi Assist, are essential in decreasing human errors by cross-checking various data sources to ensure that pilots land on the intended runway. The integration of AI-based solutions based on ADS-B can decrease runway incursions. Notably, regulations are a hurdle to AI implementation, such as NLP in ATC communication, because of the existing standards implemented to ensure clarity. Stringent FAA standards for ATC communication clarity could be addressed by proving that NLP streamlines pilot-ATC communication. Stakeholder resistance because of concerns about AI's reliability and the extensive budget requirement associated with the adoption of technology can be mitigated by supporting that the innovation will promote aviation safety. Transparency in the application and anticipated outcomes of adopting AI can help in decreasing skepticism among stakeholders. The application of AI in the aviation industry, particularly in the mitigation of runway incursions, is still in research or early development. The integration of AI into systems such as ASDE-X could provide a hybrid solution, promoting aviation safety. The recommendation for the FAA is to engage in industry collaboration to create an AI adoption roadmap for preventing runway incursions. The roadmap could standardize peril management and support AI innovation in approaches for preventing runway incursions. In the roadmap, clear budget requirements, deliverables, and timelines should also be outlined. Additionally, the FAA needs to implement specific policies, such as mandating the use of AI-enhanced runway alerts by 2028 and assigning budgets to airports to promote adoption. In essence, the adoption of AI can mitigate human errors and promote situational awareness, preventing runway incursions. Conversely, despite the potential application of AI, stakeholder collaboration, a regulatory framework, and rigorous validation are still needed. It will be important to balance innovation with reliability, ensuring that AI complements ATS's and pilots' roles.

REFERENCES

Bartulovic, D., and Steiner, S. (2023). Predictive analysis of airport safety performance: Case study of Split Airport. *Aerospace* 10(3): Article 303. https://doi.org/10.3390/aerospace10030303

Chen, J., and Pan, W. (2021). Study on airport runway incursion monitoring based on computer vision. *International Conference on Civil Aviation Safety and Information Technology* 1(1): 1328–1333. https://doi.org/10.1109/ICCASIT53235.2021.9633593

Chen, Z.H., and Juang, J.C. (2019). Mitigation of runway incursions by using a convolutional neural network to detect and identify airport signs and markings. *Sensors & Materials* 31(12): 3947–3958. https://doi.org/10.18494/SAM.2019.2303

Demir, G., Moslem, S., and Duleba, S. (2024). Artificial intelligence in aviation safety: Systematic review and biometric analysis. *International Journal of Computational Intelligence Systems* 17(1): 1–30. https://doi.org/10.1007/s44196-024-00671-w

Federal Aviation Administration. (2022). *Runway incursions*. FAA.

Federal Aviation Administration. (2024). *FAA rolls out new technology for controllers to improve surface safety at the nation's airports. FAA.*

Federal Aviation Administration. (2025a). *Runway safety statistics*. FAA.

Federal Aviation Administration. (2025b). *FAA statements on aviation accidents and incidents. FAA.*

Koc, E., and Cınar, E. (2025). An examination of serious runway incursion incidents resulting from air traffic control services. *Journal of Aviation* 9(1): 64–81. http://dx.doi.org/10.30518/jav.1552352

Odisho, E.V., Truong, D., and Joslin, R.E. (2022). Applying machine learning to enhance runway safety through runway excursion risk mitigation. *Journal of Aerospace Information Systems* 19(2): 98–112. https://doi.org/10.1109/ICNS52807.2021.9441554

Omosebi, O., Azimi, M., Olowokere, D., Wanyan, Y., Zhao, Q., and Qi, Y. (2023). Investigating runway incursion incidents at United States airports. *Future Transportation* 3(4): 1209–1222. https://doi.org/10.3390/futuretransp3040066

Pang, Y., Kendall, A.P., Porcayo, A., Barsotti, M., Jain, A., and Clarke, J.P. (2025). From voice to safety: Language AI-powered pilot-ATC communication understanding for airport surface movement collision risk assessment. *arXiv Preprint* 1(1): 1–10.

Song, I., Cho, I., Tessitore, T., Gurcsik, T., and Ceylan, H. (2018). Data-driven prediction of runway incursions with uncertainty quantification. *Journal of Computing in Civil Engineering* 32(2): Article 04018004. http://dx.doi.org/10.1061/(ASCE)CP.1943-5487.0000733

U.S. Department of Transportation Office of Inspector General. (2025). *FAA has taken steps to prevent and mitigate runway incursions, but work remains to improve data analytics and implement key initiatives*. DOT OIG.

Universal Avionics. (2024). *Universal Avionics enhances awareness beyond cockpit with augmented reality and artificial intelligence.*

Moving Towards Sustainable Businesses and Developing More Resilient Economies – Rashid and Annansingh-Jamieson (Eds)
© 2026 The Author(s), ISBN: 978-1-041-08875-2

Urban public transportation demand, pricing, and smart mobility

Clifford N. Opurum
Department of Business & Economics, School of Business & Information Systems, York College, City University of New York, USA

ABSTRACT: The metropolitan areas have continued to experience population explosions, and a larger percentage of that growth tends to concentrate in the urban centers. Mobility in urban areas has been a major challenge to transportation authorities. With the ever-increasing volume of activities associated with the rapid population growth, the need for environmentally friendly means of mobility in the city centers cannot be overemphasized. This research critically examines the various pricing policies and congestion mitigation measures in selected cities. The objective is to understand the rationale behind such policies and their feasibility. Equitable transit fare policy and flexible congestion tolls will improve urban mobility and air quality.

Keywords: Congestion pricing, Congestion relief zone, Electronic road pricing (ERP), Price elasticity of demand, Urban public transportation, Demand and pricing, Mass transit, Smart urban mobility, Traffic congestion, Air pollution, Central business district (CBD), Congestion mitigation

1 INTRODUCTION

Mobility is essential for the economic success of any region, and more so, for the urban economy. The role of urban public transportation in the economic vitality of cities and nations cannot be overemphasized. The goal of public transportation is safe, on-time arrival at the least cost. Today, however, that goal has been expanded to include minimum pollution and sustainability, and together, they represent key performance measures of any transportation system. A major concern regarding this trend is the increasing level of traffic congestion and the associated atmospheric pollution, which, together, have continued to negatively impact the economic and social well-being of our societies, as well as destroying the quality and ambience of the natural environment.

This research focuses on how we could shift the modal choice of urban travelers from the less efficient modes of travel to more energy-efficient and sustainable smart modes of urban transportation. To this end, the relationship between public transportation pricing and travel demand will be thoroughly explored, as well as a comparative review of the various modes of mobility in a typical urban environment, such as New York City, and their respective impacts on the social and economic well-being of the urbanites. Also, with the increasing level of concerns regarding exhaustion of our traditional fuel energy sources and the associated ill-health they cause, the need to advocate for and support mass transit becomes more urgent.

In general, urban public transportation, otherwise known as mass transit (or people's mover), is the engine that drives the urban economy. It represents one of the observable elements (artifacts) of urban centers' cultures and has developed from its infant stage of horse-drawn carriages or the horsecar era (1855-1890) to present-day jet speed rail systems (Opurum 2012). Without mass transit, the urban economy will be paralyzed.

Pricing of public transportation service is a major operating issue. The process of determining a realistic exchange value of a product, expressed in monetary terms, otherwise known as pricing, has been a very challenging issue for the public transportation industry.

DOI: 10.1201/9781003647300-9

Equitable pricing policies could help towards making the contribution of public transportation to the socioeconomic well-being of our society more effective by encouraging ridership or patronage. Evidently, over-pricing or under-pricing the service has some economic implications for both the operators and users of public transportation services, alike. Logically speaking, a broader review of public transport pricing is necessary for a better understanding of its relationship to travel demand. In other words, we first of all need to fully understand the system itself, and then examine price (fare) elasticity of transit travel demand and the effect of changes in fare on ridership and revenue. But first and foremost, we must understand the characteristic nature of scheduled urban public transportation.

2 THEORETICAL RATIONALE OF THE RESEARCH

The need to protect and sustain the environment has become absolutely necessary as the size of many metropolitan regions continues to grow in terms of their populations and economic activities. The air and noise pollution caused by vehicular traffic congestion in the central business districts (CBDs) of many major urban centers have contributed to the increasing respiratory and other health problems in our society. The objective is to identify the most efficient, cost-effective, and sustainable means of travel in the CBDs of major cities around the globe and the efforts cities are making to mitigate congestion and air pollution in their central business districts.

3 METHODOLOGY

To gain a full understanding of the pricing practices and environmental pollution mitigation measures that exist in the public transportation industry, the fare policies and vehicular atmospheric pollution measures of known major public transportation operators and cities in different parts of the world were critically reviewed. A comparative analysis of congestion mitigation schemes in selected major world cities (New York City, London, Stockholm, and Singapore) is made using data obtained from the New York Metropolitan Transportation Authority (MTA) and the Tri-State Transportation Campaign.

4 REVIEW OF RELATED LITERATURE

The literature review focused on the characteristics of public transportation and the pricing and congestion mitigation practices used by major public transport operators and cities in developed economies. First, an examination of the nature of urban public transportation and the various pricing practices was thoroughly performed, as featured in the following sections.

4.1 *The characteristic nature of urban public transportation*

There are four prominent characteristics of scheduled urban public transport services. First, it is a highly perishable product sold in the form of seat-miles or vehicle-miles, and it is wasted if not used instantly, once supplied. Unsold seat-miles can never be offered again for sale; they can be offered for sale only in one place, and at one occasion. In other words, the same service cannot be offered for sale twice.

Second, the use of local public transport in urbanized areas vis-à-vis rural environments is relatively high, and this arises from a complicated interaction of effects (Nash, 1982). The factors involved in this respect include tougher traffic and parking regulations in the city centers, relatively high density of population, which makes it possible to provide a good-quality public transport compared with rural areas, and greater accessibility of transit facilities to the pedestrians, which leads to lower car ownership for a given level of income. In addition to this, urban public transport operates in a local market and is, therefore, characterized with relatively low mean trip lengths, although this varies from location to location.

Third, transit service is a business affected by a wide range between peak and off-peak demands. It deals, as a rule, with large masses of people traveling in one direction in the morning hours and in the opposite direction in the late hours of the afternoon. Between peak and off-peak periods during weekday when traffic conditions make its use most convenient, the private automobile renders an increasing service for urban travel. This leads to the problem of utilization of personnel, facilities and equipment during off-peak. As Nash (1982) emphasized, the problem of the peak has been getting worse, as the city centers become more exclusively white collar with common hours of work, and as work and school hours move even closer together.

Four, the transit industry possesses only the roughest means of measuring the service, which it sells to the public (Vickers, 1934). Traditionally, the closest unit of measurement that has been used is that of zoning by which it is usually understood that a passenger may travel between two fixed points for a certain price or cover any part of the distance between those two fixed points at the same price. This means that the passenger can purchase a whole unit of service for a certain price but any part of that unit costs him the same price. It is obvious that the establishment of fixed zones gives, in no sense, a scientific metering, such as are used in the public utility industry. For instance, if a zone is a mile long, there is no means of knowing whether the passenger traveled one-tenth of a mile or the full distance, but he is charged the same fare irrespective of the length of ride he/she takes within the unit distance.

Nash (1982) stated that, "the combination of these characteristics throws up a set of problems in terms of pricing, planning services and integration of modes, and investment appraisal which are to a considerable extent unique to urban areas". Since the transit business lacked in devices to measure the service rendered, this must be kept in mind not only as a practical matter, but also as something fundamental and characteristic of its operation. Therefore, the development of any economically sound fare structure cannot be looked for in the direction of metering or approximating at all closely a charge for the individual service rendered. Furthermore, it has been evidenced in a recent study (Bresson *et al.* 2003) that public transport demand is still relatively sensitive to fare changes and that "policy measures aimed at fare reduction can play a substantial role in encouraging the use of public transport".

Travel by urban metro systems seems to be less elastic than bus trips and, in general, fare elasticities at off-peak periods may be about twice as large as peak demand elasticities. This must be interpreted as indicating that work-related travel by transit is less elastic than shopping-related and other leisure-related trips, i.e., discretionary trips, in the short-run. In the long-run, however, fare elasticity for peak travel tends to be higher compared to its short-term level, a trend which has been verified by White (2002) in his work on longer-term elasticities. This trend exists because it takes several years for the effect of fare changes to take effect since people usually need some time to decide on where they would live or work as the result of changes in travel cost.

The problem of determining the value of any given ride on an urban public transport system is a very difficult one. Hence, the public feeling against discrimination between different groups of riders or between residents of different parts of a city has limited experimentation. It has also had the effect of bringing about increases of fares on transit lines that were already paying well simply because the return on the whole system was insufficient. But the nature and causes of the problems of urban transport systems are becoming better understood and transport agencies are therefore encouraged to experiment and to apply the principles of merchandising in a way that was not true when the original departure from the initial fare was implemented.

Transit riders can be classified into necessity riders, i.e., captive riders or monopoly patrons (particularly in the short-run) and discretionary or freewill riders. The first group are mostly peak riders, and are particularly those who live too far from their work site, and who do not own, nor have private automobile at their disposal for transportation. The second group travel mostly during the off-peak periods, when scheduled public transport service face more competition with other transport modes, particularly with the private automobile.

There are certain precedents, which justify higher charges to those who fall within the category of necessity riders who utilize the peak service. That might be justified on the basis of cost on the assumption that the plant equipment, which is owned and operated, is called for by the peak service. Therefore, such charges as interest, depreciation, maintenance, etc., of the cars and equipment, which remain idle in the off-peak hours, are to be charged in full against the time during which they are operating. One may add that even if these rolling stock and equipment are operated in the off-peak periods, most of the capital cost might be charged to the peak.

Transit service might be regarded as something that mainly exists for service for eight hours during every twenty-four-hour period, i.e., four hours each during morning and evening peak periods, with service at other hours of the day as secondary. If the principle of sharing the costs with the various groups concerned were followed, the bulk of the charges would have to be assessed against the peak riders. This will assure that at the off-peak hours, the system might be enabled to enter into the competitive field at the rates, which would be attractive to the public, but not necessarily fully competitive, if charged on the same basis as to those in the monopoly field of the business. The operator will no doubt be better off, in terms of operating cost, to charge fares that are significantly below cost during off-peak than earning no passenger revenue at all during that period[1]. In so far as these competitive rates are promotional, and improve the load factor, they can be expected to react to the advantage of the peak rider through reductions in cost of service.

"Segmentation of transit pricing by different markets places emphasis on peak-load pricing as a means to level out the peaks and troughs in the demand profile in each market in order to save capacity costs, and raise the rate of capacity utilization in off-peak periods. This could also be seen as a way of pricing the service according to costs incurred. It has been noted that the greatest reform of potential of the pricing of transit services is in the differentiation of the fare structure by time of day" (Opurum 2012). However, there are some urban locations, including New York City, where differentiation of fare structure by time of day is not practiced as of this study.

In the case of New York City, the argument has been that transit service is a social service available to every social and economic class of the public, and that any fare structure that tends to favor one group against another would be socially discriminatory and unacceptable [Opurum, 2012]. It is very clear that the financial base of the transit industry is strongly supported by peak-load ridership. Furthermore, most peak period travelers do so as a matter of necessity, i.e., such trips are mostly work-related or non-discretionary as against leisure or shopping trips, which are mostly discretionary in nature.

4.2 *The principles of public transportation pricing*

First and foremost, it should be clearly stated that price is the mechanism by which scarce resources are efficiently allocated between competing uses. "For consumers, price encourages a purchase if the benefit of making the purchase exceed the benefit of alternatives. For producers, prices provide incentives for resources to move to those uses which people value most highly by informing firms how much to produce, which products to produce, when and where to sell the products, and when, where and how to invest" [Toner, 1997]. The pricing of public transportation services follows various principles and practices. In this section, we review some of the pricing principles and practices used in the public transportation industry today.

According to consumer theory, the demand for a product is determined by its price, the price of alternative goods, income and non-price attributes such as quality [Berechman, 1993]. With respect to transit, travel time components, together with the monetary price for travel, comprise the generalized cost of travel. Non-price service attributes in this case refer to measurable characteristics of transit supply which affect user's travel costs. The demand for transportation is a derived demand arising from the purpose of the trip and not for the sake of riding on the vehicle. To this end, work-related trips or business trips are considered as essential trips and are therefore price inelastic or insensitive to changes in price. On the other hand, recreational trips are not essential and so are categorized as inelastic in nature. The nature of travel demand, i.e., elastic or inelastic, is a major factor in transportation pricing policy.

4.3 *Basic pricing principles*

Public transport pricing theory suggests, under first-best pricing rule, that price be determined by marginal producer costs (MPC) and by marginal user costs (MUC) resulting from the travel time increase caused by boarding and fare collecting time of an additional passenger. Usually, these factors are more significant for bus than for rail and in the case of New York City, fare collection is transacted off-vehicle for subway trains and in-vehicle for the bus transit. In a bus/ train integrated transit fare environment, as applicable to this study, first-best pricing policy also suggests that the cost of transferring a trip is greater than the cost of a trip without a transfer.

Basically, "the economically efficient price can be stated to be equal to the marginal cost, since, if any other price is charged, it is possible to make both producers and consumers better off by switching to marginal cost pricing and redistributing the surpluses" (Toner 1997). Without government intervention, a perfectly operating market system achieves a set of prices equal to marginal cost, and by definition, all other sectors of the economy are expected to be in long-run equilibrium under first-best pricing, with price (P) equal to marginal cost (MC) which ideally may be taken to be the cost of providing one additional seat-mile. Of course, the assumption in this case is that the transit system is operating in a perfect market condition, and that all the seats in the rolling stock are occupied by fare-paying passengers.

For the transit industry, this also means that price should be set at the point where marginal social cost (MSC) equals marginal social benefits (MSB). This is because, by definition, marginal cost has two components in this respect, i.e., it is equal to marginal resource cost of production and also, equal to marginal user opportunity cost (which itself is equal to foregone benefits). It is economically understood that marginal cost is an avoidable cost, which could be diverted to an alternative use. First-best pricing requires an ideal economic state in which all markets are perfectly competitive with fixed tastes, but without external interventions, and all markets ensure complete resource allocation.

However, "equity pricing" or non-discriminatory pricing forbids the application of the kind of pricing rule discussed under first-best pricing, hence, the prices must be the same once public transport is integrated and a transfer is part of the service contract. Moreover, the resulting increase in ridership following a given reduction in fare may, in turn, reduce service quality as the transit vehicle eventually becomes overcrowded. In addition, the boarding and alighting of additional passengers tend to cause some reduction in the overall vehicle speed, thereby resulting in a reduction of user benefits. Under a constrained transit capacity, the marginal cost of a long-distance trip is much greater than that of a short-distance trip, and in which case, a graduated fare becomes more appropriate.

4.4 *Second-best pricing rules*

The first-best principles stated above apply only when all other sectors satisfy the rules for optimality as previously stated. If this condition does not hold, e.g., where for political reasons, the possibility of providing some subsidy to finance a deficit in public transport operations is obstructed, then a second-best world in which the application of first-best rules does not guarantee a welfare improvement is in effect [Toner, 1997]. When as the result of budget constraint, the marginal cost pricing (i.e., first-best pricing) cannot be practically applied, second-best pricing in some form of price discrimination may be introduced. In this case, the Ramsey pricing, i.e., to charge different prices for different price elasticities, and non-uniform prices such as fare cards can be cautiously applied.

The theory of second-best suggests that where one good is priced below marginal cost, substitute goods should also be priced below marginal cost. In the case of urban transport, both bus and rail are believed to have positive cross elasticities with respect to the price of car travel and are therefore substitutes (Preston and Nash, 1994). The Theory of second-best also states that if price is not equal to marginal cost somewhere in the economy, then, even if equality of price and marginal cost in other sectors is attainable, it is not necessarily optimal.

With second-best pricing, once there is inequality between price and marginal cost in any other sector of public transport, there is a loss in social benefit or welfare.

For optimal second-best conditions, public transport should be subsidized up to the point where marginal welfare loss on public transport equals the marginal welfare gain on private transport. From the results of their simulation test, Preston and Nash (1994) concluded that optimal second-best price for train and bus should be below the respective marginal costs. They also suggested that when there are institutional constraints on private transport at or above marginal cost, "then the second-best price for public transport should be set in such a way that the marginal net welfare loss for public transport should be equal to the marginal welfare gain to private transport".

It is well known that most public transport schemes are subsidized (with various public funds) and in such cases, prices may be set below marginal costs. Preston and Nash [1994] stated that "where schemes have been forecast to be commercially unviable and external benefits have been estimated to be at least the size of the financial deficit, the government is willing to consider the provision of subsidy up to the size of the projected financial deficit." They also stated that there is, though, a constraint on achieving the theoretical second-best optimum in the pricing of an urban rail scheme in that there should be no intervention in the commercial bus market. A comprehensive second-best solution would imply that both bus and rail prices should be held below marginal cost, given that the two modes are substitutes, with cross elasticities.

Lastly, second-best theory suggests that in situations where the policy maker cannot control prices in either the private transport market or the market for a given mode of public transport (e.g., bus), then there are no simple rules concerning the optimal price of the alternative public transport (e.g., train). In such situations, second-best theory suggests that the optimal rail price may be either above or below marginal social cost (MSC), and which of these should hold is an empirical matter [Toner, 1997].

4.5 *Peak load pricing*

In actuality, the goal of the peak load problem is to find the socially optimal peak and off-peak prices such that the capacity of the system is optimal, in the sense that social surplus is maximized. The solution to this problem [Tudela, 1995] is a particular application of the principle of marginal cost pricing, taking into account the operative marginal cost and the marginal cost of providing an additional capacity to accommodate the extra 'peak' demand. In general, it is imperative for us to understand that the higher the quality of service, the more expensive it is to provide. Therefore, we must relate the marginal cost of transit service to its service frequency in order to simultaneously optimize fares and service (Winston and Shirley, 1998).

The basic idea of peak-load pricing is to level out the peaks and troughs in the demand profile in each particular market to save capacity costs and raise the rate of capacity utilization in off-peak periods. As Nash [1982] pointed out, if the objective were to maximize social surplus with no financial constraints, fares would only be charged at times and places where there was pressure on capacity, but the benefits of increasing capacity did not justify the costs. In other words, fares would be charged in peak periods over heavily used stretches of the route, which in most cases is the inner city.

Normally, the capacity of a transport system is determined by the level of demand in the period when the maximum (or peak) quantity demanded occurs. This means that with the time variation of the demand levels, during the off-peak there will be a partial under-utilization of the total capacity available. This problem exists mostly in the case of non-storable products, or when the cost of storage is very high. However, "the optimal pricing in every period will be the marginal operating cost plus a fraction of the marginal capacity cost. The proportion of the latter cost category will depend on the number of periods under analysis, the sensitivity of the users' benefits to a change on the capacity and if demand equalizes to the capacity" [Tudela, 1995].

Similarly, White [2002] stated that a major determinant of (public transport) cost is the level of service provided during the peak period. He argued that this is because most of the vehicles and personnel (crews) needed to satisfy demand during the peak are not likely to be fully utilized at other times. This is true in the case of New York City (and perhaps other large cities), where in some instances the train and bus crews are paid for a full day work regardless of the number of hours they actually worked in a given workday. White [2002] suggested two main approaches of looking at peak costing. Thus, "either most costs are allocated to the day's services as a whole, on a time and/or distance basis, with only the extra peak output costed wholly to the peak, or the peak output can be seen as the reason for the service, with all the costs of providing it allocated initially to the peak, with extension of service to other parts of the day seen as incremental cost." However, he concluded that, "neither of these two approaches can be seen as the only (right) option, but that whatever basis is selected should be used consistently for calculation".

As evidenced in Webster and Bly [1980], the lower elasticity of peak travel suggests that a shift from a uniform (flat fare) structure to a differential fares system charging higher fares in the peak period than in the off-peak is likely to increase ridership for the same overall revenue, or increase revenue from the same overall ridership. In other words, they suggest that the lower elasticity of peak travel makes a case for charging higher fares at peak periods than at off-peak periods. However, they concluded that where such a differential fares scheme has been brought about through reducing fares in the off-peak (rather than increasing them in the peak), there has been loss of revenue in almost all cases. In addition to this, a shift of ridership from peak to off-peak might enable a reduction in capacity during the peak, thereby saving on operating cost, while a higher fare in the peak can, in some cases, be justified to passengers by the very high cost of providing peak service.

4.6 *Other alternative pricing practices*

In addition to peak load pricing, there are other transit fare differentiation practices in use. In general, there are five main fields for fare differentiation in urban transport fare structures, and they include time of day (i.e., peak and off-peak), length of trip, route or area, mode or service type, and type of passenger (Nash, 1982). In sum, price differentiation, particularly by time of day and length of trip, seems to be more efficient than a flat fare structure. Fare differentiation by time of day has previously been reviewed under peak load pricing. We will briefly review the other areas of fare differentiation in this section.

With respect to distance-based fare differentiation, since short-distance trips are more elastic than long-distance trips, with flat fares system, a given percentage rise in fare will bear even more heavily on short-distance travelers who will already be paying much more per unit distance traveled than the long-distance passengers. Consequently, an even larger proportion of short trips will be lost than for the same percentage rise imposed across all fare values in a graduated scheme. Conversely, and as Webster and Bly (1980) have stated, the longest distances in a flat-fare scheme will be less affected than in the graduated scheme.

Obviously, differentiation of fares between routes and areas does have equity considerations. "Whilst it is hard to justify the view that equity requires complete uniformity of fares, use of price discrimination to charge high fares where there is heavy captive traffic to cross-subsidize routes and areas of low traffic may well be thought objectionable, especially as the latter areas may well be more affluent than the former" (Nash, 1982).

With respect to fare differentiation based on mode or quality of service, Nash (1982) stated that where services giving different degrees of speed, comfort or reliability operate between the same pair of points, the difference in quality of service may lead to a difference in demand elasticities and hence in the optimal fare to charge. Lastly, differentiating the fare based on the type of passenger has been more of a socio-political issue rather than an economic policy. Discount fares of various kinds, such as half-fares to the physically challenged, senior citizens, students, and children, fall into this category. Nash (1982) cautioned that the problem with discriminating by type of passenger is that the category into which any individual passenger falls must be readily identifiable.

Furthermore, according to a 2012 research survey analysis (Opurum, 2012), travel frequency of public transportation patrons increases with a decrease in the fare level provided in the form of fare discounts and free transfers from one public transportation mode to another. This finding is particularly the case with discretionary riders, who unlike the captive, journey-to-work riders (commuters), have the discretion to use other private modes of transportation for their daily trips. In the case of New York City, the travel pattern suddenly changed following the introduction of free inter-modal (bus/train) transfer benefits for the transit users who pay their fare with the automated fare card, Metrocard. That survey analysis results (Opurum, 2012) also indicated that transit users prefer a flat fare policy to any other form of graduated fare structure. Approximately 90% of the surveyed New York City Transit patrons prefer a flat fare policy over a distance-based fare policy. Furthermore, the economic principle of price elasticity of demand teaches us that the higher the household income level, the less sensitive people are to changes in the public transportation fare level. In other words, the high-income group (household income of $80,000 and above) shows a very high level of insensitivity or inelasticity of demand with respect to changes in public transportation fare.

In the case of the New York City Transit system (NYCTA), the fare is not graduated. Rather, a flat fare is charged for as much as the patron desires to ride for a distance of approximately 38 miles (on the rapid transit system, the Subway) from the farthest train station in the New York City Borough of The Bronx to the last stop in Far Rockaway in the Borough of Queens. In addition to the flat fare pricing policy, a free transfer benefit is also provided between the Subway and the Bus System. The regular fare for the New York City Bus and Subway as of this work is $2.90, and $7 for a ride on the Express Buses. Also, discounted fares (half of the regular fare) are available for the physically-challenged and senior citizens. For the Express Buses, reduced fare is not available during the morning peak hours (6 am to 10 am) and afternoon/evening peak hours (3 pm to 7 pm). It is also noteworthy that the New York City Transit System is subsidized by up to 40% with the tax-payers' dollars, meaning that for every $1 the NYCTA spends to provide the service, the riders (patrons) pay $0.60. The NYC transit system is the only transit system in the world that operates on a 24/7 schedule (twenty-four hours per day, seven days a week), and one of the few transit systems with a flat fare pricing policy. The current medium of fare payment on the NYC Transit is the OMNY Fare Card, which replaced the MetroCard beginning in 2024.

4.7 *Smart urban mobility*

Mobility in urban centers is essential for the economic success of any region. The modes of mobility or the means of moving from point "A" to point "B" have evolved since the history of the world. The first and the most environmentally safe means or mode of mobility is walking, otherwise known as the "Foot-Run" instead of a Citron. The evolution of modern urban public transportation started with horse-drawn carts and continued in stages to the present-day jet speed trains (Opurum 2012). Historically, traditional means of urban public transportation included trolleys, trams (cable cars), ferries, buses, regional rails, rapid transit trains, and taxicabs. Today (in the 21st Century), various modes of mobility in urban centers include walking, bicycles, tricycles, motorcycles, mopeds, scooters, trams, taxis (including Uber), mass transit vehicles (including buses, rapid transit trains in the form of subways and suburban rails).

As a component of the process of decarbonizing transportation, smart urban mobility aims to encourage the use of cost-effective, less polluting, efficient modes of transportation in urban centers. To this end, efforts are made to discourage or minimize the use of high air-polluting (including carbon monoxide-emitting), non-mass transit vehicles in the central business districts of major urban environments. Mass transit continues to be the most efficient means of mobility in the central business districts, given its high performance over other means of mobility. In 2017, for instance, the New York City transit system had over

2.5 billion trips on its trains (Subway) and buses. The use of bicycles and shared ride on taxicabs are also smart means of travel in urban centers. The use of bicycles for daily commuting has been a key to mitigating the congestion problem in Japan and other major cities in Asia. In New York, the Citi Bike program is receiving more attention, and bicycle trips have continued to grow. According to the New York City Department of Transportation (NYCDOT), 30,000 additional bicycle trips were made in the CBD between 2016 and 2017 (NYCDOT Mobility Report, 2019). Taxis and for-hire vehicles account for much of the traffic in the CBD due to their tendency to circulate in search of passengers (fares).

Overall, walking, bicycling, and mass transit remain the most sustainable modes of travel in urban centers, and programs geared towards decongesting the central business districts (CBDs) are changing mobility patterns and resulting in fewer trips into the CBD, as has been evidenced in New York City, London, Stockholm, and Singapore, to name but a few.

4.8 *Congestion and air pollution mitigation initiatives*

Traffic congestion is very detrimental to the economic and physical environments, and ultimately, to the well-being of the people. Economically speaking, the cost of traffic congestion can be enormous, ranging from the time lost in traffic, the fuel energy wasted in slow or idling speed, to the health bills for the victims of the polluted air in the area. According to the New York Metropolitan Transportation Authority (MTA), New Yorkers lose an estimated 117 hours on average sitting in traffic every year, costing them an average of $2,000 in lost productivity and wasted time (Rivera, 2024).

Congestion pricing is a transportation policy aimed at mitigating the environmental (noise and air) pollution caused by various categories of vehicles in traffic in urban centers. It aims to redirect mobility in the central business districts from private automobiles to public transportation systems and to use the funds generated from the scheme to improve the urban public transportation system. The socio-economic consequences of traffic congestion could be overwhelming in some urban locations and indeed, cannot be over-emphasized.

According to Fox 5 Good Day New York morning news on Tuesday, May 27, 2025, the New York Metropolitan Transportation Authority (MTA) reported that the Congestion Pricing (implemented on January 5, 2025, in New York City's central business district, CBD), generated a total sum of $500 million in the First Quarter (the first three months) of the year. A similar statement by the Regional Plan Association (June 2025) gave very encouraging developments in and around New York City of the newly implemented Congestion Pricing Program. According to the Regional Plan Association (RPA), congestion declined in May 2025 by 25% in Manhattan (New York, NY), and by 10% in one of the outer boroughs of New York City, The Bronx. According to a New York City Congestion Pricing Report in July 2025 (NBC News 4, July 25, 2025), between 8 a.m. and 6 p.m. on a weekday, 44% of the roadways in the CBD experienced faster times, 40% had no discernable change, while 16% were slower on average. Also, a new study which compared data from January through May 2024 to the same period in 2025 (Russo-Lennon, 2025) shows that the Manhattan Congestion Zone is seeing 431 fewer large trucks, known as GVWR Classes 3-8, but an increase of 1,526 of multi-purpose vehicles, such as last-mile delivery trucks during the same period. Earlier in the year, it was reported that congestion in the New York City central business district (CBD) declined by 11% in February 2025 compared to the same period in 2024 (News 12 Westchester). These socioeconomic benefits represent some examples that justify the investment in congestion mitigation initiatives.

As of 2024, New York City led the world in urban automobile traffic congestion, despite having a rapid transit system that operated twenty-four (24) hours per day, seven (7) days a week (The Economist, November 21, 2024). With a population of over 8 million, the commercial capital of the United States, New York City, is the nation's most populous city, with most commercial and social activities operating 24/7. Over the years, congestion mitigation efforts have been focused within the Manhattan central business district, and on January 5,

2025, the Congestion Pricing Program (also known as the Central Business District Tolling Program, CBDTP) was finally implemented.

The New York Metropolitan Transportation Authority's (MTA's) Congestion Pricing Program (the first of its kind in the United States) is an initiative that aims to reduce gridlock traffic, improve air quality, and generate an estimated $15 billion in revenue to improve New York City public transportation programs by charging vehicles entering the congestion relief zone in Manhattan. According to the MTA, an average of 700,000 vehicles enter the Manhattan CBD daily. In June 2025, the MTA reported that 2,076,163 fewer vehicles entered the congestion relief zone (CRZ) in May 2025 alone (Russo-Lennon, 2025). The agency (MTA) added that the baseline historical daily average of vehicles entering the CRZ is 647,200 in the month. Furthermore, in May 2025, with congestion pricing, the average daily vehicle entries into the CRZ declined to 580,227. In terms of revenue, New York City's congestion pricing program's total net revenue, as of June 2025 stands at $219 million (Russo-Lennon, 2025). The MTA stated that the funds will be used for public transit improvements, including better accessibility at subway stations, more battery-electric buses with complementary charging infrastructure, and structural enhancements such as track upgrades, bridge repairs, and customer communication systems. It is hoped that the MTA will appropriate the generated net revenue as stated. Otherwise, there will be criticisms and oppositions from the public towards MTA and the congestion pricing scheme.

However, the CBDTP has remained a controversial issue and an object of political battle between New York State, the neighboring states (New Jersey and Connecticut), and the Federal Government. The New York Metropolitan Transportation Authority (MTA) and the New York City Department of Transportation (NYCDOT) are also facing intense pressure from various non-public transportation advocacy groups in and around the city to either reduce or discontinue the congestion tolls.

The New York City CBD is the area in Downtown Manhattan stretching east to west from the East River to the Hudson River, and north to south from Battery Park to 60th Street. Also known as the Congestion Relief Zone (with the exclusion of the West Side Highway, the FDR Drive, and the Hugh L. Carey Tunnel), the New York City CBD attracts large volumes of mixed vehicular traffic daily, and the congestion pricing applies mostly to most non-mass transit motor vehicular traffic using the area. The idea is to discourage the use of non-mass transit vehicles and encourage the use of mass transit within the CBD or what is known as modal shift. This will not only help to decongest the roadways in the CBD and reduce the air pollution, but also generate the revenue needed for the capital development/improvement projects of the mass transit system.

A breakdown of the New York City congestion toll is as follows:

- Passenger cars and small commercial vehicles entering the Congestion Relief Zone, including SUVs, pick-up trucks, and small vans, are charged $9 if they enter the zone between 5 a.m. and 9 p.m. on weekdays and $2.25 during overnight periods, except if they are exempted.

Figure 1. New York City congestion relief zone and access points. Courtesy of Colleen G. Scott, colleenscott.pages.dev.

- Motorcycles are charged $4.50 during the peak period and $1.05 during overnight periods.
- Small trucks and buses registered with the New York State Department of Motor Vehicles (DMV) pay $14.40 during the peak period and $3.60 overnight, while large trucks pay $21.60 during the peak, and $5.40 overnight.
- Transit buses and other registered emergency vehicles (as defined by New York State Vehicles and Traffic Law) are exempted from paying the congestion toll (mta.info/tolls/congestion-relief-zone/discounts-exemptions/).

Also, passenger cars and motorcycles are charged only once per day in the congestion relief zone. Specifically, the list of vehicles exempted from the New York City CBD congestion toll include:

- Buses providing scheduled commuter services open to the public
- School buses contracted with the New York City Department of Education
- Specialized government vehicles
- Commuter vans licensed by the New York City Taxi & Limousine Commission
- Qualifying authorized emergency vehicles (fire service vehicles, ambulances, etc.)
- Qualifying vehicles transporting people with disabilities.

The following table (Table 1) shows how different categories of vehicles were traveling into the Manhattan congestion relief zone (CRZ) in New York City during the weekday peak period on the first day of the congestion toll implementation.

According to the New York Metropolitan Transportation Authority (MTA, Jan. 30, 2025), "with the implementation of the Central Business District Program, also known as congestion pricing, New York began an exciting effort to reshape how people and vehicles share the public space of our city streets". As Table 1 also shows, within a 10-minute time interval, most of the vehicles (cars, pickup trucks, and vans) entering Manhattan via the Brooklyn Bridge made more trips on the excluded roadways than they did with the congestion relief zone entries. With the implementation of the congestion toll, motorists are devising some strategies to avoid paying the toll. This is also presenting a major vehicle parking space problem for the residents of Upper Manhattan, who live in the immediate neighborhoods outside of the congestion relief zone. In the meantime, the Federal Government of the United States has continued to oppose the New York City Congestion Toll and has threatened to end the program. "The day before the latest deadline from the Trump administration for New York to kill off its controversial congestion pricing program in Manhattan, a federal judge issued a temporary restraining order to keep the U.S. Department of Transportation (U.S. DOT) from making good on its threats to block funding. U.S. District Judge Lewis Liman's May 27 order keeps the tolls in place through at least June 9" (Lockridge, 2025). The temporary restraining order bars the U.S. DOT from withholding federal funding from New York as the legal fight continues.

Table 1. Sample of New York City Congestion Relief Zone (CRZ) data.

Toll date	Toll 10-minute interval	Time period	Vehicle category	Detection group	CRZ entries	Excluded roadway trips
Jan. 5, 2025	10:40 am	Peak	Motorcycles	Manhattan bridge	2	0
Jan. 5, 2025	10:40 am	Peak	Cars, pickups and vans	Brooklyn bridge	129	159
Jan. 5, 2025	10:50 am	Peak	Cars, pickups and vans	Manhattan bridge	171	0

Source. MTA, The most detailed view of the NYC traffic (so far). Updated January 30, 2025 12:00 p.m.

On the contrary, the Governor of the State of New York has challenged the federal government, insisting that the congestion relief program would be socially and economically beneficial to New York by generating revenue for mass transit revitalization, decongesting the roadways in the Manhattan CBD, improving vehicle travel speed, and reducing travel time, particularly for the bus transit. The neighboring states of New Jersey and Connecticut have also joined the federal government to oppose the New York City congestion relief program, citing that their residents who travel into the zone would bear the brunt of the congestion toll since they would have already paid tolls to enter New York City. It would be premature at this time to fully determine the socioeconomic and environmental impact of the New York City congestion pricing program. It will take at least a period of one year for the full impact of the program to be realized.

In the United Kingdom, the City of London's congestion mitigation program, implemented by Transport for London in 2003, is older and more costly than the New York City model. Under the Congestion Charge Zone (CCZ) program, Transport for London, TfL (the administrator of the program), charges a fee on most cars and motor vehicles driven within the CCZ in Central London between 7:00 a.m. and 6:00 p.m. Monday to Friday and between 12 noon and 6:00 p.m. Saturday and Sunday, effective February 17, 2003. The congestion charge does not apply between Christmas Day (December 25) and New Year's Day (January 1). The standard charge (for both weekday and weekend, including Bank Holidays) is 15 Pounds Sterling (approximately 20.55 US Dollars at the current exchange rate). Enforcement is primarily based on automatic number-plate (license plate) recognition (ANPR) and has been operated by a third party, IBM, since 2009 (Transport for London, 2015).

In July 2013, a discount program (a more stringent emissions control standard measure), the Ultra Low Emissions Discount (ULED) was introduced in London to limit the free access to the CCZ to all-electric cars, some plug-in hybrids, and any vehicle that emits 75 grams per kilometer or less of carbon monoxide (CO_2) and meets the Euro 5 standards of air quality (Green Car Congress, 2013). A 10% decline in traffic volume, and an 11% reduction in vehicle kilometers (vehicle miles) in Central London from the period 2000 to 2012 were mostly attributed to the Congestion Relief Zone program (Givoni, 2011).

Besides New York and London, many other major cities have experimented, or implemented one form of congestion relief program or the other. A few examples include the City of Stockholm, Sweden, where a 20-25 percent reduction in traffic volumes (on most congested roads) and a 14 percent decrease in vehicle-miles traveled within the congestion relief zone were achieved on a trial basis between January 2006 and July 2006. The scheme was fully launched in 2007 by the Swedish Transport Authority. In Singapore, the Singapore peak-period pricing scheme was introduced first in Downtown Singapore during the morning rush hours in 1975 by the Singapore Land Transport Authority, and in the spring of 1998, the city shifted the program to a fully automated electronic road pricing (ERP) scheme. The Singapore system is the first in the world, and has reduced traffic by 13 percent and increased vehicle speed by 22 percent (US Department of Transportation). The following table (Table 2) is a comparative summary of the congestion pricing schemes in the three major cities outside the United States, i.e., London, Stockholm, and Singapore, as discussed above.

A comparison of the London, Stockholm, and Singapore congestion pricing schemes shows some similarities in their design and primary goals, but the hours and days of operation differ among the three. The Singapore ERP scheme (launched in 1998) is the oldest of them all and the only one that varies the toll rates based on the road used and local traffic conditions, in addition to the time-of-day factor. Both the London and Stockholm schemes are not in effect on weekends (Saturday and Sunday), public holidays, and during night hours, quite unlike the system in Singapore, which operates from 7 am to 8 pm Monday through Saturday. In terms of the costs and revenues of the schemes, the Stockholm model with an initial capital investment of $236.7 million is the most expensive, followed by London and Singapore at $214 million and $110 million, respectively (see Table 2 and Figure 2). The operating costs of the schemes show that the London system has the highest operating cost of $172 million. On the other hand, both the Stockholm and Singapore

Table 2. Road pricing matrix: London, Stockholm, and Singapore.

	Congestion pricing scheme		
City & Year Scheme Launched (Transport Authority)	Description	Primary Goals	Auxiliary Transportation & Policy Improvement
London 2003 (Transport of London)	The cordon pricing scheme uses automatic number plate recognition in the 8 sq. ml area. Vehicles are registered automatically by the number plates. The system consists of overhead cameras at all entrance points, pavement markings, and street signage.	Reduce congestion, improve air quality and public health, improve travel time reliability for car users, and create a long-term funding source for public transit improvements.	300 new buses, Updated bus routes, Improved frequency of buses, 8,500 park-and-ride spaces, and Bike/ pedestrian Infrastructure.
Stockholm 2007. Successfully piloted first in 2006. (Swedish Transport Authority)	The cordon congestion tax scheme uses automatic number plate recognition in a 13 sq. mile area. Vehicles are registered automatically by cameras that photograph the number plates. The system consists of overhead gantries, cameras at all entrance points, pavement markings, and street signage.	Reduce congestion, improve air quality and public health, and improve travel time reliability for car users.	197 buses. 16 new bus routes. 2,800 new regional park-and-ride spaces. Bike and pedestrian infrastructures. Taxi and for-hire vehicles, such as Uber, also pay the tax.
Singapore 1998 (Land Transport Authority)	The electronic road pricing (ERP) scheme is fully automatic on specific routes, times of day, and directions, with variable pricing designed to respond to congestion in real-time. Vehicles are required to have an in-vehicle unit on the dashboard and a smart card with fare stored on it. Overhead gantries detect the type of vehicle, the congestion of the route at specific times, and deduct the variable fee from the smart card. The ERP was launched in 1998, replacing a cordon pricing scheme that was first implemented in 1975.	Reduce congestion. Improve journey time reliability for car users.	Parking fees inside the restricted zone were doubled. Buses and bus frequency increased. HOV+4 lanes were established. 15,000 were established outside of the restricted zone.

Source: Tri-State Transportation Campaign (2018), Mobilizing the Region, Congestion Pricing Report 1-4-18: Road Pricing in London, Stockholm, and Singapore.

Payments, costs, and revenue				
Payment	Hours	Initial Investment	Annual Operating Cost	Annual Net Revenue
First daily fee of 11.50 British pound sterling ($15.21 USD). Payments can be made by telephone, text message, online, by post, or via by auto pay.	7 a.m.– 6 p.m. Monday-Friday. There is no charge on weekends, Bank Holidays, or the days between Christmas and New Years Day, nor during the night hours (6:00 p.m. to 6:59 a.m.)	161.7 million British pound sterling ($214 million USD)	130 million British pound sterling ($172 million USD)	137 million British pound sterling ($182 million USD)
Vehicle pricing based on time of day. Highest peak period cost per passage is 35 krona ($4.14 USD). The owner of the vehicle is sent a monthly invoice for the total charge incurred. Payments can be made by mail, online or by direct debit from a bank account.	6:30 a.m.– 6:30 p.m. Monday-Friday. There is no charge on weekends, public holidays, nor during night hours (6:30 p.m. to 6:29 a.m.), nor during the month of July	2 billion krona ($236.7 million USD)	100 million krona ($11,8 million USD)	1.3 billion krona/ yr. ($155 million USD)
$0-$4.00 are collected on a per-pass basis at over 50 points within the surrounding central business district. Rates vary for different roads and time periods depending on local traffic conditions. The in-vehicle unit costs $150.00 ($111.00 USD).	7:00 a.m.– 8:00 p.m. Monday -Saturday. There is no charge on Sundays, public holidays, or after 1 pm the day before public holiday.	$200 million ($110 million USD).	$25 million ($18.5 million USD)	$150 million/year ($100 million USD).

systems have comparably very low operating costs than the London system. This could be attributed to some location-specific factors, such as labor cost and the size of the metropolitan area, of which London is comparably higher and larger than the other two locations. Surprisingly, the London congestion pricing scheme, though with the highest operating cost and a high initial capital investment, outperformed both Stockholm and Singapore with an annual net revenue of $182 million. Respectively, Stockholm and Singapore netted $155 million and $100 million in annual revenues. This is likely because the London peak period congestion toll ($15.21) is significantly higher than those of Stockholm ($4.14) and Singapore ($0-$4, which vary for different roads and time periods, depending on the local traffic conditions). Also, the Singapore congestion toll is collected on a per-pass basis at over 50 points within the surrounding central business district.

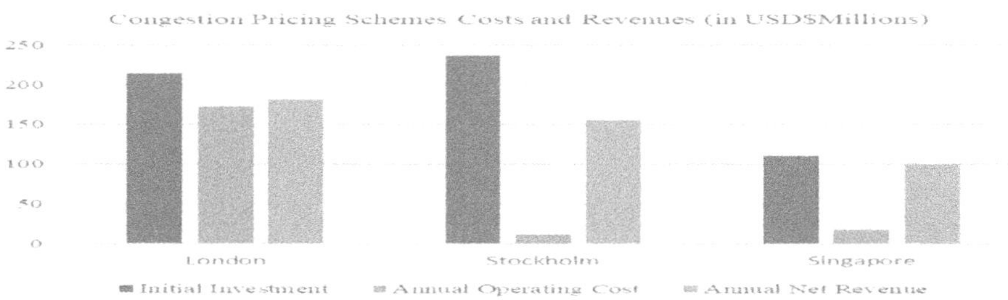

Figure 2. Congestion pricing schemes costs and revenues (in millions of US dollars). Data Source: Tri-State Transportation Campaign, Congestion Pricing Report, 2018).

In terms of metropolitan area population (Table 3), following the implementation of the road pricing schemes, Singapore experienced the highest percentage growth of 44% compared to 19% and 15% for London and Stockholm, respectively. Compared to these three cities, the New York City congestion pricing program has the longest hours of operation from 5 am to 9 pm Monday through Friday, in addition to operating during night hours and on weekends. As stated earlier in this section, it would be too soon at this time to know the full impact of the congestion pricing scheme in New York City and to be able to realistically compare it with those in similar urban environments.

Table 3. Metropolitan area population and congestion pricing scheme: London, Stockholm, and Singapore.

	Metropolitan area population		
	Year scheme launched	In 2016	% Change since launch
London	7.3 million (in 2003)	8.7 million	19%
Stockholm	1.9 million (in 2007)	2.1 million	10%
Singapore	3.9 million (in 1998)	5.6 million	44%

Source: Tri-State Transportation Campaign (2018), Mobilizing the Region, Congestion Pricing Report 1-4-18: Road Pricing in London, Stockholm, and Singapore.

5 SUMMARY

The demand for transportation is a derived demand arising from the purpose for using the service. Travel demand can be classified as either price elastic (sensitive to price) or inelastic (insensitive to price). In general, business-related trips or journey-to-work (non-discretionary trips) are price inelastic, while non-business-related trips or discretionary trips (recreation or leisure trips) are sensitive to price and so are said to be price elastic.

Travel by urban metro systems (rail rapid transit) seems to be less price elastic than bus trips and in general, fare elasticities at off-peak periods may be about twice as large as peak demand elasticities since off-peak riders are mostly discretionary riders. In New York City, demand for transit service is said to be relatively price inelastic and more or less a journey-to-work service whereby people are moved from residential neighborhoods to business districts and vice versa. This trend allows the transit authority to generate more revenue above and beyond the budgeted level with any small increase in the transit fare, other things being equal. Nevertheless, any increase in the New York City Transit fare must first go through the public hearing process before its implementation. Hence, the transit system operation is subsidized with the New York City tax-payers money and therefore, must go through that process by law.

The principles of public transportation pricing show that there are three major different rules in pricing the service: first-best pricing (marginal cost pricing) rule, second-best pricing rule (a form of price discrimination), and peak-load pricing rule. Most successful urban public transportation services are based on peak-load pricing to recover the system capacity cost. Nevertheless, equitable pricing policies could help towards making the contribution of urban public transportation to the socioeconomic well-being of our society most effective by encouraging ridership. The aim is to make the use of mass transit attractive so that a shift from the use of non-mass transit vehicles to mass transit in the CBDs becomes realistic and thereby mitigate traffic congestion and the pollution it causes. Obviously, urban centers cannot do without vehicular movements within their central business districts. Hence, the role of transportation in the urban economy cannot be overemphasized. Its contribution to the gross domestic product (GDP) in many nations is quite significant.

However, the use of non-mass transit vehicles in the central business districts of many major cities is doing more harm than good, and so, the need to design and implement appropriate transportation policies, such as congestion pricing, to mitigate the environmental pollution (air and noise pollution) arising from vehicular traffic congestion in these areas becomes necessary. The increasing number of vehicular traffic in the CBDs is indeed a major concern, given the environmental and health issues the traffic congestion poses to our society. The New York City CBD Congestion Pricing or CBD Toll Pricing program (CBDTP) is a typical measure to discourage the use of non-mass transit vehicles (and particularly for non-business-related trips during the peak-day) in the CBD. The implementation of the Congestion Pricing program in the Congestion Relief Zone in New York City is, actually, transforming the area from a gridlock to a free-flow travel environment. Congestion relief pricing is indeed a major component of any comprehensive urban transportation sustainable plan.

6 CONCLUSION AND RECOMMENDATIONS

It would be reasonable to state that the demand for public transport is relatively sensitive (relatively elastic) to changes in fare (price). However, the level of sensitivity involved depends on whether the trip is discretionary or non-discretionary, as well as the income level (the socio-economic status) of the trip-maker. This research also found that any policy aimed at fare reduction is likely to encourage use of the transit. Bresson *et al.* (2003) expressed that "the effects of such measures will be greater in the long-run than in the short-run, but the adjustment is relatively rapid, with 99% of the total effect realized within 6 years".

Studies (Bresson *et al.* 2003) also show that "there is some indication that the response to fare changes increases with the fare level so that fare reductions will have a greater impact on demand when fares are high". As Toner [1997] concluded, "in an ideal world, an optimal state would be reached by having all prices equal to the marginal social costs. These social costs would consider not only the monetary cost of providing the transport service but also factors such as damage to the environment caused in the process of producing such service".

Overall, it should be realized that the economic and demographic environment in which a given transit system operates influences demand elasticity, all else being equal (ceteris paribus). It should also be noted that fare elasticities are comparatively higher for bus transit, short-distance trips, and for peak travel than they are, respectively, for metro (rail rapid) transit, long-distance trips, and for off-peak travel. Also, the less frequently people use public transport, the more sensitive they are to changes in price (fare) and quality of service. With respect to commuters, fare sensitivity is more in the case of price increases than of decreases, and when the service is poor than when it is good. In terms of income, the proportion of the transit patron's budget spent on transit fare will determine their sensitivity to changes in the fare level. The smaller the percentage of their budget spent on transit fare, the more inelastic is their demand for transit service and vice versa, other things being equal. Notwithstanding, transit users are about twice as sensitive to changes in travel time as they are to changes in fare.

Nevertheless, it has been empirically proven that country-specific factors have a strong influence on the size of elasticity. It is obvious, however, that if fare levels are low so that, when deciding whether to travel by transit or not, most passengers pay little or no attention to the fare they would pay, fare elasticities should be relatively small. If on the other hand, fares are very high and therefore tend to dominate in travel decisions, high fare elasticity would be expected. The implementation of the Congestion Pricing program in the Congestion Relief Zone in New York City is, doubtless, transforming the CBD from a gridlock to a free-flow travel environment. The number of vehicles entering the Central Business District in Manhattan has declined significantly since the implementation of the Congestion Pricing, thereby resulting in higher vehicle travel speed and less pollution. Walking, bicycling, and mass transit are the most sustainable, cost-effective means of mobility in the commercial centers of major urban environments.

More emphasis is needed on the use of electric vehicles (EVs). To further encourage more use of electric vehicles, it is suggested that the "Buy America" campaign incorporate the exemption of those who buy electric vehicles (EVs) from sales tax and vehicle registration fees. New York City should follow the London traffic congestion relief model and consider providing some discount benefits to motorists who use low-carbon-dioxide (CO_2)-emitting vehicles in the congestion relief zone. More investments would be needed to encourage growth in the use of electric vehicles in urban areas by establishing more charging stations and building vehicles with more electric power storage capacity. A major drawback of the EV program is inadequate/insufficient charging facilities across the nation.

Nevertheless, more investments are needed for ongoing improvements on pedestrianization, bicycle infrastructures, electric vehicles (EVs), and mass transit to make them more environmentally friendly and to encourage their use. Since one of the objectives of congestion pricing is to generate revenue to revitalize the mass transit and make it more attractive to potential users, the system administrators must ensure that the funds are appropriately disbursed for the right purposes. Mass transit authorities should consider time-of-day-based (peak and off-peak) fare policy. This would encourage more ridership during the off-peak periods (including the late-night hours in the case of the New York City Transit system, which operates on a 24/7 schedule). This will not only help to avoid underutilization of the rolling stock (trains and buses) during off-peak, but also encourage ridership from discretionary riders who would otherwise not. Everything possible should be done to make the mass transit attractive to the public. Without improving the mass transit services, it would be difficult to influence any mobility shift from automobiles (particularly, single-occupancy vehicles) to mass transit.

On August 1, 2025, Governor Hochul of New York announced plans to move forward with a major new expansion of transit service in Brooklyn and Queens: The Interborough Express (IBX) to serve currently underserved neighborhoods in Brooklyn and Queens. The planning study for the project was completed in January 2023. The 14-mile light rail project, which will connect the outer boroughs of Brooklyn and Queens, is estimated to cost $5.5 billion and to be completed in about six years. When completed, the IBX will feature 19 station stops, connect to 17 Subway Lines and the Long Island Rail Road (LIRR), and serve more than 100,000 New Yorkers (MTA Press Release, August 1, 2025). If this light rail project (see Figure 3) eventually comes to fruition, it would be a step in the right direction to attract more ridership on the transit system, while justifying any fair fare increases by the MTA. Presently, Brooklyn and Queens residents who use the mass transit will take a train into Manhattan first before connecting to either of the two outer boroughs. Other expected benefits of the IBX include, direct public transit option between Brooklyn and Queens, faster commute (with end-to-end rides expected to take 40 minutes), and new transit options in underserved locations where more than one-third of the residents live under the federal poverty line.

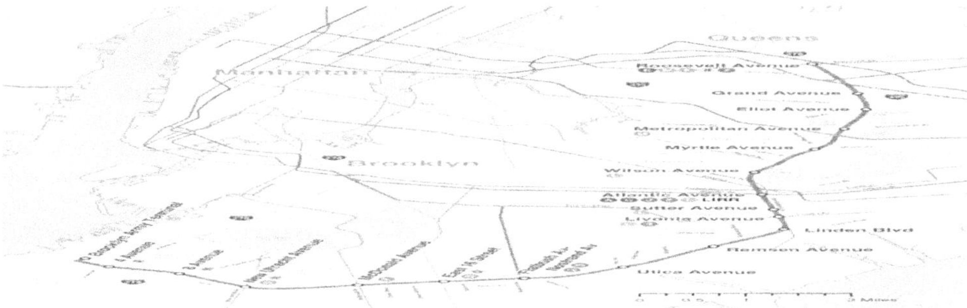

Figure 3. Map of The Brooklyn-Queens Interborough Express (IBX). Source: MTA Press Release, ICYMI, August 1, 2025.

We need to increase our level of consciousness on how to slowly move away from the overused traditional energy sources and the less efficient modes of mobility to safer and more accessible alternative sources and more economically efficient, reliable, and sustainable high-occupancy modes of travel. Particularly, it is absolutely necessary that we explore the various alternative means of intelligently encouraging the urbanites to transact their businesses remotely without contributing to the existing level of congestion and the environmental pollution they cause in our urban centers. In other words, any policy aimed at reducing the number of vehicles operating during the peak periods (morning and evening on weekdays) in the city centers or the central business district (CBD) would help significantly in mitigating the environmental pollution problems that have become a major issue in our society. More emphasis on telecommuting and flexi-time programs is needed.

Efforts should be focused on encouraging the use of mass transit in the central business district. Any improvement in the transit travel time and on-time performance would, to a large extent, encourage more ridership, particularly for business-related (journey-to-work) trips. In terms of service reliability, the New York City (NYC) rapid transit operations schedule should be adjusted to allow for adequate maintenance of the rolling stock during the late-night hours to minimize the distance between failures. (As revealed in one of the earlier sections, the NYC Transit is the only public transit system in the world that operates on a 24/7 schedule. This does not allow for enough time to properly maintain the fleet.)

From the environmental protection perspective, free inter-modal bus/train (rapid transit and suburban rails) transfers would be very encouraging to urban and suburban travelers, and help in reducing the level of emissions caused by automobiles, which some members of this group could be using otherwise. It is also recommended that public transportation authorities should continue to design and implement more effective and realistic policies that assure minimum environmental pollution and better quality of life in urban areas.

Lastly, transportation policies should be closely monitored to ensure that they are not creating problems but rather, achieving their objectives. On July 30, 2025, the New York Metropolitan Transportation Authority (MTA) unveiled its plan to increase the transit fare by approximately 3.45% from $2.90 to $3.00 on subway and buses, 4.4% on the suburban railroads (Metro-North and Long Island railroads), and tolls by 7.5%. effective January 4, 2026 (WPIX, 2025). By law, the MTA's proposal is required to go through a series of public hearings before the final decision is made to determine the implementation. If implemented, this fare policy will not only impact the congestion pricing program adversely, but could also result in more fare evasion on the buses and at the subway turnstiles, which has remained a major operating challenge to the transit agency. Also, any increase in transit fare must be justified with a commensurate improvement in transit service. Failure to do so would result in some decline in ridership, particularly in terms of the discretionary transit users. Besides fare evasion, the New York City Transit operating revenue short-fall could be attributed to its flat fare policy, which dates back to the transit system's inception in 1904. Also, because the transit is uniquely established as a social service affordable to all New Yorkers, any effort to change the fare policy from its traditional flat fare to a pay-as-you-go (distance-based) or time-of-day fare policy would be met with political/public opposition. The congestion pricing program will therefore represent a major funding source for the New York City mass transit.

In general, policies are designed and are meant to solve their intended problems, but sometimes, some policies create additional problems instead. The MTA must be very cautious while designing and implementing its transportation policies. Ultimately, the need to decongest the central business districts of major urban centers from vehicular traffic cannot be overemphasized. Nevertheless, more research is needed for a more equitable mass transit pricing policy and the most efficient means of moving people in urban centers.

NOTE

1. In New York, for instance, the MTA Metro-North Commuter Railroad, a subsidiary of the New York Metropolitan Transportation Authority, charges fares that are significantly much lower than the regular fare during off-peak. Particularly, for reverse peak operations, the railroad would rather collect minimal fares than run empty trains several kilometers from the suburban counties to the city center for the peak service.

REFERENCES

Ahlstrand, I. (2001), The politics and economics of transport investment and pricing in Stockholm, *Journal of Transport Economics and Policy*, vol. 32 (3), pp. 437–70.

Batty, Michael, Peter Hall, and David Starkie (1974), *The Impact of Fares-Free Public Transport Upon Urban Land Use and Activity Patterns*, University of Reading, Department of Geography, Reading, England.

Bresson G., J. Dargay, J-L. Madre and A. Pirotte (2003), The main determinants of the demand for public transport: a comparative analysis of England and France using shrinkage estimators, *Transportation Research Part A*, Vol. 37 (7), pp 605–27.

Cervero, Robert (1986), *Time-of-day Transit Pricing: Comparative US and International experiences, London, Transport Reviews*, Vol. 6 (4), October-December, pp.347–64.

Daniel, Fleishman, et al. (1996), *Fare Policies, Structures, and Technologies*, National Academy Press, Washington, D.C.

Dargay, J. and P. Goodwin (2000), *Changing Prices: A Dynamic Analysis of the Role of Pricing in Travel Behaviour and Transport Policy*, Landor Publishing Ltd., UK.

De Rus, Gines (1990), Public transport demand elasticities in Spain, *Journal of Transport Economics & Policy*, vol. 24 (2), May, pp. 189–201.
Fox 5 Good Day New York (Tuesday, May 27, 2025), Morning News, New York City Congestion Pricing, New York.
Givoni, M. (2011), Re-assessing the results of the london congestion charging scheme. *Urban Studies*, 49(5), 1089–1105.
Grayling, T. and S. Glaister (2000), *A new fares contract for London, Institute of Public Policy Research*, London, January.
Green Car Congress (April 24, 2013), London to introduce new ultra low emission discount for congestion charge scheme, countering dieselization.
Grey, Alexander (1975), *Urban Fares Policy, Saxon House, Haunts, England and Lexington Books*, D.C. Heath & Company, Lexington, Massachusetts.
Hoel, Lester A. (1992), *Public Transportation,* 2nd Edition, Prentice-Hall, Englewood Cliffs, New Jersey.
Lockridge, Deborah (2025), Trucking: Trump Administration Fight New York Congestion Pricing, *Fleet Management*, May 27, 2025.
Lovelock, Christopher H. et al. (1987), *Marketing Public Transit: A Strategic Approach,* Praeger Publishers, New York.
Metropolitan Transportation Authority (2021), *Annual Performance Metrics Report, Calendar Year* 2019
Mohring, Herbert (ed) (1994), *The Economics of Transport*, E. Elger Publications, Aldershot, Hants., England.
Metropolitan Transportation Authority (2023), *Annual Performance Metrics Report, Calendar Year* 2022.
Metropolitan Transportation Authority (2025), *The Most Detailed View of NYC Traffic (so far)*, Updated January 30, 2025.
MTA (2025), *Press Release, ICYMI: Governor Hochul Announces Plans to Move Forward with Major New Expansion of Transit Service in Brooklyn and Queens: The Interborough Express*, August 1, 2025.
MTA (2025). New York City Congestion Relief Zone. https://mta.info/tolls/congestion-relief-zone/discounts-exemptions/emergency-vehicles.
Nash, C.A (1982), *Economics of Public Transport*, Longman Inc., New York.
New York City Department of Transportation (August 2019), *New York City Mobility Report.*
News 12 Westchester (March 22, 2025), *Congestion in the New York City CBD.*
NBC News 4, New York (Friday, July 25, 5025), *New York City Congestion Pricing Report Channel 4 News at 6.*
Opurum, Clifford N. (2012), *Automated Fare Collection System and Urban Public Transportation: An Economic and Management Approach to Urban Transit Systems,* Trafford Publishing Co., USA.
Preston, J. and Chris A. Nash (1994), *An Application of the Second-Best Pricing Theory, Technical Note 1, Institute for Transport Studies, University of Leeds*, Leeds, U.K.
Regional Plan Association (June 2025), *Congestion in New York City*, New York.
Rivera, Alexandra (2024), Can You Avoid Congestion Pricing? *Rockland/Westchester Journal News*, Dec. 5, 2024
Russo-Lennon, Barbara (2025), New Study: Manhattan sees fewer trucks, *AMNY*, July 24, 2025.
The Economist (November 21, 2024), Congestion Pricing in New York gets the go-ahead after all. Maybe.
Toner, Jeremy P. (1997), Transport Pricing Principles, a review paper, Institute for Transport Studies, University of Leeds, Leeds, U.K.
Transport for London (2015), Congestion Pricing Official Report.
Tri-State Transportation Campaign (2018), Mobilizing the Region, Congestion Pricing Report 1-4-18: Road Pricing in London, Stockholm, and Singapore.
Tudela, Alejandro (1995), *Review: Peak Load Pricing, a review paper*, Institute for Transport Studies, University of Leeds, Leeds, U.K.
US Department of Transportation, Congestion Pricing: Examples Around the World. 1200 New Jersey Avenue, Washington, DC 20590.
Vickers, Leslie (1934), *Fare Structures in the Transit Industry*, Columbia University, New York
Webster, F.V. & P.H. Bly (joint editors) (1980), *The Demand for Public Transport: Report of The International Collaborative Study of The Factors Affecting Public Transport Patronage, Transport and Road Research Lab.*, United Kingdom.
WPIX (2025), More fare increases at MTA, Channel 11 News at 10, July 30, 2025,
White, P.R. (2002), *Public Transport: Its planning, management and operation*, 4th edition, Spon Press, London and New York.
White, P.R. (1984), User response to price changes: application of the threshold concept, *Transport Reviews*, vol. 4, No. 4, pp. 367–86.

Moving Towards Sustainable Businesses and Developing More Resilient Economies – Rashid and Annansingh-Jamieson (Eds)
© 2026 The Author(s), ISBN: 978-1-041-08875-2

An investigation into the relationship between workplace bullying and employee turnover intentions in Carib Trust Bank Limited Trinidad and Tobago: The mediating role of emotional exhaustion

TW Williams, DE Esdelle, IH Hosein, MS Singh, and SA Abraham
The University of the West Indies, Tammy

JR Ramdhan
School of Practical Accounting and Management

ABSTRACT: The existing research into the relationship between workplace bullying and employee turnover has focused on developing countries and, more recently, emerging economies. However, few studies have focused on workplace bullying in the Caribbean region within a multicultural framework. Moreover, few studies have integrated the Conservation of Resources Theory to analyze the effects of workplace bullying on employee turnover intentions. This study developed and tested a conceptual model linking bullied employees' emotions and perceptions to turnover intention. Primary data was collected from 126 employees at Carib Trust Bank in Trinidad and Tobago. Linear Multiple Regression Analysis was used for statistical analysis, and the findings revealed a positive relationship between work-related bullying and employee turnover intention. Additionally, employee emotional exhaustion played a significant mediating role between work/person-related bullying and employee turnover intentions. This study adds value to the existing literature on workplace bullying and employee turnover intentions in Trinidad and Tobago.

Keywords: Work-Related Bullying, Person-Related Bullying, Physical-Related Bullying, Conservation of Resource Theory, Employee Turnover Intention, Emotional Exhaustion

1 INTRODUCTION[1]

Boxall and Purcell (2008) define Human Resource Management as the policies and mechanisms associated with managing work and employees in firms or organizations. Moreover, human capital and human capital management are considered to be the most important factors and the driving forces that account for productivity levels and are crucial for the medium and long-term goals of all organizations. Furthermore, every possible human resource policy and framework is geared to ensure that employees are engaged and become loyal, since profits are only realized when turnover is reduced. In fact, turnover of talented workers has been a major concern for organizations and scholars in the human resource literature since recruiting is very expensive (Tan *et al.* 2019). Employees often feel satisfied when the work environment is engaging, friendly, fair, and encourages upward mobility. Some of the main reasons for employee turnover include work climate, management deficiencies, excessive job demands, poor pay, and, finally, workplace bullying (Wali and Zekeriya 2013). However, over the past decades, human resource management scholars have identified workplace bullying as the "silent epidemic" (Ciby and 2015; Ramdeo *et al.* 2020).

DOI: 10.1201/9781003647300-10

Adams (1997) posits that workplace bullying is an activity geared to degrade an employee's or employees' confidence and self-esteem through the use of negative figures of speech and actions. In fact, Gary Namie of the Workplace Bullying Institute (WBI) in the United States has indicated that approximately 30% of American employees are constantly abused at work, while 49% are severely affected. Workplace bullying is considered a major social phenomenon that is generated by specific forms of social stressors and social losses. These stressors and social losses often result in severe biopsychosocial stress reactions and health risks for the employees involved. In fact, many studies in management have identified the association between workplace bullying and its impact on employees and organizations (Einarsen *et al.* 2018; 2018; Bergbom *et al.* 2015; Ramdeo *et al.* 2020). Einarsen *et al.* (2018) posit that workplace bullying impacts about 10 to 20% of the global workforce annually.

2 LITERATURE REVIEW

According to Glambek *et al.* (2014 p. 33) workplace bullying is defined as "*the process in which an employee is subjected to persistent resentful acts prolonged for relatively long periods of time.*" Furthermore, the term workplace bullying varies across countries with terms such as mobbing, emotional abuse and harassment being used interchangeably. Zapf (1999) categorized bullying into five areas in his study: work-related, social isolation, personal attacks, verbal threats and spreading rumors. An individual who is a blustering, browbeating person who is harsh, insulting, or threatening to others who are weaker, smaller, or vulnerable in some way is considered to be a bully. However, there is a criterion necessary for this act to be classified as bullying such as repeated and regular occurrences (weekly) for a specified time period (six or more months) and the acknowledgement of power imbalance. It is viewed as an escalating process which results in the target being placed in an inferior position subject to systematic negative social acts. (Matthiesen *et al.* 2010).

According to Glambek *et al.* (2014 p. 33) workplace bullying is defined as "*the process in which an employee is subjected to persistent resentful acts prolonged for relatively long periods of time.*" Furthermore, the term workplace bullying varies across countries with terms such as mobbing, emotional abuse and harassment being used interchangeably. Zapf (1999) categorized bullying into five areas in his study: work-related, social isolation, personal attacks, verbal threats and spreading rumors

Bullying is utilized in countries like the United Kingdom and Australia, the term '*aggression*' is preferred in the USA, while '*mobbing*' is used in France and Germany (Saunders *et al.* 2007). Leymann (1996) further suggested that '*mobbing*' is used to illustrate that negative bullying behaviors is considered to be more subtle and not as physical as perpetuated by the term '*bullying*'.

According to Hossam (2014) turnover intention is an employee's projected likelihood of leaving a company or the employee's readiness to retire, while Abbasi and Hollman (2008) state that employee turnover intention can be quite expensive for a company. According to Hinkin and Tracey (2000), to remain competitive, businesses must invest in and retain their human capital. Turnover intentions can have a negative impact on organizations, as they incur costs associated with recruiting and developing new employees (James and Matthew 2012). Due to the detrimental effects that high voluntary turnover has on organizations, employers and professionals are always working to identify the workplace elements that cause turnover intention (Van Dyk 2016).

2.1 *Work related bullying and turnover intentions*

According to studies by (Faheem, Rasool, and Aruzu 2013), work-related bullying has a positive effect on employees' intentions to quit their jobs, while Mobley (1997) found that workplace bullying was a strong predictor of employee turnover intention. Giorgi *et al.*

(2016) found that individuals who experienced work-related bullying were less efficient at work and felt more exhausted, thus creating emotional exhaustion that led to employees contemplating leaving the job. Moreover, work-related bullying is a negative event that impacts the physiological and emotional well-being of the targets, and these targets, according to COR theory, will apply all resources until emotional exhaustion sets in, at which point employees contemplate leaving the job. Therefore, there is a positive relationship between work related bullying and turnover intent. Thus, the first hypothesis for this study is postulated: H1: There is a positive relationship between work-related bullying and employee turnover intentions among employees at Carib Trust Bank Trinidad and Tobago.

An employee who is the target of bullying at work will be driven to conserve resources (Hobfoll 1989, 2001), which could lead to an intention to leave the organization. Research has shown that workplace bullying has a negative impact on behavioural factors like job satisfaction (Devonish 2013) and team performance (Frick *et al.* 2018), which increases the likelihood that employees who have been bullied at work will have higher turnover intentions. Given the aforementioned, there is a positive relationship between person-related bullying and turnover intentions thus the following hypothesis is postulated: H2 there is a positive relationship between person-related bullying and employee turnover intentions among employees employed at Carib Trust Bank, Trinidad and Tobago.

Martins *et al.* (2023) investigated the impacts of workplace harassment on turnover intention within the banking industry and found a statistically significant positive relationship, mediated by mental stress and employee silence (Martins *et al.* 2023). Therefore, in light of the foregoing the third hypothesis is postulated: H3 there is a positive relationship between physical intimidating bullying and employee turnover intentions among employees at Carib Trust Bank Trinidad and Tobago.

Increased absenteeism and a pessimistic outlook on organizations and jobs are among the effects of emotional exhaustion, which also includes anxiety, lower self-esteem, and feelings of powerlessness (Ogungbamila *et al.* 2014; Cropanzano *et al.* 2003). Hobfoll (2001) states that negative emotions deplete personal resources, and employees will take steps to protect their resources. According to Marchand and Vandenberghe (2016) the most serious consequence of emotional exhaustion is turnover intention. Researchers have found a positive and significant correlation between emotional weariness and employees' intention to leave (Noh *et al.* 2019; Blankertz and Robinson 1997; Ogungbamila *et al.* 2014). According to Parzefall and Shapiro (2011), negative events which are short and few do not always have detrimental effects, but if they occur frequently and for an extended period of time, they can lead to violations. This explains emotional exhaustion as a mediating factor. Wu *et al.* (2017) demonstrated the link between customer orientation and the desire to leave, as well as the role of emotional tiredness as a mediator. H4 emotional exhaustion mediates the relationship between work-related bullying and employee turnover intentions among employees at Carib Trust Bank, Trinidad and Tobago Limited. H5 emotional exhaustion mediates the relationship between person-related bullying and employee turnover intentions amongst employees at Carib Trust Bank, Trinidad and Tobago Limited. H6 emotional exhaustion mediates the relationship between physically intimidating bullying and employee turnover intentions among employees at Carib Trust Bank, Trinidad and Tobago Limited

This study seeks to identify the link between three derivatives of workplace bullying, namely work-related, person-related, and physically intimidating bullying, and their impact on employee turnover intentions in both a developing and multicultural context.

3 METHODOLOGY

In undertaking this research paper, a quantitative approach to data collection and analysis was utilized to explore the empirical relationship between workplace bullying and employee turnover intention.

Moreover, the questionnaire used in this study has been employed in numerous studies on workplace bullying. In fact, Einarsen *et al.* (2001) have utilized the 22-item Negative Acts Questionnaire (NAQ) in workplace bullying studies since this scale focuses on behaviours that characterize workplace bullying. The survey questionnaire was divided into five sections. Employee demographics made up the first section. The second, third, and fourth sections were intended to collect information on work-related bullying, person-related bullying and physically intimidating bullying. respectively. The fourth section measured turnover intentions using the anticipated Turnover Scale developed by Hinshaw and Atwood (1978), West and Nash (2001) and Hart (2005). The final section comprised emotional exhaustion using the Maslach Burnout Inventory. However, while the Maslach Burnout Inventory Scale consists of 22 items which covers components of personalization and accomplishment, for the purpose of this study only the emotional exhaustion component was utilized since the other components were not related to this study or research hypotheses. Linear Multiple Regression Analysis (LMRA) was used to identify the hypothesized relationships between workplace bullying and turnover intent mediated by emotional exhaustion.

4 RESULTS AND DISCUSSION

4.1 *Normality assumptions*

The Kolmogorov-Smirnov/Shapiro-Wilk test returned $p < .05$, indicating that the distributions in this study were not normal

Table 1. Demographic characteristics of respondents (N = 126).

Category	Sub-category	n	%
Gender	Male	54	42.9%
	Female	72	57.1%
Age	18–30 years	17	13.5%
	31–40 years	70	55.6%
	41–50 years	29	23.0%
	51–59 years	10	7.9%
Marital status	Single	45	35.7%
	Married	71	56.0%
	Divorced	8	6.3%
	Common-law	2	1.6%
Education level	Secondary school	52	41.3%
	Associate degree	17	13.5%
	Bachelor's degree	48	38.1%
	Master's degree	9	7.1%
	PhD	0	0.0%
Current position	Supervisor	32	25.4%
	CSR/Clerk	83	65.9%
	Other	11	8.7%
	Manager	0	0.0%
Years of service	1–5 years	10	7.9%
	5–10 years	7	5.6%

4.2 *Current state of workplace bullying*

In this study, the independent variables of work-related bullying, person-related bullying, and physically intimidating bullying all had variance explained scores of 68%, 80% and 78%

respectively. Employee exhaustion and turnover variance scores were 93% and 76% respectively. The reliability scores for work-related bullying, person-related bullying, and physically intimidating bullying were 73% 94% and 85% respectively. The mediating variable of emotional exhaustion and the dependent variable of turnover intent were also above the accepted benchmark of 70% being 98% and 74%.

4.3 *Direct relationship (Workplace bullying and turnover intentions)*

The relationship between work related bullying and turnover intent is positive and significant ($\beta = .219$ and $p < .05$). The relationship between person related bullying and turnover intent is positive but insignificant ($\beta = .121$ and $p > .05$ thus the second hypothesis that there is a positive relationship between person related bullying and employee turnover intentions amongst is not supported in this study. Finally, the relationship between physical intimidating bullying is positive but insignificant ($\beta = .195$ and $p > .05$), indicating that the third hypothesis that there is a positive relationship between physical intimidating bullying and employee turnover intentions amongst employees employed at Carib Trust Bank, Trinidad and Tobago Limited, is not supported in this study.

4.4 *Mediation effect analysis (Workplace bullying and emotional exhaustion path A)*

Workplace bullying was statistically associated with turnover intentions indirectly through emotional exhaustion ($\beta =.328$ and $p < 0.05$). Person-related bullying was not statistically associated with turnover intentions indirectly through emotional exhaustion ($\beta = 0.042$ and $p > 0.05$). Physical intimidating bullying was also not statistically associated with turnover intentions indirectly through emotional exhaustion ($\beta = 0.270$ and $p > 0.05$).

4.5 *Mediation effect analysis (Emotional exhaustion and turnover intentions Path B).*

Workplace bullying predictors were not statistically associated with turnover intentions; however, emotional exhaustion was statistically significant in predicting employee turnover intent ($\beta = 0.228$, $p < 0.05$). This result indicates that emotional exhaustion did play a mediated role between workplace bullying and turnover intentions with an interaction effect = 0.09 (Product of Paths A and B; thus supporting the fourth, fifth and sixth hypotheses that emotional exhaustion mediates the relationship between work related bullying, person related bullying and physically intimidating bullying and employee turnover intentions amongst employees employed at the bank.

In summary, the current state of workplace and person-related bullying shows that workplace bullying is much more dominant than person-related bullying in the bank.

4.6 *Discussion of findings and hypothesized relationships*

In this study, there was a positive and statistical association between workplace bullying and turnover intent; thus, the first hypothesis, which postulated that there is a positive relationship between work-related bullying and employee turnover intentions amongst employees employed at Carib Trust Bank, Trinidad and Tobago Limited, is supported. This result was not unexpected as Zapf and Gross (2011) posited that workplace bullying may cause its targets to consider leaving their jobs to avoid mental burden thus impacting turnover intent. This finding also supports studies by Faheem, Rasool and Arzu (2013), who also found that work-related bullying had a positive effect on employees' intentions to leave their jobs once emotional exhaustion stepped in. Furthermore, workplace bullying can be a significant stressor, so employees often react to the bullying in an attempt to cope with the stress that is created, along with other organizational measures, which may also exacerbate the employees' stressors (Einarsen *et al.* 2018). In underpinning COR theory, once workplace bullying generates that negative feeling amongst the target employees, these employees will utilize all necessary resources to exile themselves from the work place bullying such as requesting transfers to lateral positions or they may apply for internal positions out of their geographical locations just to remove themselves from being the target of work place bullying thus giving up the resources they once utilized to gain their current positions.

4.7 *Person related bullying and turnover intent*

Unlike workplace bullying, which derived a positive and significant association with turnover intent, this was not the same direction for person-related bullying. In fact, person-related bullying was found to be positive but not statistically significant; thus, the second hypothesis, which postulated a positive relationship between person-related bullying and employee turnover intentions among employees at Carib Trust Bank Trinidad and Tobago, is not supported in this study. This may be attributed to effective bullying policies instituted by the bank. The policies may buffer or dissuade persons from person related bullying.

4.8 *Physically intimidating bullying and turnover intent*

The third and final hypothesized relationship that was tested in this study was the relationship between physically intimidating bullying and turnover intent. The findings showed that physically intimidating bullying was positive but not significant; thus, the third hypothesis that predicted a relationship between physically intimidating bullying and employee turnover intentions amongst employees employed at Carib Trust Bank, Trinidad and Tobago, is not supported in this study. Similarly, the bank's bullying policies may also deter this type of behaviour.

4.9 *Mediating effects of emotional exhaustion*

This study attempted to investigate whether an employee's emotional exhaustion has an indirect or direct relationship with workplace bullying (work-related, person-related bullying, and physically intimidating bullying) and employee turnover intent among employees of Carib Trust Bank Ltd's South Cluster of branches. Furthermore, the mediating role of emotional exhaustion allowed for explaining the real relationship between workplace bullying and turnover intentions. The findings in this study showed that emotional exhaustion did play a positive and significant mediating role with an interaction effect of (0.09) between workplace bullying and turnover intentions thus supporting the hypothesized relationships (H4, H5 and H6). While the interaction may be minimal, this result is well documented in the literature as studies by (Noh 2019; Blankertz and Robinson 1997; Ogungbamila *et al.* 2014) have found positive correlations between emotional burnout and turnover intentions. Moreover, COR can be supported here as Hobfoll (2001) states that burnt-out emotions will also cause the depletion of the employee's resources and thus employees will often find methods of intervention to protect their resources. Moreover, While the results indicate a statistically significant mediation effect, the effect size (0.09) is relatively small and should be interpreted with caution (Preacher and Hayes 2008). This suggests that although emotional exhaustion plays a role in shaping turnover intent, its impact in this context may be limited. One possible explanation for this modest effect lies in the organizational and cultural environment. In Caribbean workplaces, including Trinidad and Tobago, strong interpersonal networks and managerial intervention may serve as protective factors that buffer the negative consequences of bullying (Marchand and Vandenberghe 2016).

It is also noteworthy to mention that while the focus of this study concentrated on workplace bullying and turnover intentions mediated by employee exhaustion, there exist other factors that will create emotional exhaustion in addition to workplace bullying. In fact, when employees attempt to balance their work-life relationships, emotional exhaustion can set in. Moreover, supervisory support can be another factor that contributes to emotional exhaustion, as a supportive supervisor can reduce emotional tiredness, which is linked to reduced work satisfaction and eventual turnover intent (Maslach and Jackson 1981; Hagen 1989). Further research can attempt to investigate the role of supervisor support as a moderating variable between workplace bullying and turnover intent employees who have been bullied in the workplace receives caring and supervisory support will have significantly less intention to leave their job as against employees who do not receive supervisory support.

5 CONCLUSION

This study has shown that workplace bullying is a notable factor influencing employee turnover intentions, with emotional exhaustion emerging as a mediating variable in this relationship. These findings align with previous research by Einarsen *et al.* (2003) and Attar and Al Sharqi (2021), which highlight the psychological impact of bullying in the workplace. In this context, work-related bullying was positively and significantly associated with turnover intention, while person-related and physically intimidating bullying did not demonstrate statistically significant relationships. These results suggest that specific organizational and cultural factors at Carib Trust Bank may influence how bullying is experienced and reported by employees. While the mediating effect of emotional exhaustion was statistically significant, it was modest in size (0.09), and its practical implications should be interpreted cautiously. The findings indicate that emotional exhaustion may contribute to turnover intent but should not be overstated in terms of its standalone predictive power.

From a managerial standpoint, these insights reinforce the need for proactive interventions to reduce workplace bullying and mitigate its effects. Employees at Carib Trust Bank reported concerns such as excessive monitoring and unmanageable workloads, which may impact morale and retention. To address these challenges, the organization may consider revisiting workload distribution and operational processes. Forming cross-functional "Think Tank Teams" made up of managers, supervisors, and staff can facilitate dialogue and innovation, particularly in revising bureaucratic procedures that may contribute to stress. Furthermore, leveraging both intrinsic and extrinsic motivational tools can promote a more engaged workforce. To support employees' psychological well-being, the bank should ensure the presence of clearly communicated anti-bullying policies, provide training on identifying and reporting bullying behaviors, and offer access to mental health support. These measures not only help create a healthier work environment but also contribute to reducing turnover and strengthening organizational resilience

NOTE

1. The name CaribTrust Bank Ltd is a pseudonym used to protect the confidentiality of the organization in this study.

REFERENCES

Abbasi, S.M., and Hollman, K.W. (2000). *Turnover: The real bottom line. Public Personnel Management*, 29(3), 333–342. https://doi.org/10.1177/009102600002900303

Adams A. (1997) *Bullying at Work – How to Confront and Overcome it*. Virago Press, London.

Bergbom, B., Vaananen, M., and Kinnunen, U. (2015). Immigrants and natives at work: Exposure to workplace bullying. *Employee Relations, 37*(2), 158–175.

Blankertz, L.E. and Robinson, S.E. (1997), Turnover intentions of community mental health workers in psychosocial rehabilitation services, *Community Mental Health Journal*, Vol. 33 No. 6, pp.

Boxall, Peter, and John Purcell. (2008). *Strategy and Human Resource Management.* Hampshire, Palgrave Macmillan

Ciby, M. and Raya, R.P. (2015), Workplace bullying: a review of the defining features, measurement methods and prevalence across continents, *IIM Kozhikode Society & Management Review*, Vol. 4 No. 1,

Cropanzano, R., Rupp, D.E. and Byrne, Z.S. (2003), The relationship of emotional exhaustion to work attitudes, job performance, and organizational citizenship behaviors, *Journal of Applied Psychology*, Vol. 88 No.

Devonish, D. (2013), Job demands, health, and absenteeism: does bullying make things worse?, Employee Relations, Vol. 36 No. 2, pp. 165–181.

Einarsen, S., Skogstad, A., Rørvik, E., Lande, A.B. and Nielsen, M.B. (2018), Climate for conflict management, exposure to workplace bullying and work engagement: a moderated mediation analysis, *The International Journal of Human Resource Management*, Vol. 29 No. 3, pp.

Einarsen, S., Skogstad, A., Rørvik, E., Lande, Å. B., and Nielsen, M.B. (2016). Climate for conflict management, exposure to workplace bullying and work engagement: A moderated mediation analysis. *The International Journal of Human Resource Management, 29*(3), 549–570. https://doi.org/10.1080/09585192.2016.1164216.

Faheem, Rasool, and Arzu, E. (2013). Turnover Intention and Voluntary Turnover: The Moderating roles of Locus control and Group Cohesion. *JAP*, 90

Frick, S.E., Fletcher, K.A., Ramsay, P.S. and Bedwell, W.L. (2018), Understanding team maladaptation through the lens of the four R's of adaptation, *Human Resource Management Review*, Vol. 28

Giorgi, G., Mancuso, S., Fiz Perez, F., D'Antonio, A., Mucci, N., Cupelli, V. and Arcangeli, G. (2016), Bullying among nurses and its relationship with workplace bullying and organizational climate, *International Journal of Nursing Practice*, Vol. 22 No. 2, pp. 160–168.

Glambek, Mats, Stig Berge Matthiesen, Jørn Hetland, and Ståle Einarsen. (2014) Workplace bullying as an antecedent to job insecurity and intention to leave: a 6-month prospective study. *Human Resource Management Journal* 24, no. 3 : 255–268

Hagen, Jan L. (1989), Income maintenance workers: Burned-Out, dissatisfied, and leaving, *Journal of Social Service Research*, 13 (1), 1989.

Hinkin and Tracey. (2000). The role of the change in the relationship between job commitment and turnover. *JAP,* 92(42).

Hobfoll, S.E. (1989). Conservation of resources: A new attempt at conceptualizing stress. *American Psychologist*, 44:

Hobfoll, S.E. 2001. The influence of culture, community, and the nested self in the stress process: Advancing conservation of resources theory. *Applied Psychology: An International Review*, 50: 337–370

Hossam, M. and Abu, E. (2014) An exploratory study on turnover Intention Among private Sector employees., *IJBM*, 5(8)

James, L., and Mathew, L. (2012). Employee retention strategies: IT industry. *SCMS Journal of Indian Management*, 9(3), 79–87

Leymann, Heinz. The content and development of mobbing at work. (1996). *European Journal of Work and Organizational Psychology* 5, no. 2

Marchand, C. and Vandenberghe, C. (2016), Perceived organizational support, emotional exhaustion, and turnover: the moderating role of negative affectivity, *International Journal of Stress Management*, Vol. 23 No. 4, p. 350

Martins, J.M., Shahzad, M.F., and Javed, I. (2023). Assessing the impact of workplace harassment on turnover intention: Evidence from the banking industry. *Emerging Science Journal*, 7(5), 1699–1722. https://doi.org/10.28991/ESJ-2023-07-05-016

Maslach, Christina and Susan E. Jackson (1981), The Maslach Burnout Inventory, Palo Alto: Consulting Psychologists Press.

Mobley. (1997). How job dissatisfaction leads to employee turnover. *Journal of Business Psychology*, 2(3)

Naseer, S. and Raja, U. (2016), POS and emotional dissonance as resource depletion mechanisms in workplace bullying and job strains, *Academy of Management Proceedings*, Vol. 2016 No. 1, p. 13833.

Noh, M., Jang, H. and Choi, B.J. (2019), Organisational justice, emotional exhaustion, and turnover intention among Korean IT professionals: moderating roles of job characteristics and social support, *International Journal of Technology Management*, Vol. 79 Nos 3–4, pp. 322–344.

Ogungbamila, B., Balogun, A.G., Ogungbamila, A. and Oladele, R.S. (2014), Job stress, emotional labor, and emotional intelligence as predictors of turnover intention: evidence from two service occupations, *Mediterranean Journal of Social Sciences*, Vol. 5 No. 6, p. 351.

Parzefall, M.R. and Coyle-Shapiro, J.A. (2011), Making sense of psychological contract breach, *Journal of Managerial Psychology*, Vol. 26 No. 1, pp. 12–27.

Ramdeo, S., Balwant, P., Cowell, N. and Persadie, N., (2020). A moderated mediation model of bullying, support, justice, and organizational outcomes. *International Journal of Employment Studies*, 28(1), pp.48–81.

Saunders, Paula, Amy Huynh, and Jane Goodman-Delahunty. (2007). Defining workplace bullying behaviour professional lay definitions of workplace bullying. *International journal of law and psychiatry*

Tan, K., Lew, T.Y. and Sim, A. (2019), An innovative solution to leverage meaningful work to attract, retain and manage generation Y employees in Singapore's hotel industry, *Worldwide Hospitality and Tourism Themes*, May, doi: 10.1108/WHATT-11-2018-0075

Van Dyk, J. (2016). The mediating effect of a psychological well-being profile in the bullying and turnover intention relation. Unpublished doctoral thesis, University of South Africa, Pretoria, South Africa.

Wali and Zekeriya. (2013). Effects of Family Structure on Organizational Commitment and Turnover Intention. *Academy of Management Journal*, 42(12).

Wu, X., Shie, A.J. and Gordon, D. (2017), Impact of customer orientation on turnover intention: mediating role of emotional labour, *International Journal of Organizational Analysis*, Vol. 25 No. 5, pp.

Zapf, Dieter. (1999). Organizational, work group related and personal causes of mobbing/bullying at work. *International Journal of Manpower*. 20. 70–85. 10.1108/01437729910268669

Zapf and Gross. (2011). The effects of workplace bullying behaviour on employee turnover intention. *Annual Review of Psychology*, 41(17).

Moving Towards Sustainable Businesses and Developing More Resilient Economies – Rashid and Annansingh-Jamieson (Eds)
© 2026 The Author(s), ISBN: 978-1-041-08875-2

AI analysis of psychological biases in German stock market investments

O. Idrizi
Mediterranean University of Albania, Tirana, Albania, AUTO1 Group, Berlin, Germany

M. Kazo
Business Consultant, Payments at msg for Banking, Munich, Germany

ABSTRACT: Investment decisions in financial markets are often influenced by psychological biases, leading to deviations from rational economic factors. This research tends to explore the impact of such biases on investment decision-making in the German stock market by leveraging Artificial Intelligence (AI) and Machine Learning (ML) models. It attempts to address how Artificial Intelligence can help financial planners consider their behavioral biases and proposes the adoption of AI in financial planning to avoid behavioral biases. To achieve this, we will examine survey data gathered from German investors, aiming to reveal correlations between five significant psychological biases (overconfidence, herding behavior, loss aversion, mental accounting, and anchoring) and the success rates of investments, which traditional statistical approaches may overlook. Beyond contributing to the academic purpose, the implications of this study extend to practical applications for investors and financial advisors, policymakers by emphasizing the necessity of incorporating psychological considerations in investment strategies.

Keywords: Artificial intelligence, machine learning, psychological behaviors, investment decision, stock market

1 INTRODUCTION

The decisions made by investors play a critical role in determining their investment performance. Numerous studies, although limited in number for the German market, have consistently shown that psychological biases significantly influence investors' decision- making processes. Therefore, investigating the impact of these biases on success rates holds great importance, as it offers a new viewpoint on the field of behavioral finance. This research paper aims to investigate the potential correlation between five well-known psychological biases (overconfidence, loss aversion, mental accounting, anchoring, and herding behavior) and the rate of success in investment decisions on the German stock market applying AI and ML to detect complex patterns in investor behavior that may be overlooked by traditional statistical approaches and also to contribute to the evolving literature on the use of AI in behavioral finance. Using a combination of quantitative analysis and empirical research methodology, data will be gathered through a survey distributed to German stock market investors. In this paper, a comprehensive literature review will be presented, introducing the psychological biases from different authors perspective.

DOI: 10.1201/9781003647300-11

2 LITERATURE REVIEW

Behavioral finance has emerged as a significant development from the traditional financial paradigms that emphasize rationality and market efficiency. According to Schiller, an important aspect of behavioral finance is its focus on market anomalies that are not accounted for by the efficient market theory (Shiller 2003).

Given the implication of biases in financial decision-making and recognizing the constraints of clients' psychographic classification methods and the digitalization of financial planning in addressing these biases, we advocate for the integration of AI into financial planning services. The financial planners will employ AI to address human biases to attain optimal financial judgments for their clients (Jarrahi *et al.* 2022). AI-driven financial planning services can aid financial planners in creating risk-efficient portfolios by managing the market timing and mitigating the behavioral biases of both clients and planners. Recent advances in AI have opened new opportunities for analyzing unstructured behavioral data and investor sentiment, further expanding the toolkit available for behavioral finance research. This study focuses on five biases: loss aversion, anchoring, mental accounting, overconfidence, and herding behavior. To proceed, the study will conduct an in-depth literature review, followed by an empirical research analysis.

2.1 *Behavior finance*

In the field of finance, conventional theories assume that investors are rational and that markets function efficiently. However, instances of irrational behavior among investors have been revealed through real-world economic crises and price variations.

According to Shefrin, behavioral finance examines the psychological influences on financial decision-making and the market, emphasizing the interplay between financial behavior and psychology. While the efficient market hypothesis assumes that all investors have equal and simultaneous access to available information and news, this assumption is also acknowledged within the field of behavioral finance (Shefrin 2000).

Kourtidis *et al.* explain that while traditional financial theories focus on how individuals aim to maximize their wealth, behavioral finance studies how individuals behave in real financial situations. It examines the psychological factors that influence the interactions of individuals and organizations with financial markets (Kourtidis *et al.* 2011).

2.2 *Psychological factors impacting behavioral finance/ investor decision making*

Cognitive and emotional processes affect how investors make decisions about investments, which can lead to psychological or behavioral biases. These biases affect all investors, although the degree to which they do so may depend on the investor's traits. Pompian categorizes them as either cognitive or emotional. Cognitive biases refer to mental tendencies that can affect decision-making, including overconfidence, anchoring, and mental accounting. On the other hand, emotional biases commonly observed include loss aversion, overconfidence, and herding behavior (Pompian 2012).

2.2.1 *Loss aversion*

The concept of loss aversion bias was initially introduced within the framework of prospect theory by Kahneman and Tversky (Tversky and Kahneman 1974). The essence of this matter is that investors do not assign equal importance to profit and loss. To mitigate the risks associated with loss, investors affected by this bias tend to make decisions based on potential gains rather than potential losses. Loss aversion is a phenomenon experienced by investors who perceive avoiding losses on their stock market investments as equivalent to making profits.

2.2.2 *Anchoring*

Anchoring, a cognitive bias introduced by Amos Tversky and Daniel Kahneman, is a significant factor in human decision-making. The anchoring effect refers to individuals relying greatly on an initial piece of information, known as the anchor, when making subsequent judgments or decisions (Tversky and Kahneman 1974). Typically, investors use their initial purchase price as a reference point and react to price changes relative to their initial purchase price.

Anchoring bias, despite its valuable contributions to decision-making research, presents risks when it comes to financial contexts. Investors often tend to focus on past performance, assuming that it will continue in the future, even when faced with stagnant markets (Juneja 2015).

Upon further examination of his study, it becomes evident that the anchoring bias phenomenon leads individuals to tend to postpone the sale of their investments.

2.2.3 *Overconfidence*

The psychological bias of overconfidence is a phenomenon where an individual has an excessive level of confidence in their knowledge and abilities. The investor who shows overconfidence tends to rely on their own ideas and intuitions rather than seeking advice from others, believing that this approach leads to greater success (Bouteska and Regaieg 2020).

According to Razek's definition, overconfidence refers to the tendency to overestimate the likelihood of a particular set of events. The argument put forth by the author concerns to the operational reflection of a concept through a comparison of the assigned probability with the proportion of correct assessments associated with said probability (Razek 2011). According to Agrawal's findings, individuals who exhibit overconfidence tend to overestimate their level of knowledge, underestimate potential risks, and overestimate their capacity to exert control over events. According to the author, the source of overconfidence can be traced back to individuals' prejudiced assessment of evidence (Agrawal 2012).

2.2.4 *Mental accounting*

In the field of behavioral finance, mental accounting is an interesting phenomenon that helps explain how individuals subjectively assign value and categorize their financial resources.

Thaler observed that investors often exhibit a tendency to persist with underperforming investments due to their aversion to recognizing losses. They frequently incorporate the practice of selling underperforming assets, known as losers, to limit the experience of regret to a single temporal interval. In addition, it is common for investors to distribute the sale of profitable stocks over an extended period to sustain a positive outcome (Thaler 1980). Later perspective from Thaler, mental accounting represents a cognitive bias that influences investors' ability to manage, assess, and monitor their financial transactions. The author implies that mental accounting is comprised of three components: firstly, the act of documenting how decisions are made and assessed; secondly, the categorization of activities into multiple accounts; and thirdly, the regularity with which each account is evaluated (Thaler 1999).

Thaler again highlights the significance of considering an alternative perspective, emphasizing the importance of making financial decisions based on a rational assessment of their implications for an individual's overall wealth status (Kahneman and Thaler 2006).

2.2.5 *Herding behavior*

Herding behavior refers to the tendency of people or investors to follow the activities of others, often without doing their own research or analysis. People who exhibit herding behavior make decisions based on what a bigger group or the market consensus thinks, rather than their own assessments of important variables or information (Shiller 2004).

Investors prefer to put their own private and personal needs first when making investment decisions, even when the market changes. They use shared market knowledge to help them make their selections. So, during times of market instability, herding is likely to happen more often. When investors herd together, it can lead to market inefficiencies since it can change the values of securities and make them not reflect their genuine value (Devenow and Welch 1996).

3 RESEARCH METHODOLOGY: MACHINE LEARNING ANALYSIS OF BEHAVIORAL BIASES

This methodology enables a thorough evaluation of investor behavior and its correlation with market results. We utilized a random sampling method to make sure the sample was representative. The study's target group was individual investors who were actively trading on the German stock market. The goal was to show how different the investor community is by dividing the sample into groups based on things like age, gender, education, job, income, profession, investment experience, and more. There were 82 people in the study's sample size. We have implemented the power analysis and the observed power for each correlation. Using Fisher's z transform for testing Pearson correlations (two-tailed, α = 0.05). With n = 82 we have about 80% power to detect correlations with absolute magnitude $\approx$ 0.31 or greater.

There were two parts to the questionnaire. Eight questions in the first portion were meant to get broad background information about the investors. It was meant to learn about the demographic parameters that made up the group of investors who filled out the questionnaire, such as their age, gender, occupation, and other traits. The second part of the assessment includes all the questions that indirectly address behavioral biases. The response rate is a five-point Likert scale (1-5), which is a commonly used rating scale for gathering opinions and attitudes. This scale was used to find out how much individual investors agreed that behavioral issues affected their investment decisions. These points show how much you agree or disagree: strongly disagree, disagree, neither agree nor disagree, agree, and highly agree. The questionnaire consisted of validated scales and items that were specifically related to overconfidence, loss aversion, herding behavior, anchoring, and mental accounting biases that have been identified in the existing literature. The five-point Likert scale model was based on a previous study conducted by Waruingi in 2011. The survey was done online using Google Forms, which made it easy for a lot of investors to take part and for the results to be collected quickly. The link was sent out to German stock market participants through investing forums, professional networks, and specific social media groups.

Two Machine Learning techniques were employed to gain a better understanding of the background of the investors and examine the relationship between behavioral biases and investment decisions after collecting the data from the questionnaire. First, Regression analyses. Ordinary Least Squares (OLS) was applied to Dependent variable: Success Rate and Independent variables: Overconfidence, Herding, Loss Aversion, Mental Accounting, Anchoring. It was generated Reports for Coefficients, p-values, R^2. Additionally, another analysis was Clustering model. We have applied K-Means Clustering which has used as input five bias scores, tested k = 2 to 4 based on Mean bias scores and Mean success rate.

3.1 *Regression analysis*

The Figure 1 indicate the linear regression model which had low explanatory power ($R^2 \approx 0.186$), reflecting the complexity of investment outcomes. The overconfidence coefficient, on the other hand, was positive and statistically significant ($\beta \approx +0.1259$, $p \approx 0.112$). Herding's coefficient is positive($\beta \approx 0.2211$) and not significant ($p \approx 0.011$). Loss aversion, mental accounting, and anchoring are not statistically significant.

```
                                                      OLS Regression Results
==================================================================================================================================================
Dep. Variable:     What success rate would you attribute to your investments in the stock market over the past year?   R-squared:              0.186
Model:                                                                                                          OLS   Adj. R-squared:         0.124
Method:                                                                                               Least Squares   F-statistic:            3.014
Date:                                                                                              Sun, 10 Aug 2025   Prob (F-statistic):    0.0164
Time:                                                                                                      11:52:59   Log-Likelihood:       -38.950
No. Observations:                                                                                                72   AIC:                    89.90
Df Residuals:                                                                                                    66   BIC:                    103.6
Df Model:                                                                                                         5
Covariance Type:                                                                                          nonrobust
======================================================================================
                         coef    std err          t      P>|t|      [0.025      0.975]
--------------------------------------------------------------------------------------
const                  1.8977      0.371      5.120      0.000       1.158       2.638
Overconfidence         0.1259      0.078      1.610      0.112      -0.030       0.282
Herding                0.2211      0.085      2.607      0.011       0.052       0.390
Loss Aversion         -0.1173      0.082     -1.432      0.157      -0.281       0.046
Mental Accounting      0.0197      0.072      0.273      0.786      -0.125       0.164
Anchoring             -0.0017      0.096     -0.018      0.986      -0.193       0.190
==============================================================================
Omnibus:                        9.694   Durbin-Watson:                   1.880
Prob(Omnibus):                  0.008   Jarque-Bera (JB):                7.276
Skew:                          -0.658   Prob(JB):                       0.0263
Kurtosis:                       2.166   Cond. No.                         56.7
==============================================================================
```

Figure 1. OLS regression results.

The OLS model explains about 18.6% of the variance in self-reported investment. The F-test is significant indicating that at least one predictor contributes to explaining success. In summary, among this survey of German stock investors, only Overconfidence and hading have a statistically reliable association with reported investment success. Our results are in line with what behavioral finance says: overconfidence and herding behaviour align investment decisions based on the self reported investment success from the dataset. Other variables show no statistically significant effect in the model. Based on this results we can have a comparative view and can say that this results for heading behaviors are elaborated also from Bikhchandani, S., Hirshleifer, D., & Welch, I. on 1992.

3.2 *Clustering analysis*

We have generated the Table 2 analysis applying k-means clustering to the five bias scores to see if distinct investor "types" emerge. With k=2, the algorithm partitioned investors into:

Cluster 0 ("Lower-bias" group, n=28): generally lower scores on all biases (means: Overconfidence≈2.70, Herding≈2.50, Mental≈3.07, etc.). Mean success ≈2.57. Cluster 1 ("Higher-bias" group, n=54): higher scores across the board (means: Overconfidence≈3.61, Herding≈3.74, Mental≈4.15, etc.). Mean success ≈2.89. Thus, the high-bias cluster showed a slightly higher average success rate.

Table 2. Sample output table: Cluster summary (k=2).

Cluster	Overconfidence	Herding	Loss aversion	Mental accounting	Anchoring	Avg. success
0	2.78	2.45	3.08	3.22	3.34	2.53
1	3.61	3.74	3.52	4.08	4.15	2.89

Cluster analysis therefore indicates that psychological factors group investors into distinguishable types, and these types differ modestly in performance. Notably, high-overconfidence, high-herding, high-mental accounting profiles were associated with relatively higher success. Herding was less clearly positive: in regression it had a negative sign, but in clustering it aligned with the high-success group, highlighting the complexity of multiple biases interacting.

This investigation indicates that German investors form identifiable behavioral profiles, with variable success rates among them.

3.3 *Analysis of the variance inflation factor (VIF)*

We used the Variance Inflation Factor (VIF) to check if there is multicollinearity.

VIF is calculated as: $VIFi=1/(1-R^2)$. Where R^2 is the coefficient of determination from regressing predictor Xi on all other predictors. A VIF value greater than 10 is generally considered indicative of problematic multicollinearity. The VIF results reveal that all predictors substantially exceed the conventional threshold of 10, with several values exceeding 30. This indicates severe multicollinearity, meaning many behavioural variables are highly correlated. Such multicollinearity can inflate standard errors, destabilise coefficient estimates, and reduce the interpretability of the model. To address this, subsequent modelling in the future we will incorporate dimensionality reduction techniques (e.g., Principal Component Analysis or Exploratory Factor Analysis) to extract uncorrelated latent constructs from the behavioural measures.

4 RESULTS CONCLUSION AND FUTURE DIRECTIONS

The primary purpose of this research paper was to examine the potential relationship between five psychological biases – overconfidence, herding behavior, loss aversion, mental accounting, and anchoring – and the success rate of investors on the German stock market, based on ML techniques like Regression and Clustering analyzes, as a performance measurement instrument. Overconfidence and herding had a big positive effect on reported gains, while other biases didn't had any effect. Regression analysis showed that people who were more afraid of losing money and more likely to follow the crowd had less success with their investments. On the other hand, modest degrees of overconfidence, when combined with a lot of education or expertise in investing, were linked to higher self-reported outcomes.

Clustering showed that there are different types of investors based on how biased they are. It's important to remember that asking investors to rate how successful their investments have been may lead to biased answers. The K-Means clustering study found four main groups of investors with varied psychological traits. These groups were mostly different in how likely they were to be affected by biases including overconfidence, loss aversion, herding, and mental accounting. These clusters show that investors tend to act in certain ways and that bias combinations are not spread out at random.

There should be a lot of support for adding AI to systems that give financial advice. Banks and other financial institutions should deploy AI-powered technologies that can analyze how investors respond in real time, uncover patterns that imply psychological biases like overconfidence or herding, and give investors individualized, data-driven advice to help them make smarter choices.

Partnerships between the public and private sectors can aid with ongoing research into AI and behavioral finance. Building anonymized data repositories and benchmarking initiatives can also assist in making sure that AI models are fully tested and developed in a variety of markets and demographics. Finally, regulations and policies should be flexible to evolve and adjust. As AI technology and investors change, the rules that govern them must also shift. Regulators should find means to examine and change policies on a regular basis. They should also think about leveraging AI to build early warning systems that can find new behavioral dangers, such market bubbles generated by group biases, and let everyone in the market and the government know about them as soon as they happen.

REFERENCES

Agrawal, K., (2012). A conceptual framework of behavioral biases in finance. *The IUP Journal of Behavioral Finance*, 9(1), pp. 7–18.

Balcilar, M., Demirer, R. and Hammoudehc, S., (2013). Investor herds and Regime-Switching: Evidence from Gulf Arab stock markets. *Journal of Financial Markets, Institutions and Money*, 23(1), pp. 295–321. https://doi.org/10.1016/j.intfin.2012.09.007

Barber, B. and Odean, T. (2000). Trading is hazardous to your wealth: The common stock investment performance of individual investors. *Journal of Finance*. https://doi.org/10.1111/0022-1082.00226

Barber, B. and Odean, T. (2001). Boys will be boys: Gender, overconfidence, and common stock investment. *Quarterly Journal of Economics*. https://doi.org/10.1162/003355301556400

Bikhchandani, S., Hirshleifer, D., and Welch, I. (1992). A theory of fads, fashion, custom, and cultural change as informational cascades [J]. *The Journal of Political Economy*, 100, 992–1026. https://doi.org/10.1086/261849

Bouteska, A. and Regaieg, B., (2020). Loss aversion, overconfidence of investors ad their impact on market performance evidence from the US stock markets. *Journal of Economics, Finance and Administrative Science*, 25(50), pp. 455–465. https://doi.org/10.1108/JEFAS-05-2019-0077

Chen, Y., Wang, J., and Li, H., (2023). Explainable AI in behavioral finance: A review and future directions. *Journal of Behavioral and Experimental Finance*, 39, 100785. doi:10.1016/j.jbef.2023.100785

Devenow, A. and Welch, I., (1996). Rational herding in financial economics. *European Economic Review*, 40 (3/5), pp. 603–615. https://doi.org/10.1016/0014-2921(95)00073-9

García, D., and Denev, A., (2024). Machine learning for behavioral bias detection in retail investing: Evidence from European markets. *European Journal of Finance*, 30(2), pp. 145–167. doi:10.1080/1351847X.2023.2256789

Jarrahi, M.H., Lutz, C., and Newlands, G. (2022). Artificial intelligence, human intelligence and hybrid intelligence based on mutual augmentation. *Big Data & Society*, 9(2), 1–6. doi:10.1177/20539517221142824

Juneja, P., (2015). *MSG Management Study Guide.*

Kahneman, D. and Riepe, M.W., (1998). Aspects of investor psychology. *The Journal of Portfolio Management*, 24(4), pp. 52–65. https://doi.org/10.3905/jpm.1998.409643

Kahneman, D., and Tversky, A. (1972). Subjective probability: A judgment of representativeness. *Cognitive Psychology*, 3(3), 430–454. https://doi.org/10.1016/0010-0285(72)90016-3

Kahneman, D. and Thaler, R.H., (2006). Anomalies: Utility Maximization and Experienced Utility. *Journal of economic perspectives*, 20(1), pp. 221–234. https://doi.org/10.1257/089533006776526076

Kim, S., and Lee, J., (2024). Deep learning approaches to investor sentiment and stock market prediction: A cross-market analysis. *Expert Systems with Applications*, 237, 121235. doi:10.1016/j.eswa.2023.121235. https://doi.org/10.1016/j.eswa.2023.121235

Kourtidis, D., Sevic, Z. and Chatzoglou, P., (2011). Investors' trading activity: A behavioural perspective and empirical results. *The Journal of Socio-Economics*, 4(5), pp. 548–557. https://doi.org/10.1016/j.socec.2011.04.010

Razek, Y.H.A., (2011). *Behavioral Finance and Revisiting the Behavioral Life Cycle Theory*, s.l.: SSRN. https://doi.org/10.2139/ssrn.1971311

Shefrin, H., (2000). *Beyond greed and fear. Understanding behavioral finance and the psychology of investing*, s.l.: Greece: *Benou Publishing Company*.

Shiller, R.J., (2003). From efficient markets theory to behavioral finance. *Journal of Economic Perspectives*, 17(1), pp. 83–104. https://doi.org/10.1257/089533003321164967

Shiller, R.J., (2004). Behavioral economics and institutional innovation. *Southern Economic Journal*, 72(2), pp. 269–283. https://doi.org/10.2307/20111813

Statman, M., (2008). *What is behavioral finance?, s.l.*: John Wiley & Sons.

Thaler, R., (1980). Towards a positive theory of consumer choice. *Journal of Economic Behaviour and Organization*, 1(1), pp. 39–60. https://doi.org/10.1016/0167-2681(80)90051-7

Thaler, R., (1999). Mental accounting matters. *Journal of Behavioral Decision Making*, 12(3), pp. 183–206. https://doi.org/10.1002/(SICI)1099-0771(199909)12:3<183::AID-BDM318>3.0.CO;2-F

Tversky, A. and Kahneman, D., (1974). *Judgment under uncertainty: Heuristics and biases. Science*, 185(4157), pp. 1124–1131. https://doi.org/10.1126/science.185.4157.1124

Vrontis, D., Christofi, M., Pereira, V., Tarba, S., Makrides, A., and Trichina, E. (2022). Artificial intelligence, robotics, advanced technologies and human resource management: *A systematic review. International Journal of Human Resource Management*, 33(6), 1237–1266. doi:10.1080/09585192.2020.1871398

Zhou, L., and He, M., (2024). Large language models for behavioral finance: Opportunities and challenges. *Frontiers in Artificial Intelligence*, 7, 1198452. doi:10.3389/frai.2024.1198452

Moving Towards Sustainable Businesses and Developing More Resilient Economies –
Rashid and Annansingh-Jamieson (Eds)
 ISBN: 978-1-041-08875-2

Secure precision agriculture throughout the agribusiness value chain leveraging 5G RedCap IoT and blockchain protocols

E.U. Ogbodo
National Institute of Telecommunication, Santa Rita do Sapuca, MG, Brazil

A. Kamruzzaman
School of Business and IS, York College, The City University of New York (CUNY), NY, USA

L.L. Mendes
National Institute of Telecommunication, Santa Rita do Sapuca, MG, Brazil

ABSTRACT: The integration of digital technologies into precision agriculture is transforming traditional agribusiness into an intelligent, data-centric ecosystem. However, achieving secure, energy-efficient, and scalable communication in remote and infrastructure-poor environments remains a critical challenge. This study introduces a novel framework combining fifth generation (5G) communication reduced capability (RedCap) internet of things (IoT) devices, edge AI analytics, and blockchain-enabled lightweight cryptographic protocols to secure the agribusiness value chain. We propose a two-part system: (1) a threat-aware RedCap deployment model incorporating anomaly detection and zero-trust enforcement, and (2) a RedCap relay mesh (RRM) framework that extends network coverage in off-grid communication zones using peer-assisted relaying. RRM enables RedCap nodes to form energy-aware, multi-hop mesh networks in regions with sparse or absent base stations. Telemetry security and traceability are enforced via a lightweight blockchain and elliptic curve cryptography (ECC)-based cryptographic scheme. Performance evaluations demonstrate improved reliability, reduced energy consumption, and robust threat detection across large-scale agricultural deployments. This integrated approach strengthens precision agriculture infrastructures aligned with global goals for food security and digital transformation.

Keywords: 5G Redcap, IoT, Agribusiness, Blockchain, Precision Agriculture, Edge AI, Confidence Interval, Paired t-test

1 INTRODUCTION

Precision agriculture has emerged as a transformative paradigm in global food production, driven by advances in artificial intelligence (AI), the Internet of Things (IoT), and modern communication networks. Real-time telemetry from smart soil probes, weather stations, UAVs, and autonomous machinery now feeds predictive analytics that improve yield estimation, irrigation scheduling, pest management, and farm logistics (Bilal and Ahmed 2024). Despite these capabilities, adoption in rural and remote regions remains limited due to persistent infrastructural barriers—namely unreliable connectivity, energy constraints, and data-security vulnerabilities (Mahmoud and Rahman 2021).

Many agricultural areas suffer from weak mobile coverage, minimal fiber backhaul, and intermittent power supply, making traditional cellular architectures impractical. Fixed base stations, centralized trust models, and high deployment costs are poorly suited for fragmented farmlands. Even where connectivity exists, constrained IoT devices often lack the

 DOI: 10.1201/9781003647300-12

computational capacity and battery resources to support conventional cryptographic protocols, compromising secure communication and data authenticity (Singh and Lopez 2023). These gaps undermine the reliability of precision irrigation systems, supply-chain monitoring, and regulatory reporting.

To address this divide, we introduce the Reduced Capability (RedCap) Relay Mesh (RRM), a lightweight, peer-assisted communication layer extending 5G RedCap for off-grid agricultural environments. RRM enables RedCap devices to autonomously forward data through multi-hop paths until reaching an edge gateway or base station. Inspired by device-to-device (D2D) strategies used in vehicular and disaster-response networks, RRM is adapted for low-power agribusiness applications and medium-rate Industrial IoT (IIoT) workloads (Ogbodo and Adnan 2024). Importantly, off-grid here denotes zones lacking mobile-network infrastructure—not necessarily electricity, which may be supplied by solar microgrids or battery systems (Costa *et al.* 2020).

Each RedCap node in the RRM system dynamically evaluates its proximity, signal strength, and power budget to identify optimal forwarding paths. The mesh self-heals in real time, bypassing faulty nodes and adjusting for environmental changes, thus ensuring data delivery from deep-field sensors to the network edge. This approach eliminates the bottleneck of relying solely on base station coverage, making it especially suitable for large, fragmented farming regions where centralized architectures are neither scalable nor economical (Silva and Gomes 2021).

Security within the RRM architecture is achieved through integration with blockchain-backed lightweight cryptographic protocols. Devices authenticate each other using Elliptic Curve Cryptography (ECC), while telemetry is encrypted with ChaCha20-Poly1305 and logged via SHA-256 digests to a private blockchain hosted at the edge. Smart contracts validate the authenticity and timestamp of incoming data packets before transmission to the cloud, ensuring integrity, non-repudiation, and traceability across the agricultural value chain (Chatterjee and Bhattacharjee *et al.* 2024; Wang and Chen 2022). Furthermore, anomaly detection models deployed on edge gateways assess behavioral patterns using unsupervised learning algorithms, allowing for early detection of spoofing, firmware tampering, or sensor drift (Johnson and Silva 2023).

The convergence of 5G RedCap, blockchain security, and edge AI within the RRM framework represents a resilient and cost-effective infrastructure model for digital agriculture. It not only extends the geographic reach of precision farming but also enhances the reliability and accountability of data transmission, critical for sustainable agricultural innovation in the Global South. Building on these capabilities, this study addresses the central research question: "How does the RRM-based IoT improve connectivity and security in off-grid agricultural zones?" The paper presents the design, implementation, and performance analysis of the proposed architecture, offering practical insights for governments, agribusinesses, and rural technology providers striving to close the connectivity gap in farming systems.

2 IOT ARCHITECTURE, CHALLENGES, CLASSIFICATION, AND CRYPTOGRAPHIC ALGORITHMS

This section presents the foundational IoT architecture for smart agriculture, explores its key challenges, classifies constrained devices, and introduces lightweight cryptographic algorithms tailored for secure, energy-efficient operations in rural deployments.

2.1 *IoT architecture and challenges*

IoT systems in agriculture are structured across four functional layers: Application, Middleware, Network, and Perception. Each layer plays a critical role in enabling intelligent monitoring and actuation while simultaneously exposing the system to unique security threats (Pandey and Bhushan 2024). At the Application Layer, which handles user interfaces, analytics, and decision support, common attacks include buffer overflow, SQL injection, phishing, and cross-site scripting (Mohammad and Vishal 2021).

The Middleware Layer, acting as a bridge between applications and lower-level communications, faces threats such as unauthorized access, replay attacks, and sleep deprivation attacks (Chifor *et al.* 2017).

The Network Layer, responsible for routing and connectivity, is vulnerable to DDoS, spoofing, and man-in-the-middle attacks, while the Perception Layer, comprising sensors and actuators is susceptible to jamming, battery draining, and physical tampering. Table 1 explains attacks in various IoT Layers. The IoT architecture is depicted in Figure 1, which the authors conceptually designed.

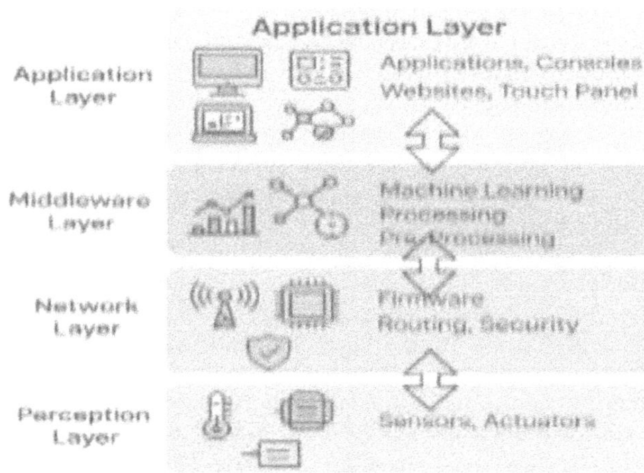

Figure 1. IoT architecture diagram.

Table 1. Summary of attacks in various IoT layers (Pandey and Bhushan 2024).

Layer	Attack	Severity of attack	Objective of attack
Application layer	Buffer overflow	High	Overwriting memory beyond allocated bounds
	Cross site scripting	Low	Injecting malicious code into web pages
	SQL injection	High	Manipulating database queries through malicious input
	Phishing	Low	Deceptive tactics to steal personal information
Middleware layer	Malware and Ransom (Bhattasali *et al.* 2023)	High	Malicious software compromising systems or data
	Sleep deprivation	Low	Disrupting system or human performance through sleep deprivation
Network layer	DoS (Chordiya *et al.* 2018)	High	Overwhelming a system to render it inaccessible
	DDoS	High	Simultaneous, coordinated DoS attacks from multiple sources
	Man-in-the-middle	High	Manipulating communication between parties

(*continued*)

Table 1. Continued

Layer	Attack	Severity of attack	Objective of attack
	Sinkhole	Low	Diverting network traffic to unauthorized destination
	Traffic analysis	Low	Monitoring and analyzing network traffic to extract information
Perception layer	Jamming	Low	Disrupting wireless communication through interference signals
	Physical capture or damage	High	Physically compromising or damaging IoT devices
	Battery draining	Low	Draining the power source of IoT devices
	Device cloning	High	Creating unauthorized copies of IoT devices

2.2 *IoT classification and cryptographic protocols*

In terms of device capabilities, IoT hardware is classified based on memory constraints—specifically, RAM (Random Access Memory) and ROM (Read-Only Memory). Devices fall into three major categories: Class 0 devices, with <1 KB RAM and <100 KB ROM, include ultra-constrained sensors like temperature and humidity probes. Class 1 devices, with around 10 KB RAM and 100 KB ROM, support moderate computation such as protocol translation or gateway functions. Class 2 devices offer ~50 KB or more RAM and support advanced operations such as cloud interfacing, data analytics, or blockchain validation as explained in Table 1.

This classification framework guides the selection of lightweight cryptographic techniques and secure communication protocols suitable for heterogeneous agribusiness environments (Ammar *et al.* 2018).

Traditional cryptographic protocols, such as RSA or AES, are computationally expensive and unsuitable for constrained devices that populate IoT environments. Lightweight cryptography (LWC) offers a secure alternative, tailored to devices with limited RAM, ROM, and processing power. These techniques include symmetric ciphers like PRESENT and PRINCE, and asymmetric schemes such as ECC and Ring-ExpLWE, which are increasingly adopted across multiple IoT sectors, including smart healthcare, IIoT, and agriculture (Pandey and Bhushan 2024).

Additionally, recent advances in smart agriculture IoT systems highlight the feasibility of secure, lightweight deployments. For instance, Prvulović *et al.* (2021) proposed a layered wireless sensor network architecture that is both energy-efficient and suitable for evaluating lightweight cryptographic performance in agriculture. Itoo *et al.* (2023) introduced a privacy-preserving agreement protocol for agricultural monitoring, while Saini *et al.* (2023) presented a hash-based key negotiation system using elliptic curve cryptography tailored to constrained agricultural sensor networks.

While recent advances have demonstrated the feasibility of secure and lightweight deployments in smart agriculture, the proposed architecture offers a more holistic and scalable solution. For example, the layered sensor network by Prvulović *et al.* (2021) focuses primarily on cryptographic evaluation, and the protocols by Itoo *et al.* (2023) and Saini *et al.* (2023) are tailored for isolated security functions, such as key agreement and privacy preservation, within constrained environments. In contrast, the proposed framework integrates connectivity extension via RRM, end-to-end lightweight cryptographic security (ECC + ChaCha20), blockchain-based traceability, and real-time AI anomaly detection into a unified, deployable system. It addresses not only data confidentiality and authentication but also network resilience, mesh adaptability, and trust decentralization, which are critical for operating in remote, infrastructure-scarce agricultural zones. The proposed architecture

Table 2. Categories of IoT devices (Pandey and Bhushan 2024).

Category	RAM	Flash	Description	IoT devices
Class 0 (Jain *et al.* 2022)	Less than 1 KB	Less than 100 KB	Communicate and sense data through protocols for light-weight communication	Temperature sensors, light sensors, motion sensors, proximity sensors, humidity sensors, accelerometers, pressure sensors, gas sensors, magnetic sensors, and actuators.
Class 1 (Ammar *et al.* 2018)	About 10 KB	About 100 KB	Rest over low-end IoT devices in order to enhance the capabilities of class 0 node devices	Smart home hubs, industrial gateways, edge computing devices, cellular gateways, data concentrators, and protocol converters.
Class 2 (Anuradha *et al.* 2022)	About 50 KB	About 250 KB	Devices with a mass number of resources in terms of flash memory, CPU, and RAM	Cloud servers, IoT platform servers, data storage servers, application servers, edge cloud servers, and data analytics servers.

Table 3. Metrics for evaluating LWC algorithms (Suryateja *et al.* 2024).

Metric	Description
Security level	The security level is the logarithmic measure of the fastest known computational attack and is measured in bits. In most cases, the security level is the length of the key
Hardware technology	It is measured using the Gate Equivalent (GE) metric or logic gates count, which is calculated by dividing the layout area of implementation in m^2 by the area of a NAND2 gate
Throughput	It is measured in KB per second, the data processed by the encryption or decryption at a specific processor frequency. In general, the frequency considered for hardware implementation is 100 KHz, and for software implementation is 4 MHz
Latency	It is the number of clock cycles required for processing a single block by the encryption or decryption operation
Power and energy consumption	The power is measured in W. Power is measured based on the hardware technology used and the GE for hardware implementations. The average power of 0.004 W for 8-bit and 0.00135 W for 16-bit microcontrollers is considered for software implementations. Energy consumption per bit for both software and hardware implementations is measured using the formula given below: Energy = (Latency $\times$ Power) / (block size) (in μJ)
RAM/ROM	The amount of memory in RAM for storing the intermediate state is considered in bytes. The amount of memory in ROM for storing the actual code of the implementation is considered in bytes
Efficiency	It indicates the trade-off between the implementation size and performance. For hardware implementations, efficiency is calculated using the formula given below: Hardware Efficiency = Throughput / Complexity (in kg GE) For software implementations efficiency is calculated using the formula given below: Software Efficiency = Throughput / Code Size (in KB)
Figure of merit	Figure of Merit (FOM) represents the system's performance and includes the power consumption. It is independent of the process involved. FOM can be calculated using the formula given below. FOM = T/A^2, where T is the throughput and A is the implementation area which is measured in GE

advances beyond cryptographic feasibility and offers a complete, field-deployable solution for secure, intelligent agribusiness in off-grid communication settings.

3 PROPOSED SECURE PRECISION AGRICULTURE ARCHITECTURE

In addressing the connectivity and security demands of precision agriculture, an RRM-based IoT architecture is introduced. This helps to overcome the challenges in fragmented or rural farm landscapes where cellular base station density is low or entirely absent. Direct communication with the edge or cloud becomes infeasible. The proposed framework incorporates an RRM, a decentralized, peer-assisted communication extension model that enables RedCap devices to form dynamic, multi-hop relay paths. Each device evaluates parameters such as local signal quality, neighbor proximity, and energy availability to forward telemetry toward the nearest reachable edge node. This results in a self-healing mesh that expands coverage across off-grid communication zones without requiring additional infrastructure. The proposed layered architecture, conceptually designed by the authors, is illustrated in Figure 2. It consists of layered components, each performing critical roles in enabling secure, resilient, and intelligent precision agriculture operations.

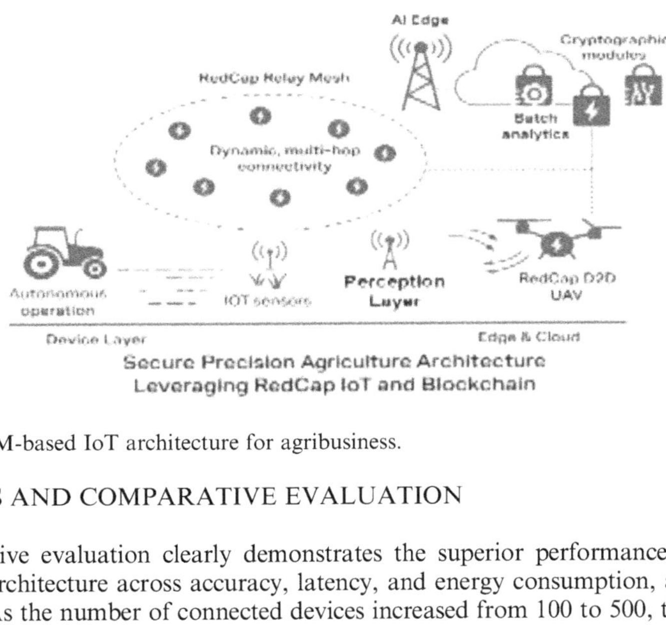

Figure 2. RRM-based IoT architecture for agribusiness.

4 RESULTS AND COMPARATIVE EVALUATION

The comparative evaluation clearly demonstrates the superior performance of the RRM-enabled IoT architecture across accuracy, latency, and energy consumption, as illustrated in Figures 3–5. As the number of connected devices increased from 100 to 500, the RRM curve consistently diverged from the traditional baseline, maintaining higher detection accuracy and lower latency and energy usage across all deployment scales. In Figure 3, the architecture achieves a 10.4% improvement in detection accuracy, reflecting its enhanced ability to isolate anomalies and correctly interpret sensor-generated data patterns. This improvement is driven by the dynamic resource allocation and context-aware processing embedded within the RRM framework, which becomes particularly important in smart agriculture and remote sensing environments where decision accuracy is mission-critical.

Latency improvements are highlighted in Figure 4, where the RRM model demonstrates a 39.8% reduction in response time. This is achieved through optimized communication pathways and intelligent task distribution between the edge and the network core, resulting in faster feedback loops. Such reductions are essential for time-sensitive agricultural applications such as irrigation automation, equipment coordination, and real-time environmental monitoring.

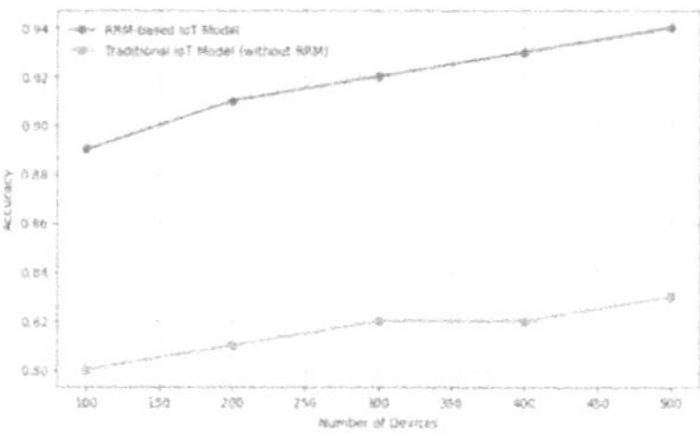

Figure 3. Detection accuracy of RRM-based IoT and traditional IoT models under increasing device load.

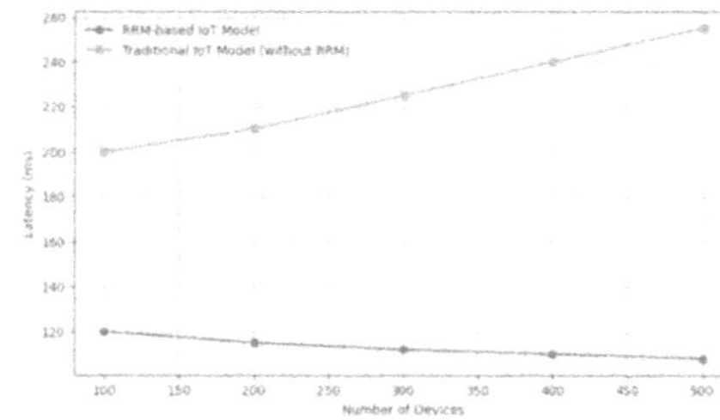

Figure 4. Latency comparison of RRM-based IoT and traditional IoT models in IoT networks.

Energy efficiency, shown in Figure 5, marks the most substantial improvement. Through adaptive scheduling, optimized wake cycles, and reduced redundant transmissions, the architecture achieves a 47.2% reduction in energy consumption. These savings directly extend device lifetime in battery-powered deployments and support the scalability of sustainable IoT infrastructures.

Statistical tests confirm the robustness of these results, with significant p-values and narrow confidence intervals validating RRM's consistent superiority across all deployment conditions.

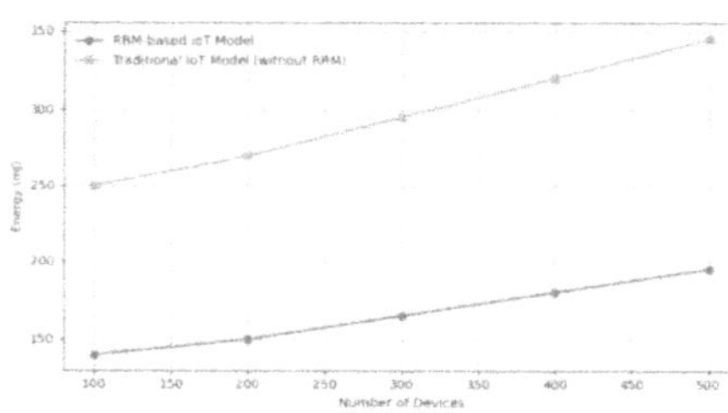

Figure 5. Energy consumption trends for RRM-based IoT model and traditional IoT model.

5 CONCLUSION

This paper presented a secure, energy-efficient, and scalable IoT architecture built around Relay-enabled Reduced Capability (RedCap) Radio Resource Management (RRM) devices, combined with elliptic-curve cryptography (ECC) and blockchain-supported telemetry. By embedding mesh-capable RedCap nodes that autonomously relay traffic, exchange keys locally, and forward data securely, the proposed system mitigates fundamental weaknesses in traditional centralized IoT deployments. Simulation results demonstrated significant improvements over baseline models, including a 10.4% increase in detection accuracy, 39.8% lower latency, and 47.2% reduced energy consumption, confirming the architecture's suitability for constrained and battery-powered environments. Lightweight ECC ensures efficient encryption compatible with low-power devices, while blockchain enhances data integrity through decentralized, tamper-resistant logging. The mesh-based design further improves resilience and throughput as the network scales toward 500 devices—an essential capability for smart agriculture, where fragmented terrain and connectivity gaps remain prevalent. Collectively, these features position the architecture as a forward-looking model for secure, sustainable IoT deployments across rural and industrial settings. Future work will focus on real-world validation through containerized Open5GS private-5G deployments, interoperability with low Earth orbit (LEO) satellite backhaul, and field trials across multiple farm sites.

NOTE

This work has been funded by the following research projects: Brasil 6G Project with support from RNP/MCTI (Grant 01245.010604/2020-14), xGMobile Project code XGM-AFCCT-2024-2-15-1 with resources from EMBRAPII/MCTI (Grant 052/2023 PPI IoT/Manufatura 4.0) and FAPEMIG (Grant PPE-00124-23), SEMEAR Project supported by FAPESP (Grant No. 22/09319-9) and Scholarship Process No. 2023/15030-4), Ciência por Elas with resources from FAPEMIG (Grant APQ-04523-23), Fomento à Internacionalização das ICTMGs with resources from FAPEMIG (Grant APQ-05305-23), Programa de Apoio a Instalações Multiusuários with resources from FAPEMIG (Grant APQ-01558-24), and Redes Estruturantes, de Pesquisa Científica ou de Desenvolvimento Tecnológico with resources from FAPEMIG (Grant RED-00194-23). This work has also been supported by CNPq-Brasil.

REFERENCES

Ammar, M., Daniels, W., Crispo, B., and Hughes, D. (2018). SPEED: Secure provable erasure for class-1 IoT devices. *In Proceedings of the Eighth ACM Conference on Data and Application Security and Privacy* (pp. 111–118). https://doi.org/10.1145/3176258.3176337

Bhattasali, T., Chaki, R., and Sanyal, S. (2023). *Sleep deprivation attack detection in wireless sensor networks. arXiv:1203.0231*. https://doi.org/10.48550/arXiv.1203.0231

Bilal, A., Shabbir, H., Naqvi, S.R., and Peng, L. (2024). Smart agriculture: Current state, opportunities, and challenges. *IEEE Access*, 12, pp.144456–144478. https://doi.org/10.1109/ACCESS.2024.3471647

Chatterjee, S., Bhattacharjee, P.P., and Koley, C. 2024. Cybersecurity analysis for monitoring of hybrid blockchain-based eco-friendly power-generating units. *In 2024, 3rd International Conference on Applied Artificial Intelligence and Computing (ICAAIC)*. IEEE, pp. 1531–1537. DOI:10.1109/ICAAIC60222.2024.10575315.

Chifor, B.-C., Bica, I., and Patriciu, V.-V. (2017). Mitigating DoS attacks in publish–subscribe IoT networks. *In 9th International Conference on Electronics, Computers and Artificial Intelligence (ECAI)*. IEEE. https://doi.org/10.1109/ECAI.2017.8166463

Costa, C.C., Bolfe, I.S.L., Jorge, L.A.A.D.C., Sanches, I.D.A., Luchiari Junior, A., Victoria, D.D.C., and Ramirez, A.R.R., (2020). Precision and digital agriculture: adoption of technologies and perception of Brazilian farmers. *Agriculture*, 10(12), 653. https://doi.org/10.3390/agriculture10120653

Farha, F., Ning, H., Ali, K., Chen, L., and Nugent, C. (2021). SRAM-PUF-based entities authentication scheme for resource-constrained IoT devices. *IEEE Internet Things J.*, 8(7), 5904–5913. DOI:10.1109/JIOT.2020.3032518

Johnson, T., and Silva, H. (2023). Edge AI for real-time threat detection in IoT. *AI Secur. Syst.*, 11(2), 89–104. https://doi.org/10.3390/fi17040179

Mohammad, A., Vishal, A., and Khandaker, M.R.A. (2021). Lightweight cryptography algorithms for resource-constrained IoT devices: A review, comparison, and research opportunities. *IEEE Access*, 9, 28177–28193. 10.1109/ACCESS.2021.3052867

Ogbodo, E.U., Abu-Mahfouz, A.M., and Kurien, A.A. (2024). 5G RedCap enhancement towards improved cellular LPWAN/5G-IoT for smart cities and industrial IoT using genetic algorithm-based neural network. *International Journal of Sensors, Wireless Communications and Control*, 15(1), pp. 14–29. https://doi.org/10.2174/0122103279312219240520053431

Oliveira, J., and Rangel, E. (2023). Energy-aware IoT frameworks in remote agriculture. *Green Comput. J.*, 7 (1), pp. 14–30.

Pandey, S., and Bhushan, B. (2024). Recent lightweight cryptography (LWC) based security advances for resource-constrained IoT networks. *Wireless Networks*, 30(4), 2987–3026. https://link.springer.com/article/10.1007/s11276-024-03714-4

Silva, A., and Gomes, L. (2021). Private 5G networks and RedCap evolution. *J. Next-Gen Wirel. Syst.*, 3(2), pp. 120–134.

Singh, A., and Lopez, J. (2023). Threat modeling for IoT-based smart farming. *J. Cybersecurity Technol.*, 7(1), 1–20. DOI: 10.1109/STI53101.2021.9732597

Suryateja, P.S., and Rao, K.V. (2024). A survey on lightweight cryptographic algorithms in IoT. *Cybernetics and Information Technologies*, 24(1), 21–34. DOI: https://doi.org/10.2478/cait-2024-0002

Wang, Y., and Chen, F. (2022). ChaCha20 vs AES-GCM for secure telemetry. *J. Cryptogr. Eng.*, 8(4), PP. 310–322.

Moving Towards Sustainable Businesses and Developing More Resilient Economies – Rashid and Annansingh-Jamieson (Eds)
© 2026 The Author(s), ISBN: 978-1-041-08875-2

Cohesion in remote teams

N. Belušić
Student, RIT Croatia, Zagreb, Croatia

M. Vidović
Ph.D., Professional Studies Professor, RIT Croatia, Zagreb, Croatia

ABSTRACT: Remote work is a common work setting in a day-to-day business operations. The flexibility of this type of work is particularly appealing to both employers and employees. However, remote work also presents challenges such as reduced managerial oversight, decreased transparency in individual work processes, and the increased risk of employee alienation. This information suggests the need to have clear rules and expectations to ensure the companies meet their objectives while fostering employee job satisfaction. This paper contributes to the understanding of the challenges that arise from remote work as well as common strategies used to overcome these challenges. Analyzing data from in-depth interviews with HR experts working with remote teams, the paper focuses on the strengths and weaknesses of remote work and the key insights in producing highly effective remote teams. Overall, the results emphasize the importance of maintaining personal connections, building trust, and resolving conflict. Additionally, the study also examines the importance of celebrating achievements and inclusivity as crucial components of organizational culture. Finally, the paper points out the significance of leadership in shaping organizational culture and outlines the most common platforms used to organize remote work settings. The paper also analyzes company remote work policies, including the number of in-office and remote workdays, as well as the size of the teams or groups affected by these policies. Moreover, the results highlight the importance of coaching methods and their contribution to team cohesion and individual contribution. Furthermore, HR experts share areas for improvement in managing remote teams that could enhance overall team cohesion.

1 INTRODUCTION

1.1 *Overview of remote work*

The rise of remote work has fundamentally reshaped how organizations and teams function, particularly in the aftermath of the COVID-19 pandemic. Remote work can take many forms, including telecommuting, virtual teaming, and distributed work, where employees perform their assignments outside the traditional office (Leonardi *et al.* 2024). What started as a temporary response to a crisis, has now become a permanent feature of many organizations. As many companies continue to use this type of work arrangement, traditional perception of in-office work settings is shifting (Monte *et al.* 2023).

Many employees recognize the benefits of remote work, such as flexible working hours, reduced commuting time, and the ability to adjust the work setting. At the same time, there are several downsides to this work arrangement, including social isolation, reduced connections between employees, and difficulties in separating personal and professional life (Kłopotek 2017). This leads to the conclusion that remote work creates a paradox for team

 DOI: 10.1201/9781003647300-13

cohesion. It offers flexibility and independence but makes it harder to maintain personal connections and smooth collaboration. Additionally, productivity in remote setups also varies. While some people thrive with flexibility, others are distracted by their home environment (Ahmed 2024).

Team cohesion can be defined as the level of commitment of members to each other and to shared team goals. For measuring team cohesion, Salas and colleagues (2015) suggest observing it as a multidimensional construct of task cohesion, social cohesion, and group pride. Same authors suggest prioritizing task and social cohesion when measuring cohesion, indicating that more research is needed on group pride. Cohesion of a team is highly important in any work setting, and particularly in a remote one. Research shows that virtual teams often have weaker social connections than teams that work together in person. Their social networks are more fragmented, with fewer informal interactions. Personal or "expressive" ties, like casual chatting or social bonding, are most affected, while task-related or "instrumental" ties are generally easier to maintain (Roth and Doehne 2023). What we are observing is that when teams first switch to remote work, cohesion can drop. Over time, however, teams can rebuild their connection through deliberate actions such as regular check-ins, virtual team-building activities, and clear collaborative practices (Baker *et al.* 2024). This highlights the importance of managers actively supporting team cohesion in virtual settings.

1.2 *Factors influencing cohesion in remote teams*

Several factors shape cohesion in remote teams. Two of the most important are trust and communication. Trust helps team members feel safe and supported, making collaboration easier. Communication strengthens that trust and keeps team members engaged and aligned (Paul *et al.* 2016). Rainey (2024) argues that trust in teams allows employees to share ideas, collaborate, and respect each other, especially in remote settings where there is less interaction daily between employees. Teams with frequent and transparent communication, shared decision-making, and clear leadership tend to have stronger cohesion (Patel *et al.* 2020; Mathieu *et al.* 2015).

Shared team identity also plays a key role in maintaining cohesion in remote teams. Teams that regularly engage in discussions, collaborative problem-solving, or shared projects feel a stronger sense of belonging (Patel *et al.* 2020). Management practices such as flexible scheduling, using digital tools effectively, and organizing occasional social events also help build cohesion (Baker *et al.* 2024; Sharma 2023).

1.3 *Overview of known strategies and best practices for cohesion in remote teams*

Cohesion is more than just a "nice-to-have" team feature. Studies consistently show that cohesive teams perform better, including in virtual environments (Chaudhary *et al.* 2022; Grossman *et al.* 2021; Mathieu *et al.* 2015; Braun *et al.* 2020; Chiocchio and Essiembre 2009). This relationship works both ways: when teams perform well, cohesion grows stronger, and strong cohesion then reinforces high performance (Mathieu *et al.* 2015; Braun *et al.* 2020). Best practices for building cohesion in remote teams combine technology, management, and soft skills. In general, teams need clear communication, shared expectations, and regular feedback, and managers play a central role in creating trust and accountability. Specifically, remote team functioning can be enhanced through clear communication, awareness of cultural differences, and project coordination (Paul *et al.* 2016), clear expectations, and frequently checking in on employees (Taylor 2025), as well as frequent video meetings and periodic in-person gatherings (Johnston and Rosin 2011). Having soft skills as a remote employee can significantly impact the team, and some of these skills include accountability, conflict management, and communication (Perna 2022).

Even with these strategies, managing remote teams is challenging. Any novel work arrangement requires adequate training and support from the company and its management.

Only 28% managers possess the essential skills to lead a remote team, which harms the overall culture of the organization (Goldberg 2022). This also impacts the training that incoming remote employees receive, as nonverbal communication is not sophisticated enough (Yonatan 2021; Fischer *et al.* 2013). Lack of informal, nonverbal communication makes it harder for new employees to learn and feel included. In today's globalized work environment, it is common for a firm to operate within different time zones, where interactions between employees are even less present. Although tools like Learning Management Systems and calendar features can help overcome these difficulties, management still faces a significant challenge (Yonatan 2021).

2 RESEARCH METHODOLOGY

To expand on the literature review and better understand how remote work affects team cohesion, this study used a qualitative research design. Data was collected through semi-structured interviews with 13 human resource (HR) professionals who currently manage remote teams. Participants were chosen to represent organizations of varying sizes and from diverse industries, offering a broad perspective on the practices and challenges of fostering cohesion in distributed teams.

2.1 *Data collection*

Interviews were all conducted online via Zoom and lasted between 30 and 60 minutes. The discussion was guided by a predefined set of 12 open-ended questions. Key topics included remote work policies and team structures, challenges and strategies for maintaining team cohesion, communication practices, trust-building, and conflict resolution, approaches to strengthening personal connections and team morale, and perceived areas for improvement in remote collaboration. All interviews were being recorded and transcribed using Zoom's transcription feature, ensuring accuracy in data capture.

2.2 *Data analysis*

The transcribed interviews were subjected to iterative coding to identify patterns, recurring challenges, and best practices. Following thematic analysis, the initial coding was performed to categorize responses according to the predefined topics, but also capture emerging themes.

2.3 *Reliability and validity*

To ensure the reliability of the findings, all interviews followed the same semi-structured protocol, which ensured that each participant was asked the same set of core questions, and in the same order. Interviews were recorded and transcribed verbatim, which minimized the risk of misinterpretation.

To ensure the validity of the findings, data triangulation was used by including participants from different industries and company sizes. This approach allowed for diverse perspectives on remote team cohesion, as well as the identification of possible industry-specific circumstances

3 RESEARCH RESULTS

3.1 *Remote work policies in place*

Most organizations have a hybrid policy in place that allows employees to work remotely for part of the week. The most common arrangement seems to be three days in the office and two days working from home. This structure was mostly introduced after the COVID-19 pandemic, around 2021 or later, once companies realized that remote work could still be productive. In more flexible companies, there is no strict limit on how many days employees can work remotely, and employees are free to choose what works best for them and their teams. Some teams are fully remote and have never had a physical office, so there is no fixed policy in place, meaning they just work from wherever they are. These variations show how remote work has become an accepted and normalized part of work culture. As one manager explained:

> *"Before COVID, we never had the work from home option ... After COVID had passed ... we wanted to allow the flexibility to continue" (Participant 1)*

On the other hand, one manager reflected:

> *"We were always fully remote ever since the company got started 10 years ago ... There is no mandatory time in the office because there is no office." (Participant 2)*

One partner noted:

> *"It is highly recommended for staff to come into the office a few days a week, but it is not mandated. Partners and senior management have a requirement of 3 days a week." (Participant 13)*

The size of teams impacted by remote policies depends on the type of company and the roles involved. In a lot of situations, the entire company is affected, especially if it is a virtual company or heavily based in IT or consulting. Some organizations have hundreds or even thousands of employees, and only specific departments, such as HR, office staff, or administration, have the flexibility to work remotely. Other companies have small core teams that are fully remote, and then a broader network of global teams. Even within larger companies, remote policies usually apply to all non-operational teams, like marketing, finance, or support roles. It is clear that these policies go beyond individuals and often apply to whole departments or entire companies.

3.2 *Challenges of remote work*

One of the main challenges of remote work is that employees feel disconnected from each other. Without casual conversations in the office, there are fewer chances to connect with colleagues. As our managers reflected:

> *"The main roadblock or disadvantages of work from home are the connections between the employees." (Participant 5)*

> *"In a Zoom call, it feels a lot more structured — you can't just casually drop by someone's desk to ask a quick question." (Participant 2)*

> *"There are a lot of people who don't feel connected to their team." (Participant 7)*

This can make it harder to feel like part of a group, especially when most communication is scheduled and specific to work. Also, as one manager explains, the dissemination of information can suffer with remote work:

> *"The downside is mostly related to the information flow ... By just passively hearing some discussion ... you are learning about the company ... when you are at home, of course, you are not exposed to [that]." (Participant 4)*

Another problem is not being able to read body language or tone during virtual meetings, which can lead to misunderstandings. To deal with these issues, teams are using strategies such as virtual coffee breaks, online team-building activities, and regular check-ins just to talk about non work related topics. Some teams also make an effort to meet in person once in a while for workshops or team events. These activities help bring back the human side of work that remote environments can sometimes lack.

Additionally, there is always a question of work productivity with remote teams, as one manager reflected:

> *"One of the challenges ... was figuring out who's doing what from home, what actually can be done from home, and organizing your workload in a way where it makes sense" (Participant 1)*

3.3 *Employee perceptions of remote work*

Team members see both benefits and downsides to working remotely. On the positive side, remote work allows for more flexibility, less commuting, and a better balance between personal and professional life. As one manager observes:

> *"Strength is of course work life balance. You can rearrange your time ... you don't need to commute to work. So, it's always you save some time one hour, 2-3 depending on where everybody lives." (Participant 6)*

Many employees said they can focus better without the usual office distractions. Note a comment from one of our managers:

> *"Sometimes when working from home, people can maybe be even more focused." (Participant 8)*

At the same time, the biggest weakness is the lack of personal interaction. When teams do not meet often, it can be hard to build trust and work together creatively. Some participants also mentioned that onboarding new employees is more difficult because they do not get the chance to learn from others. So while remote work has strong individual benefits, team cohesion can suffer if relationships and communication are not actively maintained. Another interesting perspective comes from one of the interviewed managers:

> *"The more senior you get, the more benefits you can have from being remote ... The more junior you are, the more you are losing out — because learning comes from being around people." (Participant 2)*

One manager noted:

> *"It is essential to recognize the importance of team spirit and invest in teambuilding activities." (Participant 12)*

3.4 *Strategies for staying connected while working remote*

Even though employees are not in the same physical space, teams have found ways to stay personally connected. Some groups schedule virtual lunches, where everyone eats together over Zoom. Others use internal chat platforms to share personal updates, like weekend plans or favorite movies. These small interactions help make work more enjoyable and build stronger relationships. In some cases, teams organize speed networking or informal "buddy chats" to encourage employees from different departments to connect. These connections matter because they make it easier to ask for help, share feedback, and collaborate on bigger projects. When employees feel like they know each other personally, it is easier to work together professionally. As one manager describes:

> *"We have a weekly team meeting to touch base... just so the whole team connects and sees each other." (Participant 1)*

"That hybrid strategy of having employees in the office helps . . . keep that connection." (Participant 5)

Teams rely heavily on digital tools to stay connected in remote settings. Zoom and Microsoft Teams are the most common for meetings, while Slack, WhatsApp, or internal platforms are used for quick messages and chats. For example, our managers noted:

"We have a WhatsApp group that's open all day, and we shoot messages through the group all the time." (Participant 1)

"We use Zoom. We use Outlook, and we use WhatsApp. That's it . . . Most of it happens via email and in-person meetings happen on Zoom." (Participant 2)

"We use Teams mostly." (Participant 6)

Some teams also use shared calendars, project management tools, or online boards for collaboration. These tools make it easier to work across different time zones and keep everyone on the same page. But they can also be overwhelming. Participants mentioned getting tired of constant notifications or back-to-back video meetings, also known as "Zoom fatigue." So, while communication tools are necessary, they have to be used in a way that supports collaboration without burning employees out. One manager even reflects:

"Tools cannot replace human connection. So as soon as there's too many emails floating around or text messages, we would always say, you know, just pick up the phone and have the conversation or have a meeting." (Participant 3)

3.5 *Challenges of managing remote teams*

Coaching and development in remote teams take more planning, but they are still possible with the right tools. Since managers can not observe their team in person, they often use scheduled video calls to give feedback or offer support. Some companies have set up learning platforms where employees can complete training modules, track their progress, and even earn certificates. Others have regular one-on-one meetings that are focused not just on tasks but also on personal growth. These coaching practices are important because they show employees that their development still matters, even when they are not physically in the office. When employees feel supported, they are more likely to stay engaged and connected to the team. In a reflection of one managers, we get a better insight about the importance of empathy:

"Empathy is a big one that maybe isn't touched upon enough because it's considered more of a soft skill . . . I think we're moving away from calling them soft skills to just calling them leadership skills." (Participant 3)

Trust plays a big role in how well remote teams function. In successful teams, trust is built by giving employees freedom to do their work in the way that suits them best. Managers in these teams do not micromanage but still stay available for support and check-ins. When employees feel trusted, they are more motivated and confident. On the other hand, if a team has low trust, managers might try to control everything, which makes remote work more stressful and less effective. Trust also encourages employees to communicate more openly and to help each other out. This has an impact on collaboration because employees are more willing to share ideas and take initiative when they feel supported. As one manager reflects:

"Everything hinges around flexibility but also trust. In an organization where there's a lot of trust between team members you can make remote work." (Participant 2)

"Trust can be built remotely. What I've seen it really elevate is when there's that in-person connection from time to time, whether it's once or twice a year or if it's a hybrid approach." (Participant 3)

Handling conflict remotely can be difficult because employees might not notice tension until it becomes a bigger issue. In the office, you can usually tell if something is not right, but online, these signals are easier to miss. To manage this, teams try to create open environments where it is acceptable to speak up. Some use video calls to talk through issues face-to-face, while others have structured ways to give feedback, like regular team reviews or anonymous surveys. One useful practice is to always assume good intent in digital messages, since tone can easily be misread. The most effective teams deal with conflict early and with respect which helps them stay cohesive even when disagreements happen.

Celebrating wins is an important part of keeping high morale in remote teams. Many teams use chat platforms or emails to celebrate or post about accomplishments. Some organize virtual celebrations or team games, while others send small gifts for appreciation. In-person meetups are also used to recognize milestones when possible. These moments of recognition help people feel seen and appreciated. When achievements are celebrated, it reminds everyone that their work matters and that they are part of a team. This has a positive effect on motivation and keeps employees emotionally connected to their colleagues. On the other hand, there is a slight issue with recognizing the work well done by employees working remotely, as one manager stated:

"Those folks who are visible ... in close proximity in the office ... have a better chance of being promoted ... out of sight, out of mind." (Participant 3)

One manager reflected:

"We have weekly all-team meetings where we often mention something good that has happened." (Participant 10)

Remote teams are finding ways to make sure that everyone feels included in discussions and decisions. This is especially important because some employees are naturally quieter or may feel left out if they are in a different location or time zone. As one manager reflects:

"Remotely... people get shy to say something, interrupt. You don't have a good connection and this could maybe worsen communication." (Participant 8)

One common strategy is to rotate meeting leaders so everyone gets a chance to speak. Others use written follow-ups, chat channels, or anonymous input forms to collect feedback. This way, employees who do not feel comfortable speaking out loud still have a voice. Inclusivity is also encouraged through cultural awareness and scheduling meetings at fair times for all members. When employees feel heard, they are more likely to contribute and stay engaged. One of the managers noted:

"There's always that quiet kid in class, that quiet kid in the team ... not very talkative. ... She has amazing ideas, but she's the one who's not talking. ... So this is where my boss always comes and says okay, everyone said what they wanted to say. Maria, now you." (Participant 7)

3.6 *Areas for improvement in managing remote teams*

There are still areas where remote teams should improve. One common issue is onboarding, where new employees often feel lost without physical guidance. To fix this, teams are asking for more structured training and better introductions to team culture. Others said they want more fun, social activities to make up for the lack of in-person bonding. Some employees also mentioned the need for clearer expectations, especially around working hours and availability. As one manager commented:

"It's probably the way I see it's not that polite to just call somebody out of the blue on Teams and expect them to answer the phone or the call right away." (Participant 5)

"One area of improvement is to focus on how to maintain professionalism and kindness." (Participant 11)

Better equipment and more leadership training were also suggested. Overall, employees want to feel more connected and supported in their remote roles, and small changes in communication and planning can make a big difference. One manager sees great value in enhancing the onboarding process as well:

"We have a longer ... onboarding process ... they found it a bit long and boring at first, but then they all discovered that we feel more connected." (Participant 7)

One manager made an interesting point:

"Remote work can only work if it's not only remote work; you need some time together." (Participant 9)

4 DISCUSSION

Overall, the initial literature review supports the findings from the interviews conducted in this research. The main positive and negative sides of remote work, as well as common leadership challenges and strategies, are aligned between primary and secondary research. Yet, the qualitative research provided richer insights into specific practices and challenges. Specifically, we have learned that the shift from in-office to remote work has fundamentally reshaped how teams interact and maintain cohesion. Everyone acknowledges the importance of open and clear communication, and frequent contact. It might even seem that we have re-discovered the need to communicate and build cohesion by being exposed to the lack of it via remote work. Further, while the virtual means of communication via available tools allow teams to remain functional, they seem to fail in fully replicating the dynamics of face-to-face collaboration. It would seem that online meetings tend to focus on tasks and actions, and less on people, interactions, and building culture. This type of transactional team culture surely brings efficiency, but calls for caution in ensuring the connections are still being built. Managers have historically played an important role in organizations, and this era of remote work settings seems to rely heavily on the managers as well. Proactive practices such as regular check-ins, virtual team-building activities, clear expectations, and clear communication can mitigate the social gaps created by remote work. For the teams that rely solely on remote contact, it might be advisable to rely even more intensely on deliberate efforts to stay connected and maintain team cohesion. Finally, hybrid work models seem to provide a middle ground option. These allow employees to retain some of the flexibility, while they still offer enough natural opportunities for informal in-person interactions. As we've seen from this study, a few in-person days each month can reinforce trust, shared identity, and team spirit.

4.1 *Conclusions*

The aftermath of the COVID-19 pandemic has brought a rise in remote work, with clear benefits of increased flexibility and work-life balance, but it can challenge the social fabric of teams. Trust and cohesion seem to be challenged in virtual environments, and require managers to spend additional time and effort to cultivate connections through deliberate communications, team-buildings, and occasional face-to-face interactions. Additionally, adopting hybrid models allows organizations to reap the benefits of both worlds, and enables flexibility while prioritizing social connections.

REFERENCES

Ahmed, H. (2024, September 12). *The future of remote work: Trends and challenges*. LinkedIn. https://www.linkedin.com/pulse/future-remote-work-trends-challenges-hossain-ahmed–ajamc/

Baker, A., Salman, R., Zaur, E., and Fahmi, A. (2024). The impact of remote work on team dynamics and management strategies. *Journal of Ecohumanis.*

Braun, M., Kozlowski, S., Brown, T., and DeShon, R. (2020). Exploring the dynamic team cohesion–performance and coordination–performance relationships of newly formed teams. *Small Group Research*, 51, 551–580.

Chaudhary, M., Chopra, S., and Kaur, J. (2022). Cohesion as a cardinal antecedent in virtual team performance: a meta-analysis. *Team Performance Management: An International Journal.*

Chiocchio, F., and Essiembre, H. (2009). Cohesion and Performance. *Small Group Research*, 40, 382–420.

Fischer, U., Mosier, K., Orasanu, J., Fischer, U., Morrow, D., Miller, C., ... and Orasanu, J. (2013, September). Exploring communication in remote teams: Issues and methods. *In Proceedings of the Human Factors and Ergonomics Society Annual Meeting* (Vol. 57, No. 1, pp. 309–313). Sage CA: Los Angeles, CA: SAGE Publications.

Goldberg, E.L. (2022). Managing hybrid/ remote teams is A key capability, are your team leaders ready? *Leadership Excellence*, *39*(4), 30–32. https://ezproxy.rit.edu/login?url=https://www.proquest.com/trade-journals/managing-hybrid-remote-teams-is-key-capability/docview/2655172518/se-2

Grossman, R., Nolan, K., Rosch, Z., Mazer, D., and Salas, E. (2021). The team cohesion-performance relationship: A meta-analysis exploring measurement approaches and the changing team landscape. *Organizational Psychology Review*, 12, 181–238.

Johnston, K.A., and Rosin, K. (2011, May). Global virtual teams: How to manage them. *In 2011 International Conference on Computer and Management (CAMAN)* (pp. 1–4). IEEE.

Kłopotek, M. (2017). The advantages and disadvantages of remote working from the perspective of young employees. *Organizacja i Zarządzanie: kwartalnik naukowy*, (4), 39–49.

Leonardi, P.M., Parker, S.H., and Shen, R. (2024). How remote work changes the world of work. *Annual Review of Organizational Psychology and Organizational Behavior*, *11*(1), 193–219.

Mathieu, J., Kukenberger, M., D'Innocenzo, L., and Reilly, G. (2015). Modeling reciprocal team cohesion-performance relationships, as impacted by shared leadership and members‘ competence.. *The Journal of Applied Psychology*, 100 3, 713–34.

Monte, F., Porcher, C., and Rossi-Hansberg, E. (2023). *Remote work and city structure* (No. w31494). National Bureau of Economic Research.

Patel, H., Damush, T., Miech, E., Rattray, N., Martin, H., Savoy, A., Plue, L., Anderson, J., Martini, S., Graham, G., and Williams, L. (2020). Building cohesion in distributed telemedicine teams: findings from the Department of Veterans Affairs National Telestroke Program. *BMC Health Services Research*, 21.

Paul, R., Drake, J.R., and Liang, H. (2016). Global virtual team performance: The effect of coordination effectiveness, trust, and team cohesion. *IEEE Transactions on Professional Communication*, *59*(3), 186–202.

Perna, M.C. (2022, May 17). *The top 25 soft skills remote workers need—And 3 ways to get them. LinkedIn.* https://www.linkedin.com/pulse/top-25-soft-skills-remote-workers-needand-3-ways-get-them-mark-perna/

Rainey, C. (Host). (2024, December 19). *Everything you need to know about remote teams in 2025* (Episode 735) [Audio podcast episode]. *In HR Leaders. HR Leaders Media.* https://podcasts.apple.com/hr/podcast/hr-leaders/id1263992083?i=1000680983651

Roth, P., and Doehne, M. (2023). Cohesion is lower in virtualized collaborations: A comparison of teams' network structure. *Small Group Research*, 55, 560–594.

Salas, E., Grossman, R., Hughes, A., and Coultas, C. (2015). Measuring team cohesion. *Human Factors: The Journal of Human Factors and Ergonomics Society*, 57(3), 365–374.

Sharma, A. (2023). Managing remote teams in organisations: best practices for effective collaboration and communication. *Psychology and Education.*

Taylor, P.(2025, January 30). *It's a whole new world!! A manager's guide to managing remote teams in growth organizations.* LinkedIn. https://www.linkedin.com/pulse/its-whole-new-world-managers-guide-managing-remote-teams-taylor-gbqtc/

Yonatan, R. (2021). *The challenges of managing remote teams and tools to help.* San Jose: Newstex. Retrieved from https://ezproxy.rit.edu/login?url=https://www.proquest.com/blogs-podcasts-websites/challenges-managing-remote-teams-tools-help/docview/2576684570/se-2

Moving Towards Sustainable Businesses and Developing More Resilient Economies – Rashid and Annansingh-Jamieson (Eds)

The impact of fraudulent SMS notifications on marketplace adoption of digital payment systems in developing countries

Abdulmumini Yinka Ajia
School of Business, Lincoln University, Missouri, Unites States

ABSTRACT: Digital payments have expanded financial access in many developing countries, but marketplace adoption remains fragile when users perceive payment channels as insecure. This paper examines how fraudulent short message service (SMS) notifications commonly used in phishing and "smishing" schemes shape traders' trust and willingness to accept digital payments in informal market settings. Drawing on a mixed-methods design, the study synthesizes prior evidence on trust driven technology adoption and presents primary data from Nigeria, semi-structured interviews with market traders in Lagos and a structured survey administered to traders in Ilorin and Ibadan (n = 258; 67% response rate). Results showed high reported digital payment acceptance (81%), alongside widespread exposure to fraudulent SMS (89%). Most respondents (90%) reported that fraudulent notifications significantly reduced their willingness to accept digital payments, and the same share highlighted network delays and unreliable confirmations as major deterrents. Interview themes reinforced these patterns, emphasizing trust erosion, dispute resolution gaps, and reversion to cash after fraud experiences. The paper concludes with practical recommendations for regulators and payment providers, including stronger transaction verification, phased migration from SMS alerts to encrypted in-app notifications with inclusive alternatives for low connectivity users, targeted fraud awareness campaigns, and clearer merchant redress mechanisms.

Keywords: fraudulent SMS, smishing, digital payments, marketplace adoption, consumer trust, developing countries

1 INTRODUCTION

Digital payment systems ranging from mobile money to card and account to account transfers have become central to financial inclusion strategies in developing economies. The World Bank's Global Findex Database reported that 1.4 billion adults remained unbanked in 2021, underscoring the scale of unmet demand for accessible financial services (World Bank 2022). For informal market traders, digital payments can reduce cash handling risks, broaden customer reach, and improve recordkeeping. Yet these gains depend heavily on trust in transaction integrity and confirmation mechanisms.

Short message service (SMS) alerts are widely used to confirm transfers and provide account updates because they operate on basic phones and do not always require mobile data. However, SMS is vulnerable to spoofing and social engineering. Fraudsters can send convincing, fake payment confirmations to induce merchants to release goods or services with the hope that the payment is in the bank. This "false confirmation" pathway is distinct from classic credential theft smishing and is especially damaging in face to face marketplace transactions where speed and certainty matter.

DOI: 10.1201/9781003647300-14

Despite growing public concern about SMS based fraud across multiple countries, there remains limited empirical evidence on how fraudulent SMS notifications specifically influence marketplace adoption decisions among informal sector merchants, and how this interacts with infrastructure constraints such as network delays. This study addressed this gap using Nigeria as a focal case.

2 RESEARCH OBJECTIVES

1) Assess how fraudulent SMS notifications influence traders' trust in digital payments and their willingness to accept such payments.
2) Document prevalence and perceived severity of fraudulent SMS experiences in marketplace settings.
3) Identify actionable technological and policy interventions especially verification and notification redesigns that can reduce fraudulent transactions.

3 LITERATURE REVIEW

Trust is a repeat driver of digital finance adoption. Research on technology acceptance emphasizes that perceived security and reliability shape behavioral intention and continued use, particularly where users face meaningful downside risk from system failures or fraud (McKnight *et al.* 2002; Gefen *et al.* 2003). In informal markets, the reliance on rapid settlement and immediate confirmation can raise the salience of trust cues.

SMS based fraud ("smishing") leverages both technical vulnerabilities and psychology. Attackers often imitate trusted brands or institutions and use urgency, authority cues, and time pressure to trigger compliance (Krombholz *et al.* 2015). The SMS channel itself offers limited native authentication and is not end to end encrypted, which can make spoofing and interception plausible in some contexts (Kumar *et al.* 2018).

Empirical and policy-oriented work has linked secure infrastructure to adoption of mobile money and digital payments, suggesting that user protection and reliability are not optional add ons but prerequisites for scaling (Jack and Suri 2011; Ozili 2018; Arner *et al.* 2020). In this backdrop, fraudulent SMS notifications represent a direct threat to perceived system integrity, and therefore to adoption in marketplace environments.

4 METHODOLOGY

The study used a mixed methods design to triangulate patterns in adoption behavior and perceived fraud risk. Primary qualitative data came from semi-structured interviews with market traders in Lagos. Primary quantitative data came from a structured survey administered to traders in Lagos, Ilorin and Ibadan. Secondary sources were used for context and instrument design.

A total of 385 questionnaires were distributed and 258 were returned, yielding a 67% response rate. Response rates at this level are commonly considered robust for field based social research (Baruch and Holtom 2008).

Instrument development followed standard validation steps. Survey items were derived from prior constructs on trust and perceived security (McKnight *et al.* 2002) and on SMS fraud mechanisms (Kumar *et al.* 2018). Face validity checks were conducted with academics and practitioners in digital finance, and responses were coded using predefined binary and ordinal scales aligned with the research objectives (Creswell and Creswell 2018).

5 RESULTS

5.1 *Respondent demographics*

Demographic summaries are presented in Tables 1–3. Due to item-level nonresponse on some demographic questions, totals in the demographic tables reflect n = 254 where indicated.

Table 1. Percentage distribution of respondents by gender.

Gender	Frequency	Percentage (%)
Male	187	73.6
Female	67	26.4
Total	254	100.0

Note: n = 254 due to item nonresponse.

Table 2. Percentage distribution of respondents by age group.

Age group	Frequency	Percentage (%)
18–25	23	9.1
26–35	73	28.7
36–45	114	44.9
46–55	37	14.6
55 and above	7	2.8
Total	254	100.0

Note: n = 254 due to item nonresponse.

Table 3. Percentage distribution of respondents by education level.

Level of education	Frequency	Percentage (%)
Primary	16	6.3
Secondary	60	23.6
Post-secondary	80	31.5
Bachelor's degree	85	33.5
Master's degree	12	4.7
None	1	0.4
Total	254	100.0

Note: n = 254 due to item nonresponse.

5.2 *Adoption, fraud exposure, and perceived deterrents*

Self reported use of digital payments was relatively high: 81% of respondents indicated that they frequently accept digital payments, while 19% reported that they rarely do. At the same time, exposure to fraudulent SMS notifications was widespread: 89% reported having experienced fraudulent SMS notifications associated with loss of goods or services. Most respondents (90%) stated that fraudulent notifications significantly reduced their willingness to accept digital payments. In addition to fraud, 90% reported that network instability and delayed confirmations were major deterrents.

Table 4. Summary of adoption, fraud exposure, and key deterrents.

Indicator (survey)	Result
Frequently accepts digital payments	81%
Rarely accepts digital payments	19%
Experienced fraudulent SMS notifications	89%
Fraud significantly reduced willingness to accept digital payments	90%
Network/delayed confirmation is a major deterrent	90%
Surveys returned/distributed	258/385 (67%)

Note: n = 258 unless otherwise indicated.

5.3 *Interview themes*

Interview analysis identified recurring themes consistent with the survey patterns: (a) trust erosion after fraud experiences; (b) reluctance to release goods without immediate, verifiable confirmation; (c) reliance on cash when network delays made "proof of payment" ambiguous; and (d) frustration with limited dispute resolution pathways and the perceived difficulty of recovering losses.

6 DISCUSSION

These findings highlight a marketplace paradox. Many traders reported frequent use of digital payments, yet the same population reported high exposure to fraudulent SMS and strong deterrence effects. In informal markets, where transactions are time sensitive and often completed face to face, even a small probability of false confirmation can have outsized consequences. This reinforces prior work that frames trust and perceived security as central to adoption and continued use (McKnight *et al.* 2002; Gefen *et al.* 2003).

Infrastructure constraints compounded the problem. With 90% of respondents citing network delays and confirmation uncertainty as deterrents, the SMS channel can become both a convenience and a vulnerability, it is ubiquitous and lightweight, but also difficult to authenticate. These patterns are consistent with broader evidence that reliable payment platforms and user protections are key to scaling digital finance (Jack and Suri 2011; Ozili 2018).

7 POLICY AND DESIGN RECOMMENDATIONS

(1) Strengthen transaction verification at the point of sale: Encourage merchant facing verification tools like in-app confirmation, QR based receipts, or provider short codes tied to authenticated sessions so that "payment proof" is not solely an SMS message.
(2) Reduce reliance on SMS for critical confirmations: Where feasible, migrate from SMS alerts to encrypted in-app push notifications; where connectivity is limited, implement secure USSD or hybrid models with cryptographic tokens to reduce spoofing risk.
(3) Implement targeted trader education and fraud awareness campaigns: Partner with market associations and local language media to teach common fraud patterns and safe confirmation practices, focusing on the "false confirmation" scam pathway.
(4) Improve redress and complaint resolution: Create clearer merchant dispute channels, standardized reporting templates, and time bound resolution steps to reduce the perceived irrecoverability of fraud losses.

8 LIMITATIONS AND FUTURE RESEARCH

The study relied on self-reported data and focused on selected Nigerian cities, which may limit generalizability across all regions. Future work should extend sampling to additional zones and employ longitudinal or experimental designs to quantify causal impacts of specific anti-fraud interventions, particularly notification redesign and merchant verification tools.

9 CONCLUSION

Fraudulent SMS notifications represent a practical, trust damaging barrier to marketplace adoption of digital payments in developing countries. In this sample, exposure to fraudulent SMS was widespread and most traders reported that it materially reduced their willingness to accept digital payments. Because marketplace transactions depend on fast and credible confirmation, security and reliability improvements, especially around authentication and notification channels are essential for sustaining adoption. Coordinated action by regulators, payment providers, telecom operators, and market associations can reduce spoofing opportunities, improve redress, and strengthen merchant confidence in digital commerce.

REFERENCES

Arner, D.W., Buckley, R.P., Zetzsche, D.A., and Veidt, R. (2020). Sustainability, FinTech and financial inclusion. *European Business Organization Law Review*, 21(1), 7–35.

Baruch, Y., and Holtom, B.C. (2008). Survey response rate levels and trends in organizational research. *Human Relations*, 61(8), 1139–1160. https://doi.org/10.1177/0018726708094863

Creswell, J.W., and Creswell, J.D. (2018). *Research design: Qualitative, quantitative, and mixed methods approaches* (5th ed.). SAGE Publications.

Demirgüç-Kunt, A., Klapper, L., Singer, D., and Van Oudheusden, P. (2018). *The Global Findex Database 2017: Measuring financial inclusion and the fintech revolution. World Bank.*

Donovan, K.P. (2012). Mobile money, more freedom? The impact of M-PESA's network power on development as freedom. *International Journal of Communication*, 6, 1–23.

Dos Santos, P.L., and Harvold Kvangraven, I. (2017). Better than cash, but beware the costs: electronic payments systems and financial inclusion in developing economies. *Development and Change*, 48(2), 205–227.

Gefen, D., Karahanna, E., and Straub, D.W. (2003). Trust and TAM in online shopping: An integrated model. *MIS Quarterly*, 27(1), 51–90.

Government Accountability Office. (2024). *Payment scams: Information on financial industry efforts* (GAO-24-107107). U.S. Government Accountability Office.

GSMA. (2019). *The Mobile Economy 2019*. GSM Association.

Jack, W., and Suri, T. (2011). Mobile money: The economics of M-PESA (NBER Working Paper No. 16721). *National Bureau of Economic Research.*

Krombholz, K., Hobel, H., Huber, M., and Weippl, E. (2015). Advanced social engineering attacks. *Journal of Information Security and Applications*, 22, 113–122.

Kumar, A., Rajput, N., and Agarwal, S. (2018). SMS phishing and mitigation approaches. *International Journal of Computer Applications*, 179(1), 1–6.

McKnight, D.H., Choudhury, V., and Kacmar, C. (2002). Developing and validating trust measures for e-commerce: An integrative typology. *Information Systems Research*, 13(3), 334–359.

Ozili, P.K. (2018). Impact of digital finance on financial inclusion and stability. *Borsa Istanbul Review*, 18(4), 329–340.

Statista. (2024). *Digital payments: Transaction value worldwide*. Statista.

Tade, O., and Adeniyi, O. (2020). Dimensions of electronic fraud and governance of trust in Nigeria's cashless ecosystem. *International Journal of Offender Therapy and Comparative Criminology*, 64(16), 1717–1740.

World Bank. (2022). *The Global Findex Database 2021: Financial inclusion, digital payments, and resilience in the age of COVID-19*. World Bank.

Moving Towards Sustainable Businesses and Developing More Resilient Economies – Rashid and Annansingh-Jamieson (Eds)
© 2026 The Author(s), ISBN: 978-1-041-08875-2

Neo Banking in India – A paradigm shift

B K Suresh and P Paramashivaiah
Dr. Sadananda Maiya School of Commerce & Management, Tumkur University

Y Muniraju
Department of Commerce, Mangalore University

M Venkateshwarlu
Vice Chancellor, Tumkur University

ABSTRACT: The emergence of neo banking in India marks a transformative shift in the country's financial ecosystem, redefining how individuals and businesses interact with banking services. Unlike traditional banks, neobanks operate entirely online, offering seamless, user-centric experiences through mobile and web platforms. This study explores the rapid rise of neobanks such as Jupiter, Niyo, Open, and Fi Money, driven by growing smartphone penetration, digital adoption, and demand for personalized, real-time financial solutions. The abstract highlights how neobanks are disrupting legacy banking models through innovations in AI, automation, and API-based services while facing regulatory challenges under the Reserve Bank of India (RBI). With their focus on underserved segments like millennials, salaried professionals, and SMEs, neobanks are reshaping customer expectations and financial inclusion. This paradigm shift signals a new era of digital banking, where convenience, transparency, and innovation redefine the future of finance in India. In India, Niyo Solutions is among the pioneering companies in this field.

Keywords: Neo bank, Niyo, digital financial entities, digital adoption, disrupting legacy, innovation, future of finance

1 INTRODUCTION

From 2018 to 2022, neobanks saw their transaction value rise from \$0.45 trillion to \$3.21 trillion, while their user base grew from 32.61 million to 188.4 million globally during the same timeframe (Statista 2023). The remarkable growth potential of neobanks can largely be attributed to their cost-effective model for consumers, which often entails minimal or no monthly fees associated with banking services such as maintaining minimum balances, and making deposits and withdrawals. Elements like quicker loan approval and funding processes in comparison to conventional banks, along with lower interest rates through banking apps, are propelling market growth. Key factors influencing the expansion of neobanks—primarily linked to regulatory environments, consumer preferences, and competitive pressures—are likely to persist in the coming decades. Besides providing online services, neobanks are transforming the financial sector. In 2021, neobank Chime was recognized as one of the top 10 banks in the United States with over 13 million clients. Currently, it boasts more than 21 million users. As neobanks expand, it's crucial to grasp their nature and influence on the worldwide financial landscape.

Over the last ten years, neobanks have effectively established a unique position for themselves by continuously broadening the array of services available to their clientele

 DOI: 10.1201/9781003647300-15

(Bradford 2020). The growth and embrace of neobanks are showing no signs of abating, with Statista's (2023) projections forecasting a global user base of 376.9 million by 2027, representing a twenty-fold increase from 18.95 million users in 2017. These trends signify a changing landscape in banking, although the degree to which neobanks compete with traditional banks is still uncertain. The remarkable growth potential of neobanks can largely be attributed to their cost-effective model for consumers, which often entails minimal or no monthly fees associated with banking services such as maintaining minimum balances, and making deposits and withdrawals. Neobanks are entirely digital financial entities that resemble banks. Their service offerings are generally more limited when compared to traditional banks. This streamlined approach often enables neobank users to benefit from lower fees, competitive interest rates, and personalized products.

2 SIGNIFICANCE OF NEO BANKS

The remarkable expansion of neobanks and fully digital banks has led to a fundamental transformation in the banking system, resulting in a significant shift in the delivery of financial services to consumers (OECD 2020). They set themselves apart through a completely digital approach and modern, innovative business strategies, rendering physical branches unnecessary for their operations (Buchi *et al.* 2019). For a substantial part of the 20th century, traditional banking institutions held a dominant position in the financial services sector. These institutions initially provided services such as deposits, lending, and wealth management. As the 20th century progressed, traditional banking experienced a trend toward consolidation and notable deregulation, leading to the rise of large multinational banks. In the 21st century, these organizations effectively utilized technology to improve efficiency and expand their operations (Gorton 2015). Despite the significant impact of digitalization on the structure and functions of conventional banking, many still rely heavily on physical branches and personal interactions as part of their customer service offerings. Neobanks represent a new banking paradigm that emerges from changing customer preferences and requirements. Emerging in the early 2010s, they are entirely reachable via the internet or mobile devices, employing technology to deliver a customer experience that includes services such as account creation, mobile payments, deposit options, savings and investment management tools, and various loan offerings. They also facilitate access to trading markets, including the stock market, commodities market, and cryptocurrency markets (Martinčević *et al.* 2022). Although several studies, including those by Gulieva *et al.* (2019) and Temelkov (2020), examine how neobanks' business models could potentially compete with traditional banks, statistics indicate that neobanks remain in a developmental stage. Consequently, academic research on this subject should continue to advance. The rapid growth of neobanks, the launch of new services, and emerging trends have created a gap in theoretical understanding regarding the current and future competitive landscape within the banking sector, as well as changes in customer preferences and behaviors. Therefore, a significant gap persists in the literature that evaluates the emerging opportunities for neobanks in the financial services sector, the potential risks they pose due to their newly established roles, how they differentiate themselves to customers, and their interactions with traditional banks.

3 OBJECTIVES OF THE STUDY

a) To understand the concept and evolution of neo banking in India.
b) To analyze the key drivers and enablers behind the growth of neo banks in India.
c) To evaluate customer perception, trust, and satisfaction with neo banking services.

d) To assess the regulatory challenges and policy landscape impacting neo banks.
e) To identify the opportunities and risks associated with neo banking in the Indian context.
f) To recommend strategies for sustainable growth and adoption of neo banks in India.

4 CHARACTERISTIC APPEARANCES

Key characteristics and advancements provided by neobanks Neobanks represent a unique category of financial entities that exclusively operate online, usually without any physical locations. They offer their banking services through mobile applications and websites, prioritizing an easy, user-friendly, and completely digital experience for their clients. To implement innovative features such as instant transaction alerts, budgeting and investment tools, simple account registration processes, and access to a wide range of trading markets, including cryptocurrency and stock exchanges, neobanks often rely on technological progress (Gulieva *et al.* 2019). In contrast, traditional banks are well-established financial institutions with physical branch networks. They provide a variety of banking services, including savings and time deposit accounts, loans, mortgages, and select investment options. Thanks to their physical presence and Automated Teller Machines (ATMs), customers can access the services of traditional banks in person. Additionally, they typically offer a wide range of supplementary services such as wealth management, insurance, and financial planning.

In this way, neobanks provide several distinctive features and innovations that differentiate them from traditional banks. The primary defining characteristic of neobanks is their mobile-centric approach. They are designed for use primarily on mobile devices, making them more convenient for customers who are frequently on the move. Another important aspect is their emphasis on user experience. Neobanks are crafted to be straightforward and easy to navigate, with intuitive interfaces that facilitate financial management for customers. They also provide a variety of innovative services such as budgeting tools, savings objectives, and real-time alerts. Neobanks are also recognized for their affordability and accessibility. They do not incur the same overhead expenses as traditional banks, enabling them to offer more favorable rates to their clients. Lastly, neobanks are known for their rapid and effective customer service. They utilize technology to deliver prompt responses to customer inquiries and issues.

5 KEY PLAYERS IN THE INDIAN NEO BANKING:

Several neo banks have emerged in India, each offering unique value propositions. Some of the prominent players include:

a) *Niyo*: Offers digital savings accounts, international debit cards, and wealth management services.
b) *InstantPay*: Provides business banking solutions, including current accounts, payment processing, and expense management.
c) *Jupiter*: Focuses on personal finance management with features like goal-based savings, spending insights, and reward programs.
d) *RazorpayX*: Targets businesses with services such as corporate accounts, payroll management, and automated payouts.

6 METHODOLOGY

Neo banking Market Share & Trends in India – User base Growth

Year	Neobank users (approx.)
2020	0.8 million
2022	5.1 million
2024	12+ million
2025 (Projected)	18–20 million

Source: BCG & FICCI Report (2022–2023)

Jupiter	22%	Retail banking, youth-focused UX
Niyo	18%	International cards, salaried class
Fi Money	15%	Smart saving and salary accounts
Open	20%	SMEs and business accounts
RazorpayX	12%	Payment integration and payroll
Others (Zolve, InstantPay, etc.)	13%	Niche services

Source: BCG & FICCI Report (2022–2023)

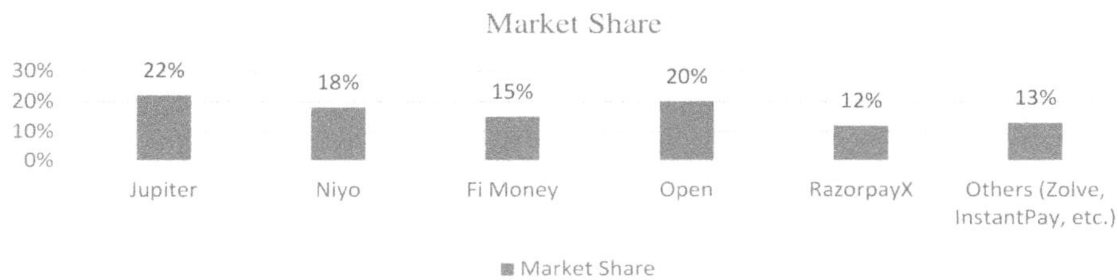

In the 2024 Indian neo banking landscape, Jupiter leads with a 22% market share, owing to its strong appeal among youth through a sleek, user-friendly interface and retail banking features tailored for digital natives. Open follows with 20%, dominating the SME and business banking segment with its integrated financial tools. Niyo captures 18%, driven by its popularity among salaried professionals and frequent travellers due to international card offerings. Fi Money holds 15%, focusing on smart savings and salary-linked accounts for urban millennials. RazorpayX, with 12%, specializes in payment integration and payroll solutions for startups and small businesses. The remaining 13% is held by players like Zolve and InstantPay, which cater to niche markets such as cross-border banking and API-driven services, collectively showcasing a dynamic and segmented neobank ecosystem in India.

7 FUTURE OUTLOOK FOR NEOBANKS

The future possibilities for neobanks appear to be very promising. The main factor contributing to the increasing popularity of neobanks is their entirely digital nature and the ease of their services. These offerings allow customers to conduct banking activities from the comfort of their homes or any other location of their preference, removing the necessity of visiting physical branches (Padmanabhan 2021). Despite the trend toward digitization in traditional banks, they still hold a substantial market share in the banking sector. However, recent trends and studies suggest a steady migration of clients towards banks that offer "online-only" solutions (Statista 2023). The global neobank market is projected to expand at a CAGR of approximately 46.5% from 2019 to 2026, potentially generating around USD 394.6 billion by 2026. Factors such as the rising adoption of smartphones, the increasing demand for digital banking solutions, and the growing number of collaborations between traditional banks and fintech firms are driving the growth of the market. Some of the future opportunities for neobanks are highlighted below:

7.1 *Market expansion*

With the rising trend of internet access and smartphone usage, neobanks are anticipated to attract more customers, particularly among the younger demographic, who are more inclined to utilize digital banking services (Nasir and Rizvi 2020). Additionally, neobanks are strategically positioned to extend their offerings to unbanked and underbanked communities in developing markets (Demirgüç Kunt *et al.* 2018).

7.2 *Technological innovation*

The area of efficiency has seen significant changes due to the introduction of modern and advanced technology. Banks have managed to automate a large portion of their operations, decreasing their reliance on manual labor, which has led to improved efficiency and a streamlined cost structure (Gulieva *et al.* 2019). Currently, banks are heavily utilizing Artificial Intelligence (AI) for various functions, including fraud detection and customer service automation (Digalaki 2022). In this light, neobanks are set to continue leading the charge in adopting cutting-edge technologies like Artificial Intelligence, blockchain, and biometrics to deliver more efficient and secure banking solutions (Jabbari and Ouerghi 2020). For example, AI can be applied for enhanced risk assessment and tailored financial advice.

7.3 *Partnerships and ecosystem development*

Neobanks often depend on collaborations and partnerships with other financial service providers to deliver their offerings for multiple reasons. A primary reason is that these institutions typically lack the necessary infrastructure, regulatory approvals, and licenses to directly provide services like loans and credit cards. They are able to offer such services through their alliances with established financial entities, allowing them to do so without the need to invest in the necessary infrastructure or secure regulatory approvals independently (Koibichuk *et al.* 2021). They are likely to develop a comprehensive ecosystem through partnerships with fintech companies, traditional banks, and non-financial organizations to deliver a wider array of services, including lending, insurance, retail, and travel (Chen 2020).

7.4 *Novel revenue generation models*

Neobanks implement various methods for generating revenue and monetizing their services. A common model involves charging fees for specialized services such as overdraft protection, foreign currency exchanges, and ATM withdrawals. Some neobanks also impose charges on certain types of transactions, like wire transfers. Many of them entice customers with high-yield savings accounts that allow customers to earn interest on their deposits. Additionally, some neobanks offer investment opportunities such as mutual funds and Exchange-Traded Funds (ETFs), facilitating customers in investing their savings. Others partner with retail businesses to provide cashback incentives when customers use their debit cards for shopping. Other collaborations may include fintech firms to deliver supplementary services such as insurance products.

The future outlook for neobanks appears promising, they are projected to continue expanding rapidly in the coming years, driven by various factors like the increasing adoption of smartphones, the rising demand for digital banking services, and the growing collaborations between traditional banks and fintech companies. Neobanks are also likely to gain from the enhanced utilization of AI and ML technologies as well as blockchain advancements.

8 KEY REGULATORY CONSTRAINTS

Regulatory Area	Implication
RBI licensing	Neobanks cannot hold banking licenses independently and must partner with licensed banks (e.g., Federal Bank, ICICI, SBM).
Credit offering restrictions	Neobanks cannot issue credit cards directly or lend without NBFC partners, limiting their revenue models.
KYC norms	RBI-mandated full KYC processes restrict remote onboarding for some services, especially for NRI users.
Data privacy & localization	Must comply with DPDP Act (2023) and ensure local data storage, which increases compliance costs.

9 CHALLENGES FACED BY NEOBANKS

Though neobanks possess numerous benefits compared to traditional banks, they encounter several challenges. Given that the adoption of neobanks and digital banking is a relatively recent phenomenon, various potential hurdles exist.

9.1 *Security concerns and cyber threats*

Cybercrime and hacking represent significant challenges or risks that can impact the banking sector and other online businesses (Larisa *et al.* 2019). The banking industry is especially susceptible to cyber threats because of the large volume of sensitive financial data it manages; unauthorized exposure of this information could result in serious ramifications. Ahsan *et al.* (2022) outline some of these risks, including malware attacks, Distributed Denial of Service (DDoS) attacks, phishing attacks, and insider threats.

9.2 *Limited brand recognition*

Another issue is the limited brand recognition. As neobanks are newcomers to the market, many individuals remain unfamiliar with them. This lack of familiarity can hinder neobanks in their efforts to draw in new clients. Additionally, an over-reliance on a partner may introduce various risks, such as potential conflicts of interest, diminished control over customer experiences, and total lack of brand visibility (Leffert 2022).

9.3 *Inconsistent customer loyalty*

With the surge in neobanks and digital banking platforms, a primary hurdle these modern banks face is the lack of consistent customer loyalty. This poses a significant challenge when it comes to maintaining a stable customer base (Corander 2021).

9.4 *Regulatory obstacles*

Adhering to various regulatory requirements is another challenge that neobanks must navigate. Like their traditional counterparts, they are legally obligated to comply with the same regulations, which can be both resource-intensive and time-consuming. Additionally, they must emphasize strong security measures to protect their customers' information. Another complication for neobanks is the necessity of implementing appropriate laws and regulations for effective banking operations. Kokh and Kokh (2020) discuss the licensing challenges faced by numerous neobanks, which often leads them to register their businesses and partner with traditional banks, creating another issue—an over-reliance on such collaborations.

9.5 *Profitability and scalability challenges*

Most neobanks are still in their growth phases and have not yet reached profitability. Achieving scalability while upholding a lean cost structure presents a notable challenge (Stoughton and Nagar 2019). Providing services at lower prices, a strategy frequently adopted by many neobanks, can undermine their capacity to generate and maintain revenue. Moreover, their operational frameworks require substantial investments in technology, resulting in high expenditures.

9.6 *Intense competition*

In a saturated market, competition is fierce. Neobanks must continuously innovate and distinguish their offerings to retain existing customers and attract new ones (Nasir and Rizvi 2020). Traditional banks have begun providing digital banking services that closely resemble those offered by neobanks. Additionally, other fintech firms are entering the market, making it increasingly challenging for neobanks to differentiate themselves.

10 USER GROWTH: NEOBANKS VS. TRADITIONAL BANKS IN INDIA (2019–2024)

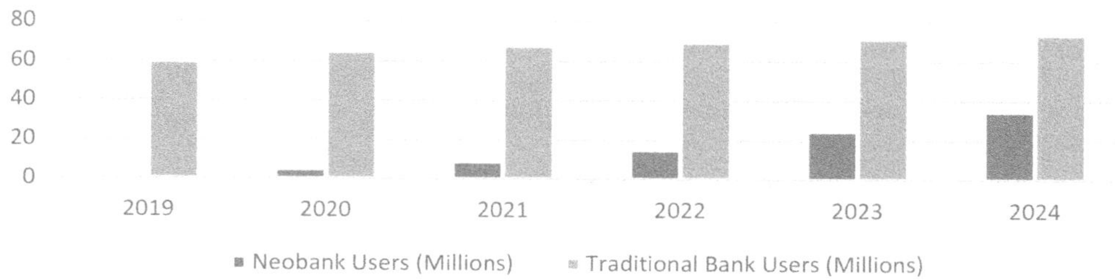

Between 2019 and 2024, neobanks in India have witnessed exponential user growth, expanding from just 2 million to 35 million users—a remarkable 17.5-fold increase—driven by digital-first strategies, app-based banking experiences, and appeal among tech-savvy millennials and SMEs. In contrast, traditional banks such as SBI, HDFC, and ICICI have shown steady but slower growth, rising from 60 million to 74 million users over the same period. While traditional banks continue to dominate in terms of overall user base and regulatory trust, the rapid adoption of neobanks reflects a significant shift in consumer preferences toward convenience, personalization, and digital innovation in financial services.

11 STRATEGIES FOR TACKLING CHALLENGES

Despite the various obstacles and security risks facing the neo banking sector, there are numerous actions that neobanks can take to alleviate or avoid these issues. Some of these are elaborated below:

(i) Establishing robust compliance and risk management frameworks: It is crucial for neobanks to comply with all applicable regulations and implement strong security protocols to protect their clients' information. Additionally, they must recognize potential threats and develop plans to manage them efficiently.
(ii) Fostering strong customer connections and engagement: Neobanks should work towards cultivating strong relationships with their clients to promote trust. This can be accomplished by providing exceptional customer support, being transparent about charges and fees, and innovating their product and service offerings.
(iii) Exploring novel revenue streams and partnerships: Neobanks should seek out fresh revenue opportunities and partnerships. This could mean working alongside other firms to offer supplementary services or designing new products tailored to their customers' preferences.
(iv) Enhancing customer acquisition and retention strategies: Neobanks must create effective approaches for gaining and retaining clients. This may involve providing incentives for opening accounts, ensuring excellent customer service, and implementing loyalty initiatives.
(v) Focusing on improved cybersecurity and data protection: Neobanks need to prioritize investments in cybersecurity to safeguard their clients' data. Like other sectors, banking is continuously evolving to find ways to protect itself from the ongoing threat of cyberattacks. Some protective strategies include: increasing cybersecurity awareness among staff and providing appropriate training (Abdulrahman *et al.* 2020), utilizing data encryption (Lakhani 2018), applying multi-factor authentication (Ometov *et al.* 2018), planning for incident response (Ghelani *et al.* 2022), and managing third-party risks (Serkebayev 2023).

12 TARGETED AI APPLICATIONS FOR COMPETITIVE EDGE

Use Case	Description	Benefits
AI-powered personal finance advisory	Tools like "AskFi" can be scaled to offer personalized budgeting, saving, and investing advice using user transaction data.	Improves customer engagement and retention, builds trust.
AI credit scoring models	Use alternative data (rent, bill payments, subscriptions) to develop credit scores for thin-file or gig economy users.	Enables micro-lending and expands user base.
Chatbots for customer support	Deploy multilingual NLP chatbots for faster, 24/7 customer service across Tier II/III cities.	Cuts down support costs, boosts satisfaction.
Fraud detection engines	Real-time anomaly detection using machine learning to flag suspicious activity.	Reduces compliance risk, supports RBI mandates.

13 CONCLUSION

Neobanks in India are navigating tight regulatory environments by focusing on experience innovation and partnership-driven growth. While they cannot offer full-stack banking like SBI or HDFC, they excel in niche differentiation, user experience, and digital agility. As the

RBI moves cautiously on digital-only bank licenses, the battle between traditional banks and neobanks will be defined by tech adaptability, trust-building, and strategic collaborations. Neobanks have the capacity to transform the banking landscape through technological advancements and customer-focused strategies. Undoubtedly, neobanks have surfaced as a revolutionary force within the banking sector. Nevertheless, they confront several hurdles, such as regulatory adherence, cybersecurity challenges, and difficulties in customer acquisition and retention. Despite these obstacles, the future appears promising for neobanks. To maintain growth and compete effectively, they must tackle issues like regulatory compliance, scalability, cybersecurity, and differentiation. They are ideally situated to capitalize on the increasing demand for digital banking solutions. As a rising number of consumers embrace mobile banking and other digital services, their growth and expansion will likely continue. To gain an edge in competition, they must innovate and create new offerings. Furthermore, they should establish strong connections with their clients and earn their trust. By doing so, they can navigate the challenges they encounter and continue to progress and prosper in the years to come.

Niyo emphasizes wealth management tools and global banking features, catering to the salaried class and frequent travelers by offering zero forex markup cards and integrated investment platforms. In contrast, Jupiter focuses on a youth-oriented user experience, leveraging gamified budgeting, instant rewards, and intuitive design to attract urban millennials. Open targets SMEs by bundling invoicing, tax filing, and banking into a single platform, while Fi Money appeals to digital natives with smart salary-linked savings features. These diverse strategies reflect how neobanks are carving out niches in the competitive landscape, each aiming to deepen customer loyalty and increase financial product adoption through tailored digital experiences. To sustain growth and gain a competitive edge, Indian neobanks should adopt targeted AI applications for personalized financial insights, fraud detection, and customer service automation, enhancing user engagement and operational efficiency. Forming strategic regulatory partnerships with the RBI and legacy banks can help navigate compliance hurdles while building trust among users. Collaborations to launch co-branded products, such as zero-balance salary accounts or investment platforms, can widen their service offerings. However, implementation challenges remain, including high RBI compliance costs, evolving digital banking norms, and the need for robust cybersecurity frameworks. Balancing innovation with regulatory alignment will be crucial for neobanks to scale sustainably in India's complex financial ecosystem.

REFERENCES

Abuladze, B. (2022). The future of neo banking. *Business Administration Research Papers*, 7.

Alaeddine Ziouache, Mohamed Bouteraa, (2023), Descriptive approach of neo banking system: conception, challenges and global practices, *International Journal of Business and Technology Management*, ISSN: 2682-7646, Vol. 5.

Bataev, A., and Bataeva, K. (2021, October). Challenger banks performance model. *In Proceedings of the 3rd International Scientific Conference on Innovations in Digital Economy* (pp. 425–433).

Bradford, T. (2020). Neobanks: Banks by any other name. *Federal Reserve Bank of Kansas City, Payments System Research Briefing*, August, 12, 1–6.

Danevska, B.A. (2021). Reinvention of new banking business models in republic of North Macedonia. *Trends in Economics, Finance and Management Journal (TEFMJ)*, 3(2), 42–52.

Dhanraj Jaglan, (2021), NEO BANKS - The rise of banking industry, *International Journal of Management and Commerce Innovations*, Issue 1, Vol. 9.

Dokania, Y. (2020). Neo bank- revolution in indian banking sector- A critical analysis. *International Journal of Law Management & Humanities*, 03(06), 361–374.

Elroy Monis and Ramesh Pai, (2023), Neo Banks: A paradigm shift in banking, *International Journal of Case Studies in Business*, ISSN: 2581–6942, Vol. 7.

Ganeshkumar, (2022), Neo Banking: The future of banking in India, *International Journal of Creative Research Thoughts*, Issue 1, Volume 10

Kavya Shabu, R. Vasanthagopal, (2022), Neo banking in India: Opportunities and challenges from customer perspective, *International Conference on Innovative Computing & Communication..*

Lindström, V., and Nilsson, O. (2023). *The sudden rise of neobanks and the threat it poses upon the traditional banking system.*

Monis, E., and Pai, R. (2023). Neo banks: A paradigm shift in banking. *International Journal of Case Studies in Business, IT and Education (IJCSBE)*, 7(2), 318–332.

Priya Raman, Angad Tiwary, 2022, Neo Banks: Future Of Indian Banking System, *UGC Care Group 1 Journal*, ISSN: 0378 – 4568.

Rangaswamy, E., Nadipilli, N., and Nawaz, N. (2022). Retracted Chapter: A comparative study of Traditional Bank A and Digital Bank B from an organizational innovation perspective. *In Communication and Intelligent Systems: Proceedings of ICCIS 2021* (pp. 489–507). Singapore: Springer Nature Singapore.

Ravichandran, S. Muralidhar and N.R. Naresh, (April: 2022), Neo banks, fintech, and banking -the changing landscape – a perspective – on dangers, Growth, opportunities – a critical study, *International Journal of Multidisciplinary Educational Research*, ISSN: 2277-7881, VOLUME:11,ISSUE:4 (6).

Reepu, R. (2023). Banking of the upcoming age: Neo Banks. In Cultural Marketing and Metaverse for Consumer Engagement (pp. 38–50). IGI Global.

Sardar, S., and Anjaria, K. (2023). The future of banking: how neo banks are changing the industry. *International Journal of Management, Public Policy and Research*, 2(2), 32–41.

Sibanda, W., Ndiweni, E., Boulkeroua, M., Echchabi, A., and Ndlovu, T. (2020). Digital technology disruption on bank business models. *International Journal of Business Performance Management*, 21(1–2), 184–213.

Umme Asma, Johnsy Mary Johnson and Gisa George, (2022), A Study On Challenges And Future Of Neobanks In India, *International Journal of Early Childhood Special Education*, ISSN: 1308–5581, Vol 14, Issue 04.

Yasmin. A. Barodawala, (July – September 2022), Neo banking: an innovative window of banking arena, GAP Interdisciplinarities, *A Global Journal of Interdisciplinary Studies*, Volume – V, Issue III.

Moving Towards Sustainable Businesses and Developing More Resilient Economies – Rashid and Annansingh-Jamieson (Eds)

A study of implications of goods and services tax in India

P Paramashivaiah
Senior Professor & Dean, Dr. Sadananda Maiya School of Commerce & Management, Tumkur University. Karnataka, India

ABSTRACT: India has witnessed major reforms in taxation since 1991. Introduction of VAT was a major breakthrough in the reforms of indirect taxes in India. But both CENVAT and VAT also have shortcomings. The Goods and Service Tax (GST) is one of the biggest taxation reforms in India, the decision on which is pending in Parliament since March 2011. The central idea behind this form of taxation is to replace existing levies like value-added tax, excise duty, service tax, and sales tax by levying a comprehensive tax on the manufacture, sale and consumption of goods and services in the country. GST is expected to unite the country economically as it will remove various forms of taxes that are currently levied at different points. The present paper attempts to highlight the major implications of the introduction of GST in India. The study, based on secondary data, highlights the impact of GST on micro and macro level of the economy. It is suggested that GST need to be implemented at the earliest to reap the benefit of it.

Keywords: VAT, CENVAT, GST, impact, revenue

1 INTRODUCTION

Any country should maintain optimization of equity and efficiency in the system of taxation for Socio-economic growth. Models of taxation should enhance the rate of growth of tax revenue by preventing adverse effects of taxes and by promoting natural compliance and making broad based taxation system. The models of taxation in India over the last 60 years were characterized by cascading and distortionary tax on production and distribution of goods and services that lead to misallocation of resources and hampered economic growth. Moreover, these models inhibit voluntary compliance. These models have a negative effect on the size of tax base and dampen the process of revenue mobilization. To address these problems, Central Value Added Tax (CENVAT) was introduced in 2000.

Introduction of VAT was a major breakthrough in the reforms of indirect taxes in India. But both CENVAT and VAT also have shortcomings. CENVAT does not cover the input value added in the supply chain before the production. Several central taxes such as additional excise duty, custom duties, surcharge etc have not been subsumed in the CENVAT. Therefore, the benefits of input tax and service tax set-off have not reached the producers and traders. Several state taxes such as entertainment tax, luxury tax etc. have not been subsumed in the VAT. Even after various initiatives by the various machineries at the centre the present taxation system is complicated and unfriendly. In this perspective, Dr Vijay Kelkar suggested a rational, scientific, simplified and modern unified tax system in tune with developed nations form the base behind the introduction of Goods and Service Tax (GST) in India.

DOI: 10.1201/9781003647300-16

2 THE CONCEPT OF GST

GST is a broad based, single, comprehensive tax levied on goods and services at each point of sale of goods or provision of service, in which, the seller or service provider may claim the input credit of tax which he has paid while purchasing the goods or availing the service; the final consumer will thus bear only the GST charged by the last dealer in the supply chain. With the introduction of GST at the State level, the additional burden of CENVAT and services tax would be comprehensively removed and all the indirect taxes of the centre and the sates will get subsumed into GST. This will reduce the multiplicity of taxes. GST is a major improvement over the previous system of VAT. GST will help-widening the coverage of tax base and improve tax compliance. This may lead to higher revenue which further results in lowering of tax burden. Although there are many hurdles to be crossed before the implementation of GST like consensus over rates, constitutional amendment, compensation mechanism for States losing out on revenue, varying models, dispute resolution etc. the Central government has reiterated its commitment towards the adoption of a unique, transparent, flawless, GST for enhancing the international competitiveness of India consequent to globalization and liberalization. There are many impediments to the proposed transition. Therefore it is pertinent to study its possible implications. It is in this perspective; the present paper aims to understand the features of the proposed GST and its impact.

3 KEY FEATURES OF GST

(i) The GST would be applicable to all transactions of goods and services made for a consideration except the exempted goods and services, goods which are outside the purview of GST.

(ii) GST will be paid to the accounts of the Centre (Central GST) and the States (State GST) separately, rates for which would be prescribed appropriately, reflecting revenue considerations and acceptability.

(iii) Since the Central GST and State GST are to be treated individually, taxes paid against the Central GST shall be allowed to be taken as input tax credit (ITC) for the Central GST and could be utilized only against the payment of Central GST.

(iv) The GST will be levied on import of goods and services into the country

(v) The rules for taking and utilization of credit for the Central GST and the State GST would be aligned.

(vi) To the extent feasible, uniform procedure for collection of both Central GST and State GST would be prescribed in the respective legislation for Central GST and State GST.

(vii) Each taxpayer would be allotted a PAN-linked taxpayer identification number with a total of 13/15 digits. This would bring the GST PAN-linked system in line with the prevailing PAN-based system for Income tax, facilitating data exchange and taxpayer compliance

(viii) The taxpayer would need to submit common format for periodical returns, to both the concerned Central and State GST authorities.

4 BENEFITS OF GST

For business and industry

(i) Easy compliance

(ii) Removal of cascading

(iii) Improved competitiveness

(iv) For Central and State Governments

(v) Simple and easy to administer

(vi) Better controls on leakage

(vii) Consolidation of tax base
(viii) Higher revenue efficiency
(ix) For the consumer
(x) Single and Transparent tax proportionate to the value of goods and services
(xi) Reduction of prices

5 SHORTCOMING OF GST

States are not having any right to make any changes in rate, it reduce the fiscal autonomy of states therefore autonomy should be given to states to change rate so that they can meet out their revenue crisis. States should be allowed to adjust their rates according to the social & economic objectives of states so that they can use the tax system as a tool for achieving their social & economic objectives

6 REVIEW OF LITERATURE

Value added tax was first introduced by a French economist Maurice Laure, in 1954. The tax was designed such that the burden is borne by the final consumer. Since VAT can be applied on goods as well as services it has also been termed as goods and services tax (GST). During the last four decades VAT has become an important instrument of indirect taxation of 130 countries resulting in one- fifth of the world's tax revenue. Tax reform in many of the developing countries has focused on moving to VAT. Most of these countries have gained thus indicating that other countries would gain from its adoption (Keen and Lockwood, 2007).

Hamilton *et al.* (1991) use a general equilibrium model to analyse the impact of GST on economic growth in Canada. The federal sales tax (FST) in Canada, as in 1989, created several distortions. One of the important distortions refers to tax applied on capital goods used in production process. It was about 4 per cent on capital goods. The removal of taxes from capital goods would, over time, lower the cost of capital to domestic producers. This would lead to increases in investments, productivity and domestic real output. The GST reforms would have substantial impacts on real output, particularly for sectors which rely heavily on taxed inputs and those which compete in the international markets – either exports or importcompeting domestic products. The GST reform would increase the real output of the Canadian economy by approximately 1.4 per cent, i.e. about $9 billion over 1989.

Devarajan *et al.* (1991) analyse the impact of introducing 10 per cent VAT in Thailand using a general equilibrium model to identify gainers and losers and the effect on output, prices and incomes. Though the paper provides an overall view of the changes in aggregate exports and imports it does not bring out sectoral changes therein. It does not provide reference to the type of the model used.

Meagher and Parmenter (1993) analyse short-run implications of Australia's tax reforms of 1992 proposed as Fightback (Liberal and national Parties, 1992). Fightback was a radical economic reform package and incorporated move to 15 per cent GST. They use a general equilibrium model for their analysis. The conclusion states that: "The GST does not discriminate between imports and domestic commodities and affects exports only in a minor indirect way. Hence, its impact on cost-sensitive industries exposed to international competition is smaller than the impacts of other taxes. Hence the implications of the GST for output and employment are relatively small". However, the paper does not lay out changes in the composition of Australia's foreign trade.

Dixon and Rimmer (1999) use a general equilibrium model to analyse the impact of Australia's tax reforms contained in Treasury Paper (ANTS) of 1998. ANTS programme proposed tax reforms including move to 10 per cent GST. The paper concludes that the longrun resource allocation gains flowing from the proposed tax changes will be negligible.

Terms-of-trade effect would be negative. Composition of exports would change away from services and in favour of goods. For example, the package would harm tourism and benefit traditional exporters like iron ore.

Wittwer and Kym (2002) use a computable general equilibrium model (CGE) to analyse the impact of the GST and wine tax reform on Australia's wine industry introduced in 2000. It is concluded that export-oriented premium segment would gain at the expense of non-premium segment of wine industry. The implicit message is that such gains would originate from increased prospects of exports of the premium wine segment.

McLure (2003) outlines characteristics of a well designed indirect tax regime in the context of Canada. While consumers should be taxed at single rate sales of inputs to business should not carry any tax liability. With regard to exports the tax should be levied under the destination principle, i.e. exports should be tax-free and imports should be taxed at the same rate as domestic products.

Vasanthagopal, (2011) in his study "GST in India: A Big Leap in the Indirect Taxation System", found that the positive impacts are dependent on a neutral and rational design of the GST, balancing the conflicting interests of various stakeholders, full political commitment for a fundamental tax reform with a constitutional amendment, the switchover to a flawless GST would be a big leap in the indirect taxation system and also give a new impetus to India"s economic change. It is also noted that, buoyed by the success of GST, more than 140 countries have introduced GST in some form to other and is fast becoming the preferred form of indirect tax in the Asia Pacific region.

Girish Garg, (2014) in his study "Basic Concepts and Features of Good and Service Tax in India", found that GST is the most logical steps towards the comprehensive indirect tax reform in our country since independence. GST creates a single, unified Indian market to make the economy stronger. Experts say that GST is likely to improve tax collections and Boost India's economic development by breaking tax barriers between States and integrating India through a uniform tax rate. Under GST, the taxation burden will be divided equitably between manufacturing and services, through a lower tax rate by increasing the tax base and minimizing exemptions.

7 OBJECTIVES OF THE STUDY

The following are the objectives of the present study.

(i) To understand the concept of Goods and Service Tax
(ii) To know the benefit of Goods and Service Tax
(iii) To understand the possible impact of GST

8 METHODOLOGY

The present paper is exploratory and based on secondary sources of available data from journals, magazines, articles and reports. The objectives of the study require descriptive research design. Keeping in view of the set objectives, this research design was adopted to have greater accuracy and in depth analysis of the research study. The analysis of the impact of GST on various areas has been made by reviewing the reports and available literature. An hypothetical example of comparative impact of GST on consumer price has also been exhibited.

9 ANALYSIS OF IMPACT

9.1 *Impact of GST on agriculture*

Through a comprehensive and wider coverage of input and service taxes set-off, subsuming of several Central and State taxes in the GST and phasing out of CST, the GST could increase the prices of agricultural produce between 0.61 and 1.18 per cent. This price increase would be a boon to millions of farmers in India (Thirteenth Finance Commission, 2009).

9.2 *Impact of GST on manufacturing industry*

Unlike the present multistage taxation, a flawless GST can help manufacturing sector to reduce their cost to the extent of almost 50 per cent. This will help them to compete with their counterparts in the west. In the words of Vijay L Kelkar, Even a two per cent reduction in production cost will increase profits by over 20 per cent, giving headroom for reducing prices and benefitting end-users (Kelkar,Vijay,2009). It is estimated that the implementation of GST would reduce the overall prices of all manufacturing sectors between 1.22 and 2.53 per cent (Thirteenth Finance Commission, 2009).

9.3 *Impact of GST on MSMEs*

The existing threshold of goods under State VAT is Rs. 5 lakh for a majority of bigger States and a lower threshold for North Eastern States and Special Category States. The present GST proposal is that the enterprises above the turnover threshold Rs. 10 lakh both for goods and services will have to be registered. Again, keeping in view the interest of micro, small and medium enterprises and to avoid dual control, the States consider that the threshold for Central GST for goods may be kept at Rs.1.5 Crore and the threshold for services should also be appropriately high (Empowered Committee of Finance Ministers, 2009). Therefore the Increase in threshold will adequately protect the interests of small traders and industries.

9.4 *Impact of GST on housing sector*

At present, stamp duty on land and other indirect taxes on inputs are included in the value of a constructed property. On registration of the property, stamp duty is payable on the entire cost including the embedded taxes. There is no mechanism for complete set-off of these taxes which results in an increase in the overall cost of the property. The GST provides for including within its scope the transactions in real estate. Therefore, for a registered real estate builder, all taxes on inputs (including that of land) will be off-set against the tax payable on the constructed property. This will reduce cost of housing to the extent of embedded taxes and Hence will benefit the poor.

9.5 *Role of GST in poverty alleviation*

At present, primary food articles like rice and wheat are liable to tax by many States either at the time of purchase or at the time of sale at a lower rate. But under the GST, all food items covered under the public distribution system including rice and wheat are proposed to be exempted. As a result primary food items like rice and wheat would be exempted from GST. Since expenditure on food constitutes a large proportion of the total consumption expenditure of the poor, the GST acts as a poverty reduction tool. Moreover, basic health and education services are also intended to be fully exempted. In any case, these services will continue to be exempted from tax and therefore no additional burden will arise on account of implementation of GST (Thirteenth Finance Commission (2009).

9.6 *Role of GST on employment generation*

GST contributes to increased growth of income and output in various sectors of the economy. On account of this increase in higher growth, there will be large scale employment opportunities.

9.7 *Role of GST in price reduction*

GST is a regressive tax system as it minimizes the number of tax rates to a single (dual) rate. However, there is allegation that the subsuming of major Central and State taxes in GST, continuous chain of set-off of input goods and services and phasing out of CST the commitment of taxes on goods would come down under GST. It is anticipated that, other things remaining the same, this would encourage manufacturers and distributors to reduce the prices of their produce and ultimately benefit the consumers. Hence, it is argued that GST would be pro-poor and not regressive.

9.8 *Impact of GST on international trade*

It is sought that the export of taxes to other countries to be eliminated through duty drawback on the basis of estimated incidence of embedded taxes. By considering the weaknesses of the present system, the GST requires that exports from the taxing jurisdiction would be tax free and imports into the jurisdiction would be taxed at the same rate as products produced and consumed within the jurisdiction. Consequently, both export-oriented industries and import-substituting industries would become internationally more competitive. As a result, while exports can be expected to register an increase, imports are likely to decrease. The gains in exports are expected to vary between 3.2 and 6.3 per cent and imports are expected to gain somewhere between 2.4 and 4.7 per cent (Thirteenth Finance Commission, 2009).

9.9 *Impact of GST on GDP*

The implementation of GST on goods and services is expected to induce India's Gross Domestic Product somewhere within a range of 0.9 to 1.7 per cent. Again, these additional gains in GDP would be earned during ever year over and above the growth in GDP which would have been achieved otherwise.

9.10 *Impact GST on government revenue*

Since all goods and services come under GST, the number of exemptions would reduce very much. Again, the tendency of tax evasion by producers and distributors will be low as to the single and low rate of tax proposed under GST. Further, increased GDP, indirect positive impact on direct tax collections, gain for the government on account of reduction in the price level of a large number of goods and services consumed by the government. As a result, GST contributes to the increase in government revenue.

Table 1. Analysis of price under present tax system & under GST.

A	Manufacturer to wholesaler	Under Present taxes (Rs)	Under GST (Rs)
	Cost of production	100000	100000
	Margin of profit @20%	20000	20000
	Price	120000	120000
	Central excise @ 14%	16800	NIL
	VAT @ 12.5%	17100	NIL
	Central GST at assumed rate of 12%	NIL	14400
	State GST at assumed rate of 8%	NIL	9600
	Total price of manufacturer	153900	144000

(continued)

Table 1. Continued

B	Wholesaler to retailer		
	Cost of goods to Wholesaler (after input tax)	136800	120000
	Margin of profit @ 5%	6840	6000
	Price	143640	126000
	VAT @ 12.5%	855	NIL
	Central GST at assumed rate of 12%	NIL	720
	State GST At assumed rate of 8%	NIL	480
	Total price of wholesaler	144495	127200
C	Retailer to final consumer		
	Cost of goods to retailer	144495	127200
	Margin of profit @ 10%	14449.5	12720
	Total	158944.5	139920
	VAT @ 12.5%	1806.1875	NIL
	Central GST at assumed rate of 12%	NIL	1526.4
	State GST At assumed rate of 8%	NIL	1017.6
	Total price to final consumer	160750.6875	142464
	Tax component in the price to the final consumer	36561.20	27744
	Total price excluding taxes	124189.5	114720

(Source: Authors own computation)

The GST must be applied on all sectors both tradable and non-tradable. Thus all services must fall under the preview GST and that the export should be fully tax rebated. The countries now introducing GST without weaknesses of the past would get benefits of expansion of their international trade with special affect on exports. Along with prudent accounting policies, transparency and the support of electronic controls, introduction of GST brings down the peak rates of taxation and enhance revenue growth. The Table 1 exhibits the comparison of the present rate of tax and the proposed GST

10 SUGGESTIONS AND CONCLUSION

GST is a single national uniform tax levied across India on all goods and services. In GST, all Indirect taxes such as excise duty, octroi, central sales tax (CST) and value-added tax (VAT) etc. will be subsumed under a single regime. Introduction of The Goods and Services Tax (GST) will be a significant step towards a comprehensive indirect tax reform in the country. It is expected that GST brings about efficiency and transparency in the indirect tax system in India. GST will also encourage an unbiased tax structure that is neutral to business processes and geographical locations. Recognizing its positive implication on various sectors in India, it requires a consensus among all political parties and state governments. Due to lack of consensus among the States and Centre on various aspects relating to limiting fiscal autonomy of the States, the implementation of GST has been delayed several times. In India, Implementation of GST would greatly help in removing economic distortions caused by present complex tax structure and also will help in development of a common national market. Therefore, the governments shall make consensus effort to implement GST and reap the benefit of it. The switch over to a flawless GST would strengthen the indirect tax system gives a new impetus to India's economic change. The positive impact of GST depends on its neutral and rational design balancing the conflicting interests of various stakeholders. It depends on complete political will for a fundamental tax reform with necessary constitutional amendment. On the success of GST more than 130 countries including Asia pacific region have introduced in some form or the other. There are several issues and challenges in the introduction of GST. While some of these are short-term issues, some others are long term issues and thus have a lasting impact on the business. An understanding of potential issues is imperative for timely implementation of measures to overcome these issues and avoid potential impediments.

REFERNCES

Chen and Mintz (2003): "How Canada's Tax System Discourages Investment". No. 68, C.D. Howe Institute.

Desai, Mihir A. and James R. Hines (2002): "Value-Added Taxes and International Trade: The Evidence".

Devarajan *et al.* (1991): "A Value-Added Tax (VAT) in Thailand: Who Wins and Who Loses?", TDRI Quarterly Review, 6(1).

Dixon, Peter B. and Maureen T. Rimmer (1999): "The Government's Tax Package: Further Analysis based on Monash Model" General Paper No. G-131, CPSIP, Monash University.

Dungan *et al.* (2008): "Growth Oriented Sales Tax Reform for Ontario", C.D. Howe Institute.

Dr. R. Vasanthagopal (2011), "GST in India: A Big Leap in the Indirect Taxation System", *International Journal of Trade, Economics and Finance*, Vol. 2, No. 2, April 2011

Empowered Committee of Finance Ministers (2009). *First Discussion Paper on Goods and Services Tax in India*, The Empowered Committee of State Finance Ministers, New Delhi.

Garg, Girish. "Basic Concepts and Features of Good and Service Tax in India." *International Journal of Scientific Research and Management*, vol. 2, no. 2, Feb. 2014, ijsrm.net/index.php/ijsrm/article/view/66.

Goods and Services Tax (GST) - A step forward (2013) available at http://articles.economictimes.indiatimes.com/2015-01-13/news/41374977_1_services-ta -state-gst-goods-and-services

Hamilton, Bob and Chun-Yan Kuo (1991): "The Goods and Services Tax: A General Equilibrium Analysis", *Canadian Tax Journal*, 39(1).

Kelkar, Vijay (2009). *GST Reduces Manufacturing Cost and Increases Employment*, Times of India, October 13.

McLure, Charles E. (2003): *"Harmonising the RSTs and GST: Lessons from Canada from Canadian Experience"*, Hoover Institution, Stanford University.

Meagher, G.A. and Brian R. Parmenter (1993): *"Some Short-Run Implications of Fight back: A General Equilibrium Analysis"*, General Paper No. G-101, CPSIP, Monash University.

Report on Reform of Domestic Trade Taxes in India, *National Institute of Public Finance and Policy*, New Delhi, 1994

Thirteenth Finance Commission (2009). *Report of the Task Force on Goods and Services Tax*, New Delhi.

Wytter, Glyn and Kym Anderson (2002): "Impact of the GST and Wine Tax Reform on Australia's Wine Industry: A CGE Analysis", *Australian Economic Papers*, Blackwell Publishing Limited.

Moving Towards Sustainable Businesses and Developing More Resilient Economies – Rashid and Annansingh-Jamieson (Eds)
© 2026 The Author(s), ISBN: 978-1-041-08875-2

Perceived workplace bullying, job satisfaction, and work engagement in selected South African banks: The moderated-mediation role of psychological empowerment

N. Khumalo, A. Mapuko, and B.R. Olaleye
North-West University Business School, Potchefstroom, South Africa

ABSTRACT: Workplace bullying significantly affects employee well-being and organizational success, especially in high-pressure settings like banking. This study examined the relationships between psychological empowerment (PE), job satisfaction (JS), work engagement (WE), and perceived workplace bullying (PWB) among South African bank employees, using the job demands-resources (JDR) and conservation of resources (COR) theories. Data from 271 employees, analyzed with PLS-SEM, showed that perceived bullying is negatively linked to job satisfaction ($\beta = -0.396$; $p < 0.05$) and work engagement ($\beta = -0.212$; $p < 0.05$). It also revealed that psychological empowerment both mediates and moderates the relationship between PWB, JS, and WE, thereby reducing employees' sense of control, purpose, and competence at work. Practically, banks should adopt a dual strategy: actively decrease bullying through policy and cultural reforms, and enhance empowerment through inclusive practices, clear communication, autonomy, and meaningful tasks.

Keywords: Workplace bullying, Job satisfaction, Work engagement, Psychological empowerment, JD-R theory

1 INTRODUCTION

Workplace bullying has emerged as a substantial challenge within modern organisational settings, exerting adverse effects on employee well-being and the overall success of the organisation (Goodboy *et al.* 2017; Olaleye and Lekunze 2024). Workplace bullying can be described as a persistent and extended mistreatment of one or more employees by supervisors and/or colleagues, whereby the victims struggle to defend themselves against the harassment (Einarsen *et al.* 2020). Although workplace bullying has been shown in numerous studies worldwide to have negative effects on employee health, organisational performance, and mental wellbeing, further research is necessary to explore the causes and impacts of bullying in South Africa (Lutgen-Sandvik 2006). Additionally, there is a lack of empirical studies focusing on the prevalence and consequences of bullying in the South African workplace, despite increasing global recognition of this issue as a significant psychosocial risk. While research links workplace bullying to negative outcomes, there's limited, rigorous evidence specifically for South African banks. The sector's unique pressures, characterized by frontline customer demands, hierarchy, regulation, and digital change, may cause different effects. Workplace bullying could harm satisfaction and service quality, increase absenteeism and turnover, and damage reputational costs (Makumbe *et al.*. 2025). This study will examine the complex nature of workplace bullying in South Africa, investigating its prevalence and the particular issues related to its mitigation in this region. Therefore, it is imperative to look into how job resources such as psychological empowerment can be strategically used to promote engagement and job satisfaction among banking employees.

 DOI: 10.1201/9781003647300-17

2 LITERATURE REVIEW AND HYPOTHESES DEVELOPMENT

2.1 *Theoretical framework*

This study utilizes the principles of the Job Demands-Resources (JD-R) model and Conservation of Resources (COR) theory to examine the interactions between workplace bullying and employees' work outcomes. The Job Demands-Resources model has proven to be an effective framework for analyzing the complex relationships among workplace stressors, resources, and employee results. The theory suggests that job characteristics can be divided into two categories: job demands and job resources (Bakker and Demerouti 2017). Job demands involve aspects of the job that require sustained physical or psychological effort, leading to specific physiological and mental costs (Bakker *et al.* 2023).Workplace bullying functions as a resource depletion process within the framework of Conservation of Resources (COR) theory: it diminishes employees' psychological, social, and material resources, thereby reducing job satisfaction and decreasing work engagement.

2.2 *Workplace bullying and job satisfaction*

Prolonged exposure to bullying can result in detachment, emotional weariness, and a decrease in one's level of accomplishment (Kim *et al.*. 2019). Reduced productivity, higher absenteeism and turnover, and a decline in staff morale are some of the organisational repercussions. Given the widespread prevalence of perceived workplace bullying, there is a pressing need for efficient intervention techniques to lessen its detrimental effects and promote a more positive work environment (Hodgins *et al.*. 2020). We argue that unpleasant experiences like workplace bullying can greatly undermine job satisfaction. Bullying at work has also been proven to have a negative correlation with job satisfaction since persistent bullying and disrespect lower employee morale and satisfaction (Rojas and Nabe 2025). Thus, the following hypothesis is proposed.:

H_1: *Perceived workplace bullying (PWB) has a negative and significant effect on employees' Job satisfaction*

2.3 *Perceived workplace bullying and work engagement*

Workplace bullying negatively affects social interactions, creates an uncomfortable work environment, and diminishes organizational effectiveness. It has far-reaching consequences that impact not only the bullied but also overall employee morale and retention (Fountain 2016). Moreover, workplace bullying damages employee work engagement, which is crucial to both individual and organizational success (Goodboy *et al.*. 2017). Work engagement is a positive and stimulating psychological state related to work, characterized by vitality, dedication, and absorption. However, a high prevalence of workplace bullying can significantly reduce work engagement. Research indicates that bullying directly causes employee disengagement by undermining their autonomy and relatedness needs, which decreases their motivation to perform well (Goodboy *et al.* 2020). Based on these findings, the following hypothesis is proposed:

H_2: *Perceived workplace bullying (PWB) has a negative and significant effect on employees' Work engagement*

2.4 *The mediating role of psychological empowerment*

Psychological empowerment denotes an individual's conviction in their ability to affect their work environment and attain desired results (Siegall and Gardner 2000). It is a multi-faceted construct comprising four cognitive dimensions: meaning, competence, self-determination, and influence (Spreitzer 1996). Employees experiencing psychological empowerment are more inclined to exhibit initiative, demonstrate innovation, and persevere when confronted with adversity. Psychological empowerment serves a crucial mediation role in the association between job satisfaction and work engagement by amplifying individuals' intrinsic motivation and sense of significance in their job. As a mediator, psychological empowerment establishes the essential psychological conditions for converting the pleasant emotions linked to job satisfaction into enduring engagement behaviours (May *et al.* 2004). Therefore, the subsequent hypotheses are examined.

H_3: *Psychological empowerment (PE) significantly mediates the relationship between perceived workplace bullying and job satisfaction*

H_4: *Psychological empowerment (PE) significantly mediates the relationship between perceived workplace bullying and work engagement*

2.5 *The moderating role of psychological empowerment*

Psychological empowerment is characterised by an individual's perception of control, competence, and significance in their workplace. It is widely acknowledged as a crucial determinant of job satisfaction and work engagement (Chompukum and Vanichbuncha 2025). Psychological empowerment acts as a buffer against the negative effects of workplace bullying, reducing how much bullying impacts job satisfaction and work engagement. Empowerment augments job satisfaction by cultivating a sense of ownership and control over one's work, hence enhancing intrinsic motivation (Jo and Shin 2025). Subsequently, the following hypotheses are tested:

H_5: *Psychological empowerment (PE) significantly moderates the relationship between perceived workplace bullying and job satisfaction*

H_6: *Psychological empowerment (PE) significantly moderates the relationship between perceived workplace bullying and work engagement*

Following the discussion above, this study proposes the conceptual model in Figure 1 below:

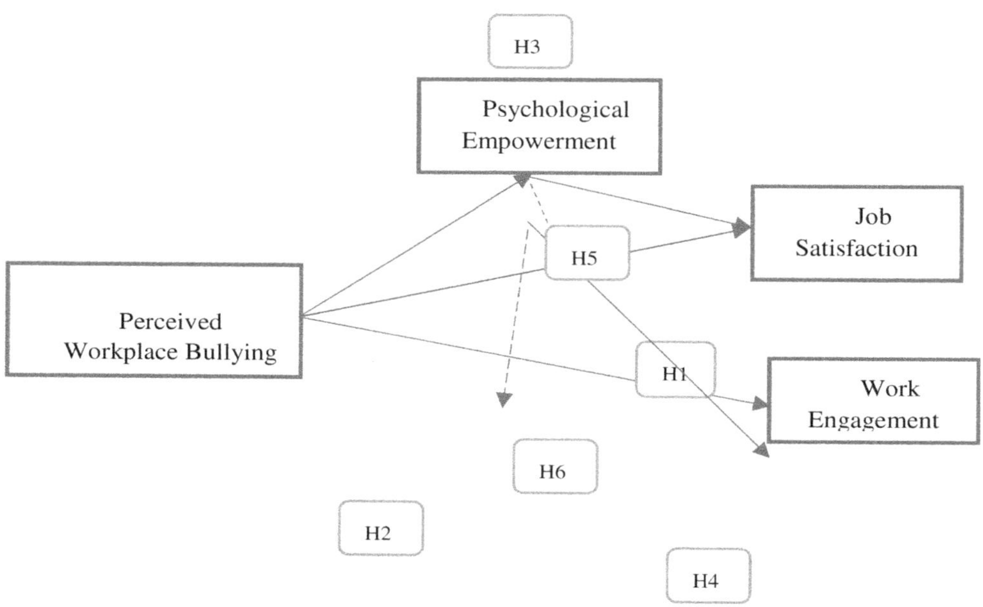

Figure 1. Research model. Source: authors' research compilation.

3 METHODOLOGY

3.1 *Design, population, and sampling procedure*

The study employed a quantitative research approach and a descriptive cross-sectional survey design to gather empirical insights on industry type. The target population comprised bank employees in three South African provinces that host several banks with large employee populations. A convenience sampling technique was applied. This choice was due to bank access constraints, and knowledgeable bank employees consented to participate in the study. An online survey was conducted to collect information from respondents after they were informed about the study. The response rate was 279 valid responses, of which 8 were excluded as outliers, resulting in a final sample of 271 respondents, for a response rate of 67.8%.

3.2 *Measures and analytical techniques*

Workplace bullying was assessed using the NAQ-R, an improved version of the original NAQ by Einarsen *et al.*. (2020). Job satisfaction was measured using the scale by Al-Muallem and Al-Surimi (2019). Work engagement was measured with the Utrecht Work Engagement Scale (UWES-9) by Schaufeli and Bakker (2003). Psychological empowerment was evaluated using the scale by Spreitzer (1996). To ensure the instrument's validity, feedback was solicited from expert academics and professionals, leading to improvements in the questionnaire's style and structure. The scales also used a 5-point Likert scale. PLS-SEM analyzed measurement and structural models, suitable for small samples with both formative and reflective constructs.

4 RESULTS

4.1 *Assessing the model using PLS*

We used the PLS-SEM method to analyze the research framework because it is effective for moderation, mediation, small samples, multicollinearity, and missing data (Rehman *et al.*. 2023). The measurement and structural models show loadings ranging from 0.565 to 0.933, all of which exceed 0.50 (Hair *et al.*. 2019). The findings presented in Table 1 indicate that all Cronbach's alpha and CR values for the first-order latent variables —workplace bullying, work engagement, job satisfaction, and psychological empowerment —range from 0.908 to 0.968, all of which surpass the threshold of 0.7, indicating internal consistency.

Furthermore, all AVE values surpass the 0.5 threshold except for perceived workplace bullying, for which the sister indicators (CR and rho_A) are above 0.7, providing satisfactory evidence of convergent validity, signifying that the measurement items effectively captured the latent constructs' shared variance (Hair *et al.*. 2021). SMARTPLS 3.0 confirmed the absence of multicollinearity issues (Table 2).

Table 1. Reliability test.

Factors	CA	CR	Rho_A	AVE
Workplace bullying	0.947	0.951	0.958	0.476
Job satisfaction	0.965	0.968	0.968	0.673
Work engagement	0.956	0.963	0.959	0.742
Psychological empowerment	0.908	0.923	0.920	0.575

Table 2. Collinearity test.

Factors	JS	PWB	PE	WE
Job satisfaction (JS)	-	-	-	-
Perceived workplace bullying (PWB)	1.537	-	1.000	1.537
Psychological empowerment (PE)	1.527	-	-	1.527
Work engagement (WE)	-	-	-	-

4.2 *Regression model test*

The SRMR was 0.053, well below the 0.080 threshold, and NFI was 0.837, nearing one (Henseler *et al.*. 2015). The study tested two direct, two mediating, and two moderating hypotheses using bootstrap resampling (5,000 iterations) with bias-corrected and accelerated confidence intervals, reporting t- and p-values. Figure 2 shows the structural model. PWB negatively related to job satisfaction ($\beta = -0.396$; $t = 6.102$; $p < 0.05$) and work engagement ($\beta = -0.212$; $t = 3.610$; $p < 0.05$), confirming H1 and H2.

In addition, psychological empowerment plays a significant role in the relationship between perceived workplace bullying and job satisfaction ($\beta = -0.364$; $t = 6.255$), thus supporting hypothesis H3. The study found a negative correlation between perceived workplace bullying and work engagement ($\beta = -0.411$; $t = 7.226$), supporting hypothesis H4. The study found that higher psychological empowerment attenuated the negative connection between PWB and JS. The statistical analysis revealed a significant negative correlation, with a beta coefficient of −0.176, p-value of 0.000, and t-value of 5.246, supporting Hypothesis H5. This indicates a notable relationship between perceived workplace bullying and work engagement. Additionally, the analysis shows that the beta coefficient (β) is −0.077, with a p-value of 0.013 and a t-value of 2.499, thus confirming Hypothesis H6. Table 3 provides a detailed overview of the enhancements regarding the negative correlation among PWB, JS, and WE.

Finally, the coefficient of determination (R^2) for job satisfaction and work engagement showed a moderate level, with adjusted R^2 values of 0.752 and 0.689. This indicates that PWB accounts for 75.2% and 68.9% of the variance in JB and WE, respectively. According to Cohen (1988), there are three levels of f2: small ($f2 \geq 0.02$), medium ($f2 \geq 0.15$), and high effect ($f2 \geq 0.35$). Table 4 and Figure 2 highlight that PWB, as well as the moderating role of PE on the connection, has a negligible effect on work engagement. At the same time, PWB has a high effect on JS ($F^2 = 0.409$). Finally, the moderating role of PE has a medium effect on perceived workplace bullying and job satisfaction

Table 3. Hypothesis outcomes (direct effect).

Hypothesis Path	β	*t*-values	*p*-values	R^2	F^2	Supported
PWB -> JS	−0.396	6.102	0.000	0.752	0.409	Yes
PWB -> WE	−0.212	3.610	0.000	0.689	0.089	Yes

Table 4. Hypothesis outcomes (indirect effects).

PLS-Path	β	*t*-values	*p*-values	F^2	Supported
PWB -> PE -> JS	−0.364	6.255	0.000	Partial mediation	Yes
PWB -> PE -> WE	−0.411	7.226	0.000	Partial mediation	Yes
PE _Moderates -> PWB -> JS	−0.176	5.246	0.000	0.170	Yes
PE _Moderates -> PWB -> WE	−0.077	2.499	0.013	0.025	Yes

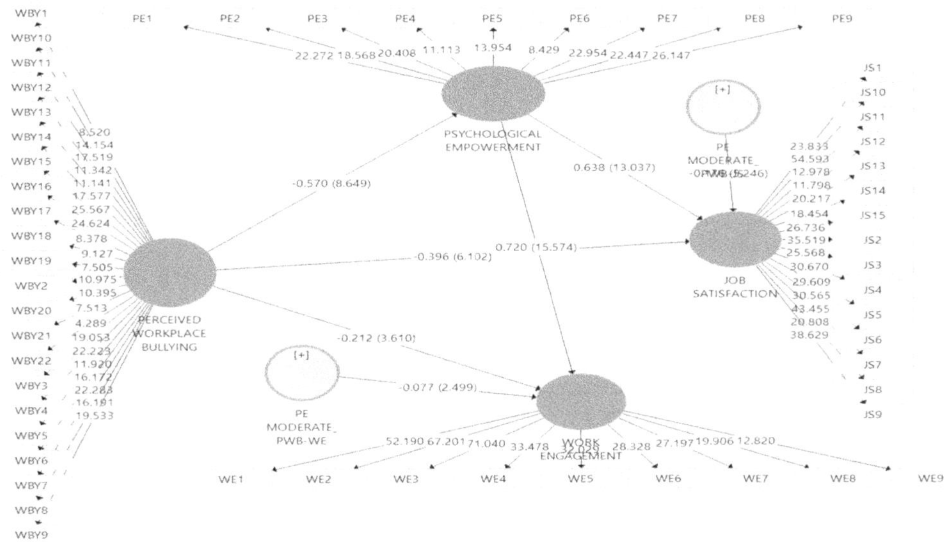

Figure 2. Path analysis and t-statistic.

5 DISCUSSION AND CONCLUSION

The study explored the relationships between perceived workplace bullying, job satisfaction, and work engagement among employees in South African banks, with psychological empowerment as a dual function: moderator and mediator. Consistent with large-scale reviews, workplace bullying, defined as repeated exposure to harassment, social exclusion, and intimidation, relates strongly and negatively to job satisfaction and psychological well-being. By hypothesis one (H1), participants who reported higher exposure to workplace bullying, such as persistent social exclusion, excessive monitoring, and professional belittlement, consistently reported lower job satisfaction. Bernstein and Trimm (2016) found that bullying significantly reduced job satisfaction, psychological well-being, and increased turnover intentions. Perceived workplace bullying was also significantly negatively associated with work engagement, as stated in H2. Bullying depletes personal and job resources, undermines vigor, dedication, and absorption dimensions of work engagement, as argued in JD–R and COR theory literature. Empirical studies in comparable banking sectors (Goodboy *et al.*. 2020) confirm that bullying links to increased employee silence and decreased engagement. In line with H3 and H4, findings depict PE as a cogent mediator between WPB, WE, and JS. Studies (Fountain 2016) show that psychological empowerment serves as a personal resource, increasing engagement and mitigating the effects of perceived bullying. Results revealed from the final testable hypotheses (H5 and H6) showed a significant association. Drawing on COR theory and JD-R perspectives, empowerment also moderates stressor–outcome links by serving as a resource caravan passageway, reducing depletion from bullying. Thus, the adverse effect of bullying on satisfaction and engagement should be weaker among employees with high empowerment than among those with low empowerment.

5.1 *Implications, limitations and future research*

First, the study expands the Job Demands-Resources model and Conservation of Resources (COR) theories by positioning psychological empowerment as both a personal resource and a moderator within a bullying context, illustrating its buffering and mediating functions. In addition, the moderating stress processes and extending Conservation of Resources (COR) theory, empowerment helps safeguard internal resources amid bullying stressors, aligning with research that shows resilience can mitigate bullying consequences. Managers should focus on developing knowledge-based empowerment strategies by promoting autonomy, role clarity, meaningful decision-making, and feedback to boost psychological empowerment, which in turn can enhance engagement and reduce the impact of bullying (Al-Romeedy and Khairy 2024). Additionally, implementing transparent reporting systems and providing leadership training on anti-bullying practices becomes imperative to foster a supportive organisational climate that can aid South African banking institutions in adapting their policies to diverse hierarchical contexts, including anti-bullying initiatives and cultural reforms. This research offers valuable insights; however, it also has several limitations that future studies could address. Firstly, the cross-sectional design restricts causal inferences. Therefore, longitudinal or experimental designs would better clarify the directionality among bullying, empowerment, satisfaction, and engagement over time. Furthermore, other possible moderators (e.g., emotional intelligence, psychological safety) or mediators (e.g., burnout, anxiety, and social support), as well as contextual factors such as current leadership styles, were not included but could significantly influence the outcomes.

5.2 *Conclusion*

This study demonstrated that workplace bullying has a significant impact on both job satisfaction and work engagement among bank employees in South Africa. Psychological empowerment serves as a crucial personal resource, helping to mitigate and moderate these adverse effects, thereby supporting employee well-being in challenging environments. From a theoretical perspective, these findings advance JD–R theory by highlighting the complex role of empowerment and providing a deeper understanding of bullying dynamics within South African banking culture. Practically, banks should combine efforts to reduce bullying through cultural change, policies, and leadership initiatives, while also strengthening empowerment through autonomy, meaningful work design, and inclusive management practices.

REFERENCES

Al-Muallem, N., and Al-Surimi, K.M. (2019). Job satisfaction, work commitment and intention to leave among pharmacists: a cross-sectional study. *BMJ open*, *9*(9), e024448.

Al-Romeedy, B.S., and Khairy, H.A. (2024). The impact of authentic leadership on workplace bullying in the tourism and hotel industry: The mediating roles of psychological empowerment and organizational health. *Journal of Human Resources in Hospitality & Tourism,* 23(4), 561–591.

Bakker, A.B., and Demerouti, E. (2017). Job demands–resources theory: Taking stock and looking forward. *Journal of occupational health psychology*, *22*(3), 273.

Bakker, A.B., Demerouti, E., and Sanz-Vergel, A. (2023). Job demands–resources theory: Ten years later. *Annual review of organisational psychology and organisational behaviour*, *10*(1), 25–53.

Bernstein, C., and Trimm, L. (2016). The impact of workplace bullying on individual wellbeing: The moderating role of coping. *SA Journal of Human Resource Management, 14*(1), a792.

Chompukum, P., and Vanichbuncha, T. (2025). Building a Positive Work Environment: The Role of Psychological Empowerment in Engagement and Intention to Leave. *Behavioral Sciences*, 15(2), 131. https://doi.org/10.3390/bs15020131.

Einarsen, S., Hoel, H., Zapf, D., and Cooper, C.L. (2020). *Bullying and Harassment in the workplace. Theory, research and practice* (3rd ed.). CRC Press.

Fountain, D.M. (2016). Relationships among work engagement, drivers of engagement, and bullying acts in registered nurses working in hospital settings (Doctoral dissertation, Rutgers University-Graduate School-Newark).

Goodboy, A.K., Martin, M.M., and Bolkan, S. (2020). Workplace bullying and work engagement: a self-determination model. *Journal of Interpersonal Violence*, *35*(21–22), 4686–4708.

Goodboy, A.K., Martin, M.M., Knight, J.M., and Long, Z. (2017). Creating the boiler room environment: The job demand-control-support model as an explanation for workplace bullying. *Communication Research*, *44*(2), 244–262. https://doi.org/10.1177/0093650215614365

Hair, J.F., Hult, G.T.M., Ringle, C.M., Sarstedt, M., Danks, N.P., Ray, S. (2021). Partial Least Squares Structural Equation Modelling (PLS-SEM) Using R. *Springer International Publishing*. https://doi.org/10.1007/978-3-030-80519-7

Hodgins, M., MacCurtain, S., and McNamara, P. (2020). Power and inaction: why organisations fail to address workplace bullying. *International Journal of Workplace Health Management*, 13(3), 265. https://doi.org/10.1108/ijwhm-10-2019-0125

Jo, H., and Shin, D. (2025). The impact of recognition, fairness, and leadership on employee outcomes: A large-scale multi-group analysis. PLoS One, 20(1). https://doi.org/10.1371/journal.pone.0312951.

Kim Y, Lee E, Lee H (2020). Association between workplace bullying and burnout, professional quality of life, and turnover intention among clinical nurses. *PLoS One* 15(1): e0228124. https://doi.org/10.1371/journal.pone.0228124

Lutgen-Sandvik, P. (2006). Take this job and quitting and other forms of resistance to workplace bullying. *Communication Monographs, 73*(4), 406. https://doi.org/10.1080/03637750601024156

Makumbe, W., Khumalo, N., Ntsizwane, L., and Lisita, T. (2025). Workplace bullying and employee hopelessness in the healthcare industry: A mediation–moderation model. *SA Journal of Human Resource Management/SA Tydskrif vir Menslikehulpbronbestuur*, *23*(0), a3241. doi: https://doi.org/10.4102/SAJHRM.v23i0.3241

May, D.R., Gilson, R.L., and Harter, L.M. (2004). The psychological conditions of meaningfulness, safety and availability and the engagement of the human spirit at work. *Journal of occupational and organisational psychology*, *77*(1), 11–37.

Olaleye, B.R. and Lekunze, J.N. (2024), "Emotional intelligence and psychological resilience on workplace bullying and employee performance: a moderated-mediation perspective", *Journal of Law and Sustainable Development*, 12 (1), 2159, https://doi.org/10.55908/sdgs.v12i01.2159

Rojas, E.G., and Nabe, N. (2025). Examining the relationship between ethical climate, workplace bullying, organizational justice, and academic job satisfaction among criminology instructors. *Journal of Interdisciplinary Perspectives, 3(8), 893–899.*

Schaufeli, W.B., Bakker, A.B., and Salanova, M. (2003). Utrecht work engagement scale-9. *Educational and Psychological Measurement*. https://doi.org/10.1037/t05561-000

Siegall, M., and Gardner, S. (2000). Contextual factors of psychological empowerment. *Personnel review, 29* (6), 703–722.

Spreitzer, G.M. (1996). Social structural characteristics of psychological empowerment. *Academy of Management Journal*, *39*(2), 483–504.

Moving Towards Sustainable Businesses and Developing More Resilient Economies – Rashid and Annansingh-Jamieson (Eds)
© 2026 The Author(s), ISBN: 978-1-041-08875-2

Managing the crisis facing health professionals in the health sector

A.G. Alshareef
University of Jeddah, Jeddah, Saudi Arabia

ABSTRACT: Health professionals' fear of the coronavirus is a growing concern in the health system, as the disease's spread throughout staff and patients can have a crisis-like impact both inside and outside facilities. COVID-19 is a disease that can spread over a large area throughout hospitals and the community. A quantitative study was conducted to gain a description of health professionals' fear of the coronavirus. The sample (n = 213) consisted of health professionals from different departments in public hospitals in Al-Madinah city in Saudi Arabia. A 35-item questionnaire addressed the fear of the coronavirus, workload, hazards, job satisfaction, and intent to stay. This study strongly indicates that poorly regulated hospital policies that fail to develop preparedness plans for protecting health professionals and reducing levels of fear due to coronavirus have played a significant role in influencing health professionals' intention to stay and job satisfaction.

Keywords: Health professionals, workload, hazard, fear od the coronavirus, job satisfaction

1 INTRODUCTION

The fear of the coronavirus disease (COVID-19) plays a critical role in the maintenance of health workers' well-being, job demand, job satisfaction, and intention to stay in their job. The COVID-19 pandemic has had a dramatic impact on the health system. The International Council of Nurses reports that in prior to May 2020, approximately 6% of all confirmed cases of COVID-19 worldwide were healthcare workers (The International Council of Nurses 2020). ICN states that there are thousands of nurses who have been infected with COVID-19 around the world but there is a lack of specific data available as governments did not collect that information. Concerns about being infected with COVID-19 are compounded not just for nurses but also other healthcare professionals in the Saudi Arabian healthcare system, as they are not only responsible for providing health care but are also in the frontlines of the pandemic response. The first Saudi nurse died from COVID-19 in June 2020 while working in one of the hospitals in Al-Madinah city in Saudi Arabia. On 8 August 2021, the Saudi Arabian government announced that the family of healthcare professionals who died from COVID-19 would be granted US$133,300 (Saudi Press Agency 2021). Healthcare professionals can be defined as "all people primarily engaged in actions with the primary intent of enhancing health" (WHO 2006). Healthcare has been listed among the most dangerous professions for infection as it involves deeply personal interactions with people, especially patients and other healthcare providers, who also worry about getting infected (Mohanty *et al.* 2019). High levels of fear concerning COVID-19 may lead to intention to leave or job dissatisfaction.

DOI: 10.1201/9781003647300-18

2 THE PRESENT RESEARCH

The fear of the coronavirus disease (COVID-19) plays a critical role in the maintenance of health workers' well-being, job demand, job satisfaction, and intention to stay in their job. The COVID-19 pandemic has had a dramatic impact on the health system. Determining the fear levels of the health workforce in the health sector is of great importance for providing quality health services and protecting the well-being of health professionals. Fear is a syndrome that threatens many of the dynamics of daily life, thus establishing the importance of this research. Fear has various definitions in academic and scientific literature. This research uses the American Psychological Association's definition of fear, which describes it broadly as "a basic, intense emotion aroused by the detection of imminent threat, involving an immediate alarm reaction that mobilizes the organism by triggering a set of physiological changes" (American Psychological Association 2020). Health workers may become distant from their family environment as a consequence of fear and they can experience problems in interpersonal relationships due to ongoing worry about being infected with COVID-19 and fear that their family members may get infected (Schimmenti, Billieux and, Starcevic 2020). Many recent studies (e.g., Chen *et al.* 2020; Labrague, and de Los Santos 2021; Mertens *et al.* 2020) have shown that the health workforce has experienced psychological distress, worry, health anxiety, high turnover, and decreased work satisfaction as a result of the coronavirus pandemic. Fear of the coronavirus is recognized as a severe problem among health workforces.

This study aims to examine the relative influence of the fear of the coronavirus on healthcare workers and work-related outcomes (workload, hazards, job satisfaction, and intent to stay) as shown in Figure 1. The consequences of fear include experiencing health problems and having to deal with psychological difficulties. Fear has negative effects both inside hospitals and outside the workplace, including affecting individual's social lives and personal relationships. Therefore, it is a phenomenon that needs to be tackled at both the individual and organizational levels.

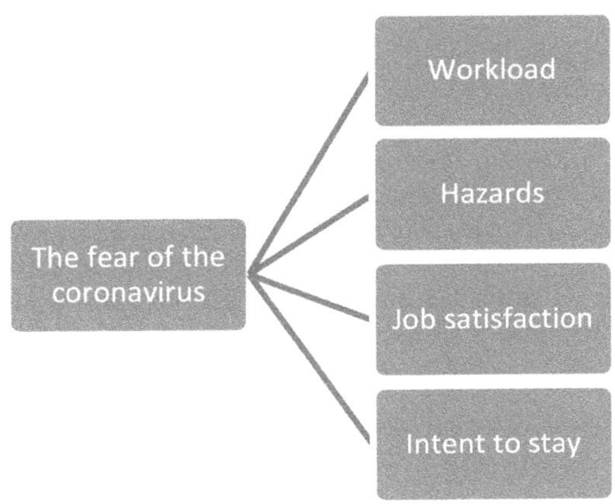

Figure 1. Theoretical model from current literature.

3 METHOD

A cross-sectional study was constructed and administered to health professionals. As the research and analyzed data was collected at one time, a web survey on Microsoft Forms was used. Data were collected from January to August 2022 from a public hospital in

Al-Madinah city that treated patients with COVID-19. The unit of analysis of the current study was health professionals who worked at a public hospital that dealt with COVID-19. The survey response rate was 61% (the response rate of 213 out of 350). The survey was written in English, since staff who work in hospitals in Saudi Arabia use English as the primary language of communication. The participants met the criteria for taking part in the study, which was working during the COVID-19 pandemic in one of the selected public hospitals. The aim of these criteria is to identify the specific challenges, including the workload, hazard, job satisfaction, and intent to stay within the hospitals, that affect the level of fear of the coronavirus experienced by health professions in order to decrease the level of fear of the coronavirus and increase intention to stay and job satisfaction among health professionals.

3.1 *Measurements and analysis*

The study measured four exogenous variables: workload, hazard, job satisfaction, and intent to stay, and one endogenous variable, which was the fear of the coronavirus. A survey consisting of 35 items was arranged into three sections. The response set was designed in accordance with five-point Likert scales. In the first section, a demographic questionnaire was developed by the researcher that collected data on age, education level, marital status, gender, and ethnicity. In the second part, three questions were designed to explore the perception of health professionals in regard to awareness of existing protocols related to COVID-19, if they had been infected by the coronavirus, and their attendance of coronavirus training, which is awareness training about the virus and how to protect oneself from it. The third part comprised the four exogenous variables: workload, hazard, job satisfaction, and intent to stay, and the endogenous variable, which was the fear of the coronavirus. Fear of the coronavirus was measured by seven indicators on a five-point Likert scale, ranging from strongly disagree to strongly agree, using the Fear of the Coronavirus Scale (FCS) developed by Ahorsu in 2020 to study nurses' concern about COVID-19. For the purpose of this research, three items were used to obtain data to measure hazards, which were defined as the extent to which employment is physically dangerous. In regard to the Job Satisfaction Scale (JSS), seven items were used and Cronbach's alpha was used to measure reliability (Kim *et al.* 1996). The intent to stay scale was measured using four items to assess health professionals' intent to stay in their job during COVID-19 (Price 2001). The quantitative data were collected through a questionnaire using SPSS and structural equation modelling (SEM) to examine the relationships among the study variables (Kline 2015). In addition, the goodness of fit index (GFI) and adjusted goodness of fitness index (AGFI) were used. The Tucker-Lewis index (TLI) and normed fit index (NFI) are used if the GFI and AGFI do not provide researchers with satisfactory results. Descriptive statistics from SPSS showed frequency tables and the distribution of variables. For the purpose of the study, a statistical analysis of the demographic characteristics of health professionals and their response to the fear of the coronavirus, workload, hazard, job satisfaction, and intent to stay was undertaken.

4 RESULTS

The study measured four exogenous variables: workload, hazard, job satisfaction, and intent to stay, and one endogenous variable, which was the fear of the coronavirus. A survey consisting of 35 items was arranged into three sections. Table 1 displays the demographic characteristics of the respondents. The participants were asked to provide information about their ethnicity, religion, age, educational qualifications, gender, job title, and marital status. All the participants reported their job title on the survey (nurses = 101, physicians = 30, pharmacists = 25, allied health personal = 18, and other = 38). Overall, there were more nurse participants (48%) than physicians (14%) and pharmacists

(12%). Of the 213 respondents, the majority were female (128; 60%). This is typical for the health workforce, which is majority female. A majority of all participants (65%) were married. Exactly half of the respondents had a bachelor's degree (50%), followed by a master's degree (16%), diploma (14%), and (11%) postgraduate certification. Less than 10% of respondents had a doctorate. The majority of respondents identified as Arab (54%). The next most common ethnicities identified were Asians (31%), Indian (10%), and African (5%); see Table 1 for the frequency distribution highest level of education level of participants. Analysis of the age question on the survey indicated that the largest group were aged between 30–40 years (47%) and 41–45 (31%). Only 13% were aged over 51 years of age and 10% were aged between 20–29 years.

Table 1. Characteristics of respondents of the study.

	Number (%)
Gender	
Men	85 (40%)
Women	128 (60%)
Marital status	
Married	131 (62%)
Single	77 (36%)
Divorced	5 (2%)
Job Titel	
Nurses	101 (48%)
Physicians	30 (14%)
Pharmacists	25 (12%)
allied health	18 (8%)
Other	38 (18%)
Ethnicity	
Arab	115 (54%)
Asian	65 (31%)
Indian	18 (10%)
African	10 (5%)
Education	
Diploma	38 (14%)
Bachelor's degree	82 (50%)
Postgraduate certificate	25 (11%)
Master's degree	42 (16.0%)
Doctorate	26 (9%)

When asked whether they were constantly following all news updates regarding the virus, almost 75% of the participants responded that they were constantly following all news updates regarding the virus. This suggests the health professionals' fear of the coronavirus is influenced by news and media, which can be overwhelming and contribute to feelings of the fear of the coronavirus or fear of being infected. When asked whether they were aware of existing protocols related to COVID-19, almost 93% of participants responded that they had knowledge of existing protocols related to COVID-19 in the hospital. Moreover, when the participants were asked whether they had attended COVID-19 training, the majority commented that their hospital had only provide a small number of training courses related to COVID-19. In response to the question asking whether they had been infected by COVID-19 while working at their hospital during the COVID-19 pandemic, most of those surveyed reported that they had not been infected by the coronavirus, suggesting they were aware of and followed protocols related to COVID-19 and they had enough information to know how to deal with COVID-19 to minimize the chances of becoming infected. Fear of the coronavirus was measured by the FCS, using seven items to study health professionals' concern about COVID-19 (Ahorsu 2020). The first item, FCS1, asks if participants are very worried about the coronavirus outbreak. As shown in Table 2, 62% (132) of participants agreed they were worried about a coronavirus outbreak. Item FCS2 asks if participants are taking precautions to prevent infection. Most (86%; 183) respondents indicated they were taking precautions to prevent infection, such as avoiding contact with infected people, washing their hands, and avoiding touching door handles. Item FCS4 asked if participants believe the virus to be more dangerous than the seasonal flu. As shown in Table 2, 73% (155) of respondents stated that the virus was much more dangerous than the seasonal flu. Furthermore, when asked whether they were worried that their friends or family would be infected, almost 70% (148) of participants responded that they were worried that their friends or family would be infected. In the final part of the FCS, respondents were asked if they felt that the health authorities were doing enough to deal with the virus. The results showed that 71% (150) of respondents did not think health authorities were doing enough.

Table 2. Characteristics of respondents of Covid 19-related questions (n = 213).

	Number (%)
Attended to COVID-19 training	
No	64 (30%)
Yes	148 (70%)
Awareness of existing protocols related to COVID-19	
No	15 (7%)
Yes	197 (93%)
Infected by the coronavirus	
No	179 (84%)
Yes	33 (16%)
Worried about the coronavirus	
No	81 (38%)
Yes	132 (62%)
Worried that friends or family will be infected	
No	65 (30%)
Yes	148 (70%)

For the current study, FCS scores were analyzed according to personal factors. Participants were divided into nurses, physicians, pharmacists, allied health personnel, and other according to their job title. Job title was found to be statistically associated with the fear of the coronavirus using analysis of variance (ANOVA). A statistically significant difference in the fear of the coronavirus was found comparing allied health personnel, nurses, and pharmacists ($p = 0.006$). However, there were no differences in the fear of the coronavirus comparing nurses and physicians ($p = 0.886$). This indicates that nurses and physicians were less likely to fear the coronavirus in comparison to allied health personnel, pharmacists, and other people who work in administrative areas.

In regard to participants' marital status, no significant difference in the fear of the coronavirus was found based on marital status. As shown in Table 2, there was no significant difference in mean scores comparing married participants ($M = 2.966$, $SD = 0.4121$) and single participants ($M = 3.032$, $SD = 0.4332$) ($t(477) = -0.919$, $p = 0.322$). This result suggests that marital status did not influence the fear of the coronavirus among participants in the current study. Regarding participants' gender, no significant difference in the fear of the coronavirus was found based on gender. As shown in Table 2, there was no significant difference in mean scores comparing male participants ($M = 2.987$, $SD = 0.4312$) and female participants (M = 2.983, SD = 0.4332) (t (488) = -0.137, p = 0.392). This result suggests that gender does not influence the fear of the coronavirus among participants in the current study. Regarding participants' education level, there was significant difference associated with the fear of the coronavirus (F (489) = 3.762, p = 0.006). Post-hoc Tukey honestly significantly different (HSD) tests show that there was a statistically significant difference in fear of the coronavirus between participants who had doctorate and those with a master's degree (p = 0.016) as well as nurses who had bachelor's degree and master's degree (p = 0.004). However, there were no differences in the fear of the coronavirus between participants who had diplomas and postgraduate certificates (p = 0.997).

The current study's hypothesis proposed that workload, hazards, job satisfaction, and intent to stay were related to the fear of the coronavirus of participants in their current job. For example, decreased workload and hazards were associated with a decrease in the fear of the coronavirus among participants in hospitals. The SEM results indicate a good fit between the study's hypothesized model and the data. As shown in Table 3, these goodness-of-fit statistics show that the study's model fits very well with the data.

Table 3. Criterion for validation of models.

(X2/df)	P	RMSEA	GFI	CFI	TLI
1.983	0.017	0.056	0.977	0.980,	0.961

The total variance in the fear of the coronavirus accounted for in the four predictors is 36%.

Workload had a significant negative affect on the fear of the coronavirus of participants in their current job ($\beta = -0.27$, $p < .01$). The negative regression coefficient suggests that a decrease in workload will decrease the fear of the coronavirus of participants in their current job. The hazards factor is defined as the extent to which employment is physically dangerous. The results broadly support the work of other studies in this area linking workload, hazards, and job satisfaction with the fear of the coronavirus (Labrague, and de Los Santos 2021; Satici *et al.* 2021).

The SEM results indicated that job satisfaction had a significant negative effect on the fear of the coronavirus among participants ($\beta = -0.24$, $p < .01$). This means that as the participants' job satisfaction increases, the fear of the coronavirus will decrease. Intent to stay also had significant negative affect on the fear of the coronavirus among participants ($\beta = -0.19$, $p < .01$). The negative regression coefficient indicates that a decreased level of fear of the coronavirus was associated with an increased level of intent to stay among participants in their job.

Table 4. Regression statistic of the factors on fear of the COVID-19.

Indicators	Standardised Regression Weight	Unstandardised Regression Weight	Standard Error	CV/	p
Workload	−.275	−.142	.039	−3.609	***
Job satisfaction	−.240	−.213	.034	−6.318	***
Hazards	−.201	−.106	.023	−4.672	***
Intent to stay	−.193	−.131	.037	−3.507	***

5 CONCLUSIONS

The current study was designed to investigate the impact of the fear of the coronavirus among health workers on workload, hazards, job satisfaction, and intent to stay. The results of this investigation indicate that the majority of participants were worried about a coronavirus outbreak and were worried that friends or family would also be infected. They believed the virus to be much more dangerous than the seasonal flu (Mertens *et al.* 2020). Furthermore, the spread of a disease such as COVID-19 throughout a hospital's staff or patients can have crisis-like impact inside and outside the hospital's facilities. COVID-19 is a disease that can spread over a large area, throughout hospitals and the community (Koh 2020; World Health Organization 2019). The results of this study suggest that attending COVID19 training courses may help prevent participants from being worried about or infected by COVID19 as well as result in a decreased level of fear of COVID-19 among health workers. These results reflect those of Labrague and de Los Santos (2021), who also found that attendance of coronavirus-related training was a significant predictor of a decrease in fear of the coronavirus. Management can handle crises that are due to COVID-19 by ensuring that staff have training on clearly identified policies and procedures that are established to ensure protection for both patients and staff. Hospital management also needs to be prepared to deal with staff's fear concerning a possible outbreak of COVID-19.

One of the more significant findings to emerge from this study is that the higher the workload reported by participants, the higher their levels of fear of the coronavirus. These results are consistent with those of other studies (Asmundson, and Taylor 2020; Santos, and Labrague 2021; Lai *et al.* 2020; Zhou *et al.* 2020) and suggest that hospital management assign health professionals workloads that are hard to handle (Campos *et al.* 2022; Zhang *et al.* 2021; Alshareef *et al.* 2020). A possible explanation for these results may be the lack of staff and support from colleagues or related to hospitals being understaffed and having a high patient ratio during COVID-19. Additionally, hospital staff may not know about existing protocols related to COVID-19 in their hospital. Regarding participants' gender and marital status, no significant difference in the fear of the coronavirus was found based on gender and marital status. This means that gender these factors were not predictive of increase fear of the coronavirus. This outcome is consistent with Mertens *et al.* (2020) who found that gender was not significantly associated with fear of the coronavirus. However, in contrast to other researchers, Labrague and de Los Santos. (2021) found statistically significant association between personal factors and health professionals' fear of the coronavirus, including health professionals' gender and marital status.

Contrary to expectations, this study did find a significant difference between job title and the fear of the coronavirus, with nurses and physicians less likely to fear of the coronavirus than allied health personal, pharmacists, and other employees who work directly in administrative areas. It seems possible that these results are because nurses and physicians were awareness of existing protocols not just related to COVID-19 but also existing protocols for disease more generally. It is very important to understand that protocols are essential in health systems and all health professionals should be aware of them, not just nurses and physicians. This suggests that hospitals should ensure policies are in place that support a safe work environment. Additionally, the provision of infection control supplies is vital to support health professionals and lower the level of fear of the coronavirus.

In this study, the fear of the coronavirus was found to cause intent to leave. This finding is in agreement with Santos and Labrague's (2021) findings, which showed addressing the fear of the coronavirus may result in increased intent to stay in the profession. These findings suggest that in general the fear of the coronavirus decreases intent to stay and decreases job satisfaction.

5.1 *Implications for health management*

This research contributes to existing knowledge about the fear of the coronavirus by providing strategies to health professionals, hospital administrators and policymakers in the health system to manage and reduce levels of fear of the coronavirus. There are several important areas where this study makes an original contribution concerning fear of the coronavirus. First, it is very important for hospitals to develop awareness training about the virus to help educate health professionals on how to prepare and protect themselves from the coronavirus. Furthermore, it is important to train health professionals on how to identify reliable sources of COVID-19 information and which sources of COVID-19 can be trusted. This study indicates that following news and social media regarding the coronavirus can be overwhelming and contribute to feelings of fear of the coronavirus or fear of being infected. This study suggests that there is a need to consider the source and whether the information related to the coronavirus is based on evidence. This means that hospital management needs to develop training sessions for several reasons. Firstly, to help educate health professionals on how to protect themselves from the coronavirus, and secondly, to educate health professionals on what resources they should use to stay informed regarding COVID-19 in order to reduce the level of fear of the coronavirus among health professionals.

It is very important for hospitals to provide current knowledge about the coronavirus to staff and to share accurate information on the issues about which health professionals working in a hospital need to be informed. The evidence from this research suggests that in order to reduce fear of the coronavirus, the dissemination of information about the disease should be focused, with correct and up-to-date knowledge provided so that health professionals understand the danger of COVID-19 in hospitals. This will provide the key elements of hospital management policies that can help with avoid misleading news that can cause a sense of fear.

This study has shown that workloads in the hospitals where participants work have reached a critical level and need to be reduced urgently to both decrease the staff's fear of being infected or infecting others as well as the fear of failing to provide passable care for patients due to limited resources. An increase in the visibility of management, increasing the number of health professionals and support from colleagues may be improve the sense of safety and support alleviate fear in health professionals.

Based on current study findings, the researcher recommends training content that includes infection control protocols and media literacy. For staffing solutions, the researcher suggests implementing optimal nurse-to-patient ratios. The current study's limitations include its single-city focus, and the researcher proposes future research directions, such as longitudinal studies, to further explore the relationships between variables. One of the important limitations of the study is that it only concentrated on the healthcare area. It is possible that healthcare delivery may have different dynamics than other service areas, such education and law enforcement. Future studies may examine whether case management may enhance organizational performance in other areas.

REFERENCES

Alshareef, A.G., Wraith, D., Dingle, K., and Mays, J. (2020). Identifying the factors influencing Saudi Arabian nurses' turnover. *Journal of Nursing Management, 28*(5),1030–1040. https://doi.org/10.1111/jonm.13028

American Psychological Association. APA dictionary of psychology: fear. Am Psychol Assoc (2020). Available online at: https://dictionary.apa.org/fear (accessed October 10, 2020).

Asmundson, G.J.G., and Taylor, S. (2020b). How health anxiety influences responses to viral outbreaks like COVID-19: What all decision-makers, health authorities, and health care professionals need to know. *Journal of Anxiety Disorders,* 71, 102211. https://doi.org/10.1016/j.janxdis.2020.102211.

Campos, A.T., Dos Santos, C.H., Gabriel, G.T., and Montevechi, J.A.B. (2022). Safety assessment for temporary hospitals during the COVID-19 pandemic: A Simulation Approach. *Safety Science, 147*, 105642.
Chen, Q., Liang, M., Li, Y., Guo, J., Fei, D., Wang, L., ... and Zhang, Z. (2020). Mental health care for medical staff in China during the COVID-19 outbreak. *The Lancet Psychiatry,* 7(4), e15–e16.
De los Santos, J.A.A., and Labrague, L.J. (2021). The impact of fear of COVID-19 on job stress, and turnover intentions of frontline nurses in the community: a cross-sectional study in the Philippines. *Traumatology,* 27 (1), 52.
International Council of Nurses. (2020). ICN calls for data on healthcare worker infection rates and deaths. Retrieved from ICN calls for data on healthcare worker infection rates and deaths | ICN - International Council of Nurses https://www.icn.ch/news/icn-calls-data-healthcare-worker-infection-rates-and-deaths#:~:text=ICN%20has%20gathered%20further%20information,than%20260%20nurses%20have%20died.
Kline, R.B. (2015). Principles and practice of structural equation modeling (4th ed.). New York: Guilford Publications.
Kim, S.W., Price, J.L., Mueller, C.W., and Watson, T.W. (1996). The determinants of career intent among physicians at a US Air Force hospital. *Human relations*, 49(7), 947–976.
Koh, D. (2020). Occupational risks for COVID-19 infection. *Occupational medicine,* 70(1), 3–5. https://doi.org/10.1093/occmed/kqaa036
Labrague, L.J., and de Los Santos, J.A.A. (2021). Fear of Covid-19, psychological distress, work satisfaction and turnover intention among frontline nurses. *Journal of nursing management,* 29(3), 395–403.
Lai, X., Wang, X., Yang, Q., Xu, X., Tang, Y., Liu, C., ... and Chen, H. (2020). Will healthcare workers improve infection prevention and control behaviors as COVID-19 risk emerges and increases, in China? *Antimicrobial Resistance & Infection Control,* 9(1), 1–9.
Mertens, G., Gerritsen, L., Duijndam, S., Salemink, E., and Engelhard, I.M. (2020). Fear of the coronavirus (COVID-19): Predictors in an online study conducted in March 2020. *Journal of anxiety disorders,* 74, 102258. https://www.icn.ch/news/icn-calls-data-healthcare-worker-infection-rates-and-deaths
Mohanty, A., Kabi, A., and Mohanty, A.P. (2019). Health problems in healthcare workers: A review. *Journal of Family Medicine and Primary Care,* 8(8), 2568.
Price, J.L. (2001). Reflections on the determinants of voluntary turnover. *International Journal of Manpower,* 22(7), 600–624. https://doi.org/10.1108/EUM0000000006233
Satici, B., Gocet-Tekin, E., Deniz, M.E., and Satici, S.A. (2021). Adaptation of the Fear of COVID-19 Scale: Its association with psychological distress and life satisfaction in Turkey. *International Journal of Mental Health and Addiction,* 19, 1980–1988.
Saudi Press Agency. (2020). Families of Health Workers in Saudi Arabia Who Die of COVID-19 Start Receiving SAR 500,000. Retrieved from Families of Health Workers in Saudi Arabia Who Die of COVID-19 Start Receiving SAR 500,000 (spa.gov.sa)
Schimmenti A, Billieux J, Starcevic V. The four horsemen of fear: an integrated model of understanding fear experiences during the COVID-19 pandemic. *Clin Neuropsychiatry.* (2020) 17:41–5. doi: 10.36131/CN20200202
World Health Organization. (2019). Coronavirus disease (COVID019) advice for public. Retrieved from Advice for the public (who.int)
Zhang, M., Zhang, P., Liu, Y., Wang, H., Hu, K., and Du, M. (2021). Influence of perceived stress and workload on work engagement in front-line nurses during COVID-19 pandemic. *Journal of Clinical Nursing,* 30(11–12), 1584–1595.
Zhou, Y., Wang, W., Sun, Y., Qian, W., Liu, Z., Wang, R., ... and Zhang, X. (2020). The prevalence and risk factors of psychological disturbances of frontline medical staff in China under the COVID-19 epidemic: workload should be concerned. *Journal of Affective Disorders,* 277, 510–514.

Moving Towards Sustainable Businesses and Developing More Resilient Economies – Rashid and Annansingh-Jamieson (Eds)

Net neutrality for the Indian marginalized community to transact on e-commerce platforms

Y. Muniraju
Senior Professor & Former Dean, Department of Commerce and Management, Mangalore University, Karnataka, India

B K. Suresh
Associate Professor & Chairman, DOSR in Commerce (Information Systems), Tumkur University

ABSTRACT: The global economy is witnessing a transformational change in digital sectors. All the countries are promoting and encouraging their citizens to use digital platforms and discouraging physical transactions, in this direction very effectively implement the net-neutrality policy of almost all countries in the world. Indian economy is also doing well in this direction, the respondents very effectively used E-Commerce platforms.

Keywords: Zero-rating, UPI, Net-Neutrality, Cognitive Ability, Scalability, Q-Commerce

1 INTRODUCTION

The world is moving very fast towards a borderless business world. Physical boundaries focused on social, political and religious based segments. However, the movements of money, materials, men, information and ideas absolutely free and fair in the global order, and it is a still the major concerns of the users. It is further swift in the recent transformational change in digital sectors, the goal of this online in industry is to improve the quality of life and quality of time (Elias M Awad 2015). India is also embrace the information, communication and technology and digital aspects and in a mass movement Indian government (including state governments) are promoting and encouraging their citizens to optimum use of digital products and discouraging the brick and mortal transactions. To support this movement, Green Revolution, Yellow Revolution, Blue Revolution, White Revolution and more importantly Commercial Revolution, Demand Revolution, Emotional Revolution, People Movement Revolution and Consumption Revolution are witnessing in India (Y M Raju 2012). India is the land of heritage, multiple-culture, multiple-religions and more importantly land of festivals. Indian land is popularly called unity in diversity. In the recent years analphabets Indian became smarter, adapt various skills, and digital learners and capacity to aspiring cultural maturity (Appa Desai 2024).

India is racing towards a digitally empowered in the present and future situations. The digital transformation has changed very rapidly, and unschooled people are using digital platforms. Particularly online payments through purchased the goods from E-Commerce, M-Commerce and Quick-Commerce platforms. These platforms have served as a very powerful platforms to easy to buy and pay by the consumer. These platforms are empowering the illiterates. Internet and smart phones are becoming an integral part of everycitizen in the world (Bhat *et al.* 2025) The significant note is low-income people, analphabets, are frequently purchasing goods by using the internet, evaluating E-Commerce functionality is proved that this platform is focus on Customer Quality Service (Loiacono, E Leanor 2004).

DOI: 10.1201/9781003647300-19

Against this background, this research article makes an attempt to know the role of net-neutrality policy. Effective and efficient functioning of E-Commerce, M-Commerce and Quick Commerce platforms and unified payment interface systems support the illiterate migrated kannada language speaking people are working in the mickey-mouse jobs in Bangalore, Mangalore and Mysore cities, State of Karnataka, India. In the bakery and small business enterprises currently attracts GST notices by crossing their turnover more than Rs.40 lakhs per year. The greater number of marginalized communities purchased the bakery items and payment through online mode is the reason of small business units earned more than 40 lakhs per year.

2 FOCUS OF THE STUDY

This study examines the role of net-neutrality policy and marginalized community benefited from this principle. Particularly E-Commerce, M-Commerce and Q-Commerce platforms in the state of Karnataka, India. It also focused on the life styles in the three cities of the state.

Indian marginalized communities are special and they possessed the significant characteristics from their respective parents and families particularly inherent intellectual skills. These segments are not privileged class and particularly, economically, exclusion class. However, they are dutiful and responsible citizen of the country. Not only dutiful and responsible Indian citizens they practice many moral-ethical principles in this quotidian life styles. They are:

Honesty and integrity citizen of the country, Commitment, Disciplined citizens, Healthy and happier citizens, Not greed and big ambition in the life.

3 SCOPE OF THE STUDY

This study is focused on marginalized community domicile in Karnataka state, Karnataka is situated in the Southwestern region of India. It is one of the most prosperous states in India. The per capita income of the state is number one in the country and more than Rs.2 lakhs (Ministry of Finance 2005) Karnataka has made tremendous progress in the field of education, industry, agriculture, IT and its capital is called Silicon Valley of Asia for this information revolution era. The literacy rate of the state is 75 percent and IT hub of India. Marginalized community are frequently using the E-commerce, M-Commerce and Quick-Commerce, platforms and payments made through online, and benefited from net neutrality principle. *Net-Neutrality principle,*

4 OBJECTIVES OF THE STUDY

a) To study the socio-economic profile of the respondents.
b) The analyze the advantages and benefits from net-neutrality, E-Commerce, M-Commerce, and Q-Commerce platforms to the vulnerable section of society.
c) To know the usage patterns of E-Commerce platforms and online payment system of the marginalized community.
d) To suggest a suitable system of online transactions of the innocent section of the society and protect the marginalized community.

5 METHODOLOGY

This study was conducted in three famous districts and these districts are attracted more and more migrated community in the state of Karnataka, India. The three districts are

Bangalore, capital city of the state and Mangalore and Mysore. These districts are continuously growing in terms of construction sectors and there is a demand of construction workers. The major parameters used to draw the respondents are: possessed the 5G mobile phones, illiterates or studied up to 5th standard, school drop outs and age is more than 25 years and deprived of KARBWWB facilities and even they are not aware about the board.

Migrated marginal people are bread winner of the family and worked in the construction sectors. This is an empirical study: the sample used in the study consist of 350 respondents drawn through snow ball sampling techniques under non-probability methods. Administered the structured questionnaire and personally collected the primary data. The researcher went to the construction sites of Bangalore, Mangalore and Mysore and even their residential areas in the 3 districts and read the questionnaire. The questionnaire was written in the kannada language (official language of the state) and then asked the other construction workers address and went that respondents. Like that primary data was collected. In the questionnaire nearly 15 questions were asked to the respondents. The Karnataka state consists of 30 districts and the respondents are last 10 years construction sectors is growing and great demand the blue-collar jobs under this parameters 150 respondents drawn from Bangalore and 100 respondents in each districts.

6 AGE OF THE RESPONDENTS

Table 1. Age of the respondents.

Cities	25-30 years	31-40 years	41-50 years	Total
Bangalore	106 (30.29%)	33 (9.43%)	11 (3.14%)	150 (42.86%)
Mangalore	26 (7.43%)	42 (12%)	32 (9.14%)	100 (28.57%)
Mysore	21 (6%)	36 (10.29%)	43 (12.29%)	100 (28.57%)
Total	153 (43.71%)	111 (31.71%)	86 (24.57%)	350 (100.00)

Source. Primary data.

The table depicts that majority of the respondents are below 40 years.

7 EDUCATIONAL ACCOMPLISHMENTS OF THE RESPONDENTS

Table 2. Formal educational qualification of the respondents.

Cities	analphabets	School dropouts (1-4th std)	School dropouts (5th- 8th std)	Total
Bangalore	81 (23.14%)	42 (12%)	27 (7.71%)	150 (42.86%)
Mangalore	69 (19.71%)	13 (3.71%)	18 (5.14%)	100 (28.57%)
Mysore	64 (18.29%)	17 (4.86%)	19 (5.43%)	100 (28.57%)
Total	214 (61.14%)	72 (20.57%)	64 (18.29%)	350 (100%)

Source. Primary data.

Table 2 illustrates that more than 20 percent of the respondents studied up to 4th standard and nearly 60 percent of the respondents are analphabets.

8 MIGRATED POPULATION

Table 3. Migrated to Bangalore, Mangalore and Mysore.

Cities	5 years ago	5-10 years ago	Above 10 years	Total
Bangalore	40 (11.43%)	89 (25.43%)	21 (6.00%)	150 (42.86%)
Mangalore	14 (4.00%)	63 (18.00%)	23 (6.57%)	100 (28.57%)
Mysore	22 (6.29%)	59 (16.86%)	19 (5.43%)	100 (28.57%)
Total	76 (21.71%)	211 (60.29%)	63 (18.00%)	350 (100%)

Source. Primary data.

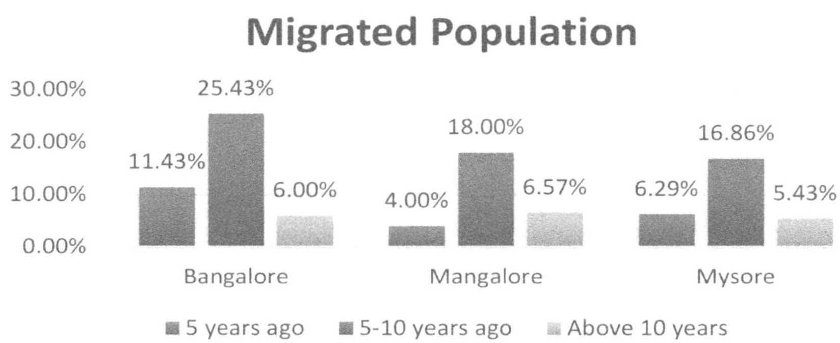

The above table and graph depicts that nearly 80 percent of the respondents migrated 10 years ago from their native place.

9 GENDER OF THE MIGRATED PEOPLE

Table 4. Gender of the respondents.

Cities	Male	Female	Total
Bangalore	58 (16.57%)	92 (26.29%)	150 (42.86%)
Mangalore	66 (18.86%)	34 (9.71%)	100 (28.57%)
Mysore	62 (17.71%)	38 (10.86%)	100 (28.57%)
Total	186 (53.14%)	164 (46.86%)	350 (100.00)

Source. Primary data.

The table demonstrates that female also migrated to 3 cities.

10 PURCHASED GOOD THROUGH E, M AND Q-COMMERCE

Table 5. Purchased Goods through E-Commerce and M-Commerce & Q-Commerce mode.

Cities	Frequently	Rarely	Not at all	Total
Bangalore	117 (33.43%)	20 (5.71%)	30 (3.71%)	150 (42.86%)
Mangalore	88 (25.14%)	05 (1.4)	07 (1.96)	100 (28.57%)
Mysore	92 (26.29%)	03 (0.84)	05 (1.4)	100 (28.57%)
Total	288 (84.86%)	22 (8%)	15 (7.14%)	350 (100.00)

Source. Primary data.

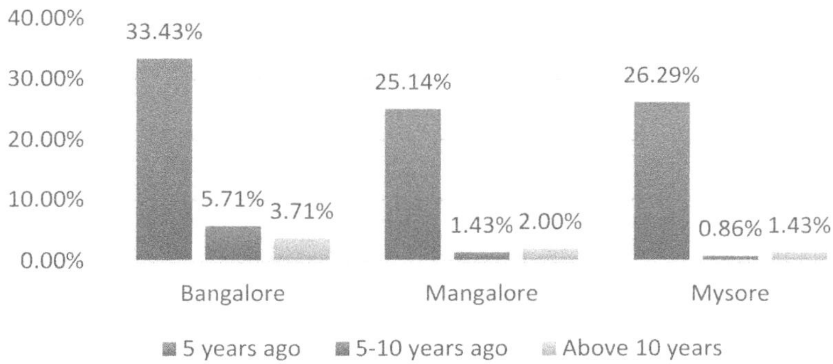

The above table and chart no.5 shows that nearly 85 percent of the respondents are frequently purchased the goods from the online platforms.

11 ELECTRONIC PAYMENT SYSTEM

Table 6. Payment through electronic modes.

Cities	Yes	Taken help from others	No	Total
Bangalore	94 (26.86%)	53 (15.14%)	03 (0.86%)	150 (42.86%)
Mangalore	76 (21.71%)	17 (4.86%)	07 (2%)	100 (28.57%)
Mysore	72 (20.57%)	23 (6.57%)	05 (1.43%)	100 (28.57%)
Total	242 (69.14%)	93 (26.57%)	15 (4.29%)	350 (100.00)

Source. Primary data.

The above table highlights that nearly 70 percent of the respondents made payment through digital mode.

12 FINDINGS OF THE STUDY

(i) More than 75 percent of the innocent migrated community (villagers) and in their productive age spent in working in the cities as a construction work and daily wage earners.
(ii) Bangalore, Mangalore and Mysore cities in the state of Karnataka attracted analphabets to construction sectors. It is a great demand in the construction sector and shortage of labour in this sector.
(iii) According the survey, more than 50 percent of the respondents are never enrolled their formal education system even for the 1st standard in the schools and they taken care of their aged parents.
(iv) Majority of the respondents are in the age group of 25 to 40 years are living in the city slums and loss their productive life and suffers a lot.
(v) The survey reveals that, more than 80 percent of the respondents are migrated to cities 5 to 10 years ago.
(vi) It is evident that, more than 40 percent of the migrated respondents are females.
(vii) According to the survey, more than 85 percent of the respondents purchased the products through online and payments are made through electronic payment system.

13 SUGGESTIONS

(i) Rich countries and rich people across the world, contribute the fund for this welfare to this community. The migrated community and their wards. Their contribution is enormous to build the roads, dams and buildings to sacrifice their growth and their families.
(ii) The special drive particularly holidays and Sundays for adult education in the to the migrated community or Monday to Saturday, any one day weekly two hours training for reading and writing skills to this community.
(iii) Across the countries come together and providing training centers to migrated community for how to use the mobile phones, online platforms like E-commerce, M-Commerce and Q-Commerce in the cyber crime era.
(iv) Dynamic youngsters are migrated cities and towns. To stop this and create job opportunities in village and taluk levels (PURA, APJ Abdul Kalam 2011).
(v) A special provision for this community and their children like basic facilities to provide to ensure dignity, peace, equality and justice in the slum areas.
(vi) Any accidents took place in the construction sites immediate action and compensation shall be given with in the week to that families.
(vii) A special provision for female construction workers, who were working more than 18 hours a day and union govt. and state government appoint the construction workers correspondence to monitor their status.
(viii) Provide social and emotional support system to create counselors. This robust system shall be created by NGOs, state government and builders association in India.
(ix) All Gram panchayaths have a broadband connectivity under Bharath Net Mala Scheme in the state of Karnataka. So that the village panchayaths should maintain the data about the migrated people and villagers must informed the panchayath administrative officer over the phone are whatsapp, when they are leaving their villages.

14 CONCLUSION

Digital platforms such as E-Commerce, M-Commerce, and Quick-Commerce have similarly played a transformative role in empowering marginalized communities in India. These platforms are not only inclusive by design but also accessible and beneficial to socially and economically disadvantaged community.

REFERENCES

(2021) Food retail supply chain resilience and the Covid-19 pandemic: A digital twin-based impact analysis and improvement directions, *Transport.Res.E Logist. Transport. Rev.*, 152(2021), Article 102412.

Alats Syed Farid (2022), Political economics of knowledge production on and around academic dependency. *Journal of Historical Sociology*, Volume (35), 14–23.

Alats Syed Hussein (2000) Intellectual imperialism: Definition, traits and problems, *Asian Journal of Social Science* Volume 28, PP.23–25.

Ambuj D. Sagar Adil Najamib (1998), *The Human Development Index: Critical Review* (Elsvier Ecological Economics).

Anusha Natarajan *et al.* (2022), *Key Facts About Recent Trends in Global Migration: Pew Research centre*, pp 201–220.

APJ Abdul Kalam and Srijan Pal Singh (2011), *Target 3 Billion: PURA: Innovation Solution Towards Sustainable Development*. Penguin India.

Appa Desai A (2024), *The Capacity to Aspire in Cultural and Public Action*, Rao Edited Standferd Press.

Appadurai, Arjun (2006), *The Right to Research Globalization Sciences and Education*, Vol.4, Number 2, PP 167–177.

Bhat A S, Kansana K and Khan J M (2025), *Asian Journal of Technology and Management*, ISSN, 22490892, Vol.6, Issue 1, pp 16–21.

Bommireddipalli, R T Bommireddipalli, (2022) What's next for Q-Commerce: the golden child of E-Commerce?

Burgos and Ivanov, D. Burgos, D. Ivanov Burns, Holly (December 26, 2024), Why your new year's resolutions should involve your interpersonal relationships (https://www.nytimes.com/2024/12/26/style/new-years-resolutions-relationships-loved-ones-html). The New York Times. Retrieved January 5, 2025.

Chen H. Chen, Z. Hu, S. Solak, (2021) Improved delivery policies for future drone-based delivery systems, *Eur.J.Oper.Res.*, 294(3)(2021), pp.1181–1201.

Christian Hildebrandt and Luka Wiewiorra (2023), The past present and future of net-neutrality: A state of knowledge review and research Agenda, *Journal of Information Technology*, Vol 39, Issue 11, pp 167–193.

Deborach Philips and David Robinson (2015), Reflections on migration, community and place, *Journal of Population, Space, Place*, No.21, PP 409–420.

Elias M Awad (2015), Electronic commerce from vision to fulfillment, PHI Learning Pvt. Ltd.

Forbes, (2022), https: // www.forbes.com /councils /forbestechcouncil /2022/02/08/whats-next-for-q-commerce-the-golden-child-pf-e-commerce, accessed 20th Aug 2024.

Gund and Daniel, HP Gund, J Daniel, (2023) Q-Commerce or E-Commerce? A systematic state of the art on comparative last- mile logistics greenhouse gas emissions literature review, *Int. J. Indus. Eng. Operat. Manag.*, 6(3) (2023), pp.185–207.

Havish Madhrapathy and Shiva Goyal (2014), Net neutrality-A Look at the Future of Internet, *IOSSR Journal of Computer Engineering*, ISSN 2278-8728, Vol 16, Issue 4, pp 71–77.

Hong J H, BC Kim, KS Park, (2019) Optimal risk management for the sharing economy with stranger danger and service quality, *Eur.J.Oper.Res.*, 279(3), pp.1024–1035.

Human Development Index Report (2025), *The Annual Publication by the United Nations Development Programme*, edited by Vajiram and Ravi.

Koncius, Jura (July 11, 2016), Find Your Inner Calm by Containing Your Clutter(http://www.chron.com/news/article/Find-your-inner-calm-by-containing-your-clutter-8352343.php). Houston Chronicle. Org. Washington Post. Retrieved may 13, 2017.

Lam H Y Lam, GTS Ho, D Y Mo, V. Tang, (2023) Responsive pick face replenishment strategy for stock alocation to fulfil E-commerce order, *Int.J.Prod.Econ.*, 264(2023), Article 108976.

Larson, Sarah (August 17, 2015), *Better Living Through Podcasts* (https://www.newyorker.com/culture/sarah-larson/better-living-through-podcasts). The New Yorker, retrieved April 21, 2019.

Lewis Kurt (1946), Action research and minority problems *Journal of Social Issues*, Vol 12, Number 4, PP: 34–46.

Lightner, Nancy J. (2004), Evaluating E-commerce functionality with a focus on customer service, *Communications of the ACM* (pp 88–92).

Loiacono, Eleanor (2004), Cyberaccess: Web accessibility and corporate America. *Communications of the ACM* (8387)
Ministry of Finance (2025), india.gov.in
Ozok, A A, Olden Burger, K and Salvendy G. (2007), Impact of consistency in customer relationship management on e-commerce shoppers performance, *Journal of Organizational Computing and Electronic Commerce*, Vol 17, issue 4, pp 283–309.
Pahwa and Jaller, (2022). A cost-based comparative analysis of different last-mile strategies for E-commerce delivery, transport. *Res.E Logist. Transport. Rev.*, 164(2022), Article 102783.
Pyun C S, Scruggs-L and Nam K (2002), Internet banking in the US, Japan and Europe, *Multinational Business Review*, pp 73–81.
Raju Y M (2012), SCM and ICT: A cornerstone to sustainable development of Agribusiness: An analytical study. *Driving the economy through innovation and Entrepreneurship: Emerging Agenda for Technology Management*. Springer, pp 715–725.
Saani Soloman *et al.* (2022), Impact of E-commerce platforms on consumer mindset, *International Research Journal of Modernization in Engineering and Science*, pp 601–620.
Yan Chan *et al.* (2003), Putting teams in to the gig economy: A filed experiment at a ride sharing platform Management Science, vol. 69, no.9.

Moving Towards Sustainable Businesses and Developing More Resilient Economies –
Rashid and Annansingh-Jamieson (Eds)
© 2026 The Author(s), ISBN: 978-1-041-08875-2

Breaking barriers: Diversity, equity, and inclusion initiatives for employees with disabilities

Ume Sumayya and Sajjad Nawaz
Iqra University, Karachi, Pakistan

Ume Amen
University of Health Sciences, Karachi, Pakistan

ABSTRACT: The foundation of the study is based with a qualitative study design and semi structured interviews carried out in Karachi, Lahore and Islamabad, it can demonstrate how corporate DEI (Diversity, Equity, and Inclusion) initiatives are perceived by employees with disabilities in Pakistan. Although global principles of HR-driven inclusion are intended to support any kind of identity, the study indicates the great differences in how the same practices are applied in various local settings. Using first-hand information, it finds that strong practices–including performance-based appraisal, monthly Pakistani Sign Language (PSL) training, and customized-onboarding–help foster an inclusive and caring workplace culture. However, there remain serious lapses when it comes to multilingual communication, accessibility to digital and assistive tools, and factors involving infrastructure. The evidence shows that DEI performance depends on localisation of global frameworks to local capacities and sensitivities: inclusion cannot be transferred equally in all settings. The study reveals that inclusion policies are supposed to be based on cultural flexibility, employee responses and ongoing feedback instead of top-down comprehensive requirements.

Keywords: Disability, DEI, HR practices, Inclusion, Organization equity

1 INTRODUCTION

In the current competitive and globalized world, workforce diversity has been taken as a strategic strength and not a mere compliance issue as it used to be before. Diversity is a broad term encompassing such a wide variety of features: gender, age, ethnicity, physical ability, and needs to be met with well-organized policies in order to make meaningful contribution to all the employees (Dessler 2017). Nevertheless, the consideration of the inclusion of the differently abled (DA) is not always given much focus and most organizations do not offer a fair opportunity and accommodations. Despite the increasing advocacy, employees of DA still encounter the structural barriers, stigma, and systemic issues that do not allow them to advance in their careers and make contributions (Kalargyrou and Volis 2014; Fraser 2009). The studies have shown that the increased employee commitment, innovation and overall productivity are the positive aspects of the disability-inclusive workplaces and the philosophical and strategic significance of the necessity to encourage inclusion (Kimball 2020).

This paper analyzes the DEI practices of DA workers in Karachi-based, Lahore-based, and Islamabad-based organizations, to evaluate the effectiveness of the policy, highlight the obstacles, and learn about the real experience of the employees. It provides practical policy gaps by getting insights straight off the workers with disabilities and subsequently make recommendations to enhance inclusive HR practices. The study highlights the importance of

DOI: 10.1201/9781003647300-20

ability diversity and the necessity of human-centered solutions that build equitable, resilient, and inclusive organizational cultures, which ensures meaningful inclusion of all the employees despite physical ability differences.

2 LITERATURE REVIEW

Human Resource Management (HRM) is an area based on essential theoretical views behind Diversity, Equity, and Inclusion (DEI). The Diversity Theory is based on the importance of diversity embracing different identities like disability, gender and ethnicity in order to boost innovation and organizational performance. The Equity Theory emphasises the importance of equality in resource distribution in that the perception of employees in matters of justice is based on the correspondence between the input and the wage. Inclusion Theory is based on the idea of providing the environment, in which everyone feels appreciated and included, especially those who represent historically marginalized groups. All these frameworks highlight the role of organizational culture and climate on job satisfaction, commitment, and overall involvement of employees including those with disabilities (Shore *et al.* 2018; Thomas and Ely 1996; Dobbin *et al.* 2015).

Empirical studies indicate that, despite enabling disabilities to work hard in an organization, those with disabilities are more likely to commit, be creative and adaptable, but do not always receive favorable treatment in terms of stereotypes and structural obstacles (Kalargyrou and Volis 2014; Fraser 2009). Such policies as accessible job advertising, blind recruitment, inclusive onboarding, mentorship, and skill development targeted can decrease discrimination and ensure fair career progression (Kulkarni and Lengnick-Hall 2011; Bengisu and Balta 2011; Poerwanti 2017). Also, accessibility, assistive technology, and long-term inclusion, as well as participation are backed by DEI measures and employee feedback tools, which increase the autonomy of employees with disabilities (Nevala 2014; Bonaccio *et al.* 2020).

In spite of the increasing awareness of DEI, companies face such issues as insufficient funding, lessening leadership efforts, and the discrepancy between the declared policies and operational life (Johnson 2021; Buttner and Lowe 2017; Williams 2019). Pakistan National efforts to support disability-inclusive practices with the help of assistive technologies are reflected in such initiatives as ReLAB-HS and the Technology for Inclusion Summit, but there are still gaps in infrastructure and benchmarking (CERB 2023; NUST and Pak-Everbright 2021). DEI plans should be also oriented to the demands of the sector, as well as cultural standards, and healthcare should value patient accessibility, and manufacturing should prioritize ergonomic adjustments, which makes the consideration of context-sensitive and culture-specific HRM policies a crucial issue (Kaplan and Donovan 2013). Together, the literature upholds the necessity of localized, disability-focused DEI activities and outlines the ongoing obstacles, which determines the justification of the current research.

3 METHODOLOGY

This research used an interpretivist, inductive inquiry of the qualitative paradigm to explore the experiences of employees with disabilities on Diversity, Equity and Inclusion (DEI) practices in major Pakistan cities acknowledging the socially constructed and subjectively perceived nature of organizational realities. The qualitative design provided qualitative in-depth information and data based on the lived experiences of participants (Merriam 2009), 12 participants who included undergraduates to doctorate students, in various industries, occupations, and family backgrounds were recruited through disability based online networks and references in Karachi, Lahore, and Islamabad, with the chosen participants being assured of confidentiality and diversity. Data were gathered using 60-minute face-to-face interviews in Karachi and using Zoom to interview remote participants and structured around the themes of diversity, equity, and inclusion to gather rich personal stories and provide a voice to marginalized voices (Goodley and Clough 2004). The process of conducting interviews was audio-taped with consent, transcribed word-for-word and conducted either in English or Urdu based on the preferences of the participants to be able to express themselves more truthfully, and the thematic analysis was an inductive, iterative procedure of coding that was enhanced by field notes and reflexivity notes. Ethical protection, such as informed consent, voluntary involvement and sensitivity of disability-related questions were closely respected. Despite the lack of generalizability due to the qualitative, city-specific approach, triangulation, reflexivity, and data saturation (Guest *et al.* 2021) allowed delivering strong and context-based results that shed light upon the intersectionality of disability, employment, and organizational inclusion in Pakistan.

4 RESULTS AND FINDINGS

Table 1 provides a summary of the participants involved in this study, showcasing the diversity of their backgrounds, disabilities, and three major cities of Pakistan. Twelve participants with various disabilities (e.g. physical, visual, neurodivergent, hearing) took part across Karachi, Lahore, and Islamabad. They had tenures of less than a year, four years, and were qualified working in different Industries.

Table 1. Demographic details of participants.

Participant ID	City	Disability	Qualification	Tenure
P1	Karachi	Physical disability	Bachelor's degree	1 year
P2	Karachi	Multiple disabilities	Bachelor's degree	3 years
P3	Karachi	Hearing impairment	Master's degree	1 year
P4	Karachi	Mobility impairment	Master's degree	1.5 years
P5	Lahore	Cognitive disability	Master's degree	3 years
P6	Lahore	Visual impairment	Bachelor's degree	7 months
P7	Lahore	Neurodivergence	Master's degree	1.5 years
P8	Lahore	Psychiatric disability	Master's degree	2 years
P9	Islamabad	Multiple disabilities	Bachelor's degree	1 year
P10	Islamabad	Physical disability	Bachelor's degree	2.5 years
P11	Islamabad	Visual impairment	Master's degree	4 years
P12	Islamabad	Auditory impairment	Master's degree	1.6 months

Thematic analysis was used to analyze the interview data with respect to 6 phase model introduced by Braun and Clarke (2006) including familiarization, coding, theme development, review, definition, and final reporting. Inductively, themes were developed, and memos written in a reflexive manner to record the assumptions, decision process, and changing interpretations made by the researcher in the process. The theme building and coding process was iterative and previous transcripts were revisited and recoded as novel knowledge emerged. Credibility was achieved by use of methodological triangulation which is a combination of interviews, observations and field notes as recommended by Denzin (1970). Selective use of member checking also allowed the subject of validation or clarification of interpretations of their point of view by the participants.

The results showed that the recognition of the inclusive HR practice was always positive, such as performance appraisals, personalised onboarding, regular trainings, and most importantly, monthly Pakistani Sign Language (PSL) sessions, which made close communication between hearing and non-hearing employees stronger. Participants stressed that the programs like Inspire (to deaf employees) and Insight (to blind employees) made accessibility and sense of belonging much better, and several participants reported about fair performance evaluation and successful post-training assessment. Although overall satisfaction was large, the same recurrent challenges arose associated with language access, insufficient digital accommodations, and inadequate assistive technologies, which was indicative of larger national disparities in the infrastructure that is disability-inclusive. Workers mentioned HR as being helpful and receptive but noted logistical setbacks and the need to have more assertive management consciousness. The recommendations revolved around further PSL refresher training, empathy training, involvement of the leadership and institutional affiliations. When put collectively, the findings indicate a workplace culture where employees with disabilities are empowered and structural gaps that support the general studies on disability inclusion in Pakistan are identified, which necessitates long-term, context-based DEI interventions.

5 CONCLUSION

As the current research shows, performance-based assessments, monthly training in the Pakistani Sign Language (PSL), and individualized onboarding are the examples of well-designed DEI practices that can help increase the level of belonging, communication, and psychological safety among employees with disabilities in the largest urban work environment in Pakistan and correspond to the aspect of the inclusive workplace that was suggested by Shore *et al.* (2018) and the principles of equity and organizational justice used in Equity Theory. Although the participants confirmed the importance of culturally competent HR practices, and disability-specific initiatives like Inspire and Insight, the systemic flaws highlighting the lack of access to Urdu-based means of communication, limited assistive tools, and poor access to digital opportunities indicate the presence of the perception gap as described by Buttner and Lowe (2017), wherein intentions to be inclusive surpass their practical accessibility. The findings resonate with the evidence at regional and international levels that the concept of sustainable inclusion implies that leaders should show their determination, ensure ongoing training, and reorganize the infrastructure (Robbins and Judge 2017; Bonaccio *et al.* 2020; CERB 2023). The feedback of the participants on the continuation of PSL refresher courses, mentorships, assisting devices, available digital tools, and cross-organizational partnerships promotes disability-inclusive research in HRM that should focus on non-charitable approaches to the issue (Diemer *et al.* 2020; Kulkarni and Lengnick-Hall 2011). In general, the research validates that DEI is a long-term organizational change initiative that is an iterative process that requires structural support, multi-language communication, and leadership responsibility, in line with recent discoveries regarding inclusive work design and disability accommodation (Derbyshire *et al.* 2024). As the work shows that DEI has a powerful positive effect, the researchers note that that the implementation models and pathways that can be scaled to ensure the connection between policy and practice in the corporate sector in Pakistan require greater clarity.

6 LIMITATIONS AND FUTURE IMPLICATIONS

The research is useful in terms of understanding disability-centered DEI practices in Pakistan, but there are a number of limitations to the applicability of the results. The small purposive sample (n=12) and the use of one organizational case only limit generalizability because DEI cultures and resources differ across sectors and regions, and the purposive sample (n=12) was too small to represent across the departments, roles, and types of disabilities. The use of self-reported interviews also increases the potential of the social desirability effect, and scarce observational evidence and lack of longitudinal evidence do not help to understand how inclusion practices change over time. Also, there was the possibility of communication problems, especially with multilingual and the necessity to have interpreters during the interaction with hearing-impaired or sight-impaired participants, which could have influenced the in-depthness of responses. The research should be expanded in future to include industries, cities, and seniority, use mixed methods to reinforce the measurement validity, and investigate the long-term effect of DEI interventions with changing technologies and policies. Future research on the overlap of gender and disability and the application of trained interpreters and alignment of organizational practices to national policy frameworks like the Pakistan ICT Rights of Persons with Disabilities Act (2020) can produce better insight on a representative sample and actionable insights into sustainability on inclusive workplaces in Pakistan.

REFERENCES

Bengisu, M., and Balta, S. (2011). Employment of the workforce with disabilities in the hospitality industry. *Journal of Sustainable Tourism, 19*(1), 35–57. https://doi.org/10.1080/09669582.2010.499172

Boehm, S. A., Kunze, F., and Bruch, H. (2014). Spotlight on age-diversity climate: The impact of age-inclusive HR practices on firm-level outcomes. *Personnel Psychology, 67*(3), 667–704.

Bonaccio, S., Connelly, C.E., Gellatly, I.R., Jetha, A., and Martin Ginis, K.A. (2020). The participation of people with disabilities in the workplace across the employment cycle: Employer concerns and research evidence. *Journal of Business and Psychology, 35*(2), 135–158. https://doi.org/10.1007/s10869-018-9602-5

Braun, V., and Clarke, V. (2006). Using thematic analysis in psychology. *Qualitative Research in Psychology, 3* (2), 77–101. https://doi.org/10.1191/1478088706qp063oa

Buttner, E.H., and Lowe, K.B. (2017). Addressing internal stakeholders' concerns: The role of transformational leadership in implementing diversity initiatives. *Journal of Leadership & Organizational Studies, 24* (2), 199–210. https://doi.org/10.1177/1548051816662612

Centre of Excellence in Responsible Business (CERB), ConnectHear, and Bokhari, R. (2023). *Landscape Analysis of Disability Inclusion in Corporate Pakistan.* Pakistan Business Council.

Denzin, N.K. (1970). *The Research Act: A Theoretical Introduction to Sociological Methods.* Aldine. Dessler, G. (2017). *Human Resource Management* (15th ed.). Pearson. (No DOI)

Derbyshire, K., Jeanes, E., Khedmati Morasae, E., Reh, S., and Rogers, M. (2024). Employer-focused interventions targeting disability employment: a systematic review. *Social Science & Medicine, 347*, 116742. https://doi.org/10.1016/j.socscimed.2024.116742

Dobbin, F., Schrage, D., and Kalev, A. (2015). Rage against the iron cage: The varied effects of bureaucratic personnel reforms on diversity. *American Sociological Review, 80*(5), 1014–1044. https://doi.org/10.1177/0003122415596416

Effendi, M. (2017). Workplace accommodations and their effect on employee performance: Evidence from disability-inclusive organizations. *International Journal of Human Resource Studies, 7*(3), 1–15. https://doi.org/10.5296/ijhrs.v7i3.11477

Fraser, R.T. (2009). Vocational rehabilitation and employment outcomes for people with disabilities. *Rehabilitation Counseling Bulletin, 52*(3), 146–159. https://doi.org/10.1177/0034355208320061

Goodley, D., and Clough, P. (2004). Researching life stories: Method, theory and analyses in a biographical age. *Identity: An International Journal of Theory and Research, 4*(1), 63–82. https://doi.org/10.1207/s1532706xid0401_5

Guest, G., Namey, E., and Chen, M. (2021). A simple method to assess and report thematic saturation in qualitative research. *PLoS ONE, 15*(5), e0232076. https://doi.org/10.1371/journal.pone.0232076

Hernandez, B., and McDonald, K. (2010). Exploring the rights of persons with disabilities: The contribution of the United Nations Convention on the Rights of Persons with Disabilities. *Journal of Disability Policy Studies, 21*(1), 1–7. https://doi.org/10.1177/1044207309350567

Johnson, K.R. (2021). Leadership support in disability-inclusive workplaces. *Equality, Diversity and Inclusion: An International Journal, 40*(5), 545–562. https://doi.org/10.1108/EDI-03-2020-0064

Kalargyrou, V., and Volis, A.A. (2014). Disability inclusion initiatives in the hospitality industry: An exploratory study of industry leaders. *Journal of Human Resources in Hospitality & Tourism, 13*(4), 430–454. https://doi.org/10.1080/15332845.2014.888512

Kaplan, D.M., and Donovan, M. (2013). The inclusion of people with disabilities in workplace diversity: Theory, practice, and training. *Journal of Diversity Management, 8*(1), 1–13. https://doi.org/10.19030/jdm.v8i1.7865

Kimball, L. (2020). Linking inclusion to innovation and employee well-being. *Harvard Business Review.*

Kulkarni, M., and Lengnick-Hall, M.L. (2011). Socialization of employees with disabilities: A conceptual framework. *Journal of Managerial Psychology, 26*(4), 307–322. https://doi.org/10.1108/02683941111124858

McCoy, R. (2021). Organizational learning in diversity and inclusion initiatives: Lessons from corporate practice. *Equality, Diversity and Inclusion: An International Journal, 40*(6), 694–710. https://doi.org/10.1108/EDI-09-2020-0257

Merriam, S.B. (2009). *Qualitative Research: A Guide to Design and Implementation.* Jossey-Bass.

Michàl, M. B. (2000). *Managing Diversity: Toward a Globally Inclusive Workplace.* Sage Publications.

Milian, R.P., and Wijesingha, R. (2023). Organizational learning and diversity practice diffusion: Exploring cross-company influence in inclusive employment. *Journal of Business Ethics.* https://doi.org/10.1007/s10551-023-05438-2

Mondy, R.W. (2016). *Human Resource Management* (14th ed.). Pearson. (No DOI)

Nevala, N., Pehkonen, I., Koskela, I., Ruusuvuori, J., and Anttila, H. (2014). Workplace accommodation among persons with disabilities: A systematic review of its effectiveness and barriers or facilitators. *Journal of Occupational Rehabilitation, 25*(2), 432–448.

Nishii, L.H., Khattab, J., Shemla, M., and Paluch, R. (2018). A multi-level process model for understanding diversity practice effectiveness. *Academy of Management Annals, 12*(1), 37–82.

Robbins, S.P., and Judge, T.A. (2017). *Organizational Behavior* (17th ed.). Pearson. (No DOI) Roberson, Q. M. (2019). Diversity in the workplace: A review, synthesis, and future research agenda. *Annual Review of Organizational Psychology and Organizational Behavior, 6*(1), 69–88.

Schur, L., Kruse, D., and Blanck, P. (2005). Corporate culture and the employment of persons with disabilities. *Behavioral Sciences & the Law, 23*(1), 3–20.

Shahzada Irfan Ahmed. (2019). Assistive technologies and workplace inclusion: Cost and implementation. *Pakistan Journal of Rehabilitation, 12*(3), 45–60.

Shier, M., Graham, J.R., and Jones, M.E. (2009). Barriers to employment as experienced by disabled people: A qualitative analysis in Calgary and Regina, Canada. *Disability & Society, 24*(1), 63–75.

Shore, L.M., Cleveland, J.N., and Sanchez, D. (2018). Inclusive workplaces: A review and model. *Human Resource Management Review, 28*(2), 176–189.

Thomas, D.A., and Ely, R.J. (1996). Making differences matter: A new paradigm for managing diversity. *Harvard Business Review, 74*(5), 79–90.

Westmorland, M., and Williams, R. (2005). Barriers to work for people with disabilities in the UK. *European Journal of Disability Research, 2*(1), 69–85.

Williams, M. (2019). Leadership's role in sustaining disability-inclusive culture. *Equality, Diversity and Inclusion: An International Journal, 38*(5), 551–567. https://doi.org/10.1108/EDI-12-2017-0283

Moving Towards Sustainable Businesses and Developing More Resilient Economies – Rashid and Annansingh-Jamieson (Eds)

Innovation in firm enterprise and female ownership effects: Evidence from selected sub-Saharan African countries

O.A. Adediran
University of South Africa, School of Business Leadership, Department of Sustainable Livelihoods, South Africa

ABSTRACT: This paper investigates the impact of female business owners on innovation in selected sub-Saharan African countries using a dataset from the World Bank Firm Enterprise from 2007 to 2024. The study created an index of innovation using multiple correspondence analysis (MCA) from categorically measured improvement-related variables in production, organisational structure, and access to the website. The primary independent variable was derived from a dichotomised categorical question of female business ownership. The study employed a fixed effects estimator to control for unobserved and time-invariant components. The results reveal that female business ownership has a significantly positive effect on innovation. Examining the effect of firm size, medium-scale enterprises contribute the most, followed by small-scale enterprises. The study suggests that corporations and activities can enhance sustainable innovation in business enterprises.

1 INTRODUCTION

Innovation in the firm may be defined as a process by which a business introduces new or improved ideas, products, processes, organisation, marketing, logistics, research and development (Aarstad *et al.* 2019; Xu *et al.* 2025) or business models that may increase efficiency, competitiveness, value creation and performance (Kijkasiwat & Phuensane 2020; Szuper & Wołoszyn, and 2020; Kaur and Kaur 2021). It is a key driver of firm growth, as well as economic growth (Huarng *et al.* 2020; Szuper and Wołoszyn 2020), and long-term sustainability in continuously changing markets (Hysa *et al.* 2020; Surya *et al.* 2021). It is crucial to note that Africa is often cited as a continent that lags behind in innovation. Gender inequality may have a potential adverse effect on innovation and international trade (Ryu and Nam 2024). Gender diversity in leadership or ownership is likely to have a positive influence on innovation (del Mar Fuentes-Fuentes *et al.* 2023). Studies have highlighted that socio-cultural factors and inexperience are the most significant factors affecting women's ability to own a business (Coleman 2002; Hora 2014), which may include low self-esteem and negative beliefs that discourage and reduce women's potential.

Relevant barrier determinants to new business may also be associated with the inability of women to own businesses, such as limited financial capital (Fairlie and Robb 2009), lack of education and experience, regulations (Rashad 2025), and access to innovation, among others. According to the publications on the Focus2023 website, 93% of girls, compared to 94% of boys aged 15-24, were literate in 2023. Approximately 26% of women and 26% of men in paid employment worked in agriculture in 2023. Approximately 2.3% of employed women and 5% of men held company management positions. Only 2% of women, compared to 4% of men, held a management-level position in a company. Women own about 33% of businesses worldwide (https://focus2030.org/Overview-of-data-resources-on-gender-equality-across-the-world).

DOI: 10.1201/9781003647300-21

It is essential to note that innovation plays a significant role in contributing to firm performance and economic growth.

While the current study focuses on innovation from new production, processes, organisation, website, and marketing. Innovation may occur due to technological advancement in firms. Firms that make significant innovations are likely to be better positioned to influence the market with new or improved products, attract consumer demand, and sustain productivity gains over time. (Zhang 2023; Xu, *et al.* 2025). The theoretical understanding of the intersection between innovation in firm enterprise and female business ownership can be analysed from the mirror theories of entrepreneurship, innovation, and gender economics. Schumpeter presented his view on the mechanism of economic change, where "innovation implies doing things differently in the realm of economic life". Innovations are initiated by entrepreneurs, and innovators are assumed to be the leaders. (Sweezy 1943; Śledzik 2013). This can be applied to all factors of production. Time preference is a factor that is lagging in Schumpeter's theory. The current study builds on existing theory by hypothesising that an innovative improvement in one nation should be replicated in another country and yield the same outcomes.

We observed that varying economic crises have undermined and reduced the relevance of Schumpeter's theory for what capitalist entrepreneurs face nowadays. Hence, Schumpeter's theory may be less applicable to the current study, as women have a unique nature that the theory has not previously considered (Śledzik 2013). Notwithstanding, female business owners may also be agents of innovation. Empirically, there is an increase in the study of female business ownership and innovation (Dohse *et al.* 2019; Machado *et al.* 2023; Biswas 2025). Female entrepreneurs have made significant contributions to efficient and improved job creation and economic development (Sajjad *et al.* 2020; Quak *et al.* 2022; Gulvira *et al.* 2024) in both developed and developing economies. Despite the importance of innovation to firm growth, economic development, and policymaking, there is a paucity of studies that attempt to answer the question of whether female business ownership of firms improves innovation in selected countries in sub-Saharan Africa.

The study also examines the impact of women entrepreneurs on the distribution of innovation. The current study makes a significant contribution to the body of knowledge by utilising scientific tools, such as multiple correspondence analysis (MCA), to create an index of innovation from a battery of innovation variables, including website innovation, introduction of new products, and new, improved organisational structures. The study employed a fixed effect estimator with a time effect to control for unobserved and time-invariant components. The results reveal that female business ownership has a significantly positive effect on innovation. Additionally, the results indicate that female business ownership has a heterogeneous effect on innovation, as determined by bootstrapped quantile regression. The study findings have direct policy relevance for female entrepreneurs and innovation policies in Sub-Saharan Africa (SSA). The remaining part of the study includes Section 2 for data and methods, Section 3 which presents empirical results, section is the discussion of results, and Section 4 is the conclusion.

2 DATA AND METHODS

The current study utilises a dataset from the World Bank Enterprise Surveys, covering various countries and years from 2007 to 2024. The World Bank Enterprise Surveys (WBES) are conducted across many countries and cover diverse firm-level data on the business environment, including conditions that affect firms. The study selected 10 countries in sub-Saharan Africa, which include the Central African Republic, Ethiopia, Ghana, Kenya, Lesotho, Nigeria, Rwanda, Sierra Leone, South Africa, and Tanzania. The survey uses standardised questionnaires and uniform sampling methods. The study creates an index of innovation from innovation-related questions, including those from the establishment's own website, a new or significantly improved product introduced in the last three years, and a new or significantly improved organisational structure introduced in the last three 3 years.

The study employs multiple correspondence analyses (MCA) to create an index of innovation. MCA is an appropriate tool for the restructuring of batteries of variables that exceed two. If there are only two variables, correspondence analysis is the suitable choice, rather than multiple correspondence analysis (MCA).

One of the independent variables is sales growth, and it was computed following Shekar (2025). The sales growth was calculated by subtracting the establishment's sales 3 years ago (previous sales) from the total annual sales for all products and services (current sales). The study generated sales dollar conversion for both current and previous sales. Sales growth was calculated by dividing the current year's sales by the previous year's sales, minus the difference between the two years. Other variables include firm age, access to finance, firm size (i.e., micro, small, medium, and large firms), and legal status (i.e., shareholder-owned and non-shareholder-owned). Industries are listed as dummy variables.

2.1 *Summary statistics*

Table 1 presents the summary of the dependent variable and the independent variables. Approximately 52% of the females in the sample are business owners. The innovation index has a mean of -0.10 and a standard deviation of 0.83, with a minimum value of -2.74 and a maximum value of 7.15. Aside from sales growth, computed and firm age are continuous variables.

Table 1. Descriptive statistics.

Variable	Obs.	Mean	Std. Dev.	Min	Max
Female business owners	11827	0.524	0.499	0	1
Innovation index	12309	-0.103	0.832	-2.743	7.149
Website innovation	12309	0.288	0.453	0	1
Production innovation	6496	0.401	0.49	0	1
Organization innovation	6496	0.316	0.465	0	1
Sales growth	11620	-0.048	0.987	-1	36.283
Legal status	12309	0.084	0.278	0	1
Firm size	.	.	.	.	.
Micro	11699	0.53	0.499	0	1
Small	11699	0.294	0.456	0	1
Medium	11699	0.121	0.326	0	1
Large	11699	0.056	0.23	0	1
Finacc	12309	0.618	0.486	0	1
Firm age	12309	16.948	14.339	0	220
Expert	11018	0.095	0.294	0	1

Source: Compiled by the Author, 2025; Note: Legal status implies shareholder and non-shareholder.

2.2 *Methods*

Firstly, the study employs ordinary least squares (OLS) regression, robust to heteroskedasticity, to investigate the relationship between innovation and female business ownership, as well as other control variables in the model. Secondly, we employed a fixed effect estimator with a robust standard error to control for unobserved and time-invariant components. Thirdly, the study used a quantile regression bootstrapped to examine the heterogeneous effect of female business ownership on the innovation index. The model is as follows;

$$innovation = \beta_0 + \beta_1 FBO_{it} + \beta_2 X_{it} + \varepsilon_{it}$$

Where FBO_{it} denote female business ownership; X_{it} denote other independent variables. β_0 is an intercept or a constant. β_1 and β_2 the coefficients of the variables.

3 EMPIRICAL RESULTS

3.1 *Correlation and variance inflationary analysis*

Table 2 displays the correlation analysis of the innovation index and independent variables. The correlation analysis reveals a positive correlation between the innovation index and female business ownership (r = 0.018). Innovation index and firm age are positively correlated (r = 0.082). Additionally, the innovation index and the expert are positively correlated (r = 0.19). The innovation index and the legal status are positively correlated (r = 0.074). The innovation index and access to finance are positively correlated (r = 0.078). While innovation and sales growth are negatively correlated (r = -0.046). The VIFs of the independent variables are moderately correlated, as they meet the general guidelines. The guideline for the variance inflation factor (VIF) states that VIFs should be below 10. If this is not the case, it indicates a potential issue of multicollinearity in the analysis.

Table 2. Matrix of correlations and Variance Inflation Factor (VIF).

Variables	(1)	(2)	(3)	(4)	(5)	(6)	(7)	VIF
(1) innovation index	1.000							
(2) Female bus. owner	0.018	1.000						1.063
(3) Firm age	0.082	−0.122	1.000					1.079
(4) Expert	0.187	−0.057	0.228	1.000				1.085
(5) Legal status	0.074	−0.054	0.088	0.150	1.000			1.041
(6) Access to finance	0.078	−0.209	0.132	0.125	0.092	1.000		1.074
(7) Sales growth	−0.046	0.093	−0.029	−0.072	−0.112	−0.076	1.000	1.025
Mean VIF								1.061

Source: Computed by the Author, 2025.

3.2 *Estimation of innovation and female business ownership using FE robust*

Table 3 column (1) shows that female business ownership has a significant positive impact on the innovation index. The expert also has a significant positive effect on innovation. Column (2) revealed that female business ownership has a significant positive effect on innovation for micro-scale firms. Also, legal status has a significant positive effect on innovation. While sales growth has a significant negative effect on innovation. Column (3) shows that female business ownership has a significant positive effect on innovation for small-scale firms. Also, legal status has a significant positive effect on innovation. Column (4) indicates that female business ownership has a significant positive impact on innovation for medium-sized firms. Also, legal status has a significant positive effect on innovation. Column (5) indicates that female business ownership has a statistically insignificant positive impact on innovation for large-scale firms. The sales growth has a significant positive impact on innovation for large-scale firms. This is a unique and accurate portrayal of technology innovation, which can only thrive in large-scale enterprises due to its high capital intensity.

Table 3. Female business ownership on innovation: Fixed effects robust.

Variables Firm size	(1) Panel Innovation index	(2) Micro Innovation index	(3) Small Innovation index	(4) Medium Innovation index	(5) Large Innovation index
Female bus. owner	0.172***	0.106**	0.207**	0.353**	0.289
	(0.0189)	(0.0346)	(0.0661)	(0.119)	(0.158)
Firm age	0.00166	-0.000204	3.03e-06	0.00189	-0.00246
	(0.00126)	(0.00145)	(0.00110)	(0.00115)	(0.00152)
Expert	0.418***	0.341***	0.374***	0.262***	0.297
	(0.0471)	(0.0632)	(0.0973)	(0.0687)	(0.133)
Legal status	0.134	0.175*	-0.0356	0.0504	-0.00105
	(0.0777)	(0.0813)	(0.0588)	(0.168)	(0.103)
Access to finance	0.0707	0.0449	0.0310	-0.0707	-0.0639
	(0.0617)	(0.0310)	(0.0637)	(0.133)	(0.0260)
Sales growth	-0.0142	-0.00788*	0.0244	0.157	1.489**
	(0.00961)	(0.00342)	(0.0148)	(0.138)	(0.187)
Constant	-0.338***	-0.380***	-0.190**	0.00243	0.410***
	(0.0458)	(0.0229)	(0.0742)	(0.174)	(0.0373)
Observations	9,851	4,994	2,947	1,319	591
R-squared	0.041	0.019	0.028	0.046	0.052
Number of years	9	8	9	8	3
sigma_u	0.203	0.251	0.249	0.209	0.790
sigma_e	0.781	0.635	0.860	0.935	0.814
rho	0.0633	0.135	0.0771	0.0478	0.485

Robust standard errors in parentheses: *** $p<0.01$, ** $p<0.05$, * $p<0.1$; Source: Computed by the author 2025

4 CONCLUSION AND RECOMMENDATIONS

The current study investigates the impact of female business ownership on innovation in the case of sub-Saharan African countries using a dataset from WBES. The study selected 10 countries in sub-Saharan Africa, which are growing economies in terms of gross domestic product (GDP). Although the effect of gender bias toward females may not be over-emphasised, we hypothesised that female business ownership is likely to have a positive influence on technology innovation. The results revealed that female ownership of businesses enhances innovation. Overall, the results highlight the strategic importance of women in technological innovation and as catalysts for improving firm performance and national growth in sub-Saharan African countries. The study suggests that policymakers should implement policies that encourage innovation and the establishment of female-owned businesses.

Despite the valuable insights the study provides into the investigation of the impact of female business owners on innovation, several limitations must be noted. The country-level dataset (the World Bank Enterprise Surveys (WBES)) used is cross-sectional in nature, which makes it challenging to produce a dynamic panel analysis. The study utilised significant variables relevant to innovation, but may not accurately capture the quality of innovation activities, especially at the micro-firm level. The study controls for unobserved characteristics. However, it is unable to control for the endogeneity issue. Future research may utilise a longitudinal dataset to examine the long-term impact of female business ownership on innovation and correct for the endogeneity issue by employing an appropriate instrumental variable.

REFERENCES

Aarstad, J., Kvitastein, O.A., and Jakobsen, S.E. (2019). What drives enterprise product innovation? Assessing how regional, national, and international inter-firm collaboration complement or substitute for R&D investments. *International Journal of Innovation Management*, 23(05), 1950040.

Biswas, S. (2025). Her presence matters–female owners and firm innovation in India. *Journal of Economic Studies*.

Coleman, S. (2002). Constraints faced by women small busines owners: Evidence from the data. *Journal of Developmental Entrepreneurship*, 7(2), 151.

del Mar Fuentes-Fuentes, M., Quintana-García, C., Marchante-Lara, M., and Benavides-Chicón, C.G. (2023). Gender diversity, inclusive innovation and firm performance. *Sustainable Development,* 31(5), 3622–3638.

Dohse, D., Goel, R.K., and Nelson, M.A. (2019). Female owners versus female managers: Who is better at introducing innovations?. *The Journal of Technology Transfer*, 44(2), 520–539.

Fairlie, R.W., and Robb, A.M. (2009). Gender differences in business performance: evidence from the Characteristics of Business Owners survey. *Small Business Economics*, 33(4), 375–395

Gulvira, A., Ainash, M., Sagynysh, M., Meiramgul, A., and Aliya, K. (2024). The Impact of Female Entrepreneurship on Economic Growth in Developing and Developed Economies. *ECONOMICS-Innovative and Economics Research Journal*, 12(2), 145–162.

Hora, E.A. (2014). Factors that Affect Women's Participation in Leadership and Decision-Making Positions. *Asian Journal of Humanity, Art and Literature*, 1(2).

Huarng, K.H., Rey-Martí, A., and Guaita-Martínez, J.M. (2020). Knowledge, business, and innovation: Economies and sustainability of future growth. *Journal of Business Research*, 112, 236–239.

Hysa, E., Kruja, A., Rehman, N.U., and Laurenti, R. (2020). Circular economy innovation and environmental sustainability impact on economic growth: An integrated model for sustainable development. *Sustainability*, 12(12), 4831.

Kaur, N., and Kaur, P. (2021). What drives innovation in micro, small, and medium enterprises?. *Journal of Public Affairs*, 21(2), e2336.

Kijkasiwat, P., and Phuensane, P. (2020). Innovation and firm performance: The moderating and mediating roles of firm size and small and medium enterprise finance. *Journal of Risk and Financial Management*, 13 (5), 1–15.

Machado, D., Braga, V., Correia, A., Braga, A., and Silva, C. (2023). How female entrepreneurship may boost business innovation and internationalization. *Global Business and Organizational Excellence*, 42(5), 91–110.

Quak, E.J., Barenboim, I., and Guimaraes, L. (2022). Female entrepreneurship and the creation of more and better jobs in sub-Saharan African countries.

Rashad, A. (2025). Breaking Barriers: Investigating the Effects of 100% Foreign Ownership on Business Entry in Dubai. *Journal of Entrepreneurship and Public Policy*.

Ryu, D., and Nam, H.J. (2024). Impacts of Gender Inequality on International Trade and Innovation. *Finance Research Letters*, 63, 105366.

Sajjad, M., Kaleem, N., Chani, M.I., and Ahmed, M. (2020). Worldwide role of women entrepreneurs in economic development. *Asia Pacific Journal of Innovation and Entrepreneurship*, 14(2), 151–160.

Śledzik, K. (2013). Schumpeter's view on innovation and entrepreneurship. Management Trendsin Theory and Practice,(ed.) Stefan Hittmar, Faculty of Management Science and Informatics, University of Zilina & Institute of Management by University of Zilina.

Surya, B., Menne, F., Sabhan, H., Suriani, S., Abubakar, H., and Idris, M. (2021). Economic growth, increasing productivity of SMEs, and open innovation. *Journal of Open Innovation: Technology, Market, and Complexity*, 7(1), 20.

Sweezy, P.M. (1943). Professor Schumpeter's theory of innovation. *The Review of Economics and Statistics*, 25 (1), 93–96.

Szuper, K., and Wołoszyn, K. (2020). Innovation & enterprise innovation strategies. Zeszyty Naukowe. Organizacja i Zarządzanie/Politechnika Śląska.

Xu, S., Chen, S., Jiao, W., and Chen, M. (2025). State-owned enterprises shareholders and innovation of private enterprises: Evidence from China. *Technovation*, 140, 103144.

Zhang, K. (2023). Optimisation models for member firms selection to build an embedded innovation ecosystem. *Managerial and Decision Economics*, 44(6), 3696–3705.

Moving Towards Sustainable Businesses and Developing More Resilient Economies – Rashid and Annansingh-Jamieson (Eds)

Leveraging artificial intelligence in business decision-making: A study on predictive analytics in retail management

Md Sharfuddin
Management Information System, International American University, Los Angeles, California, USA

Nazmul Islam and Omor Fahad
Digital Communication in Media Multimedia, Westcliff University, Irvine, California, USA

ABSTRACT: In today's dynamic business landscape, sustainable practices and resilient strategies are essential for long-term success. This study examines how Artificial Intelligence (AI) enhances decision-making in retail management, with predictive analytics as a key enabler of operational efficiency and strategic growth. AI-enabled predictive analytics allows retailers to analyse vast datasets, forecast consumer behaviour, optimise inventory levels, and mitigate risks. These insights enable more informed decisions that support sustainability goals while ensuring economic resilience. The research highlights the practical applications of AI-driven tools in retail to streamline operations, minimise waste, and enhance customer satisfaction. Furthermore, it emphasises the importance of integrating AI to address challenges such as supply chain disruptions and fluctuating consumer demands. Overall, the findings demonstrate that predictive analytics not only drives profitability but also fosters sustainable business practices, allowing organisations to thrive in an increasingly competitive market.

Keywords: Artificial Intelligence (AI), Predictive Analytics, Retail Management, Sustainable Business, Decision-Making

1 INTRODUCTION

Artificial Intelligence (AI) is a rapidly evolving business aspect sweeping through industries, and retail is one of the biggest beneficiaries. In modern, information-based, and dynamic markets, companies must integrate smart technologies to remain competitive (Samikannu *et al.* 2024). One of the key AI applications, predictive analytics, provides the decision-maker with practical insights to forecast trends, consumer behavior, and operational risks (Srinivasa Reddy Vuyyuru 2023). Retailers face challenges such as fluctuating demand, supply chain disruptions, and sustainability pressures (Darshan *et al.* 2024). Traditional decision-making methods are inadequate due to their reliance on static models and limited access to data. AI overcomes these limitations by offering real-time insights, optimizing operations, predicting demand, enhancing efficiency, and reducing uncertainty (Hossam *et al.* 2024; Agarwal 2024). However, AI adoption faces hurdles, including aligning technology with strategic goals and ensuring data integrity (Ganguly and Mukherjee 2024). Balancing profitability with sustainability is another priority amid growing consumer expectations for eco-friendly practices (Viswanathan 2024). To address these issues, the role of AI in decision-making must be explored to promote economic resilience and environmental stewardship (Munsaka *et al.* 2024). This research examines how AI-powered predictive analytics enhances retail management by improving efficiency,

DOI: 10.1201/9781003647300-22

reducing waste, and boosting customer satisfaction (Samikannu *et al.* 2024). The study focuses on three objectives: analyzing AI-driven tools in retail, assessing predictive analytics' impact on profitability and sustainability, and identifying strategies to integrate AI solutions into existing retail frameworks.

2 LITERATURE REVIEW

The retail industry is being transformed by artificial intelligence, which occasionally utilises chatbots, personalised marketing plans, demand prediction, and inventory management. This approach leverages consumer-behaviour data to boost productivity and Customer satisfaction (Samikannu *et al.* 2024; Nirupam *et al.* 2023). Predictive analytics enhances decision-making through scrutiny of past data as well as the application of machine-learning models to forecast trends and condition prices, predict churn, and make more efficient inventory selections, in turn, improving efficiency by up to 20% (McKinsey and Company 2023; Agarwal 2024; Hossam *et al.* 2024). Data-intensive resources can help merchants to quickly adjust to changes in consumer tastes and mobilize business (Srinivasa Reddy Vuyyuru 2023; Darshan *et al.* 2024).

AI is also conducive to sustainability, which can be achieved by reducing waste, limiting overstocking, and mitigating carbon emissions, as well as enhancing resiliency to supply-chain disruptions in support of the Sustainable Development Goals (SDGs) and mitigating the effects of unintended consequences (Viswanathan 2024; Munsaka *et al.* 2024). Machine-learning models also help optimize sales projections, which leads to environmental and financial security (Ganguly and Mukherjee 2024).

However, significant gaps remain in integrating predictive analytics, sustainability, and resilience into a unified retailing model. Current literature tends to focus on each element separately, and the way their intersection can drive overall retail management is minimally addressed (Haque *et al.* 2024). The current research aims at bridging this gap by examining the overlap of these dimensions and offering prospective guidance on lucrative and sustainable AI-enabled retail operations (Sudharshan 2021).

3 METHODOLOGY

3.1 *Research design and methods*

This study adopts a mixed-methods approach that integrates quantitative time-series modelling with a qualitative literature synthesis to examine how AI-driven predictive analytics supports retail decision-making. The research employs a deductive design, testing theoretical assumptions about the impact of AI on retail using historical sales and economic data. Quantitatively, ARIMA models are applied to generate retail sales forecasts, while qualitatively, a systematic review of studies published between 2020 and 2025 was conducted.

3.2 *Data collection and data pre-processing*

Two primary datasets support the analysis: the UK Retail Sales Index (1970–2025) from the Office for National Statistics (Office for National Statistics 2025) and the Kaggle Walmart Weekly Sales Dataset (2011–2020), providing real-world benchmarks for forecasting accuracy.

3.2.1 *Check of missing values*

Missing values were identified using the DataFrame *df.isnull().sum()*, which returned the count of null entries in each column. Columns that did not contribute meaningful information to the analysis were removed based on project requirements. A refined DataFrame was then created by retaining only relevant columns, and the remaining missing values were handled using *df.dropna (inplace=True)*.

3.3 *Model specification*

Forecasting Retail sales was performed using the AutoRegressive Integrated Moving Average (ARIMA) model, a well-known time-series prediction model. The data were split into two parts: 80% of the training data (1970-2019) and 20% of the testing sample (2020-2025); the forecast horizon was considered to be 12 months. Three traditional measures of error were used to determine model performance (Root Mean Square Error (RMSE), Mean Absolute Error (MAE), Mean Absolute Percentage Error (MAPE). These measures provide both indicators of absolute and relative accuracy, thereby facilitating a strict comparison of time-series forecasting models (Hyndman and Athanasopoulos 2021).

Table 1. Evaluation metrics used for forecast accuracy assessment (Source: Hyndman and Athanasopoulos 2021).

Metric	Formula
RMSE (Root Mean Square Error)	$\text{RMSE} = \sqrt{\frac{1}{n}\sum_{i=1}^{n}\left(\gamma_i - \bar{\gamma}_i)^2\right)}$
MAPE (Mean Absolute Percentage Error)	$\text{MAPE} = \frac{100\%}{n}\sum_{i=1}^{n}\mid\frac{(\gamma_i - \bar{\gamma}_i)}{\gamma_i}\mid$
MAE (Mean Absolute Error)	$\text{MAE} = \frac{1}{n}\sum_{i=1}^{n}\lvert\gamma_i - \bar{\gamma}_i\rvert$

3.4 *Literature search strategy*

Initial keyword search strings included: “Artificial Intelligence in Retail”, “Predictive Analytics for Retail Management”, “AI-driven sustainability in retail”, “Retail Forecasting with AI”, “Economic resilience through AI”. Boolean operators (AND, OR), and phrase searching for precision. A systematic search was conducted across major academic databases, including Google Scholar, PubMed, IEEE Xplore, and ScienceDirect, using keywords such as AI in retail, predictive analytics, sustainable business practices, and resilient economic strategies. Industry-specific sources, such as McKinsey Insights and Statista data, were also utilised to obtain current statistics and market trends (McKinsey and Company 2023).

3.5 *Eligibility criteria*

3.5.1 *Inclusion criteria*

While 40 articles were initially deemed eligible for inclusion, the final selection of 20 sources was made to ensure a focused and coherent analysis aligned with the study’s objectives. Table 2 shows specific inclusion criteria established for the study.

Table 2. Inclusion criteria for the study.

Category	Criteria
Study Type	Peer-reviewed journals, empirical case studies, and validated industry reports
Focus	AI in retail management, predictive analytics, sustainability, and resilience
Data/Tools	Studies using actual datasets or discussing tools like ARIMA
Metrics	Includes KPIs: sales, inventory accuracy, carbon impact, customer churn
Publication Year	2020–2025

3.5.2 *Exclusion criteria*

The methodology also followed clearly defined exclusion criteria (Table 3).

Table 3. Exclusion criteria for the study.

Criteria Type	Description
Scope Mismatch	Studies not related to the retail industry or not focused on predictive analytics or AI applications
Redundancy	Duplicate studies or retracted articles from the same authors with overlapping content
Non-Peer Reviewed	Content from vendor blogs, marketing brochures, unpublished preprints, or opinion pieces
Accessibility	Studies whose full text could not be retrieved due to access restrictions

3.6 *Study selection process*

The literature review employed a step-by-step methodology to enhance rigour and transparency, as illustrated in Figure 1, ensuring best practice in scholarly research.

4 FINDINGS AND DISCUSSION

4.1 *Inventory optimisation*

The forecasting models of artificial intelligence, such as ARIMA, help retail stores accurately predict sales trends and adjust stock accordingly. According to McKinsey & Company (2023), the use of AI-powered demand forecasting at Walmart resulted in a 50% reduction in overstock levels, leading to cost savings and improved shelf availability. These returns are based on the adoption of machine learning and deep learning instruments in supply chains. AI assists in optimization of inventory, lessening holding expenses, preventing inventory out-of-stock and other operations (Agarwal 2024). Ganguly and Mukherjee (2024) also emphasise the necessity of relying on data-focused forecasting models to bring the inventory into consistency with customer demand. Figure 2(a) illustrates simulated sales for 2011 and 2025 on a weekly basis, encompassing both seasonal and long-term retail trends.

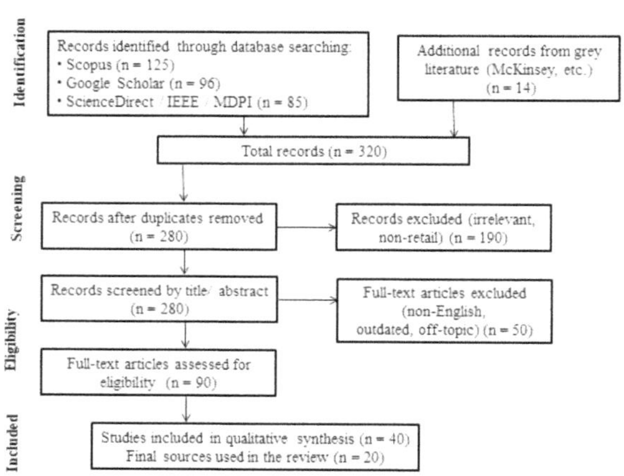

Figure 1. Systematic review process for identifying and selecting studies on ai in retail management (Source: Author).

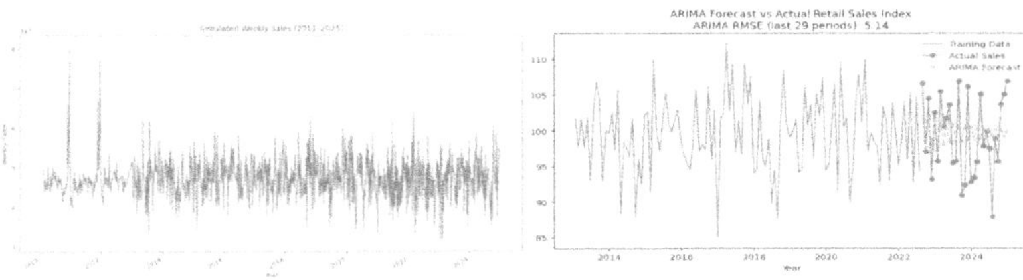

Figure 2. (a) Simulated Weekly Sales (2011–2025) (Data source: Walmart Sales Dataset: https://www.kaggle.com/datasets/mikhail1681/walmart-sales); (b) ARIMA forecast vs. actual retail sales based on the ONS Retail Sales Index (1970–2025) (Data source: Office for National Statistics 2025).

A real-world dataset from the Office for National Statistics (2025) demonstrates the effectiveness of ARIMA in forecasting retail sales. Figure 2 (b) illustrates that the model was trained on approximately 80% of the UK Retail Sales Index data (2013–2025) and tested on the most recent 29 months. The ARIMA model achieved an RMSE of 5.14, an MAE of 4.44, and a MAPE of 4.52%. The index generally ranges from 85 to 115 units; these error rates indicate strong predictive accuracy. The results highlight ARIMA's ability to capture underlying sales trends and adapt to market fluctuations.

4.2 *Consumer behaviour forecasting*

AI enables retailers like Amazon to recommend items based on collected customer data, creating conversions and loyalty (Viswanathan 2024). Predictive models adapt to shifting preferences among Gen Z and millennials who gain a personalised shopping experience. For example, AI-powered recommendation engines utilise previous purchase history, web browsing history, and demographics to recommend relevant items, enhancing customer satisfaction and retention (Srinivasa Reddy Vuyyuru 2023). Additionally, predictive analytics helps identify emerging consumer trends and guide targeted marketing strategies (Munsaka *et al.* 2024). Figure 3 (a) illustrates the evolution of consumer purchasing behaviour and economic resilience over time, aligning with AI-driven forecasting models.

4.3 *Supply chain risk mitigation*

COVID-19 exposed the weakest links in the supply chain, prompting retailers to introduce predictive analytics to support proactive logistics planning and risk simulation, as illustrated in Figure 3 (b) (Oosthuizen *et al.* 2021). AI-powered platforms reduce delays and costs associated with surges by detecting potential disruptions and proposing alternative sourcing solutions. For example, Ananth Raja Muthukalyani (2023) emphasises the benefits of using AI in supply chain operations, which increase resilience through forecasting bottlenecks and resource allocation. These technologies optimise logistics and guarantee consistency even in an increasingly volatile global market (Goffer *et al.* 2025).

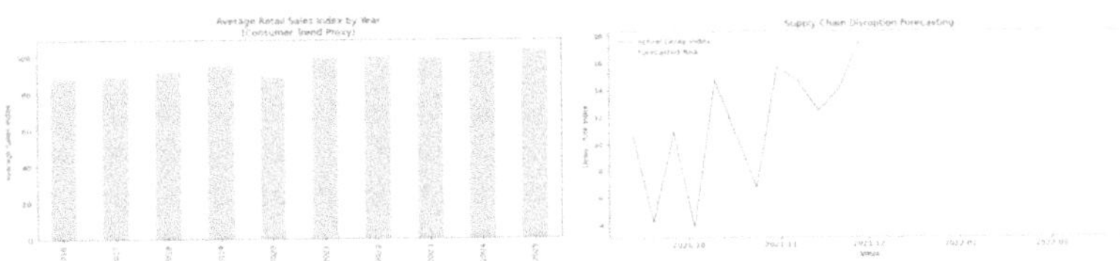

Figure 3. (a) Average UK Retail Sales Index by Year (2015–2024) (Data source: Office for National Statistics, 2025); (b) Supply Chain Disruption Forecasting (Data source: Office for National Statistics 2025).

4.4 *Enhancing strategic decision-making*

AI enables executives to explore a situation in real-time, leveraging faster and less biased dashboards (Mahmud *et al.* 2025; Kim and Lee 2022). The predictive insights are utilised to inform decisions regarding promotions, staffing, and pricing. Alternative strategies are simulated using hybrid machine learning models combined with business intelligence systems, helping the company to be more responsive to market dynamics (Das *et al.* 2025; Sang *et al.* 2022). Cohesive MIS systems also make the retail operation more agile (Das *et al.* 2025). Figure 4 (a) illustrates an AI-driven simulation that demonstrates how forecasted sales inform promotional timing and workforce planning.

4.5 *Aligning with sustainability goals*

Retailers are also using AI to minimise waste and impact on the environment. For example, H&M relies on data-driven demand predictions to avoid excess production (Malenkov *et al.* 2021). Predictive models track energy usage and carbon emissions, contributing to ESG compliance and sustainable operations (Gazi *et al.* 2025). Comparing the emissions at naive overproduction with those at AI-informed production is illustrated in Figure 4 (b). AI-based logistics optimisation significantly reduces the ecological footprint of the retail industry and attracts environmentally oriented customers (Shawon *et al.* 2025).

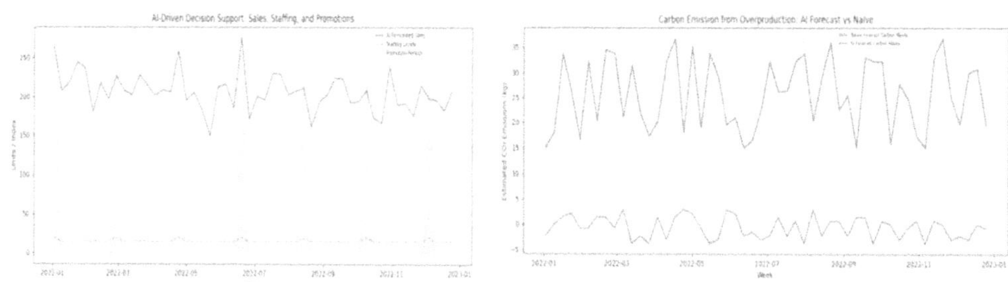

Figure 4. (a) AI-Driven Decision Support: Sales, Staffing, and Promotions (Data source: Office for National Statistics 2025); (b) Sustainability Impact of Forecasting vs Overproduction (Data source: Office for National Statistics 2025).

4.6 *Challenges and limitations in adoption*

AI-based predictive analytics faces numerous obstacles related to the retail environment, particularly for small and medium-sized enterprises (SMEs), which can be attributed to higher implementation costs associated with both infrastructure and software, as well as the need for skilled staff (Haque *et al.* 2024). Ethical factors and data privacy risks arise when retailers must process large amounts of data containing sensitive information relevant to consumers, thereby increasing their susceptibility to data leaks and biased model results. Lack of transparency affects consumer confidence and predictive models that were trained using past information and are prone to over-fitting, leading to false predictions. The digital competencies also limit the successful adoption of AI (Sudharshan 2021), and weak leadership and inappropriate sustainability priorities exacerbate the issue (Oosthuizen *et al.* 2021). Table 4 highlights key retail areas that benefit from AI-powered predictive models, along with relevant examples and references.

Table 4. Applications of AI-powered predictive analytics across retail functions.

Retail Function	AI Application	Example	Reference
Inventory Management	Sales forecasting using ARIMA	Walmart, Target: 30% reduced overstock	Hossam *et al.* 2024; Gangulyand Mukherjee 2024
Consumer Behavior	AI recommendation engines	Amazon: Personalised product suggestions	Viswanathan 2024; Munsaka *et al.* 2024
Supply Chain	Risk simulation and logistics planning	Alternate sourcing, resource allocation	Oosthuizen *et al.* 2021; Vuyyuru 2023
Strategic Decision-Making	Real-time dashboards and scenario simulation	Pricing, staffing, promotions	Kim and Lee 2022; Sang *et al.* 2022; Das *et al.* 2025
Sustainability	Environmental tracking and demand alignment	H&M: Waste reduction and ESG compliance	Malenkov *et al.* 2021; Shawon *et al.* 2025
Adoption Challenges	Bias mitigation, privacy and training needs	SMEs face infrastructure limitations	Haque *et al.* 2024; Jäger *et al.* 2022; Sudharshan 2021

5 CONCLUSION

Predictive analytics powered by artificial intelligence is rapidly transforming the retail industry through maximising the effectiveness of operations, facilitating mass personalisation, and sustainability efforts. Retailers can predict consumer behaviour, anticipate supply-chain disruptions, and optimise resource allocation by analysing large volumes of data. The capabilities minimise waste, enhance customer satisfaction and enhance profitability and environmental sustainability. The current study serves three main purposes: (1) to examine AI usage in the retail setting; (2) to evaluate how predictive analytics can affect the profitability and sustainability rates; and (3) to outline implementation strategies that will mitigate ethical risks, such as favouritism, privacy issues, and inclusivity loopholes. Small and medium-sized companies are progressively implementing solutions based on the cloud through subsidized training and agreements with other companies. The additional value of AI-driven environmental, social, and governance (ESG) within the project, composed of carbon accounting, advanced demand forecasting, and automated transparency reporting, is available. Future longitudinal studies are necessary to determine the best ways to further supplement supply-chain resilience over the long term, particularly in markets with underrepresentation, utilising AI.

REFERENCES

Agarwal, R. (2024). AI-driven retail analytics: Leveraging predictive models for consumer goods and retail optimisation. *Journal of Artificial Intelligence General Science*, 2(1). https://doi.org/10.60087/jaigs.v2i1.235

Ananth Raja Muthukalyani. (2023). Analysing the adoption and influence of AI in retail supply chain operations. *International Journal of Artificial Intelligence Research and Development*, 1(1), 43–51. https://iaeme-library.com/index.php/IJAIRD/article/view/IJAIRD_01_01_004

Darshan, M.S., Jaisachin, B., and NithinRaj, N. (2024). Integrating data mining and predictive modeling techniques for enhanced retail optimisation. *arXiv*. https://doi.org/10.48550/arXiv.2409.19248

Das, N., Rahman, H., Siddiqa, K. B., Barikdar, C. R., Hassan, J., Bhuiyan, M. M. R., and Mahmud, F. (2025). The strategic impact of business intelligence tools: A review of decision-making and ambidexterity. *Modern Trends*, Article 307. https://doi.org/10.52710/mt.307

Ganguly, P., and Mukherjee, I. (2024). Enhancing retail sales forecasting with optimised machine learning models. *arXiv*. https://doi.org/10.48550/arXiv.2410.13773

Gazi, M.S., Barua, A., Karim, F., Siddiqui, M.I.H., Das, N., Islam, M.R., Zeeshan, M.A.F., Rahman, M.A., and Al Montaser, M.A. (2025). Machine learning-driven analysis of low-carbon technology trade and its economic impact in the USA. *Journal of Ecohumanism*, 4(1), 49–61. https://doi.org/10.62754/joe.v4i1.6412

Goffer, M.A., Uddin, M.S., Kaur, J., Hasan, S.N., Barikdar, C.R., Hassan, J., ... Hasan, R. (2025). AI-enhanced cyber threat detection and response: Advancing national security in critical infrastructure. *Journal of Posthumanism*, 5 (3), 1667–1689. https://doi.org/10.63332/joph.v5i3.965

Haque, A., Akther, N., Khan, I., Agarwal, K., and Uddin, N. (2024). Artificial intelligence in retail marketing: Research agenda based on bibliometric and content analysis (2000–2023). *Informatics*, 11(4), 74. https://doi.org/10.3390/informatics11040074

Hossam, A., Ramadan, A., Magdy, M., Abdelwahab, R., Ashraf, S., and Mohamed, Z. (2024). Revolutionising retail analytics: Advancing inventory and customer insight with AI. *arXiv*. https://doi.org/10.48550/arXiv.2402.00023

Hyndman, R.J., and Athanasopoulos, G. (2021). *Forecasting: Principles and Practice* (3rd ed.). OTexts. https://otexts.com/fpp3/

Jäger, S., Flick, A., Sanchez Garcia, J.A., von den Driesch, K., and Biessmann, F. (2022). GreenDB: A dataset and benchmark for the extraction of sustainability information of consumer goods. *arXiv*. https://doi.org/10.48550/arXiv.2207.10733

Kim, H., and Lee, J. (2022). Designing an analytics dashboard for knowledge extraction in the retail industry using descriptive and predictive analytics. *Journal of Industrial Services and Sustainable Development*, 10 (2), 45–59. http://dx.doi.org/10.62870/jiss.v10i2.27900

Mahmud, F., Barikdar, C.R., Hassan, J., Goffer, M.A., Das, N., Orthi, S.M., ... Hasan, R. (2025). AI-driven cybersecurity in IT project management: Enhancing threat detection and risk mitigation. *Journal of Posthumanism*, 5(4), 23–44. https://doi.org/10.63332/joph.v5i4.974

Malenkov, Y., Kapustina, I., and Kudryavtseva, G. (2021). Digitalisation and strategic transformation of retail chain stores: Trends, impacts, prospects. *Journal of Open Innovation: Technology, Market, and Complexity*, 7(2), 108. https://doi.org/10.3390/joitmc7020108

McKinsey and Company. (2023). *The power of AI and data analytics in retail*. https://www.mckinsey.com/business-functions/mckinsey-digital

Munsaka, J., Vlačić, I., and Anttiroiko, A.-V. (2024). AI-driven predictive analytics in retail: Emerging trends and customer engagement strategies. *International Journal of Management & Entrepreneurship Research*, 6(2), 307–321.

Niropam Das, Jahid Hassan, Habiba Rahman, Kazi Bushra Siddiqa, Shuchona Malek Orthi, Clinton Ronjon Barikdar, and Md Alamgir Miah. (2023). Leveraging management information systems for agile project management in information technology: A comparative analysis of organizational success factors. *Journal of Business and Management Studies*, 5 (3), 161–168. https://doi.org/10.32996/jbms.2023.5.3.17

Office for National Statistics. (2025). *Retail Sales Index: All Businesses, Seasonally Adjusted, Monthly (1970–2025)* [Dataset]. https://www.ons.gov.uk/datasets/retail-sales-index-all-businesses/editions/time-series/versions/25

Oosthuizen, K., Botha, E., Robertson, J., and Montecchi, M. (2021). Artificial intelligence in retail: The AI-enabled value chain. *Australasian Marketing Journal*, 29 (3), 264–273. https://doi.org/10.1016/j.ausmj.2020.07.007

Samikannu, R., Jeon, S., Li, J., Gnanamurthy, S., and Gamariel, G. (2024). AI-powered predictive analytics for retail trends. *Journal of Unmanned System Technology*. https://www.ojs.unsysdigital.com/index.php/just/article/view/1267

Sang, G., Xu, L., and de Vrieze, P.T. (2022). 360° retail business analytics by adopting hybrid machine learning and a business intelligence approach. *Sustainability*, 14 (19), 11942. https://doi.org/10.3390/su141911942

Shawon, R.E.R., Hasan, M.R., Rahman, M.A., Ghandri, M., Lamari, I.A., Kawsar, M., and Akter, R. (2025). Designing and deploying AI models for sustainable logistics optimisation: A case study on eco-efficient supply chains in the USA. *arXiv*. https://doi.org/10.48550/arXiv.2503.14556

Srinivasa Reddy Vuyyuru. (2023). Unlocking future consumer insights: Using predictive analytics and AI to shape proactive retail strategies. *European Journal of Advances in Engineering and Technology*, 10 (3), 110–115. https://doi.org/10.5281/zenodo.15560633

Sudharshan, P. (2021). AI-enabled demand sensing and forecasting in retail: Integrating IoT and big data analytics. *African Journal of Artificial Intelligence and Sustainable Development*, 1(2). https://africansciencegroup.com/index.php/AJAISD/article/view/139

Viswanathan, J. (2024). Artificial intelligence: Transforming the future of retail. *International Journal of Science and Research*, 13 (9). https://doi.org/10.21275/SR24901234506

Walmart Sales Dataset. Retrieved from https://www.kaggle.com/datasets/mikhail1681/walmart-sales

Moving Towards Sustainable Businesses and Developing More Resilient Economies – Rashid and Annansingh-Jamieson (Eds)
 ISBN: 978-1-041-08875-2

A conceptual investigation into graduates' employability attitudes: The significant role of protean career attitudes

Muhammad Latif Khan, Tasawar Kamran, Suad Al Kindi, and Zakia AL Abri
Global College of Engineering & Technology, Muscat Oman

ABSTRACT: The idea of a "traditional" career in an organization is being challenged by the current unpredictable business environment in support of the protean career perspective, which holds that people have strong personal identities and beliefs that shape their professional choices. Although the protean career concept's applicability, empirical study hasn't provided much insight into its origins and consequences for those who are just beginning their professions. This study seeks to provide information on the psychological predispositions for protean career attitudes and explore the link between protean career attitudes and graduates employability with help of organizational career management.

Keywords: Self-Directed career Attitudes, Value Driven career Attitudes, Organizational career Management, Perceived graduates Employability

1 INTRODUCTION

Long-term employment relationships have been impacted by changes in the nature of work, the workforce, and access to technology, which have all led to organizations rethinking their old employee management structures and methods (Lin 2015a; Park *et al.* 2022). Employees are implementing new career management and advancement methods in response to this development in order to increase their chances of finding career success. One of them, the protean career notion, has been defined as having a career orientation driven by values as defined by an individual and career management style that is built in accordance with those personal value (Hall 1996b). Several studies have highlighted the significance of the protean career notion and its role as a factor in professional success. (De Vos and Soens 2008; Gubler *et al.* 2014; Hall 1996b), and new information is emerging in the literature recently (Chui *et al.* 2022; Cortellazzo *et al.* 2020). A significant amount of attention is being paid to this field since employees' perceptions and confidence must be shaped by a flexible mindset in today's highly volatile and unreliable employment market. Every worker prefers to take advantage of the dynamic economic environment when there are many job opportunities available and strives to become a versatile talent. In order to maintain their employability and value to both their present and potential employers, protean talents typically have a strong protean attitude that enables them to work with several organizations over the course of their careers in transactional interactions (Haenggli *et al.* 2021; Tee *et al.* 2022).

Because of today's unstable and tumultuous employment environment, career pathways and expectations are highly ambiguous (Arbona *et al.* 2021). Careers are increasingly being managed by the individual rather than the organization in order to deal with this ambiguity. They are also being influenced by intrinsic values as opposed to extrinsic reasons. Protean career attitudes, a novel strategy that (Hall 1976), was the first to name, is an individual attitude in which job decisions are individualized and serve as the foundation for the pursuit

DOI: 10.1201/9781003647300-23

of self-fulfillment. In contrast to normal jobs centered on upward mobility, income increases, and responsibilities across a few organizations, a protean career is conceived of as being self-directed. (Briscoe *et al.* 2006); As a result, it is the employee that chooses their own personal career objectives. goals that may extend beyond corporate boundaries (Arthur *et al.* 2005). Additionally, protean career attitudes is value-driven in the sense that an individual's own values serve as their career's guide and yardstick for success (Briscoe *et al.* 2006). According to (Wesarat *et al.* 2014; Zhou 2022), people have a propensity to hunt for employment that fulfills their life demands as well as their professional ones, giving the word "career" a broader definition of self-realization.

2 PROBLEM STATEMENT

Rapid global development creates a brand-new environment marked by rising economic inequality and disparity as well as an uncertain future. Vocational psychologists, educational institutions, and educators are advised to address the challenges of employability in response to this unstable and unpredictable work environment, where people are required to focus on their own professions and steady long-term employment is not granted for everyone. Young individuals entering the workforce in the twenty-first century must be prepared for the workforce, employable, and able to maintain that employment. (Marock 2008; Rios *et al.* 2020). Their employability is characterized by a sense of personal action or self-direction in securing or maintaining employment. This is based on a set of personal career-related characteristics that are typically promoted by employers and researchers as a substitute for job stability in a climate of uncertain employment. (Bezuidenhout 2011; Harrison *et al.* 2021).

Many people are still searching for a career that fits their abilities, despite the fact that many policymakers and institutions have worked hard to educate graduates and individuals for the demands of the workplace. Significant gaps are created between companies and recent graduates seeking career growth as a result of this mismatch (Belwal *et al.* 2017a; Mirza and Karolak 2019). The similar concept was highlighted by Al Hinai *et al.* (2020), who stated that close cooperation between academic institutions is necessary.

In this context, protean career attitudes have been connected with self-directed and value-driven career attitudes, which ultimately contribute to career advancement, despite the fact that numerous scholars have offered numerous ideas and solutions to address this issue. According to Hall (2004) and Briscoe *et al.* (2006), individuals with protean career attitudes take charge of their own professional destiny.

This paper addresses that gap by conceptually exploring how behavioral competencies contribute to the development of protean career attitudes and how these, in turn, shape perceptions of graduate employability. It also examines the role that organizational career management (OCM) may play in bridging these elements. By developing a theoretical framework around these constructs, the paper aims to enrich current understandings of employability in an increasingly dynamic and uncertain global labor market.

3 RESEARCH QUESTIONS

(1) *Is there any relationship between protean career attitude (value-driven attitudes and self-directed career attitude) student's perceived employability?*
(2) *What is the role organizational career management as a mediating factor between students' protean career attitudes, namely, value-driven and self-directed and perceived employability?*

4 RESEARCH OBJECTIVES

(1) *To know whether protean career attitudes (value-driven attitudes and self-directed career attitude) have impact on student's perceived employability.*
(2) *To know either organizational career management play mediating role in between students' protean career attitudes, specifically value-driven and self-directed orientations and perceived employability.*

5 LITERATURE REVIEW

5.1 *Conceptualization and definition of protean career attitudes*

To address the shifting nature of job trajectories, seasoned researcher Hall first proposed the idea of a protean career in 1976. The term "protean" comes from the Latin word Proteus, denoting an individual's remarkable ability to adapt the shape of something when faced with uncertainty (Briscoe *et al.* 2006). Hall (1976) describes the concept of a protean career as follows: It's a contemporary approach where individuals take control of their own career instead of relying on organizational structures.

Protean career attitudes are characterized by two key features: being self-directed and being values-driven. Self-direction refers to the extent to which individuals strategically manage their own careers (Briscoe *et al.* 2006; Mirvis and Hall 1994). On the other hand, a values-driven approach involves individuals being highly conscious of their personal priorities, using them as standards for decision-making and evaluating success (Hall and Mirvis 1996; Mirvis and Hall 1994).

5.2 *Self-directed career attitude*

This part of the idea of protean careers emphasizes the habits and dispositions that come with having a mindset of protean careers. Those with a protean career orientation take charge of their career trajectory in harmony with their professional aspirations (Briscoe *et al.* 2006). Proactivity, engagement in long-term career strategizing, reflective assessment of career decisions and experiences, executing plans to achieve career objectives, and nurturing networks and relationships are valued attributes among individuals embracing a protean approach (Briscoe *et al.* 2006).

Fully comprehending protean career attitudes poses a challenge, as there are various research paths to explore in uncovering self-directed behaviors. However, not much research has been done on how people develop self-directed professional perspectives. Professional self-management is generally prioritized by many career development specialists by those with a protean career perspective. Career self-management entails individuals proactively taking responsibility for their own career paths (Cortellazzo *et al.* 2020; Lin 2015b). Those with such a perspective actively seek information and make timely decisions about their future. Notable characteristics prevalent among practitioners of career self-management include continuous on-the-job learning and a tendency towards boundaryless career approaches (Downs *et al.* 2024).

Recent research has employed various scales to gain comprehensive insights into career self-management. These scales gauge different attitudes and behaviors individuals adopt to address their career management challenges, these strategies, including skill enhancement, networking, opportunity creation, and seeking career guidance, collectively contribute to individuals' overall management of their careers (De Andrade *et al.* 2023; De Vos *et al.* 2009; Kim *et al.* 2023; Purohit and Jayswal 2024).

5.3 *Values-driven career attitude*

The relevance of value-driven professional attitudes cannot be overlooked, since self-directed career attitudes significantly contribute to individual career success. Briscoe and Hall (2006) argue that value-driven career attitudes, as a component of protean career attitudes, reflect individuals' internal values, principles, and beliefs. These values serve as guiding principles for their career success, with individuals prioritizing their own principles and values in decision-making processes (Briscoe *et al.* 2006). Those with a value-driven approach are highly attuned to their career priorities, using their values as benchmarks for decision-making and performance evaluation (Hall 1996a).

Numerous studies underscore the significance of norms, values, and principles in career decision-making (Bolat and Odacı 2017; Katz and Kahn 2015). (Schwartz 1994), defines values as beliefs regarding desirable end states or conduct modes that transcend specific situations, guiding behavior, people, and event evaluation in order of importance. (Rokeach 1973), posits that values are central principles individuals use to evaluate their daily performance.

5.4 *Perceived employability*

In a broad sense, employability encompasses an individual's capacity to secure, maintain, and transition between jobs or industries (Forrier and Sels 2003) . (Vanhercke *et al.* 2014), describe it as the ability to pursue career advancement within and outside of one's current organization. Clearly, having employability enhances the prospects of employment success, showcasing an individual's ongoing marketability throughout their professional journey. Consequently, the perception of one's employability, reflecting a personal confidence in future career pursuits, is considered pivotal for achieving career success, which is evaluated based on past accomplishments. This perceived employability is seen as a key determinant in securing employment and subsequent career advancement. It is often understood as comprising external and internal employability components (Silva *et al.* 2023).

5.5 *Organizational career management*

"Organizational Career Management (OCM) refers to the support and resources provided by an organization to facilitate the career growth and development of its employees".

Organizational career management (OCM) also known as programs and other forms of career development opportunities offered by employing organization to support employees' career success (Verbruggen *et al.* 2007; Wesarat *et al.* 2014). Employee career management programs are also called organizational career development (Verbruggen *et al.* 2007). (Bagdadli and Gianecchini 2019), on the other hand, define organizational career management as a course of action where employees continually monitor career strategies and objective. Further research in career management defines Organizational Career Management (OCM) as a process through which individuals engage with organizational support systems to plan, develop, and navigate their career paths within the company.

OCM is a continuous chain of proper activities by employees to enhance their career success that will also increase the chances of obtaining organizational objectives (Arnold 1996; Moon and Choi 2017). Many organizational policies in which the purpose is to improve the career of employees are linked to organizational career management (Orpen 1994). The literature suggests that organizational career activities often include structured career progression paths, opportunities for job enrichment, employee development programs, and broader initiatives aimed at supporting career growth. Within the scope of Organizational Career Management (OCM), the organization's role can also extend to supporting employees in managing their own careers, encouraging greater individual involvement in self-directed career development. Organizational career management may help employees in job-matching discussions, job rotation and the transfer of employees in different departments, job search, all of which will enhance their employability inside and outside an organization (Bridgstock 2009).

5.6 *Career management – critical analysis*

Fast-paced economic shifts and technological innovations have been major forces behind organizational change. To remain ahead in the competition, companies need to swiftly adjust to the changing demands of the market. In today's globalized business culture is vibrant and individual careers are volatile (Donald *et al.* 2020). Researchers like (Akkermans *et al.* 2021), have suggested that organizations are no longer ready for employee's career management and consequently employees have become the actor of their own career. Nevertheless, the importance of organizations in employee's career management cannot be ignored (Dachner *et al.* 2021). Baruch (2006) proposes the balanced view of career management where the both parties are responsible for career management (De Vos and Cambré, 2017). (Soares and Mosquera, 2021) suggests that the joint efforts for career management do work in organizations. The change in career systems does not mean that organizations need to lose their role in managing careers; rather, they can support and develop their human assets (Baruch, 2006). This balanced perspective highlights that both organizations and individuals share responsibility for managing careers. When both parties work together effectively, it can lead to greater success for employees and in turn, benefit the organizations that employ them.

At an individual level, career management aids undergraduate students in understanding their career possibilities and prompts them to consider their career decisions and paths (Hirschi and Koen, 2021). Work, career management skills also play a role in shaping one's identity, as the nature of our work influences our social status and provides a framework for self-identification and societal recognition (Greco and Kraimer, 2020). In the long term, career management skills have been shown to positively impact employee wellbeing, self-efficacy, goal attainment, resilience, personal growth, and work engagement (Baluku *et al.*, 2021). Additionally, (Karaca-Atik *et al.* 2023) highlighted the link between effective career self-management and the ongoing development and maintenance of a positive self-concpt, aligned with evolving strengths and weaknesses, changing beliefs and attitudes, and future aspirations.

Figure 1. A model of organizational career management.

At an individual level, career management aids undergraduate students in understanding their career possibilities and prompts them to consider their career decisions and paths (Hirschi and Koen, 2021). Work, career management skills also play a role in shaping one's identity, as the nature of our work influences our social status and provides a framework for self-identification and societal recognition (Greco and Kraimer, 2020). In the long term, career management skills have been shown to positively impact employee wellbeing, self-efficacy, goal attainment, resilience, personal growth, andwork engagement (Baluku *et al.* 2021). Additionally, (Karaca-Atik *et al.* 2023) highlighted the link between effective career self-management and the ongoing development and maintenance of a positive self-concept, aligned with evolving strengths and weaknesses, changing beliefs and attitudes, and future aspirations.

5.7 *Protean career attitudes and perceived employability*

Protean career attitude is a helpful psychological tool employed by protean talents in their quest of psychological professional success. It was first proposed by Hall (1996). Protean career attitude is defined by two dimensions: value-driven career attitude and self-directed career attitude, and it is based on an individual's attitude toward career management (Briscoe and Hall 2006; Hall 2002). People with a protean worldview frequently steer clear of organizational norms in favor of personal beliefs, and they are self-directed in controlling their professional behavior (Hall 2004). People with protean career attitudes, sometimes referred to as people who are at ease establishing an active career-oriented relationship beyond organizational borders, are thought of as having a wide range of skills (Briscoe and Hall 2006). Favor a career that demands real physical mobility, such as switching jobs (Briscoe *et al.* 2006). According to empirical research (Kiong and Yin-Fah 2016; Volmer and Spurk 2011; Waters *et al.* 2014), a protean career attitude is positively connected to numerous work-related outcomes like career growth, career success, and job enhancement. Protean career attitudes are comparable to the "demand" part of the Job Demands-Resource Model (Xanthopoulou *et al.* 2007), which was developed to manage job needs and, in the end, push people to seek better through self-directed and value-driven career attitudes.

People's perceptions of their employability become crucial in a time when the workplace is extremely vulnerable to change because how they perceive a situation can have a favorable or negative impact on their behavior, feelings, and thoughts. An individual's opinion of his or her chances of finding new, equal, or better employment is known as perceived employability (Berntson 2008). Perceived employability is viewed as a resource or benefit for employees, allowing them to approach job prospects with more assurance and fostering a sense of well-being and career autonomy (De Cuyper *et al.* 2011). According to studies (D. J. Chen and Lim 2012; H. Chen2022), increased perceptions of employability may result in better employment outcomes like an improved capacity to adjust to a changing work environment, job search behaviors, and subjective well-being, and health. Internal and external employability, which refer to two distinct facets, are components of perceived employability in a work environment. Internal employability relates to a worker's desire to stay with their current employer, whereas external employability signifies the capacity and willingness to shift to comparable or different employment in another company (Juhdi *et al.* 2010).

According to the conversion of resources (COR theory) and job demand resource (JD-R model), people with a more prodigious career attitude are more likely to be self-driven to acquire skills that improve their employment prospects, which in turn has a positive impact on how employable they are perceived to be. JD-R model could be used as a lens through which to explain protean professional mindset and its effects (Xanthopoulou *et al.* 2007). According to the JD-R paradigm, every work environment consists of both job demands and job resources. In the workplace, protean career attitudes (self-directed and value driven career attitudes) is a requirement that forces employees to put up effort to acquire such resources (Cortellazzo *et al.* 2020; Li 2018; Lisá and Valachová 2023). Each person acquires these resources in accordance with their own intuitive understanding (i.e. their career goal). Effective career planning is produced as a result of the changing demand, assisting in the construction of numerous resources . They establish a "resource caravan" by strengthening their social, human, and psychological resources through meticulous career planning and they also enhance a vital resource known as the "perceived notion" of their employability. According to the COR theory, perceived employability is viewed as a personal resource (Meerman *et al.* 2022; Tee *et al.* 2022). Depending on the employee's perceived market opportunities and career goals, employability perceptions may be internal or external. It truly piques the authors' interest to examine whether personnel with a flexible career mindset predict internal or external employability.

6 THE UNDERLYING THEORIES OF THE STUDY

6.1 *Social cognitive theory*

Career scholars have emphasized more and more that career growth is a collaborative process rather than just an individual one as interest in protean career attitudes continues to grow. Given the growing interest in flexible career attitudes, career researchers have proposed that both individuals and organizations can manage a person's career. It is anticipated that both the organization and the individual will have a major impact on learning experiences and, in turn, on how each person choose to manage their career.

The match between organizational and individual values is explained by Bandura's social cognitive theory (1986), which may have an impact on an individual's behavior and desire for career success. The social cognitive theory (SCCT) has identified three distinct factors: (i) the formation of career interests, (ii) choice and goals, and (iii) performance accomplishment. These three distinct conceptual models are linked to demonstrate the connection between organizational and personal elements (Lent *et al.* 1994). The three key elements that influence a person's career decision are self-efficacy, result expectations, and career success aim, according to social cognitive theory (SCCT). It is anticipated that anyone who is confident in their ability to achieve favorable job outcomes will also become interested in their work. Protean career attitudes have been linked to the same elements of self-efficacy and self-career management (Quigley and Tymon Jr 2006).

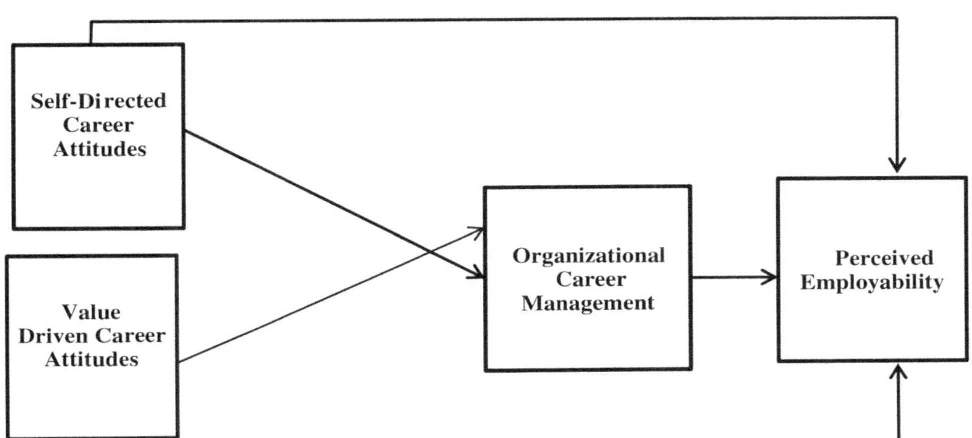

Figure 2. Proposed research model.

The research framework for this study, which is based on a review of the literature on the study variables on organizational career management, protean career attitudes, and organizational career management, was based on social cognitive theories (1986). The research paradigm states that employees with protean career perspectives will have a favorable and direct impact on their perceived employability and professional performance. The conceptual framework to describe how organizational goals match with personal values is thus emphasized by social cognitive theory (1986), which may have an impact on an individual's interest in and conduct related to professional achievement.

7 METHODLOGY

This paper adopts a conceptual research approach, grounded in a comprehensive and critical review of existing academic literature. Rather than collecting empirical data, the study synthesizes theories, models, and prior empirical findings to construct a theoretical framework that explains the relationship between protean career attitudes, organizational career management, and perceived employability.

The methodological foundation of this paper rests on **secondary data** drawn from peer-reviewed journals, academic books, and credible theoretical publications. A focused search strategy was employed to identify relevant literature published over the past two decades, with particular attention to studies on protean career orientation, self-directed learning, value-driven attitudes, organizational career management (OCM), and graduate employability. Databases such as Scopus, Web of Science, and Google Scholar were used to retrieve relevant literature using search terms like "protean career," "graduate employability," "organizational career management," and "self-directed career attitude."

This conceptual inquiry applies **theoretical reasoning and thematic analysis** to integrate various strands of literature into a cohesive framework. Key theoretical underpinnings such as Social Cognitive Career Theory (SCCT), Conservation of Resources (COR) theory, and the Job Demands-Resources (JD-R) model serve as guiding lenses for interpretation and framework development. Through this synthesis, the paper offers novel insights into how protean career attitudes influence graduate employability, mediated by organizational support mechanisms.

While the study does not involve primary data collection, it builds a strong foundation for future empirical testing by proposing a testable research model and a set of research questions. This method allows for the development of theory in an area where empirical investigation is still emerging, particularly in the context of transitional economies such as Oman and the broader GCC region.

8 RESULTS

The literature strongly supports the positive relationship between protean career attitudes and employability outcomes. Recent research continues to validate these associations, especially in increasingly dynamic and uncertain job markets. Studies have shown that individuals with strong self-directed and value-driven traits are more proactive in career development and resilient to labor market fluctuations. For instance, Chen *et al.* (2022) found that graduates with protean traits demonstrated better job fit and faster employment transitions. Similarly, Alavi and Yaghoob Nejad (2021) emphasized that career self-management behaviors—rooted in protean values—are instrumental in enhancing perceived employability among university students. Furthermore, Kim and Park (2023) highlighted that such attitudes are particularly impactful in collectivist cultures when supported by organizational learning opportunities. These findings reinforce the argument that protean career attitudes not only empower individuals but also interact positively with external structures like organizational career management (OCM), shaping employability perceptions in diverse economic contexts.

Table 1. Extended summary of key studies on protean career attitudes and employability.

Author(s)	Context	Main Findings	Relevance to This Study
Briscoe and Hall (2006)	US	Introduced PCA and linked it to individual career agency	Established theoretical foundation
Baruch (2014)	UK	PCA positively influences career satisfaction and mobility	Highlights employability relevance
De Vos and Soens (2008)	Belgium	OCM enhances career outcomes when aligned with PCA	Supports mediation role of OCM
Nabi *et al.* (2018)	Multi-country	Protean attitudes predict perceived employability	Supports central hypothesis
Khapova and Arthur (2011)	Netherlands	Career self-management linked to employability perceptions	Reinforces PCA-employability link
Chen *et al.* (2022)	China	Graduates with PCA traits had better job transitions	Confirms role of PCA in employability
Alavi and Yaghoob Nejad (2021)	Iran	Career self-management behaviors enhance employability	Validates role of value-driven traits
Kim and Park (2023)	South Korea	PCA interacts with OCM to improve outcomes in collectivist contexts	Shows cross-cultural relevance

9 DISCUSSIONS AND RECOMMENDATIONS

In recent years, the concept of graduate employability has undergone a significant shift. No longer can students rely solely on their academic credentials to secure meaningful employment. The modern job market places increasing value on those who actively manage their own career development (Monteiro *et al.* 2022). This study has highlighted how protean career attitudes specifically, self-direction and value-driven decision-making can enhance a graduate's ability to navigate this evolving landscape. When institutions and organizations support these attitudes through appropriate structures and programs, the outcome is a more confident, adaptable, and employable graduate. Moving forward, there is a need for stronger collaboration between higher education institutions, industry, and government (Cheng *et al.* 2022).

Universities, for example, should rethink the way they prepare students for life beyond graduation. This could include tailored training sessions focused on long-term career planning, exposure to real-world work environments through internships or consulting projects, and opportunities for students to reflect on their personal goals and values. Employers also play a crucial role. They can introduce mentoring initiatives and flexible learning pathways that support continuous growth, especially for young professionals still finding their footing. At the policy level, government agencies might consider offering support to organizations that invest in early-career talent whether through funding, tax incentives, or formal partnerships with universities.Naturally, there are obstacles. Not all companies have the capacity to implement structured career development plans, and budget constraints are real in both private and public sectors. However, these barriers are not insurmountable (Kim*et al.* 2024) .

In higher education institutions, the Human Resources (HR) department holds significant potential to influence and nurture protean career attitudes among staff. By creating an environment that encourages personal initiative, continuous learning, and career adaptability, HR can support employees in developing the mindset and competencies required to stay competitive in an ever-changing job landscape. Encouraging this kind of professional growth not only enhances the individual's ability to manage their own career paths but also contributes to the institution's broader success by fostering a more engaged, agile, and forward-thinking workforce.

Many of the recommended actions such as career counseling, digital mentorship, and collaborative training platforms can be introduced at low cost and scaled as needed. By removing some of these roadblocks and reinforcing the connection between education and the workplace, graduates will be far better positioned to meet the demands of today's fast-changing professional world. The Gulf countries, which have significant issues pertaining to youth, might test the same conceptual framework. In addition to the mediating variable (organizational career management), parental training may also be examined to see whether or not it affects an individual's employability. According to one study (Jannesari*et al.* 2024), parents' support plays a crucial role in fostering protean career attitudes, and these attitudes in turn influence how employable a person is judged to be.It demonstrates that parental education enhances a person's perceived employability in addition to fostering sociability. It's important to remember that the relationship between perceived employability and protean career attitudes might be moderated by parental career support. To determine if people with self-directed and value-driven career attitudes may succeed in their careers, professional success can be utilized as a dependent variable between protean career attitudes.

Self-confidence can be explored further as either a moderating or mediating variable to better understand its influence on both actual and perceived employability outcomes. It may serve as a crucial psychological factor that enhances or explains the relationship between protean career attitudes and employability. Recent research by Wujema, Mohd Rasdi, Zaremohzzabieh, and Ahrari (2022) provides compelling evidence that self-confidence positively contributes to graduates' employability, suggesting that individuals who believe in their capabilities are more likely to succeed in today's dynamic job market. This insight reinforces the critical role educational institutions must play—not only in equipping students with technical knowledge and career management strategies but also in nurturing essential soft skills such as communication, adaptability, and self-assurance. Institutions must adopt a more holistic approach to career development, ensuring that graduates are not only informed about how to navigate their professional paths but are also empowered with the confidence to do so effectively in real-world settings.

REFERENCES

Akkermans, Jos, Spurk, Daniel, and Fouad, Nadya. (2021). Careers and career development *Oxford Research Encyclopedia of Psychology*.

Arbona, Consuelo, Fan, Weihua, Phang, Ayoung, Olvera, Norma, and Dios, Marcel. (2021). Intolerance of uncertainty, anxiety, and career indecision: A mediation model. *Journal of Career Assessment, 29*(4), 699–716.

Arnold, John. (1996). The psychological contract: A concept in need of closer scrutiny? *European Journal of Work and Organizational Psychology, 5*(4), 511–520.

Arthur, Michael B, Khapova, Svetlana N, and Wilderom, Celeste PM. (2005). Career success in a boundaryless career world. *Journal of Organizational Behavior: The International Journal of Industrial, Occupational and Organizational Psychology and Behavior, 26*(2), 177–202.

Bagdadli, Silvia, and Gianecchini, Martina. (2019). Organizational career management practices and objective career success: A systematic review and framework. *Human Resource Management Review, 29*(3), 353–370.

Baluku, Martin Mabunda, Mugabi, Eriphase Nsaale, Nansamba, Joyce, Matagi, Leonsio, Onderi, Peter, and Otto, Kathleen. (2021). Psychological capital and career outcomes among final year university students: The mediating role of career engagement and perceived employability. *International Journal of Applied Positive Psychology, 6*, 55–80.

Berntson, Erik. (2008). *Employability perceptions: Nature, determinants, and implications for health and well-being.* Psykologiska institutionen.

Bezuidenhout, Mareli. (2011). *The development and evaluation of a measure of graduate employability in the context of the new world of work.* University of Pretoria.

Bolat, Neslihan, and Odacı, Hatice. (2017). High school final year students' career decision-making self-efficacy, attachment styles and gender role orientations. *Current Psychology, 36*, 252–259.
Bridgstock, Ruth. (2009). The graduate attributes we've overlooked: Enhancing graduate employability through career management skills. *Higher education research & development, 28*(1), 31–44.
Briscoe, Jon P, Hall, Douglas T, and DeMuth, Rachel L Frautschy. (2006). Protean and boundaryless careers: An empirical exploration. *Journal of vocational behavior, 69*(1), 30–47.
Chen, Don JQ, and Lim, Vivien KG. (2012). Strength in adversity: The influence of psychological capital on job search. *Journal of Organizational Behavior, 33*(6), 811–839.
Cheng, M., Adekola, O., Albia, J. and Cai, S., (2022). Employability in higher education: a review of key stakeholders' perspectives. *Higher Education Evaluation and Development*, 16(1), pp.16–31.
Chen, Huaruo, Liu, Fei, and Wen, Ya. (2022). The influence of college students' core self-evaluation on job search outcomes: Chain mediating effect of career exploration and career adaptability. *Current Psychology*, 1–12.
Chui, Hazel, Li, Hui, and Ngo, Hang-yue. (2022). Linking protean career orientation with career optimism: career adaptability and career decision self-efficacy as mediators. *Journal of Career Development, 49*(1), 161–173.
Cortellazzo, Laura, Bonesso, Sara, Gerli, Fabrizio, and Batista-Foguet, Joan M. (2020). Protean career orientation: Behavioral antecedents and employability outcomes. *Journal of Vocational Behavior, 116*, 103343.
Dachner, Alison M, Ellingson, Jill E, Noe, Raymond A, and Saxton, Brian M. (2021). The future of employee development. *Human Resource Management Review, 31*(2), 100732.
De Andrade, Alexsandro Luiz, Teixeira, Marco Antônio Pereira Teixeira, and de Oliveira, Manoela Ziebell. (2023). The Brazilian Portuguese adaptation of Protean Career Orientation Scale: invariance, correlates, and life/career stages. *International Journal for Educational and Vocational Guidance, 23*(3), 615–633.
De Cuyper, N, Van der Heijden, BIJM, and De Witte, H. (2011). Associations between employability and employee and organizational outcomes: A matter of psychological contracts. *International Journal of Human Resource Management, 22*(7), 1486–1503.
De Vos, Ans, and Cambré, Bart. (2017). Career management in high-performing organizations: A set-theoretic approach. *Human resource management, 56*(3), 501–518.
De Vos, Ans, Dewettinck, Koen, and Buyens, Dirk. (2009). The professional career on the right track: A study on the interaction between career self-management and organizational career management in explaining employee outcomes. *European Journal of Work and Organizational Psychology, 18*(1), 55–80.
De Vos, Ans, and Soens, Nele. (2008). Protean attitude and career success: The mediating role of self-management. *Journal of Vocational behavior, 73*(3), 449–456.
Donald, William E, Baruch, Yehuda, and Ashleigh, Melanie J. (2020). Striving for sustainable graduate careers: Conceptualization via career ecosystems and the new psychological contract. *Career Development International, 25*(2), 90–110.
Downs, Carolyn, Mughal, Farooq, Shah, Uzair, and Ryder, Mike. (2024). Are undergraduate internships worth the effort? Time to reconceptualize work-based learning for building protean meta-competencies. *Studies in Higher Education, 49*(1), 84–97.
Forrier, Anneleen, and Sels, Luc. (2003). The concept employability: A complex mosaic. *International journal of human resources development and management, 3*(2), 102–124.
Greco, Lindsey M, and Kraimer, Maria L. (2020). Goal-setting in the career management process: An identity theory perspective. *Journal of Applied Psychology, 105*(1), 40.
Gubler, Martin, Arnold, John, and Coombs, Crispin. (2014). Reassessing the protean career concept: Empirical findings, conceptual components, and measurement. *Journal of Organizational Behavior, 35*(S1), S23–S40.
Haenggli, Madeleine, Hirschi, Andreas, Rudolph, Cort W, and Peiró, José María. (2021). Exploring the dynamics of protean career orientation, career management behaviors, and subjective career success: An action regulation theory approach. *Journal of vocational behavior, 131*, 103650.
Hall, Douglas T. (1976). *Careers in organizations*: Goodyear Publishing Company.
Hall, Douglas T. (1996a). *The Career Is Dead–Long Live the Career. A Relational Approach to Careers. The Jossey-Bass Business & Management Series*: ERIC.
Hall, Douglas T. (1996b). Protean careers of the 21st century. *Academy of management perspectives, 10*(4), 8–16.
Hall, Douglas T, & Mirvis, Philip H. (1996). The new protean career: Psychological success and the path with a heart. *The career is dead: Long live the career, 23*, 15–45.

Harrison, Jennifer A, Budworth, Marie-Hélène, & Halinski, Michael %*J Career Development International*. (2021). Trait gratitude and job search: the mediating role of perceived employability.

Hirschi, Andreas, & Koen, Jessie. (2021). Contemporary career orientations and career self-management: A review and integration. *Journal of Vocational Behavior, 126*, 103505.

Jannesari, Milad, Sullivan, Sherry E, & Baruch, Yehuda. (2024). The effect of parents' support, protean career orientation and self-perceived employability on the school-to-work transition. *Career Development International*, 29(4), 494–509.

Juhdi, Nurita, Pa'Wan, Fatimah, Othman, Noor Akmar, & Moksin, Hanifah. (2010). Factors influencing internal and external employability of employees. *Business and Economics Journal, 11*(1–10).

Karaca-Atik, Ayşegül, Meeuwisse, Marieke, Gorgievski, Marjan, & Smeets, Guus. (2023). Uncovering important 21st-century skills for sustainable career development of social sciences graduates: A systematic review. *Educational Research Review, 39*, 100528.

Katz, Daniel, & Kahn, Robert. (2015). The social psychology of organizations *Organizational Behavior 2* (pp. 152–168): Routledge.

Kim, Sujin, Creed, Peter A, Hood, Michelle, & Bath, Debra. (2024). Protean career processes in young adults: Relationships with perceived future employability, educational performance, and commitment. *International Journal for Educational and Vocational Guidance*, 24(3), 1–24.

Kim, Sujin, Creed, Peter A, Hood, Michelle, & Bath, Debra. (2023). Protean career processes in young adults: Relationships with perceived future employability, educational performance, and commitment. *International Journal for Educational and Vocational Guidance*, 1–24.

Kiong, Tee Poh, & Yin-Fah, Benjamin Chan. (2016). Exploring factors towards career success in Malaysia. *International Business Management, 10*(17), 3936–3943.

Lent, Robert W, Brown, Steven D, & Hackett, Gail. (1994). Toward a unifying social cognitive theory of career and academic interest, choice, and performance. *Journal of vocational behavior, 45*(1), 79–122.

Li, Yongzhan. (2018). Linking protean career orientation to well-being: The role of psychological capital. *Career Development International, 23*(2), 178–196.

Lin, Yi-chun. (2015a). Are you a protean talent? The influence of protean career attitude, learning-goal orientation and perceived internal and external employability. *Career Development International.*

Lin, Yi-chun. (2015b). Are you a protean talent? The influence of protean career attitude, learning-goal orientation and perceived internal and external employability. *Career Development International, 20*(7), 753–772.

Lisá, Elena, & Valachová, Michaela. (2023). Dispositional employability and self-regulation in antisocial and prosocial personalities: different contributions to employability. *BMC psychology, 11*(1), 7.

Marock, Carmel. (2008). Grappling with youth employability in South Africa.

Meerman, Jan, Van Casteren, Patricia AJ, Brouwers, Evelien PM, Van Dam, Arno, & Van Der Klink, Jac JL. (2022). A capability perspective on sustainable employability: A Dutch focus group study on organizational, work and personal conversion factors. *Plos one, 17*(10), e0274000.

Mirvis, Philip H, & Hall, Douglas T. (1994). Psychological success and the boundaryless career. *Journal of organizational behavior, 15*(4), 365–380.

Monteiro, Sílvia, Almeida, Leandro, Gomes, Cristiano, & Sinval, Jorge. (2022). Employability profiles of higher education graduates: a person-oriented approach. *Studies in higher education*, 47(3), 499–512

Moon, Jae Seung, & Choi, Suk Bong. (2017). The impact of career management on organizational commitment and the mediating role of subjective career success: The case of Korean R&D employees. *Journal of Career Development, 44*(3), 191–208.

Orpen, Christopher. (1994). The effects of organizational and individual career management on career success. *International journal of manpower, 15*(1), 27–37.

Park, Yoonhee, Lee, Jin Gu, Jeong, Hong Jeon, Lim, Min Sub, & Oh, Mi-Rae. (2022). How does the protean career attitude influence external employability? The roles of career resilience and proactive career behavior. *Industrial and Commercial Training.*

Purohit, Divyang, & Jayswal, Rachita. (2024). Developing and validating protean and boundaryless career scale for college passing out students. *European Journal of Training and Development, 48*(1/2), 23–40.

Quigley, Narda R, & Tymon Jr, Walter G. (2006). Toward an integrated model of intrinsic motivation and career self-management. *Career development international, 11*(6), 522–543.

Rios, Joseph A, Ling, Guangming, Pugh, Robert, Becker, Dovid, & Bacall, Adam %J Educational Researcher. (2020). Identifying critical 21st-century skills for workplace success: A content analysis of job advertisements. *49*(2), 80–89.

Rokeach, Milton. (1973). *The nature of human values*: Free press.

Schwartz, Shalom H. (1994). Are there universal aspects in the structure and contents of human values? *Journal of social issues, 50*(4), 19–45.
Silva, Ana Maria, Gomes, Jorge FS, & Monteiro, Sílvia. (2023). Perceived employability in a situation of crisis: the influence of the external context and perceived financial threat. *Higher Education, Skills and Work-Based Learning, 13*(6), 1054–1072.
Soares, Maria Eduarda, & Mosquera, Pilar. (2021). Linking career management practices with individual outcomes: The mediating role of perceived employability. *Journal of Business Research, 124*, 547–559.
Tee, Poh Kiong, Cham, Tat-Huei, Low, Mei Peng, & Lau, Teck-Chai. (2022). The role of perceived employability in the relationship between protean career attitude and career success. *Australian Journal of Career Development, 31*(1), 66–76.
Vanhercke, Dorien, De Cuyper, Nele, Peeters, Ellen, & De Witte, Hans. (2014). Defining perceived employability: a psychological approach. *Personnel Review, 43*(4), 592–605.
Verbruggen, Marijke, Sels, Luc, & Forrier, Anneleen. (2007). Unraveling the relationship between organizational career management and the need for external career counseling. *Journal of Vocational Behavior, 71*(1), 69–83.
Volmer, Judith, & Spurk, Daniel. (2011). Protean and boundaryless career attitudes: Relationships with subjective and objective career success. *Zeitschrift für ArbeitsmarktForschung, 43*(3), 207–218.
Waters, Lea, Briscoe, Jon P, Hall, Douglas T, & Wang, Lan. (2014). Protean career attitudes during unemployment and reemployment: A longitudinal perspective. *Journal of Vocational Behavior, 84*(3), 405–419.
Wesarat, Phathara-on, Sharif, Mohmad Yazam, & Majid, Abdul Halim Abdul. (2014). A review of organizational and individual career management: A dual perspective. *International Journal of Human Resource Studies, 4*(1), 101.
Wujema, Baba Kachalla, Mohd Rasdi, Roziah, Zaremohzzabieh, Zeinab, & Ahrari, Seyedali. (2022). The role of self-efficacy as a mediating variable in CareerEDGE employability model: The context of undergraduate employability in the North-East Region of Nigeria. *Sustainability*, 14(8), 4660.
Xanthopoulou, Despoina, Bakker, Arnold B, Dollard, Maureen F, Demerouti, Evangelia, Schaufeli, Wilmar B, Taris, Toon W, & Schreurs, Paul JG. (2007). When do job demands particularly predict burnout? The moderating role of job resources. *Journal of managerial psychology*.
Zhou, Jie. (2022). Influence of Career Decision Ambiguity Tolerance Preference on Career Adaptability: The Role of Individual and Organizational Career Management. *Psychological Reports*, 00332941221092648.

Moving Towards Sustainable Businesses and Developing More Resilient Economies – Rashid and Annansingh-Jamieson (Eds)
© 2026 The Author(s), ISBN: 978-1-041-08875-2

Innovation management in practice: Framework analysis of Walmart and Microsoft

Akhmadbek Bakhtiyorov
University of Exeter, Exeter, United Kingdom

ABSTRACT: The world today is heavily influenced by high technologies and artificial intelligence, which makes digital transformation very essential for businesses to grow sustainably. Since terms such as digital transformation and advanced technologies integration all fall under the broader theme of innovation, this report examines innovation management in two core areas and demonstrates two major companies as examples, through analytical framework models. The first is Exploration and/or Exploitation, which explores whether businesses are innovatively responding to evolving customer demand or continuing to rely on traditional practices, and the analysis, in turn, will be maintained through the Simplified Model of the Innovation Process in order to critically evaluate innovation management strategies at diverse levels. Accordingly, Walmart, the world's largest retailer, serves as the subject of analysis for this framework, and it presents a compelling example of an organisation that has leveraged its scale and operational prowess while simultaneously investing in digital innovation, automation, and supply chain transformation.

1 INTRODUCTION

It is important to note that the world today is heavily influenced by high technologies and artificial intelligence, which makes digital transformation very essential for businesses to grow sustainably. Terms such as digital transformation and advanced technologies integration all fall under the broader theme of innovation. However, competitive pressure to innovate and rapid digital transformation must not compromise environmental sustainability or ethical integrity. Thus, this report examines innovation management in two core areas and demonstrates two major companies as examples, through analytical framework models as they have actively engaged with these concepts. The analysis, in turn, will be maintained through the Simplified Model of the Innovation Process in order to critically evaluate innovation management strategies at diverse levels, from strategic intent to implementation and organisational learning. The second concept is Responsible Innovation, and it illustrates how businesses assess or respond to environmental, ethical, and societal impacts in the innovation process. Microsoft is selected for analysis due to its notable outcomes by its responsible strategic approaches in product development, particularly in spheres of artificial intelligence and sustainability.

2 BACKGROUND

Innovation – understood as strategic breakthrough – is considered a high-value strategy for businesses. Exploration refers to a process of inventing new ways to success by the combination of several key aspects. By contrast, exploitation is considered highly effective

 DOI: 10.1201/9781003647300-24

for cost-competitive strategies as the system works on established systems without any new tremendous changes. Nevertheless, the competitive global business environment is full of risks, and organisations unwilling to take that risk and adopting less innovative strategies can increase the risk of failure as customers today are interested in new products more. Companies are recommended to choose both explorative along with exploitative frameworks, as ambidextrous for long-term survival. Therefore, those companies are nine times more likely to create innovative products and processes than non-ambidextrous firms – while sustaining or even improving their existing operations. Ultimately, Walmart has consistently improved its supply chain and in-store efficiency, while also embracing AI, automation, and digital services to meet evolving customer needs and market conditions. The company's digital development can be outlined through its major transformation phases as shown in Diagram 1.

Diagram 1. Walmart digital transformation timeline.

	Period	Focus Area	Key Developments
1	2013-2015	Initial Digitalization & In-Store Tools	Pilot online sales channels, mobile apps, digital kiosks; gather customer behaviour data
2	2016-2017	E-Commerce & Omni-Channel Integration	BOPIS (Buy Online, Pick Up In-Store); Acquired Jet.com to expand e-commerce
3	2018-2020	Supply Chain Innovation & Customer Services	AI & ML for inventory; Walmart+ for customer loyalty; IoT integration in warehouses
4	2021-2023	Post-Pandemic Digital Optimization	Expanded digital tools; same-day delivery via app; AI for customer behaviour analytics
5	2024-present	AI, Sustainability & Personalized Services	Autonomous delivery, generative AI for recommendations, sustainability-driven logistics

Responsible Innovation plays a key role in the contemporary business world. Therefore, innovations must be purpose-oriented and include risk monitoring systems, user-centred and value sensitive design, clear morale justification and provide transparency to avoid further detrimental effects. In general, responsible innovation management encourages customer trust, stakeholder engagement and environmentally sustainable approaches. Microsoft achieved notable business growth and advanced digital technologies globally as one of the key players. Its carbon-negative pledge and AI for Good programs also prove how innovation can be both competitive and conscientious. Finally, Microsoft serves as a representative case for responsible innovation in practice, aligned with global calls for sustainable digital leadership. Microsoft's progress in responsible innovation is also reflected in its continuous strategic milestones presented in Diagram 2.

Diagram 2. Microsoft responsible innovation timeline.

	Period	Focus Area	Key Developments
1	2013-2015	Foundation for Cloud & AI Ethics	Launch of Azure cloud platform; early talks on AI ethics
2	2016-2017	Responsible AI Principles	Establishment of Microsoft's AI and Ethics in Engineering and Research (AETHER)
3	2018-2020	Sustainability & Global AI Access	AI for Earth initiative; sustainability goals (carbon-negative by 2030)
4	2021-2022	Responsible Tech Frameworks	Launch of Responsible AI Standard and ecosystem-wide toolkits
5	2023-2024	Expansion & Regulation Alignment	EU AI Act preparation compliance; Open-source governance tools; AI transparency

In summary, both companies demonstrate that sustained innovation and responsibility together define long-term competitiveness in the modern digital economy.

3 LITERATURE REVIEW

The Literature Review demonstrates why exploration and exploitation are pivotal for business and indicates aspects of responsible innovation to balance potential benefit and harms of novel innovations. Exploration and exploitation are considered diverse concepts such as processes or outcomes in various contexts as stated in a research paper by Li-Ying, Vanhaverbeke, and Schoenmakers (2008). In this context, ambidexterity should be supported by developing exploration and exploitation in both domains through strategic knowledge search across different distances and functions. Nevertheless, regardless of any definition given for the concepts, companies should emphasize integrating existing competencies with radical innovations to achieve tremendous success eventually.

As a foundation for exploration and exploitation, prior research on managing innovation within firms widely discussed key points to implement such a system that supports exploration and exploitation – innovation management – well. In this context, Ron Adner (2006) emphasizes that the importance of ecosystem lies not only in internal effects but also requires well-balanced external involvement. Firms should make strategic decisions regarding the evaluation of risk, including integration as well as interdependency, and managers should identify clear plans to avoid detrimental effects in advance.

O'Reilly III and Tushman (2004) argued that companies that integrate current competencies with innovative initiatives – ambidextrous organisations – are nine times more likely to show better results in the market. Ambidextrous organisations should strategically separate new innovations from core business units and accelerate tight integration at the senior executive level to share critical resources without allowing the traditional culture to dominate.

Applying these insights to the context of emerging economies, Moreira (2022) highlighted the significance of ambidextrous companies with evidence from Mozambican SMEs. The research found that exploitative decisions better manage the relationship than explorative ones in terms of short-term incremental development. However, explorative initiative accelerates the direct growth of export performance and positively affects the whole emerging economy. Thus, integrating exploration as well as exploitation is thought as a feasible solution for success, especially in resource-scarce economies.

While exploration and exploitation are essential for organisational success in today's competitive business landscape, companies must adhere to social, ethical as well as environmental norms. Consequently, the concept of responsible innovation has become a heated topic among experts due to its core principles and framework for measurement. Tait (2021) also suggests that responsible innovation inspires businesses to create a well-structured evaluation system for potential benefit and harm of novel innovations for which traditional standards are not fully ready yet. Stilgoe, Owen, and Macnaghten (2013) also argued that there is a lack of structured framework for responsible innovation assessment, particularly in government regulations. Further innovative initiatives should be governed based on potential risks throughout the entire process rather than emphasizing only a final output.

In conclusion, the literature review illustrated the importance of balancing exploration and exploitation to achieve substantial growth for businesses, while responsible innovation ensures that such progress remains ethically and environmentally sustainable.

4 ANALYSIS

4.1 *Exploration and exploitation: Walmart*

There are myriad organisations structuring their exploration and exploitation strategies, and a suitable example for analysis is Walmart. The remarkable outcomes achieved through strong innovation management policies within the company have inspired millions of satisfied customers worldwide. Walmart is a leading American multinational retail corporation known for its cost leadership strategy, global scale, and continuous innovation across supply chain management, technology integration, and customer experience. The current paragraph indicates the way how explorative and exploitative actions are balanced within Walmart's innovation process, critically assessing these dynamics through the Simplified Model of the Innovation Process.

There are myriad organisations structuring their exploration and exploitation strategies, and a suitable example for analysis is Walmart. The remarkable outcomes achieved through strong innovation management policies within the company have inspired millions of satisfied customers worldwide. Walmart is a leading American multinational retail corporation known for its cost leadership strategy, global scale, and continuous innovation across supply chain management, technology integration, and customer experience.

Search element of the Simplified Model of the Innovation Process is linked with discovering unfamiliar spaces to enable breakthroughs and refining available capabilities for efficiency improvement. Walmart strategically integrated both components, as the company has been developing its supply chain management as well as data systems with emerging technologies. In addition, significant investments in Artificial Intelligence, Augmented Reality (AR), and robotics also clearly support explorative initiatives. Exploitative activities encompass continuous development in supply chain management such as the refinement of its Retail Link platform along with the integration of RFID technologies. Therefore, Walmart has chosen sustainable integration of exploration and exploitation for its search for the latest advancements to provide its competitive advantage in the current dynamic business landscape.

Strategic Selection is a process of choosing appropriate innovative initiatives in order to minimize uncertainty risk and effectively allocate limited resources. Walmart shows excellence in the selection of innovations by strategically aligning them with its core principles and tests modern technologies before scaling, where balancing new tech with proven cost-saving projects support this strategy. Thus, Walmart's selection strategy enables its innovation management strong due to balanced exploration and exploitation operations.

Agile Implementation refers to the implementation of the selected idea within the firms through fast experimentation and adaptation of required components. At Walmart, the agile implementation process starts by piloting novel ideas and assessing them in selected limited locations, which eventually enables the company to scale up successful practices. This approach is considered agile compared to slow traditional R&D systems. Meanwhile, the organization integrates tested explorative initiatives exploiting them to support operational efficiency aligning with strategic goals.

Walmart emphasized implementing an innovation-supportive culture rather than just installing technology. Heavy investments in employee involvement, adaptation, and open innovation programs like WIN support the company's recent digital transformation efforts to involve internal cultural change towards agility. Business development and innovation-driven strategies require better partnerships with external stakeholders, including suppliers and universities to strengthen existing capabilities. Accordingly, Walmart leverages partnerships with suppliers and technology firms, supporting consistent collaborative innovation for its success. Walmart develops evolving capabilities by leveraging data analytics, AI-driven insights, and agile employee training programs, allowing continuous adaptation to changing customer needs and market dynamics.

In conclusion, only ambidextrous companies are more likely survive in the current business environment. Implementing balanced explorative and exploitative initiatives on innovation management policy requires careful emphasis on integrating multiple innovation aspects, challenging the innovation framework development.

4.2 *Responsible innovation: Microsoft*

Responsible Innovation is considered as the process of preventing the potential harms and increasing the benefits of innovation initiatives through stakeholder engagement. The main aim aims to deliver sustainable outcomes that support ethical, social and environmental values. The Business Model Canvas examines the strategy of innovation management frameworks established in the firms and describes the structure of value prepositions in business though nine major elements. Thus, this section critically analyses Microsoft's Responsible Innovation principles according to its innovation management policy based on the Business Model Canvas components.

Value proposition strategy emphasizes providing people, businesses and other institutions with novel ideas development while accounting for ethical, environmental and social norms to foster digital transformation improvements. Innovations such as AI, cloud computing or cybersecurity software supported by Microsoft are directed toward overcoming digitalization process challenges and addressing customer needs responsibly and transparently.

Customer segments encompass large enterprises, small and medium-sized businesses, government institutions, educational organizations, and individual consumers. Diverse customer segmentation scale would have been tricky to cope with without appropriate responsible innovation which drives products and services that meet the ethical, security, and sustainability needs of each segment. Customer relationships are shaped by transparency, data privacy, and ethical AI practices to ensure long-term and trustworthy engagement. These are supported by self-service platforms, personalized support, and collaborative innovation initiatives.

Revenue streams, key resources, and key partners reflect how Microsoft aligns its innovation process with sustainability and responsibility. Microsoft generates revenue through cloud service subscriptions, software licensing, and AI solutions, ensuring that revenue growth aligns with ethical, sustainable, and socially responsible innovation practices. The company usually works with OpenAI, governments, academic institutions, nonprofit organizations, and technology providers who play a pivotal role in supporting collaborative ecosystem for responsible innovation in AI development, cybersecurity, sustainability initiatives, and digital inclusion programs.

Key activities and cost structure emphasize Microsoft's investments in R&D for responsible AI, cloud infrastructure development, cybersecurity advancements, sustainability programs, and employee training to drive its ethical and inclusive innovation commitment. In conclusion, Microsoft's global success stems from its internal policy which integrates its business model with sustainable value creation and drives ethical practices across all operations.

5 CONCLUSIONS

The innovation management framework consists of diverse specific aspects, and the report highlighted two main themes out of them. Exploration and exploitation perspectives are core drivers of open innovation and require various development systems which ultimately deliver distinct positive outcomes eventually. Hence, ambidextrous firms that could achieve a balance of new initiative integration with existing capabilities maintain higher results in the current competitive business landscape.

As an example, Walmart clearly provided a solid strategy on balancing its heavy investment in agile innovation and existing system development, and Retail Link platform along with the integration of RFID technologies or AI based customer support systems are vivid examples of this statement. Moreover, Walmart demonstrates a commitment to fostering radical innovations, such as AI and robotics, and simultaneously improves its existing supply chain operations. Strategic selection also ensures that only scalable innovations are pursued. Proactive linkages with partners, internal culture of innovation, and evolving capabilities have positioned the company to support global market leadership through flexible technological and customer shifts.

Responsible innovation, in turn, inspires ethical and sustainable innovation accountability within the firms. Thus, Microsoft's innovation management strategy was evaluated based on the Business Model Canvas. The company aligned its core principles, particularly value propositions with such norms and facilitates strategic partnerships, sustainable key activities, and trustworthy customer relationships emphasizing transparency and privacy. Accordingly, the business model also demonstrated long-term resilience driven by organizational revenue streams, cost structures, and key resources. Walmart and Microsoft innovation management frameworks' comparison highlighted the key role of responsible and balanced innovation strategies, including efficiency as well as creativity or achieving future success. Therefore, exploration without exploitation leads to unsustainable risk, and innovation without ethical considerations erodes trust. Structured and responsible innovation approaches shape competitive advantage for businesses to positively contribute to society. Innovation is no longer about only product development, it is now about sustainable value creation, as well as future impact.

REFERENCES

Adner, R. (2006). Match your innovation strategy to your innovation ecosystem. *Harvard Business Review*, 84(4), 98–107. https://hbr.org/2006/04/match-your-innovation-strategy-to-your-innovation-ecosystem

Alabdulhadi, A. (2023). Analysis of Microsoft's innovation and technology development strategies. *International Journal of Research and Innovation in Social Science (IJRISS)*, 7(3), 650–654. https://doi.org/10.47772/IJRISS.2023.73132

Alonso, T. (2022, November 25). Strategy study: The Microsoft growth study. Cascade. https://www.cascade.app/studies/how-microsoft-innovations-made-it-technology-giant

Basker, E. (2007). The causes and consequences of Wal-Mart's growth. *Journal of Economic Perspectives*, 21(3), 177–198. https://doi.org/10.1257/jep.21.3.177

Bogers, M., Chesbrough, H., and Moedas, C. (2018). Open innovation: Research, practices, and policies. *California Management Review*, 60(2), 5–16. https://doi.org/10.1177/0008125617745086

Budden, P., and Murray, F. (2022). Strategically engaging with innovation ecosystems. MIT Sloan Management Review. https://sloanreview.mit.edu

Chesbrough, H.W. (2003). Open innovation: The new imperative for creating and profiting from technology. Harvard Business School Press. https://www.researchgate.net/publication/280211463_Open_Innovation_The_New_Imperative_for_Creating_and_Profiting_from_Technology20041Henry_W_Chesbrough_Open_Innovation_The_New_Imperative_for_Creating_and_Profiting_from_Technology_Boston_MA_Harvard_Bus

Cho, Y.S., and Linderman, K. (2020). Resource-based product and process innovation model: Theory development and empirical validation. *Sustainability*, 12(3), Article 913. https://doi.org/10.3390/su12030913

Diorio, S. (2023, June 1). Harnessing a wave of AI innovations to expand Microsoft's markets. Forbes. https://www.forbes.com/sites/stephendiorio/2023/06/01/using-innovation-to-expand-microsofts-markets/

Dziallas, M., and Blind, K. (2019). Innovation indicators throughout the innovation process: An extensive literature analysis. *Technovation*, 80–81, 3–29. https://doi.org/10.1016/j.technovation.2018.05.005

Fakieh, B., Al-Ghamdi, A., and Ragab, M. (2022). The effect of utilizing Business Model Canvas on the satisfaction of operating electronic business. *Complexity*, 2022, 1–10. https://doi.org/10.1155/2022/1649160

Freeman, R.B., Nakamura, A.O., Nakamura, L.I., Prud'homme, M., and Pyman, A. (2011). Wal-Mart innovation and productivity: A viewpoint. *The Canadian Journal of Economics / Revue canadienne d'Economique*, 44(2), 486–508. https://www.jstor.org/stable/41336371

Gartner. (2024). Magic Quadrant for Cloud Infrastructure and Platform Services. https://www.gartner.com

Gurzawska, A. (2021). Responsible innovation in business: Perceptions, evaluation practices and lessons learnt. *Sustainability*, 13(4), 1826. https://doi.org/10.3390/su13041826

Holgersson, M., Baldwin, C.Y., Chesbrough, H., and Bogers, M. (2022). The forces of ecosystem evolution. *California Management Review*, 64(3), 5–23. https://doi.org/10.1177/00081256221086038

Horrocks, I., and Walker, S. (2025). Technology, innovation and management. The Open University. https://www.open.edu/openlearn/mod/oucontent/view.php?id=27445&printable=1

Jacobides, M.G. (2022). How to compete when industries digitize and collide: An ecosystem development framework. *California Management Review*, 64(3), 99–123. https://doi.org/10.1177/00081256221083352

Li-Ying, J., Vanhaverbeke, W., and Schoenmakers, W. (2008). Exploration and exploitation in innovation: Reframing the interpretation. *Creativity and Innovation Management*, 17(2), 107–126. https://doi.org/10.1111/j.1467-8691.2008.00477.x

MacCormack, A., and Iansiti, M. (2004). Intellectual property, architecture, and the management of technological transitions: Evidence from Microsoft Corporation [Working paper]. Harvard Business School. https://www.hbs.edu/ris/Publication%20Files/03-020.pdf

McKinsey and Company. (2023). Digital strategy trends in 2023: A global outlook. https://www.mckinsey.com/business-functions/mckinsey-digital/our-insights

Microsoft Corporation. (2023). Annual report 2023. https://www.microsoft.com/investor/reports/ar23/index.html Microsoft+2Microsoft+2Microsoft+2

Microsoft Corporation. (2024). Annual report 2024. https://www.microsoft.com/investor/reports/ar24/

Moreira, A.C., Navaia, E.C., and Ribau, C. (2022). The importance of exploration and exploitation innovation in emerging economies. *Journal of Open Innovation: Technology, Market, and Complexity*, 8(3), 140. https://doi.org/10.3390/joitmc8030140

Mujtaba, B.G., and Maxwell, S. (2007). Wal-Mart in the global retail market: Its growth and challenges. *Journal of Business Case Studies (JBCS)*, 3(2), 55–66. https://doi.org/10.19030/jbcs.v3i2.4837

Murray, A., and Scuotto, V. (2015). The Business Model Canvas. Symphonya. Emerging Issues in Management, 3(94), 13–21. https://doi.org/10.4468/2015.3.13murray.scuotto

Muwafak, B.M., Mokadem, W., and Abdeldayem, M.M. (2021). Business Model Canvas (BMC) as a tool of planning and implementing entrepreneurial projects: A case study of Google Business Model Canvas. *Global Scientific Journal*, 9(5), 1245–1260. http://www.globalscientificjournal.com

Nathan, G. (2015). Innovation process and ethics in technology: An approach to ethical (responsible) innovation governance. *Journal on Chain and Network Science*, 15(2), 119–134. https://doi.org/10.3920/JCNS2014.x018

O'Reilly III, C.A., and Tushman, M.L. (2004). The ambidextrous organization. *Harvard Business Review*, 82(4), 74–81. https://hbr.org/2004/04/the-ambidextrous-organization

Pandey, R., Dillip, D., Jayant, J., Vashishth, K., Nikhil, T.J.Q., Mui Hung Kee, D., Cai Mei, T., Yong Kai Xin, R., and Yong Qhi, L. (2021). Factors influencing organization success: A case study of Walmart. *Journal of Business Management and Economic Research*, 4(2), 112–120. https://www.researchgate.net/publication/353433894_Factors_Influencing_Organization_Success_A_Case_Study_of_Walmart

Stilgoe, J., Owen, R., and Macnaghten, P. (2013). Developing a framework for responsible innovation. *Research Policy*, 42(9), 1568–1580. https://doi.org/10.1016/j.respol.2013.05.008

Tait, J., Brown, A., Lalinde, I.C., Barlow, D., Chiles, M., and Mason, P. (2021). Responsible innovation: Its role in an era of technological and regulatory transformation. *Engineering Biology*, 5(1), 2–9. https://doi.org/10.1049/enb2.12005

Tiwari, R., Buse, S., and Herstatt, C. (2007). Innovation via global route: Proposing a reference model for chances and challenges of global innovation processes (Working Paper No. 49). Hamburg University of Technology, Institute for Technology and Innovation Management. http://www.tu-harburg.de/tim/downloads/arbeitspapiere/Working_Paper_49.pdf

Udell, G.G., Bottin, R.R., and Glass, D.D. (1993). The Wal-Mart Innovation Network: An experiment in stimulating American innovation. *Journal of Product Innovation Management*, 10(1), 23–34. https://doi.org/10.1016/0737-6782(93)90051-Q

Walmart's Integration of AI. (2023). Forbes Insights Report.

Wonglimpiyarat, J. (2012). Technology strategies and standard competition — Comparative innovation cases of Apple and Microsoft. *Journal of High Technology Management Research*, 23(2), 90–102. https://doi.org/10.1016/j.hitech.2012.06.005

Yeboah, A. (2023). Innovation process model: An integration of innovation costs, benefits and core competence. *Cogent Business & Management*, 10(1), Article 2176445. https://doi.org/10.1080/23311975.2023.2176445

Zhang, W. (2024). An analysis of Walmart based on its internal and external environment. *Proceedings of the 3rd International Conference on Business and Policy Studies*, 142–146. https://doi.org/10.54254/2754-1169/77/20241609

Zhao, B. (2022). Microsoft's overview and development strategies based on multiple analyses. *BCP Business & Management FEMS*, 19, 73–77. https://www.researchgate.net/publication/361795676_Microsoft's_overview_and_development_strategies_based_on_multiple_analyses

Moving Towards Sustainable Businesses and Developing More Resilient Economies – Rashid and Annansingh-Jamieson (Eds)
© 2026 The Author(s), ISBN: 978-1-041-08875-2

Ethical AI lending practices: Ensuring fairness and resilience in USA mortgage approvals

M.A. Hasan
Feliciano School of Business, Montclair State University, Montclair, New Jersey, USA

M.T.R. Mazumder
School of Information Technology, Washington University of Science and Technology, Alexandria, Virginia, USA

M.S.H. Shourov
School of Information Technology, Webster University, Webster Groves, Missouri, USA

S. Nashid
Graduate School of Technology, Touro University, Manhattan, New York, USA

ABSTRACT: The advancement of artificial intelligence (AI) is reshaping mortgage lending in the USA by enhancing efficiency and forecasting accuracy. However, its application in high-stakes financial decisions raises concerns about fairness and transparency. This study empirically evaluated the ethical dimensions of AI-supported mortgage approval using Home Mortgage Disclosure Act (HMDA) data from 2019–2023. Through descriptive statistics, fairness metrics (disparate impact and demographic parity), and logistic regression, it examined whether race, gender, and income influence loan approval outcomes when controlling for credit-relevant factors. The findings revealed persistent demographic disparities, suggesting that AI may reinforce historical biases when unregulated or opaque. The paper advocated fairness-aware algorithm design, institutional transparency, and regulatory safeguards. Positioned within the discourse on financial ethics and socio-technical governance, the study focuses on sustainable and inclusive innovation in business ecosystems, supporting the development of equitable AI systems in mortgage lending.

Keywords: Artificial intelligence, Mortgage approval, Mortgage lending, Sustainability, Business ecosystem, Bias mitigation, Algorithm fairness

1 INTRODUCTION

Artificial Intelligence (AI) is transforming financial decision-making by improving predictive accuracy, minimizing human bias, and increasing the speed and scale of credit evaluations. Machine learning and advanced statistical techniques enable AI systems to detect complex patterns in large datasets, thereby enhancing credit scoring, risk assessment, and fraud detection and monitoring. These technologies also broaden financial inclusion by incorporating non-traditional data sources into lending assessments (Piacentino 2025). In mortgage lending, AI-enabled Automated Underwriting Systems now influence applicant evaluation, pricing, and loan approvals (Adewale *et al.* 2022). However, these innovations raise critical

DOI: 10.1201/9781003647300-25

ethical concerns regarding fairness, transparency, accountability, and regulatory compliance, particularly in high-stakes credit decisions (Barocas *et al.* 2019).

Persistent inequities in U.S. mortgage lending rooted in redlining, exclusionary zoning, and discriminatory credit practices continue to shape contemporary outcomes (Rothstein 2017). Despite safeguards under the Equal Credit Opportunity Act and the Home Mortgage Disclosure Act, research shows that algorithmic lending can replicate historical biases when models rely on data that is embedded with structural inequalities (Kim 2020). Proxy variables such as ZIP code and employment patterns frequently correlate with protected attributes, enabling unintended discrimination. The opaque "black-box" nature of many machine-learning models further complicates oversight and limits applicants' ability to contest adverse decisions (Pasquale 2015). This study examined demographic disparities in AI-mediated mortgage approvals using HMDA data from 2019 to 2023 through descriptive analysis, disparate-impact metrics, and multivariate logistic regression. Given the mortgage market's scale (over $12 trillion in assets) (Federal Reserve Bank 2023), ensuring the ethical deployment of AI is essential for promoting economic equity, strengthening community stability, and safeguarding opportunities for intergenerational mobility (Benjamin 2019).

1.1 *Research questions*

Do AI-supported mortgage approval processes produce disparate outcomes across demographic groups such as age, race, gender, ethnicity, and income level; To what extent can algorithmic bias in mortgage lending be detected and quantified using fairness metrics such as the disparate impact ratio and demographic parity; Do demographic characteristics significantly predict mortgage approval outcomes when controlling for financial indicators such as income, debt-to-income ratio, and loan size; How have patterns of algorithmic bias in mortgage lending evolved temporally from the pre-COVID era (2019) through the post-pandemic recovery period (2023)?

2 REVIEW OF LITERATURE

Artificial intelligence (AI) has revolutionised credit scoring by employing advanced computational techniques that enhance predictive accuracy, streamline risk assessment, and expand financial inclusion. Traditional scoring models, which rely heavily on formal financial documentation and linear statistical relationships, often fail to capture the complexity of contemporary financial behaviour (Sudjianto & Zhang 2024). AI-driven systems, utilising machine learning and deep learning, analyse diverse borrower data more efficiently; however, concerns remain regarding fairness, transparency, and data governance, underscoring the need to strike a balance between efficiency and ethical accountability in lending (Piacentino 2025). Mortgage underwriting has similarly evolved through the use of automated systems that replace manual assessments of income, credit history, and loan-to-value ratios, thereby improving decision speed and consistency (Mhlanga 2021). Rule-based systems, such as Desktop Underwriter and Loan Product Advisor, have been supplemented by non-linear machine learning models and alternative data sources, thereby expanding credit evaluation capacity (Berg *et al.* 2020). However, empirical evidence showed that automated lending can reproduce historical inequities. Black and Hispanic borrowers face higher denial rates despite comparable financial profiles (Bartlett *et al.* 2019). Proxy variables such as ZIP code reinforce structural segregation, while fairness metrics remain limited because no single standard fully captures equity objectives (Chouldechova 2017). Scholars warn that without robust institutional safeguards, AI may exacerbate systemic inequality, prompting renewed calls for transparency and accountability (OSTP 2022).

3 RESEARCH METHODOLOGY

3.1 *Research design and process*

The study employed a quantitative, non-experimental research design that utilised secondary data analysis. The dataset included variables captured and grouped into four categories: Demographic, Financial, Geographic, and the Lending Process. The primary dependent variable was loan approval status, coded as a binary variable: 1 for approved and 0 for denied.

3.2 *Method of data analysis*

To address the research objectives, several analytical techniques were employed:

3.2.1 *Descriptive statistics and Chi-Square tests (Objective 1)*

Descriptive statistics were used to calculate group-wise loan approval rates. Cross-tabulations were followed by Chi-Square tests to determine the significance of differences:

$$\chi^2 = \sum \frac{(O_i - E_i)^2}{E_i}$$

Where: - O_i is the observed frequency - E_i is the expected frequency

3.2.2 *Fairness metric analysis (Objective 2)*

The study employed fairness auditing techniques, including:

Disparate Impact Ratio (DIR):

$$DIR = \frac{P(\text{Approved} \mid \text{Protected Group})}{P(\text{Approved} \mid \text{Reference Group})}$$

DIR < 0.8 or > 1.25 signals potential bias.

Demographic Parity Difference:

$$DP = \left| P\left(\widehat{Y} = 1 | A = 0\right) - P\left(\widehat{Y} = 1 | A = 1\right) \right|$$

3.2.3 *Logistic regression modeling (Objective 3)*

To assess whether demographic predictors remain significant after controlling for financial factors, the following logistic model was estimated:

$$\log\left(\frac{P(Y = 1)}{1 - P(Y = 1)}\right) = \beta_0 + \beta_1 X_1 + \beta_2 X_2 + \ldots + \beta_k X_k$$

Where: $Y = 1$ if approved, $X_1, X_2, \ldots, X_k$ include income, race, DTI, age, gender, and other covariates

3.2.4 *Temporal and COVID-19 impact analysis (Objective 4)*

To evaluate fairness trends and the impact of COVID-19, two models were used:

Interrupted Time Series (ITS):

$$Y_t = \beta_0 + \beta_1 Time_t + \beta_2 PostCOVID_t + \beta_3 TimeAfter_t + \epsilon_t$$

Y_t: outcome at time t, $PostCOVID_t = 1$ from 2020 onward, 0 otherwise, $TimeAfter_t$: time since 2020

Difference-in-Differences (DiD):

$$Y_{it} = \alpha + \beta_1 Treatment_i + \beta_2 Post_t + \beta_3 (Treatment_i \cdot Post_t) + \epsilon_{it}$$

Where: $Treatment_i$: protected group indicator, $Post_t$: binary for post-COVID period

4 ANALYSIS AND RESULTS

4.1 *Sample characteristics and descriptive statistics*

- *Demographic Distribution*

Results showed that white applicants comprised 82.4% of the sample; Black and Asian applicants each made up 8.8%. Males represented 63.9%, females 36.1%. Most applicants fell within the age range of 25 to 54. Hispanics accounted for 9.6%, with small subgroup shares. These demographic imbalances were critical for interpreting fairness in mortgage approval outcomes.

4.2 *Objective 1: Disparate outcomes across demographic groups*

This section examined whether mortgage approval outcomes varied across demographic groups. The analysis covered race, gender, age, and income (Table 1 and Table 2).

- *Mortgage Approval Rates by Demographics*

Table 1. Mortgage approval rates by race.

Race	Total Applications	Approved Applications	Approval Rate (%)
White	1992840	1649053	82.75
Asian	215625	169357	78.54
Black	215566	145487	67.49

Table 2. Mortgage approval rates by gender.

Gender	Total Applications	Approved Applications	Approval Rate (%)
Male	1550077	1269572	81.90
Female	873954	694325	79.45

Meanwhile, younger applicants under 25 years had the highest approval rate at 89.30%, followed by those aged 25–34 (87.51%) and 35–44 (82.89%). Approval rates declined steadily with age, reaching 70.38% among applicants aged 74 years or older. High-income applicants had an 85.55% approval rate, compared to 67.21% for low-income applicants, representing an 18.34 percentage point gap. Approval rates were also lower for Black, Hispanic, female, older, and low-income applicants (Figure 1).

- *Intersectional Analysis*

Intersection analysis by Race and Gender (Table 3 and Figure 1) revealed that White males had the highest approval rate (83.35%), while Black females had the lowest (67.16%), marking a 16.19-point gap. Across all races, females had slightly lower approval rates than males.

Table 3.

Race	Gender	Total Applications	Approved Applications	Approval Rate (%)
Asian	Male	147727	117904	79.81
	Female	67898	51453	75.78
Black	Male	110575	74974	67.80
	Female	104991	70513	67.16
White	Male	1291775	1076694	83.35
	Female	701065	572359	81.64

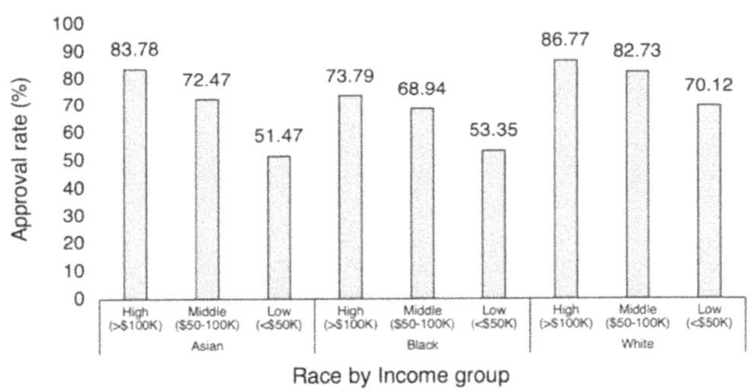

Figure 1. Mortgage approval rates (%) by race and income category.

4.3 *Objective 2: Algorithmic bias quantification*

- *Fairness Metrics Analysis*

White applicants had an 82.75% approval rate (DIR = 1.0), Asian applicants had an 78.54% approval rate (DIR = 0.949), and Black applicants had a 67.49% approval rate (DIR = 0.816). Black applicants had a demographic parity difference of 0.1526 when compared to White applicants, indicating significant bias. Asian applicants had a smaller difference of 0.0421[1]. Similar patterns were observed in the ethnic subgroups. Cuban applicants had the largest parity difference, at 0.3282, followed by Mexican (0.2389), Other Hispanic or Latino (0.2003), and Puerto Rican (0.1688) applicants. In Table 4, the gender-based DIR shows that male applicants served as the reference group with an approval rate of 81.90% and a DIR of 1.0. Female applicants had an approval rate of 79.45%, resulting in a DIR of 0.970. This value falls comfortably within the accepted range of 0.8 to 1.25, indicating no evidence of disparate impact based on gender.

4.4 *Objective 3: Demographic predictors with financial controls*

A multivariate logistic regression model (Table 5) was employed to examine the impact of income, debt-to-income ratio, loan amount, applicant demographics, and other relevant

Table 4. Disparate impact ratio analysis by gender and race.

		Total Application	Approved	Approval Rate (%)	DIR	DIR Interpretation
Gender	Female	873954	694325	79.45	0.970	No Disparate Impact (0.8 ≤ DIR ≤ 1.25)
	Male	1550077	1269572	81.90	1.0	Reference Group
Race	Black	215566	145487	67.49	0.816	No Disparate Impact (0.8 ≤ DIR ≤ 1.25)
	White	1992840	1649053	82.75	1.0	Reference Group
	Asian	215625	169357	78.54	0.949	No Disparate Impact (0.8 ≤ DIR ≤ 1.25)

factors on the likelihood of loan approval. The Regression results confirmed that income, race, age, and DTI significantly affect the odds of loan approval. Low-income applicants (OR = 0.326) were 67% less likely to be approved than high-income peers. Black applicants (OR = 0.501) also faced substantial disadvantages, even when controlling for credit-relevant variables. Lower DTI ratios (<36%) were associated with an improved likelihood of approval (OR = 2.515). Age showed a declining approval trend, with the oldest group (>74) at OR = 0.399. Some Hispanic subgroups exhibited higher odds (e.g., Puerto Rican OR = 3.252).

Table 5. Multivariate logistic regression - loan approval probability.

Variable	Odds Ratio	Std. Error	Z-Value	P-value	Sig.
(Intercept)	1,980,931,597.020	64.98733	0.33	0.742	
Income category					
Low (<$50K)	0.326	0.01276	-87.73	<0.001	***
Middle ($50-100K)	0.608	0.00860	-57.91	<0.001	***
Debt-to-income-ratio					
Low (<36%)	2.515	0.00871	106.69	<0.001	***
Moderate (36-43%)	3.504	0.00982	127.95	<0.001	***
Loan amount	1.000	0.00000	47.96	<0.001	***
Tract to MSA income percentage	0.993	0.00009	-78.89	<0.001	***
Rate Spread					
Normal	0.778	68.64277	0.00	0.9971	
Applicant Race					
Black	0.501	0.01641	-42.29	<0.001	***
White	0.996	0.01178	-0.37	0.7142	
Applicant sex					
Male	1.086	0.00780	11.08	<0.001	***
Applicant ethnicity					
Hispanic	3.465	0.18479	6.73	<0.001	***
Mexican	1.501	0.20363	2.00	0.0459	*
Not Hispanic	4.286	0.18452	7.89	<0.001	***
Other Hispanic or Latino	1.908	0.19565	3.30	<0.001	***
Puerto Rican	3.252	0.21416	5.51	<0.001	***

(continued)

Table 5. Continued

Variable	Odds Ratio	Std. Error	Z-Value	P-value	Sig.
Applicant age					
25-34	0.733	0.03131	-29.73	<0.001	***
35-44	0.600	0.02514	-12.38	<0.001	***
45-54	0.499	0.02479	-20.64	<0.001	***
55-64	0.462	0.02490	-27.91	<0.001	***
65-74	0.433	0.02523	-30.58	<0.001	***
>74	0.399	0.02663	-31.34	<0.001	***

Nagelkerke $R^2 = 0.164$*; Hosmer-Lemeshow* $\chi^2 = 96.7$ $(p = 0.00)$*; Odds ratios (OR) > 1 indicate increased odds of mortgage approval; OR < 1 indicate decreased odds; Statistical significance levels: *** p<0.001, ** p<0.01, * p<0.05, p<0.1*

4.5 *Objective 4: Temporal evolution analysis (Pre-Covid and Post-Covid Era)*

The analysis used Disparate Impact Ratios (DIRs)[2] to track differences in approval rates between protected groups and their respective reference groups. This supports Objective 4 by examining how fairness levels changed before, during, and after the COVID-19 pandemic (Figure 2 (a). Figure 2 (b) reported DIR values for underwriting systems (LP vs. DU) hovered around 1.0, indicating minimal bias. However, Vantage 3.0 scores showed potential adverse impact in 2020 (0.792) and 2022 (0.791) compared to FICO 04, suggesting that credit score type may contribute to bias, particularly during economic fluctuations.

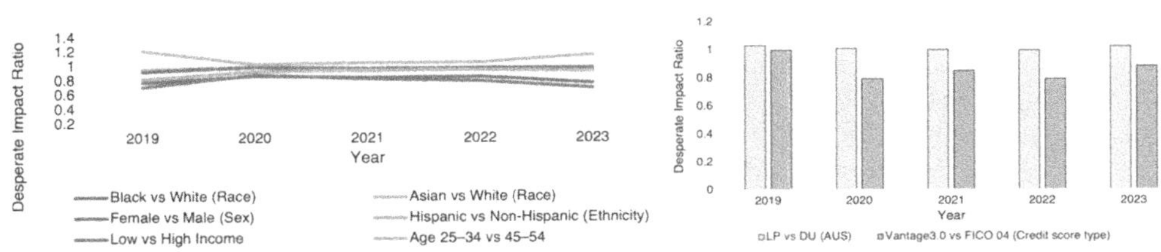

Figure 2. (a) Disparate impact ratios by year; (b) Disparate impact ratios by AUS and credit score type.

5 DISCUSSION

Significant disparities in mortgage approvals from 2019 to 2023 demonstrate persistent inequities in AI-mediated lending. Black applicants had a 67.5% approval rate compared to 82.75% for White applicants, with Hispanic and Native American borrowers also experiencing higher denial rates. Although the Disparate Impact Ratio (DIR) for Black applicants (0.816) met the EEOC's 0.80 guideline, it still reflected structural disadvantage, consistent with Bartlett *et al.* (2019), who found Black and Hispanic borrowers remain 40–80% less likely to receive mortgages even after controlling for financial factors. Gender gaps were narrower but still present, while applicants over the age of 65 faced disproportionately high denials, illustrating "asynchronous bias" arising from underrepresentation in model training (Wachter *et al.* 2017). Income disadvantage further compounds these patterns, consistent with intersectionality theory (Crenshaw 1991). Fairness metrics revealed additional layers of inequity. While DIR suggested formal compliance, the demographic parity difference (0.153) exceeded widely accepted thresholds, indicating practical harm. Aggregated measures also masked subgroup disparities. For example, among Puerto Rican and Native American applicants (Kearns *et al.* 2019). Given incompatibilities between fairness definitions such as demographic parity and equalized odds, scholars highlight the need for clearer regulatory prioritization (Chouldechova 2017). Regression analysis confirmed that race and income were significant predictors, even after adjusting for financial characteristics: Black applicants (OR = 0.781) and low-income borrowers (OR = 0.326) faced substantially lower approval odds. The lack of statistical significance in gender likely reflects indirect proxy effects, highlighting the limitations of "fairness through unawareness," as models often infer race through variables such as ZIP code.

Temporal trends revealed temporary improvements in fairness during the COVID-19 pandemic, attributed to federal protections, but subsequent deterioration, underscoring the need for sustained governance (Barocas *et al.* 2023). Transparency gaps in proprietary scoring models and Automated Underwriting Systems persist (Binns 2018), while rural and minority communities continue to face disproportionate denials (Federal Reserve Bank of Minneapolis 2023). Fairness optimization techniques, explainability tools such as SHAP and LIME (Nannini *et al.* 2023), and institutionalized audits remain essential for equitable AI-based lending.

6 CONCLUSION

This study examined the fairness of AI-driven mortgage lending using HMDA data (2019–2023) and identified persistent disparities affecting Black, Hispanic, low-income, and elderly applicants, indicating that algorithmic systems may reproduce entrenched inequities despite financial controls. Ensuring equity, therefore, requires stronger federal oversight. Agencies such as the FHFA and CFPB should adopt standardized, publicly audited credit scoring models to reduce lender-specific variability that disproportionately impacts underserved groups (CFPB 2023). Accountability can be improved through periodic, independent fairness audits of automated underwriting systems, aligned with national AI governance principles (OSTP 2022). Expanding HMDA reporting to include intersectional identity categories and mandating interpretable explanations for adverse decisions would further strengthen transparency and due-process protections. However, the study has limitations. HMDA excludes certain small lenders and lacks prequalification denial data, underrepresenting rural and marginalized borrowers. It also omits intersectional identifiers, while proprietary AUS models restrict transparency. Unobserved factors, such as credit scores and employment histories, may also affect fairness assessments. Future research should incorporate real-time bias monitoring, intersectional diagnostics, and causal inference techniques to effectively identify and address hidden discrimination.

NOTES

1. *Demographic Parity > 0.1 indicates significant bias. Measures absolute difference in approval rates. DIR < 0.8 indicates adverse impact; DIR > 1.25 indicates favorable impact relative to Not Hispanic applicants*
2. Disparate Impact refers to the deviation from statistical parity in predictions, measured by the ratio of the probability of a positive classification for different subgroups within a demographic group.

REFERENCES

Adewale, G.T. Umavezi, J.U. & Olukoya, O. (2022). Innovations in lending-Focused FinTech: Leveraging AI to Transform Credit Accessibility and Risk Assessment.

Barocas, S. & Selbst, A.D., (2016). Big data's disparate impact. *California Law Review*, 104(3), pp.671–732. https://doi.org/10.2139/ssrn.2477899

Bartlett, R., Morse, A., Stanton, R., & Wallace, N. (2019). Consumer-lending discrimination in the fintech era. *Journal of Financial Economics*, 143(1):30–56. https://doi.org/10.1016/j.jfineco.2021.05.047

Benjamin, R. (2019). *Race After Technology: Abolitionist Tools for the New Jim Code*. Political Press.

Berg, T., Burg, V., Gombović, A., & Puri, M. (2020). On the rise of fintechs – credit scoring using digital footprints. *Review of Financial Studies*, 33(7):2845–2897. https://doi.org/10.1093/rfs/hhz099

Binns, R. (2018). Fairness in machine learning: Lessons from political philosophy. *Proceedings of the 2018 Conference on Fairness, Accountability and Transparency*, 149–159.

Chouldechova, A. (2017). Fair prediction with disparate impact: A study of bias in recidivism prediction instruments. *Big Data*, 5(2), 153–163.

Consumer Financial Protection Bureau (CFPB), (2023). CFPB issues guidance on credit denials by lenders using artificial intelligence. [online] *Consumer Financial Protection Bureau.* Available at: https://www.consumerfinance.gov/about-us/newsroom/cfpb-issues-guidance-on-credit-denials-by-lenders-using-artificial-intelligence/.

Crenshaw, K. (1991). Mapping the margins: Intersectionality, identity politics, and violence against women of color. *Stanford Law Review*, 43(6):1241–1299. https://doi.org/10.2307/1229039

Federal Reserve Bank. (2023). Quarterly report on household debt and credit. Retrieved from https://www.federalreserve.gov/

Home Mortgage Disclosure Act (HMDA) | FFIEC. Available at: https://www.ffiec.gov/data/hmda (Accessed: 12 July 2025).

Kearns, M. & Roth, A., (2020). The ethical algorithm: The science of socially aware algorithm design. Oxford: Oxford University Press.

Kim, P.T. (2020). Data-driven discrimination at work. *William & Mary Law Review*, 58(3):857–936.

Mhlanga, D. (2021). Financial inclusion in emerging economies: The application of machine learning and artificial intelligence in credit risk assessment. *International Journal of Financial Studies*, 9(3):39.

Nannini, L., Balayn, A. & Smith, P., (2023). Explainability and policy alignment in high-stakes AI. *arXiv preprint arXiv*:2304.11218. https://doi.org/10.48550/arXiv.2304.11218

Office of Science and Technology Policy (OSTP), (2022). Blueprint for an AI bill of rights: Making automated systems work for the American people. [online] The White House. Available at: https://bidenwhitehouse.archives.gov/ostp/ai-bill-of-rights/

Pasquale, F. (2015). The Black Box Society: The secret algorithms that control money and information. Harvard University Press.

Piacentino, L., (2025). The transformative role of artificial intelligence in financial decision-making: Main applications in corporate and personal finance, impacts and future prospects (Doctoral dissertation, Politecnico di Torino).

Rothstein, R. (2017). The color of law: A forgotten history of how our government segregated America. Liveright Publishing.

Sudjianto, A. & Zhang, A., (2024). Model validation practice in banking: A structured approach for predictive models. *arXiv preprint arXiv*:2410.13877

Wachter, S., Mittelstadt, B., & Floridi, L. (2017). Why a right to explanation of automated decision-making does not exist in the general data protection regulation. *International Data Privacy Law*, 7(2):76–99. https://doi.org/10.1093/idpl/ipx005

Moving Towards Sustainable Businesses and Developing More Resilient Economies – Rashid and Annansingh-Jamieson (Eds)

Integrating artificial intelligence in IT project management: A review of tools, techniques, and use cases

Kh Maksudul Hasan
Management Department, St Francis College, Brooklyn, New York, USA

Md Sazzad Hossen
Technology Management, University of Arkansas Pulaski Technical College, North Little Rock, Arkansas, USA

Ariful Islam
Business Analytics and Systems, University of Bridgeport, Bridgeport, Connecticut, USA

Al Akhir
The Ernest C. Trefz School of Business, University of Bridgeport, Bridgeport, Connecticut, USA

ABSTRACT: This PRISMA-guided systematic review examines AI adoption in IT project management using data from Scopus, Web of Science, and Google Scholar, as well as industry data from 2018 to 2025. The findings indicate that tools like Asana, Monday.com, and Jira can improve efficiency by 12% to 40% and reduce failures by 25%. Although a 2021 McKinsey study noted that 65% of project managers intended to implement AI within 3 to 6 months, evidence of returns on investment is limited. The study's findings revealed major obstacles, including data silos, difficulties in integrating legacy systems, resistance to change, and costs associated with adopting AI in IT project management. We proposed the SAFE-PM framework to facilitate human-AI partnerships, support the integration of legacy systems, and promote sustainability accounting through the EcoResilience Ratio (ERR). This approach aims to strike a balance between operational efficiency and environmental impact, while promoting ethical governance.

Keywords: AI, IT, Project Management, Sustainability, Systematic Literature Review, SAFE-PM

1 INTRODUCTION

1.1 *Crisis of complexity in IT projects*

Historically, IT projects have faced significant challenges, particularly the trifecta problem of budget overruns, missed deadlines, and poor-quality products. Traditional project management (PM) methodologies tend to be relatively rigid and linear (Tanim and Ahmad 2025). Consequently, organisations struggle to keep pace with changing risks and diverse stakeholder needs. Hosseini and Seilani (2025) noted that artificial intelligence (AI) has emerged as a strategic imperative in recent years, with generative models and autonomous agents becoming increasingly capable of automating repetitive tasks, generating insights, and increasing productivity. Industry forecasts suggest that by 2030, 80% of project

 DOI: 10.1201/9781003647300-26

management will involve the use of AI, resulting in unprecedented efficiency and improved project management outcomes (Gartner 2019).

1.2 *AI-PM evidence gap*

According to a global survey by PwC and IPMA, 65% of project managers have either initiated an AI implementation plan or scheduled one within 3 to 6 months (Figure 1); however, only 23% have utilised AI in project management (IPMA 2021).

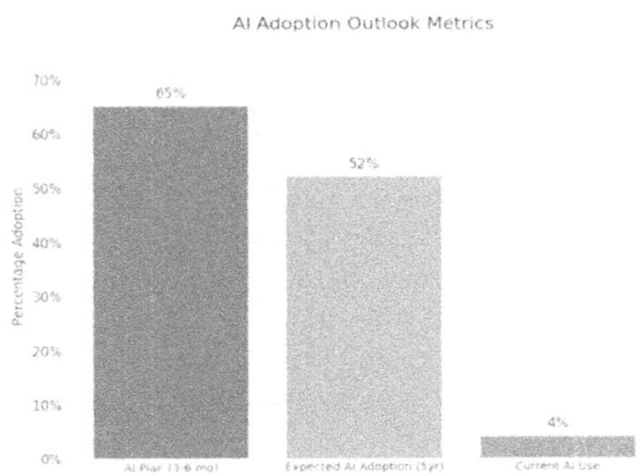

Figure 1. AI adoption metrics in project management (Adopted from IPMA 2021).

Yet, amidst rapid vendor innovation, industry projections, and managerial enthusiasm, studies indicate that the promise of AI-driven efficiency collides with the possibility of poor adoption outcomes and a void in empirical evidence of return on investment (Hunady 2025). This crisis presents an evidence vacuum and a perpetual cycle of speculative adoption, where vendor hype often eclipses empirical validation. Trinh *et al.* (2024) pointed out the immense potential of AI to revolutionise IT project management, but further warned that when left unchecked, the integration could lead to a myriad of challenges, including heightened resource consumption and energy demand, as well as issues of algorithmic bias. To replace hype with evidence, the study aims to address the following research question:

- RQ1: What are the prominent AI tools in IT project management?
- RQ2: What empirical evidence exists regarding the impact of AI tools on key IT project delivery metrics and sustainability?
- RQ3: What are the existing technical and organisational barriers that limit AI adoption, and what framework can be proposed to address these barriers with suitable ethical oversight and sustainability accounting?

2 LITERATURE REVIEW

The integration of AI into IT project management has evolved from a theoretical discussion to a necessary practice (Martins 2023). It has evolved from early rule-based systems (2018–2021), basic natural language processing (2022-2024), to generative AI and autonomous agents, which enable flexible scheduling, automatic content creation, and proactive monitoring of projects.

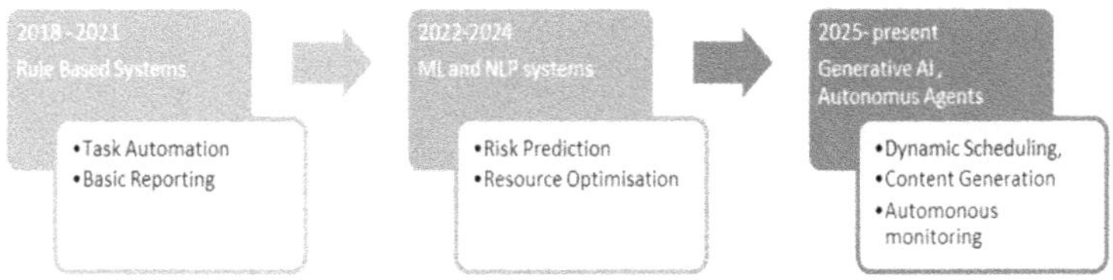

Figure 2. Evolution of AI in project management.

The use of generative AI models, such as GPT-4, for historical data analysis, market trends, feasibility analysis, and scope definition has been discussed in several studies (Barcaui and Monat 2023). In the planning stage, ML algorithms are gaining adoption in predicting timelines and resource needs by finding patterns in both past data and current constraints (Aggrawal and Thomas 2024). According to Pereira *et al.* (2024), although very few PMs understand the capabilities and potential of AI agents, over 79% of them hope to find helpful AI agents for support in project management. Given the growing ability of AI agents to track project progress, spot deviations, and identify potential problems in real-time, AI agents are poised to gain increased adoption in execution and monitoring (Pereira *et al.* 2024). Table 1 presents a comparison of prominent AI tools, including Wrike and ClickUp AI (Ivanova 2024).

Table 1. Comparison of prominent AI project management tools.

Tool	Core AI Capabilities	Primary Use Cases	Key Industries	URL
ClickUp AI	Task automation, predictive risk	Centralised project tracking	IT, Healthcare	clickup.com
Wrike	Risk prediction, resource alerts	Risk/resource optimisation	IT, Healthcare	wrike.com
Monday.com	Risk analysis, bug categorisation	DevOps/Compliance workflows	IT, Healthcare	monday.com
Asana	Task prioritisation, smart routing	Cross-functional project execution	IT, Healthcare	asana.com
Notion AI	Autofill, knowledge management	Collaborative documentation	IT, Healthcare	notion.com
Trello	Automation (Power-Ups), AI integrations	Visual team coordination	IT, Healthcare	trello.com
MS Project	Predictive scheduling, risk analytics	Complex project management	IT, Healthcare, Const.	Microsoft.com/project
Airtable	AI data automation	Structured data tracking	IT, Healthcare, Research	airtable.com
Jira	Predictive issue tracking	Software development lifecycle	IT, Healthcare, Tech	atlassian.com

Similarly, in non-IT fields such as healthcare project management, AI is being increasingly utilised for tasks like predicting patient care needs, enhancing operational workflows, and managing clinical projects (Wilson *et al.* 2021). However, healthcare AI projects face unique challenges, particularly regarding data privacy, diverse stakeholders, regulations (e.g., FDA), and the need for clinical validation (Lämmermann *et al.* 2024). In contrast, IT project management often focuses on operational efficiency and automation, working with stakeholders who generally have more technical backgrounds, which invariably leads to the smoother integration of AI tools. Despite the potential of AI in IT project management, several barriers hinder the widespread and sustainable adoption of AI.

3 METHODOLOGY

This systematic literature review follows the PRISMA 2020 guidelines to ensure transparency, reproducibility, and minimisation of selection bias.

3.1 *Literature search strategy*

The research methodology follows a multi-source search strategy to identify relevant articles and case studies for the study. The study utilised Scopus, Web of Science, and Google Scholar, as well as industry insights from PMI and McKinsey (Table 2).

Table 2. Search Query for different databases.

Database	Search String
Scopus	TITLE-ABS-KEY(((“artificial intelligence” OR “AI” OR “machine learning”) AND (“project management” OR “software development”) AND ((“tool adoption” OR “ROI” OR “cost savings”) OR (“technical barriers” OR “data quality” OR “system integration”))) AND PUBYEAR > 2017 AND PUBYEAR < 2026
Web of Science	TS=((“artificial intelligence” OR “AI” OR “machine learning”) AND (“project management” OR “software development”) AND ((“tool adoption” OR “ROI” OR “cost savings”) OR (“technical barriers” OR “data quality” OR “system integration”))) AND PY=(2018-2025)
Google Scholar	(“artificial intelligence” OR “AI” OR “machine learning”) AND (“project management” OR “software development”) AND ((“tool adoption” OR “ROI” OR “cost savings”) OR (“technical barriers” OR “data quality” OR “system integration”))

3.2 *Eligibility criteria*

Table 3 shows specific inclusion and exclusion criteria established for the study.

Table 3. Inclusion criteria for the study.

Category	Criteria
Study Type	Empirical studies (case studies, experiments, surveys), systematic reviews, peer-reviewed technical reports, as well as independently audited industry whitepapers (e.g., McKinsey, Gartner)
Focus	AI, machine learning, and generative AI in IT and software project management contexts (e.g., agile teams, DevOps, software delivery lifecycle)
Metrics	Reports quantitative project metrics (schedule variance, defect density, ROI) OR qualitative insights on adoption barriers/sustainability trade-offs, Tools, as well as best practices
Publication Source	Peer-reviewed journals, conference proceedings, industry reports from established firms (McKinsey, PMI, Gartner), and government/NGO technical reports.
Timeframe	January 2018 – April 2025.

3.3 *Study selection process*

The selection process of this study, following the PRISMA 2020 four-phase flow, is presented in Figure 3.

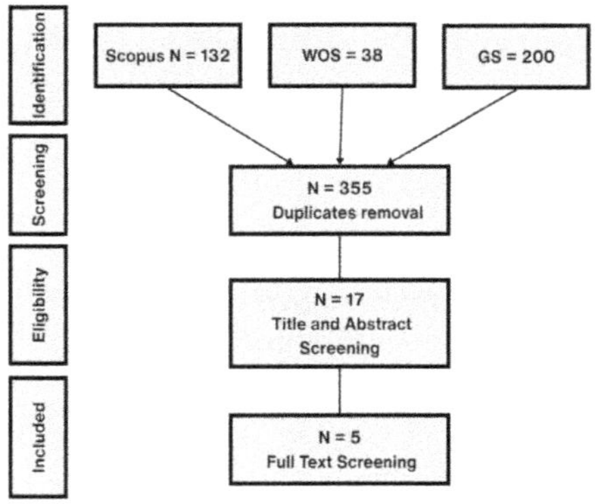

Figure 3. PRISMA methodology for the study.

4 RESULTS

4.1 *Study characteristics and overview*

The analysis identified five strong studies from 2024 to 2025. These studies employed various methods, ranging from experimental design to systematic literature reviews, case studies, and mixed-method approaches, and provided solid evidence for integrating AI in IT project management. The study sizes varied, ranging from controlled experiments to large-scale projects that tracked over 12,424 issues over extended periods.

4.2 *Prominence and Effectiveness of AI tools in IT project management*

AI Tool Adoption, Performance and Barriers: The studies suggest that several tools have gained prominence in IT project management (Table 4 and Figure 4), offering various functionalities, including task automation, real-time monitoring, predictive analytics, data visualisation, and fully integrated project management.

Table 4. Key Findings from selected studies.

Aspect	Key Findings
Popular IT Project Management Tools	Asana, Jira, Monday.com, Wrike, eazyBI, Tableau, Power BI, Clickup offer automation, real-time monitoring, predictive analytics, and visualization (Dwivedi *et al.* 2021).
AI-Powered Platform Performance	Jira: 49% task completion, 90% auto task assignment, 51% unresolved issues; Monday.com: 95% task automation; Asana: 20% full and 30% partial automation. (Das *et al.* 2025)
Strategic Decision-making Impact	AI tools reduced project failures by 25%; improved sprint planning by 30%; cut infrastructure costs by 40%; reduced delays by 35%.
Case Study Outcomes	A multinational bank improved deadline adherence by 30%; a tech company optimized cloud resource allocation with reinforcement learning, saving costs and enhancing system stability.
Barriers to AI Integration	Salimoghadam *et al.* (2025) identified integration with legacy systems as primary technical issue due to complexity and data silos. Thirumal *et al.* (2024) highlight financial barriers from upfront costs (training, hardware/software, infrastructure). Data quality and completeness are critical, with poor data causing inaccurate AI predictions and weak decisions

(*continued*)

Table 4. Continued

Aspect	Key Findings
	(Ding and Li 2018). Human factors such as cultural resistance (Hashfi and Raharjo 2023)
Environmental Impact Gap	Limited studies on AI's environmental impact in IT project management despite rising use (2018–2025). Training foundational models consumes massive energy (e.g., GPT-3 ~1,287 MWh) and generates significant CO_2 (192 lbs per Transformer model; up to 626,155 lbs in neural architecture search) (Tabbakh *et al.* 2024; Strubell *et al.* 2019)

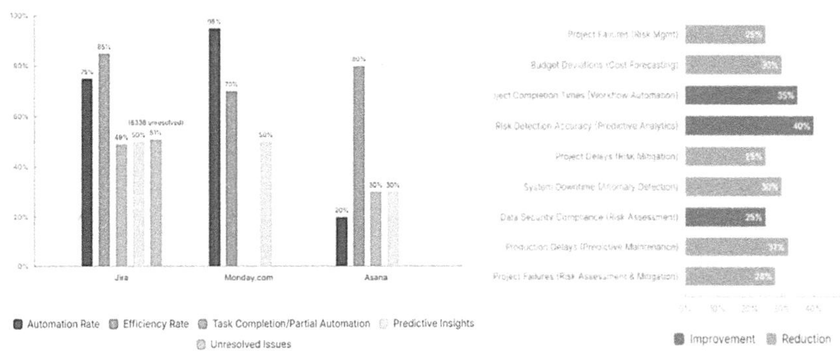

Figure 4. Comparison and empirical outcomes of AI Project management tools (2024 – 2025).

4.3 *Barriers, challenges and best practices*

Some recommended best practices, as presented in the studies, are listed in Table 5.

Table 5. Challenges and best practices.

Challenges	Description	Best Practices	Benefits
Technological Barriers	Integrating AI with existing systems, poor data quality to Hossain *et al.* (2024)	Prioritise Data Governance	25-40% efficiency gains, 32% reduction in AI scheduling errors
Financial Limitations	High upfront investments	Phased Integration, Pilot Programs	Reduced risk, refined workflows
Human Resistance	Fears of job loss, lack of AI understanding	Change Management, Stakeholder Engagement	Smoother adoption, increased ROI
Sustainability	Environmental impact of AI	Embed Sustainability in Procurement and Operations	Reduced carbon footprint, transparent vendor assessment

5 SUSTAINABILITY ADAPTIVE FRAMEWORK FOR ETHICAL PROJECT MANAGEMENT WITH AI (SAFE-PM)

The systematic review reveals a significant gap in the IT project management (ITPM) literature, as there is no comprehensive framework that addresses operational efficiency, human-AI collaboration, and sustainability in the adoption of AI. Current models, such as PMBOK 7, Agile-AI hybrids, and AI maturity models (AIMM), tend to be fragmented (Fukas *et al.* 2021). They focus on task automation but overlook challenges related to legacy integration, ethical governance, and environmental responsibility. The SAFE-PM Framework, or Sustainability-Adaptive Framework for Ethical Project Management with AI, aims to fill this gap (Figure 5).

5.1 *Theoretical underpinnings and core principles*

Structuration Theory (Kolasi 2020): AI and a company's rules need to adapt to each other. Socio-technical Systems Theory (Abbas and Michael 2025): Technology (like AI) and people (like teams) must work together smoothly. Ecological Modernisation Theory (Gibbs 2017): Technology should be used to make projects more efficient without harming the environment.

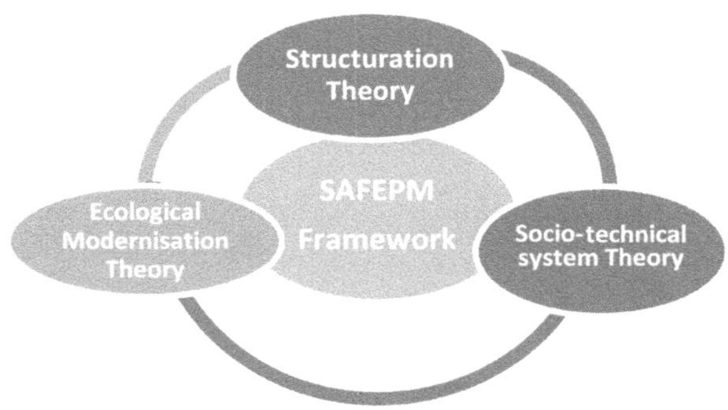

Figure 5. Proposed SAFE-PM framework.

5.2 *SAFE-PM principles*

Contextual Sovereignty: AI autonomy is situational. High-risk decisions (such as ethical judgments and stakeholder conflicts) are typically delegated to human project managers, while repetitive tasks (such as schedule optimisation and anomaly detection) utilise AI.

Legacy-Inclusive Design: Overcome integration barriers using "wrappers" (APIs, middleware) to translate between legacy systems and modern AI.

Embedded Sustainability Accounting: Environmental impact (energy, carbon, e-waste) is a core Key Performance Indicator monitored in real-time.

Negotiated Resilience: Balance economic benefits against ecological costs using the EcoResilience Ratio (ERR).

5.3 *Component architecture & cycles*

Cycle 1: *Symbiosis (Human-AI Co-Evolution)*

A dynamic role allocation engine assigns task "sovereignty" based on context, risk, and ethics, allowing AI Autonomy as well as human override. Performance feedback refines allocation, raising the Symbiosis Index (SI) (percentage of tasks correctly reassigned).

Cycle 2: *Adaptivity (Legacy Integration & Learning)*

Uses containerised APIs and data harmonisation layers to integrate legacy systems. Success is tracked with the Legacy Adaptivity Score (LAS):

$$\mathbf{LAS} = (\mathbf{1} - (\mathbf{Failed\ Integration\ Events/Total\ API\ Calls})) \times \mathbf{100}$$

Cycle 3: *EcoResilience (Sustainability & Economic Balance)*
A Green AI Impact auditor estimates environmental impact. These metrics feed a Risk-Sustainability Tradeoff Optimiser that computes the EcoResilience Ratio (ERR):

$$\text{ERR} = (\text{Economic Value Gain})/(\text{Environmental Impact} + \text{Social Risk Cost})$$

Table 6. Key metrics and proposed timeline in the SAFE-PM framework.

Pillar	Metric	Calculation	Timeline	Key Actions
Symbiosis	Symbiosis Index (SI)	(Correct Auto-Reallocations / Total Context-Shift Tasks) × Ethical Weight	Months 1-6	Deploy to 10 teams; map a Sovereignty matrix target >75% Symbiosis Index (SI).
Adaptivity	Legacy Adaptivity (LAS)	(1 - (Integration Failures / Total API Calls)) × 100	Months 7-18	Scale to 50 teams using containerised APIs; target >90% Legacy Adaptivity Score (LAS).
Sustainability	Carbon Intensity (CI)	$kgCO_2e$ per AI-Driven Task Output (Tiers 1-3)	Months 19-30	Roll out to 100+ teams; integrate carbon accounting; optimize using EcoResilience Ratio (ERR).
EcoResilience Ratio (ERR)	ERR	(Cost Savings + Schedule Gain) / (CI + Social Risk)		

Recent industry estimates suggest that implementing an AI-enabled system, such as the SAFE-PM framework, which includes software licensing, system integration, initial setup, and training, typically costs between $100,000 and $500,000 for mid-sized projects. This amount varies based on the complexity and scope (Walturn 2024).

6 CONCLUSION

This literature review confirms AI‘s potential in IT project management, demonstrating 12-40% improvements in efficiency, risk detection, and cost control. However, significant barriers remain, including implementation costs, data quality issues, and a critical oversight of environmental impacts, such as AI's substantial energy consumption. To address this, we propose the SAFE-PM framework, which introduces three core innovations: a dynamic human-AI task allocation system measured by a Symbiosis Index; legacy integration scaffolds to overcome technical debt; and a built-in sustainability auditor that uses an EcoResilience Ratio (ERR) to ensure efficiency gains do not come at an excessive environmental cost. SAFE-PM thus transforms AI from a fragmented tool into a holistic system that delivers measurable economic and ecological resilience.

REFERENCES

Abbas, R., Michael, K., (2025) *Socio-Technical Theory: A Review*, in: Papagiannidis, S. (Ed.), *TheoryHub Book*.

Aggrawal, S., Thomas, P., (2024). *Investigating the Industry Perceptions and Use of AI Tools in Project Management: Implications for Educating Future Engineers.* https://doi.org/10.18260/1-2–47700

Barcaui, A., Monat, A., (2023). Who is better in project planning? Generative artificial intelligence or project managers? *Proj. Leadersh.* Soc. 4, 100101. https://doi.org/10.1016/j.plas.2023.100101

Das, J., Elegbe, I., Coffie, L., Khadka, R., Chen, L., Ji, Y., IEEE, (2025). AI-Powered IT project management: Analyzing the Effectiveness of Advanced Project Management Tools to Ensure Project Efficiency,

in: University System of Georgia. Presented at the southeastcon 2025, pp. 1554–1559. https://doi.org/10.1109/SOUTHEASTCON56624.2025.10971718
Ding, J., Li, X., (2018). *An Approach for Validating Quality of Datasets for Machine Learning*. https://doi.org/10.1109/BigData.2018.8622640
Dwivedi, Y.K., Skandali, D., Magoutas, A., Tsourvakas, G., *others*, (2021). Artificial Intelligence (AI): Multidisciplinary perspectives on emerging challenges, opportunities, and agenda for research, practice and policy. *Int. J. Inf. Manag.* 57, 101994. https://doi.org/10.1016/j.ijinfomgt.2019.08.002
Fukas, P., Rebstadt, J., Remark, F., Thomas, O., (2021). *Developing an Artificial Intelligence Maturity Model for Auditing*.
Gartner, (2019). Gartner Says 80 Percent of Today's Project Management Tasks Will Be Eliminated by 2030 as Artificial Intelligence Takes Over. *Gart. Newsroom*.
Gibbs, D., 2017. Ecological Modernization. https://doi.org/10.1002/9781118786352.wbieg0434
Hashfi, M.I., Raharjo, T., (2023). Exploring the challenges and impacts of artificial intelligence implementation in project management: A systematic literature review. *Int. J. Adv. Comput. Sci. Appl. IJACSA* 14, 366–375 ; Note: End page is estimated; adjust if known.
Hossain, Q., Hossain, M.A., Nizum, M.Z., naser, S., (2024). *Influence of Artificial Intelligence on Customer Relationship Management (CRM)* 16, 653–662.
Hosseini, S., Seilani, H., (2025). The role of agentic AI in shaping a smart future: A systematic review. *Array* 26, 100399. https://doi.org/10.1016/j.array.2025.100399
Hunady, J., (2025). *Factors Affecting Adoption of Artificial Intelligence in SMEs and its Impact on Firm's Skills Needs*. https://doi.org/10.5281/zenodo.14693236
IPMA, (2021). Report: More than half of project management professionals see the adoption of Artificial Intelligence in their profession [online]. URL https://ipma.world/report-more-than-half-of-project-management-professionals-see-the-adoption-of-artificial-intelligence-in-their-profession-in-the-next-5-years/
Ivanova, N., (2024). 10 AI project management tools every team needs [Online. URL https://instituteprojectmanagement.com/blog/10-ai-project-management-tools-every-team-needs
Kolasi, K., (2020). *Structuration Theory*. https://doi.org/10.1007/978-3-319-74336-3_360-1
Lämmermann, L., Hofmann, P., Urbach, N., 2024. Managing artificial intelligence applications in healthcare: Promoting information processing among stakeholders. *Int. J. Inf. Manag.* 75, 102728. https://doi.org/10.1016/j.ijinfomgt.2023.102728
Martins, M., (2023). Project management evolution: From traditional IT implementations to AI-Driven projects. *Int. J. Sci. Res. Manag. IJSRM* 11, 5011–5028. https://doi.org/10.18535/ijsrm/v11i07.em03
Pereira, L., Nobre, R., Dias, Á., d, R., Costa, a, Gonçalves, R., (2024). Artificial intelligence and project management: exploring the contributions and implications. *Int. J. Logist. Syst. Manag.* 47, 432–467. https://doi.org/10.1504/IJLSM.2024.138916
Strubell, E., Ganesh, A., McCallum, A., (2019). Energy and policy considerations for deep learning in NLP. *Presented at the Proceedings of the 57th Annual Meeting of the Association for Computational Linguistics, Association for Computational Linguistics*, Florence, Italy, pp. 3645–3650. https://doi.org/10.18653/v1/P19-1355
Tabbakh, A., Al Amin, L., Islam, M., Mahmud, G.M.I., Chowdhury, I.K., Mukta, M.S.H., (2024). Towards sustainable AI: A comprehensive framework for Green AI. *Discov. Sustain.* 5, 408. https://doi.org/10.1007/s43621-024-00641-4
Tanim, S., Hussain, Ahmad, M.S., (2025). AI driven strategic decision-making in IT project management: Enhancing risk assessment, cost control, and efficiency. *World J. Adv. Res. Rev.* 25, 247–268. https://doi.org/10.30574/wjarr.2025.25.2.0366
Thirumal, S., Udawatta, N., Karunasena, G., Al-Ameri, R., (2024). Barriers to adopting digital technologies to implement circular economy practices in the construction industry: A systematic literature review. *Sustainability* 16. https://doi.org/10.3390/su16083185
Trinh, E., Funke, M., Lago, P., Bogner, J., (2024). Sustainability integration of artificial intelligence into the software development life cycle, in: 8th *International Workshop on Green and Sustainable Software* (GREENS'24).
Walturn, (2024). The cost of implementing AI in a business: A comprehensive analysis [Online]. URL https://www.walturn.com/insights/the-cost-of-implementing-ai-in-a-business-a-comprehensive-analysis
Wilson, A., Saeed, H., Pringle, C., Eleftheriou, I., Bromiley, P., Brass, A., (2021). Artificial intelligence projects in healthcare: 10 practical tips for success in a clinical environment. *BMJ Health Care Inf.* 28, e100323. https://doi.org/10.1136/bmjhci-2021-100323

Moving Towards Sustainable Businesses and Developing More Resilient Economies – Rashid and Annansingh-Jamieson (Eds)
 ISBN: 978-1-041-08875-2

Generative AI: Ethical governance and strategic innovation

Shokhrukh Komilov
University of Exeter, Exeter, United Kingdom

ABSTRACT: Living in a time and age that is characterized by blistering technological change coupled with an increase in scrutiny on the part of society, innovation is no longer simply an issue of capacity. The paper addresses the aspect of generative artificial intelligence (AI) and ethical governance and how they are transforming the management of innovation based on a comparative case study of two tech giants in the world NVIDIA and Tesla. With the construction of integrated ecosystems in hardware, software, and cloud-based environments (e.g. DGX Cloud, CUDA-X AI), NVIDIA has shifted its business model to AI-as-a-service. Comparatively, Tesla innovation strategy examined through Simplified Innovation Process illustrates the conflict between speed in the production of new products and ethical control.

Keywords: Generative AI, Responsible Innovation, Business Model Canvas, Innovation Governance, Tesla, NVIDIA

1 INTRODUCTION

Today, innovation management transcends the traditional business boundaries and takes a turn as a strategic necessity driven by the relentless technological disruption and societal expectations that are constantly on the rise. The systematic analysis of the emerging technologies, market transformations, and ethical considerations has been conducted throughout the BEMM178 Innovation Management module. In this academic foundation, which is as keen about competitive strategic foresight as it is about technological leadership, success in innovation is not connected to the technological dimension exclusively, nor to the strategic dimension, but also to the relational dimension. In this light, this report tries to further critically assess how two frontier themes, such as generative artificial intelligence (generative AI) and responsible innovation, are remaking the organizational models and innovation processes at work in practice, drawing on two global giants—NVIDIA and Tesla.

Generative AI is the first of the two topics because it is one of the most radical technological shifts of the 21st century. Using advanced large language models such as GPT-4 and GPT-4.5, which are being referred to as generative AI systems, the data that they learn from goes into learning how to produce novel outputs (text, images, designs, etc.) from it (Ransbotham and Westerman, 2023). The creation of these new business models, customer experiences, and operational processes was expedited by this technology.

2 BACKGROUND

2.1 *Justification for topic selection*

The theory prompts the selection of the focal themes of this report, namely Generative Artificial Intelligence (Generative AI) and Responsible Innovation, as they represent the

DOI: 10.1201/9781003647300-27

fundamental matters relating to the evolution of innovation management. Both topics are powerful and complementary forces that are shaping how organizations create value, manage risk, and secure sustainable competitive advantage in a more volatile environment.

Organizations are discovering that generative AI opens a new era in which they can go beyond the analytics of discerning the past into the automation of innovative outputs. Today, such LLM systems, namely OpenAI's GPT-4 as well as Google DeepMind's Gemini (Deepmind, 2024), are driving breakthroughs in every major industry, from drug discovery to entertainment (McKinsey, 2023). According to the report from Gartner (2024), this year, by 2026, more than 80 percent of enterprises will have deployed generative AI applications across business functions, from less than 5 percent in 2023.

Responsible innovation is no longer something to 'add on' to the existing ethical mess but an integral part of a new (process) of innovation. It is now more widely recognized (Stilgoe, Owen and Macnaghten, 2013; OECD, 2023) that the deployment of technology unchecked carries risks of use of data (Salter and Morris, 2013); environmentally destructive effects (Kinross *et al.*, 2012); inequality (Barnes *et al.*, 2012); as well as regulatory backlash and loss of public trust (Coles, 2000; Foray, 2004; for a recent example, see the statement on AI authored by Oxford 21 scientists in October 2023 as they convene for In line with the World Economic Forum (2024), the number provides nearly 70 percent of consumers globally demanding companies showing clear responsibility in how they 'develop and deploy new technologies.'

2.2 *Topics in the context of real-world organisation*

NVIDIA and Generative AI

Generative AI is exemplified in NVIDIA's transformational potential to reshape the corporate strategy and business model design. NVIDIA was always known as the one offering high-performance graphics processing units (GPUs) for gaming and visualization sectors and has pivoted into becoming a leader in AI computing.

Some of the greatest generative AI applications are now powered by NVIDIA's AI infrastructure, including the DGX systems, TensorRT-LLM platforms, and the Omniverse ecosystem. In 2024, NVIDIA's AI-related businesses contributed \$26 billion of its \$26 billion quarterly revenue, or 50 percent of the total, up from less than 10 percent five years before (NVIDIA Annual Report, 2024). Strategic partnerships with OpenAI, Microsoft Azure, and Recursion Pharmaceuticals (the display listed above) have underpinned this transformation.

In addition, NVIDIA's strategic evolution goes far beyond its historical position as a hardware giant and now includes software and AI ecosystem from end to end. By providing access to generative AI capability through Omniverse, DGX Cloud, and CUDA-X AI, NVIDIA has made generative AI democratized and accessible all around the globe for developers, enterprises, and research institutions. Not only is this reflected in the company's positioning in the strategic sense, but also its revenue structure. The figure (Figure 1) illustrates that the data center processors for analytics and AI revenue increased from 25% in 2019 to an astonishing 78% in 2024, while revenues from traditional GPUs for computers also dropped significantly from 53.3% to 17.1% over the same timeframe.

Tesla and Responsible Innovation

The implementation of responsible innovation at Tesla exists as a complex yet persuasive example. As a company devoted to "accelerating the world's transition to sustainable energy," Tesla has accomplished multiple environmental achievements through EV adoption and large- scale battery storage, along with Solar Roof solutions. The customers of Tesla have experienced more than 20 million metric tons of CO_2 emission reduction worldwide since 2024, according to the Tesla Impact Report of 2024.

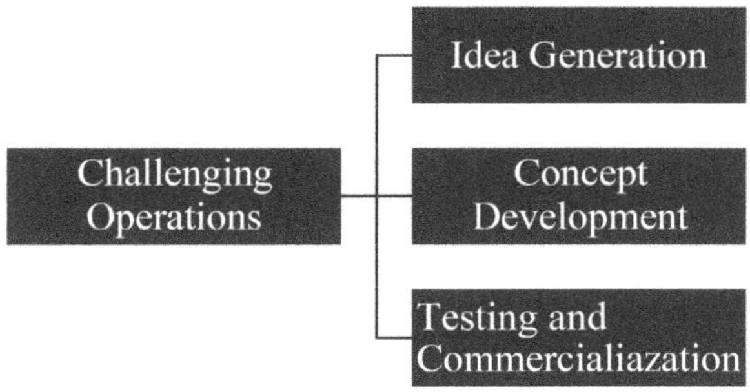

The Simplified Model of the Innovation Process demonstrates the responsible innovation issues that Tesla faces within its various operational sectors. The idea generation stage of Tesla demonstrates occasional poor stakeholder involvement with its emphasis on revolutionary. sustainable technologies. The process of testing and commercialization produced cases such as Autopilot deployment at an early stage that exposed issues concerning public risk communication and transparency (Financial Times, 2024).

3 LITERATURE REVIEW

3.1 *Introduction*

The generation of Generative Artificial Intelligence (Generative AI) is of paradigmatic importance in today's global innovation world. Generative AI goes much beyond automation with systems capable of creating original content, ideas, and designs without human involvement, stated Ransbotham and Westerman (2023). Within this regime, firms like NVIDIA and Tesla are exemplars of technological leadership, but with different innovation philosophies. Critical to the exploration of the role disruptive innovation and responsible innovation play in intermingling with the vanguard of innovation in AI ecosystems lies NVIDIA's strategic repositioning from a GPU maker to an orchestrator of AI ecosystems and Tesla's (bold and, quite honestly, controversial) use of AI in a consumer product.

3.2 *NVIDIA and the strategic evolution of generative AI ecosystems*

Beyond their roots in high-performance graphic processors, NVIDIA has played a significant role in the Generative AI boom. In the past few years, it has become an indispensable enabler for AI research and commercialization through an end-to-end platform comprised of accelerated computing, model libraries, service microservices, and an applications deployment system (NVIDIA, 2024; Westerman, 2023). This is in line with the "AI Stack" formulated by MIT Sloan researchers, who mark this as an era where the future of AI innovation will relate not to the developers of algorithms but rather to those who can dictate the whole innovation infrastructure (Bughin *et al.*, 2023).

By platformizing Generative AI, it also grants strategic advantages in developer lock-in, ecosystem-driven network effects, and market defensibility (McKinsey, 2023). In addition, it introduces ethical challenges as well:

- Algorithmic Bias: Biases may be strengthened by uncontrolled model scaling (Floridi and Cowls, 2019).
- Energy Consumption: Carbon emissions have become an issue when large-scale models are trained on NVIDIA infrastructure (OECD, 2023).

- Data Governance: Ownership issues with training datasets are still not sufficiently resolved (World Economic Forum, 2024).

As NVIDIA continues to support Responsible AI research with growing amounts of funding, critics claim that voluntary initiatives do not suffice in the absence of a structural governance that permeates layers of its ecosystem (Cath *et al.*, 2020).

3.3 *Tesla's approach to disruptive and responsible innovation*

Tesla's trajectory for automotive innovation has been well documented as disruptive. It has made an early adoption in full self-driving (FSD) capabilities, advanced battery management systems, and AI on production optimization entities, a sign of their passion to reshape industries (Jatavallabha, 2024). However, Tesla, having a vested interest in the rapid scaling of its business, often finds itself at odds with responsible innovation norms (MIT Technology Review, 2016).

Applying Stilgoe *et al.*'s (2013) Four Dimensions of Responsible Innovation:

Anticipation	Weak – Limited public forecasting of unintended impacts
Reflexivity	Low – Minimal internal reflection processes published
Inclusion	Weak – Limited third-party ethical auditing
Responsiveness	Reactive – Responses follow public controversies

Therefore, even if Tesla is a prime example of technological audacity, it falls short in integrating responsible innovation procedures during crucial stages of innovation.

3.4 *Comparative insights*

A comparative analysis between NVIDIA and Tesla demonstrates the different strategic ways of running innovation and responsibility management. NVIDIA successfully orchestrates its ecosystem through an infrastructure-led model, which creates pathways for modular ethical interventions across the entire AI development stack (Ransbotham and Westerman, 2023; Bughin *et al.*, 2023). Nvidia can bridge hardware, frameworks, libraries, and platforms, which enables ethical safeguards like bias detection, carbon footprint monitoring, and model transparency audits to be systematically rolled in across layers of the AI innovation stack (NVIDIA, 2024). This matches OECD's (2023) definition of modular governance, which is necessary for large-scale technological deployment.

3.5 *Conclusion*

Based on this literature review, how leading firms NVIDIA and Tesla manage innovation and responsibility challenges in generative AI and disruptive technology is discussed. What is shown by the comparative analysis is that although both companies have made great technological breakthroughs, they are varying greatly in their approaches to responsible innovation, and the different strategic implications generated are important.

4 METHODOLOGY

The methodology used in this study is a comparative, qualitative case study design that attempts to critically pose questions regarding the transformation in the organizational approaches to innovation and ethical governance frameworks that are occasioned by the emergence of frontier technologies, in this case, generative artificial intelligence (AI). The methodological design is theoretically based and exploratory in nature and consistent with immediate traditions whose focus is on contextual interpretation, rather than generalization, being statistically represented by concepts rather than by persons.

4.1 *Analytical strategy*

The review has been developed around three interconnecting theoretical frameworks that are both descriptive and evaluative:

(1) The Business Model Canvas (Osterwalder and Pigneur, 2010) is applied as the model that was reduced to nine canonical blocks to decompose the strategic transformation of NVIDIA as a de facto hardware company to an AI-as-a-service company per the creation, capture, and delivery of value.
(2) Simplified Innovation Process Model (Tidd and Bessant, 2020) was used to evaluate the integrity and responsiveness of the innovation pipeline of Tesla at the stages of ideation, selection, implementation and diffusion.
(3) Responsible Innovation Framework (Stilgoe *et al.* 2013) was used to assess particularly the ethical approaches of both companies by reference to the four defining dimensions: anticipation, reflexivity, inclusion, and responsiveness.

5 RESULTS

5.1 *Introduction to frameworks*

In this section, two foundational frameworks of innovation management are applied to one of the case organizations, Tesla and NVIDIA, respectively, with the Simplified Model of the Innovation Process and the Business Model Canvas (BMC). Innovation is a dynamic, iterative flow through four main stages (Tidd and Bessant, 2020): search, select, implement, and capture, each of the four having two contingent layers of organizational learning, evolving capabilities, strategic integration, and collaboration. On the other hand, the Business Model Canvas (Osterwalder and Pigneur, 2010) allows you to see and analyze how an organization creates, delivers, and takes value at nine interdependent building blocks.

5.2 *NVIDIA and the business model canvas*

5.2.1 *Customer segments*

Strategic expansion into generative AI has brought NVIDIA's customer base to a far greater degree than ever before. Traditionally, segments of the GPU market were made up of gamers and other professionals looking for high-performance GPUs, but these days the market is more segmented by professional content creators, data visualization, AI developers, researchers, enterprise software companies, cloud service providers, and autonomous technology firms. As such, companies like Microsoft Azure, AWS, and Meta, as well as many startups building generative AI applications in the finance, healthcare, robotics, and language technologies industries, NVIDIA is now the AI infrastructure provider of choice.

NVIDIA Offers Differentiated Value to Each Segment

Gamers	**Content Creators**	**AI Developers and Enterprises**
Unmatched GPU Performance and Visual Fidelity	Advanced Graphic Rendering Tools	Integrated AI Solutions through the NVIDIA AI Platform

5.2.2 *Channels*

One of NVIDIA's customer reaches is through both physical and digital distribution channels. Similar to retail stores, physical products such as GPUs are distributed through authorized partners as well as OEM channels. Now, NVIDIA's AI solutions are being delivered increasingly through digital and cloud (e.g., Microsoft Azure, AWS) channels, including directly through its official website and enterprise partnerships. DGX Cloud and NVIDIA AI Enterprise provide organizations with the ability to access NVIDIA's capabilities on demand. With this hybrid channel structure, either the consumer-oriented business or enterprise-scale AI deployment can be supported.

6 DISCUSSIONS

This comparison of NVIDIA and Tesla leads to discovery of two very diverse institutional logics of innovation and ethical responsibility when applied to generative artificial intelligence (AI). As the two companies have an equal position at the technological frontier, a large contrast can be observed in the architectural organization of innovation ecosystems, approaches to involving stakeholders, and anticipatory governance systems.

NVIDIA is an embodiment of a platform-based, infrastructure-led innovation paradigm that is based on the rationale of ecosystem orchestration and modular scaling. Formally, and empirically, this is done with its shift, as a GPU-focused hardware provider, to enabling AI infrastructure and a full-stack through its DGX platform and the CUDA libraries, TensorRT and domain-specific APIs (NVIDIA, 2024; BCG, 2024). This vertical integration has enabled NVIDIA to integrate ethical protections- e.g. auditing on fairness, model explainability policies, and measures of energy-efficiency into their technology stack.

7 CONCLUSION

This report critically examined how the organizations operating in complex, high-stakes industries have been actively changing their strategic architecture and innovation dynamics through frontier innovation (generative artificial intelligence and responsible innovation). However, seeing how it is to innovate today through the 'Simplified Model of the Innovation Process' and how NVIDIA is in business through the Business Model Canvas, innovation today is not a pure linear process dominated by technology. It is; however, a very integrated, sociotechnical process that requires a coincidence between what the organization's business objectives are, collaboration with the ecosystem, stakeholder values, and the long-term societal impact.

NVIDIA is an example of how generative AI is a disruptive technology that completely reorganizes the business logic. NVIDIA used to be an active component-based hardware supply company but now has become a full-stack AI infrastructure provider. The business model has come to a paradigm shift on almost every building block—from who it is serving (AI labs, enterprises, developers) to its new sales streams, which are based around recurring cloud subscriptions and partners. NVIDIA's platform-centric approach—spinning up software, hardware, and AI frameworks—enables it to sprinkle ethical interventions that are modular at various stages of the AI value chain.

On the other hand, Tesla takes a visionary but frisky attitude toward innovation. The Simplified Innovation Process was applied to the company, showing that its search and selection stages are driven by an ambitious mission and principles of first principles thinking, but there is often a lack of ethical deliberation and inclusivity with stakeholders. In areas such as autonomous driving, battery production, and the software for full self-driving, Tesla's fast-scaling strategies have also turned the company to criticism regarding governance, transparency, and accountability after the deployment. Nevertheless, Tesla's model exposes the limits of a disruption-first strategy when reflexivity, inclusion, and anticipation are not fully institutionalized within the innovation architecture.

REFERENCES

Bohnsack, R., Pinkse, J., and Kolk, A. (2014). Business models for sustainable technologies: Exploring business model evolution in the case of electric vehicles. *Research Policy,* 43(2), 284–300. https://doi.org/10.1016/j.respol.2013.10.014

BCG, (2024). Where's the Value in AI? *Boston Consulting Group.* Available at: https://media-publications.bcg.com/BCG-Wheres-the-Value-in-AI.pdf

Bughin, J., Seong, J., Manyika, J., Chui, M. and Joshi, R., (2023). *The State of AI in 2023: Generative AI's Breakout Year. McKinsey & Company.* Available at: https://www.mckinsey.com/capabilities/quantumblack/our-insights/the-state-of-ai-in-2023-generative-ais-breakout-year

Cath, C., Wachter, S., Mittelstadt, B., Taddeo, M. and Floridi, L., (2020). Artificial intelligence and the 'good society': the US, EU, and UK approach. *Science and Engineering Ethics*, 26(5), pp.505–533. https://doi.org/10.1007/s11948-017-9901-7

DeepMind, (2024). Introducing Gemini: Next-generation AI models. Available at: https://www.deepmind.com/blog/introducing-gemini

Financial Times, (2024). US to loosen rules on self-driving vehicles criticised by Elon Musk. *Financial Times,* 26 April. Available at: https://www.ft.com/content/4758aea9-dddd-444e-a1d3-f6fea0e28100

Floridi, L. and Cowls, J., (2019). A unified framework of five principles for AI in society. *Harvard Data Science Review,* 1(1). https://doi.org/10.1162/99608f92.8cd550d1

Gartner, (2024). Hype Cycle for Generative AI, 2024. Available at: https://www.gartner.com/en/articles/hype-cycle-for-genai

Jatavallabha, A., (2024). Tesla's Autopilot: Ethics and tragedy. arXiv 2409.17380. https://doi.org/10.48550/arXiv.2409.17380

McKinsey and Company, (2023). *The Economic Potential of Generative AI: The Next Productivity Frontier.* Available at: https://www.mckinsey.com/capabilities/mckinsey-digital/our-insights/the-economic-potential-of-generative-ai-the-next-productivity-frontier

MIT Technology Review, (2016). *Tesla Autopilot. MIT Technology Review*, 23 February. Available at: https://www.technologyreview.com/2016/02/23/161972/tesla-autopilot/

NVIDIA Corporation, (2024). Annual Report 2024. Available at: https://investor.nvidia.com/financial-info/annual-reports-and-proxies/default.aspx

OECD, (2023). *Responsible Innovation. Paris: Organisation for Economic Co-operation and Development.* Available at: https://www.oecd.org/innovation/responsible-innovation.htm

Osterwalder, A. and Pigneur, Y., (2010). *Business Model Generation: A Handbook for Visionaries, Game Changers, and Challengers.* Hoboken, NJ: Wiley.

Ransbotham, S. and Westerman, G., (2023). The state of AI in 2023: Generative AI's breakout year. MIT Sloan Management Review. Available at: https://sloanreview.mit.edu/article/the-state-of-ai-in-2023-generative-ais-breakout-year/

Stilgoe, J., Owen, R. and Macnaghten, P., (2013). Developing a framework for responsible innovation. *Research Policy*, 42(9), pp.1568–1580. https://doi.org/10.1016/j.respol.2013.05.008

Tesla, Inc., (2024). Impact Report 2024. Available at: https://www.tesla.com/ns_videos/2023-tesla-impact-report-highlights.pdf

Tidd, J. and Bessant, J., (2020). *Managing Innovation: Integrating Technological, Market and Organisational Change.* 6th ed. Hoboken, NJ: Wiley.

World Economic Forum, (2024). *Shaping Tomorrow: Responsible Innovation for a Brighter Future.* Geneva: WEF. Available at: https://www.weforum.org/publications/shaping-tomorrow-responsible-innovation-for-a-brighter-future/

Moving Towards Sustainable Businesses and Developing More Resilient Economies – Rashid and Annansingh-Jamieson (Eds)
© 2026 The Author(s), ISBN: 978-1-041-08875-2

Design and deployment of a fuel logistics information system

Mohamed Loutis
Sorbonne Université, Paris, Île-de-France, France

Esma Aïmeur
Université de Montréal, Montreal, Quebec, Canada

ABSTRACT: This paper presents a centralized information system for managing fuel logistics processes. Designed to overcome the limitations of conventional SCADA and decentralized supply chains, the platform integrates Industry 4.0 technologies such as IoT and cloud computing to provide end-to-end data integration and real-time visualization across production, supply, replenishment, and marketing stages. It resolves data fragmentation, reduces manual operations, and supports distributed monitoring. Validation results show up to 50% reduction in supply delays, a 70% decrease in manual interventions, and a forecasting accuracy of 95% under simulated scenarios, demonstrating significant gains in transparency, responsiveness, and system resilience.

Keywords: Information systems modeling, Fuel logistics, Supply chain, IoT, Relational database management system, Software deployment

1 INTRODUCTION

Many oil and gas operators still rely on traditional Supervisory Control and Data Acquisition (SCADA) architectures that are fragmented, vendor-locked, or misaligned with current requirements. Recent studies on intelligent decision-support in control rooms and enhanced SCADA architectures that combine advanced visualization, programmable control logic, and Machine Learning (ML) show promising gains in situational awareness and automation at the terminal level (Enemosah 2021; Fang *et al.* 2025; Rashad *et al.* 2022). Empirical work on pipeline operations further emphasizes the role of Industry 4.0 technologies such as Internet of Things (IoT), cloud computing, and Artificial Intelligence (AI) in enabling automated, distributed monitoring (Taifa *et al.* 2025). However, these advances typically address local subsystems rather than providing end-to-end, real-time visibility across the entire fuel supply chain, so data fragmentation and operational inefficiencies persist.

In this context, we design and deploy a centralized digital platform specifically tailored to the fuel logistics process. The system combines a structured relational database with a unified interface that connects refineries, depots, and transport modes. By standardizing data collection, enabling real-time visualization of key indicators, and automating core reporting functions, the platform improves transparency, coordination, and analytics-driven decision-making across the fuel distribution network.

The fuel logistics process follows a structured, sequential flow from production at refineries to final distribution at consumption sites. Production converts crude oil into fuel products that are temporarily stored at loading ramps. The subsequent supply and

 DOI: 10.1201/9781003647300-28

replenishment stages transport fuel from refineries to primary depots and then to secondary depots closer to end users, using a combination of pipelines, maritime shipping, rail, and road to balance flexibility, security, and cost. The final marketing stage delivers fuel from secondary depots to service stations and industrial customers. Depots thus act as critical hubs for intermediate storage, regional redistribution, and demand balancing. Figure 1 summarizes this four-phase flow and the main transport links.

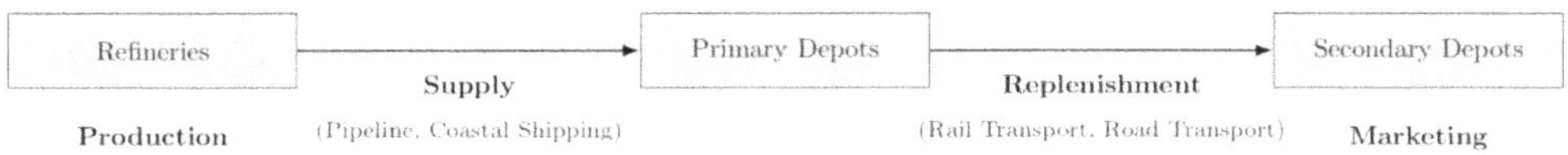

Figure 1. Fuel logistics process from production at refineries to final marketing through a structured flow of supply and replenishment.

At each stage, the process generates critical data, including stock volumes, transport timings, delivery confirmations, and depot occupancy rates, which, in many existing systems, are spread across heterogeneous platforms or collected manually. The proposed platform addresses this limitation by supporting centralized data collection, continuous monitoring, and performance analysis across the entire fuel logistics chain.

2 CHALLENGES AND OBJECTIVES

Although the fuel logistics process is structured around clearly defined stages, several persistent weaknesses limit its performance. A key issue is the lack of integrated, end-to-end visibility: SCADA systems, even when enhanced through advanced electronics and full data visualization (Fang *et al.* 2025), are often fragmented or vendor-locked, preventing real-time insight across facilities. Similarly, many petroleum terminals rely on conventional Programmable Logic Controller (PLC) ladder logic without scalable abstraction layers. Approaches based on Add-On Instructions (AOI) combined with ML classifiers (Gonçalves and Carrilho da Cunha 2021; Rashad *et al.* 2022) highlight that automation remains constrained in flexibility, adaptability, and diagnostic capability. As a result, tracking daily supply operations from refineries to primary depots, monitoring replenishment flows between primary and secondary depots, estimating fuel autonomy, and consolidating real-time reporting across stages all suffer from limited synchronization, transparency, and coordination. These gaps reduce operational responsiveness and undermine strategic planning.

In response, this study aims to design a digital platform tailored to the fuel logistics process, providing a foundation for integrated monitoring, performance evaluation, and strategic planning. The proposed system consolidates operational data from refineries and depots into a centralized interface, offers real-time visibility on storage capacities, stock levels, and transfer operations, and automates the generation of daily operational reports across production, supply, and replenishment. By reducing delays by 50%, improving forecasting accuracy to 95%, decreasing manual interventions by 70%, and lowering manual errors by 40% after deployment, the platform directly addresses the costs and risks associated with manual data entry and decentralized reporting emphasized in supply chain management literature (Chopra and Meindl 2016). At the systemic level, the unified data backbone supports accurate demand forecasting and calibrated safety stock policies (Mardiana 2023), while enabling the integration of IoT endpoints, cloud services, and advanced analytics. Together, these elements create conditions for a more predictive, resilient, and efficiently managed fuel distribution network.

3 SYSTEM DESIGN

3.1 *System architecture and infrastructure*

The proposed system adopts a layered client–server architecture that combines smart field devices with a modern PLC/SCADA stack. Multiple user roles interact with a centralized data server, ensuring unified access, real-time visibility, and secure coordination across refineries and depots. This design follows object-oriented principles and contemporary IoT–SCADA topologies, where edge devices and programmable controllers relay data to centralized or cloud-hosted dashboards for monitoring and control (Ahmed *et al.* 2023). Figure 2 summarizes the client–server topology and the distribution of user roles.

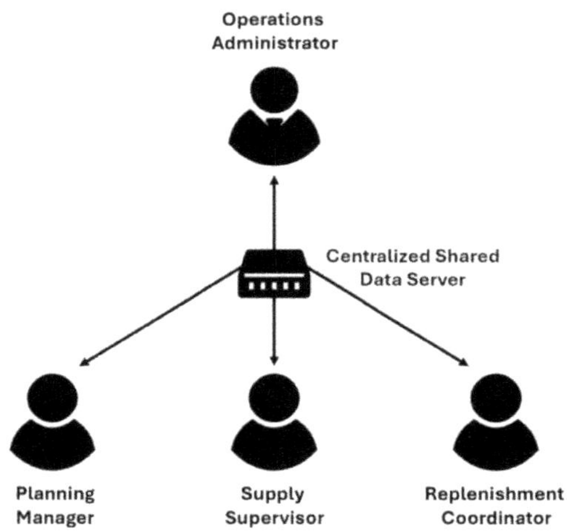

Figure 2. Client–server architecture with distributed roles for monitoring the fuel logistics process.

Four user profiles access the platform: a Planning Manager, responsible for production forecasts and strategic planning; a Supply Supervisor, who creates supply orders and manages transfers from refineries to primary depots; a Replenishment Coordinator, who manages replenishment orders to secondary depots and produces daily operational reports; and an Operations Administrator, who oversees system-wide activities with full access rights for comprehensive performance assessment. At the infrastructure level, a centralized server hosts the relational database, executes application logic, and provides shared services such as reporting and authentication. User workstations serve as terminals for data entry, supervision, and report generation, while industrial-grade networking links these terminals to embedded controllers. PLCs and FPGA-based units ensure deterministic control of fuel-level processes and real-time signal acquisition, forwarding cleaned and time-stamped data to the central platform.

This architecture enables real-time data collection and visualization, centralized and secure storage, and automated generation of daily reports and historical records, thereby improving traceability and reducing manual aggregation. Deploying such an infrastructure entails a non-trivial initial investment in PLCs, networking, and server equipment, as well as skilled personnel capable of integrating AOI logic and SCADA interfaces. However, the platform is designed for scalability and flexibility: cloud-based services and modular database extensions support centralized management of large networks of depots, allowing the system to grow with the infrastructure without compromising performance or data integrity.

3.2 *Conceptual data model*

The Conceptual Data Model (CDM), derived from the European information systems design methodology Merise (Avison 1991; Arab *et al.* 2018), provides a structured foundation that aligns the information architecture with the strategic objectives of fuel logistics. It identifies the main domain entities, formalizes their interrelationships, and specifies the rules governing system behavior.

Following Merise and Soft Systems Methodology (SSM), the model combines two complementary perspectives (Manggiasih and Hidayatno 2023): a static view, which structures information via entity–association diagrams for depots, refineries, products, supply flows, and related objects; and a dynamic view, which captures how users and data flows interact across processes. Together, these views ensure that the database schema and process logic remain consistent with operational requirements. A selection of the most critical data structures is presented below. Table 1 lists the core entities and their attributes, while Table 2 summarizes the main associations and cardinalities between them.

Table 1. Entities and their attributes.

Entity	Identifier	Attributes
Depot	depot_code	depot_name, depot_address, storage_capacity, occupied_volume
City	city_code	city_name
District	district_code	district_name
Depot_type	depot_type_code	depot_type_description
Product	product_code	product_name, product_abbreviation, unit_volume
Refinery	refinery_code	refinery_name, refinery_address
Region	region_code	region_name
Supply_order	supply_order_number	supplied_quantity, supplied_elements_count, start_date, end_date, notes_supply_order
Transfer_Type	transfer_code	transfer_description
Production_Record	production_record_code	production_date, quantity_produced, remaining_quantity
Replenishment_Order	replenishment_order_code	quantity_delivered, delivered_elements_count, cost_per_element, total_cost, loading_date, unloading_date, notes_replenishment_order
Transporter	transporter_code	transporter_name
Movement_Type	movement_code	movement_description

Table 2. Entity associations and cardinalities.

Association	Entities Involved	Cardinality	Attributes
Belongs_to	Depot × City	(1,1) : (1,N)	—
Managed_by	Depot × District	(1,1) : (1,N)	—
Has_type	Depot × Depot_Type	(1,1) : (1,N)	—
Benefits_from	Depot × Supply_Order	(1,N) : (1,1)	—
Includes	City × Region	(1,1) : (1,N)	—
Executed_by	Supply_Order × Transfer_Type	(1,1) : (1,N)	—
Supplies	Supply_Order × Product	(1,1) : (1,N)	—
Sent_by	Supply_Order × Refinery	(1,1) : (1,N)	—
Linked_to	Supply_Order × Production_Record	(1,1) : (1,N)	—
Stores	Depot × Product	(1,N) : (1,N)	stock_quantity

(continued)

Table 2. Continued

Association	Entities Involved	Cardinality	Attributes
Produced_by	Production_Record × Refinery	(1,N) : (1,1)	—
Contains	Production_Record × Product	(1,1) : (1,N)	—
Issues	Depot × Replenishment_Order	(0,N) : (1,1)	—
Receives	Replenishment_Order × Depot	(1,1) : (0,N)	—
Refuels	Replenishment_Order × Product	(1,1) : (1,N)	—
Carried_by	Replenishment_Order × Transporter	(1,1) : (1,N)	—
Performs	Transporter × Movement_Type	(1,1) : (1,N)	—

The relationship constraints expressed as cardinalities in Table 2 define the minimum and maximum connections between entities and provide a precise framework for mapping real-world associations into the database. Data integrity and business logic are enforced through a set of information system rules, including logical constraints on entity behavior and computational expressions for costs, inventory balances, and quantities; these are applied in the implementation but omitted here for brevity. The current CDM assumes that each supply or replenishment order refers to a single product type per transaction and does not explicitly support multi-product or multi-modal shipments. These simplifications enhance model clarity and performance, while leaving room for future extensions as operational requirements evolve.

3.3 *Logical data model*

Following the conceptual modeling phase, the data structure is translated into a logical schema suitable for implementation in a Relational Database Management System (RDBMS). This Logical Data Model (LDM) organizes information into normalized tables with clearly defined primary and foreign keys, preserving referential integrity and supporting efficient querying. Table 3 lists the logical tables of the system, each corresponding to an entity or association derived from the conceptual model.

Table 3. Tables of the logical data model.

Table	Attributes
Depot	***depot_code**, depot_name, depot_address, storage_capacity, occupied_volume, ****city_code**, ****district_code**, ****depot_type_code**
City	***city_code**, city_name, ****region_code**
District	***district_code**, district_name
Depot_type	***depot_type_code**, depot_type_description
Product	***product_code**, product_name, product_abbreviation, unit_volume
Refinery	***refinery_code**, refinery_name, refinery_address
Region	***region_code**, region_name
Supply_order	***supply_order_number**, supplied_quantity, supplied_elements_count, start_date, end_date, notes_supply_order, ****transfer_code**, ****refinery_code**, ****production_record_code**, ****product_code**, ****depot_code**
Transfer_Type	***transfer_code**, transfer_description
Production_Record	***production_record_code**, production_date, quantity_produced, remaining_-quantity, ****refinery_code**, ****product_code**
Replenishment_Order	***replenishment_order_code**, quantity_delivered, delivered_elements_count,

(continued)

Table 3. Continued

Table	Attributes
	cost_per_element, total_cost, loading_date, unloading_date, notes_replenishment_order, ****depot_code_emitter**, ****depot_code_receiver**, ****product_code**, ****transporter_code**
Transporter	***transporter_code**, transporter_name, ****movement_code**
Movement_Type	***movement_code**, movement_description
Stores	***depot_code**, ***product_code**, stock_quantity

***: Primary keys; **: Foreign keys.**

Once this logical schema is defined, it specifies precisely how data is stored and accessed in the database, ensuring that all entities and relationships from the conceptual design are implemented in a consistent and operationally optimized manner.

4 DEPLOYMENT OF THE INFORMATION SYSTEM AS A SOFTWARE APPLICATION

After completing the design phases, namely the system architecture, the CDM, and the LDM, the project moves into deployment, where the relational schema is implemented and connected to a graphical user interface. The application links the database to forms for data entry, processing, search, and reporting, while defining table structures, data types, indexing, and storage constraints to ensure scalability, performance, and consistency. The software is developed in Embarcadero RAD Studio 12.3 (Embarcadero Technologies 2025), using Delphi for object-oriented and event-driven programming. RAD Studio provides visual components for user interface design and seamless database integration, enabling rapid development and high-performance compilation. Microsoft SQL Server 2022 (Microsoft Corporation 2025) is used as the RDBMS, with data operations implemented in Transact-SQL (T-SQL). Stored procedures, triggers, and optimized indexes support secure and efficient real-time processing throughout the fuel logistics workflow. The application is developed and tested on a modern workstation with a multi-core processor and 16 GB of RAM, representative of typical deployment environments. It is a generalized, framework-based application delivered with an empty database that can be customized for specific organizations. The complete source code, which comprises 46 nested windows organized through a structured toolbar, along with deployment and configuration instructions, is available on a public GitHub repository: https://github.com/mloutis/fuel-information-system/.

To ensure long-term reliability and resilience, the platform adopts an information security risk management approach aligned with ISO/IEC 27005 and NIST recommendations (International Organization for Standardization & International Electrotechnical Commission 2022; National Institute of Standards and Technology 2010, 2020). Layered security controls are applied across the application, database, and infrastructure, and SQL Server's Maintenance Plan Wizard is used to configure scheduled backups and documented recovery procedures, following a Defense-in-Depth strategy that maintains service continuity and data integrity. Once deployed, the platform is evaluated against the project's operational objectives through a series of empirical and simulated tests covering data integration, real-time monitoring, automated reporting, stock forecasting, alerting, usability, security, and scalability. Simulated multi-source data injections confirm correct data integration with less than 2% data loss, while virtual event scenarios show that dashboards update within 10 seconds. Automatically generated daily reports match manual references with processing times below one minute per report, and historical data replay yields stock forecasts with a Mean Absolute Percentage Error (MAPE) of 5% or better. Virtual threshold breaches trigger alerts within 30 seconds, usability tests indicate that more than 90% of typical operational tasks can be completed without assistance, and role-based access control tests block all unauthorized actions. Under stress tests with five times the nominal data volume, the system remains stable with response times under three seconds, demonstrating that the platform fulfills its main operational objectives and offers a scalable option for real-world deployment.

5 CONCLUSION

This study presents the design, development, and deployment of a centralized digital platform tailored to fuel logistics in petroleum operations. Built on a structured engineering methodology that spans architecture design, conceptual and logical data modeling, and implementation in Embarcadero RAD Studio and Microsoft SQL Server, the system addresses operational complexity and fragmented data flows by providing real-time monitoring, traceable inventory control, and automated reporting across refineries and depots. Empirical validation confirms that the platform meets its core objectives, with delivery delays reduced by up to 50%, forecasting accuracy around 95%, manual interventions decreased by 70%, and manual errors reduced by 40% under simulated scenarios. These results, combined with multi-layered security and documented backup and recovery procedures, provide a solid foundation for gradually integrating Industry 4.0 technologies such as IoT, predictive analytics, cloud-based services, and AI-driven decision support into increasingly complex fuel distribution networks.

REFERENCES

Ahmed, S., Pathan, A., Sohu, F.K., Shah, S.H., Arain, D.M. and Mangi, R.A. (2023). FPGA-based implementation of SCADA system for fuel management. *QUEST Research Journal* 21(2): 21–28. https://doi.org/10.52584/QRJ.2102.03

Arab, I., Bourhnane, S. and Kafou, F. (2018). Unifying Modeling Language–Merise integration approach for software design. *International Journal of Advanced Computer Science and Applications* 9(4): 6–12. https://doi.org/10.14569/IJACSA.2018.090402

Avison, D.E. (1991). Merise: A European methodology for developing information systems. *European Journal of Information Systems* 1(3): 183–191. https://doi.org/10.1057/ejis.1991.33

Chopra, S. and Meindl, P. (2016). *Supply Chain Management: Strategy, Planning, and Operation* (6th ed.). Pearson.

Embarcadero Technologies. (2025). RAD Studio 12.3 – Press Releases – Embarcadero. Accessed June 26, 2025. https://www.embarcadero.com/press-releases/rad-studio-12-3-released

Enemosah, A. (2021). Intelligent decision support systems for oil and gas control rooms using real-time AI inference. *International Journal of Engineering Technology Research and Management* 5: 236–255. https://doi.org/10.5281/zenodo.15362005

Fang, F., Sun, T., Zheng, M., Feng, Y., Zhang, L., Sun, L. and Wang, W. (2025). Enhancing SCADA systems in oil and gas pipelines through electronics and full data-type publishing technology. *Australian Journal of Electrical and Electronics Engineering* 19(2): 1–11. https://doi.org/10.1080/1448837X.2025.2459491

Gonçalves, M. and Carrilho da Cunha, A.E. (2021). Scheduling tank trucks at a fuel distribution terminal using max-plus model-based predictive control. *Journal of Process Control* 103: 8–18. https://doi.org/10.1016/j.jprocont.2021.05.005

International Organization for Standardization and International Electrotechnical Commission. (2022). ISO/IEC 27005:2022 – Information security, cybersecurity and privacy protection – Guidance on managing information security risks. https://www.iso.org/standard/80585.html

Manggiasih, A. and Hidayatno, A. (2023). Evaluating the conceptual model of the fuel supply chain from terminal to small-scale fuel stations using a Soft System Methodology approach. *In Proceedings of the 2023 IEOM Society Conference*. IEOM Society International. https://doi.org/10.46254/AF04.20230054

Mardiana, S. (2023). Gasoline policy simulation to increase responsiveness using system dynamics: A case study of Indonesia's gasoline downstream supply chain. *International Journal of Energy Economics and Policy* 13(6): 109–118. https://doi.org/10.32479/ijeep.14933

Microsoft Corporation. (2025). Microsoft SQL Server 2022. Accessed June 26, 2025. https://www.microsoft.com/en-us/sql-server

National Institute of Standards and Technology. (2010). *Contingency planning guide for federal information systems* (NIST SP 800-34 Rev. 1). U.S. Department of Commerce. https://nvlpubs.nist.gov/nistpubs/Legacy/SP/nistspecialpublication800-34r1.pdf

National Institute of Standards and Technology. (2020). *Security and privacy controls for information systems and organizations* (NIST SP 800-53 Rev. 5). U.S. Department of Commerce. https://csrc.nist.gov/pubs/sp/800/53/r5/upd1/final

Rashad, O., Attallah, O. and Morsi, I. (2022). A smart PLC-SCADA framework for monitoring petroleum products terminals in Industry 4.0 via machine learning. *Measurement and Control* 55(7–8): 830–848. https://doi.org/10.1177/00202940221103305

Taifa, I.W., Mahundi, R.A. and Mahabi, V. (2025). Exploring the applicability of Industry 4.0 technologies in oil and gas pipeline leakage monitoring: Results from an empirical study. *Journal of Industrial Information Integration* 46: 100857. https://doi.org/10.1016/j.jii.2025.100857

Moving Towards Sustainable Businesses and Developing More Resilient Economies – Rashid and Annansingh-Jamieson (Eds)
 ISBN: 978-1-041-08875-2

Navigating interconnected risks in the creative industry: A case study on the relationship between operational risks and cyber, financial, human, strategic, and reputational risks

A.A.P. Jaquias, G.E. Ceballos, B.T. Melchor, J.A.A. Santiago, E.T. Untalan, J.M. Abad, and J.T. Tenerife
Industrial Engineering Department, Technological Institute of the Philippines, Quezon City, Philippines

ABSTRACT: This study assessed the operational risks of a private creative firm in the National Capital Region of the Philippines. Qualitatively, these risks were placed under six general categories: Operational, Cyber, Financial, Human, Reputational, and Strategic. This classification provided a systematic process of understanding the relationship of the risks that affect company operations. Thematic analysis was conducted on data from in-depth and written interviews with key individuals, which provided significant information on the perception and management approaches used by decision-makers towards these risks. The study showed that human-related risks have the most significant impacts, as the creativity, competence, and inputs of staff are most important in the success and viability of the organization. This study contributes to existing literature regarding risk management. It is especially relevant to industries in developing countries like the Philippines, where such industries might be accorded less priority or attention than more traditional service and manufacturing industries.

Keywords: Advertising, Creative Industry, Risk Interdependencies, System Analysis

1 INTRODUCTION

This study looks at the case of BBX, a creative firm that was established in 2015 in Quezon City, Philippines, and focuses on medical and experiential marketing, hybrid experiences, and end-to-end brand design. BBX strikes a balance between flexibility, hybrid work, and professional development, and the demands of work-life balance, complicated projects, and rapidly changing technologies. It serves both domestic and international clients in a range of industries. The study identifies six interrelated risk areas—operational, cyber, financial, human, strategic, and reputational—supported by thematic analysis and causal loop diagrams based on in-depth and written interviews with creatives, managers, and leaders. Strong risk resilience is necessary for BBX‘s work in branding, events, and digital engagement, particularly since ICT dependence raises operational and cyber risks, client-dependent revenues raise financial risk, brand credibility shapes reputational risk, and employee motivation and skills affect human risk. In the end, the study suggests a systems-based strategy to assist creative companies in anticipating risks and making better decisions.

2 LITERATURE REVIEW

Cyber, financial, human, operational, reputational, and strategic risks are just a few of the risks that organizations must deal with in today's quickly changing business environment in order to maintain performance and sustainability. This review of the literature highlights the

 DOI: 10.1201/9781003647300-29

significance of effective risk management strategies by looking at these risks, their causes, effects, and the role of stakeholders in managing them.

Table 1. Summary of current literature on interconnected risks in the creative industry.

Theme	Key Insights	Representative Studies
Cyber Risk*	Strong cybersecurity and thorough financial risk assessment are necessary because the rise in digital marketing has increased cyber threats due to globalization and new technologies, resulting in an increase in data breaches, ransomware, phishing, and malware.	Kurolov and Esanova (2024)
Financial Risk*	Effective financial risk management enhances profitability, competitiveness, and stability, whereas late customer payments can compromise cash flow and potentially lead to insolvency. ERM enables an organization to effectively identify, make informed decisions about, and proactively allocate resources to specific risks.	Sun (2024)
Human Risk*	Organizations that are talent-based have much to lose when talent is managed badly, resulting in stagnation, reduced innovation, and weak adaptability.	Castañeda et al., (2022)
Operational Risk*	Resolves potential issues in everyday operations, procedures, and systems, usually resulting from human error due to employee action or decision.	Segal (2024)
Reputational Risk*	Most closely tied to operational and stakeholder risk, it encompasses controlling factors like trust and is generally researched in close association with broader risk analysis.	Nobanee *et al.* (2023).
Strategic Risk*	Aligns risk management with strategy by articulating common threats and opportunities influencing strategy execution.	Sharma (2024)
Key Stakeholders*	Accordingly, the governance of operational risk is handled by the CEO and the Operations Senior Manager, while financial risk is managed by the Finance Manager, the CEO, and the CTO. Strategic risk is managed by the CEO, the COO, the CTO, and the CCO. Reputational risk is covered by the CEO, COO, and CCO; cyber risk, by the CEO; and human risk, which covers employee well-being, ethics, and safety, by HR and the CEO.	Mitchell, 2024); Yasmina (2024); Lagace *et al.* (2025)

The six main risk categories—financial, human, operational, reputational, cyber, and strategic—as well as their causes, consequences, and mitigation techniques, are listed in Table 1. Digitalization creates cyber risks, cash flow problems and delayed payments create financial risks, and skill gaps or disengagement create human risks. Daily process mistakes give rise to operational risks, stakeholder trust issues give rise to reputational risks, and misaligned objectives or inadequate technological preparedness give rise to strategic risks. Key executives (CEO, COO, CTO, CCO) and department heads in operations, finance, and human resources oversee risk management.

3 METHODOLOGY

This qualitative case study used IDIs and WIs to investigate organizational risk. Thematic analysis examined lower-level risk factors and interdependencies, with SAMS employed in order to go beyond the typical set of isolated analyses of each individual risk. Capturing dynamic interdependencies among operational, cyber, financial, human, reputational, and strategic risks provides a framework for innovative firms to anticipate compound risks, apply proactive interventions, and strengthen long-term organizational resilience.

3.1 *Participants*

The CEO, COO, CTO, CCO, Finance Manager, Operations Senior Manager, HR Manager, and four male (57%) and three female (43%) senior leaders took part. The central executive team (CEO, COO, and CCO) had ten years of experience, while the other positions had been filled within the previous three years. The ages ranged from 39 to 46.

3.2 *Measures*

Six major risks—operational, financial, cyber, human, strategic, and organizational—were identified, prioritized, and managed throughout the project life cycle using interview protocols for IDIs and WIs. Workflows, quality control, budgeting, funding distribution, negotiating client payments, data security, employee welfare, talent retention, organizational culture, communication, teamwork, competitive positioning, and market flexibility were all covered in the questions. A thorough and proactive approach to risk analysis was made possible by the presentation of intricate risk maps, causal loop diagrams, and system dynamics models using a SAMS framework.

3.3 *Data gathering procedure*

Key personnel from the operations, finance, and executive departments were selected to provide a thorough understanding of organizational risks. Executives managed client relations and strategy, Finance managed viability and resources, and Operations managed partners and project execution. Reputational, operational, financial, human, strategic, and cyber risks were all covered in a structured interview guide. Participants were interviewed either in person or virtually after being chosen based on their areas of expertise and given an overview of the project. The interviews were videotaped, recorded, and carefully analyzed.

3.4 *Data analysis*

This study approach, called thematic analysi,s looks for and analyzes patterns or themes in a dataset, typically yielding fresh data and insights (Naeem *et al.*, 2023). Otter AI, an artificial intelligence-assisted transcription program, was used to transcribe the study's interviews. Thematic analysis was used to code the transcribed IDI data throughout the study in an attempt to find and classify significant trends and themes. To fully immerse themselves in the data, the researchers first listened intently to audio recordings, participant narratives, interview transcripts, and observational notes. In order to create overarching themes, the researchers also arranged recurring themes from different accounts. The systematic review of the data allowed researchers to arrange and analyze the information into important conclusions.

Table 2. Perspectives on the interconnectedness of risks.

Interview Questions	Accounts	Common Themes	Major Themes	Direct Quotes from the Respondents
How does the agency stay competitive in a rapidly evolving experiential marketing industry by differentiating itself	Deep understanding of clients and audiences Innovation, research, and agility	Purpose-driven and market-centric strategy - aligns organizational goals with market needs and societal impact to drive	Strategic client-centered services and specialization in the industry The two aspects align tailored, data-driven solutions	Strategic client-centered services: "We have our own distinct collaboration process and communication frameworks that we

(*continued*)

Table 2. Continued

Interview Questions	Accounts	Common Themes	Major Themes	Direct Quotes from the Respondents
from competitors, evaluating new opportunities amid market uncertainties, and continuously adapting to emerging trends to ensure agility?	Expertise and credibility in medical marketing Operational excellence and scalable growth	meaningful and competitive growth. Strategic investment in people and culture prioritizes talent development and a strong workplace culture to enhance performance and long-term sustainability.	with client needs while leveraging niche expertise and credible talent to deliver high-value, market-specific outcomes.	use with our clients to determine the best communication plan, given the situation they are facing and the current data we have in the market." Specialization in the industry: "It is one of the things you have to understand, but you also have to know that trends may or may not fit your business. So those are the things you have to be cautious about—just because it is trending with another business or client does not mean it will fit yours if you do not check."
How does the company ensure financial sustainability while maintaining high-quality execution amid market fluctuations and client-related challenges?	Financial management Operational excellence Strategic growth Client and revenue management	Financial resilience and budgeting - focused on proactive planning, risk forecasting, and smart budget allocation to ensure long-term stability. Operational excellence and compliance center on tech-driven quality assurance and efficient processes to maintain performance and adaptability.	Market reach diversification and strategic financial management. Involve expanding across sectors while maintaining financial stability through careful budgeting, risk forecasting, and secure revenue practices.	Market reach diversification: "We mitigate financial risk during low-demand periods by maintaining a diversified client base, ensuring a steady flow of projects across sectors. We also build financial buffers through conservative cash flow management and reserve funds." Strategic financial management: "We use forecasting models to project revenues, manage expenses, and identify future cash needs. This allows us to make proactive decisions, such as adjusting

(*continued*)

Table 2. Continued

Interview Questions	Accounts	Common Themes	Major Themes	Direct Quotes from the Respondents
				pricing strategies, reallocating resources, or exploring new revenue streams."
How do employee retention, work setups, and well-being affect your company, and what strategies support mental health, work-life balance, and motivation in a fast-paced industry?	Impact of employee turnover and role disruption Work arrangement and flexibility Culture, engagement, and recognition Employee wellness and mental health support	Holistic employee care and flexible work enhance well-being through mental health, wellness, and balanced work setups. Turnover, role disruption, and engagement – manage changes by boosting engagement to maintain team stability and performance.	Employee well-being and work setup flexibility This theme emphasizes employee wellness through mental health support, positive culture, and flexible work, while addressing turnover, role shifts, and engagement for stability and productivity.	Employee well-being: "Employee well-being is critical to the company's success because our people drive our creativity, collaboration, and client satisfaction. –We believe caring for our employees' mental and emotional health is essential for retention and sustainable, high-quality work." Work setup flexibility: "We focus on building a supportive and transparent culture, maintaining open channels for feedback, and developing policies that are people-first but aligned with business needs."
Why is contingency planning vital for managing unforeseen issues and minimizing risks during large-scale event execution?	Structured execution and contingency planning Team capability and support Continuous improvement	Project preparedness and risk management – Ensures smooth delivery through structured planning and proactive risk handling. Capability building and continuous improvement – Strengthens performance through team growth, mentorship, and ongoing learning.	Operational resilience and performance sustainability Ensure smooth project delivery through planning and risk management, while building long-term effectiveness through team growth and continuous improvement.	Operational resilience: "Regardless of nature, are scheduled and planned out until delivery, are tasked to come up with countermeasures which include but are not limited to extending the workforce through support external manpower, replacing materials with easily accessible assets, etc."

(continued)

Table 2. Continued

Interview Questions	Accounts	Common Themes	Major Themes	Direct Quotes from the Respondents
				Performance sustainability: "Our company approaches large-scale activations with a layered risk assessment process. Each project undergoes a comprehensive pre-production phase and a post-mortem or debriefing."
How does your company protect sensitive client data and secure virtual or hybrid event platforms against cyber threats and unauthorized access?	Data access control and confidentiality Cybersecurity infrastructure and protection Third-party engagement for system integrity	Data security and confidentiality - safeguard information through controls and cybersecurity. System integrity and third-party management - ensures reliability via secure systems and vendor oversight.	Data protection and expert-driven cybersecurity Ensures data safety and system defense through strong protection measures and expert-driven cybersecurity.	Expert-driven cybersecurity: "We hire experts to do it for us. We check their credentials, and they present their risk mitigation strategies to us. We also present that to our clients, and if it meets their requirements, then that is what we go with. It is always about getting the right people with the best experience and qualifications for the job to make the work possible."
How does your company manage client dissatisfaction, negative publicity, and online presence through proactive communication to protect and maintain its reputation?	Transparency and accountability Communication and expectation management Reputation and risk management	Organizational accountability and communication – ensure trust through clear, transparent communication. Brand trust and risk mitigation – safeguards reputation via trust-building, feedback, and issue resolution.	Proactive reputation and relationship management This theme centers on trust and strong client relationships through transparency and early risk management.	Proactive reputation and relationship management: "We try to approach it in the most legal way possible. It is not about managing or exposing anything publicly; it is about being mature, sitting down, having clear meetings with these people, and making sure our side is as clear as theirs."

Thematic Synthesis: *The agency manages interrelated risks through a client-focused, results-driven approach emphasizing creativity and specialist skills. It is financially secure by diversifying in the marketplace, strategically planning, and budgeting in advance. Employee welfare is enhanced by flexible work schedules, mental health programs, and a positive company culture. Careful planning and continuous team building are key components of business resilience. Specialist-led cybersecurity processes and open communication procedures safeguard information security and organizational reputation.*

4 RESULT AND DISCUSSION

IDIs and WIs with stakeholders in leadership, project management, and creative roles were used to collect data. Sub-risk factors and their effects were found through thematic analysis, which guided the creation of CLDs to show how risks are balanced and reinforced. Future system dynamics simulations will use these diagrams as a basis to model scenarios and forecast the evolution of risk.

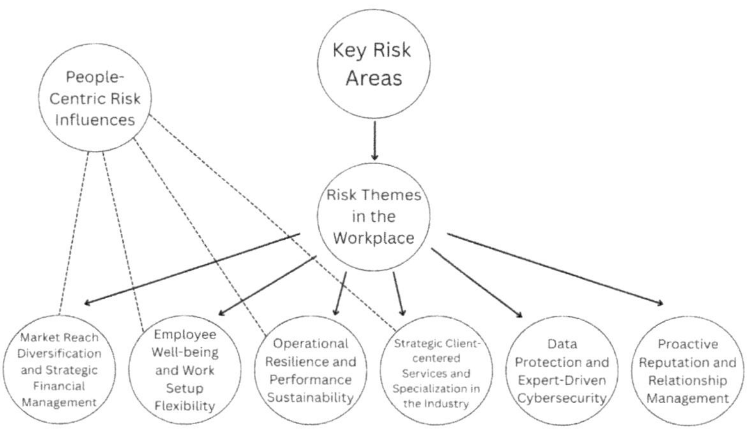

Figure 1. Causal loop diagram of risk themes and people-centric workplace influences.

Workplace hazards in advertising function as a networked system that promotes adaptability, creativity, and long-term success. While sound financial management and cybersecurity stabilize operations and foster client trust, flexible work increases balance, creativity, and productivity. By keeping employees during the 2020 lockdowns, implementing hybrid work, providing subsidies and mental health support, and fostering a flexible, trust-based environment, BBX is a prime example of a human-centered culture. With the help of a matrix-hybrid structure that improves scalability and clarity, it has expanded from six to fifty-two employees since 2015. BBX, which is based on the theory of human capital, employs worldwide specialists and makes investments in staff training to uphold high standards. The agency welcomes positive risk by implementing a "guess-and-test" strategy, launching new services, and reacting to market shifts. BBX's outstanding reputation is a result of its excellent communication, data-driven storytelling, and customer-focused service. Through strategic partners, emergency funds, a diverse clientele, frugal budgeting, and precise forecasting, its financial stability allows it to manage unforeseen circumstances and maintain high-quality results.

5 CONCLUSION

In order to manage the human risks connected with the fast-paced creative industry, BBX invests in talent development, mental health support, and flexible work arrangements because it considers human capital to be its most valuable asset. Collaboration, creativity, and resilience are made possible by the hybrid matrix structure and trust-based culture, which help BBX maintain solid client relationships and deal with outside obstacles like the COVID-19 pandemic. BBX anticipates possible threats and implements proactive mitigating strategies in response with the aid of qualitative risk analysis, scenario planning, and stakeholder input. The foundation for managing interrelated human, strategic, financial, operational, cyber, and reputational risks is the application of system dynamics, agent-based simulations, and network analysis. This strategy is regularly assessed for employee programs by Kuzior, Ober, and Karwot (2022), global adaptation with succession planning by Gillespie and Swan (2022), and financial diversification with emergency fund availability by Chit and Rizov (2023). BBX is able to secure viability, agility, and a competitive advantage in a dynamic and complex industry through such integration.

6 DIRECTIONS FOR THE FUTURE RESEARCH

Future research could compare the efficacy of risk management in niche and non-niche markets using quantitative metrics and look at how various work modalities affect productivity. Increased generalizability and the identification of sector-specific risk patterns can result from more comprehensive geographic and interindustry comparisons. Quantitative metrics such as effect size, probability, and impact ratings can be integrated with qualitative evaluations to improve interpretation while maintaining depth. Feedback-loop identification and decision-making can also be enhanced by using testing tools, such as causal loop diagrams (CLDs), across organizations of varying sizes. The creation of flexible, evidence-based risk management models will result from additional research on financial, operational, market, and human-related risks across various industries and geographical areas.

7 CONFLICT OF INTEREST, DECLARATION OF ETHICAL COMPLIANCE, AND DECLARATION OF AI USAGE

There are no conflicts of interest disclosed by the writers. Every interview was conducted in accordance with ethical standards, and participants were guaranteed confidentiality and informed of their rights. Audio recordings were accessed with consent, and identifiable data was only used for academic purposes. The study's concepts were unaffected by generative AI; AI was only utilized for human-supervised language improvement.

REFERENCES

Castaneda, J.M., Japos, G., and Wenifreda Templonuevo. (2022). Effects of hybrid work model on employees' and staff's work productivity: A literature review. *JPAIR Multidisciplinary Research*, 50(1), 159–178. https://doi.org/10.7719/jpair.v50i1.537.

Chit, M.M., and Rizov, M. (2023). SMEs' diversification of financing sources: Strategy or desperation? *International Journal of Finance & Economics.* https://doi.org/10.1002/ijfe.2822.

Gillespie, K., and Swan, K.S. (2022). *Global Marketing* (5th ed.). Routledge. https://doi.org/10.4324/9781003141709.

Kurolov, M.O., and Esanova, S.U. (2024). Quantifying the impact of cybersecurity risks on digital marketing ROI: A case study analysis. *Lecture Notes in Computer Science*, 387–397. https://doi.org/10.1007/978-3-031-60994-7_33.

Kuzior, A., Ober, J., and Karwot, J. (2022). Employee attitudes towards employee evaluation systems in the utility sector: A case study of sewage and water supply Ltd., Rybnik, Poland. *Sustainability*, 14(19), 12436. https://doi.org/10.3390/su141912436

Lagace, L., Garcia, R., Herrity, J., and Eads, A. (2025). What is a chief creative officer? (With how-to and skills). *Indeed.* https://ca.indeed.com/career-advice/finding-a-job/what-is-chief-creative-officer.

Mitchell, M. (2024). Stakeholder: How Ed Freeman's Vision for Responsible Business Moved From Theory to Reality – Darden Report Online. Darden Report Online. https://news.darden.virginia.edu/2024/05/16/stakeholder-how-ed-freemans-vision-for-responsible-business-moved-from-theory-to-reality/

Naeem, M., Ozuem, W., Howell, K., and Ranfagni, S. (2023). A step-by-step process of thematic analysis to develop a conceptual model in qualitative research. *International Journal of Qualitative Methods*, 22. https://doi.org/10.1177/16094069231205789.

Nobanee, H., Elsaied, F.A., Alhajjar, M., Abushairah, G., and Al Harbi, S. (2023). Reputational risk: A bibliometric review of relevant literature. *Emerging Science Journal*, 7(2), 654–675. https://doi.org/10.28991/esj-2023-07-02-025.

Segal, T. (2024). Operational risk: Overview, importance, and examples. *Investopedia.* https://www.investopedia.com/terms/o/operational_risk.asp.

Sharma, M. (2024). Embracing emerging trends in risk management. *LinkedIn.com.* https://www.linkedin.com/pulse/day-26-embracing-emerging-trends-risk-management-manoj-sharma-ppgjc.

Sun, W. (2024). Research on corporate financial risk management and countermeasures. *International Journal of Global Economics and Management*, 3(1), 59–65. https://doi.org/10.62051/ijgem.v3n1.07.

Yasmina. (2024). Meaning of the acronyms CEO, COO, CMO, CIO, and CTO. *Beyond by Esade.* https://www.esade.edu/beyond/en/c-level-executives-what-do-the-acronyms-ceo-coo-cmo-cio-and-cto-stand-for/

Moving Towards Sustainable Businesses and Developing More Resilient Economies – Rashid and Annansingh-Jamieson (Eds)

Leadership perceptions and strategic readiness: A multivariate and qualitative study on AI figintegration in industry

P. Hernandez, J. Tenerife, J. Flores, J.A. Padullon, M.T. Landicho, R.A. Dela Cruz, M.L. Belen, J.C. Candaza, N.L. Tabasa, and M. Navarro
Department of Industrial Engineering, Technological Institute of the Philippines, Quezon City, Philippines

ABSTRACT: Artificial Intelligence (AI) is transforming industries by enhancing efficiency, user experience, and decision-making. This study examines AI adoption across four key sectors: education, manufacturing, healthcare, and services in the Philippines, National Capital Region (NCR). Using the user gratification framework, it explores how organizational needs influence technology choices. A mixed-methods approach, combining interviews and surveys with 150 leaders and managers, was employed. Thematic and multivariate analyses identified persistent challenges like inefficient data collection, manual processes, limited statistical skills, and poor data visualization. AI tools effectively addressed these issues by improving data management, automation, and digital competence. Structural equation modeling confirmed a strong model fit, while descriptive results showed high consensus on AI's positive impact on operational performance. The study offers insights for leaders, educators, and policymakers aiming to build AI capabilities. It contributes to research on AI adoption, digital transformation, and Industry 4.0 in developing countries, particularly within the Philippine context.

Keywords: Adoption, Artificial Intelligence, Decision-making, Efficiency, Readiness

1 INTRODUCTION

The industry is significantly changing for increased efficiency, innovation, and growth with the emergence of AI. This research concentrates on the insights of executives and managers in the Philippines, specifically in the National Capital Region (NCR). Leaders and decision-makers influence the successful initiation of AI in an organization. It is important to note that their perspective can make or break the successful integration of AI and its impact on strategic planning, operations, and customer satisfaction. Given the tremendous pace at which AI is being adopted, the study is coming from the premise that a comprehensive needs analysis is needed. Without a clear understanding of industry-specific challenges and objectives, AI will never meet critical performance indicators (KPIs) in an organization, which results in operations being disrupted or, in some cases, increased costs. The study uses multivariate and qualitative methods to assess the perceptions of leaders and decision-makers to understand strategic preparedness towards integrating AI across all select industries considered in the study. The study seeks to understand the key needs, perceived limitations or challenges, and AI's potential in ensuring customer satisfaction and goals in specific industries. The current literature suggests that effective AI deployment requires a clear understanding of its boundaries and how it can be applied in modern industries. AI can significantly enhance workplace efficiency by automating tasks, streamlining processes,

DOI: 10.1201/9781003647300-30

managing inventory, and improving organizational operations [1]. Its impact continues to expand across sectors [2], particularly in management, where AI enhances operational performance, supports data collection, and fosters future advancements [3]. These recent works further underscore the significance and potential impact this study can have on organizations nationwide. It will also fill in the gap by providing a guide and a survey tool for identifying industry needs in integrating or enhancing systems with AI.

2 METHODOLOGY AND RESEARCH DESIGN

This study used a mixed-method approach. It combined insights from non-uniform qualitative patterns with quantitative techniques to provide a more complete view of the subject. The first phase involved in-depth interviews with selected industry leaders and decision-makers, chosen for their experience and expertise. These interviews aimed to surface key issues, highlight recurring themes, and draw out practical concerns faced by different sectors, especially within the Philippine context. Afterward, thematic analysis was applied to the qualitative data, allowing the researchers to identify recurring patterns and meaningful themes. These insights guided the development of a structured survey instrument, which was later used to gather quantitative data from a broader group of respondents. This step-by-step process ensured that the survey items were grounded in real-world perspectives and reflected the actual experiences of professionals in the field. The survey was built around specific constructs, which served as key measures in the study (see Table 1). Structural Equation Modeling (SEM) was used to test how these constructs relate and interact.

2.1 *Participants and key informants*

A structured survey was designed and carried out in the Philippines' National Capital Region (NCR). A total of 150 participants from key sectors, 18% Finance and service, 17% manufacturing, 16% Information technology, 10% communication and education, and 4.7% healthcare industry, participated in the survey. Among them, 42% were from lower management, 46.7% from middle management, and 11.3% from top management. This mix allowed the study to capture a well-rounded view of how AI is perceived and approached across different levels of decision-making and operational roles in organizations. For the qualitative part, with a total of 3 interviewees, in-depth interviews were conducted with leaders and key decision-makers from three strategically selected sectors: Information Technology (IT), Heavy Robotics, and Business Process Outsourcing (BPO). These sectors were deliberately chosen because of their strong involvement in AI-related initiatives, making them ideal sources for insights on strategic perspectives and actual applications of the technology in the local context.

2.2 *Quantitative measures and interview questions used in the study*

The study highlighted key developments in the constructs used to assess how people perceive and expect AI to grow. Table 1 shows a breakdown of these constructs and the specific indicators tied to different areas like data handling, AI integration, and user experience. It also outlines significant challenges and improvements observed during the study and how many items were used to measure each construct. Among the recurring issues were: difficulty in collecting accurate and complete data; repetitive manual tasks that are time-consuming and prone to human error; and problems with statistical analysis, especially in understanding and interpreting data correctly.

Table 1. Constructs and measures.

Constructs	Items	Description
Difficulties in Data Collection	7	Challenges in retrieving data, reliance on manual processes, and insufficient training for data collectors.
Repetitive Manual Work	7	Issues with manual tasks are causing delays, inefficiency, fatigue, and decreased motivation among employees.
Challenges in Statistical Treatment	7	Problems in statistical treatment due to manual processes, errors, and handling large volumes of data.
Difficulties in Data Visualization	7	Struggles with interpreting poor data visualizations, lacks creativity, and has insufficient training on visualization tools.
Lack of AI Knowledge & Familiarity	7	Limited understanding and familiarity with AI tools lead to AI adoption and integration challenges.
Challenges in Technology	3	General difficulties related to data handling, statistical treatment, visualization, and AI integration.
Improved Data Management System	7	Benefits of a system that improves data retrieval, processing, and decision-making capabilities.
AI Automation	7	The role of AI in improving monitoring, decision-making, workflow, and overall efficiency.
Improved AI Assistance	7	AI assistance enhances operations, reduces human error, and improves communication and data accessibility.
User-friendly	7	There is a need for AI systems to be intuitive, easy to navigate, and adaptable to user needs.
Requirement	3	Incorporating user requirements into the design and development of AI systems is essential.
Gratification	3	The impact of addressing challenges and user needs on user satisfaction and efficiency improvements.

Note: *The study examines challenges like data collection difficulties, repetitive tasks, and limited AI knowledge. It also highlights solutions, including improved data systems, AI automation, and user-friendly tools. Addressing these issues enhances AI adoption, user satisfaction, and overall efficiency. Based on the IDI with Leaders and Decision-makers.*

Key informants shared several concerns during the interviews. One of the common issues raised was difficulty in visualization—unclear visuals made it hard to draw insights and communicate findings effectively. Another primary concern was the limited knowledge and familiarity with AI, which often results in poor understanding and underutilization of AI tools in actual work settings. Among the identified needs were better data management systems to strengthen AI automation and improve operational flow, and smarter assistance for handling more complex tasks. Informants also highlighted the need for user-friendly systems, emphasizing the importance of having interfaces that are easy to navigate and accessible to all levels of users. The interviews mainly focused on perceived effectiveness and trust in AI, how AI is used in daily work processes, and the features and integration that users hope to see in future AI systems.

2.3 *Data gathering procedure*

The data-gathering process involved administering a structured online survey to 150 leaders and decision-makers in NCR. Using convenience sampling supported by the snowball technique, the survey reached respondents across key sectors, including education, healthcare, service, and manufacturing. Participants were briefed on the study's objectives and assured of confidentiality. The questionnaire comprised multiple-choice, Likert-scale, and narrative questions aimed at exploring perceptions of AI about the identified constructs and measures. Data collection was conducted over two weeks, yielding an 85% response rate. The key informants were interviewed online. In the process of gathering data, the researcher adhered to ethical standards. Key informants in this study signed consent forms and used role-based pseudonyms Task Leaders, Section Managers, and Operations Supervisors—to ensure confidentiality while reflecting their roles accurately. Participants were fully informed of the study's purpose, assured of their voluntary participation, and guaranteed confidentiality. Informed consent was obtained before the survey, and the data collected were treated anonymously.

2.4 *Data analysis*

For the qualitative data, thematic analysis was used to give meaning to the responses of the key informants. Thematic analysis is a qualitative research method for identifying, analyzing, and interpreting patterns or themes within textual data [64]. The analysis followed a clear and structured process. First, the researchers read and re-read the responses to become thoroughly familiar with the data. After that, they started generating initial codes to capture key points or meaningful sections from the interviews. These codes were then reviewed to find recurring patterns or common themes. Once the themes began to emerge, they were further refined, modified, and clearly defined to ensure they genuinely reflected the participants‘ perspectives. Finally, the researchers interpreted these themes and drew insights based on the study's goals, particularly focusing on how participants experience and perceive the use of AI in their work environments (see Table 3).

Table 2. Summary of the accounts from the key informants from the in-depth interviews.

Focus	Thematic Integration of Key Informant Insights
Perceived Effectiveness and Trust in AI	1. AI enhances decision-making through timely and accurate insights. AI tools help leaders make better choices by giving updated, reliable data when needed most. 2. AI builds trust across roles by supporting performance tracking. Managers and supervisors trust AI to monitor progress and give clear feedback on team performance. 3. Predictive features of AI aid long-term planning and process control. AI forecasting tools help task leaders and managers stay ahead and keep processes on track. 4. Real-time analytics and visualizations support informed decisions. Fast data analysis and clear visuals make it easier to understand what's happening and decide what to do next. 5. AI streamlines workflows and boosts operational efficiency. AI helps simplify repetitive tasks and improve productivity, especially on the operations floor.
AI in Daily Work Processes	1. AI supports daily operations and more intelligent decisions. Task Leaders use AI to make monitoring easier and decisions faster in everyday work. 2. Real-time tracking through AI keeps KPIs in check. Section Managers depend on AI to stay updated on progress and meet performance goals. 3. AI simplifies data handling and reduces manual work. Operations Supervisors benefit from AI in managing big data quickly and accurately. 4. AI forecasting helps with strategy and process control. Task Leaders use predictions for planning, while Section Managers use them to fine-tune operations. 5. Routine tasks are automated, boosting team focus and output. With AI doing repetitive work, all roles can concentrate on more important and productive tasks.

(*continued*)

Table 2. Continued

Focus	Thematic Integration of Key Informant Insights
Desired AI Features and Integration	1. Easy-to-use AI is a top priority. All roles want AI tools that are simple, intuitive, and accessible in daily tasks. 2. Real-time data matters for better decisions. Everyone values AI that updates instantly, helping them act on current information. 3. Clear visuals help make sense of complex data. Section Managers especially need AI with strong visualization features for better analysis. 4. Automation saves time and boosts efficiency. AI should handle repetitive tasks so teams can focus on more important work. 5. AI must fit specific roles and workflows. All roles prefer AI tools that they can customize to match their unique tasks and processes.

Note: *Key informants trust AI to enhance decision-making, track performance, and streamline operations. AI supports daily tasks by automating routines, improving efficiency, and enabling real-time insights. All roles prefer intuitive, customizable AI tools with clear visualizations and up-to-date data to better integrate into workflows.*

Table 2 presents a comprehensive thematic integration of key insights from informants regarding AI use across various managerial and decision-making roles. It highlights three main areas: perceived effectiveness and trust in AI, its role in daily work processes, and desired features for future integration. One key question explored was: "To what extent do decision-makers trust AI to support accurate and timely decisions in their roles?" This theme pointed to strong confidence in AI, especially in enhancing employer-employee interactions. Another guiding question was: "How does AI fit into the actual day-to-day work of different roles?" Here, the responses differentiated between simply recognizing AI's effectiveness and applying it in specific job contexts. Finally, the question "What AI features do professionals wish to see improved or added?" surfaced demands for more intuitive, role-specific, and automation-focused tools. These themes reveal current experiences and forward-looking expectations about AI integration in the Philippine workplace setting.

The qualitative analysis reveals strong trust in AI's role in improving decision-making across Task Leaders, Section Managers, and Operations Supervisors. Task Leaders value AI for its ability to deliver accurate, timely data that leads to reliable insights. One Task Leader noted that AI "enhances decision-making through accurate, timely data, [and] reliable insights across roles," showing how AI supports long-term outcomes through predictive decision-making. Section Managers also showed strong confidence in AI, especially in generating real-time data visualizations that help them make sense of complex information. For them, AI enables "informed decision-making" by providing precise, actionable data.

On the other hand, Operations Supervisors see AI as a key tool for quickly generating valuable insights, which helps streamline operations. As one Supervisor said, AI helps with "optimizing operations" by delivering fast, relevant information that makes workflow management easier. These perspectives confirm that AI is essential in improving operational performance through timely, predictive, and real-time decision support.

The data also suggests that AI improves productivity and the quality of decision-making, especially in routine day-to-day operations. For instance, Task Leaders use AI to streamline performance monitoring and assist with timely decision-making. One Task Leader shared that AI helps "streamline performance monitoring and decision-making," showing how it reduces the need for manual data analysis and improves task productivity. Section Managers, on the other hand, rely heavily on AI's "real-time tracking capabilities" to monitor critical business processes and make sure key performance indicators (KPIs) are consistently met. This allows them to respond quickly and stay on target with operational goals.

Meanwhile, Operations Supervisors benefit from AI's ability to handle large datasets and promptly produce valuable insights. One Supervisor explained that AI supports "quickly interpreting results," which speeds up decision-making and cuts down on manual work. Together, these roles demonstrate how AI is vital in improving daily work efficiency and enabling more accurate, faster decisions.

Multivariate analysis, specifically Structural Equation Modeling (SEM), was used for the quantitative data. SEM is a multivariate statistical analysis technique that can simultaneously analyze multiple relationships among variables. SEM provides the study with options to test complex models containing various independent and dependent variables and the direct and indirect effects [65]. Thus, SEM is excellent in helping the study understand how different factors are interrelated and how they jointly affect the results that they are studying. In this case, SEM would permit you to assess the interconnections between perceptions about generative AI and its adoption in the workplace under a much wider lens. In the context of SEM, the results in Figure 1 could be framed as a model where the identified industry challenges (e.g., data collection issues, statistical analysis struggles, and technological unfamiliarity) are considered latent variables, or constructs. These constructs would be connected by hypothesized relationships, with arrows indicating how one challenge may influence another or the outcome. The study hypothesizes that outdated systems lead to repetitive tasks, affecting managerial satisfaction with AI integration. Similarly, a lack of familiarity with emerging technologies might be linked to difficulties in adopting AI tools, impact on development, and satisfaction. SEM allows these relationships to be tested statistically, estimating the strength and direction of the connections between the variables. It also allows the study to assess the fit of the proposed model to the data, ensuring that the diagram effectively represents the real-world dynamics observed in the interviews. Using SEM, the study can quantify how these challenges are interrelated and guide the development of AI solutions to address them, enhancing workplace efficiency and satisfaction.

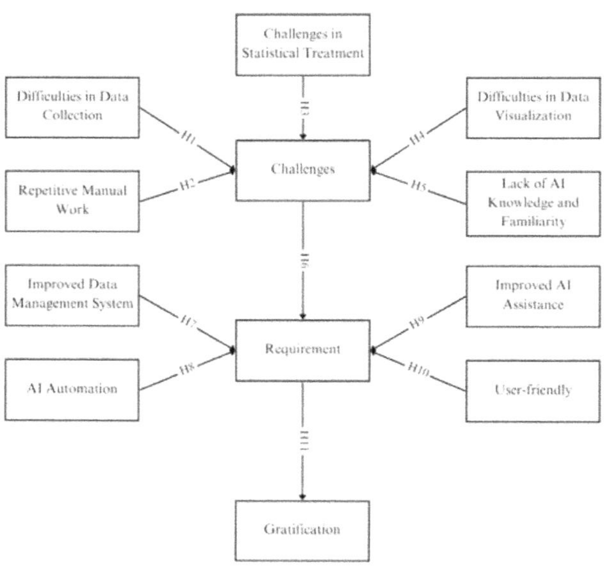

Figure 1. The industry-AI gratification model (IAGM).

Figure 1 shows that in today's fast-paced and data-driven work environments, organizations face numerous challenges that hinder productivity and decision-making. These challenges, ranging from data collection and statistical analysis difficulties to integrating emerging technologies such as AI, can create significant barriers to organizational efficiency. As AI continues to emerge as a transformative tool in various industries, it is crucial to understand the factors that impact its integration and effectiveness. This study explores how specific workplace challenges influence the need for AI solutions and how improved systems and AI technologies can enhance productivity and satisfaction. The following hypotheses address these challenges and the potential role of AI in overcoming them.

2.4.1 *Difficulties in data collection*

Managers rely heavily on data for informed decision-making, and any inefficiencies or hurdles in data collection can seriously disrupt these processes. Once data collection directly affects decision-making accuracy, challenges in the area should, in turn, be detrimental to organizational efficiency. Thus, the study posits: Hypothesis 1 (H1): That difficulties in data collection reduce workplace efficiency because inefficient data collection processes hinder the creation of well-informed decisions by managers, with adverse implications for organizational performance.

2.4.2 *Repetitive manual work*

Repetitive manual jobs typically involve working quite a lot and, hence, usually tend to tire employees; all the more, these employees lose motivation to work and become less productive. This results in the opposite cycle that might trigger even more stress on the employees and create disengagement, whereupon the employees themselves would find it hard to meet company objectives. For all the above reasons, the study hypothesizes: Hypothesis 2 (H2): That repetitive manual work will adversely affect productivity, as employees performing repetitive tasks are unlikely to perform efficiently, leading to greater errors and reduced total output.

2.4.3 *Challenges in statistical treatment*

Employees who lack the required mathematical knowledge or statistical expertise can find themselves even more unable to interpret data accurately. A lack of an alternative view on the understanding grounds may cause errors in data analysis, adversely affecting business decisions. Therefore, the study proposes that: Hypothesis 3 (H3): Challenges in statistical treatment can hinder practical workplace analysis. When statistical knowledge is lacking, data may be misinterpreted, leading to flawed decisions that could result in undesirable outcomes for the organization.

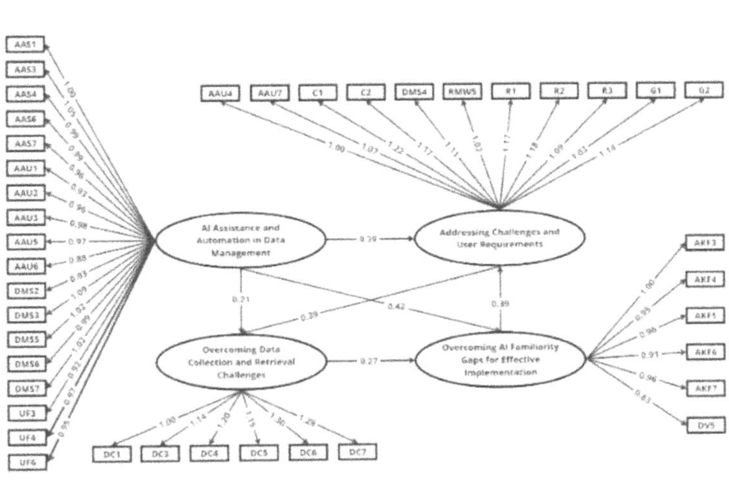

Figure 2. Factor analysis SEM.

2.4.4 *Difficulties in data visualization*

Data visualization is vital in converting complex data into accessible and actionable insights. If employees find difficulties in interpreting or creating compelling data visualizations, then the clarity of the information is reduced, which impedes good decision-making. This study's hypothesis states: Hypothesis 4 (H4): Problems in data visualization can lead to poor decision-making, as ineffective visualization tools hinder the clear communication of insights, resulting in substandard decisions and missed opportunities.

2.4.5 *Lack of AI knowledge and familiarity*

For AI to be effectively integrated, employees must possess at least rudimentary knowledge of AI technologies. Without such knowledge, employees will find it challenging to fit AI systems into their workflows, which can adversely affect the implementation and utility of AI functions. Based on this premise, the study reports: Hypothesis 5 (H5): Limited AI knowledge presents challenges to AI integration in the workplace, as employee unfamiliarity with AI tools and processes can reduce the effectiveness of implementation.

Table 3 highlights four critical dimensions of AI influence in the realm of data management that were assessed in this study for their reliability and validity by measuring internal consistency using Cronbach's alpha. The value of at least the alpha above for reliability is 0.70 [58]. The first dimension is AI Assistance and Automation in Data Management, where 18 items achieved an internal consistency of 0.952, thus indicating excellent reliability. The second variable is Addressing Challenges and User Requirements, with an array of 11 items, showing 0.941, verifying very high stability in capturing the users' capabilities and requirements. The third item, Overcoming Data Collection and Retrieval Challenges, consists of 6 indicators, with the recording of 0.893 indicating strong internal consistency. Last among those with six items was Overcoming AI Familiarity Gaps, with an alpha of 0.866, thus confirming reliability in identifying gaps in knowledge. Accordingly, results have shown that the variables are adequate from the reliability standpoint, and they improve the instrument's relevance in capturing the industry's challenges about AI automation.

2.4.6 *Evaluating the impact of AI on data management: Results from four key tests*

This study explored the role of AI in addressing challenges in data management. By conducting four AI tests, it aims to assess how AI can improve efficiency in data collection, automation, and user familiarity, ultimately enhancing decision-making processes in the workplace. The results provide valuable insights into the potential of AI to overcome common data management hurdles and its effectiveness in real-world applications. In the context of data management analysis, Figure 2 displays results from four AI tests. These tests assess different facets of the effect of AIs on data management challenges. The alpha coefficient for Test 1, AI Assistance, and Automation. It has a value of 0.42, based on 18 items ranging from 1.05 to 0.88. This implies a relatively moderate internal consistency regarding AI assistance and automation items. Test 2 reports an average score of 0.47 over 11 items in the relationship between Addressing Challenges and User Requirements. The item scores vary from 1.22 (C1) to 1.00 (AAU4), indicating the extent of variability of challenges and user needs addressed by the AI system. Test 3, measuring Overcoming and Effectiveness in Challenges of Data Collection and Retrieval, scored 0.61, proving a higher possibility of the score. The item individual factors, that is, DC6 (1.30), DC5 (1.20), DC4 (1.10), DC3 (1.10), DC2 (1.10), and DC1 (1.00), suggest a relatively strong association with overcoming data management challenges. Lastly, Test 4, which concerns the overcoming gaps of AI familiarity, presents a score of 0.83, with values ranging from 1.00 (AKF3) to 0.83 (DV5), indicating that greater consistency applies to the issue. The measurement, via these correlations between the tests, suggests how these different AI dimensions interact. Such correlations include those found between Test 1 and Test 4 (0.42), Test 2 and Test 4 (0.39), Test 3 and Test 4 (0.21), Test 2 and Test 3 (0.26), and Test 3 and Test 4 (0.27) as they relate to user challenges as a result of performance. The latest research considered the model fit through various fit indexes concerning SEM. For instance, the fitting indices were used in the CFI, RMSEA, and CMIN to judge how well the model fits the data. While a CFI of 0.816, RMSEA of 0.086, and CMIN/DF of 2.106 fall well within the ranges of acceptable criteria for a good model fit, they also go further to validate the model as accurately representing responses to the survey *(see* Table 2). These findings indicate that the model proposed is effective in casting relationships between AI capabilities and challenges in data management, hence providing crucial insights regarding the impact of AI on workplace processes.

Table 3. Model fit summary.

SEM Goodness of Fit Measures	Parameter Estimates	Minimum Cut-Off
CFI	0.816	$\geq$ 0.80
RMSEA	0.086	$\leq$ 0.10
CMIN/DF	2.106	$\leq$ 3

Note: *The model's fit was assessed using key SEM indicators. The Comparative Fit Index (CFI) scored 0.816, meeting the acceptable threshold of 0.80. The RMSEA was 0.086, within the $\leq$ 0.10 cut-off, and the CMIN/DF ratio was 2.106, falling below the maximum recommended value of 3. These results indicate a good model fit.*

Additionally, the KMO test yielded a value of 0.890, indicating excellent sampling adequacy for factor analysis. Also, Bartlett's Test of Sphericity (χ^2 = 9879.383, p = 0.000) confirmed that the variables were significantly correlated, justifying factor analysis. Descriptive statistics were computed to summarize survey responses from 150 managers, leaders, and decision-makers. Means and standard deviations of each construct examined on a 7-point Likert scale. The construct *"AI assistant and data management"* average score stood at 5.94 (SD = 0.79), indicating strong agreement on AI's effective use for data management. This result correlates with [53] and [54], who link AI use with productivity improvement and favorable business outcomes. The *"Workplace Challenges and Requirements"* construct recorded an equal score of 5.94 (SD = 0.70), showing that operational barriers need urgent attention, a point alluded to by [54] concerning digital transformation. The construct *"Data collection and Retrieval"* produced a mean of 5.78 (SD = 0.77), thereby showing strong support for AI enhancing efficiency, like that which was found by [55] concerning data accessibility and resource optimization. Lastly, the *"AI Familiarity Gap"* registered a mean score of 5.32 (SD = 0.94), suggesting moderate familiarity among respondents but considerable gaps in understanding. This accords with [56]'s suggestion for targeted skill development programs to facilitate the acceptance and integration of AI.

Table 4. Test of reliability and validity.

Latent Variables	Cronbach's Alpha	AVE	CR
AI Assistance and Automation in Data Management	0.952	0.757	0.96
Addressing Challenges and User Requirements	0.941	0.718	0.95
Overcoming Data Collection and Retrieval Challenges	0.893	0.656	0.90
Overcoming AI Familiarity Gaps for Effective Implementation	0.866	0.788	0.88

Note: *Cronbach's Alpha assesses the internal consistency or reliability of a group of items within a construct. A value above 0.70 is generally accepted as indicating a reliable measurement. Meanwhile, Average Variance Extracted (AVE) measures the variance captured by the construct about the variance attributed to measurement error. An AVE value greater than 0.50 suggests the construct demonstrates adequate convergent validity. Lastly, Composite Reliability (CR) evaluates the overall reliability of a latent variable, with values above 0.70 indicating that the construct reliably reflects the underlying factor it is intended to measure.*

3 RESULTS AND DISCUSSIONS

This study used the user gratification framework to understand how organizations in the Philippines choose technologies to meet the growing demand for artificial intelligence (AI) integration. One hundred fifty respondents from various sectors — including finance, manufacturing, information technology, communication, education, and healthcare — participated by answering an online questionnaire with 84 distributed through Google Forms. The structural equation model (SEM) developed in this study highlights meaningful relationships that help explain how leaders and managers perceive and adopt AI to improve data management and tackle modern business challenges. This insight is timely, as more and more organizations rely on AI to stay competitive, efficient, and adaptable.

This framework studied four key factors: AI assistance and automation in data management; addressing challenges and user requirements; overcoming data collection and retrieval issues; and bridging gaps in AI familiarity to support smooth implementation. Each factor has a unique role in shaping how organizations get ready for AI integration.

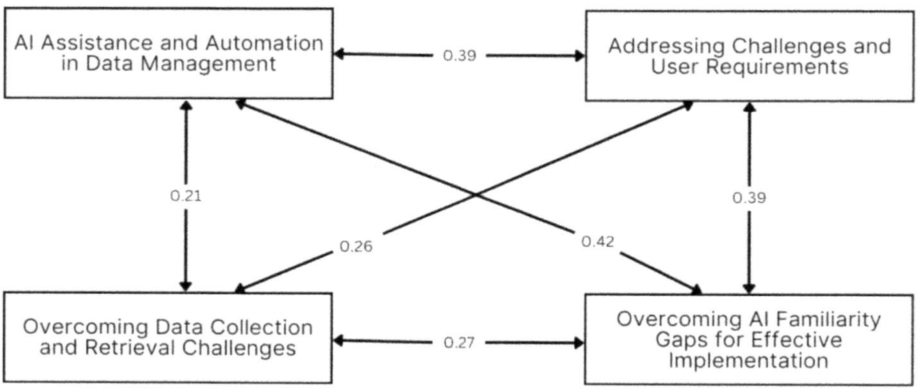

Figure 3. Key correlations in the final model: AI assistance, workplace challenges, and user familiarity.

Figure 3 shows the interrelationship of AI assistance, data management, and workplace challenges, which conceptual model illustrates from the key correlation shown in Figure 3. AI assistance, data management, and workplace challenges have a notable correlation of 0.39, which supports past studies [59,60] that describe the function of AI in relieving repetitive tasks and increasing efficiency in decision-making and operational terms, respectively. Appropriately, the strongest correlation of 0.42 connects AI assistance to the gap in user familiarity, endorsed by [61] observation that the lack of understanding of technology dramatically inhibits the benefit of automation at work. Moreover, a correlation of 0.26 between addressing user needs and overcoming data collection challenges aligns with [62], which emphasizes that aligning AI frameworks with employees' specific needs plays a crucial role in promoting AI adoption and boosting productivity. Finally, the correlation of 0.27 between familiarity with data tools and resolving data collection issues underscores [63]'s recommendation for comprehensive training programs to unlock AI's full potential, emphasizing the need for a well-prepared workforce to maximize AI's benefits in data-driven environments.

Moreover, the results show that successful AI integration in industries depends on balancing technological investments with human-centered strategies. This balance helps improve data quality, automate repetitive tasks, and effectively meet user needs. For companies to be ready, they should create open communication channels where team leaders, managers, and supervisors can openly discuss AI-related challenges and shared expectations. Organizing workshops, pilot programs, and setting clear policies can help organizations adapt more easily and reduce possible risks. A phased approach to AI adoption is also recommended, allowing employees to gradually get used to automation without fearing AI advancement.

In the Philippines, AI use is increasingly growing as more organizations realize its power to boost efficiency, accuracy, and organizational competitiveness. This study confirms that all the proposed hypotheses were supported. The results highlight that the user gratification framework positively influences and directly affects key aspects such as AI perceptions, strategic readiness, and user acceptance within various industries. Organizations can ensure smoother integration of AI technologies into their operations by addressing user needs, enhancing familiarity, and overcoming data-related challenges. This shows the importance of aligning AI tools with real user expectations and work contexts to maximize benefits and minimize resistance. This study's SEM model supports the idea that AI can effectively transform industry operations. By understanding these interconnections, organizations can better prepare, align strategies with user needs, and develop a workforce ready to embrace AI innovations.

4 CONCLUSION AND RECOMMENDATIONS

The study used factor analysis, thematic analysis, SPSS, and SEM [65] to achieve its objectives. Interviews with three managers highlighted AI's role in improving customer satisfaction through actionable insights and simplified data presentation. [64] A thematic analysis informed the development of a theoretical framework, focusing on challenges and solutions for effective AI integration. A survey was then distributed to managers and leaders in the NCR region to explore AI implementation challenges, data processing, and user requirements. Validated using SPSS [66], the survey provided insights into AI's impact on operational efficiency, error reduction, and user-friendly data management. SEM analysis identified key factors for successful AI adoption, including addressing workplace challenges, data obstacles, and familiarity gaps. Results showed that AI improves decision-making, productivity, and user engagement, while emphasizing the need for tailored training programs. The study met its objectives: (1) gathering perspectives on AI challenges and improvements, (2) developing and validating a survey tool for AI integration, and (3) using SPSS and SEM to ensure reliable findings. These insights contribute to the development and implementation of AI across industries. Thus, it is imperative to first understand the needs or the end users of an organization before implementing or upgrading AI functions, based on findings, training and continued learning through seminars will help users or employees keep up with evolving challenges and technology.

5 DIRECTIONS FOR FUTURE RESEARCH

The study focused on multiple industries; future studies can dive into a more focused discussion or AI integration in a specific sector, such as critical industries like education and health. Further, as AI continues to expand and advance, this comes with ethical implications, and determining the perceptions of industry leaders in this matter is one direction worth exploring for future research.

AUTHOR CONTRIBUTION STATEMENT

The authors' contributions to the study are as follows: Prince Hernandez led the team, managed task assignments, conducted factor analysis and structural equation modeling, and made key decisions. Jaypy Tenerife provided expertise in both quantitative and qualitative analysis. He also provided directions for improvement and edited the manuscript. Janelle Flores handled literature reviews and assisted with factor analysis. Jacel Allia Padullon and Michaela Theresa Landicho developed the survey tool and interpreted the results. Rochelle Ann Dela Cruz wrote the methodology, while Miguel Louis Belen and Justin Carl Candaza prepared the introduction and conclusions. Nikko Louis Tabasa double-checked all sections and assisted with structural equation modeling. As an adviser, Maricar Navarro guided content, methodology, and overall study improvements.

ACKNOWLEDGEMENT

The researchers would like to acknowledge everyone who has made this study possible, especially with all the respondents who gave their time to answer the survey and the interviewees who shared their experience and insights. The study would not have been successful without the information and data provided.

DECLARATION OF CONFLICT OF INTEREST, RESEARCH ETHICS, AND USE OF ARTIFICIAL INTELLIGENCE IN THE RESEARCH WRITING PROCESS

The paper's authors affirm that no part or content of the paper is generated by artificial intelligence (AI), all content and thoughts of the paper are from the authors, and that AI was solely used for grammar checking and improving the paper's readability.

REFERENCES

[1] Jan Z., F. Ahamed, W. Mayer, N. Patel, G. Grossmann, M. Stumptner, and A. Kuusk, (2023) Artificial intelligence for industry 4.0: Systematic review of applications, challenges, and opportunities, *Expert Systems with Applications*, vol. 216, p. 119456

[2] A. Bhimdiwala, R.C. Neri, and L.M. Gomez, (2021) Advancing the design and implementation of artificial intelligence in education through continuous improvement, *International Journal of Artificial Intelligence in Education*, vol. 32, no. 3, pp. 756–782.

[3] S. Malik, K. Muhammad, and Y. Waheed, (2024). Artificial intelligence and industrial applications—a revolution in modern industries, *Ain Shams Engineering Journal*, vol. 15, no. 9, p. 102886.

[4] Malik, A.S. (2024, January 4). Top 7 challenges in data visualization and how to overcome them.. Platform 3 Solutions. Available: https://platform3solutions.com/top-7-challenges-in-data-visualization-and-how-to-overcome-them/.

[5] S. Russel and D. Susskind, 6 Positive AI visions for the future of work, *World Economic Forum*, Sep. 10. [Online]. Available: https://www.weforum.org/stories/2021/11/positive-artificial-intelligence-visions-for-the-future-of-work/.

[6] Challenge noun - Definition, pictures, pronunciation and usage notes, *Oxford Advanced Learner's Dictionary*, Oxford Learner's Dictionaries. [Online]. Available: https://www.oxfordlearnersdictionaries.com/us/definition/english/challenge_1.

[7] B. Hawash, M. Mukred, U.A. Mokhtar, and M.I. Nofal, (2023). The influence of big data management on organizational performance in organizations: The role of Electronic Records Management System Potentiality, *Interdisciplinary Journal of Information, Knowledge and Management*, vol. 18, pp. 059–086.

[8] IBM, What is intelligent automation? *IBM*, Aug. 15, 202. [Online]. Available: https://www.ibm.com/topics/intelligent-automation.

[9] M. Mabungela, (2023). Artificial Intelligence (AI) and automation in the world of work: A threat to employees? *Research in Social Sciences and Technology*, vol. 8, pp. 135–146.

[10] E.C. Ling, I. Tussyadiah, A. Liu, and J. Stienmetz, (2023). Perceived intelligence of artificially intelligent assistants for travel: Scale development and validation, *Journal of Travel Research*, vol. 0, no. 0.
[11] User-friendly, *Merriam-Webster Dictionary*, (2024). [Online]. Available: https://www.merriam-webster.com/dictionary/user-friendly.
[12] Acropolium, (2024). AI use cases in major industries: Elevate your business with disruptive technology, *Acropolium Spol. S R. O.* [Online]. Available: https://acropolium.com/blog/ai-use-cases-in-major-industries-elevate-your-business-with-disruptive-technology/.
[13] M. Bae, (2018). Understanding the effect of the discrepancy between sought and obtained gratification on social networking site users' satisfaction and continuance intention, *Computers in Human Behavior*, vol. 79, pp. 137–153.
[14] S. Ibrihich, A. Oussous, O. Ibrihich, and M. Esghir, (2022). A review on recent research in information retrieval, *Procedia Computer Science*, vol. 201, pp. 777–782.
[15] F. Pervaiz, A. Vashistha, and R. Anderson, (2019). Examining the challenges in development data pipeline, in *Proceedings of the 2nd ACM SIGCAS Conference on Computing and Sustainable Societies*.
[16] V. Di Pasquale, S. Miranda, W.P. Neumann, and A. Setayesh, (2018). Human reliability in manual assembly systems: A systematic literature review, *IFAC PapersOnline*, vol. 51, no. 11, pp. 675–680.
[17] C. Coombs, D. Hislop, S.K. Taneva, and S. Barnard, (2020). The strategic impacts of Intelligent Automation for knowledge and service work: An interdisciplinary review, *The Journal of Strategic Information Systems*, vol. 29, no. 4, p. 101600.
[18] J.M. Diefendorff, M.E. Kenworthy, F.C. Lee, and L.K. Nguyen, (2022). Work motivation, *Oxford Research Encyclopedia of Psychology*.
[19] S.R. Fletcher, T. Johnson, T. Adlon, J. Larreina, P. Casla, P.J. Alfaro, and M. Del Mar Otero, (2020). Adaptive automation assembly: Identifying system requirements for technical efficiency and worker satisfaction, *Computers & Industrial Engineering*, vol. 139, p. 105772.
[20] K. Barchard and L. Pace, (2011). Preventing human error: The impact of data entry methods on data accuracy and statistical results, *Computers in Human Behavior*, vol. 27, pp. 1834-1839.
[21] N. Corbett, R. Sibbald, P. Stockton, and A. Wilson, (2015). Gross Error Detection: Maximising the Use of Data with UBA on Global Producer III (Part 2), *3rd International North Sea Flow Measurement Workshop*.
[22] B. Alabdullah, N. Beloff, and M. White, (2018). Rise of Big Data – Issues and Challenges, *2018 8th International Conference on Next Generation Computing (NCG)*, pp. 1-6.
[23] Z.A. Al-Sai, R. Abdullah, and M.H. Husin, (2019). A review on big data maturity models, *2019 IEEE Jordan International Joint Conference on Electrical Engineering and Information Technology (JEEIT)*.
[24] S. Friedrich, G. Antes, S. Behr, H. Binder, W. Brannath, F. Dumpert, K. Ickstadt, H.A. Kestler, J. Lederer, H. Leitgöb, M. Pauly, A. Steland, A. Wilhelm, and T. Friede, (2021). Is there a role for statistics in artificial intelligence? *Advances in Data Analysis and Classification*, vol. 16, no. 4, pp. 823–846.
[25] S. Lee, (2016). Avoiding negative reviewer comments: common statistical errors in anesthesia journals, *Korean Journal of Anesthesiology*, vol. 69, no. 3, pp. 219–226.
[26] L. Ashour, (2024). A review of user-friendly freely available statistical analysis software for medical researchers and biostatisticians, *Research in Statistics*, vol. 2, no. 1.
[27] C. Burnay, F. Dargam, and P. Zarate, (2019). Special issues: data visualization for decision making an important issue, *Operational Research*, vol. 19, no. 3, pp. 853-855.
[28] E. Dimara, H. Zhang, M. Tory, and S. Franconeri, (2021). The unmet data visualization needs of decision makers within organizations, *IEEE Transactions on Visualization and Computer Graphics*.
[29] M.H. Jarrahi, (2018). Artificial intelligence and the future of work: Human-AI symbiosis in organizational decision making, *Business Horizons*.
[30] J. Manyika, M. Chui, M. Miremadi, J. Bughin, K. George, P. Willmott, and M. Dewhurst, (2017). Harnessing automation for a future that works, *McKinsey Global Institute*.
[31] Y. Xia and H. Wei, (2024). Applications of Data Visualization Technology in Artificial Intelligence, *Frontiers in Business, Economics and Management*, vol. 15, pp. 385-388.
[32] Y. Griep, I. Vranjes, M.M.L. Van Hooff, D.G.J. Beckers, and S.A.E. Geurts, (2021). Technology in the workplace: Opportunities and challenges, in *Springer eBooks*, pp. 93–116.
[33] H. Chetlapalli and T. Perumal, (2024). Driving business intelligence transformation through AI and data analytics: A comprehensive framework, *International Journal of Information Technology and Computer Engineering*.
[34] J. Darmont, B. Novikov, R. Wrembel, and L. Bellatreche, (2022). Advances on Data Management and Information Systems, *Journal of Database Management*.

[35] R. Ahmed, S. Shaheen, and S. Philbin, (2022). The role of big data analytics and decision-making in achieving project success, *Journal of Engineering and Technology Management*.
[36] O. Okuyelu and O. Adaji, (2024). AI-driven real-time quality monitoring and process optimization for enhanced manufacturing performance, *Journal of Advances in Mathematics and Computer Science*, vol. 39, no. 4, pp. 81–89.
[37] A.O. Onososen and I. Musonda, (2022). Perceived benefits of automation and artificial intelligence in the AEC sector: An interpretive structural modeling approach, *Frontiers in Built Environment*, vol. 8.
[38] S. Maruthi, S.B. Dodda, R.R. Yellu, P. Thuniki, and S.R.B. Reddy, (2022). Automated planning and scheduling in AI: Studying automated planning and scheduling techniques for efficient decision-making in artificial intelligence.
[39] N.L. Rane, S.P. Choudhary, and J. Rane, Artificial intelligence-driven corporate finance: Enhancing efficiency and decision-making through machine learning, natural language processing, and robotic process automation in corporate governance and sustainability, *Studies in Economics and Business Relations*, vol. 5, no. 2, pp. 1–22.
[40] D. Mathew, N.C. Brintha, and J.T.W. Jappes, (2023). Artificial intelligence powered automation for industry 4.0, in *Springer eBooks*, pp. 1–28.
[41] P. Budhwar, A. Malik, M.T.T. De Silva, and P. Thevisuthan, (2022). Artificial intelligence – challenges and opportunities for international HRM: A review and research agenda, *The International Journal of Human Resource Management*, vol. 33, no. 6, pp. 1065–1097.
[42] D. Talati, (2024). Virtual Health Assistance – AI-Based, TechRxiv. [Online]. Available: https://doi.org/10.36227/techrxiv.170474377.76705256/v1.
[43] S.K. Devineni, (2024). AI in Data Privacy and Security, IJAIML. [Online]. Available: https://iaeme-library.com/index.php/IJAIML/article/view/IJAIML_03_01_004.
[44] S. Balasubramanian, (2023). Integration of artificial intelligence in the manufacturing sector: A systematic review of applications and implications, *Int. J. Prod. Technol. Manag.*, vol. 14, no. 1, pp. 1–11.
[45] H. Hassani and E.S. Silva, (2023). The role of ChatGPT in data science: How AI-assisted conversational interfaces are revolutionizing the field, *Big Data Cogn. Comput.*, vol. 7, no. 2, p. 62.
[46] Zhou, C., Liu, X., Yu, C., Tao, Y., and Shao, Y., (2023). Trust in AI-augmented design: Applying structural equation modeling to AI-augmented design acceptance, Heliyon, vol. 10, no. 1, p. e23305.
[47] Diaferia, L., Blohm, I., De Rossi, L.M., and Salviotti, G., (2022). When Standard Is Not Enough: a Conceptualization of AI Systems' Customization and its Antecedents, in *Proceedings of the International Conference on Information Systems (ICIS)*, Copenhagen, Denmark, pp. 8.
[48] A. Olsson and G. Joelsson, (2019). *Requirements Analysis For AI Solutions: A Study On How Requirements Analysis Is Executed When Developing AI Solutions* (Dissertation).
[49] K. Ahmad, M. Abdelrazek, C. Arora, A.A. Baniya, M. Bano, and J. Grundy, (2023). Requirements engineering framework for human-centered artificial intelligence software systems, *Applied Soft Computing*, vol. 143, p. 110455
[50] A.I.K. Mohammed, (2024). The Role of Motivation and Job Satisfaction in Enhancing Employee Performance: Systematic review, *Psikostudia Jurnal Psikologi*, vol. 13, no. 1, p. 105.
[51] P. Singh and V. Singh, (2024). The power of AI: enhancing customer loyalty through satisfaction and efficiency, *Cogent Business & Management*, vol. 11, no. 1.
[52] M. Rožman, D. Oreški, and P. Tominc, (2023). Artificial-Intelligence-Supported reduction of employees' workload to increase the company's performance in today's VUCA environment, *Sustainability*, vol. 15, no. 6, p. 5019.
[53] T. Cao, Y.Q. Khoo, S. Birajdar, Z. Gong, C. Chung, Y. Moghaddam, A. Xu, H. Mehta, A. Shukla, Z. Wang, and R. Akkiraju, (2024). Designing towards productivity: A centralized AI assistant concept for work, in *AHFE International*.
[54] S. Anagnoste, I. Biclesanu, F. D'Ascenzo, and M. Savastano, (2021). The Role of Chatbots in End-To-End Intelligent Automation and Future Employment Dynamics, in *Springer Proceedings in Business and Economics*, pp. 287–302.
[55] L. Gkinko and A. Elbanna, (2022). The appropriation of conversational AI in the workplace: A taxonomy of AI chatbot users, *International Journal of Information Management*, vol. 69, p. 102568.
[56] A. Jurczuk and A. Florea, (2022). Future-Oriented Digital Skills for Process Design and Automation, *Human Technology*, vol. 18, pp. 122–142.
[57] U. Bhale and H.S. Bedi, (2023). Sem Model Fit Indices, Meaning, and Acceptance of Model Literature Support.
[58] K.S. Taber, (2017). The use of Cronbach's Alpha when developing and reporting research instruments in science education, *Research in Science Education*, vol. 48, no. 6, pp. 1273–1296.

[59] A. Zirar, S.I. Ali, and N. Islam, (2023). Worker and workplace Artificial Intelligence (AI) coexistence: Emerging themes and research agenda, *Technovation*, vol. 124, p. 102747.

[60] M.U. Tariq, M. Poulin, and A.A. Abonamah, (2021). Achieving Operational Excellence Through Artificial Intelligence: Driving Forces and Barriers, *Frontiers in Psychology*, vol. 12, p. 686624.

[61] A. Bewersdorff, X. Zhai, J. Roberts, and C. Nerdel, (2023). Myths, mis- and preconceptions of artificial intelligence: A review of the literature, *Computers and Education Artificial Intelligence*, vol. 4, p. 100143.

[62] T. Haipeter, M. Wannöffel, J. Daus, and S. Schaffarczik, (2024). Human-centered AI through employee participation, *Frontiers in Artificial Intelligence*, vol. 7, p. 1272102.

[63] K.K. Ramachandran, A. Srivastava, V. Panjwani, D. Kumar, N.R. Cheepurupalli, and C.R. Mohan, (2024). Developing AI-powered Training Programs for Employee Upskilling and Reskilling, *Journal of Informatics Education and Research*, vol. 4, pp. 1526–4726.

[64] N. Naeem, W. Ozuem, K. Howell, and S. Ranfagni, (2023) A step-by-step process of thematic analysis to develop a conceptual model in qualitative research, *Int. J. Qual. Methods*, vol. 22, (2023). [Online]. Available: https://doi.org/10.1177/16094069231205789

[65] R. Hidayat and N.P. Wulandari, Structural equation modelling (SEM) in research: Narrative literature review, *Open Access Indones. J. Soc. Sci.*, vol. 5, no. 6, pp. 852–858, (2022). [Online]. Available: https://doi.org/10.37275/oaijss.v5i6.141

[66] A. Rahman and M. Muktadir, SPSS: An imperative quantitative data analysis tool for social science research, *Int. J. Res. Innov. Soc. Sci.*, vol.. 5, no. 10, pp. 300–302, (2021). [Online]. Available: https://doi.org/10.47772/ijriss.2021.51012

Moving Towards Sustainable Businesses and Developing More Resilient Economies – Rashid and Annansingh-Jamieson (Eds)
 ISBN: 978-1-041-08875-2

Risk governance assessment: Analyzing the sustainable management strategies of a steel fabrication company

C.N.F. Dee, J.L.B. Dela Paz, F.N.R.A. Dimaano, S.M.L. Galit, D.A.S. Maquilan, and J.T. Tenerife
Industrial Engineering Department, Technological Institute of the Philippines, Quezon City

ABSTRACT: This study examines risk governance in a steel fabrication company, focusing on human resource, safety, environmental, and financial risks. Using a qualitative method, data were collected through in-depth interviews with key informants specializing in human resources, finance, safety, environmental, and manufacturing. Findings show that compliance risk is equal to 21.7, particularly in the Department of Labor and Employment (DOLE) guidelines and mental health programs, affecting workplace safety, operational stability, and financial performance. Key themes include labor-management communication, safety preparedness, environmental responsibility, and quality training. The study introduces a modified risk framework that links compliance with broader operational risks, emphasizing the need for integrated governance strategies. It also recommends using digital tools such as Enterprise Resource Planning (ERP) systems, AI, and digital twins to bridge the gap between risk identification and action. This framework guides organizations in improving risk governance, supporting sustainability, and promoting a safer industrial environment.

Keywords: Compliance, Environmental Risk, Financial Risk, Green HRM, Operational Risk, Risk Governance, Risk Management, Steel Fabrication, Sustainability, Workplace Safety

1 INTRODUCTION

Risk management is essential in steel manufacturing to ensure strong governance and sustainability. The industry is vital to infrastructure and medical applications, but is a major emitter of greenhouse gases due to energy-intensive operations (Ghosh *et al.* 2023). Sustainability governance involves ethical and resilient decisions that support social and environmental welfare, with management systems helping companies set goals, meet regulations, improve efficiency, and reduce risks. Challenges remain in emissions, waste, labor conditions, and community impact, requiring strategic and innovative solutions. In the Philippines, the steel sector supports national development but faces operational and occupational risks, including those in structural iron work (Jalac *et al.* 2018). These risks affect productivity and performance, especially when issues like limited training, inadequate equipment, and lack of qualified supervision are present. Larger companies also require more advanced risk management approaches. This study identifies gaps in current practices and recommends improvements to strengthen responsible industrial governance.

2 LITERATURE REVIEW

Efe (2023) compared major risk management frameworks—the Committee of Sponsoring Organizations of the Treadway Commission Enterprise Risk Management (COSO-ERM),

 DOI: 10.1201/9781003647300-31

the National Institute of Standards and Technology Risk Management Framework (NIST RMF), the International Organization for Standardization 31000 (ISO 31000), and Control Objectives for Information and Related Technologies (COBIT). COSO-ERM provides an enterprise-wide approach integrating governance and strategy, while NIST RMF offers a structured, repeatable process mainly for cybersecurity risks. ISO 31000 delivers flexible, principle-based guidelines applicable to any organization, and COBIT focuses on aligning IT governance with business objectives. ISO 9001:2015, though not a risk framework, reinforces risk-based thinking within Quality Management Systems (Yazo-Cabuya *et al.* 2025). Risk management involves identifying and controlling threats to operations, supported by tools like risk registries (Isah 2023). Common risks include safety hazards in manufacturing, environmental risks from poor waste handling, financial risks from potential losses (Lancaster and Goff 2023), and HR risks related to policies and compliance. HRM plays a central role by strengthening safety culture and reducing accidents through proper hiring and training (Al-Mekhlafi 2024), while Green HRM practices help minimize environmental risks (Ahmad *et al.* 2023). Poor safety and environmental performance increase compensation costs, operational disruptions, insurance premiums, and liabilities, making risk management essential for financial stability (Campo and Antonio 2022; Cohen 2024).

3 METHODOLOGY

A qualitative research technique was used in the study. According to Nordlof *et al.* (2015), qualitative methods offer a comprehensive overview and employ empirical strategies to gather deep insights and understand complex phenomena. To understand how people think, feel, and make decisions, the researchers conducted in-depth interviews, held in four separate company offices. Key informants on HR, environmental, safety, finance, and manufacturing were briefed and provided with interview guidelines before conducting interviews. Interviews were transcribed and analyzed using thematic analysis, a commonly used tool for identifying patterns in qualitative data (Harsch and Festing 2019).

3.1 *Participants*

Four key informants participated in the study and were chosen for their roles and areas of expertise about particular organizational risk types. The HR shared information about the risks related to human resources. The Safety and Environmental officer, whose role covered both departments, addressed safety and environmental risks. A CFO offered insightful opinions on financial risks. Finally, a civil engineer employed in the manufacturing industry was consulted to provide thorough insights into all four risk areas—financial, environmental, safety, and human resources, from the perspective of a non-managerial worker in the manufacturing industry.

3.2 *Measures*

A semi-structured interview guide was used as the primary measure to gather in-depth insights from key informants. The interview guide comprised parts on introduction, consent, study background, interview questions, conclusion, references, and researcher profiles. The interview questions focused on identifying and understanding risks in human resources, workplace safety, environmental compliance, financial operations, and overall organizational risk management practices.

3.3 *Data gathering procedure*

The study involved four key informants specializing in human resources, finance, manufacturing, and safety and environmental management. In-depth interviews were conducted based on each informant's roles and expertise in specific risk areas. The human resources representative shared insights on labor risks and training practices, the finance officer discussed financial impacts of operational issues, the manufacturing worker provided a non-managerial perspective, and the safety and environmental officer addressed workplace hazards and compliance concerns. Prior to data collection, coordination with the company ensured scheduled interview sessions across four office locations. Informants received a formal briefing and semi-structured interview guides to clarify objectives and encourage open discussion. All sessions were audio-recorded with consent and transcribed verbatim. Data were analyzed using thematic analysis to identify recurring themes and implications across risk domains.

3.4 *Data analysis*

Based on the thematic analysis of interview responses, the labor-management relations topic, the interviews revealed four key sub-themes. Communication and responsiveness emerged as essential, with one worker noting that all concerns are being tackled and addressed (*Key Informant 4, Manufacturing Worker*), reflecting trust-building through open dialogue. Safety and preventive measures were also emphasized, as reporting near-miss incidents was seen as important to prevent serious accidents (*Key Informant 2, Safety Officer*), supporting findings by (Nordlof *et al.* 2015). Legal and compliance issues showed that unresolved concerns may lead to formal complaints affecting finance (*Key Informant 3, CFO*). Lastly, adaptability and personal responsibility were evident, as workplace learning was applied both at work and at home (*Key Informant 2, Environmental Officer*). Overall, these insights reinforce open communication as a central factor in preventing safety and compliance issues.

The researchers identified four common themes in workplace safety culture. First, safety as a top priority was emphasized, with one worker noting that safety is most important because accidents can occur (*Key Informant 4, Manufacturing Worker*), reflecting the high-risk nature of steel work (Nordlof *et al.* 2015). Second, preparedness and emergency response were highlighted, as onsite medical support ensures immediate assistance during incidents (*Key Informant 2, Safety Officer*). Third, clear communication of safety protocols was stressed, with the HR manager noting that miscommunication is not allowed and protocols must be clearly communicated (*Key Informant 1, HR Manager*). Lastly, environmental and resource conservation emerged as part of safety practice, such as waste segregation to prevent hazards (*Key Informant 2, Safety Officer; Key Informant 4, Environmental Officer*). Overall, the theme focuses on prioritizing safety culture and preparedness in daily operations.

Five sub-themes were identified for Green HRM. Environmental protection and sustainability are emphasized by a manufacturing worker (*Key Informant 4, Manufacturing Officer, March 7, 2025*), who noted that proper waste and material segregation reduces accidents and operational issues, supported by Al-Mekhlafi (2024). The second sub-theme, support and encouragement from management, was reflected in how safety officers (*Key Informant 2, Environmental Officer, March 7, 2025*) shared that management provides the assistance needed to implement green practices. The third sub-theme is the impact on productivity and operations, where an HR manager (*Key Informant 1, HR Manager, March 7, 2025*) noted that Green HRM enhances daily operations and employee productivity. The fourth sub-theme, financial impact, as explained by the finance officer (*Key Informant 3, CFO, March 7, 2025*), stated that environmental impacts rarely cause significant financial effects. Lastly, as emphasized by a safety officer (*Key Informant 2, Safety Officer, March 7, 2025*), a Pollution Control Officer (PCO) helps protect the environment and ensure compliance.

In terms of high-quality training, four sub-themes are identified. First, self-initiative and meeting standards highlight how employees take responsibility for meeting company expectations (*Key Informant 4, Manufacturing Worker, March 7, 2025*). The second sub-theme, management's role in guidance, was shared by (*Key Informant 2, Safety Worker, March 7, 2025*), noting that while management assigns tasks, employees are responsible for ensuring compliance (Harsch and Festing, 2019). The third sub-theme is regular training programs and evaluations, as noted by (*Key Informant 1, HR Manager, March 7, 2025*), with monthly programs covering topics such as safety procedures and performance evaluations. The fourth sub-theme is investment in quality training, with (*Key Informant 3, CFO, March 7, 2025*) highlighting that the founder invested in employees' training to enhance skills and performance.

4 RESULT AND DISCUSSION

On-site interviews showed that the company is ISO 9001:2015–certified and uses a risk registry to identify and assess organizational risks, supporting risk-based thinking. Table 1 presents the risks recorded in the registry, which also align with themes from the thematic analysis. Likelihood and consequence ratings were taken directly from the registry, and risk factors were computed by multiplying these values. Based on the risk matrix, R 1.1, R 1.2, R 1.3, and R 1.4 fall under **very high risk**, while R 1.5 is classified as **high risk**.

Table 1. Risk assessment.

Code	Risk	Likelihood Rating (L)	Consequence Rating (C)	Risk Factor (L x C)
R 1.1	Non-Compliance with Recent DOLE Guidelines in Managing the Workplace	5.0	4.3	21.7
R 1.2	Non-Compliance with Mandatory Environment, Safety, and Health Training	5.0	4.2	20.8
R 1.3	Compliance with Mandatory Environment, Health, and Safety / Mental Health Workplace Policies and Programs	5.0	4.0	20
R 1.4	Non-Implementation of Mental Health Workplace Policies and Programs	5.0	4.3	21.7
R 1.5	Attrition / Quick Turnover / Transfer of Key Talents to Competition	4.5	3.0	13.5

DOLE is the primary agency enforcing OSH standards, making compliance essential for preventing accidents and meeting labor regulations. Compliance ensures organizational practices follow legal and internal guidelines, while non-compliance creates operational and safety risks. This reinforces why the company's compliance-related risks score very high in the registry.

Non-compliance, even when unintentional, can lead to errors, violations, and disruptions. This is especially critical in steel manufacturing, where mental health and safety programs help reduce stress and support workers in a high-risk environment. These findings explain why mental health program gaps appear as very high risks in the company's registry.

Table 2 summarizes the Risk Matrix Rating Levels, showing how likelihood and consequence scores combine to determine risk severity. The color-coded scale ranges from low to extreme and outlines the required response for each category. Scores of **1–4** are considered low and require no corrective action, while **5–9** indicate moderate risk that must be monitored. Scores of **10–16** fall under high risk and need prompt attention, whereas **17–20** are very high and require immediate, significant action. The most critical category, **21–25**, is classified as extreme risk and demands urgent intervention or stopping the activity entirely.

Table 2. Risk matrix.

LIKELIHOOD						
Very likely to occur	5				R 1.1 R 1.2 R 1.3 R 1.4	
Likely to occur	4			R 1.5		
Somewhat likely to occur	3					
Unlikely to occur	2					
Not applicable	1					
		1 Very Low	2 Low	3 Medium	4 High	5 Very High

Research shows that mental health issues are common among steel workers and worsen under harmful work conditions. The company may also face turnover risks, as employees often leave for better compensation, benefits, or career opportunities. These issues reinforce the financial and operational impact of the risks listed in the registry. Risk matrices and risk registers help evaluate the likelihood and impact of hazards and ensure risks are documented across departments. The company's registry supports the thematic findings, showing strong risk identification practices. However, the repeated appearance of the same high-level risks suggests the need for stronger implementation and follow-through.

Table 3. Risk matrix rating levels.

CONSEQUENCE	
	= 21-25: Extreme Risk – Immediate action or termination of activity required.
	= 17-20: Very High Risk – Requires immediate attention and significant action.
	= 10-16: High Risk – Requires attention.
	= 5-9: Moderate Risk – Monitor and manage.
	= 1-4: Tolerable, Low Risk – Acceptable, no action required.

5 CONCLUSION

The findings of this study demonstrate that, within a steel fabrication company, HR risks constitute financial risks due to their connection with compliance, safety, and environmental obligations. These risks are interrelated, with compliance exerting particular influence over outcomes in other areas. Although the company has a robust ISO 9001:2015-certified risk register and thorough identification methods, identification alone is insufficient. As Altomonte (2025) stated, mitigation necessitates ongoing action, and the recurring nature of the identified issues highlights gaps in implementation and execution. Therefore, the company must develop stronger capabilities not only in risk identification but also in risk control and response. The study should therefore provide clear evidence supporting more effective implementation of safety, HR, and environmental policies, particularly concerning labour-management relations and compliance. It should also address the adoption of digital technologies such as ERP systems. Evidence from AlMarri *et al.* (2025) indicates that, even with AI and digital twins, ERP platforms can enhance risk assessment, automate compliance monitoring, and enable predictive analytics to inform decisions. Integrating AI into ERP systems increases efficiency and reduces human error, leading to more reliable risk classification.

Besides, the adoption of a digital ecosystem in tandem with the philosophy of sustainable governance cements long-term resilience. According to Ghosh *et al.* (2023), ESG integration has helped organizations move beyond mere passive compliance to active leadership in sustainability on the basis of transparency through reporting and periodic assessment of ESG performance. Finally, sustainability should guide major business decisions, particularly since the steel industry is ranked among the largest contributors to emissions and resource consumption. Operationally aligning with SDG 12, SDG 9, and SDG 8 will ensure responsible production, industry growth driven by innovation, and decent working conditions, as expected from modern-day stakeholders by Depczyński *et al.* (2023).

6 DIRECTIONS FOR FUTURE RESEARCH

For future research, integrating advanced digital technologies such as ERP systems, AI-based risk prediction models, and blockchain offers significant potential to enhance risk transparency, simulation, and traceability in compliance reporting. However, existing literature lacks metrics of ERP systems applied in the steel industry. Therefore, future research may also consider tracking the quantitative performance of such systems. In addition, evaluating the effectiveness of digital ecosystems in improving decision-making and stakeholder engagement is particularly relevant in industrial settings, especially within emerging economies. To further understand these dynamics, longitudinal investigations are needed to evaluate how digital and sustainable risk governance impacts organizational resilience, innovation capacity, and long-term performance, specifically focusing on the steel manufacturing sector.

7 CONFLICT OF INTEREST, DECLARATION OF ETHICAL COMPLIANCE, AND DECLARATION OF AI USAGE

The authors affirm that there is no conflict of interest and that the study was conducted in accordance with research ethics. The researchers ensure that all information is used solely for research and that the Key Informants will remain private. The authors state that the only purpose of artificial intelligence (AI) is to enhance language clarity and readability. Grammarly's AI was used to provide grammar and style recommendations, but the authors checked and revised every change to make sure it was correct and appropriate.

REFERENCES

Abreu, P., Fernandes, V., Neto, L., and Oliveira, U. (2021). *Risk Management Applied to the Reverse Logistics of Solid Waste*. São Paulo: Springer. https://doi.org/10.1016/j.jclepro.2021.126517

Ahmad F., Ejaz F., Hossain M.B., and Mustafa K. Green (2023). *HRM Practices and Knowledge Sharing Improve Environmental Performance by Raising Employees' Commitment to the Environment*. Basel: Multidisciplinary Digital Publishing Institute. https://www.mdpi.com/2071-1050/15/6/5040

Al-Mekhlafi, A. (2024). *Effective Human Resources Management Creates A More Secure Work Environment By Improving Safety Culture*. Bahrain: Gulf University. https://tinyurl.com/vmp9ksnb

AlMarri, M., Al-Ali, M., Alzarooni, M., AlTeneiji, A., Al-Ali, K., and Bahroun, Z. (2025). *Enterprise Resource Planning Systems For Health, Safety, and Environment Management: Analyzing Critical Success Factors*. Sharjah: MDPI. https://doi.org/10.3390/su17072947

Altomonte (2025). What is Risk Mitigation? Sydney: SafetyCulture. https://safetyculture.com/topics/risk-mitigation/

Antonio, K. and Campo, B. (2022). *Insurance Pricing With Hierarchically Structured Data: An Illustration with a Workers' Compensation Insurance Portfolio*. Oxfordshire: Taylor & Francis. https://doi.org/10.1080/03461238.2022.2161413

Cohen, S. (2024). The Connection Between Environmental Risk, Financial Risk, And Data-Based Sustainability Management. New York: Columbia University School of Professional Studies. https://tinyurl.com/5cdfymbm

Depczyński, R., Secka, J., Cheba, K., D'Alessandro, C., Szopik-Depczyńska, K. (2023). *Decision-Making Approach in Sustainability Assessment in Steel Manufacturing Companies—Systematic Literature Review*. Basel: Multidisciplinary Digital Publishing Institute. https://doi.org/10.3390/su151511614

Efe, A. (2023). A comparison of key risk management frameworks: coso-erm, nist rmf, iso 31.000, cobit. *Journal of Auditing and Assurance Services.* https://tinyurl.com/5458dd93

Ghosh, R., Raut, D., Mandal, M., and Ray, A. (2023). "*Revisiting the Nexus Between Sustainable Supply Chain Management and the Performance of Steel Manufacturing*. Piscataway: Institute of Electrical and Electronics Engineers. https://doi.org/10.1109/EMR.2022.3233484

Harsch, K. and Festing, M. (2019). *Dynamic Talent Management Capabilities and Organizational Agility—A Qualitative Exploration*. Hoboken: John Wiley & Sons https://doi.org/10.1002/hrm.21972

Isah, M.A., and Kim, B.S. (2023). Development of a knowledge graph based on a risk register to support risk management of construction projects. *Retrieved from: (PDF) Development of Knowledge Graph Based on Risk Register to Support Risk Management of Construction Projects*. Dae-jeon: KSCE Journal of Civil Engineering.

Jalac, P.I., Fedilo, J.M., Sison, J.P., and Galingan, R. (2018). Work-Related Musculoskeletal Risk Assessment among Structural Iron Workers in a Steel Company in the Philippines. Bandung, Indonesia: *International Conference on Industrial Engineering and Operations Management.* https://tinyurl.com/yw6bbmfd

Lancaster, A. and Goff, S. (2023). *Financial Risk Management Fundamentals* https://tinyurl.com/45bs6r6e

Nordlof, H., Wiitavaara, B., Winblad, U., Wijk, K., and Westerling, R. (2015). *Safety Culture And Reasons For Risk-Taking At A Large Steel-Manufacturing Company: Investigating the Worker Perspective*. Gävle: Elsevier Ltd. https://doi.org/10.1016/j.ssci.2014.11.020

Yazo-Cabuya, E.J., Ibeas, A., and Rey-Caballero, R. (2025). Multi-criteria decision making for risk management in quality management systems. *Barcelona*: MDPI. https://doi.org/10.3390/su17031092

Moving Towards Sustainable Businesses and Developing More Resilient Economies – Rashid and Annansingh-Jamieson (Eds)
 ISBN: 978-1-041-08875-2

Effect of tariff on the correlation between the dollar and international investment assets

Joseph Cheng and Victor Shahnazarian
Pepperdine University, USA

ABSTRACT: For promoting fair international trade and encouraging more investment in U.S. manufacturing, the Trump administration imposed reciprocal tariff on imports from many nations. Liberation Day was declared on April 2, 2025 when sweeping reciprocal tariff was implemented across the board, causing a major shift in the landscape of world trade and international flow of investments. During the period, the value of the U.S. dollar relative to other currencies experienced substantial depreciation. Furthermore, the S&P 500 index also suffered significant declines from the market peak on February 19 to the trough on April 8. Recovery for the U.S. stock market began on April 9th due to the tariff pause. Accordingly, two sample periods were created: first part for the declining period and the second part for the recovery period. Regressions were conducted for both sample periods for estimating the values of beta for 18 International ETFs for the purpose of evaluating the correlation between International ETF's and U.S. market. The result reveals that the beta values for majority of the International ETF's declined from the first (declining period) to the second period (recovery period), indicating that most International ETFs suffered greater loss during the declining period than the gains realized from the recovery period. The result from a second regression with U.S dollar added as an additional independent variable reveals that the returns of foreign financial markets correlate negatively with the U.S. dollar, instead of positively as generally explained by traditional economics theory. This surprise finding suggests that the stronger U.S. dollar would not help foreign companies increase their import into the U.S. or to increase their profit if the strengthening of the dollar is linked to the tariff rather than to other economics factors.

1 LITERATURE REVIEW

International trade has become a major issue in 2025 due to the Reciprocal Tariff Proposal made by the U.S. government. There has been a plethora of articles emerged for discussing the impact of tariff on the world economy and financial markets.

Yilmazkuday (2025), using a structural VAR model in Finance Research Letters, quantifies the long-term effects of U.S. tariff shocks on major equity indices. A one standard deviation tariff shock reduces stock prices by 7.3%–10.1% across the S&P 500, NASDAQ, and Dow. Additionally, tariff-related uncertainty explains up to 10% of stock return variance.

Similarly, Amiti, Itskhoki, and Konings (2025), in a National Bureau of Economic Research (NBER) working paper, find that a 1% increase in tariffs is associated with a 0.23% decline in equity prices. Their analysis uses a refined measure of tariff variation to isolate the causal impact.

DOI: 10.1201/9781003647300-32

Tan (2025) develops a multivariate econometric model to assess the effects of tariff policy features—such as magnitude, scope, and timing—on stock market performance. His findings suggest strong predictive relationships between trade policy and return, supporting implications for portfolio risk management.

Ma (2025), in conference proceedings published by EWAdirect, reports immediate market reactions to U.S. tariff announcements in April 2025. The findings include stock market corrections, heightened volatility, and increased flows to safe-haven assets. Markets more exposed to U.S. trade experienced sharper declines.

2 INTRODUCTION

While there have been many articles addressing the issue of how financial markets are impacted by the tariff, there is a lack of literature addressing how the correlation or interdependency between specific foreign markets and the U.S. markets might have changed.

In this study, we divided our sample into two periods according to the performance of the U.S. stock market as represented by the S&P 500 index:

Declining period-starting from the day of market index peaking on Feb 19 to the date when the market reaching a trough on April 8; and recovery period- starting from April 9th to the end of June 2025. The recovery of the market during that time was due to the announcement of tariff pause, providing the market hope that the tariff negotiation would continue, which boosted the market in the ensuing period. Thus, the declining period was the earlier period prior to the tariff pause and the recovery period was the latter period afterward.

The reason that we chose to end the sample period on June 30th is that the Big and Beautiful Bill was passed by Congress at that time, which entails many economic proposals that would certainly have some impact on the financial markets. In order to minimize any spillover effect of the Bill on the financial markets, we ended the sample period at the end of June so that most of the movements in the financial markets in the sample period are related to the changes in tariff announcements and not to the proposals from the new bill.

In the Capital Asset Pricing Model, the beta of a stock represents the degree of market risk, which is normally estimated by regressing the stock's return on the market return, whose proxy is often the S&P returns. The higher the beta value, the greater the fluctuation of the stock relative to the S&P. The value of beta also reflects the relative co-variation or correlation between the stock and the market. In order to evaluate the covariation between the international financial markets and the U.S. market, we regressed the returns of international ETF's, which are used as proxy for the foreign financial markets, on the return of S&P. The coefficient for the S&P return would be the beta for the international ETF, which would yield information on how the international financial markets correlate with the U.S. market for both periods. Linear regressions were performed for analyzing the correlation between the daily return of 18 international ETF's and the daily return of SP for both declining and recovery periods.

3 REGRESSION RESULTS

The regression result is shown in Table 1, with p-values for the coefficients placed in parenthesis. Note that all the p-values are less than 1%, which means that all the beta coefficients are statistically significant at the 99% level.

Table 1. Beta estimate for international ETF for both sample periods.

Country	Beta (Declining Period)	t-stat (p-value)	R^2	Beta (Recovery Period)	t-stat (p-value)	R^2
China (FXI)	0.636	2.6 (.014)	.171	.627	6.81 (0)	.466
Argentina (ARGT)	1.074	5.81 (0)	.505	.817	6.83 (0)	.468
Israel (EIS)	0.74	7.82 (0)	.649	.611	6.86 (0)	.47
India (EPI)	0.576	6.46 (0)	.558	.356	4.63 (0)	.288
Australia (EWA)	0.928	8.41 (0)	.682	.729	11.3 (0)	.7
Canada (EWC)	0.838	13.37 (0)	.844	.5	11.08 (0)	.698
Sweden (EWD)	0.922	6.37 (0)	.552	.598	8.17 (0)	.558
Germany (EWG)	0.674	4.4 (0)	.37	.675	10.0 (0)	.653
France (EWH)	0.597	3.81 (.001)	.305	.366	5.66 (0)	.377
Italy (EWI)	0.792	5.35 (0)	.465	.7	10.3 (0)	.667
Japan (EWJ)	0.739	7.55 (0)	.633	.668	10.38 (0)	.67
Switzerland (EWL)	0.432	3.55 (.001)	.276	.4	6.16 (0)	.417
Malaysia (EWM)	0.509	4.33 (0)	.363	.318	4.57 (0)	.283
Singapore (EWS)	0.739	5.88 (0)	.511	.707	10.18 (0)	.662
Taiwan (EWT)	0.868	6.89 (0)	.59	.856	8.37 (0)	.569
UK (EWU)	0.606	4.86 (0)	.417	.449	8.29 (0)	.565
Mexico (EWW)	0.544	2.89 (.007)	.203	.574	6.05 (0)	.408
Brazil (EWZ)	0.61	3.57 (.001)	.279	.523	6.43 (0)	.438

Regression Result indicates that beta values of foreign ETF's are all positive, as one would expect, indicating that financial markets across the globe are all linked together.

Interestingly, when comparing the beta values of the same ETF for the two different samples periods, we noted that the magnitude of the beta values for the majority of the international ETFs' dropped from the declining period to the recovery period. This means that the beta values for the declining period are greater than the beta value for the recovery period. One possible way to interpret this result is that the loss suffered by these International ETF's relative to the U.S. market during the declining period is greater than their gains relative to the U.S. market during the recovery period. This indicates that while tariff caused losses in all financial markets, including the U.S. market, the losses in international markets tend to be even greater relative to the U.S. This suggested that the market sentiment is that the U.S. tariff imposes greater penalty on the foreign nations than on the U.S.

Another possible cause for the decline in the value of beta or covariation between the foreign markets and the U.S. market is that foreign firms exporting to the U.S. made some adjustments that might reduce their dependence on the U.S. market.

To extend this study, we continued with a second regression model with the daily return of the international ETF's remained as the dependent variable while adding a second independent variable, which is the daily change in the value of the U.S. dollar (whose data was downloaded from FRED, which is broad based index measuring the dollar's international value) in percentage terms. The coefficients for the daily change in the U.S. dollar represent the magnitude of correlation between International ETF's and the U.S. dollar. According to traditional economics theory, the correlation between USD and foreign market returns should be positive. That is because when USD rises, foreign import becomes cheaper to American Consumers, which will increase export of foreign countries into the U.S. and thus increase profit for foreign companies.

The estimating result for the second regression model with U.S. Dollar added as an additional explanatory variable is summarized in Table 2, with the first row of each ETF summarizes the statistics for the coefficient for S&P and the second row for the coefficient for the U.S.D:

Table 2. Correlation between international ETF's and the U.S. Dollar for both sample periods.

Country	Independent Variables	Estimated Coefficient (Declining Period)	t-stat (p-value)	R^2	Estimated Coefficient (Recovery Period)	t-stat (p-value)	R^2
China (FXI)	SP	0.591	3.10 (.004)	.509	0.715	8.5 (0)	.593
	USD	-3.641	-4.69 (0)		-1.737	-4.01 (0)	
Argentina (ARGT)	SP	1.043	6.89 (0)	.679	0.889	7.48 (0)	.519
	USD	-2.562	-4.16 (0)		-1.426	-2.33 (.023)	
Israel (EIS)	SP	0.730	8.22 (0)	.701	0.619	6.65 (0)	.471
	USD	-0.851	-2.35 (0.025)		-0.159	-0.33 (.74)	
India (EPI)	SP	0.562	7.385 (0)	.688	0.404	5.32 (0)	.362
	USD	-1.127	-3.63 (0.001)		-0.963	-2.46 (.017)	
Australia (EWA)	SP	0.908	10.71 (0)	.818	0.809	15.50 (0)	.824
	USD	-1.69	-4.90 (0)		-1.581	-5.89 (0)	
Canada (EWC)	SP	0.824	21.39 (0)	.943	0.557	14.96 (0)	.813
	USD	-1.168	-7.46 (0)		-1.086	-5.67 (0)	
Sweden (EWD)	SP	0.891	9.28 (0)	.809	0.684	11.22 (0)	.718
	USD	-2.561	-6.56 (0)		-1.708	-5.44 (0)	
Germany (EWG)	SP	0.642	6.09 (0)	.711	0.753	13.13 (0)	.771
	USD	-2.634	-6.15 (0)		-1.528	-5.18 (0)	
HK (EWH)	SP	0.574	4.27 (0)	.508	0.408	6.39 (0)	.445
	USD	-1.979	-3.62 (.001)		-0.826	-2.51 (.015)	
Italy (EWI)	SP	0.726	7.19 (0)	.733	0.777	13.31(0)	.775
	USD	-2.447	-5.67 (0)		-1.499	-5.00 (0)	
Japan (EWJ)	SP	0.729	7.81 (0)	.676	0.721	11.81(0)	.728
	USD	-0.785	-2.06 (.047)		-1.049	-3.34 (.002)	
Switzerland (EWL)	SP	0.412	4.14 (0)	.533	0.490	9.50 (0)	.671
	USD	-1.696	-4.19 (0)		-1.680	-6.33 (0)	
Malaysia (EWM)	SP	0.496	4.48 (0)	.452	0.404	7.16 (0)	.568
	USD	-1.026	-2.28 (.029)		-1.700	-5.85 (0)	
Singapore (EWS)	SP	0.717	7.09 (0)	.693	0.773	12.16 (0)	.74
	USD	-1.792	-4.35 (0)		-1.299	-3.97 (0)	
Taiwan (EWT)	SP	0.854	7.20 (0)	.648	0.936	9.57 (0)	.639
	USD	-1.105	-2.29 (.028)		-1.593	-3.16 (.003)	
UK (EWU)	SP	0.585	5.65 (0)	.61	0.521	12.60 (0)	.767
	USD	-1.674	-3.98 (0)		-1.430	-6.72 (0)	
Mexico (EWW)	SP	0.500	4.88 (0)	.77	0.648	7.10 (0)	.5
	USD	-3.708	-8.90 (0)		-1.449	-3.09 (.003)	
Brazil (EWZ)	SP	0.578	4.47 (0)	.6	0.567	6.93 (0)	.48
	USD	-2.669	-5.07 (0)		-0.862	-2.05 (.045)	

Note in Table 2 that the signs of the coefficient of the U.S. dollar for the international ETF's are all negative (instead of positive as had originally expected). Surprisingly, the estimated values for the coefficients for the U.S.D for all the ETFs not only turned out to be negative, they are statistically significant, which contradict to what one might had expected. One possible reason for this surprising finding is that the U.S.D can be strengthened by the tariff because tariff reduces demand for imports by American consumers which can help reduce U.S trade deficit, which in turn decrease the flow of US dollar abroad and thus increase the value of the dollar. Such kind of increase in the value of the dollar might not benefit foreign companies because this specific form of increase in the dollar value is linked to tariff rather than linked to other economic factors. And the tariff imposed by the U.S. would certainly reduce imports into U.S. and thus the profit and returns of foreign companies, which would explain the negative correlation and why the returns of the international ETF's declined as the dollar was strengthened by the tariff during this volatile period.

3 CONCLUSION

The regression results for the two sample periods surrounding the tariff saga revealed that the values of beta for majority of the international ETF's dipped from the declining period to the recovery period, which suggested that while reciprocal tariff exerted a negative impact on financial markets around the world, the market sentiment seems to indicate that the foreign markets would suffer even greater losses than the U.S. market. Another possible cause for the decline in beta or covariation of returns is that foreign firms exporting to the U.S. made some adjustments that reduced their dependence on the U.S. markets.

A surprising finding was made regarding the negative correlation between the foreign markets and the U.S.D. during both the declining and recovery periods. This negative correlation is contrary to general economic theory and is an indication that any rise in the value of the dollar due to tariff would neither boost imports into the U.S. nor increase profits for foreign firms.

REFERENCES

Benguria, F., and Saffie, F. (2025). Rounding up the effect of tariffs on financial markets: Evidence from April 2, 2025 (NBER Working Paper No. 34036). *National Bureau of Economic Research*. https://doi.org/10.3386/w34036

Ma, R. (2025). Impact of 2025 US tariff increases on stock markets and strategic responses. *Advances in Economics, Management and Political Sciences*, 200(1), 69–76. https://doi.org/10.54254/2754-1169/2025.lh25109

Tan, K.H. (2025). Modelling the impact of tariff policy shocks on stock market performance: A multivariate econometric approach [Preprint]. https://doi.org/10.13140/RG.2.2.34238.80963

Yilmazkuday, H. (2025). U.S. tariffs and stock prices. *Finance Research Letters*, 83, 107708. https://doi.org/10.1016/j.frl.2025.107708

Moving Towards Sustainable Businesses and Developing More Resilient Economies –
Rashid and Annansingh-Jamieson (Eds)
 ISBN: 978-1-041-08875-2

Analyzing the effects of weather on stock prices for investment management

John Goodermote
College of William and Mary, Williamsburg, USA

Jola Pham
Chicago, USA

Tracy Phan
New York, USA

Loyal Goodermote
College of William and Mary, Williamsburg, USA

ABSTRACT: This paper studies the effects of changes in weather variables, specifically temperatures, precipitation, and wind, on stock prices of companies in different sectors. The changes of these weather indicators are defined regarding their normal values. The stocks are selected from different sectors such as retail, energy, and sports. Experimental results show that while it seems that in general there is no effect of weather on stock price movement, when the weather changes are significantly crossing certain thresholds there are patterns of stock price movement in certain time periods of the year. These results can be used to temporarily exit or enter certain sectors/individual stocks in a portfolio to improve its performance and return.

1 INTRODUCTION

There are many factors which influence stock prices. They can be (i) fundamental, such as company earnings reports and management; (ii) technical, such as trading volume and chart patterns; (iii) economics, such as inflation and unemployment rate; (iv) psychological such as news articles and investor mood; and (v) external, such as natural disasters and election results. Weather factors such as temperatures, precipitation, humidity, wind speeds, and cloud cover can fundamentally affect the productions, services, and performance of many companies in different sectors such as energy, agriculture, sport, and retails. Weather factors can also psychologically affect market sentiment and investor behaviors. While there are many research papers investigating the effects of various fundamental, technical, economic, and psychological factors on stock performance, there are not many publications about the effects of weather on stock prices.

This paper aims to study the effects of weather factors, specifically temperature, precipitation, and wind speed, on the stock prices of companies in various sectors. The potential findings from this research can be used in making decisions about temporarily existing or entering certain stocks within a portfolio, with the goal of enhancing its performance and returns. The rest of this paper is organized as follows. First, the related work is reviewed in Section 2. Then, the design of the analytical system, data, and sources are described in Section 3. Next, the experiments and results on the effects of temperature, precipitation, and

 DOI: 10.1201/9781003647300-33

wind speed on stock prices are presented in Sections 4, 5, and 6 respectively. Finally, conclusions and future work are provided in Section 7.

2 REVIEW OF RELATED WORKS

Numerous studies have examined how fundamental factors such as earnings, and technical indicators such as trading volume influence stock prices. However, far fewer studies have explored the impact of weather on stock prices. While Kathiravan *et al.* (2021) provided a comprehensive review of research papers investigating the effects of weather on stock prices, Saunders (1993) seems to be considered the first who reported that weather might have influenced stock prices. He found a significant correlation between cloud cover in New York and stock prices: there were lower returns on cloudier days. Hirshleifer and Shumway (2003) echoed that hypothesis and reported that "sunshine is strongly significantly correlated with stock returns" across 26 international stock exchanges from 1982 to 1997. Akhtari (2011) reassessed Saunders's 1993 study, finding a significant relationship between sunshine and stock prices for over a half-century. Goetzmann *et al.* (2015) also found some evidence of how weather-induced mood affects institutional investors' decisions. In terms of temperature, Cao and Wei (2005) found a statistically significant negative correlation between temperature and stock returns across various global markets. Kathiravan *et al.* (2018) also found that temperature affects Indian stock returns and volatility using GARCH models. An *et al.* (2018) analyzed daily air-pollution data from 2005 to 2014 and found that "a contemporaneous negative and a two-day lagged positive relationship exists between air pollution levels and stock returns."

Looking beyond one single weather variable, Chang *et al.* (2006), used a threshold model with GJR-GARCH method to analyze daily data from 1997 to 2003, and found that both temperature and cloud cover significantly influence stock returns in Taiwan. Exploring more weather variables, Yoon and Kang (2009) found connections between temperature, humidity, cloud cover, and stock returns in the Korean stock market. They used MA-MSD to analyze the relationship between them. Symeonidis *et al.* (2010) found that cloudiness and the length of nighttime are inversely related to stock market volatility. In the same direction but with mixed results, Lu and Chou (2012) examined the Shanghai Stock Exchange (SSE) and found that temperature, humidity, and wind significantly impacted trading activities, through indicators such as turnover, volatility, and liquidity, while they have almost no significant impact on asset returns. Soost *et al.* (2021) provided a comprehensive study on German stock markets (2003–2017), finding air pressure as the only consistent weather variable affecting returns and trading volume. Their results showed positive effects on returns in the DAX, MDAX, and SDAX, suggesting a positive influence of improving weather conditions in the German market.

Besides directly measuring daily weather variables, some researchers measure weather through weather-related events such as storms, drought, flood, etc. Antoniuk and Leirvik (2021) examined how climate-related events impact the stock prices from different sectors. They found that "the clean energy sector benefited from events that increased awareness and support for climate change policies, while sectors like utilities, energy-intensive industries, and transportation experienced increased market risks." Recently, Li *et al.* (2024) analyzed 526 climate-related extreme weather events during 2000–2019 and found that biological (influenza or algal blooms) and hydrological (drought, wildfires, hurricanes, and floods) events negatively affected returns within the NASDAQ 100, while the climate dimension had a positive impact.

On the other hand, Kramer and Runde (1997), using German data, argued that the results in some studies on correlations between weather and stock markets likely come from data mining rather than true influence of weather on the stock market performance. Goetzmann and Zhu (2005) analyzed the trading activity of individual investor accounts in five major US cities over a six-year period. They found virtually no difference or very limited evidence for weather influencing trading behavior: buying or selling equities on cloudy days as opposed to sunny days. Keef and Roush (2007) also found mixed evidence for weather effects on Australian stock indices. Off-season temperatures were reported to have a stronger negative effect than normal temperatures while wind speed, cloud cover, and storm have mixed effects. They also highlighted that the weather effects are not uniform and can vary based on locations. Pizzutilo and Roncone (2017) completely rejected the weather effect hypothesis in emerging markets with an analysis on how temperature, cloud cover, humidity and wind affect the stock markets of nine emerging countries.

In the end, does the weather affect stock prices after all? A way to find out is to implement weather-guided stock trading mechanisms and see if we can improve investment returns with them. Dong and Tremblay (2021) tested weather-based trading strategies globally and found that sunshine has a universal positive impact on returns: "mean annual return of hedge strategy is 15.2 % relative to 6.2 % of the world index".

In summary, although some skepticism remains regarding the influence of weather on stock price movements, most empirical studies suggest that certain weather variables do exert a measurable impact on market behavior. They also try to explain these effects solely with behavioral finance theory, which suggests that weather conditions can act as mood proxies, influencing investors' decisions and potentially impacting market volatility. For example, some studies suggest that sunny weather might lead to increased optimism and risk-taking among investors, potentially driving up returns, while cloudy or rainy weather may have the opposite effect.

3 AN ANALYTICAL SYSTEM FOR MEASURING WEATHER EFFECTS

We propose a system to measure the effects of weather, specifically the temperature change, precipitation amount, and wind speed on the stock prices. Unlike most of the studies reviewed in the preceding section, which examine stock market fluctuations through broad market indices, this study aims to analyze the effects of weather on stock prices of individual companies in different sectors such as utilities, retails, energy, and sports. Our goal is to analyze stock price changes (compared to the SP500 change of the same day) against the changes of temperature (compared to normal), precipitation accumulation (rain and snow), and wind speed in New York city. The following companies in different sectors were selected for our study: Consolidated Edison (ED), Verizon Communications (VZ) in utilities, Walmart Inc (WMT) in retail, Exxon Mobil (XOM) in energy, Madison Square Garden Sports (MSGS) in sport, while Nike (NKE), Dicks Sporting Goods (DKS), and Topgolf Callaway Brands (MODG) are in a retail-sport mix.

3.1 *Data and sources*

We use weather data sets, daily and normal, for Central Park station in New York city, from the National Center for Environment Information and stock price data sets (ED, VZ, WMT, XOM, MSGS, NKE, DKS, MODG, and SP500) from Fidelity. Both weather and stock price data are from 05/21/2014 to 21/05/2025.

3.2 *System design*

Our system consists of the following components: Data Gathering, Data Preparation, Data Analysis, Data Export, Data Visualization. The Data Gathering component inputs and verifies the downloaded raw data about the weather and stock prices. The obtained weather data includes the data sets of daily temperature (minimal and maximal), precipitation (total), snow (total), and wind speed (minimal and maximal) and their normal for the given period. The obtained stock data are the daily minimal, maximal, open, and close prices for the same period. The Data Preparation component cleans and refines raw data transforming raw data into a unified or right format as well as preprocess and normalize data from different series and sets. The Data Analysis component processes the refined data implementing the data analysis methods and algorithms which are described in the next section. The Data Export component produces the results of data analysis in the right formats and in appropriate combinations for visualization. Finally, the Data Visualization component displays the output of the Data Export component in charts. Most of these components are implemented in Python while the current Data Visualization component is a plug-in to outsource the output of the Data Export component to Excel for charts.

3.3 *Methodology for data analysis*

The obtained weather data includes daily temperature (minimal and maximal), total daily rain fall, total daily snow fall, and wind speeds (minimal and maximal) and their normal for the given period from 05/21/2014 to 05/21/2025.

3.3.1 *Measuring weather*

To measure the changes of temperatures we calculate the daily relative changes in temperatures of the current day compared to the normal temperature of the same day instead of calculating the absolute change of current day temperature compared with the temperature of the previous day. This is to remove the seasonal characteristics that temperatures always increase in spring and decrease in fall. The daily temperature change is defined as follows:

$$\mathrm{T}_{\mathrm{change(d)}} = \frac{\mathrm{T}_{\mathrm{current}_{\mathrm{max(d)}}} + \mathrm{T}_{\mathrm{current}_{\mathrm{min(d)}}}}{2} - \frac{\mathrm{T}_{\mathrm{normal}_{\mathrm{max(d)}}} + \mathrm{T}_{\mathrm{normal}_{\mathrm{min(d)}}}}{2}$$

In our study, the second weather indicator to be examined is the precipitation where we use the daily values themselves, instead of the changes compared with the normal or previous days, because rain and snow are rare events which themselves are significant factors enough to influence business activities and the emotions of traders and investors. The daily precipitation is defined as the total amount of rainfall and snowfall of a given day.

$$P(d) = R_{fall(d)} + S_{fall(d)}$$

The third weather indicator we use in our study is the wind speed. Similar to precipitation, we use the wind speed daily values themselves $W(d)$, instead of the changes compared with the normal or previous days.

3.3.2 *Measuring stock price changes*

To measure the changes of a particular stock price we calculate the beta of the stock price regarding the change of the stock market using SP500 index. This is to remove the general events or factors which affect the whole market for all stocks. The comparative relative change of this stock price against SP500 index value is defined as follows.

$$SwSP_{change(d,s)} = \frac{\left(S_{open(d,s)} + S_{close(d,s)} + S_{high(d,s)} + S_{low(d,s)}\right) - \left(S_{open(d-1,s)} + S_{close(d-1,s)} + S_{high(d-1,s)} + S_{low(d-1,s)}\right)}{\left(S_{open(d-1,s)} + S_{close(d-1,s)} + S_{high(d-1,s)} + S_{low(d-1,s)}\right)} - \frac{\left(SP_{open(d,s)} + SP_{close(d,s)} + SP_{high(d,s)} + SP_{low(d,s)}\right) - \left(SP_{open(d-1,s)} + SP_{close(d-1,s)} + SP_{high(d-1,s)} + SP_{low(d-1,s)}\right)}{\left(SP_{open(d-1,s)} + SP_{close(d-1,s)} + SP_{high(d-1,s)} + SP_{low(d-1,s)}\right)}$$

Where d is a given date, s is the symbol of a given stock, SP is the SP500 index value.

3.3.3 *Identifying the impact of weather on stock price*

We track the stock price movement of a given stock price against these weather indicators: temperature change, precipitation amount, and wind speed.

Temperature
For a given period of time PT=[ts,te], we calculate the frequency or its percentage of stock price increase (Si) above a stock price change threshold S_threshold, when the temperature of the day rises (Ti) above the normal temperature by a given threshold T_threshold as follows.

$$TiSi(s, ts, te) = \frac{\sum_{d=ts}^{te} BOOL\big(\big(SwSP_{change(d,s)} - S\_threshold\big) > 0\big) \cdot BOOL\ \big(\big(T_{change(d)} - T\_threshold\big) > 0\big)}{\sum_{d=ts}^{te} BOOL\big(\ \big(T_{change(d)} - T\_threshold\big) > 0\big)}$$

where, ts = starting date and te = ending date, s is a given stock symbol, BOOL is the boolean function which returns 1 when true and 0 when false.

Precipitation
For the given period of time PT=[ts,te], we calculate the frequency or its percentage of stock price increase (Si) above a stock price change threshold S_threshold, when the rainfall and snowfall amount is above a threshold P_threshold.

$$PSi(s, ts, te) = \frac{\sum_{d=ts}^{te} (BOOL\ \big(\big(SwSP_{change(d,s)} - S\_threshold\big) > 0\big) \cdot BOOL\ (R\_fall(d) + S\_fall(d) - P\_threshold) > 0)}{\sum_{d=ts}^{te} BOOL\ (R\_fall(d) + S\_fall(d) - P\_threshold) > 0)}$$

$$PSd(s, ts, te) = \frac{\sum_{d=ts}^{te} (BOOL\ \big(\big(SwSP_{change(d,s)} - S\_threshold\big) < 0\big) \cdot BOOL\ ((R\_fall(d) + S\_fall(d) - P\_threshold) > 0)}{\sum_{d=ts}^{te} BOOL\ BOOL\ ((R\_fall(d) + S\_fall(d) - P\_threshold) > 0)}$$

where, ts = starting date and te = ending date, s is a given stock symbol, BOOL is the boolean function which returns 1 when true and 0 when false.

Wind
For a given period of time PT=[ts,te], we calculate the frequency or its percentage of stock price increase (Si) above a stock price change threshold S_threshold, when the wind speed is above a stock price change threshold W_threshold.

$$WSi(s, ts, te) = \frac{\sum_{d=ts}^{te} (BOOL\big(\big(SwSP_{change(d,s)} - S\_threshold\big) > 0\big) \cdot BOOL((W(d) - W\_threshold) > 0)}{\sum_{d=ts}^{te} BOOL((W(d) - W\_threshold) > 0)}$$

$$WSd(s, ts, te) = \frac{\sum_{d=ts}^{te} \big(BOOL\ \big(\big(SwSP_{change(d,s)} - S\_threshold\big) < 0\big) \cdot BOOL\ ((W(d) - W\_threshold) > 0)\big)}{\sum_{d=ts}^{te} BOOL((W(d) - W\_threshold) > 0)}$$

where, ts = starting date and te = ending date, s is a given stock symbol, BOOL is the boolean function which returns 1 when true and 0 when false.

4 EFFECTS OF TEMPERATURE CHANGES

We conducted experiments based on the above analysis of weather and stock price changes to see if changes in temperatures (compared to normal) may affect the stock price of companies from different sectors such as retail, energy, and sports.

4.1 *Analysis of temperature effects on stock price with zero thresholds*

First, we track any change in the stock price (compared with the change in the SP500 index of the same day) when there is any change in the temperature (compared with the normal temperature of that day). Both the S_threshold and T_threshold are 0 in this case. For DKS, whenever the temperature increases (rises above the normal) 50.58% of the time during the year the stock increases (rises above the SP500 change of the same day) while 49.42% decreases, or in other words 50/50. When the temperature decreases (falls below normal) 59.73% of the time during the year the stock increases (rises above the SP500 change of the same day) while 40.27% decreases. We received similar results for all other retail-related stocks such as NKE, MODG, WMT, or utilities stocks such as ED, VZ, and almost the same for XOM in energy sector, and MSGS a local sport team stock. Therefore, our conclusion is that, in general, temperature seems to have no effects on stock price when the thresholds are 0, that is when we consider an increase or decrease by any amount, even the smallest ones, are still an increase or decrease.

4.2 *Analysis of temperature effects on stock price with significant thresholds*

In this section we investigate the effects of temperature only when the changes are significant, above a given threshold. For example, when we set the T_threshold to 7F and S_threshold to 0.5% the results lean toward a certain direction in certain months. For simplicity, in this section when we say stock increases or decreases it may mean that the given stock price increases or decreases by at least S_threshold or 0.5% over the SP500 change of the same day. When we say temperature increases or decreases it may mean that the temperature increases or decreases by at least T_threshold or 7F below the historically normal temperature of the same day. As shown in Figure 1, if the given day is in June, when the temperature decreases (by at least 7F below the normal) then 71.43% of time Dicks stock price decreases (by at least 0.5% over the SP500 change of the same day.) If the given day is in August, whenever the temperature increases (by at least 7F above the normal) then there is over 72.73% of time Dicks stock price increases (by at least 0.5% over the SP500 change of the same day.)

Month	TiSi/(TiSi+TiSd)%	TiSd/(TiSi+TiSd)%	TdSi/(TdSi+TdSd)%	TdSd/(TdSi+TdSd)%
1	55.32	44.68	58.33	41.67
2	50	50	37.5	62.5
3	44	56	52.17	47.83
4	41.94	58.06	42.31	57.69
5	48	52	33.33	66.67
6	44.44	55.56	28.57	71.43
7	46.67	53.33	50	50
8	72.73	27.27	33.33	66.67
9	65.38	34.62	40	60
10	39.66	60.34	55.56	44.44
11	51.02	48.98	60	40
12	55.81	44.19	52.94	47.06

Figure 1. Increase and decrease changes (*S_threshold = 0.5%*) of stock prices (DKS) when temperatures are above or below (*T_threshold = 7F*) the normal (New York, USA).

5 EFFECTS OF PRECIPITATION (RAIN & SNOW)

We conducted experiments to see how precipitation (defined as the total amount of rain and snow falls of the day) may affect the stock price of companies from different sectors such as retail, energy, and sports.

5.1 *Analysis of general precipitation effects on stock price (All Time)*

We track changes in the stock price (compared with the change in the SP500 index of the same day) when there is rain or snow of any amount, that is when both the S_threshold and

P_threshold are 0. Similarly to the results in the study of temperature effects, it seems that precipitation doesn't have much effect on stock price movement in this general case.

5.2 *Analysis of precipitation effects on stock price (by Months, with Thresholds)*

When we broke down the effects of precipitation by months we obtained interesting results. For each stock from our list we found that P_threshold and S_threshold with certain values can lead to clear patterns, as shown in Figure 2 (a). When the precipitation is 1" or above there is a 90.91% and 71.43% chance that DKS stock price would increase (by at least 0.5% over the SP500 change of the same day.) if the given day is in February or August respectively. However, there is a 100%, 100%, and 80% chance that DKS stock price would decrease (by at least 0.5% over the SP500 change of the same day.) if the given day is in May, June, or October respectively.

Month	PiSi	PiSd
1	41.67	58.33
2	90.91	9.09
3	42.86	57.14
4	28.57	71.43
5	0	100
6	0	100
7	60	40
8	71.43	28.57
9	57.14	42.86
10	20	80
11	50	50
12	33.33	66.67

(a)

Month	W-Si	W-Sd
1	56.52	43.48
2	41.67	58.33
3	53.12	46.88
4	36	64
5	40	60
6	100	0
7	N/A	N/A
8	0	100
9	42.86	57.14
10	40	60
11	45.45	54.55
12	33.33	66.67

(b)

Figure 2. Chances of DKS stock prices increase and decrease by month when (a) there is precipitation *P_threshold = 1*, *S_threshold = 0.5%* and (b) there is wind, *W_threshold = 8mph, S_threshold = 0.8% in* New York, USA.

6 EFFECTS OF WIND

Similarly to the study of temperature and precipitation effects, we first look at the general case tracking any change in the stock price (compared with the change in the SP500 index of the same day) and we calculate the chance of a stock increasing or decreasing based on the total frequency of all time. The results show that wind doesn't have much effect on stock prices in general. However, when we broke down the effects of wind by month we obtained interesting results. When the wind speed is 8mph or above there is a 100% chance that DKS stock price would increase (by at least 0.8% over the SP500 change of the same day.) if the given day is in June. However, there is a 100% chance that DKS stock price would decrease (by at least 0.8% over the SP500 change of the same day.) if the given day is in August. Similar results are found for other stocks (ED, VZ, WMT, XOM, MSGS, NKE, MODG) in our list.

7 CONCLUSIONS

We investigated the impact of weather variables, specifically temperature, precipitation, and wind on the stock prices of companies across various sectors such as retail, energy, and sports. The weather changes are measured relative to their typical or average values. The stock price changes are measured compared with the change of the SP500 index value of the same day to remove impacts of other factors which may affect the whole market. The experimental results suggest that, in general, if we calculate the probability of stock increase or decrease using the total frequency of all time, weather changes do not significantly influence stock price movements. However, when we break down by month and that the weather deviations exceed certain thresholds, noticeable patterns in stock behavior emerge during specific periods of the year. These findings may be leveraged to make strategic portfolio adjustments, temporarily entering or exiting certain stock positions, to potentially enhance performance and returns of an investment portfolio. For example, when the temperature decreases by 7F or more in June we should replace the position of DKS with NKE. While this paper focuses on reporting the weather effects on stock prices, future work can use the findings here to build trading and investment algorithms and strategies based on short-term weather forecasts.

REFERENCES

Akhtari, Mitra. (2011). Reassessment of the weather effect: Stock prices and wall street weather. *Undergraduate Economic Review* 7 (1): 1–2. University of California, Berkeley.

An, Nan, Bin Wang, Peng Pan, and Kai Guo. (2018). The effect of air quality index on stock market volatility: Evidence from China. *Journal of Cleaner Production*.

Antoniuk, Yuliya, and Tor Leirvik. (2021). Climate change and stock returns: evidence from the nordic markets. *Journal of Sustainable Finance & Investment*.

Cao, Melanie, and Jason Wei. (2005). Stock market returns: A note on temperature anomaly. *Journal of Banking & Finance* 29 (6): 1559–1573.

Chang, Tsangyao, Cheng-Chih Nieh, Mu-Jeng Yang, and Tzu-Ying Yang. (2006). Are stock market returns related to the weather effects? Empirical evidence from Taiwan. *Physica A: Statistical Mechanics and Its Applications* 364: 343–354.

Dong, Ming, and Alain Tremblay. (2021). Global weather-based trading strategies. *Journal of Banking & Finance*.

Goetzmann, William N., and Ning Zhu. (2005). Rain or shine: Where Is the weather effect? *European Financial Management* 11 (5): 559–578.

Goetzmann, William N., Dasol Kim, Alok Kumar, and Qian Wang. (2015). Weather-induced mood, institutional investors, and stock returns. *Review of Financial Studies* 28 (1): 73–111.

Hirshleifer, David, and Tyler Shumway. (2003). Good day sunshine: Stock returns and the weather. *Journal of Finance* 58 (3): 1009–1032.

Kathiravan, C., M. Raja, and M. Selvam. (2018). Impact of weather on stock market returns: Evidence from indian stock market. *Int. Journal of Pure and Applied Mathematics* 119(15):1445–1457.

Kathiravan, C., M. Selvam, B. Maniam, and M. Dharani. (2021). Effect of weather on stock market: A literature review and research Agenda. *Cogent Economics & Finance* 9 (1).

Keef, Stephen P., and Mark L. Roush. (2007). Daily weather effects on the returns of australian stock indices. *Applied Financial Economics* 17 (3): 173–184.

Krämer, Walter, and Ralf Runde. (1997). Stocks and the weather: An exercise in data mining or yet another capital market anomaly? *Empirical Economics* 22 (4): 637–641.

Li, Feng, *et al.* (2024). A study of impact of climate change on the U.S. Stock Market as Exemplified by the NASDAQ 100 Index constituents. *Scientific Reports*.

Lu, Jin, and Robin K. Chou. (2012). Does the weather have impacts on returns and trading activities in order-driven stock markets? Evidence from China. *Journal of Empirical Finance* 19 (1): 79–93.

Pizzutilo, Fabio, and Vincenzo Roncone. (2017). Is There a Weather Effect? Evidence from a panel of emerging countries' Stock Markets. *African Journal of Business Management*.

Saunders, Edward M., Jr. (1993). "Stock prices and wall street weather." *American Economic Review* 83 (5): 1337–1345.

Soost, Christian, *et al.* (2021). "Does Weather Still Affect the Stock Market?" *Schmalenbach Journal of Business Research* 73 (4): 571–523.

Symeonidis, Lazaros, Georgios Daskalakis, and Raphael N. Markellos. (2010). "Does the Weather Affect Stock Market Volatility?" *Finance Research Letters* 7 (4): 214–223.

Yoon, Seong-Min, and Sang Hoon Kang. (2009). "Weather Effects on Returns: Evidence from the Korean Stock Market." *Physica A: Statistical Mechanics and Its Applications* 388 (5): 682–690.

Moving Towards Sustainable Businesses and Developing More Resilient Economies –
Rashid and Annansingh-Jamieson (Eds)

An orthogonal approach to simple linear regression model

Raja R. Vatti
St John's University, Jamaica NY

ABSTRACT: The objective in developing a simple linear regression model between the dependent variable Y and the independent variable X is to minimize the sum of squared residuals between the actual Y and estimated Y by using the linear regression model in the perpendicular direction. The Least Squares technique is more commonly used. Another feasible method to minimize the sum of squared residuals is using the orthogonal residuals. The objective of the current research is to develop an Orthogonal regression model to investigate its advantage in minimizing residuals when compared with the ordinary least squares method.

Keywords: Orthogonal Regression, Ordinary Least Squares Regression, Minimization of residuals between Actual dependent variable, and forecasted dependent variable

1 INTRODUCTION

The traditional least square technique to develop a least square linear regression model between the dependent variable Y and independent variable X assumes that Y alone is the random variable. It considers residuals in the perpendicular direction only from the sample point to the fitted line. In the proposed Orthogonal model, the important assumption is that both X and Y are changing in the sample data, and residuals are developed using Orthogonal lines from the sample point to the fitted regression line. This technique results in residual components which maybe widely distributed, identical most of the time and independent.

Differences shown in Graphs between Orthogonal and Least Squares Methods

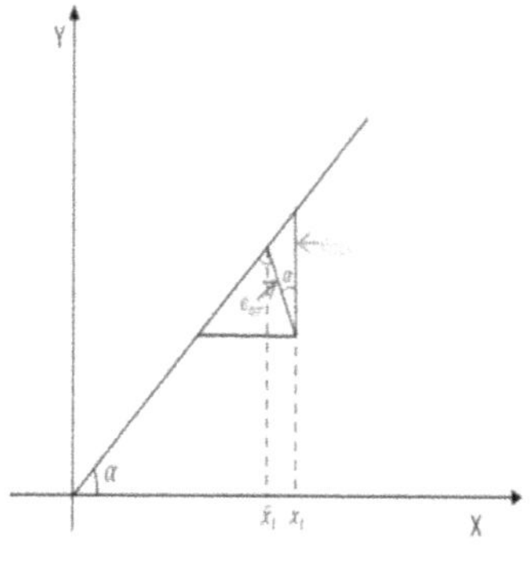

Figure 1. Orthogonal regression line [32].

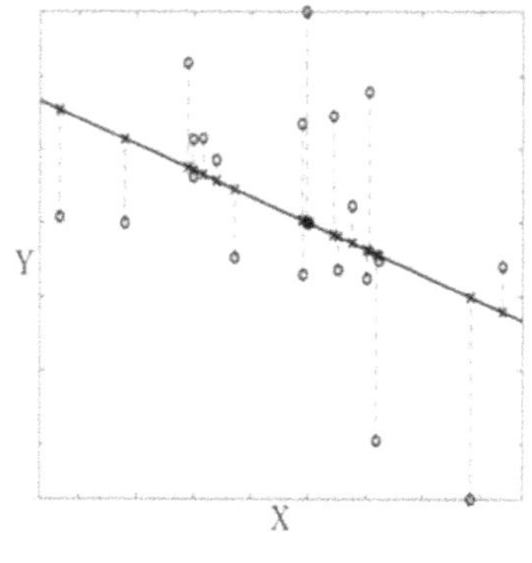

Figure 2. Least-squares estimation is depicted schematically [39].

DOI: 10.1201/9781003647300-34

2 METHODOLOGY

Minimization of the distance between the forecasted value of the dependent variable Y and the actual dependent variable Y using Orthogonal lines instead of perpendicular lines used in ordinary least squares.

2.1 *Orthogonal analysis summary*

Dependent Variable: Y
Independent Variable: X
Linear Model: Y=a +b*x
Number of observations: 15
Assumed Ratio of Error Variance: 1.0

Orthogonal Regression

	Orthogonal Estimate	Standard Error	Z Stat	P Value
Intercept	1.71535	0.89958	1.9068	0.0565
Slope	0.691903	0.0882247	7.84251	0.000

Estimated Error Variance

	Variance
Y	0.222399
X	0.222399

95% Confidence Interval for Estimates

	Lower Limit	Upper Limit
Intercept	−0.0478083	3.47851
Slope	0.518985	0.864821

2.2 *Orthogonal regression model*

Y=1.71535+0.691903*x

Orthogonal Model Statistics

	Orthogonal Model
Intercept	1.71535
Slope	0.691903
Coefficient of Determination	0.92
Standard Error of Estimate	0.4

Orthogonal Fitted Y and Residuals

X	Y	Fitted Y	Residual
8.2	7.3	7.36015	−0.06015
11.8	10.0	9.91872	0.081128
11.0	10.1	9.57677	0.52323
7.4	7.4	7.01821	0.38179
10.2	8.7	8.7492	−0.0492
10.4	8.7	8.84278	−0.14278
10.9	8.1	8.88249	−0.78249
7.5	6.9	6.90312	−0.00312
9.6	9.2	8.63033	0.56967
12.0	9.3	9.78568	−0.48568
11.9	9.7	9.86838	−0.16838
11.9	10.8	10.2245	0.5755
12.3	9.8	10.0879	−0.2879
6.6	6.0	6.19064	−0.19064
9.0	8.0	7.9611	0.0389

Orthogonal ANOVA Table

	DF	SS	MSS	F	P Value
Regression	1	23.79062	23.79062	147.0851	1.84009E-08
Residual	13	2.102715	0.161747307		
Total	14	25.89333			

3 CONCLUSIONS

- Orthogonal Regression technique appears to give smaller residuals when compared with the ordinary Least Squares technique.
- Standard Error of Regression estimate is smaller and coefficient of determination is larger with the orthogonal model.

REFERENCES

[1] Fuller, W.A., (1987). *Measurement Error Models*. Wiley, New York

[2] Kendall, M.G. and A. Stuart, (1961). *The Advanced Theory of Statistics*, Vol 2. Charles Griffin, London.

[3] Madansky, A., (1959). The fitting of straight lines when both lines are subject to error. *Journal of the American Statistical Association*, 54, 173–205.

Moving Towards Sustainable Businesses and Developing More Resilient Economies – Rashid and Annansingh-Jamieson (Eds)
 ISBN: 978-1-041-08875-2

Sustainability controlling and the limits of ESG monetization

Julius Winterhalter
The University of Applied Sciences Merseburg, Germany

Ronny Gebhardt
Professor, University of Applied Sciences Merseburg, Germany

ABSTRACT: This paper examines the changing role of sustainability controlling as a strategic management and risk governance tool. Drawing on current literature and the CSRD framework, it analyses the rationale, instruments, and limits of ESG measurement. It argues that sustainability is increasingly framed as financial risk rather than transformation, translating complex social and ecological issues into monetary terms. While this enables integration into financial logic, it narrows the normative scope and reduces sustainability to technical metrics. The paper calls for a more reflective, ethically grounded approach that maintains strategic relevance while recognising the limits of quantification and the need for societal accountability.

1 THE COMPATIBILITY OF SUSTAINABILITY WITH CURRENT ECONOMIC PARADIGMS

1.1 *New framework for non-financial reporting*

With the Corporate Sustainability Reporting Directive (CSRD), the European Commission (EC) introduces a comprehensive new framework for how companies in the EU must report on environmental, social, and governance (ESG) topics. At its core are the European Sustainability Reporting Standards (ESRS), which define in detail what must be disclosed. But the key question remains: is it the right tool to create a garment that truly fits the shape of today's complex, unequal, and ecologically fragile world?

This tension becomes particularly evident in the current transformation of the CSRD in the EU. The introduction of the CSRD by the EC (2023) marks a significant regulatory intervention in corporate reporting. Its objective is to systematically integrate ESG criteria into corporate reporting and by doing so, into decision-making processes. The directive aims to provide transparent, comparable, and reliable data that serve a broad range of stakeholders, from investors and regulators to customers, employees, and civil society. At the same time, the CSRD is a key instrument of the European Green Deal, designed to redirect financial flows toward sustainable investments. The key challenge is alignment: standardized indicators must function across heterogeneous firms, sectors, and regions, raising questions about fit and steering relevance (European Commission 2023; Kirchhoff *et al.* 2024).

1.2 *Political Ambivalence and the ESG Backlash*

This challenge comes with political and institutional setbacks. The postponement of the CSRD's application deadlines, the weakening of the European Supply Chain Act, and the fundamental public questioning of ESG by various actors under "anti-woke" narratives have

DOI: 10.1201/9781003647300-35

all contributed to growing ambivalence in sustainability governance (Sætra 2024; Imolauer 2024; London Business School 2025). ESG has become an ideological battleground, viewed in both the United States and Europe as a symbol of intrusive regulation (Sætra 2024). This development stands in contrast to the assessments of international institutions. The Task Force on Climate-related Financial Disclosures (TCFD 2017) describes climate change as one of the most mispriced systemic risks to the global financial system. The European Central Bank (ECB 2022) identifies substantial credit risks arising from environmental and social factors and warns of a continued underestimation of non-financial risks in corporate valuation.

Empirical studies underline the need for stronger ESG integration into risk management and finance. Buchmüller *et al.* (2023) show that ESG factors increasingly serve as early warning signals of business risk, and Crifo *et al.* (2022) demonstrate that long-term sustainability strategies are rewarded by capital markets, especially in times of crisis. Yet corporate implementation of ESG factors remains fragmented, constrained by political uncertainty and conceptual ambiguity. From this perspective, sustainability regulation appears not as an end in itself but as a means of strengthening economic resilience through risk prevention, reputational protection, and long-term capital allocation (Baumüller 2025; Kirchhoff *et al.* 2024; BaFin 2019). This paper therefore examines the potential and limits of sustainability controlling and outlines an empirical design to assess how ESG indicators are applied in management practice. While sustainability is often linked to normative ideals, it is increasingly interpreted by banks and companies as a matter of risk management. This translation into measurable values raises fundamental questions about the compatibility of sustainability with prevailing sustainability reporting paradigms and related controlling concepts.

2 SUSTAINABILITY CONTROLLING – CONCEPT, RELEVANCE AND STATUS QUO

2.1 *From traditional controlling to ESG integration*

Controlling supports corporate goal achievement by structuring decision-making through information, planning and monitoring (Weber and Schäffer 1999). This logic also applies to sustainability objectives, provided they are recognised as strategically relevant. In recent years, ESG controlling has gained importance in both research and practice (Schmidt 2024). Long-term integration of ESG topics is feasible only when they become part of the regular controlling system (Weber and Hastenteufel 2024). Even if ESG criteria were clearly defined and measurable—which is still rarely the case—there remains the problem of how to prioritise sustainability goals in relation to financial targets. This generates typical conflicts in multidimensional steering: while achievements such as CO_2 reduction can be measured, their relative importance compared with cost efficiency or return on investment is difficult to determine objectively (Schmidt 2024).

Sustainability controlling, as conceptualised by Colsman (2016), extends beyond traditional cost accounting and CSR reporting. It functions as a strategic management instrument that links ecological, social and economic dimensions within governance and performance measurement. Controllers are thus expected to evolve from data reporters to strategic partners who develop forward-looking indicators, assess long-term risks and translate non-financial impacts such as biodiversity, equity or reputation into managerial guidance. Tools such as the Sustainability Balanced Scorecard and the iooi model help align sustainability with value creation. Colsman (2016) also stresses that controlling must not lose sight of its normative foundation: ethical responsibility and societal legitimacy are prerequisites of lasting competitiveness.

2.2 *Risk logic, monetization, and normative tensions*

The integration of ESG factors into financial logic has reshaped how companies and financial institutions understand sustainability. Increasingly, it is framed not as a moral obligation but as a category of risk. From transition risks to reputational threats, ESG issues are analysed for their potential to affect financial performance. In this view, sustainability becomes a new language of risk management. Yet this logic requires partial monetization: as the price per ton of CO_2 provides a reference for environmental costs, similar models are sought for biodiversity loss, social inequality or workplace safety. The question remains what happens when such risks resist valuation.

Corporate and financial actors often treat sustainability as an instrument for risk minimisation, whereas society views it as a driver of social and ecological transformation. This divergence produces tensions between monetary metrics and ethical values, between compliance and responsibility. Sustainability controlling operates precisely within this field of tension, translating qualitative aspirations into managerial information without dissolving their normative ambiguity (Colsman 2016; Schmidt 2024).

2.3 *Empirical findings and the rise of engagement*

Empirical evidence suggests that solid ESG performance can strengthen economic value creation. The meta-analysis by Friede, Busch and Bassen (2015) finds that about 90 per cent of studies report neutral to positive links between ESG and financial performance. More recent work confirms correlations between robust ESG strategies, innovation capacity, cash-flow stability and reduced capital costs (Whelan *et al.* 2021; Gillan *et al.* 2021; Gibson *et al.* 2024; Budzinski *et al.* 2024). Capital markets increasingly interpret credible ESG efforts as indicators of long-term viability (Fatemi *et al.* 2020; Buallay 2019). However, there is still no differentiated model capturing the specific financial effects of individual ESRS topics.

A central obstacle is the inconsistency of ESG metrics and ratings. Divergent methodologies among rating agencies create what Berg *et al.* (2022) term "aggregate confusion", weakening the steering function of ESG assessments. The social dimension remains particularly underdeveloped. Indicators such as diversity quotas or training hours often lack depth, are often superficial and provide little real insight into social conditions inside organisations (Hale *et al.* 2019). Qualitative studies confirm this gap, showing that social sustainability initiatives are frequently decoupled from organisational transformation (Bozyazi 2022; Weber and Hastenteufel 2025).

For controlling, ESG has gained practical relevance through its effect on financing conditions. Banks now integrate sustainability risks into credit assessment alongside traditional financial metrics (Ott 2024; Breinrich-Schilly 2024). Companies with strong ESG profiles benefit from lower interest rates and better credit terms, reflecting their perceived lower default risk. Nevertheless, empirical analyses show that banks focus mainly on environmental and governance aspects, while social factors remain secondary (Fatica and Panzica 2021; Hajek *et al.* 2024). Despite regulatory calls from the European Banking Authority (2022) for full integration of ESG risks, implementation remains uneven (EBA 2022).

In sum, research demonstrates the growing financial materiality of ESG factors but also the persistence of methodological inconsistency and selective attention. For sustainability controlling, this implies a dual task: to provide reliable data for financial steering and to maintain the broader perspective of ecological and social responsibility (Klein and Kämmler-Burrak 2021; Wellbrock *et al.* 2020; VBA 2025).

3 REQUIREMENTS FOR EFFECTIVE SUSTAINABILITY CONTROLLING

3.1 *Structural and methodological foundations*

Sustainability controlling must translate a complex and normatively charged concept into management-compatible structures. This places high demands on conceptual, methodological and data-related dimensions. From Carlowitz's forestry principle (1713) to the Brundtland Report (1987) and current ESG frameworks (EU 2023), sustainability has never been a clearly definable goal but a multidimensional and contested system of values. It must therefore be embedded within an overarching framework of economic, environmental and social objectives. Such integration inevitably produces trade-offs that controlling systems must render visible, quantify where possible and use as a structured basis for managerial decisions, even under normative ambiguity or political instability. Regulatory frameworks such as the CSRD, EU taxonomy and sector-specific climate requirements increase these demands by requiring robust data, forward-looking planning and adaptive control mechanisms.

Another prerequisite is the development of interdisciplinary competencies among controllers. Alongside financial expertise, knowledge of environmental law, social impact assessment, stakeholder engagement and ESG reporting standards is becoming essential. Many organisations still lack such integrative know-how, revealing an urgent need for capacity building and cultural change within the profession (Weber and Hastenteufel 2024). Finally, the dominant focus on "green controlling" has been criticised for narrowing sustainability to environmental issues. Colsman (2016) calls for a broader perspective that includes all ESG dimensions and promotes inclusive steering systems. True sustainability requires the integration of economic, social and ecological factors; overlooking any of them risks ignoring significant opportunities and risks.

3.2 *Ethical boundaries and the limits of monetization*

Efforts to integrate ESG into financial logic encounter ethical and epistemological limits. Social dimensions such as equity, inclusion and psychological health often resist meaningful quantification. Even when proxies or composite indicators are used, valuations rest on assumptions and normative choices. This raises the question of how far sustainability should be translated into monetary terms. The drive to monetise stems largely from the logic of financial risk management, which demands comparable and ideally monetary indicators. Yet this logic can obscure or devalue aspects that are difficult to price, such as dignity, justice or ecological complexity. While carbon pricing has become a model for environmental externalities, similar metrics for social and ecological systems remain contested. Sustainability controlling thus faces a structural dilemma: it must simplify without trivialising, standardise without erasing diversity, and deliver figures while remaining aware of their constructed and political nature.

In sum, effective sustainability controlling must balance institutional pressures, normative tensions and epistemic uncertainty. It requires methodological innovation combined with reflexivity and ethical awareness, particularly regarding the limits of monetisation and the assumptions embedded in ESG metrics.

3.3 *Instruments and concepts for steering sustainability*

Achieving sustainability goals requires instruments that integrate ESG factors into strategic and operational decision-making. One of the most established approaches is the Sustainable Balanced Scorecard (SBSC), which extends the classical Balanced Scorecard (Kaplan and Norton 1992) by adding ecological and social dimensions. It links sustainability to corporate value creation and supports strategy alignment, yet implementation often faces limits in data availability, operationalisation and incentive design (Figge *et al.* 2002). Complementary instruments have emerged to measure and manage broader sustainability effects. Impact Measurement and Management (IMM) frameworks such as IRIS+, RAISE Impact and Impact Europe combine quantitative and qualitative indicators to assess both input and outcome dimensions (Upmetrics 2023; EtkiYap 2021; Impact Europe 2024). Within this logic, the Social Return on Investment (SROI) assigns monetary proxies to social or environmental outcomes using stakeholder-based valuation methods such as the Analytical Hierarchy Process (Investopedia 2024; Ohio University 2024). These approaches link ESG investments to measurable impact and strengthen the business case for sustainability even when financial returns are indirect or long term.

The Value Balancing Alliance (VBA) represents another methodological development, aiming to monetise externalities such as CO_2 emissions or health impacts and integrate them into financial reporting (VBA 2025). By connecting non-financial outcomes with traditional performance metrics, value balancing supports cost-benefit analyses and evidence-based decision-making. Similarly, scenario analysis and climate stress testing have gained importance, especially in the financial sector. The European Central Bank's Climate Stress Test (ECB 2022) and the European Banking Authority's guidelines (EBA 2022) require institutions to assess ESG-related risks across transition scenarios and integrate them into capital planning and control frameworks.

Finally, sustainability maturity models, such as Baumgartner's Sustainability Integration Model, help organisations evaluate the degree of ESG integration and guide development from basic compliance to strategic governance (Baumgartner 2010; Upmetrics 2023; Sopact 2024). Despite the diversity of these tools, their effectiveness depends on consistent implementation within planning, budgeting and incentive systems. Only when ESG indicators are embedded in core management processes can sustainability controlling evolve from reporting to genuine strategic steering.

4 INDICATOR LOGIC AND MONETIZATION OF SOCIO-ECOLOGICAL EFFECTS

4.1 *Measuring the immeasurable? ESG indicators and the limits of monetization*

A central task of sustainability controlling is to develop indicators that translate qualitative aspirations into quantifiable metrics for planning and performance evaluation. Unlike standardised financial measures such as ROI, ESG indicators often suffer from unclear definitions, inconsistent methodologies and limited comparability, which weakens both internal steering and external reporting. The CSRD and the European Sustainability Reporting Standards (ESRS) aim to standardise such measures across environmental, social and governance domains (EU 2023), yet the challenge of capturing diffuse and context-dependent effects remains. The monetisation of non-financial impacts such as biodiversity loss, social exclusion or employee well-being illustrates this difficulty. Instruments like Social Return on Investment (SROI), carbon pricing and the Value Balancing Alliance framework (VBA 2025) attempt to express these effects in monetary terms, but they rely on normative assumptions and hypothetical cost constructs. This creates an epistemic tension: monetisation facilitates integration into financial decision-making while risking simplification and misrepresentation. As Hale *et al.* (2019) note, indicators are performative—they shape realities by defining what counts as success. Measuring gender diversity, psychological safety or labour conditions always reflects ethical and political priorities.

Hence, indicator development must rest not only on measurability or efficiency but also on legitimacy, stakeholder relevance and ethical reflection. The demand to assign prices to all dimensions of sustainability is inherently limited: phenomena such as ecosystem integrity, social cohesion or human dignity lose meaning when reduced to financial equivalents. The logic of monetisation thus exposes the systemic boundaries of the economic paradigm itself. Putting a price on a human life or on the extinction of a species may help in cost–benefit models, but it cannot capture the moral value, cultural meaning, or irreversible loss involved, showing the limits of monetisation.

4.2 *Criteria, hybrid approaches, and sector-specific applications*

A promising way forward lies in hybrid indicator systems that combine monetary, quantitative and qualitative elements. Such systems recognise the limits of each measurement approach while capturing sustainability's multidimensional nature. Effective indicators require clarity, transparency and reproducibility to ensure internal usability and external credibility. Yet the proliferation of ratings and self-reported data continues to produce inconsistency and weak comparability (Berg *et al.* 2022).

Sector-specific differentiation is essential. The automotive industry focuses on CO_2 and energy efficiency, the food sector on water and waste, the textile sector on labour rights, and the technology industry on diversity, equity and inclusion (DEI). Particularly in the context of skilled-labour shortages, DEI metrics have become strategically relevant, as organisations with inclusive cultures tend to be more innovative and productive (Gläsener 2011). Indicators therefore shape not only control systems but also corporate perception and meaning. Sustainability controlling must remain aware of this performative power and use indicators as instruments for learning and transformation rather than mere compliance.

5 METHODOLOGY AND RESEARCH DESIGN

A forthcoming study by the authors will explore how ESG key performance indicators (KPIs) are used within corporate controlling and sustainability management. It is guided by the assumption that ESG indicators are socially embedded instruments that reflect organisational priorities and institutional expectations rather than neutral measures. A qualitative, exploratory design is planned. Expert interviews with practitioners from controlling and sustainability management, complemented by selected stakeholder perspectives, will provide insight into how ESG metrics influence managerial decision-making and reporting practices. These interviews will be supported by targeted document analysis to contextualise how indicators are defined and communicated. The empirical work aims to clarify how ESG indicators mediate between regulatory requirements, strategic management, and the pursuit of broader sustainability objectives. Through qualitative interpretation, the study seeks to identify key tensions, practical challenges and future directions for effective sustainability controlling.

6 CONCLUSION AND DISCUSSION

Sustainability controlling has evolved from a peripheral reporting activity into a strategic function for identifying risks, allocating capital and responding to stakeholder expectations. Yet this evolution reveals deep contradictions. Translating complex ecological and social realities into measurable indicators exposes technical, ethical and political tensions. Frameworks such as the CSRD, ESG ratings and valuation models like SROI or carbon pricing have advanced standardisation and comparability, but at the cost of reducing sustainability to what can be quantified. When value is confined to numbers, dimensions such as dignity, biodiversity or mental health risk fading from view.

The politicisation of ESG further intensifies this dilemma. What began as a governance tool has become an ideological symbol, contested between regulatory ambition and market scepticism. While institutions such as the ECB, OECD and TCFD warn of systemic risks from neglecting non-financial factors, some political actors increasingly challenge the legitimacy of sustainability frameworks. Within this tension, sustainability controlling must provide reliable data without mistaking measurement for objectivity and support risk management without dissolving its normative foundation.

Looking ahead, methodological precision must be combined with ethical reflection. Hybrid indicator systems that integrate financial and non-financial dimensions offer potential, but only if they are embedded in broader conceptions of value, legitimacy and social relevance. The social dimension of sustainability—care, inclusion, psychological wellbeing—resists commodification and calls for descriptive, context sensitive approaches that capture lived experience. Market based instruments may improve short term decision making, yet they operate within the same economic logic that sustains ecological degradation. True transformation requires rethinking valuation and governance towards models centred on resilience, solidarity and collective responsibility.

In practice, companies should strengthen stakeholder engagement, develop hybrid indicators tailored to sectoral priorities and embed sustainability metrics into planning, budgeting and incentive systems. Controlling teams must combine technical expertise with ethical awareness and interpretive judgment to ensure that sustainability data inform genuine reflection rather than serve as symbolic reassurance.

In the end, sustainability controlling demands tools, patterns and measurements, but also sensitivity to form, proportion and meaning. The frameworks and KPIs we employ may offer structure, yet they often follow templates that do not fit the asymmetric and evolving shape of our planetary reality. But it is well know that a well tailored suit follows the body, not the standard. Likewise, sustainability controlling must follow the contours of life itself, grounded in ethics, guided by responsibility and attentive to what truly matters, so that we do not mistake the stitching for the substance while the fabric of nature and society quietly frays beneath.

REFERENCES

BaFin. (2019). Nachhaltigkeit als Chance – Haltung, Regulatorik und neue Wege im Finanzmarkt. *BaFin Perspektiven* 2. [https://www.bafin.de/SharedDocs/Veroeffentlichungen/DE/BaFinPerspek tiven/2019_02/bp_19_2_Stremlau.html]

Baumgartner, R.J. (2010). Organizational culture and leadership: preconditions for the development of a sustainable corporation. *Sustainable Development* 17 (2): 102–113.

Baumüller, J. and Schönauer, K. (2025). EU-Omnibus-Paket zur Nachhaltigkeit: (sinnvolle) Vereinfachung oder (nur) Deregulierung? *RWK – Reporting & Wirtschaft kompakt* 2 (3): 74–82.

Berg, F., Kölbel, J.F. and Rigobon, R. (2022). Aggregate confusion: The divergence of ESG ratings. *Review of Finance* 26 (6): 1315–1344.

Bozyazi, E. and Kurt, D. (eds.) (2022). *Soziale Nachhaltigkeit und digitale Transformation: Für ein erfolgreiches, nachhaltiges und menschliches Business.* Stuttgart: Schäffer-Poeschel.

Buallay, A., Hamdam A. and Barone E. (2019). Sustainability reporting and firm performance: Compara tive study across emerging and developed markets. *International Journal of Productivity and Performance Management.* ahead-of-print.

Budzinski, A., Flick, L. and Semmo, L.S. (2024). Die Relevanz der Berücksichtigung von ESG-Faktoren in der Unternehmensbewertung *.INUR-Blog.* [https://inur.de]

Carlowitz, H.C. von. (1713). *Sylvicultura Oeconomica oder haußwirthliche Nachricht und Naturmäßige Anweisung zur wilden Baum-Zucht.* Leipzig.

Colsman, B. (2016). *Nachhaltigkeitscontrolling.* Wiesbaden: Springer Gabler.

Crifo, P. and Roudaut, G. (2022). Economic Crisis and Corporate Governance: How Can Board Independence and Expertise Maximize the Firm Value? *Theoretical Economics Letters* 12 (5): 1227–1258. [https://doi.org/10.4236/tel.2022.125066]

European Banking Authority (EBA). (2022). *Draft Guidelines on ESG Risk Management and Scenario Anal ysis.* [https://www.eba.europa.eu]

ECB – European Central Bank. (2022). *Report on Climate Stress Testing Practices.* [https://www.bank ingsupervision.europa.eu]

EtkiYap. (2021). *Impact Measurement and Management Framework.* [https://etkiyap.org]

Fatemi, A., Glaum, M. and Kaiser, S. (2018). ESG Performance and Firm Value: The Moderating Role of Disclosure. *Global Finance Journal* Elsevier, vol. 38(C), pages 45-64. 45: 100487.

Figge, F., Hahn, T., Schaltegger, S. and Wagner, M. (2002). The sustainability balanced scorecard: linking sustainability management to business strategy. *Business Strategy and the Environment* 11 (5): 269–284.

Gibson Brandon, R., Krueger, P. and Schmidt, P.S. (2021). ESG rating disagreement and stock returns. *Financial Analysts Journal* 77 (4): 104–127. [https://doi.org/10.1080/0015198X.2021.1963186]

Gillan, S.L., Koch, A. and Starks, L.T. (2021). Firms and social responsibility: A review of ESG and CSR research in corporate finance. *Journal of Corporate Finance* 66: 101889.

Hale, J., Legun, K., Campbell, H. and Carolan, M. (2019). Social sustainability indicators as performance. *Geoforum* 103: 47–55. [https://doi.org/10.1016/j.geoforum.2019.03.008]

Imolauer, K. (2025). Zwischen zwei Welten: ESG Backlash in den USA. *Haufe Sustainability Debatte.* [https://www.haufe.de/sustainability/debatte/zwischen-zwei-welten-esg-backlash-in-den- usa_575768_646030.html]

Kaplan, R.S. and Norton, D.P. (1992). The Balanced Scorecard: Measures That Drive Performance. *Harvard Business Review* January–February: 71–79.

Kirchhoff, K.R., Niefünd, S. and von Pressentin, J.A. (2024). *ESG: Nachhaltigkeit als strategischer Erfolgs faktor.* Wiesbaden: Springer Gabler.

Klein, A. and Kämmler-Burrak, A. (2021). *Nachhaltigkeit in der Unternehmenssteuerung: Grundlagen, In strumente, Praxisbeispiele.* Freiburg: Haufe-Lexware.

London Business School. (2025). What the ESG Backlash Reveals – and What Comes Next. *Forbes.* [https://www.forbes.com/sites/lbsbusinessstrategyreview/2025/03/25/what-the-esg-backlash-reveals-and-what-comes-next/]

Sætra, H.S. (2024). The ESG Backlash: Politics, Ideology and the Future of Sustainable Business. *SSRN.* [https://doi.org/10.2139/ssrn.4782018].

Schmidt, R.C. (2024). ESG Controlling. In Weber, S.T. and Hastenteufel, J. (eds.) *Nachhaltigkeit im Controlling.* Wiesbaden: Springer Fachmedien, 59–75.

Task Force on Climate related Financial Disclosures (TCFD). (2017). *Final Report: Recommendations of the Task Force on Climate related Financial Disclosures.*

Value Balancing Alliance (VBA). (2022). *Introduction into the Value to Business Framework (V2B).* Frankfurt am Main: Value Balancing Alliance. [https://www.value-balancing.com/en/publications.html]

Weber, J. and Hastenteufel, M. (2024). *Controlling for Sustainable Corporate Management.* Wiesbaden: Springer Gabler.

Weber, J. and Schäffer, U. (2022). *Einführung in das Controlling.* 17th ed. Stuttgart: Schäffer-Poeschel.

Whelan, T., Atz, U., Van Holt, T. and Clark, C. (2021). *ESG and Financial Performance: Uncovering the Relationship by Aggregating Evidence from 1,000 Studies Published between 2015-2020* NYU Stern Center for Sustainable Business and Rockefeller Asset Management.

Moving Towards Sustainable Businesses and Developing More Resilient Economies – Rashid and Annansingh-Jamieson (Eds)
 ISBN: 978-1-041-08875-2

Analyzing the impact of adopting IFRS S1 and S2 sustainability standards on strategic managerial accounting practices

Ghazi Maan Faisal and Saba Kareem Abbood
Post-graduate Institute for Accounting and Financial Studies, University of Baghdad, Iraq

ABSTRACT: The study aims to explore the relationship between IFRS S1, S2, and Strategic Managerial Accounting (SMA) practices by building an applied model in an environment where these standards have not yet been implemented. The study focuses on the manufacturing sector in Iraq, as it is the sector most affected by environmental issues. The content analysis methodology was used to extract quantitative indicators from companies' reports related to sustainability standards. The results showed that the adoption of the Sustainability disclosure Standards (SDS) requires incorporating this information into consolidated and financial disclosure reports. The results of implementing Material Flow Cost Accounting (MFCA) showed that this tool helps reclassify costs between positive (product outputs) and negative (non-product outputs). The analysis demonstrates a complementary relationship between the use of SMA practices and the ability to implement modern disclosure standards, thereby contributing to the generation of quantitative information necessary for their implementation. The study proposes conducting similar studies in vital sectors such as the oil, cement, and food industries to verify the suitability of Strategic Managerial Accounting Practices, such as MFCA, in different production environments and whether the findings obtained in Diyala Company apply to diverse industrial contexts. In light of the theoretical and applied analysis of Strategic Managerial Accounting Practices, and based on the results of implementing MFCA at the Diyala General Company for Electrical Industries, the following conclusions can be drawn: It is clear that the applied accounting system focuses on recording costs in general without giving sufficient importance to environmental or social costs, leading to a clear lack of comprehensive disclosure. Contrary to the requirements of IFRS S1 and S2.

Keywords: Strategic Managerial Accounting, Sustainability disclosure standards, Financial Performance, Material Flow Cost Accounting

1 INTRODUCTION

Managerial Accounting Practices is viewed as a strategic innovation that enables the company to survive and strengthen its competitive position in a competitive business environment (Alamri 2019; Rathwatta and Samudrage 2019). Adopting SMA practices to support and focus on the effectiveness of organizational flexibility and responsiveness is an approach that helps provide appropriate information and the ability to improve and develop the efficiency and effectiveness of decision-making to achieve the company's strategic objectives, improve performance and operations, and focus on achieving a clearer, more accurate, and more integrated vision of the relationship. These practices include tools for measuring performance and costs and methods for presenting information (Stormi *et al.* 2019; Nik Abdullah 2020). SMA practice is defined as an information system that focuses on providing

DOI: 10.1201/9781003647300-36

financial and non-financial data to support strategic decisions, such as analyzing the competitive environment, identifying competitive and target markets, and evaluating strategic performance (Kanakria 2020; Nik Abdullah and Said 2016). SMA practices focus on helping to identify the company's future direction, evaluating the company's strategic alternatives, and focusing on achieving a competitive advantage (Rashid *et al.* 2020). SMA practices also focus on demonstrating and clarifying the importance of identifying how these practices focus on adapting to a changing environment. The steps for implementing SMA practices are implemented by focusing on applying the steps, which include analyzing the company's internal and external environment, working on identifying and selecting the appropriate tools for application, which include the balanced scorecard, value chain analysis, target costing, data collection and analysis, and focusing on evaluating performance in the company (Boulalib 2021; Krisdiyawati and Maulidah 2024; Tran 2023). The IFRS S1 and S2 The Sustainability Disclosure Standards) SDS) issued by the ISSB of the IFRS) provides a unified global framework for the disclosure of SRI. These standards aim to enhance credibility, transparency, and accountability in financial markets, focusing on providing accurate and reliable information about the sustainability-related risks and opportunities facing companies (IFRS Foundation 2024; Grajales Gaviria *et al.* 2023). The DP represents the company's strategy and statement of its SRG in SR. These standards focus on assessing the company's performance in achieving these goals. Sustainability Disclosure (SD) is the process of providing and disseminating all company information related to sustainability performance (Stocker *et al.* 2020; Li 2024). IFRS S1 aims to define general and specific DR, clarifying and explaining all risks and opportunities that could affect a company's cash flows, its ability to obtain financing, or its cost of capital in the short, medium, and long term. IFRS S2 aims to clarify and explain sustainability and climate-related disclosures, including a focus on disclosures related to governance, strategy, risk management, climate-related metrics, and targets (IFRS S1 Foundation General Requirements 2023; IFRS S2 Foundation Climate-related Disclosures 2023; IFRS Foundation publishes Annual Report 2024). The importance of SR lies in demonstrating the company's ability to promote corporate social responsibility and achieve sustainable development. This is achieved by demonstrating focus, accuracy, reliability, credibility, and transparency in disclosing information in SR about a company's economic, environmental, and social performance. This, in turn, helps contribute to promoting long-term sustainable development, focusing on providing transparent and comprehensive information to shareholders and stakeholders, such as investors, employees, and customers, to help them understand a company's sustainable performance and its impact on economic, environmental, and social dimensions (Vitolla *et al.* 2019; Oktariyani 2024). SDS These standards also aim to outline the foundations for improving the quality, reliability, transparency, and credibility of SR by focusing on providing standardized and comparable information on sustainability, enhancing transparency and accountability, supporting the integration of sustainability and financial performance, and establishing strict disclosure standards to prevent the provision of misleading information about sustainability practices (Kusuma and Gani 2024; Amelia and Djakman 2024; Indyk 2022). The major shift in the past decade has been towards encouraging the development and improvement of work quality and focusing on enhancing the transparency and credibility of IFRS. This shift has led to significant and subtle changes in areas such as financial instruments, fair value accounting, revenue recognition, and leasing (Thijeel *et al.* 2025). The steps for implementing SDS include assessing institutional readiness by analyzing the company's readiness to adopt the standards in terms of resources, systems, and processes; identifying material issues by identifying sustainability-related risks and opportunities that are material to the company; collecting data; developing processes by establishing or improving systems for collecting sustainability-related data and ensuring their accuracy and reliability; preparing reports and disclosures by developing disclosure reports under the requirements of IFRS S1 and S2, including disclosure of governance, strategy, risk management, metrics, and objectives; and continuous improvement by regularly reviewing reports and improving processes based on feedback and changes in the regulatory environment (IFRS Foundation 2023; Dinçer 2024).

2 LITERATURE REVIEW AND HYPOTHESES DEVELOPMENT

A study (Parkinson and Chew 2022) aims to implement the recommendations of the UNDSD (2001), which focuses on environmental MA on identifying, collecting, and analyzing. This is based on identifying and examining what organizations currently report and assessing the strengths and weaknesses of such reporting. (Le and Nguyen 2023) The study focuses on assessing the impact of SMA practices on employee satisfaction in companies in Vietnam. The study relied on documents and direct interviews with relevant individuals from selected companies and organizations in Hanoi. The study recommended helping companies gain valuable insights to enhance the application of SMA practices to improve employee satisfaction, thereby enhancing their growth and competitiveness in the global market. A study (Nechyporuk *et al.* 2023) focused on the effects of SMA practice, made recommendations for improving SMA practice methodology in the complex management system of companies. The study reached the most important conclusions: SMA practices are based on various elements, such as the use of technology, the use of effective information, and public policies. A study (Tolkach 2023) aims to explain the importance of implementing new Financial Reporting Standards (FRS) under IFRS, such as IFRS 17 for US companies, in addition to IFRS S1 and IFRS S2, for developing sustainable businesses in the USA. A study (Ogundajo *et al.* 2024) aims to demonstrate and clarify the impact of SMA practices on the social and cultural value creation of listed depository banks in Nigeria. The results of the study, using pooled ordinary least squares analysis, revealed a significant impact of SMA practices on social and cultural value creation within these banks. The study recommended that bank management integrate SMA practices into their operations to enhance value creation. A study (Cojocaru and Mihăilă 2024) aims and focuses on demonstrate the extent to which these standards are applied in integrated reports by focusing on providing a coherent vision for sustainability-related disclosures. The study is based on a documentary and comparative analysis of IFRS S1 and S2 with the integrated reporting framework, based on a qualitative approach to analyze the integration between these two standards around the principles of integrated reporting. The results show that integrating IFRS S1 and S2 will provide a comprehensive concept for reporting on sustainability risks and opportunities, aligning reporting with sustainability objectives. The study hypothesis was formulated based on previous studies related to the study problem, and to achieve its objective, we assumed the following:

H1: *Adopting IFRS S1 and S2 standards enhances the level of disclosure of environmental, social, economic, and governance sustainability indicators, contributing to enhanced transparency and corporate accountability.*

H2: *The increased level of disclosure of sustainability indicators, in light of the implementation of IFRS S1 and S2 standards, contributes to improving the quality and accuracy of financial estimates within corporate budgets, thus supporting the effectiveness of strategic managerial accounting practices.*

3 METHODOLOGY

Today, global companies are witnessing a remarkable shift towards integrating sustainability principles into their various activities, which has led to the emergence of SDS as an essential part of financial and non-financial reporting. Since SMA practices are a key tool for supporting internal decisions, the adoption of sustainability standards directly impacts the nature and approach of SMA practices. However, the extent to which SMA practices respond to these standards remains unclear, especially in emerging markets. This raises questions about the extent of change in SMA practices and techniques resulting from the adoption of SD. The study aims to analyze the impact of adopting SDS on SMA practices and evaluate the extent to which SMA practices align with sustainable disclosure requirements. The importance of the study lies in enhancing disclosure transparency, thus contributing to attracting investments and increasing confidence in financial markets. The main question of the study is: *To what extent has the adoption of SDS affected* SMA practices *in companies?*

3.1 *Hypothetical model*

The study model aims to demonstrate the role of adopting IFRS S1, S2, and SDS when implementing SMA practices, as shown in Figure 1.

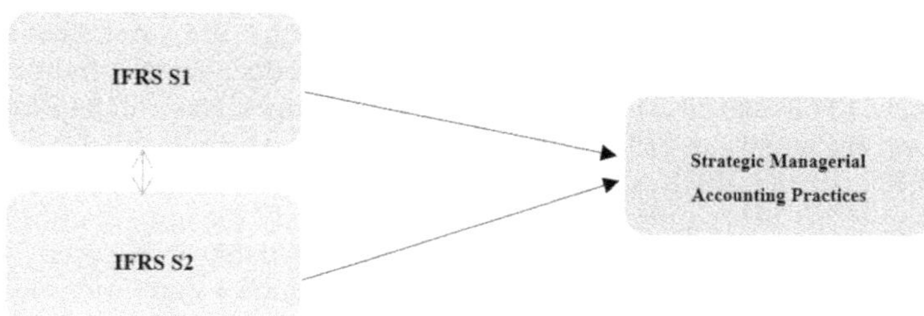

Figure 1. Study model.

3.2 *Sample*

Diyala State Company is located in Diyala Governorate on the international road linking Baqubah city center and Baghdad. The company includes production and service halls, a water treatment unit, a neutralization unit for treating the unit's liquid waste, and warehouse buildings. It is one of the formations of the Ministry of Industry and Minerals, having been established in 1974 under the name "Light Engineering Industries Complex" and at the time the "Industrial Complex", which includes production plants (Electrical Measurements Plant, Iron Plant, Spark Plug Plant, Ceiling Fan Plant), which were inaugurated in 1978 with the start of trial operation. The company aims to produce products with a competitive advantage that enables it to face competition in the market, increase the company's production capacity, meet market needs, increase capital, develop its products, increase sales volume, seek to reach new markets, and develop the skills of the company's employees.

4 RESULTS

4.1 *Determined material flow, the inputs and outputs*

Based on the previously determined material flow, the inputs and outputs for an 11/250/kVA product can be determined. Table 1 shows the costs of raw materials, semi-finished parts, auxiliary chemicals, and packaging materials involved in the manufacturing process (MP) for an 11/250/kVA product.

Table 1. Positive raw material costs for an 11/250/kVA Product for the year 2021.

Details	Quantity (kg)	Unit price (Iraqi dinars)	Product cost
Raw Material Cost	1049	2815	2952935
Semi-finished Parts Cost	104	2808	292032
Auxiliary Chemicals Cost	85.766	2000	171532
Packaging Materials Cost	48	1600	76800
Total Material Costs			3493299

Illustrated from Table 1, the accuracy of the accounting system in tracking cost components contributes to improving strategic decision-making and reducing unnecessary costs. Furthermore, dividing costs by material component helps link them to outputs and analyze waste. These costs appear in the traditional unified accounting system and are the basis for assessing product cost. Analysis of the data in Table 1 related to the costs of various raw materials, which included four main types of costs: raw materials, semi-finished parts, auxiliary chemicals, and packaging materials. The following are the most prominent results for the Arithmetic mean: (Average quantity: approximately 321.7 kg, Average unit price: approximately 2,305.75 Iraqi dinars, Average product cost: approximately 873,325 Iraqi dinars.) Maximum and minimum values: (The highest cost was for raw materials, amounting to 2,952,935 Iraqi dinars; the lowest cost was for packaging materials, amounting to 76,800 Iraqi dinars. The highest quantity used was raw materials (1,049 kg), and the lowest quantity used was packaging materials (48 kg). As for the standard deviation, the analysis showed a large variation in values, especially in the quantity and costs of materials, as the standard deviation of the product cost amounted to more than 1.38 million dinars, indicating that some materials clearly dominate the total cost. The percentage of contribution of each element to the total cost: (Raw materials constitute approximately 84.5% of the total cost, semi-finished parts constitute 8.36%, auxiliary chemicals constitute 4.91%, and Packaging materials constitute only 2.2% of the total cost).

Table 2 illustrates non-commodity outputs (industrial waste), which are considered one of the main areas of environmental disclosure under IFRS S2. The associated financial values are used to analyze their impact on the financial position. They represent costs associated with materials and energy that did not produce final outputs but rather constituted waste or environmental waste in the MP for a product of 11/250/KVA for the year 2021.

Table 2. Negative raw material costs are involved in the MP for 11/250/KVA for the year 2021.

Details	Quantity (kg)	Unit price (Iraqi dinars)	Product cost
Cost of damaged raw materials	21.411	2815	60272
Cost of damaged semi-finished parts	2.815	2808	7904
Cost of wasted chemicals	1.75	2000	3500
Cost of wasted packaging materials	0.962	1600	1540
Total costs of damaged and wasted materials			73216

When analyzing the data in Table 2, including the costs of damaged and wasted materials during the production process, including raw materials, semi-finished parts, chemicals, and packaging materials. The following is a summary of the analysis: The arithmetic mean (average quantity damaged or wasted: approximately 6.73 kg, average unit price: 2,305.75

Iraqi dinars, average cost of damage/waste: approximately 18,304 Iraqi dinars). The maximum and minimum values (the highest cost of waste: damaged raw materials, amounting to 60,272 Iraqi dinars, the lowest cost: wasted packaging materials, amounting to 1,540 Iraqi dinars, the highest quantity of damaged raw materials (21.411 kg), the lowest quantity of packaging materials (0.962 kg). The standard deviation (the cost of waste) is relatively high (28,105 dinars), indicating a significant variation in values between different types of materials. The percentage of contribution of each material to the total cost of waste (73,216 dinars): damaged raw materials: 82.3%, damaged semi-finished parts: 10.8%, wasted chemicals: 4.8%, packaging materials wasted: 2.1%. And Shows under Table 2 the outputs, which are wasted costs that do not produce added value and are therefore including environmental and social impacts related to disclosure in non-financial reports. The company's traditional system ignores this information, but the use of Material Flow Cost Accounting MFCA has enabled it to be measured quantitatively and monetarily, bringing the company closer to compliance with IFRS S2 requirements related to climate risks.

The use of MFCA, a technical tool for reallocating costs between actual production and lost production, and Table 3 shows the energy costs.

Table 3. Energy costs for producing an 11/250/kVA transformer for the year 2021.

Details	Positive cost	Negative cost	Total cost
Electricity	3495185	71330	3566515
Fuel	5016	102	5118
Oils	1566	32	1598
Total	3501767	71464	3573231

Table 3 shows the costs associated with the energy used in the production process: electricity, fuel, and oils. Costs are classified as positive (actually spent) and negative (lost or damaged). The percentage contribution of each energy component to the total cost is shown below: electricity (represents the largest proportion, reaching 98.91% of total energy costs), fuel (represents 0.63% of total costs), and oils (represent the smallest proportion, at only 0.12%). The analysis of negative costs reveals that the highest loss was recorded in electricity: 71,330 dinars, while losses in fuel and oil were very limited (102 and 32 dinars, respectively). This type of information is the basis for climate disclosure according to IFRS S2 and contributes to supporting environmental governance requirements. To measure the impact of applying strategic accounting and the MFCA tool on the sustainable performance of the 11/250/kVA transformer, the regular costs were analyzed, as shown in Table 4.

Table 4. Regular costs for the production of an 11/250/kVA transformer for the year 2021.

Details	Positive cost	Negative cost	Total cost
Environmental salaries and wages	80552080	1643920	82196000

Table 4 shows that the 2% reduction in waste reflects the positive impact of implementing the MFCA in improving energy efficiency and reducing waste. This data is essential for the climate disclosure process according to IFRS S2 and contributes to meeting environmental governance requirements, reflecting the impact of MFCA in improving energy efficiency.

4.2 Analysis of results

Based on the results shown above, the analysis of the results is as follows:

4.2.1 *Positive costs (actual production)* amounted to 3,493,299 dinars, which included the costs of raw materials, semi-finished parts, auxiliary chemicals, and packaging materials. These costs represented actual production outputs under the traditional accounting system, and these results indicate partial efficiency in resource allocation.

4.2.2 *Negative costs (manufacturing loss)* amounted to 73,216 dinars, which included the costs of damaged raw materials, damaged semi-finished parts, wasted chemicals, and wasted packaging materials. These costs were not previously disclosed, but they represent environmental waste that must be disclosed under IFRS S1 and S2, especially since they impact environmental performance.

4.2.3 *Energy costs, according to the MFCA tool,* represented a total cost of 3,573,231 dinars, which amounted to a net efficiency of 3,501,767 dinars. In comparison, the loss cost amounted to 71,464 dinars, representing 2% of the total energy. This percentage represents the potential for reducing invisible climate costs and the need to disclose them under IFRS S2.

4.2.4 *The regulatory results (salaries and environmental wages)* represented a total cost of 82,196,000 dinars, a regulatory loss of 1,643,920 dinars, and a net efficiency of 80,552,080 dinars. The loss cost is often associated with administrative weaknesses and can be disclosed in the governance section of IFRS S1.

4.2.5 *The impact of the results on the adoption of IFRS S1 and S2* is illustrated in Table 5.

Table 5. Adoption results for IFRS S1 and S.

The Outcome	Relationship to IFRS S1 AND S2
Accurately identify losses	Aligns with the full disclosure principle of IFRS S1
Measure wasted energy and emissions.	Required under the climate disclosure of IFRS S2
Link environmental costs to financials	Establishes the integration of financial and non-financial reporting
Improved efficiency and reduced waste	Strengthens internal governance and increases organizational transparency
Improved material use efficiency	Strengthens the environmental disclosure of IFRS S1
Improved energy efficiency	Strengthens climate disclosure of IFRS S2
Improved administrative efficiency	Strengthens governance disclosure of IFRS S1
Improved measured environmental costs	Strengthens support for sustainable reporting of IFRS S1 and S2
Enhanced financial disclosure transparency	Promotes trust and compliance

5 DISCUSSION OF RESULTS

Based on the results shown above, the results of the MFCA application are discussed, revealing a partially effective regulatory control structure, which is represented by the ability to measure positive and negative costs and focus on determining energy efficiency by 98%. However, this oversight still suffers from critical gaps, most notably:

5.1 *The strength of regulatory oversight in Iraqi banks compared to the KSA and the UAE*: due to the presence of a strict oversight system by the Central Bank of Iraq. However, this requires a greater role compared to the KSA and the UAE, which have effectively implemented international standards in their banks, such as IFRS 9 and IFRS 7.

5.2 *Weak narrative disclosure and banking governance.* Despite instructions from the Central Bank, narrative disclosure in Iraqi financial reports requires increased transparency compared to American MD&A reports.

5.3 *The need for increased attention to the accounting and auditing structure* in the Iraqi hotel sector to begin implementing IFRS.

5.4 *The role of international standards (IFRS and ISO):* Iraqi banks have gradually begun implementing international standards (IFRS 9). Iraqi hotels, however, do not apply IFRS, unlike hotels in the selected countries, which implement it through regulatory bodies. The USA adopts GAAP, which is subject to strict oversight by the SEC and PCAOB.

5.5 The lack of professional specialization in environmental accounting and climate impact assessment has weakened and reduced the ability of personnel to analyze environmental data comprehensively or link it to international disclosure standards such as IFRS S1 and S2.

5.6 Weak narrative disclosure: Reports focus on numerical values without adequately explaining the context of environmental and regulatory losses or analyzing their causes, which reduces the effectiveness of disclosure and undermines the confidence of company stakeholders.

5.7 Regulatory losses (1,643,920 dinars) and the lack of disclosure of environmental waste highlight the need to strengthen the oversight role of accounting and auditing, not only in tracking costs, but also in ensuring ethical and transparent disclosure of environmental performance.

These data confirm the importance of establishing professional ethics, such as integrity, objectivity, and full disclosure, to ensure that financial and environmental reports are a tool for making sustainable decisions and not merely formal compliance with standards. Positive costs totaled 3,493,299 dinars, indicating partial efficiency in resource allocation. Meanwhile, previously undisclosed negative costs amounted to 73,216 dinars, representing 2.1% of the total costs. These are environmental wastes that require disclosure according to IFRS S1 and S2. Energy losses amounted to 71,464 dinars out of 3,573,231 dinars, representing 2%, revealing potential opportunities to improve climate efficiency. The organizational loss amounted to 1,643,920 dinars out of 82,196,000 dinars, also representing 2%, indicating administrative weaknesses.

6 CONCLUSIONS

In light of the theoretical and applied analysis of SMA practices, and based on the results of implementing MFCA at the Diyala General Company for Electrical Industries, the following conclusions can be drawn: It is clear that the applied accounting system focuses on recording costs in general without giving sufficient importance to environmental or social costs, leading to a clear lack of comprehensive disclosure. Contrary to the requirements of IFRS S1 and S2 sustainability standards, the results of implementing MFCA showed that this tool helps reclassify costs between positive (product outputs) and negative (non-product outputs). This contributes to raising management's awareness of waste costs, thereby enhancing their ability to make informed decisions to improve environmental and financial efficiency. Although the company calculates wages and overhead costs, their absence from social sustainability indicators (such as impact on the local community and employee well-being) reflects a lack of effective implementation of IFRS S1 requirements in terms of governance and social SD. The results showed that environmental information such as loss, pollution, and energy consumption, was not included in official reports. However, the adoption of the new IFRS standards requires incorporating this information into consolidated and financial disclosure reports. The analysis demonstrates a complementary relationship between the use of SMA practices, particularly MFCA, and the ability to implement modern disclosure standards, as SMA practices contribute to generating the quantitative information necessary to implement disclosure standards.

REFERENCES

Alamri, A.M. (2019). Association between strategic management accounting facets and organizational performance. *Baltic Journal* of Management 18March14(2):212–234. https://doi:10.1108/bjm-12-2017-0411

Boulalib, O. (2021). The Contribution of Strategic Management Accounting to Strategic Performance Evaluation: A Case Study of Ain El Kebira Cement Company. *Journal of Advanced Economic Research*, 6 (2), 301–325. https://www.asjp.cerist.dz/en/article/178397

Cojocaru, A.-C., and Mihăilă, S. (2024). Implementation of IFRS sustainability disclosure standards into integrated reporting: a journey of future-oriented companies. *Revista de Studii Financiare*, *9*(17), 39–55. https://doi.org/10.55654/jfs.2024.9.17.03

Dinçer, B. (2024). Assessment of greenhouse gas emissions measurement within scope 1 and scope 2 in accordance with IFRS S2. *Journal of Economics, Business and International Relations. Volume: 3 Issue: 1, 136 - 154*. https://doi.org/10.58654/jebi.1478784

Grajales Gaviria, D.A., Cataño Martínez, E.M., Catellanos Polo, O.C., and Arcila, J. (2023). Accounting mechanism to measure the environmental impact of industries in the aburrá valley and its application of the general disclosure requirements related to Financial Information on Sustainability (IFRS S1) and Climate-Related Disclosures (IFRS S2). *RGSA: Revista de Gestão Social e Ambiental*, *17*(5), e03639. https://doi.org/10.24857/rgsa.v17n5-013

Amelia, M., and Djakman, C. (2024). Gap analysis in implementing IFRS S1 and IFRS S2: A case study at bank X in Indonesia. *International Journal of Economics Development Research, 5(4), 210–224*. https://doi.org/10.37385/ijedr.v5i3.5755

IFRS Foundation publishes Annual Report. (2024). IFRS - IFRS Foundation

IFRS Foundation. (2023). Effects Analysis: IFRS S1 and IFRS S2. https://www.ifrs.org/content/dam/ifrs/project/general-sustainability-related-disclosures/effects-analysis.pdf

IFRS Foundation. (2024). AP9D: Implementation Challenges and Concerns Related to IFRS S2. Agenda Paper 9D, *International Sustainability Standards Board Meeting*, November 2024. ap9d-implementation-challenges-concerns-s2.pdf

IFRS S1 General Requirements for Disclosure of Sustainability-related Financial Information. (2023). IFRS - IFRS S1 General Requirements for Disclosure of Sustainability-related Financial Information

IFRS S2 Climate-related Disclosures. (2023). IFRS - IFRS S2 Climate-related Disclosures

Indyk, M. (2022). Are the Companies Prepared for Sustainability Reporting under the ED IFRS S1 and S2? Evidence from Poland. *Audit Financiar*, *20*(168), 641–654. https://doi.org/10.20869/auditf/2022/168/022

Kanakria, Raed M. (2020). The Role of Strategic Management Accounting and Its Impact on Competitive Advantage in Jordanian Industrial Companies. *Journal of Economic and Administrative Sciences*, Vol. 26, No. 120, pp. 497-515. https://search.emarefa.net/detail/BIM-976637

Krisdiyawati, and Maulidah, H. (2024). Maximizing SME Performance through Strategic Management Accounting in a Competitive Environment (Case Study in SME Indonesia). *Asian Journal of Economics, Business and Accounting*, *24*(12), 266–276. https://doi.org/10.9734/ajeba/2024/v24i121607

Kusuma, K.N., and Gani, L. (2024). Implementation of Published IFRS S1 and S2 Standards Globally. *Dinasti International Journal of Economics, Finance and Accounting*, *5*(3), 943–954. https://doi.org/10.38035/dijefa.v5i3.2734

Kwarbai, J. (2025). Strategic Management Accounting Practices and Socio-Cultural Value Creation in Listed Deposit Money Banks in Nigeria. *Social Science Research Network*. https://doi.org/10.2139/ssrn.5048308

Le, T.T.H., and Nguyen, T.H. (2023). Influence of Strategic Management Accounting Practices on Employee Satisfaction in Businesses in Vietnam. *International Academic Journal of Accounting and Financial Management.10(1), 40-44*. https://doi.org/10.9756/iajafm/v10i1/iajafm1005

Li, Z. (2024). The Impact of IFRS S1 on Corporate ESG Disclosure: A Comparative Analysis of SMIC and MTR Corporation. *Finance & Economics*, *1*(10). https://doi.org/10.61173/5a4tgb09

Nechyporuk, N.L., Hryhorova, Z., Kvasko, A. Yu., and Avanesova, N. (2023). Strategic management accounting within the system of integrated management of enterprises. *Ekonomìka, Fìnansi, Pravo, 2*, 26–29. https://doi.org/10.37634/efp.2023.2.5

Nik Abdullah, H.N. (2020). *Assessing Strategic Management Accounting Practices in Public Interest Companies in Malaysia. Indonesian Journal of Economics, Social, and Humanities*, *2*(1), 13–25. https://doi.org/10.31258/IJESH.2.1.13-25

Nik Abdullah, H.N., and Said, J. (2016). *Strategic management accounting practices and value creation: towards good governance and accountability in government-linked companies. International Conference on Accounting Studies (ICAS). 107-114.* http://repo.uum.edu.my/20797/

Ogundajo, G.O., Kwarbai, J.D., Ogunsola, O.A., and Omidiji, D.O. (2024). Strategic Management Accounting Practices and Socio-Cultural Value Creation in Listed Deposit Money Banks in Nigeria. *European Journal of Business and Management Research*, *9*(6), 57–63. https://doi.org/10.24018/ejbmr.2024.9.6.2491

Oktariyani, A. (2024). *Analisis pengungkapan tanggung jawab sosial dan lingkungan perusahaan pertambangan di Indonesia. Journal of Economic, Accounting and Management, 2(1), 232-246.* https://doi.org/10.61994/equivalent.v2i1.375

Parkinson, A., and Chew, L. (2022). Towards an Environmental Sustainability Management Accounting Template. *The Business & Management Review*, *13*(01). https://www.researchgate.net/publication/360614693_Towards_an_Environmental_Sustainability_Management_Accounting_Template

Rashid, M.M., Ali, Md. M., and Hossain, D.M. (2020). *Strategic management accounting practices: a literature review and opportunity for future research. Asian Journal of Accounting Research.* *6*(1), 109–132. https://doi.org/10.1108/AJAR-06-2019-0051

Rathwatta, H., and Samudrage, D.N. (2019). *Generic Strategy and Strategic Management Accounting Practices: Case Study of a Sri Lankan Telecommunications Company.* *5*(2). https://doi.org/10.31357/VJM.V5I2.4197

Stocker, F., de Arruda, M.P., de Mascena, K.M., and Boaventura, J.M. (2020). Stakeholder engagement in sustainability reporting: a classification model. Corporate Social Responsibility and Environmental Management, 27(5), 2071-2080. https://doi.org/10.1002/csr.1947

Stormi, K., Laine, T. and Korhonen, T. (2019), Agile performance measurement system development: an answer to the need for adaptability?, *Journal of Accounting & Organizational Change*, Vol. 15 No. 2, pp. 231-256. https://doi.org/10.1108/JAOC-09-2017-0076

The ISSB's New Sustainability Disclosure Standards (2024). A First Look at S1 and S2. *CPA Journal.* https://www.cpajournal.com/2024/04/03/the-issbs-new-sustainability-disclosure-standards/

Thijeel, A.M., Al-Fandawi, H.H.F., and Faisal, G.M. (2025). IFRS adoption and credit rating in Iraqi banks: The mediating role of governance and implications for agricultural finance. *AgBioForum*, 27(1), 58-67. file:///C:/Users/Lenovo/Downloads/6-AgBio+27(1)2025+Revised_66010+(Final).pdf

Tolkach, V. (2023). The importance of international financial reporting standards (IFRS) and the new sustainability reporting standards, IFRS S1 and IFRS S2, in sustainable business development in the us. *V⊠da a Perspektivy.* https://doi.org/10.52058/2695-1592-2023-7(26)-282-290

Tran, N.H. (2023). Factors impacting strategic management accounting adoption: Empirical evidence from an emerging market. *International Journal of Innovative Research and Scientific Studies. 6(3), 710–717.* https://doi.org/10.53894/ijirss.v6i3.1877

Vitolla, F., Raimo, N., Rubino, M., and Garzoni, A. (2019). How pressure from stakeholders affects integrated reporting quality. *Corporate Social Responsibility and Environmental Management*, 26(6), 1591-1606. https://doi.org/10.1002/csr.1850

Moving Towards Sustainable Businesses and Developing More Resilient Economies – Rashid and Annansingh-Jamieson (Eds)
© 2026 The Author(s), ISBN: 978-1-041-08875-2

Relationship between organizational intelligent and digital transformation readiness

S. Ebrahimi Mehrabani
Contract Faculty, York University & International Business University, Toronto, Ontario, Canada

M. Shajari
Faculty of Computer Studies, Georgian College, Barrie, Ontario, Canada

ABSTRACT: The aim of this study is to investigate the effects of organizational intelligence dimensions on digital transformation readiness. Using the Karl Albrecht model of organizational intelligence, data were collected through questionnaires completed by private SMEs in Toronto, Canada. The analysis was conducted using both descriptive and inferential statistics in SPSS. The findings provide empirical evidence of a positive and significant relationship between organizational intelligence and digital transformation readiness, based on Pearson correlation analysis. Stepwise regression results identified knowledge deployment, appetite for change, and performance pressure as key predictors of digital transformation readiness. Therefore, for a successful digital transformation, organizations must pay more attention to all organizational intelligence dimensions, especially the three mentioned.

1 INTRODUCTION

One of the biggest challenges of management in the current era is to create intelligent organizations that can easily adapt to the changing environment. In the past three decades, building smart organizations did not receive much attention, but as technology improved managers paid more attention to the importance of these technologies to have smart organizations. With no doubt, at this time, one of the best ways to increase organizational effectiveness and efficiency is the use of intelligence including organizational intelligence (OI) and machine intelligence (Erfani-Khanghahi 2023). Intelligence can be seen as the ability to learn, reason, and understand.

It was explained by Tsiu *et al.* (2025) that SMEs face unique challenges which can be mitigated using business intelligence and data mining technologies. Based on reviewing 93 scholarly articles from 2014 to 2024, they found that advanced analytics like predictive modeling and machine learning are increasingly being adopted, however some challenges such as high costs, complexity, and skills gaps persist. They stated the need for empirical research to measure the actual impact of BI on SME performance (Tsiu *et al.* 2025).

The main aim of current research is to find out how organizational intelligence and its dimensions have been put into place in some random selected SMEs in Toronto. It is also to find out the relationship between organizational intelligence dimensions and digital transformation readiness in those companies.

DOI: 10.1201/9781003647300-37

2 LITERATURE REVIEW

2.1 *Organizational intelligence and digital transformation readiness*

Ly (2022 2024) emphasized that organizations must be innovative, committed, and continuously developing new skills to stay competitive. Their work identifies adaptability, learning capability, and strategic foresight as key drivers of digital transformation readiness—core aspects of organizational intelligence. This suggests that higher organizational intelligence improves an organization's readiness and success in digital transformation. As stated, "The advantages of transformation will only be fully realized once an adequate level of maturity has been attained in an organization's soft components" (Cyfert *et al.* 2025), such as digital leadership, digital competencies, and digital organizational culture.

Michelotto and Joia (2024) similarly highlighted management capability, human capability, and corporate culture as essential for digital transformation readiness, reinforcing the importance of soft skills in preparing organizations for change. Developing strong digital intelligence is also recognized as a major challenge for today's workforce (Cordes and Rosemann 2020)

Building on Albrecht's (2003) dimensions of organizational intelligence, several of these directly relate to digital transformation readiness. A clear strategic direction aligns with the strategic vision dimension, which is essential for readiness, as noted by Michelotto and Joia (2024). Cyfert *et al.* (2025) stress the importance of shared culture and values—soft components that enable successful transformation. This reinforces the need for shared fate, where employees work toward common goals. An organization's ability to innovate and adapt reflects its appetite for change, and cultivating such digital intelligence, including openness to change, is one of the major challenges in digital transformation (Cordes and Rosemann 2020). In addition, in a study on employees' well-being and digitalization highlights researchers showed that employee engagement and well-being are critical factors in the context of digital transformation (Demaria and Cavicchioli 2025). On the other hand, considering "heart" as one of the dimensions of organizational intelligence focus on employee engagement and emotion-al commitment, which are critical for sustaining transformation efforts as well.

Moreover, Jöhnk *et al.* (2021) recognized strategic alignment as a key factor in managing multiple digital transformation initiatives (Jöhnk 2020). This can reflect the relation between alignment and congruence with digital strategies. Michelotto and Joia (2024) include knowledge management and human capability as essential pillars of digital transformation readiness which can make a meaningful connection between knowledge deployment and digital transformation readiness. Finally, Cyfert *et al.* (2025) explained that performance expectations, when supported by leadership and digital competencies, can accelerate transformation and innovation. This is aligned with what is considered in organizational intelligence as performance pressure in this study.

2.2 *Digital transformation readiness*

2.2.1 *Digital-first mindset*

A digital-first mindset reflects an organizational culture where digital solutions are prioritized and embraced across all levels. It begins with leadership communicating the benefits of digital transformation, modeling digital behaviors, and incentivizing change through both monetary and non-monetary rewards. This mindset encourages employees to consider digital technologies as integral to problem-solving and innovation.

2.2.2 *Digitized practices*

Digitized practices involve the integration of digital technologies into core business operations, decision-making, and learning processes. This includes automating workflows, using data analytics for informed decisions, and fostering a culture of collaboration and experimentation. These practices aim to enhance efficiency, responsiveness, and continuous improvement within the organization.

2.2.3 *Empowered talent*

Empowered talent refers to the development and engagement of employees with the necessary digital skills and experiences. It includes equipping staff with competencies in emerging technologies, encouraging self-motivation and entrepreneurial thinking, and aligning human resources with digital transformation goals. This dimension ensures that the workforce is capable and confident in driving digital initiatives.

2.2.4 *Data access and collaboration tools*

This dimension focuses on the technological infrastructure that enables seamless communication, data sharing, and collaboration. It encompasses tools that provide real-time access to customer and operational data, integrated systems across departments, and flexible computing resources. These tools support informed decision-making and foster a connected, agile organizational environment (Kontić and Vidicki 2018).

2.3 *Organizational intelligence*

Despite several definitions of organizational intelligence, many researchers agree on the key conceptual definition of it which refers to capacity for information processing, learning and problem solving; ability to adapt to environment or reshape it; and the skill of recognizing people's feelings, thoughts and behaviours in order to find out how to act properly based on that understanding (Akgün *et al.* 2007). Karl Albrecht (2003) is on this belief that if organizations want to be more effective, they need to be more intelligent. He defines the organizational intelligence as the organizational ability and capacity to gather all available brain power and lead it to achieve the organizational goal and mission. He introduced three factors for success in business. They are smart people, smart team and smart organization. In his definition, organizational intelligence has seven dimensions. He stated that organizations must concentrate on theses seven dimensions to improve the performance and develop the organization. These dimensions represent inherent traits rather than behaviours, structural characteristics, or processes. Each trait has distinct antecedents that can help enhance that specific aspect of intelligence (Albrecht 2003). Based on the Albrecht (2003) these dimensions are included:

2.3.1 *Strategic vision*

Each organization needs a theory which defines its ideal future. Strategic vision refers to the organizational capacity to create, develop, and state the aim of the organization. Organizational intelligence assumes leaders can articulate, develop, and refine a successful strategic vision.

2.3.2 *Shared fate*

Shared fate is the collective belief that individual success is linked to the organization's success. When members share a common vision and purpose, they collaborate as if rowing in the same boat toward a unified destination. This alignment builds trust, mutual accountability, and coordinated action, enabling the organization to overcome challenges and achieve its strategic goals more effectively.

2.3.3 *Appetite for change*

In current era people understand the need to reinvent the business model to be adopted with challenges and learn creative ways of succeeding. There is a need to enough attention to adopting the variety of changes which are required for the strategic vision.

2.3.4 *Heart*

The heart's elements involve the willingness to give more than the standard. Organizational psychologists describe "heart" or discretionary effort as the extra energy employees put into their work beyond what is formally required by their job contracts. In an organization with lots of heart employees recognize their success in line with the organizational success therefore they try to do more than expected.

2.3.5 *Alignment and congruence*

In today's dynamic environment, organizations must reinvent their models to meet new challenges and drive innovation. Albrecht (2003) highlights the importance of alignment and congruence where values, strategies, and systems work in harmony. In intelligent organizations, these systems bring people together, with leaders guiding employee energy and alignment toward a shared mission. This coherence strengthens the organization's ability to adapt and succeed.

2.3.6 *Knowledge deployment*

Knowledge deployment refers to an organization's ability to effectively use its intellectual and informational resources. It requires maintaining an open flow of knowledge while balancing access to needed information with the protection of sensitive data. It also involves fostering a culture that encourages new ideas, innovation, and open-minded questioning.

2.3.7 *Performance pressure*

In the intelligent organization, each employee is responsible for their performance. Leaders can promote and support a sense of performance pressure, but it is more effective when accepted by all organizational members. In this situation there is a shared sense of imperative

3 METHODOLOGY

This study employed a quantitative research design using a structured questionnaire adapted from previously validated instruments. Data were collected from five randomly approached private SMEs located in Toronto. Due to practical constraints and limited access, a total of 44 employees, including managers and expert staff, participated in the study.

The sampling method used was non-probability convenience sampling, where participants were selected based on availability and willingness to participate. While this approach may limit generalizability, it is commonly used in exploratory research to gain initial insights into emerging topics. The sample size, though modest, was sufficient to conduct both descriptive and inferential statistical analyses and to identify meaningful patterns in the relationship between organizational intelligence dimensions and digital transformation readiness.

Although reliability metrics such as Cronbach's alpha were not calculated due to the small sample size, the questionnaire items were sourced from prior studies that had already established their validity and reliability. A set of questionnaires containing a 5-point Likert type scale-ranging from 'strongly disagree' (1) to 'strongly agree' (5) was produced to gather the data. The questionnaire was included 49 questions about organizational intelligence using Albracht (2003) organizational intelligence survey and, 32 questions from the questionnaire developed by Kontić and Vidicki (2018) in order to assess digital transformation readiness.

3.1 *Study hypotheses*

The main hypothesis of this research is: There is a positive relationship between organizational intelligence dimensions and digital transformation readiness. To find the result for this main hypothesis, 7 sub-hypotheses were posed as follows:

- There is a relationship between strategic vision and digital transformation readiness.
- There is a relationship between shared fate and digital transformation readiness.
- There is a relationship between employees' heart and digital transformation readiness.
- There is a relationship between organizational alignment and congruence and digital transformation readiness.
- There is a relationship between appetite for change and digital transformation readiness.
- There is a relationship between knowledge deployment and digital transformation readiness.
- There is a relationship between performance pressure and digital transformation readiness

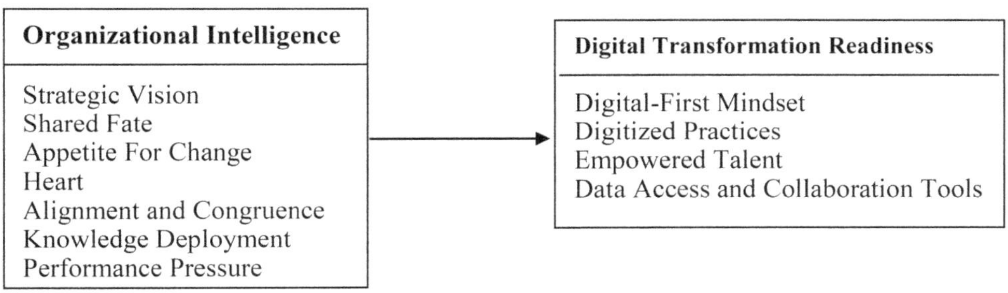

Figure 1. Conceptual framework.

4 RESULTS

At first, the level of organizational intelligence was investigated in the target companies. The results showed that about 60 percent of employees had an organizational intelligence more than average and about 40 percent of them were at the average level of organizational intelligence.

In the next step, the mean score of organizational intelligence dimensions were compared with the hypothetical mean of 3. As Table 1 shows the observed 't' of strategic vision, appetite for change, alignment and congruence, heart and, performance pressure is larger than the critical value of the table at an error level of 0.05. However, the observed 't' of shared fate and knowledge deployment is smaller than the critical value of the table at an error level of 0.05 and therefore, these two dimensions are less than average level.

Table 1. Comparison of organizational intelligence dimension means with the hypothetical mean of 3.

Organizational Intelligence	$\bar{X}$	S	Se	t
Strategic Vision	3.34	0.735	0.063	5.36
Shared Fate	2.50	0.612	0.052	−9.40
Appetite to Change	3.49	0.771	0.066	7.39
Alignment and Congruence	3.22	0.715	0.061	3.63
Heart	3.37	0.582	0.05	7.41
Knowledge Deployment	3	0.648	0.056	0.17
Performance Pressure	3.49	0.695	0.06	8.16

In the next analysis relationship between organizational intelligence dimensions and digital transformation readiness is investigated based on Pearson correlation coefficient analyses. As Table 2 shows there is a meaningful and positive relationship between organizational intelligence and digital transformation readiness and there are meaningful and positive relationships between all dimensions of organizational intelligence and digital transformation readiness. Among the organizational intelligence dimensions, the correlation coefficient of knowledge deployment with digital transformation readiness is at the higher level (0.669) and the correlation coefficient of alignment and congruence with digital transformation readiness is in the lower level (0.578).

Table 2. Correlation between organizational intelligence (and its dimensions) and digital transformation readiness.

Independent variables	Dependent Variable	Pearson correlation coefficient	Significant level
Organizational intelligence	Digital	0.775	0.001
Strategic vision	transformation	0.619	0.001
Shared fate	readiness	0.600	0.001
Appetite to change		0.646	0.001
Alignment and congruence		0.578	0.001
Heart		0.629	0.001
Knowledge deployment		0.669	0.001
Performance pressure		0.631	0.001

To provide a predictive model for digital transformation readiness, regarding to Table 2, organizational intelligence dimensions which had more correlation coefficient with digital transformation readiness were chosen for regression analysis (Table 3). Based on the Table 3 and Table 4, the best predictors for digital transformation readiness are knowledge deployment, appetite for change and performance pressure.

Table 3. Multiple correlation between organizational intelligence dimensions and digital transformation readiness.

Model	R	R2	AD R2	F CHANGE	SIG	CHANGE R
Knowledge deployment	0.669	0.447	0.443	106.77	0.001	0.447
Appetite for change	0.738	0.545	0.538	28.14	0.001	0.098
Performance pressure	0.786	0.617	0.608	24.47	0.001	0.072

Table 4 presents the results of a multiple regression analysis conducted to predict organizational intelligence and digital transformation readiness. The table highlights the extent to which selected variables contribute to explaining variations in these outcomes.

Table 4. Multiple regression predicting organizational intelligence and digital transformation readiness.

Model	Nonstandard factor β	Nonstandard factor Standard error	Standard factor β	T	P
Constant factor	45.93	5.1	——	8.99	0.001
Knowledge deployment	2.44	0.237	0.669	10.33	0.001
Constant factor	34.37	5.13	——	6.69	0.001
Knowledge deployment Appetite	1.61	0.267	0.442	6.06	0.001
for change	1.38	0.262	0.386	5.3	0.001
Constant factor	22.42	22.42	——	4.22	0.001
Knowledge deployment Appetite for	0.843	0.843	0.23	2.89	0.004
change performance pressure	1.36	1.36	0.381	5.67	0.001
	1.17	1.17	0.344	4.94	0.001

5 CONCLUSION AND RECOMMENDATIONS

The investigation into the level of organizational intelligence at the study site revealed that it is at a moderate to above-moderate level. This finding reflects a valuable capability within the organization, which managers can leverage in strategic and operational planning to achieve desired goals. However, investigating the organizational dimensions illustrated the low level of shared fate and knowledge deployment in the organization (Table 1). Therefore, having a plan for increasing these dimensions seems to be important.

The results of investigating the main hypothesis demonstrated that organizational intelligence has a meaningful and positive relationship ($r = 0.775$) with digital transformation readiness. It means with increasing the organizational intelligence, organizations will be more prepared for digital transformation. In addition, the results of testing sub hypotheses illustrated that there is the meaningful and positive relationship between all organizational intelligence dimensions and digital transformation readiness.

Positive relationship between strategic vision and digital transformation readiness shows that if managers increase their ability of problem solving, setting the priorities, using mission statement and stating the directions, the digital transformation readiness will increase.

Positive relationship between shared fate and digital transformation readiness illustrates that if employees believe that their fate is in line the organizational fate and they have a sense of belonging partnership and success, they will be ready to accept new technologies and apply them.

Positive relationship between appetite to change and digital transformation readiness demonstrate that if employees realize the challenges as the opportunities for learning the new methods and get the new experience, it can help them to be ready to accept the digital transformation easily.

Positive relationship between employee heart and digital transformation readiness means that employees with higher level of heart, work more than expected and they are ready to face new challenges and learn new technologies.

Positive relationship between alignment and congruence and digital transformation readiness shows that if organizational structure, politics, processes, methods and rules lead the organizations to achieve the organizational goals and mission, employees will lead to common goals and will accept the new goals toward digitalization.

Positive relationship between knowledge deployment and digital transformation readiness confirms that if knowledge and information be followed in the organization and organization encourage the new idea, innovation and creative questions and appreciate skills, then employee will be more ready to face digital transformation.

Positive relationship between employee pressure and digital transformation readiness illustrates that if each employee believes in the validity of organizational goals and have a suggestion and plans for performance and have commitment for achieving organizational goals, their performance toward accepting the new technology will increase. The results also showed that the best predictors of digital transformation readiness are knowledge deployment, appetite for change and performance pressures.

Therefore, organizations must consider improving organizational intelligence if they aim to digitally transform. Future studies should consider incorporating robustness checks, such as multicollinearity diagnostics, to enhance the reliability of regression results and provide deeper insights into the relationships between variables. Additionally, future research should aim to provide more actionable strategies for SMEs, such as targeted training programs or resource allocation plans, and include comparative studies across different regions or countries to enhance the practical and global relevance of the findings. Expanding the sample size and diversity of participating SMEs would also help improve the generalizability and depth of the results. Future research could explore policy recommendations tailored to SMEs, including cost estimates for digital tools, strategies to overcome budget constraints, and potential partnerships with technology hubs to support digital transformation efforts.

REFERENCES

Akgün, A.E., Byrne, J., and Keskin, H. (2007). Organizational intelligence: A structuration view. *Journal of Organizational Change Management,* 20(3), 272–289. https://doi.org/10.1108/09534810710740137

Albrecht, K. (2003). The power of minds at work: Organizational intelligence in action. *American Management Association*, New York, USA.

Cordes, A.-K., and Rosemann, M. (2020). Developing organizational digital intelligence: A design science research approach. *28th European Conference on Information Systems (ECIS 2020)*. ECIS 2020. https://aisel.aisnet.org/ecis2020_rip/7

Cyfert, S., Dyduch, W., Szumowski, W., and Prause, G. (2025). Are we ready for digital transformation? The role of organizational culture, leadership and competence in building digital advantage. *Central European Management Journal*, 33(2), 219–231. https://doi.org/10.1108/cemj-11-2024-0346

Demaria, F., and Cavicchioli, M. (2025). Employees' well-being, work-related factors, and digitalization: A decision-tree approach for imbalanced data. *Annals of Operations Research.* https://doi.org/10.1007/s10479-025-06702-9

Erfani Khanghahi, M. (2023). Organizational Intelligence. *Danesh Bonyan.*

Jöhnk, J. (2020). *Managing Digital Transformation: Challenges and Choices in Organizational Design and Decision-Making [Application/pdf]*. VII, 83 pages. https://doi.org/10.15495/EPUB_UBT_00004854

Kontić, L., and Vidicki, Đ. (2018). Strategy for digital organization: Testing a measurement tool for digital transformation. *Journal Strategic Management*, 23(1).

Ly, B. (2024). The interplay of digital transformational leadership, organizational agility, and digital transformation. *Journal of the Knowledge Economy*, 15(1), 4408–4427. https://doi.org/10.1007/s13132-023-01377-8

Michelotto, F., and Joia, L.A. (2024). Organizational digital transformation readiness: An exploratory investigation. *Journal of Theoretical and Applied Electronic Commerce Research*, 19(4), 3283–3304. https://doi.org/10.3390/jtaer19040159

Tsiu, S.V., Ngobeni, M., Mathabela, L., and Thango, B. (2025). Applications and competitive advantages of data mining and business intelligence in SMEs performance: A systematic review. *Businesses*, 5(2), 22. https://doi.org/10.3390/businesses5020022

Moving Towards Sustainable Businesses and Developing More Resilient Economies – Rashid and Annansingh-Jamieson (Eds)
© 2026 The Author(s), ISBN: 978-1-041-08875-2

AI for automating financial consolidation and reporting

Srinivas R. Gottimukkala
Deere & Company, Johnston, IA, U.S.A.

Shiva Kumar Bhuram
Dorman Products, Colmar, PA, U.S.A.

ABSTRACT: Artificial Intelligence (AI) is reshaping how companies handle financial consolidation and reporting. By bringing together tools like machine learning (ML), natural language processing (NLP), and robotic process automation (RPA), organizations can automate time-consuming tasks, reduce errors, and speed up the reporting cycle. This paper takes a closer look at how these AI technologies are being used in practice, the challenges businesses face when adopting them, and real-world examples of their impact. Ultimately, it shows how AI not only boosts the accuracy of financial reports but also supports better decision-making and more efficient operations.

1 INTRODUCTION

Financial consolidation and reporting play a vital role in helping businesses—especially large, multinational organizations—stay on top of their financial health (Saifan *et al.* 2020a). These processes ensure that data from various departments and subsidiaries align, meet regulatory requirements, and present a clear picture to stakeholders (Chopra and Ziemba 2011). But traditionally, financial consolidation has been anything but smooth. It's often slow, complex, and prone to errors, especially as businesses grow and their financial operations become more intricate (Saifan *et al.* 2020b). Manually gathering data, validating numbers, eliminating intercompany transactions, and preparing reports involves many moving parts (Roy *et al.* 2020). Each step introduces the risk of delays, inconsistencies, or mistakes—any of which can hurt the credibility of financial reports and hinder timely decision-making (Benartzi and Thaler 2001). Add to that the increasing volume and variety of data companies now handle, plus the growing demand for real-time reporting, and it becomes clear: the old ways of doing things simply aren't cutting it anymore. That's where Artificial Intelligence (AI) comes in. With technologies like machine learning (ML), natural language processing (NLP), robotic process automation (RPA), and predictive analytics, AI is helping finance teams automate repetitive tasks, reduce human error, and unlock valuable insights (Ang and Piazzesi 2003). For instance, ML can quickly flag anomalies in financial data, NLP can generate on-demand reports in plain language, and RPA can take over tedious tasks like data entry and reconciliations (Swamy 2012). Predictive analytics, meanwhile, helps organizations anticipate future trends and plan more effectively. The ability to process vast amounts of data with speed and accuracy is a major advantage in today's fast-paced business world. AI not only improves the reliability of financial reports but also frees up finance professionals to focus on more strategic, value-added work. It's no surprise, then, that AI is fast becoming a must-have in the financial toolkit.

This paper explores how AI is transforming the landscape of financial consolidation and reporting. We'll dive into specific use cases, highlight the benefits AI brings, and look at real-world examples of companies that have successfully adopted these technologies. As digital

DOI: 10.1201/9781003647300-38

transformation continues to shape the business world, understanding AI's role in finance will be key to staying competitive and agile in the years ahead.

2 RELATED WORKS

Financial consolidation and reporting are cornerstones of corporate financial management, especially for large organizations that operate across multiple regions or business units (Kanaparthi 2024). At its core, the process is about bringing together financial data from across the company to create a clear, unified picture of its financial health. But getting to that point involves several critical steps—each with its own challenges. It starts with data collection. This means pulling information from different departments, subsidiaries, or systems—often scattered across various locations and using different accounting software. Without the right systems in place, this stage can be messy and inconsistent, leading to errors down the line (Gottimukkala 2025). Next comes data validation, where the collected data is carefully reviewed to catch any mistakes, inconsistencies, or missing pieces. This step is essential to ensure that the final reports are accurate and trustworthy. For multinational companies, currency conversion is another key hurdle. Financial data reported in multiple currencies needs to be translated into a common reporting currency, often while dealing with fluctuating exchange rates and complex accounting rules. It's a sensitive step—one miscalculation can throw off the entire report. Intercompany eliminations add another layer of complexity. These are internal transactions—like sales or loans between subsidiaries—that need to be removed from the final reports to prevent double counting. It's a critical step in painting a truthful picture of the company's finances (McMillan 2017). After that, the consolidation phase brings everything together—merging the cleaned and adjusted data into a single set of financial statements, like the balance sheet and income statement. This often requires aligning different accounting policies and ensuring compliance with global standards. Finally, reporting ties it all together. Companies generate formal financial markets by MMAR by (Gottimukkala 2025) that follow regulations like GAAP or IFRS, which are then used by executives, auditors, and regulators. These reports not only drive business decisions but also ensure transparency and accountability.

Traditionally, this entire process has been labor-intensive, heavily dependent on spreadsheets, manual data entry, and repeated checks and reconciliations. It's time-consuming and prone to human error. Financial teams can spend weeks—or even months—wrangling spreadsheets, double-checking formulas, and resolving discrepancies. And with more data flowing in as businesses scale, the old manual methods are increasingly unsustainable. Inaccuracies caused by manual mistakes or inconsistencies don't just slow things down—they also pose compliance risks and can lead to significant consequences if financial statements are wrong. That's why there's a growing push toward automation in financial consolidation (Gottimukkala 2024). By reducing reliance on manual work, companies can speed up reporting, improve accuracy, and free up teams to focus on more strategic activities. (Mascarenhas, S.J. 2018) investigates the Fed's influence on global bond yields using 3-day policy windows and OLS, revealing its stronger impact than domestic policies, though limited by short time frames. (Gupta and Chen 2020) automates correlated portfolio replication using stock data from Yahoo Finance, comparing algorithms for a visualization tool, but faces challenges in volatile markets. (Ayele, Gabreyohannes, and Tesfay 2017) applies Monte Carlo simulation with variance reduction to price exotic options, highlighting efficiency gains but limited by basic techniques used. (Cliff 2021; Kurani *et al.* 2023; Cai *et al.* 2018)] explore machine learning in healthcare and fraud detection. (Alarfaj *et al.* 2022) applied ML models to detect credit card fraud using undersampling and majority voting, finding logistic regression on unbalanced data more effective. (Henrique, Sobreiro, and Kimura 2018) analyzed psychiatric medication reviews using VADER, RoBERTa, and BERT, revealing strong sentiment-rating correlations. (Kolm, Tütüncü, and Fabozzi 2014) examined psychiatric drug feedback on WebMD using sentiment and topic modeling on AWS, uncovering themes like side effects and efficacy. All highlight ML's potential, though limited by data bias and interpretation challenges. At last (Zou, Gao, and Gao 2022) proposed a study on the effects of gradient compression techniques—sparsification and quantisation—on distributed training performance. The purpose was to enhance communication efficiency without significantly compromising model accuracy. Techniques like top-k, DGC, and QSGD were tested across 1, 2, and 4-worker setups. Results showed that top-k and DGC at 50× compression reduced perplexity and improved convergence with fewer epochs, though top-k incurred higher computation due to sorting. Compression above 5000× degraded DGC performance. While communication times decreased, trade-offs in scalability and precision emerged. A key limitation is the need for technique-specific hyperparameter tuning and the computational cost of some methods in large-scale systems. Table 1 is showing traditional and AI-driven financial consolidation.

Table 1. Traditional vs AI-driven financial consolidation.

Process Step	Traditional Approach	AI-Driven Approach
Data Collection	Manual gathering from multiple systems	Automated data extraction via RPA and ML
Data Validation	Spreadsheet checks and manual reviews	ML models flag anomalies and clean data automatically
Intercompany Eliminations	Performed manually, time-consuming	RPA automates with accuracy and speed
Report Generation	Written manually by finance professionals	NLP tools generate structured, readable reports
Forecasting	Based on historical trends, limited scope	Predictive analytics offers real-time, data-driven insights

3 AI TECHNOLOGIES IN FINANCIAL CONSOLIDATIONS AND REPORTING

3.1 *Machine learning for data validation*

Machine learning (ML) is quickly becoming a game-changer in the way organizations validate financial data (Liu and Wu 2017). Traditionally, reviewing financial records for errors or inconsistencies has been a manual, time-consuming task—but ML offers a smarter, faster alternative. By learning from large volumes of historical data, ML models can automatically spot patterns and flag anything that seems out of place, often before a human would notice. One of the most valuable uses of ML in this space is anomaly detection (Gottimukkala 2025). These algorithms are trained to recognize what "normal" financial activity looks like. When something unusual shows up—like a transaction that doesn't fit past trends or expected rules—it's flagged for further review. This proactive approach helps catch potential issues early, whether they're simple mistakes, data entry errors, or signs of fraud.ML can also take on the tedious work of data cleansing. That includes fixing missing values, identifying duplicates, and standardizing formats—tasks that would otherwise eat up hours of an accountant's time as shown in Table 2. With ML handling these repetitive chores, finance teams can focus more on analysis and strategy rather than combing through spreadsheets. Ultimately, using ML for data validation not only improves accuracy but also speeds up the entire consolidation and reporting process. It reduces the reliance on manual checks, lowers the risk of errors slipping through the cracks, and helps ensure that the financial data used for reporting is trustworthy and complete. For businesses aiming to modernize their financial operations, ML is a powerful step in the right direction.

Table 2. AI technologies in financial consolidation and reporting.

AI Technology	Description	Key Benefits
Machine Learning (ML)	Learns from historical data to detect anomalies and validate data.	Early error detection, improved data quality, faster validation
Natural Language Processing (NLP)	Generates readable, standards-compliant financial reports from structured and unstructured data.	Time-saving, consistent language, audience-specific reporting
Robotic Process Automation (RPA)	Automates repetitive and rule-based tasks such as data entry and intercompany eliminations.	Reduces manual effort, fewer errors, faster processing
Predictive Analytics	Analyzes historical and external data to forecast financial trends and risks.	Better planning, proactive decision-making, risk mitigation

3.2 *Natural Language Processing (NLP) for report generation*

Natural Language Processing (NLP) is an exciting branch of AI that helps computers understand and generate human language. In the world of finance, this means NLP can take on one of the most time-consuming tasks: writing reports. Instead of manually pulling numbers from spreadsheets and turning them into narratives, AI-powered tools can now do much of the heavy lifting(Gottimukkala 2024). Using NLP, organizations can automatically extract key financial data from both structured sources (Kanaparthi 2024) (like balance sheets or income statements) and unstructured documents (like annual reports, emails, or even financial news). Once the data is gathered, NLP tools can generate clear, well-structured summaries that explain financial trends, key metrics, and performance insights in plain language. These AI-generated reports can be customized for different audiences—whether that's executives looking for a high-level overview, investors needing detailed performance analysis, or regulators checking for compliance. NLP also helps ensure that these reports meet accounting standards like IFRS or GAAP by automatically spotting missing information or inconsistencies that might raise red flags. In short, NLP helps companies produce accurate, timely, and readable financial reports with far less manual work—freeing up teams to focus on strategy rather than spreadsheets.

3.3 *Robotic Process Automation (RPA) for repetitive Tasks Robotic process automation*

RPA is another powerful AI tool that's transforming the finance function—especially when it comes to repetitive, rule-based tasks. Think of RPA as a set of digital "bots" that can mimic how a human interacts with software, but much faster and without taking breaks. In financial consolidation, RPA can handle tedious jobs like entering data into financial systems, pulling reports, and moving information between platforms. For example, instead of a person spending hours copying figures from different spreadsheets, an RPA bot can do it automatically and with fewer errors. One particularly important area where RPA shines is intercompany eliminations—removing internal transactions between different parts of a company so they don't get double-counted. This process is crucial for accurate consolidated statements, and RPA makes it faster, more reliable, and far less stressful.By automating these routine tasks, RPA allows finance teams to focus on higher-level analysis and decision-making. It's a great example of how AI can boost productivity without replacing the critical thinking and expertise that humans bring to the table.

3.4 *Predictive analytics for financial forecasting*

Predictive analytics uses AI to help businesses see what's coming—financially speaking. By analyzing patterns in past financial data, these tools can forecast future trends with impressive accuracy. Whether it's estimating next quarter's revenue, forecasting expenses, or projecting cash flow, predictive models give organizations a clearer view of what lies ahead. These forecasts aren't just based on internal data—they can also factor in broader economic indicators, seasonal trends, and market conditions to provide a well-rounded outlook. For example, predictive analytics might help a company anticipate a dip in cash flow due to supply chain delays or forecast higher sales in a seasonal peak. Beyond forecasting, predictive analytics is also a powerful tool for managing risk. It can identify warning signs—like potential liquidity issues or shifts in market demand—before they become serious problems. This gives businesses time to adjust strategies, allocate resources more effectively, and make smarter decisions. In a fast-moving business environment, the ability to forecast with confidence isn't just helpful—it's essential. Predictive analytics empowers finance teams to be more proactive, agile, and strategic in planning for the future.

4 ADVANTAGES OF AI IN FINANCIAL CONSOLIFDATION AND REPORTING

4.1 *Enhanced efficiency*

One of the biggest benefits of using AI in financial consolidation is how much it speeds up the entire process. Tasks that used to take hours—or even days—can now be done in minutes as shown in Table 3. Instead of spending valuable time on repetitive activities like data entry, reconciliation, or assembling reports, finance teams can hand these over to AI tools like machine learning systems and RPA bots. AI can pull data from different systems, clean it up, reconcile inconsistencies, and generate reports—all without constant human input. That means fewer manual errors, faster reporting cycles, and more time for finance professionals to focus on what really matters: strategic planning and financial analysis. On top of that, AI can monitor data continuously, flagging issues in real time so they can be addressed immediately. The result Smoother operations, faster decision-making, and a more responsive finance function.

Table 3. Advantages of AI in financial reporting.

Advantage	Description
Enhanced Efficiency	Speeds up tasks like reconciliation, report generation, and data validation
Improved Accuracy	Detects anomalies, removes manual errors, ensures reliable data
Cost Reduction	Cuts down on labor and consulting costs through automation
Scalability	Easily handles large data volumes and complex consolidation needs
Real-time Reporting	Delivers up-to-date financial insights, enhancing decision-making and transparency

4.2 *Improved accuracy*

Mistakes in financial data can be costly, whether they lead to poor decisions, compliance issues, or damaged credibility. AI helps tackle this problem head-on by dramatically improving accuracy. Machine learning algorithms are great at spotting irregularities—like duplicate transactions, missing values, or data that doesn't align with historical trends. AI doesn't just catch errors; it also removes the guesswork and bias that can come with manual data handling. It validates and cleans data with precision, ensuring that only correct and complete information makes it into final reports. This leads to financial statements that better reflect the true state of the business. Plus, since these AI systems follow consistent rules, the results are more objective and better aligned with standards like GAAP or IFRS. In the end, stakeholders can have more confidence in the numbers they're seeing.

4.3 *Cost reduction*

AI also helps cut costs in a big way. Traditional consolidation and reporting often require a lot of people doing a lot of manual work—especially during peak reporting periods. That means higher labor costs, overtime, and sometimes even the need to bring in outside consultants.AI changes that equation. By automating routine tasks—like pulling data from different systems, generating reports, and processing intercompany eliminations—companies can reduce their reliance on manual labor. Finance teams can be smaller and more focused, dedicating their time to high-level analysis instead of crunching numbers. AI systems also operate more efficiently than humans and can help avoid costly errors and rework. Over time, this adds up to significant savings and a leaner, more cost-effective financial operation.

Table 4. Use cases of AI technologies in finance.

Use Case	AI Technology Used	Outcome
Anomaly detection	Machine Learning (ML)	Identifies unusual transactions for review
Automated financial narratives	Natural Language Processing	Produces tailored financial summaries
Intercompany transaction removal	Robotic Process Automation	Removes duplicates to ensure accurate consolidated reporting
Revenue and cash flow prediction	Predictive Analytics	Helps organizations forecast with precision and prepare accordingly

4.4 *Scalability*

As companies grow—especially those operating in multiple regions or with numerous business units—the complexity of financial consolidation grows too. AI is built to handle this kind of scale. Whether you're consolidating data from 5 entities or 500, AI systems can adapt without missing a beat.

These tools can manage financial data across currencies, countries, and departments, all while keeping everything aligned and standardized. And when a company expands—say, through acquisitions or international growth—AI can scale up instantly to take on new data sources and consolidation rules without needing a full system overhaul. This kind of scalability keeps operations smooth, even as the organization becomes more complex.

4.5 *Real time reporting*

One of the most exciting benefits of AI is its ability to make real-time financial reporting a reality. Traditionally, financial reports are only available after lengthy consolidation and review cycles. But with AI, data can be gathered, validated, and reported continuously—giving finance teams and executives access to up-to-date insights at any time. This real-time access is a game-changer. Leaders can see how the business is performing right now—not just last month or last quarter—and make faster, more informed decisions. Whether it's managing cash flow, responding to market changes, or identifying emerging risks, real-time reporting allows businesses to be more agile and proactive. It also enhances transparency, helping internal stakeholders and external regulators get an accurate, current view of the organization's financial health.

5 CONCLUSION

AI is changing the game when it comes to financial consolidation and reporting. With tools like machine learning, natural language processing, robotic process automation, and predictive analytics, businesses are no longer stuck with slow, error-prone, and manual financial processes. Instead, they're moving toward smarter systems that can automate repetitive tasks, ensure greater accuracy, and deliver timely insights that support better decision-making. By taking the pressure off finance teams and handling complex data at scale, AI doesn't just make consolidation faster—it makes it more reliable and more strategic. Yes, implementing AI solutions comes with its own set of challenges, from system integration to upfront investment. But the long-term payoff—greater efficiency, lower costs, more accurate reporting, and the ability to work in real time—makes it a smart move for organizations looking to stay competitive. In today's fast-paced, data-driven world, the ability to quickly understand and act on financial information is a major advantage. Companies that embrace AI in their financial processes aren't just keeping up—they're getting ahead. As technology continues to evolve, AI will only become more essential in helping organizations navigate complexity, drive growth, and stay agile in an ever-changing business landscape.

REFERENCES

Alarfaj, Fawaz Khaled, Iqra Malik, Hikmat Ullah Khan, Naif Almusallam, Muhammad Ramzan, and Muzamil Ahmed. (2022). "Credit Card Fraud Detection Using State-of-the-Art Machine Learning and Deep Learning Algorithms." *IEEE Access* 10:39700–715. https://doi.org/10.1109/ACCESS.2022.3166891.

Ang, Andrew, and Monika Piazzesi. (2003). "A No-Arbitrage Vector Autoregression of Term Structure Dynamics with Macroeconomic and Latent Variables." *Journal of Monetary Economics* 50 (4): 745–87. https://doi.org/10.1016/S0304-3932(03)00032-1.

Ayele, Amare Wubishet, Emmanuel Gabreyohannes, and Yohannes Yebabe Tesfay. (2017). "Macroeconomic determinants of volatility for the gold price in Ethiopia: The application of GARCH and EWMA volatility models." *Global Business Review* 18 (2): 308–26. https://doi.org/10.1177/0972150916668601.

Benartzi, Shlomo, and Richard H. Thaler. (2001). "Naive diversification strategies in defined contribution saving plans." *American Economic Review* 91 (1): 79–98. https://doi.org/10.1257/aer.91.1.79.

Cai, Yaping, Kaiyu Guan, Jian Peng, Shaowen Wang, Christopher Seifert, Brian Wardlow, and Zhan Li. (2018). "A high-performance and in-season classification system of field-level crop types using time-series landsat data and a machine learning approach." *Remote Sensing of Environment* 210 (June):35–47. https://doi.org/10.1016/j.rse.2018.02.045.

Chopra, Vijay K., and William T. Ziemba. (2011). "The effect of errors in means, variances, and covariances on optimal portfolio choice." In *The Kelly Capital Growth Investment Criterion: Theory And Practice*, 249–57. https://doi.org/10.3905/jpm.1993.409440.

Cliff, Dave. (2021). "BBE: Simulating the microstructural dynamics of an in-play betting exchange via agent-based modelling." *SSRN Electronic Journal*, May. https://doi.org/10.2139/ssrn.3845698.

Gottimukkala, S.R. (2024). *Automating Portfolio Replication with Stock Market Algorithms*. Preprints. https://doi.org/10.20944/preprints202409.1388.v1

Gottimukkala, S.R. (2024). *Evaluating the Impact of Fed and Domestic Monetary Policies on Long-Term Government Bond Yields*. Preprints. https://doi.org/10.20944/preprints202409.1320.v1

Gottimukkala, S.R. (2024). *Optimizing Exotic Option Pricing: Monte Carlo Simulation and Variance Reduction Techniques*. Preprints. https://doi.org/10.20944/preprints202409.2256.v1

Gottimukkala, S.R. (2025, February). Applying the Multifractal Model of Asset Returns (MMAR) to financial markets: Insights and Limitations. In *2025 10th International Conference on Signal Processing and Communication (ICSC)* (pp. 277-282). IEEE.

Gottimukkala S.R., (2025). "Leveraging generative AI for real-time anomaly detection in SAP FICO: A paradigm shift in financial governance," *TechRxiv*, Jul. 31, 2025. doi: 10.36227/techrxiv.175393572.23304487/v1.

Gupta, Rubi, and Min Chen. (2020). "Sentiment analysis for stock price prediction." *Proceedings - 3rd International Conference on Multimedia Information Processing and Retrieval, MIPR 2020*, August, 213–18. https://doi.org/10.1109/MIPR49039.2020.00051.

Henrique, Bruno Miranda, Vinicius Amorim Sobreiro, and Herbert Kimura. (2018). "Stock price prediction using support vector regression on daily and up to the minute prices." *Journal of Finance and Data Science* 4 (3): 183–201. https://doi.org/10.1016/j.jfds.2018.04.003.

Kanaparthi, Vijaya. (2024). "AI-based personalization and trust in digital finance," January. https://arxiv.org/abs/2401.15700v1.

Kolm, Petter N., Reha Tütüncü, and Frank J. Fabozzi. (2014). "60 Years of Portfolio Optimization: Practical Challenges and Current Trends." *European Journal of Operational Research* 234 (2): 356–71. https://doi.org/10.1016/j.ejor.2013.10.060.

Kurani, Akshit, Pavan Doshi, Aarya Vakharia, and Manan Shah. (2023). "A comprehensive comparative study of Artificial Neural Network (ANN) and Support Vector Machines (SVM) on stock forecasting." *Annals of Data Science*. Springer Science and Business Media Deutschland GmbH. https://doi.org/10.1007/s40745-021-00344-x.

Liu, Jiaming, and Chong Wu. (2017). "A gradient-boosting decision-tree approach for firm failure prediction: An empirical model evaluation of chinese listed companies." *Journal of Risk Model Validation* 11 (2): 43–64. https://doi.org/10.21314/JRMV.2017.170.

Mascarenhas, S.J., FR. Oswald A. J. (2018). "The turbulent market of modern debt-overleveraged and promoter-dominated corporations." In *Corporate Ethics for Turbulent Markets*, 189–213. Emerald Publishing Limited. https://doi.org/10.1108/978-1-78756-187-820181007.

McMillan, David G. (2017). "Which variables predict and forecast stock market returns?" *SSRN Electronic Journal*, June. https://doi.org/10.2139/ssrn.2801670.

Roy, Sanjiban Sekhar, Rohan Chopra, Kun Chang Lee, Concetto Spampinato, and Behnam Mohammadi-Ivatlood. (2020). "Random forest, gradient boosted machines and deep neural network for stock price forecasting: A comparative analysis on South Korean companies." *International Journal of Ad Hoc and Ubiquitous Computing* 33 (1): 62–71. https://doi.org/10.1504/IJAHUC.2020.104715.

Saifan, Ramzi, Khaled Sharif, Mohammad Abu-Ghazaleh, and Mohammad Abdel-Majeed. (2020a). "Investigating algorithmic stock market trading using ensemble machine learning methods." *Informatica (Slovenia)* 44 (3): 311–25. https://doi.org/10.31449/INF.V44I3.2904.

Swamy, Dr. Vighneswara. (2012). "Impact of macroeconomic and endogenous factors on non performing bank assets." *SSRN Electronic Journal*, February. https://doi.org/10.2139/ssrn.2060753.

Zou, Yao, Changchun Gao, and Han Gao. (2022). "Business failure prediction based on a cost-sensitive extreme gradient boosting machine." *IEEE Access* 10:42623–39. https://doi.org/10.1109/ACCESS.2022.3168857.

Moving Towards Sustainable Businesses and Developing More Resilient Economies –
Rashid and Annansingh-Jamieson (Eds)

AI-driven fraud detection in accounts payable

Srinivas R. Gottimukkala
Deere & Company, Johnston, IA, U.S.A.

Shiva Kumar Bhuram
Dorman Products, Colmar, PA, U.S.A.

ABSTRACT: Fraud within accounts payable (AP) shows a major threat to companies, showcasing significant financial issues each year. Conventional rule-based solutions continuously face critical issues to detect complex and misleading fraudulent behavior. This paper explores the application of artificial intelligence (AI) in identifying AP fraud, emphasizing machine learning (ML), deep learning (DL), and natural language processing (NLP) strategies. It reviews current practices, addresses obstacles faced during practical deployment, and emphasizes the promise of AI in creating fraud detection tools that are precise, flexible, and scalable. A side-by-side review of supervised versus unsupervised learning models is presented, with recommendations for upcoming research.

1 INTRODUCTION

Fraud within the accounts payable (AP) process presents an increasingly critical challenge for organizations across industries, especially since global operations now adopt digital and integrated systems (Saifan *et al.* 2020a). Accounts payable fraud includes several deceptive methods (Chopra and Ziemba 2011) such as falsified or overstated invoices, unauthorized edits to vendor records, duplicate transactions, use of shell entities, internal and outside collusion, and manipulation of approval pipelines (Saifan *et al.* 2020b). If overlooked promptly, these incidents may result in severe financial setbacks, legal action, and harm to an organization's credibility. According to the Association of Certified Fraud Examiners (ACFE), businesses forfeit around 5% of annual earnings to occupational fraud, with billing and settlement schemes representing a major portion of such losses (Roy *et al.* 2020). Conventional techniques for detecting fraud—mainly involving manual review, rule-based tools, and simple statistical filters—are becoming less reliable in current dynamic and sophisticated financial landscapes (Benartzi and Thaler 2001). These strategies usually rely on static thresholds, such as flagging transactions above a set amount or identifying reused invoice IDs. While helpful in catching obvious fraud, they frequently miss more intricate methods that bypass basic screenings. Additionally, these processes are often time-consuming, rigid, and lead to high false-alert rates, increasing manual effort and slowing early fraud detection [6]. Modern developments in artificial intelligence (AI), particularly in fields like machine learning (ML), deep learning (DL), and natural language processing (NLP), bring new and advanced capabilities to enhance fraud detection within the AP framework. Unlike rigid systems, AI-driven models can identify trends, map associations, and detect irregular activity from historical financial records, adapting to emerging types of fraud over time (Ang and Piazzesi 2003). For instance, supervised machine learning models can be developed using labeled information to spot fraud indicators missed by humans or standard tools. Conversely, unsupervised models like anomaly detection techniques—including autoencoders and clustering frameworks—can uncover

DOI: 10.1201/9781003647300-39

hidden correlations by scanning unlabeled datasets, especially valuable when confirmed fraud cases are scarce.

In addition, enhancements in NLP allow AI systems to read and interpret unstructured and semi-structured files like PDF invoices, emails, or handwritten memos, enabling complete evaluation of invoice content, vendor communication, and payment documentation. These features can be boosted with graph-oriented strategies that visualize relationships among entities such as vendors, staff, and payments to reveal collusion and organized fraud networks hidden in tabular data. Time-aware models such as Long Short-Term Memory (LSTM) networks can track the order and timing of payments, assisting in identifying strange shifts in billing frequency or invoice timestamps. AI solutions also offer the benefit of continuous improvement, making fraud detection techniques adaptable as fraudulent behaviors evolve (Swamy 2012). Their scalability allows them to process millions of entries across multiple departments or locations without needing manual checks for every record. However, to ensure AI systems are practical, careful design is needed—addressing data integrity, algorithm selection, result transparency, and how they integrate with current financial tools and audit protocols. Since financial information is sensitive and decisions based on flagged activity carry serious risks, clarity and accountability in AI outputs are essential. To summarize, as fraud becomes more advanced and difficult to trace with traditional practices, AI-powered techniques are evolving into indispensable assets for creating resilient and intelligent financial oversight systems. By leveraging AI's strengths in pattern detection, anomaly spotting, language analysis, and network mapping, organizations can significantly boost their capacity to detect, evaluate, and stop fraud in accounts payable—safeguarding resources, enhancing operations, and promoting ethical corporate conduct.

2 RELATED WORKS

2.1 *Account payable process*

The accounts payable (AP) procedure represents a vital component of an organization's financial framework, managing payments owed to vendors and suppliers (Naimy *et al.* 2023). This routine generally follows a defined chain of steps: receiving invoices, verifying their accuracy alongside related purchase orders (POs) and goods receipts, obtaining necessary approvals, and ultimately processing the payments. Nevertheless, the AP process contains specific vulnerabilities that can be exploited for fraudulent schemes. A major problem is invoice-to-PO discrepancies, where mismatches between the invoice and the original request might remain unnoticed if validation controls are insufficient (Kanaparthi 2024). Additionally, unauthorized edits to vendor records—such as modifications to bank account numbers or contact entries—can result in funds being routed to fraudulent beneficiaries. The absence of clear segregation of responsibilities can aggravate the risk, as it might allow one employee excessive access across vital elements of the AP process, including invoice validation and payment authorization. These risks heighten the likelihood of fraud from both inside and outside actors. Because AP operations often happen in high volumes and are repeated regularly, organizations need to maintain both efficiency and oversight. This underscores the importance of adopting improved and more automated strategies for fraud identification and prevention within the AP environment.

2.2 *Traditional fraud detection techniques*

Traditional fraud detection methods in the accounts payable sector have mainly relied on deterministic rule-based approaches and basic statistical evaluations. These rule-based tools operate by checking predefined thresholds to flag potentially unusual transactions, like invoices that surpass a set limit (e.g., $50,000) without an associated purchase order (McMillan 2017), or payments directed to vendors who are not officially recorded.

While such rules are simple to apply and interpret, they remain static in structure and limited in adaptability, which makes them weak in spotting emerging or shifting types of fraud. Furthermore, these methods often struggle with handling high volumes of transactions, resulting either in too many false positives that burden auditors or in undetected fraud because of overly general rules (Gottimukkala 2024). Statistical techniques, like linear regression and z-score calculations, aim to uncover irregularities by spotting deviations from previous behavior. Yet, these techniques frequently presume data follows a normal pattern and may overlook the intricate and nonlinear trends often seen in fraud instances. They also depend heavily on proper feature engineering and the reliability of input data and typically fall short in processing unstructured information or incorporating contextual insights. Consequently, although traditional tools provide an initial layer of fraud protection, they prove inadequate in settings where fraud methods are constantly evolving and often hard to detect. This gap has sparked growing attention toward intelligent, data-driven models that can recognize and adapt to sophisticated financial behaviors.

2.3 *AI in financial fraud detection*

Artificial intelligence (AI) has become an essential tool for financial fraud detection, allowing the processing of large datasets, recognition of subtle trends, and response to evolving fraudulent actions (Aren and Aydemir 2015). In domains including credit card fraud detection, insider threat monitoring, and anti-money laundering (AML), machine learning (ML) systems have shown remarkable performance by learning through labeled examples of fraud to detect complex behavioral trends that older techniques might ignore. These systems, including supervised classifiers like random forests and support vector machines, along with deep learning structures like convolutional neural networks (CNNs) and recurrent neural networks (RNNs), are trained using extensive transaction records to predict fraudulent activity with strong precision. Nonetheless, using AI within the accounts payable (AP) sector brings specific challenges (Mascarenhas, S.J. 2018). Compared to the structured setup of credit card operations, AP platforms frequently handle unstructured or loosely structured data, such as scanned PDF bills and free-text fields. This requires natural language processing (NLP) to perform reliable data extraction and understanding. Moreover, AP fraud usually emerges gradually, making chronological analysis critical to detect abnormal patterns in payments or vendor relationships—scenarios where time-series models like LSTMs are especially effective. Beyond this, domain-level aspects like internal rules and vendor arrangements demand careful modeling. Even with these obstacles, AI shows strong potential to build intelligent, context-aware platforms that not only enhance fraud detection reliability but also adapt to shifting fraud techniques.

Several studies have advanced financial fraud detection through innovative modeling techniques. (Gottimukkala 2025) uses the Multifractal Model of Asset Returns to capture complex transactional behaviors, aligning with the need to detect volatility in accounts payable data. Study (Gottimukkala 2025) highlights the influence of systemic factors, echoing the importance of external data sources in fraud risk evaluation. (Akita *et al.* 2016) emphasizes automation and visualization, which parallels AI-driven invoice processing and vendor analysis. Meanwhile, (Gottimukkala 2024) applies Monte Carlo simulations for precision, reflecting the significance of robust model validation in fraud detection. Together, these studies reinforce the value of data-driven, interpretable, and adaptive AI systems. (Gottimukkala 2024)Recent studies support AI-driven fraud detection by showcasing machine learning's adaptability across domains. (Smita 2021) applies logistic regression and SVMs to credit card fraud, addressing data imbalance—an issue also critical in accounts payable (AP) fraud detection—achieving high ROC-AUC scores through unbalanced training. (Alarfaj *et al.* 2022) demonstrates how sentiment analysis using models like RoBERTa and BERT extracts insights from unstructured text, similar to using NLP for invoice interpretation in AP systems. (Saiktishna *et al.* 2022) explores gradient compression in distributed learning, underscoring the importance of efficient model training—a relevant consideration for scaling AI-based fraud detection across enterprise-level financial datasets.

3 METHODOLOGY

3.1 *Data sources*

The information utilized for fraud detection in the accounts payable (AP) domain originates from multiple origins, incorporating both internal data from ERP or AP systems and external data to enhance the fraud detection approach. The primary data source is the organization's ERP or AP system, such as SAP or Oracle, which stores comprehensive records of invoices, purchase orders (POs), payments, and vendor details. These platforms are vital for processing transactions, delivering the structured data required to spot issues like mismatches between invoices and POs, duplicate payments, and modifications to vendor information. Historical data on invoices and POs are critical for training machine learning algorithms, as they contain abundant past transactions and patterns of normal behavior that assist in identifying fraudulent actions. External data sources improve the fraud detection system by contributing additional context. For example, vendor blacklists and public databases can be integrated to identify known fraudulent vendors, verify vendor information, and introduce external risk elements to the dataset. Additionally, incorporating data from other sectors, such as HR or security, can aid in spotting potential employee involvement in fraud. By merging internal ERP data with external data as shown in Table 1, a more thorough perspective of the AP process is achieved, enabling the detection of not only fraudulent transactions based on historical behavior but also more complex fraud schemes that may involve unidentified participants or cooperation across organizations. Collectively, these data sources facilitate a multi-layered, AI-based approach to fraud detection, utilizing both structured and unstructured data for more trustworthy and precise fraud recognition.

Table 1. Datasets used.

Dataset Type	Description	Purpose
Simulated Dataset	10 million transaction records over three years with inserted fraud cases	To evaluate model performance in controlled, varied fraud scenarios
Real-world ERP Dataset	Actual data from a mid-sized company's ERP system with unstructured formats and complex vendor relationships	To assess model robustness and adaptability in practical, uncontrolled environments

3.2 *Data preprocessing*

Effective data preprocessing is critical for converting raw data into a format suitable for machine learning models, ensuring these models can accurately detect fraudulent activities in the accounts payable (AP) process. The first step in preprocessing includes extracting text from invoices, which often exist in unstructured formats like scanned PDFs or images. Optical Character Recognition (OCR) tools are used to transform scanned images into machine-readable text, while Natural Language Processing (NLP) methods help interpret and pull-out relevant details from the text, such as vendor names, invoice amounts, dates, and purchase order numbers. After text extraction, feature engineering is done to generate meaningful and useful attributes from the raw transaction data. Essential features include payment terms, which show when payments are made relative to invoice due dates; invoice frequency, which could uncover unusual patterns or discrepancies; and amount anomalies, which highlight invoices that deviate from standard trends. Vendor creation time is another feature that might suggest potential fraud if a vendor is registered just before submitting fraudulent invoices. Labeling the data is an important step for supervised learning, where datasets are categorized as either fraudulent or legitimate based on previous audits or synthetic data meant to simulate fraud situations. Proper labeling helps machine learning models differentiate between genuine transactions and fraudulent ones. Data preprocessing is a continuous process that involves refining features, correcting missing or inconsistent data, and ensuring the final dataset is clean and ready for model training, assisting the AI system in detecting and minimizing fraudulent activities in the AP process.

3.3 *Model architectures*

The choice of model architecture is key to the performance and effectiveness of fraud detection in the accounts payable (AP) domain. Various models offer specific benefits depending on the data characteristics and the type of fraud being targeted. Supervised learning models are frequently employed for fraud detection because they can categorize transactions as either fraudulent or legitimate based on labeled training data. Popular supervised models include Logistic Regression, Random Forests, and XGBoost, which are adept at recognizing patterns and identifying transactions that deviate from typical behavior. Deep Neural Networks (DNNs) are especially useful when dealing with complex invoice data containing many features, as they can uncover intricate, non-linear relationships between data points. On the other hand, unsupervised learning models are valuable for discovering new fraud patterns without the need for labeled data. Autoencoders model normal transaction behavior, identifying anomalies by detecting transactions that deviate substantially from expected data. Isolation Forests are effective in finding outliers by isolating anomalies in the data, while clustering techniques like DBSCAN and K-Means group similar transactions as shown in Table 2, helping to identify unusual transaction types. In the field of Natural Language Processing (NLP), transformer-based models like BERT and LayoutLM process and categorize invoice elements from unstructured text, which enhances accuracy in extracting key details such as vendor names, amounts, and PO numbers. Named Entity Recognition (NER) further improves the model's ability to pinpoint specific entities within the invoice data. Time-series models, such as Long Short-Term Memory (LSTM) networks, analyze patterns in the timing of AP transactions, enabling the detection of irregular payment cycles or invoice submission periods. Lastly, Graph Neural Networks (GNNs) are highly effective in uncovering fraudulent collaboration across vendor-employee networks by modeling relationships and interactions between different entities, such as vendors, employees, and transactions. This aids in identifying hidden fraud networks and collaborative fraudulent schemes. Each of these models offers a unique feature to the AI-driven fraud detection system, and when integrated, they provide a comprehensive, multi-faceted approach to identifying and preventing fraud in the AP process.

Table 2. Model architecture overview.

Model Type	Models/Techniques	Key Purpose
Supervised Learning	Logistic Regression, Random Forest, XGBoost	Classify transactions as fraud or legitimate using labeled data
Unsupervised Learning	Autoencoder, Isolation Forest, DBSCAN, K-Means	Detect new fraud patterns without labeled data
NLP Models	BERT, LayoutLM, Named Entity Recognition (NER)	Extract and understand invoice information from unstructured text
Time-Series Models	Long Short-Term Memory (LSTM)	Detect temporal anomalies in AP transaction patterns
Graph-Based Models	Graph Neural Networks (GNN)	Model vendor-employee relationships to detect collusive fraud schemes

4 EXPERIMENTAL EVALUATION

4.1 *Datasets*

The experimental assessment of fraud detection models in the accounts payable (AP) process utilizes two distinct datasets: simulated AP transaction logs and actual ERP logs from a mid-sized company. The simulated dataset was designed to create a large-scale setting for evaluating fraud detection models, containing 10 million records over a three-year span. This dataset facilitates controlled experiments, allowing specific fraud scenarios such as duplicate payments, invoice-to-purchase order (PO) mismatches, and vendor impersonation to be deliberately introduced for testing the models' detection capabilities. Although the simulated data provides flexibility in examining various fraud scenarios, it lacks the complexities and unpredictability of real-world financial transactions. To compensate for this, the real-world dataset, drawn from an anonymized mid-sized company's ERP system, brings in the inherent challenges of working with actual business data, including unstructured invoice formats, inconsistent data entries, and complicated vendor relationships. This dataset is employed to evaluate how effectively the models can adjust to practical, real-world conditions and assess their performance in an uncontrolled setting. Together, these two datasets offer a robust foundation for evaluating the effectiveness and precision of the fraud detection models in both controlled and real-world scenarios.

4.2 *Evaluation metrics*

The evaluation of the fraud detection models is performed using a blend of standard classification metrics and specific metrics tailored for anomaly detection. Precision, Recall, and F1-score are the primary metrics utilized to evaluate classification models, providing a complete overview of the model's ability to accurately detect fraudulent transactions while reducing false positives and false negatives. Precision indicates the proportion of correctly identified fraud cases among all predicted fraud cases, whereas Recall measures the model's ability to identify all actual fraudulent occurrences. The F1-score merges both precision and recall into one metric, offering a balance between the two. Another key metric is the Area Under the ROC Curve (AUC), which is particularly valuable for evaluating the trade-off between the true positive rate (sensitivity) and the false positive rate (1-specificity). AUC serves as a strong measure of the model's capacity to distinguish between fraudulent and legitimate transactions at various thresholds as shown in Table 3. For anomaly detection models, the Equal Error Rate (EER) is employed to identify the point where the false positive rate equals the false negative rate, offering insight into the model's ability to detect anomalies in a balanced manner. Together, these metrics provide a comprehensive assessment of the models' performance, demonstrating the accuracy, reliability, and robustness of fraud detection systems in the AP domain.

Table 3. Evaluation metrics.

Metric	Description
Precision	Correctly predicted fraud cases among all flagged fraud cases
Recall	Ability to identify all actual fraudulent cases
F1-Score	Harmonic mean of Precision and Recall, balancing both
AUC (ROC Curve)	Measures ability to distinguish between fraud and legitimate transactions across thresholds
Equal Error Rate (EER)	Point where False Positive Rate equals False Negative Rate, used for anomaly detection models

4.3 *Results summary*

The outcomes of the fraud detection models reveal notable differences in performance across various techniques, highlighting both the benefits and challenges of different machine learning methods for identifying fraudulent activities in the accounts payable (AP) process. Logistic Regression, a conventional supervised model, reached a precision of 0.72, recall of 0.65, F1-score of 0.68, and AUC of 0.81. While this model performs reasonably well, it struggles to recognize intricate fraud patterns, especially when handling unstructured or noisy data. In contrast, the Random Forest model surpassed Logistic Regression, achieving a precision of 0.85, recall of 0.78, F1-score of 0.81, and AUC of 0.92, showcasing superior handling of feature interactions and enhanced fraud detection abilities. The Autoencoder model, an unsupervised learning technique, attained an F1-score of 0.82 and an AUC of 0.89, excelling at spotting anomalies in the AP transaction logs. The LSTM network, designed to capture temporal trends, delivered the top performance, with a precision of 0.88, recall of 0.87, F1-score of 0.87, and AUC of 0.94, excelling at identifying fraud that spans multiple timeframes. The combination of LayoutLM and Graph Neural Networks (GNN) reached the highest performance, with precision and recall of 0.91 and 0.90, respectively, and an impressive AUC of 0.96. This demonstrated the power of transformer-based models and graph-based methods in understanding complex relationships and fraud patterns in the AP domain. These findings underline the potential of AI-driven approaches to significantly improve fraud detection accuracy in AP processes.

Table 4. Model performance summary.

Model	Precision	Recall	F1-Score	AUC
Logistic Regression	0.72	0.65	0.68	0.81
Random Forest	0.85	0.78	0.81	0.92
Autoencoder (Unsupervised)	—	—	0.82	0.89
LSTM Network	0.88	0.87	0.87	0.94
LayoutLM + GNN	0.91	0.90	—	0.96

5 CONCLUSION

Artificial intelligence (AI) provides a revolutionary method for detecting fraud in accounts payable by delivering scalable, data-driven, and adaptive frameworks capable of identifying fraudulent activities in intricate transactional data. By employing machine learning, natural language processing (NLP), and graph modeling approaches, organizations can decrease false positives, enhance detection accuracy, and uncover fraud patterns that may go unnoticed with traditional methods. These AI-based systems can adapt to evolving fraud tactics, boosting their efficiency over time. Nonetheless, issues like data imbalance, which may cause biased model performance, and the need for explainable AI decisions, continue to be important areas demanding attention. Guaranteeing that AI models are interpretable and their decisions understandable is crucial for securing trust from stakeholders and ensuring compliance with regulatory guidelines. Continuous research and development are essential to improve these systems, tackle these issues, and further enhance fraud detection within the accounts payable workflow.

REFERENCES

Akita, Ryo, Akira Yoshihara, Takashi Matsubara, and Kuniaki Uehara. (2016). "Deep learning for stock prediction using numerical and textual information." *2016 IEEE/ACIS 15th International Conference on Computer and Information Science, ICIS 2016 - Proceedings*, August. https://doi.org/10.1109/ICIS.2016.7550882.

Alarfaj, Fawaz Khaled, Iqra Malik, Hikmat Ullah Khan, Naif Almusallam, Muhammad Ramzan, and Muzamil Ahmed. (2022). "Credit Card Fraud Detection Using State-of-the-Art Machine Learning and Deep Learning Algorithms." *IEEE Access* 10:39700–715. https://doi.org/10.1109/ACCESS.2022.3166891.

Ang, Andrew, and Monika Piazzesi. (2003). "A No-Arbitrage Vector Autoregression of Term Structure Dynamics with Macroeconomic and Latent Variables." *Journal of Monetary Economics* 50 (4): 745–87. https://doi.org/10.1016/S0304-3932(03)00032-1.

Aren, Selim, and Sibel Dinç Aydemir. (2015). "The Factors Influencing Given Investment Choices of Individuals." *Procedia - Social and Behavioral Sciences* 210 (December):126–35. https://doi.org/10.1016/j.sbspro.2015.11.351.

Benartzi, Shlomo, and Richard H. Thaler. (2001). "Naive Diversification Strategies in Defined Contribution Saving Plans." *American Economic Review* 91 (1): 79–98. https://doi.org/10.1257/aer.91.1.79.

Chopra, Vijay K., and William T. Ziemba. (2011). "The Effect of Errors in Means, Variances, and Covariances on Optimal Portfolio Choice." In *The Kelly Capital Growth Investment Criterion: Theory And Practice*, 249–57. https://doi.org/10.3905/jpm.1993.409440.

Gottimukkala, S.R. (2024). Evaluating the Impact of Fed and Domestic Monetary Policies on Long-Term Government Bond Yields. Preprints. https://doi.org/10.20944/preprints202409.1320.v1

Gottimukkala, S.R. (2024). Optimizing exotic option pricing: monte carlo simulation and variance reduction techniques. Preprints. https://doi.org/10.20944/preprints202409.2256.v1

Gottimukkala, S.R. (2025, February). Applying the Multifractal Model of Asset Returns (MMAR) to Financial Markets: Insights and Limitations. In *2025 10th International Conference on Signal Processing and Communication (ICSC)* (pp. 277–282). IEEE.

Gottimukkala, S.R. (2024). Automating *Portfolio Replication with Stock Market Algorithms*. Preprints. https://doi.org/10.20944/preprints202409.1388.v1

Kanaparthi, Vijaya. (2024). "AI-Based Personalization and Trust in Digital Finance," January. https://arxiv.org/abs/2401.15700v1.

Mascarenhas, S.J., FR. Oswald A. J. (2018). "The turbulent market of modern debt-overleveraged and promoter-dominated corporations." In *Corporate Ethics for Turbulent Markets*, 189–213. Emerald Publishing Limited. https://doi.org/10.1108/978-1-78756-187-820181007.

McMillan, David G. (2017). "Which variables predict and forecast stock market returns?" *SSRN Electronic Journal*, June. https://doi.org/10.2139/ssrn.2801670.

Naimy, Viviane, Rim El Khoury, José María Montero, and Jana Souk. (2023). "Post-Brexit exchange rate volatility and its impact on UK exports to eurozone countries: A bounds testing approach." *Oeconomia Copernicana* 14 (1): 135–68. https://doi.org/10.24136/oc.2023.004.

Roy, Sanjiban Sekhar, Rohan Chopra, Kun Chang Lee, Concetto Spampinato, and Behnam Mohammadi-Ivatlood. (2020). "Random Forest, Gradient Boosted Machines and Deep Neural Network for Stock Price Forecasting: A Comparative Analysis on South Korean Companies." *International Journal of Ad Hoc and Ubiquitous Computing* 33 (1): 62–71. https://doi.org/10.1504/IJAHUC.2020.104715.

Saifan, Ramzi, Khaled Sharif, Mohammad Abu-Ghazaleh, and Mohammad Abdel-Majeed. (2020a). "Investigating Algorithmic Stock Market Trading Using Ensemble Machine Learning Methods." *Informatica (Slovenia)* 44 (3): 311–25. https://doi.org/10.31449/INF.V44I3.2904.

Saiktishna, Ciram, Nalam Sai Venkat Sumanth, Muppavarapu Madhu Sudhan Rao, and J. Thangakumar. (2022). "Historical Analysis and Time Series Forecasting of Stock Market Using FB Prophet." In *Proceedings - 2022 6th International Conference on Intelligent Computing and Control Systems, ICICCS 2022*, 1846–51. Institute of Electrical and Electronics Engineers Inc. https://doi.org/10.1109/ICICCS53718.2022.9788231.

Smita, Mrinalini. (2021). "Logistic regression model for predicting performance of S&P BSE30 company using IBM SPSS." *International Journal of Mathematics Trends and Technology* 67 (7): 118–34. https://doi.org/10.14445/22315373/ijmtt-v67i7p515.

Gottimukkala S.R. (2025). "Leveraging generative AI for real-time anomaly detection in SAP FICO: A paradigm shift in financial governance," *TechRxiv*, Jul. 31, . doi: 10.36227/techrxiv.175393572.23304487/v1.

Swamy, Dr. Vighneswara. (2012). "Impact of macroeconomic and endogenous factors on non performing bank assets." *SSRN Electronic Journal*, February. https://doi.org/10.2139/ssrn.2060753.

Moving Towards Sustainable Businesses and Developing More Resilient Economies – Rashid and Annansingh-Jamieson (Eds)

Using cognitive load theory as a facilitator for teaching and learning accounting

E.S. QUAYE
York College – CUNY, New York, USA

ABSTRACT: The findings of various researchers on accounting instructional studies worldwide have noted that accounting is perceived by students as a hard, boring, and difficult subject to learn and this perception negatively impacts students desire to pursue an accounting degree. Cognitive load theory (CLT) which is an important development in cognitive psychology examines the limitations faced by humans as they learn new complex information and provides guidance on how those limitations can be mitigated through the reduction of cognitive load of students during instruction and learning. CLT has been used extensively in other disciplines and gaining traction in accounting education. The purpose of this paper is to review existing research articles on instructional methods used in teaching accounting and to document the opinions of students on the effect of those instructional methods on reducing their cognitive load. The opportunities for future research using CLT is noted.

Keywords: cognitive load theory, accounting instructional methods, accounting education

1 INTRODUCTION

Cognitive load theory (CLT) relates to the extent to which human cognitive architecture process information. According to CLT, the human cognitive architecture consists of three main functions: sensory memory, working memory, and long-term memory. The sensory function filters out unnecessary information and passes on any useful information to the working memory which further processes the information received and decides which information to store in long-term memory. The working memory can normally process no more than 5 to 9 chunks of information at a given time. The long-term memory organizes the information based on how that information is used and stores them in structures called "schemas"; even highly complex schemas are classified as one "chunk" of information in the working memory. The more the information stored in schemas is used, the more developed they become and the easier it gets to recall that information (Medical College of Wisconsin. (2022). For accounting students therefore, cognitive load refers to the volume of accounting material that their sensory function will pass on as useful information to the working memory for retention in long-term memory and for recall when needed (Mostyn 2012; Sweller *et al.* 2011; Stark 2004). The motivation for this study is to review a small set of existing research on accounting students' perceptions of instructional methods, teaching tools and artifacts used in accounting instruction to determine students' evaluation or perceptions on how those tools and techniques may reduce their cognitive load.

DOI: 10.1201/9781003647300-40

2 METHODOLOGY

I reviewed 162 journal articles retrieved from SCOPUS related to cognitive load theory and accounting education. Most of the articles did not meet the criteria for the goal of the study as they did not address teaching methods and cognitive load specifically related to college level accounting courses. I selected the seven research articles listed below published between 2014 and 2018 because they provide specific tools used to teach accounting and have the potential to impact the cognitive load of accounting students. The learning strategies used in these research articles include design of textbook material, computer simulations and use of posters in teaching accounting. While the number of articles reviewed is small, they provide significant insights into instructional methods, the effects of the teaching methods on gender and provide opportunities for future research. The research findings help readers and accounting instructors to determine students' perceptions of the instructional methods used in helping the students learn accounting. The gaps noted in the research provide future researchers with opportunities to contribute to the advancement of cognitive learning theory in accounting pedagogy and accounting research.

2.1 *Cognitive load and curriculum development*

The Accounting Education Change Commission (AECC) (1993, pp. 1–2) identified curriculum design and course development as critical for the teaching-learning process in accounting. CLT requires that in course design, provision is made to activate prior knowledge or schemas so that prior knowledge is built upon by focusing on the gap between what students know and what they need to know. If effective assessment is not made of what is known and what needs to be learned, there is the potential to overload students with information they are unable to process and retain (Halabi 2004, 2006; Medical College of Wisconsin 2022). Cognitive overload can be influenced by not just the learner's natural working and long-term memory but also by social, emotional, and physical issues (Halabi 2006; Sweller *et al.* 2011; Sweller & Chandler,1994).

In designing coursework and instructional material, cognitive overload can be mitigated in several ways. First, ascertain whether prerequisite requirements have been met by enrolled students, and tutoring is available to support students. This is especially critical with large size classes and where individual instruction is not feasible. Determine through various forms of assessments such as surveys, quizzes, tests, and review of prior curriculum to determine what students already know or can do. In teaching the course breakdown problems into smaller parts as opposed to learning complex problems in a short period of time. Give adequate time for completion of assignments (Blayney *et al.* 2015; Medical College of Wisconsin 2022; Mostyn 2012; Kalyuga 2007). Seven research articles related to the human capacity to learn and teaching methods that motivate and encourage accounting students to gain the technical knowledge and other soft skills required to excel in the profession are reviewed.

Article 1: Using Cognitive Load Theory to Tailor Instruction to Levels of Accounting Students' Expertise (Blayney *et al.* 2015)

LITERATURE AND THEORY USED: The focus of this article is the use of cognitive load theory (CLT) combined with technology (excel) to develop instructional material unique to the learner's previous knowledge of the subject being taught. The article notes that human cognitive architecture relies on working memory and long-term memory to determine how learning is acquired. For learning to be effective instructors should tailor instructional material to suite a learner's unique prior knowledge in a face to face or small group learning environment.

METHOD AND STATISTICAL TEST: Experiment was conducted with 171 first year university accounting students consisting of 37% males and 63% females. Students were separated into isolated (adaptive) and interactive (non-adaptive) learning environments and ANOVA test was used to evaluate the results.

HYPOTHESES AND KEY FINDINGS:
Hypothesis 1*: Experts perform better using interactive over isolated element instructions; novices perform better using isolated over interactive elements instructions.* The findings present strong evidence that students learn more when the method of instruction is based on their levels of expertise. Hypothesis 2*: For a group of students that includes learners at different levels of expertise, learning will be facilitated if students are provided with instruction that is tailored to their level of expertise.* The findings are that novice learners need to be provided with isolated elements learning environment to compensate for their lack of long-term memory.

AREAS FOR FUTURE RESEARCH: (1) determine the type of preassessment evaluation in selection of students at any level of instruction in accounting; (2) investigate the diagnostic tests that have been proposed for monitoring student progress and alternative methods of instruction to benefit all types of learners; (3) the use of technology in identifying and addressing student learning preferences may be determined and evaluated; (4) establish internal validity by measuring and analyzing indicators of participant's cognitive load during learning and testing phases; (5) refinement of indicators for adaptation procedures are needed.

Article 2: Instructional strategies and students' performance in accounting: an evaluation of those strategies and the role of gender (Sithole 2018)

LITERATURE AND THEORY USED: The research is based on CLT and is motivated by the question: What instructional strategy is more effective for accounting students in terms of increasing performance scores and reducing mental load? Two instructional strategies and the gender differences within those strategies were examined by the researcher.

a) Split-attention: Most accounting textbooks use diagram with text below, above or on the side to explain accounting concepts e.g. the accounting cycle is presented to students with text separate from diagrams so the student must hold small segments of text relating to each step in working memory as he searches for the matching feature on the diagram. This makes learning unintelligible according to CLT because it creates unnecessary cognitive load. When text and diagrams are integrated, it reduces cognitive load and enhances the learner's performance because the learner's capacity to understand the material is related to how much cognitive load is used to understand the material.
b) Self-Managed text integrated text/diagram format with separate text and diagrams: This method guides the student on how to integrate spatially separated text and diagrams in the accounting discipline. This is a more effective way of bringing the material to the student.

METHOD AND STATISTICAL TEST: The research instrument is an experiment conducted with 74 first-year students from an Australian university enrolled in a financial accounting course. A one-way ANOVA test used to analyze both pretest and posttest experiments to explore differences across the conditions.

HYPOTHESES AND KEY FINDINGS: Hypothesis 1*: Self-management instructional materials will be superior to split-attention instructional materials.* The findings did not support this hypothesis. Hypothesis 2*: Students in the split-attention format group would report higher mental effort than students in the self-management format group.* The findings indicate that (a) participants in the self-management group had significantly higher performance scores than those in the split-attention group; (b) providing learners with guidance on self-management before the learning of new instructional material may enhance learning; (c) learners studying with the self-management format consistently reported significantly lower mental effort than the split-attention format during the first phase (learning phase) and the second phase (test phase). The hypothesis was confirmed as students studying under the self-management format incurred significantly lower cognitive load than students studying under the split-format group. The findings show students' ability to learn better with integrated materials (self-managed materials) than by requiring them to split their attention between text and diagrams. The main findings are: (a) self-management group had significantly higher performance scores than those in the split-attention group; (b) providing learners with guidance on self-management before the learning of new instructional material may enhance learning; (c) learners studying with the self-management format consistently reported significantly lower mental effort than the split-attention format.

AREAS FOR FUTURE RESEARCH:

a) Further research is needed on the reasons for the performance of females in the study which identified the following: females performed better in spatial skills than males. From the mental effort results, female students did not put in more mental effort, but they utilized the self-management techniques more than their male counterparts. It seems more likely that female students improved their spatial skills by utilizing self-management techniques more than males.
b) Research further using other accounting topics.

Article 3. Representation of knowledge on some management accounting techniques in textbooks (Golyagina & Valuckas 2016)

LITERATURE AND THEORY USED: Textbooks are expected to be neutral as they embody legitimate existing knowledge and help prepare students for professional careers. The study presents a comprehensive analysis of the coverage of four management accounting techniques in five different US and UK textbooks. The techniques are (a) activity-based costing (ABC), (b) balances scorecard (BSC), (c) economic value added (EVA) and beyond budgeting.

METHOD AND STATISTICAL TEST: No statistical experiments were conducted.
KEY FINDINGS: The five Management Accounting Textbooks researched are Bhimani *et al.*, Drury, Garrison *et al.*, Horngren *et al.*, and Seal *et al.* The main findings are: (a) all the textbooks differ in their interests of knowledge; (b) all textbooks are fundamentally concerned with the technical interest of knowledge; (c) Bhimani *et al.* seem to be concerned with discussing different aspects of management accounting techniques in different contexts the most; (d) Horngren *et al.* tend to represent management accounting techniques only within a local context. By ignoring global developments of management accounting practice, textbooks may deprive readers of imagining alternatives to the prescribed techniques.

AREAS FOR FUTURE RESEARCH: More research is needed to: (1) understand the role of textbook co-authorship in producing the content of both traditional textbooks and their adaptations; (2) examine the representation of knowledge on other subject areas and in non-mainstream textbooks; (3) investigate the evolution of textbook content over time especially the role of textbook adaptations and co-authorship.

Article 4: A Conceptual Framework for Learning Management Accounting (Spraakman & Jackling 2014)

LITERATURE AND THEORY USED:
The focus of the study is how problem-based learning (PBL) using Schoenfeld's (1985) conceptual framework for mathematics can be used to re-engineer management accounting course curricula to meet the needs of the accounting profession. PBL reinforces critical skills and the ability to provide quality advice for decision making. The accounting profession is

evolving so fast that by the time students graduate, information acquired in school is obsolete, so students need skills to learn quickly, effectively, and independently when they need it. This paper demonstrates how Schoenfeld's (1985) conceptual framework for mathematics can guide management accounting instructors in facilitating student learning by focusing on problem solving strategies.

*KEY FINDINGS:*The framework includes Heuristics: established methods for solving management accounting problems. Problems are explicitly or implicitly stated in mathematical terms. Problem solving techniques – may be financial or non-financial. Some examples can be derived from activity-based costing, balanced scorecard techniques, absorption costing and cost-volume-profit analysis. To facilitate the learning of management accounting heuristics, instructors need to explain clearly, provide examples, and test the application abilities of students. Instructors also need to get students to apply the heuristics with different datasets.

AREAS FOR FUTURE RESEARCH: More research is needed to: (1) Determine the importance of the framework in teaching and learning management accounting; (2) Understand the additional costs that will be incurred when teaching with the Schoenfeld framework; (3) The structure and processes outlined in the study paper would need to be studied carefully when instructors develop revised learning objectives and assessment techniques.

Article 5: The Use of Poster Projects as a Motivational and Learning Tool in Managerial Accounting Courses (Altintas & Aydin 2014)

LITERATURE AND THEORY USED: The purpose of the research is to introduce poster projects as an alternative method of motivating, encouraging learning and dissemination of information for managerial accounting students. The study compares the opinions of students on submitting regular term papers as opposed to poster projects. Posters have been used as a study tool in many disciplines including in the natural sciences (chemistry, biology, and math), and the social sciences (psychology, and sociology) but this may be the first ever research on use of posters in teaching managerial accounting and as a learning tool.

METHOD AND STATISTICAL TEST: The research involved 252 third year undergraduate accounting students at the School of Business, University of Istanbul. The students completed two questionnaires (a) to gather information about their perceptions of poster projects, and to collect student demographics (gender, GPA, and internships) information of the participants. (b) to gather information on students expressing their feelings and perceptions about using traditional term paper as opposed to poster projects. Frequency analysis, independent samples t-test and chi-square tests were used to analyze the results.

KEY FINDINGS: The findings for point a: 46% of the participants thought poster projects embodied the managerial accounting topics and the subjects that they had learned in managerial accounting course would be beneficial to their future business. The findings for point b - students expressing their feelings and perceptions about using traditional term paper as opposed to poster projects the findings are less than 20% of the students thought that traditional term papers are more enjoyable than poster projects whereas over 30% of the participants thought that traditional term papers embody the managerial accounting topics.

AREAS FOR FUTURE RESEARCH: (1) A research with a focus on the perceptions of males and females on use of poster projects will add value to literature. The results obtained from this research are not clear; (2) Alternative assessment tools similar to the poster projects can be used in place of more traditional approaches to motivate students. (3) Further research on the applicability of poster projects to other topics in managerial accounting and to graduate level accounting courses will be interesting.

Article 6: Bridging the Gap between Accounting Students and the Profession: A Case Study (Lightweis 2014)

LITERATURE AND THEORY USED: Various research findings indicate that accounting graduates are underprepared for this challenging career mainly because of the teaching and learning methods. Accounting Professors lecture and students memorize the information from the lectures. Accounting students need opportunities to build their professional skills through learning activities that mimic real-world situations. This purpose of this qualitative study is to determine whether computer-assisted instruction encourage critical thinking, communication, and problem-solving skills. The study was done using an auditing simulation, semi-structured interviews before and after computer use, and reflective journals provided by the participants. The auditing simulation gave students the opportunity to practice their knowledge of accounting and enhance their professional skills.

KEY FINDINGS: The findings suggest that students made a connection between concepts learned in course work and situations found in the accounting profession. The simulation-built confidence in students and motivated them to learn more about enhancing skills necessary for the accounting profession. The evidence indicates that accounting educators could use simulations as a supplemental learning tool in preparing accounting students for the profession.

AREAS FOR FUTURE RESEARCH: (1) Accounting educators can use their practitioner experience to create simulations that depict the challenges in the field. (2) For a forensic accounting instructor, a simulation game may include investigations forensic accountants undertake after a crime has been committed in a company. (3) Accounting students can design simulation games, as a course-long group project. (4) State accounting associations and societies provide a venue for accounting educators to collaborate with CPAs to determine the current needs of the profession. (5) The more aware accounting students are of the challenges in the profession while attending school, the better prepared they will be for the workplace. Instructors should make students aware of this.

Article 7. Audit workplace simulations as a methodology to increase undergraduates' awareness of competences (Bautista-Mesa *et al.* 2018).

LITERATURE AND THEORY USED: The European Commission and the European Higher Education Area (EHEA), has recently added pressure on universities to better prepare students for the workplace by increasing their employability and paying special attention to key competences required by the Accounting Profession to reduce unemployment in the European Union. The purpose of the study is to use audit workplace stimulation as a teaching tool to help accounting students improve their skills to meet the demands of the profession. The skills required include (a) technical accounting knowledge, (b) teamwork skills, (c) leadership skills, (d) communication skills.

KEY FINDINGS: Pretests and posttests were used to measure the degree of change occurring in the students as they participate in the research. During the pretest phase first year undergraduate students show lower awareness of the technical knowledge, teamwork, and communication skills than senior students. First year undergraduate students perceived communication skills as the least important, which contrasts with the current needs of the industry. Improving the awareness of younger students on communication skills still appears as a challenge for teachers in the earliest stages. Workplace simulation increased the awareness of the first-year undergraduate students. The results reveal a significant improvement in the awareness of the technical accounting knowledge as well as communication skills.

AREAS FOR FUTURE RESEARCH: (1) Future research on: (1) Possible link between interest in a subject and the engagement in it and whether the stimulation exercise may contribute to attracting younger students in accounting and auditing subjects. (2) whether this research can apply to other industries to increase undergraduate employability.

3 CONCLUSION

Awareness of cognitive learning theory by accounting educators provides the opportunity to use it in curriculum design, teaching methods and instructional materials. CLT has the potential to reduce the cognitive load of accounting students when they learn accounting concepts. Accounting educators will be encouraged to reinforce assessment materials to test for retention of accounting material in both working and long-term memory of students. The existing research has identified potential limitations of CLT and gaps in instructional methods that need further exploration. The gaps and limitation noted in this review provides ample opportunity for further research in the use of CLT in accounting education.

REFERENCES

Accounting Education Change Commission. (1993). *Objectives of Education for Accountants: Position statement number one*. American Accounting Association

Altintas, N.N., and Z. Aydin, Z. (2014). The use of poster projects as a motivational and learning tool in managerial accounting courses. *Journal of Education for Business, 89*(4), 196–201. https://doi.org/10.1080/08832323.2013.840553

Bautista-Mesa, R., Molina Sánchez, H., & Ramírez Sobrino, J.N. (2018). Audit workplace simulations as a methodology to increase undergraduates' awareness of competences. *Accounting Education, 27*(3), 234–258. https://doi.org/10.1080/09639284.2018.1476895

Blayney, P., Kalyuga, S., & Sweller, J. (2010). Interactions between the isolated–interactive elements effect and levels of learner expertise: Experimental evidence from an accountancy class. *Instructional Science*, 38(3), 277–287. doi:10.1007/s11251-009- 9105-x

Blayney, P., Kalyuga, S., & Sweller, J. (2015). Using cognitive load theory to tailor instruction to levels of accounting students' expertise. *Educational Technology & Society*, 18 (4), 199–210.

Golyagina, A., & Valuckas, D. (2016). Representation of knowledge on some management accounting techniques in textbooks. *Accounting Education, 25*(5), 479–501. https://doi.org/10.1080/09639284.2016.1211942

Halabi, A. (2004). Applying cognitive load theory concepts to the design and evaluation of CBL materials and feedback in teaching introductory accounting (Doctoral dissertation, Department of Accounting and Finance, Monash University). Retrieved from http://arrow.monash.edu.au/hdl/1959.1/9653

Halabi, A. (2006). Applying an instructional learning efficiency model to determine the most efficient feedback for teaching introductory accounting. *Global Perspectives on Accounting Education*, 3, 93–113.

Kalyuga, S. (2007). Expertise reversal effect and its implications for learner-tailored instruction. *Educational Psychology Review*, 19(4), 509–539.

Lightweis, S. (2014). Bridging the gap between accounting students and the profession: A case study. *Higher Education Studies, 4*(5), 18–27. https://doi.org/10.5539/hes.v4n5p18

Medical College of Wisconsin. (2022). *Cognitive Load Theory: A guide to applying cognitive load theory to your teaching*. Office of Educational Improvement. https://www.mcw.edu/-/media/MCW/Education/Academic-Affairs/OEI/Faculty-Quick-Guides/Cognitive-Load-Theory.pdf

Mostyn, G. (2012). Cognitive load theory: What it is, why it's important for accounting instruction and research. *Issues in Accounting Education*, 27(1), 227–245.

Paul Blayney, S.K. (2015, October). Using Cognitive Load Theory to Tailor Instruction to Levels of Accounting Students' Expertise. *Journal of Educational Technology & Society, 18*(4), 199–210.

Sithole, S.T. (2018). Instructional Strategies and Students' Performance in Accounting: an evaluation of those strategies and the role of gender. *Accounting Education,* Vol. 27(NO. 6), 613–631. Retrieved from HTTPS://DOI.ORG/10.1080/09639284.2017.1361852)

Spraakman, G., & Jackling, B. (2014). A conceptual framework for learning management accounting. *Accounting Perspectives, 13*(1), 61–81. https://doi.org/10.1111/1911-3838.12024

Stark, R. 2004. Implementing example-based learning and teaching in the context of vocational school education in business administration. *Learning Environments Research* 7: 143–163.

Sweller, J., Ayres, P., & Kalyuga, S. (2011). Cognitive load theory. New York: Springer.

Sweller, J. & Chandler, P. (1994). Why some material is difficult to learn. *Cognition and Instruction*, 12(3), 185–233

Moving Towards Sustainable Businesses and Developing More Resilient Economies – Rashid and Annansingh-Jamieson (Eds)
 ISBN: 978-1-041-08875-2

Developing and framing the influence of AAI environment on consumer buying behaviour: Consumer buying is controlled or influenced?

Md Uzir Hossain Uzir
Taylor's Business School, Taylor's University, Lakeside Campus, Selangor, Malaysia

Siti Norida Wahab
Faculty of Business Management, Universiti Teknologi MARA (UiTM), Kampus Puncak Alam, Malaysia

Ishraq Jerin
Department of Management, Putra Business School, UPM, Serdang, UPM, Malaysia

Sharmini A.P. Gopinathan and Pek Chuen Khee Pek
Taylor's Business School, Taylor's University, Lakeside Campus, Selangor, Malaysia

ABSTRACT: Consumers are generally influenced by technology while they interact. Nowadays, technological advancement and its applications have myriad impacts on consumer buying behaviour. Specially, artificial intelligence (AI) and its daily application (AAI) strengthen this drastic change. Customers are constantly interacting with AAI and building trusting regions- trust expansion or trust contraction in the AAI environment (AAI interaction- AAII and AAI Trust Contraction- AAITC). Hence, this study focuses on the development of measurement of AAI environment- AAII and AAITC. A total of 215 Malaysian-educated respondents were surveyed and the scales were found valid. The empirical test showed that marketing stimuli were found significant and in the contributory portion, AAII and AAITC have moderating effects on the relationships among the marketing stimuli. Importantly, the study categorised four major segments of the AAI environment based on the customer's interaction and trust contraction: a) Low AAII and Low AAITC- blind region; b) High AAII and Low AAITC- Moderate Region; c) Low AAII and High AAITC- Ignorance; and d) High AAII and High AAITC- Critical Region. The study contributed to the scholarly world by proposing and validating two measurements of these two concepts- AAII and AAITC of the AAI environment. Besides, the findings might contribute to the body of knowledge by supporting One: Stimulus-Organism-Response Theory. The study believes some practical insights will be available for marketing managers and brands to know whether using AAI and its implications control or influence consumer buying behaviour.

1 INTRODUCTION

1.1 *Background of study*

Depending on its application, applied artificial intelligence (AAI) can be used to both encourage and regulate consumer behaviour (Gursoy *et al.* 2019). Comparable, AAI is capable to tailor marketing messages and product recommendations based on consumer behaviour and preferences in order to motivate consumer behaviour (Davenport *et al.* 2020). Retailers, for instance, can make use of AAI to examine a consumer's past purchases and browsing behaviour in order to provide product recommendations that the consumer is

 DOI: 10.1201/9781003647300-41

likely to find interesting (Alfian *et al.* 2019). This might also encourage the consumer to buy something which they find the information is interactive, informative and in a timely manner. Using AAI to affect or sway consumer purchase decisions is necessary for influencing consumer behaviour (Hoyer *et al.* 2020). An e-commerce site, for another instance, can utilise AAI to differentiate prices by displaying various prices to various consumers all over the globe depending on their browsing history and other information (von Zahn *et al.* 2021). This may evade consumers from paying more for the same products or being unknowingly persuaded to purchase particular products (Cornish *et al.* 2020). Thus, it is crucial to remember that employing AAI to manipulate consumer behaviour is typically regarded as immoral and, in some situations, illegal (Handa and Ahuja 2022). Worth to highlight that, transparency and accountability should be prioritised when using AAI in marketing.

Consumer behaviour is generally the behavior as actions that result in the lifecycle of the product, behavior, or service (White *et al.* 2019). This behaviour or actions (activities) can be in three forms (phases): pre-purchase behaviour, during purchase, and post-purchase (usage or consumption) behaviour. These behaviors are portrayed in factors of product quality, service quality, perceived value, consumption or usage experience, product (or service) price), brand (company) image and awareness, brand (company) knowledge, consumer (customer) satisfaction, customer repurchase or loyalty. The study will focus on whether AAI tools such as ChatGPT (Open AI), BARD AI (Google-Alphabet AI), and others influence or control consumer three-phase behaviour on these factors. The study investigates if companies or business organizations or intermediaries (at any stage of the supply chain) reshape, restructure or modify the factors (aforesaid) through using AAI tool in the forms of data controlling, data managing, or data trimming whether the customer will be biased in any of the three phases (pre-, during or post-purchase).

Generally, consumers as human beings are influenced by the behavior or information of others (family members, colleagues, friends, and even the device or machine). Nowadays, besides human interaction, customers tend to use devices, tools, websites, and apps to find better products or services, check product or service reviews, compare prices, and configure product or service details. If these events are controlled or influenced by the company or websites or third parties (hackers, gamblers, etc.), what would be the ultimate results? This result is based on an ambient artificial environment which is characterized by two aspects: i) how much the consumer as a human interacts with this technology and; ii) to what extent they feel it is trustworthy. These aspects of consumer behaviour are portrayed in two applied artificial intelligence environments: consumer's AAI interaction and AAI trust contraction. The current study attempts to figure out the explore AAI environment, marketing stimuli, consumer organism and loyalty in this AAI environment, based on these multiple aspects, will offer a conceptual framework, and measurement of the two aspects of the AAI environment to evaluate the environment while a consumer intends to buy, buy actual and behave post-buying. Moreover, the study additionally presents a consumer buying matrix where the interaction and trust contraction determine the consumer pattern or character using a specific score earned.

The following sections describe AAI aspects, AAI environment, consumer behaviour, theoretical support, conceptual framework, methodology, data collection and data analysis, discussion of the findings, implications and recommendations. The manuscript concludes with conclusion and future directions.

A study by de Marcellis-Warin *et al.* (2022) highlighted that the application of AAI can influence and encourage consumer behavior through targeted advertising, tailored recommendations, and even nudging. For instance, data analytics is the foundation of AAI which uses to comprehend user preferences and behaviour patterns in order to market products and services (Nadarzynski *et al.* 2019). On the other hand, Davenport *et al.* (2020) argued that the AAI application offers consumers with possess free will and decision-making authority. Therefore, AAI can affect consumer behaviour, but ultimately, individuals must decide based on their priorities and values (Sima *et al.* 2020).

2 AAI ENVIRONMENT AND CONSUMER BEHAVIOUR

AAI environment is categorised into two perspectives namely AAI interaction and AAI trustworthy contraction. Applied artificial intelligence environment refers to the use of artificial intelligence (AI) technologies and techniques to create intelligent systems or applications in a specific environment or context (Ramos *et al.* 2008). These authors proposed ambient artificial intelligence (AI) environment where devices and humans will interact with each other. Bryndin (2021) mentioned that from an innovation of Microsoft, using an intelligent model reduces the time and money spent for searching and standard cognition is working on a standalone shopping payment system where customers can wander around the store, pick items and pay without scanning their items or interacting with an employee.

Being inspired by the concept of Bryndin (2021), this current study proposed an AAI environment from two perspectives: i) smart AAI and; ii) ethical standards. Smart AAI is conceptualized in AAI interaction and the ethical standard is conceptualized in trust contraction.

2.1 *AAI interaction*

According to Gams *et al.* (2019), the applications of AI in smart environments have encountered different challenges, for example, the task of recognizing the context that surrounds the user (detailed in several subsequent sections). The human centricity of AmI requires that the computational intelligence is closely bound to the needs and goals of the user and that the learning takes place in a rich living environment. The representation of meaning and knowledge of the environment requires semantic models of entities, activities and their relations.

As an AAI language model, it can interact with users in a variety of ways, including answering questions, providing information on a wide range of topics, generating text based on input or prompts, and engaging in conversation. To start a conversation or to share information, the users can simply ask a generative tool a question or provide a topic for discussion. The generative tool will do its best to understand users' input and provide a helpful response. If users have a specific task they like a generative tool/device to perform, such as generating a story or summarizing a long document, the user can provide the relevant details and it will use AAI's language processing capabilities to complete the task. This device or tool is designed to interact with the user in a way that's as natural and seamless as possible. Thus, users can ask anything they like or provide any input that might be relevant to their conversation.

This concept of 'AAI Interaction' surfaced two extremes: a) a high interaction with the users and it shares the best possible information, guidance, suggestions and recommendations, and the next extreme, b) users with less involvement for the best possible information, guidance, suggestions and recommendations. Figure 1 demonstrates the AAI interaction in green colour: high interaction in dark green and low interaction in light green. In the scoring matrix (Figure 1), dark green scores from 51 to 100 and light green scores from 0 to 49. A score value of 50 indicates a neutral value.

2.2 *AAI trust contraction*

According to Bryndin (2021), as a language model, AAI does not have personal relationships or engage in partnerships with human beings. However, trust is still an important concept in the context of AAI, as users need to trust that AAI systems will act in their best interests and protect their privacy and personal information. Besides, the trust should be embedded in information, guidance, suggestions and recommendations provided by the AAI. Trust in AAI can be affected by a variety of factors, including accuracy, transparency, reliability, and ethical considerations. If an AAI system consistently produces inaccurate or unreliable results, users are likely to lose trust in its ability to perform its intended function. Additionally, if an AAI system operates in a way that is opaque or difficult to understand, users may be hesitant to use it or perhaps suspicious of its motives.

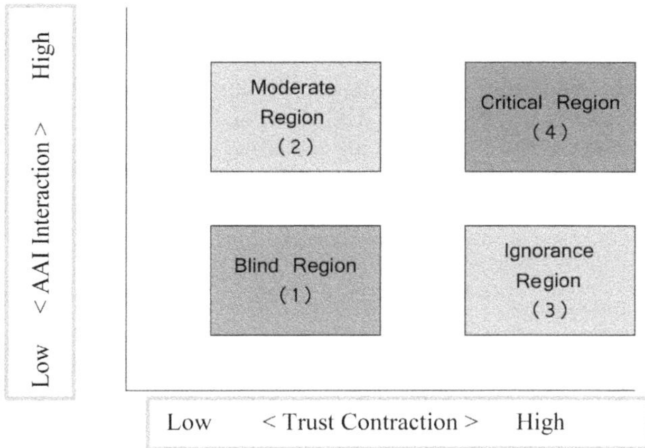

Figure 1. AI environment matrix.

3 METHODOLOGY AND TECHNIQUES

The authors have generated these measurement items of the two constructs as shown in Table 1. The questionnaire items will be used to measure AAI interaction and AAI trusts contraction on a 7-point Likert-type scale ranging from 1 (strongly disagree) to 7 (strongly agree).

Table 1. Measurement.

Construct	Items	Statement
AAI Interaction	AAI_Int1	I always seeking for help before selecting the intended product/service.
	AAI_Int2	I always utilise the AAI generative platform in identifying product/service information.
	AAI_Int3	I always follow the guidance from AAI generative tools in buying products/services.
	AAI_Int4	I always depend on the recommendation from AAI generative tools in using products/services.
	AAI_Int5	I always review the products/services from the company's website.
AAI Trust Contraction	AAI_TC1	I think the outcome that AAI generative tools provide is biased.
	AAI_TC2	I think the information that AAI tools provide is not true.
	AAI_TC3	I think the outcome that AAI tools provide is outdated.
	AAI_TC4	I think the information that AAI tools provide is not reliable.
	AAI_TC5	I think AAI tools provide information manipulated by the company.
	AAI_TC6	I think AAI tools do not maintain the users' privacy.
	AAI_TC7	I think AAI tools interaction is not friendly.

SOURCE: Authors

4 DATA ANALYSIS

4.1 *Data sample, Data collection, and Demographic information*

This study collected data from 215 respondents in Malaysia Petaling Jaya. The paper questionnaires were distributed purposely to the educated people who are informed of applied artificial intelligence (AI) its usage and use various AAI tools/devices in their daily life. Though these 215 samples are small for marketing research, this study collected these from the respondents selectively due to an aim to collect data from them who are aware of AAI. Data collection took around a month. The demography details showed that 55% males and 45 females from graduate to post-graduated people and from various nationalities such Malaysian, Nigerian, Sudanese, Bangladeshi, Indian, Pakistani, Middle East people, African, Chinese, Sri-Lankan, Nepalese, Uzbekistani, Afghan, etc. In their professional ground, they are Graduate and Post graduate students, university teachers, businesspeople, and Malaysia government and non-government officials located in Petaling Jaya, Selangor state in Malaysia. This diverse demographic profile strengthens the findings and the finding is expected to be generalised in marketing research.

Table 2. Reliability and validity.

	Items	Loading	CA	CR	AVE
AAI Interaction	AII_2	0.813	0.906	0.935	0.783
	AII_3	0.930			
	AII_4	0.926			
	AII_5	0.865			
AAI Trust Contraction	AITC_1	0.855	0.925	0.943	0.769
	AITC_2	0.895			
	AITC_4	0.868			
	AITC_6	0.864			
	AITC_7	0.901			

Reliability of these factors are determined using Cronbach's Alpha (< 0.70). In the case of new constructs such as AAI interaction and AAI trust contraction could be reliable if alpha is 0.60 and above Table 2).

5 CONSUMER AI ENVIRONMENT MATRIX AND DISCUSSION OF THE FINDING

As per second objective the study measured the AI environment in two dimensions: AI interaction and AI trust contraction. From the finding it is shown that 21% (43) respondents are in less AI interaction and less trust contraction. Similarly, 26% (53) are in less AI interaction but hight trust contraction; 25% (51) are in high AI interaction and less trust contraction; final 29%(60) are in high AI interaction and high trust contraction. The finding indicates that 21% respondents are in **blind region** because they have less AI interaction, however, they have less trust contraction (they trust AAI) e.g., ***Segment 1*** in Figure 2. This particular group of people trust the advancement of technology though they interact less in their real life. In ***Segment 2***, 25% participants have lest trust contraction (they trust AAI) though they interact highly in AAI environment. This result indicates that they interact very much with trust and confidence that AAI maintains privacy, confidentiality, and secrecy of data, information, and financial transaction, and product review results. These people are **moderate** in buying and using products and services. 26% respondents showed that they have less interaction and highly rigid in trusting AAI (***Segment 3***). Thus, they fall in the **ignorance region** of their consumer behaviour in AAI environment. Finally ***Segment 4*** showed that maximum 29% respondents are in highly interaction and highly trust contraction. It implies that though they interact more in AAI environment, they have least trust in this environment. Thus, this group of people are very **critical**.

Based on this information, AAI can recommend customised prices or provide incentives like discounts and sales to entice a consumer to make purchases (Tong *et al.* 2020). By integrating brand knowledge through tailored suggestions, targeted advertising, and education, AAI can affect consumer behaviour (Kumar *et al.* 2019). AAI systems can examine consumer data to comprehend preferences and behaviours and suggest customised products and services (Libai *et al.* 2020). AAI can also target consumers who are more interested in the business's products and services by personalising marketing messaging to reflect consumer perceptions of the brand (Sands *et al.* 2022).

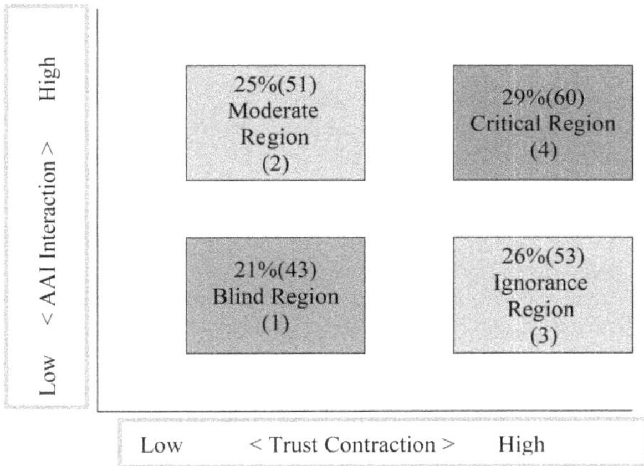

Figure 2. AI environment scoring.

Consumer satisfaction can be enhanced by using AAI in a variety of ways, including tailored suggestions, customer care chatbots, sentiment analysis, and predictive analytics (Patel and Trivedi 2020). According to Pereira *et al.* (2022), AAI systems can examine consumer data to offer tailored suggestions based on past purchases, interests, and behaviour. This helps increase consumer satisfaction by ensuring that consumers are able to see the products and services that are most pertinent to their interests (Brill *et al.* 2019).

6 IMPLICATION AND CONCLUDING REMARKS

The study investigated the conceptual framework including AAI interaction and AAI trust contraction. In theory, these two constructs were added to customer satisfaction and customer loyalty. This contribution to the body of knowledge. On the other hand, a marketing manager can find a better insight to understand the consumer and develop a strategic plan. The study focuses on consumer buying behaviour and the role of AAI considering various factors in the event of pre, post or during purchase behaviour. The literature and the current events of human (customer) involvement in using AAI tools indicate that consumers are dependent on AAI information, guidance, suggestions, and recommendation. Although it is not conclusive that a company or business organization will control consumer behaviour using AAI tools, it is obvious that their behaviour can be influenced. However, consumers are independent to select, choose, buy or use a product or consuming service. To come to an end conclusion, it is necessary to wait for observing future events and consumers' behaviour, attitude and decision-making capabilities.

Future directions for recovering the study limitation might be increase sample size up to 500 and more because marketing research 500 or 600 is acceptable. The samples are purposive such as only educated people were communicated for data collection. This study concentrated in Malaysian City area where rich and middle-class family reside. Thus, poor, rural and suburban area in developed and developing countries might be included. In this study behaviour loyalty was focused. Next research might include attitudinal loyalty and customer usage.

REFERENCES

Adam, M., Wessel, M., and Benlian, A. (2021). AI-based chatbots in customer service and their effects on user compliance. *Electronic Markets*, *31*(2), 427–445.

Ahmed, A.A.A., Agarwal, S., Kurniawan, I.G.A., Anantadjaya, S.P., and Krishnan, C. (2022). Business boosting through sentiment analysis using Artificial Intelligence approach. *International Journal of System Assurance Engineering and Management*, *13*(Suppl 1), 699–709.

Ameen, N., Tarhini, A., Reppel, A., and Anand, A. (2021). Customer experiences in the age of artificial intelligence. *Computers in Human Behavior*, *114*, 106548.

Bryndin, E. (2021). Formation of international ethical digital environment with smart artificial intelligence. *Automation, Control and Intelligent Systems*, *9*(1), 22.

Bryndin, E. (2021). Implementation of competencies by smart ethical artificial intelligence in different environments. *Software Engineering*, *8*(4), 24–33.

Chen, T., Guo, W., Gao, X., and Liang, Z. (2021). AI-based self-service technology in public service delivery: User experience and influencing factors. *Government Information Quarterly*, *38*(4), 101520.

Dash, R., McMurtrey, M., Rebman, C., and Kar, U.K. (2019). Application of artificial intelligence in automation of supply chain management. *Journal of Strategic Innovation and Sustainability*, *14*(3), 43–53.

Davenport, T., Guha, A., Grewal, D., and Bressgott, T. (2020). How artificial intelligence will change the future of marketing. *Journal of the Academy of Marketing Science*, *48*, 24–42.

Grewal, D., Motyka, S., and Levy, M. (2018). The evolution and future of retailing and retailing education. *Journal of Marketing Education*, *40*(1), 85–93.

Hoyer, W.D., Kroschke, M., Schmitt, B., Kraume, K., and Shankar, V. (2020). Transforming the customer experience through new technologies. *Journal of interactive marketing*, *51*(1), 57–71.

Kotler, P. (2012). *Kotler on marketing*. New York: Simon and Schuster: The Free Press.

Kotler, P., and Armstrong, G.M. (2018). Marketing Mix: Selected Chapters From: Principles of Marketing, Philip Kotler and Gary Armstrong. New Jersey, USA: Pearson.

Kumar, V., Rajan, B., Venkatesan, R., and Lecinski, J. (2019). Understanding the role of artificial intelligence in personalized engagement marketing. *California Management Review*, *61*(4), 135–155.

Kushwaha, A.K., Kumar, P., and Kar, A.K. (2021). What impacts customer experience for B2B enterprises on using AI-enabled chatbots? Insights from Big data analytics. *Industrial Marketing Management*, *98*, 207–221.

Kvale, K., Freddi, E., Hodnebrog, S., Sell, O.A., and Følstad, A. (2021). Understanding the user experience of customer service chatbots: what can we learn from customer satisfaction surveys?. In *Chatbot Research and Design: 4th International Workshop, CONVERSATIONS 2020, Virtual Event, November 23–24, 2020, Revised Selected Papers 4* (pp. 205–218). Springer International Publishing.

Lee, S.M., and Lee, D. (2020). Untact: a new customer service strategy in the digital age. *Service Business*, *14* (1), 1–22.

Lele, M.M., and Karmarkar, U.S. (1983). Good product support is smart marketing. *Harvard business review*, *61*(6), 124–132.

Leung, F.F., Gu, F.F., and Palmatier, R.W. (2022). Online influencer marketing. *Journal of the Academy of Marketing Science*, 1–26.

Liao, Q.V., Gruen, D., and Miller, S. (2020, April). Questioning the AI: informing design practices for explainable AI user experiences. In *Proceedings of the 2020 CHI Conference on Human Factors in Computing Systems* (pp. 1–15).

Libai, B., Bart, Y., Gensler, S., Hofacker, C.F., Kaplan, A., Kötterheinrich, K., and Kroll, E.B. (2020). Brave new world? On AI and the management of customer relationships. *Journal of Interactive Marketing*, *51*(1), 44–56.

Liljander, V. and Strandvik, T. (1993). Estimating zones of tolerance in perceived service quality and perceived service value. *International Journal of Service Industry Management,* 4(2): 6–28.

Liu, R., Gupta, S., and Patel, P. (2021). The application of the principles of responsible AI on social media marketing for digital health. *Information Systems Frontiers*, 1–25.

Loomba, A.P. (1998). Product distribution and service support strategy linkages: An empirical validation. *International Journal of Physical Distribution & Logistics Management, 28*(2), 143–161.

Luo, J.M., Vu, H.Q., Li, G., and Law, R. (2021). Understanding service attributes of robot hotels: A sentiment analysis of customer online reviews. *International Journal of Hospitality Management*, *98*, 103032.

Luo, X., Tong, S., Fang, Z., and Qu, Z. (2019). Frontiers: Machines vs. humans: The impact of artificial intelligence chatbot disclosure on customer purchases. *Marketing Science*, *38*(6), 937–947.

Machtynger, L. (2020). Artificial intelligence (AI) in strategic marketing decision-making: a research agenda. *The Bottom Line*, *33*(2), 183–200.
Menezes, C. and Devi, R. (2016). Effect of Social Media Marketing on Brand Loyalty formation from the Perspective of Online Consumer. *The IASMS Journal of Business Spectrum*, 9(1): 34–37.
Mogaji, E., Olaleye, S., and Ukpabi, D. (2020). Using AI to personalise emotionally appealing advertisement. *Digital and Social Media Marketing: Emerging Applications and Theoretical Development*, 137–150.
Mogaji, E., Soetan, T.O., and Kieu, T.A. (2020). The implications of artificial intelligence on the digital marketing of financial services to vulnerable customers. *Australasian Marketing Journal*, j-ausmj.
Mohseni, S., Jayashree, S., Rezaei, S., Kasim, A., and Okumus, F. (2018). Attracting tourists to travel companies' websites: the structural relationship between website brand, personal value, shopping experience, perceived risk and purchase intention. *Current Issues in Tourism*, *21*(6), 616–645.
Nadarzynski, T., Miles, O., Cowie, A., and Ridge, D. (2019). Acceptability of artificial intelligence (AI)-led chatbot services in healthcare: A mixed-methods study. *Digital health*, *5*, 2055207619871808.
Nguyen, T.M., Quach, S., and Thaichon, P. (2022). The effect of AI quality on customer experience and brand relationship. *Journal of Consumer Behaviour*, *21*(3), 481–493.
Nikolajeva, A., and Teilans, A. (2021). Machine Learning Technology Overview In Terms Of Digital Marketing And Personalization. *ECMS*, 125–130.
Nilashi, M., Ahmadi, H., Arji, G., Alsalem, K.O., Samad, S., Ghabban, F., ... and Alarood, A.A. (2021). Big social data and customer decision making in vegetarian restaurants: A combined machine learning method. *Journal of Retailing and Consumer Services*, *62*, 102630.
O'Guinn, T., Allen, C. and Semenik, R. (2009). *Advertising and Integrated Brand Promotion,* Mason, USA: South-Western Cengage Learning.
Pizzi, G., Scarpi, D., and Pantano, E. (2021). Artificial intelligence and the new forms of interaction: Who has the control when interacting with a chatbot?. *Journal of Business Research*, *129*, 878–890.
Ramos, C., Augusto, J.C., and Shapiro, D. (2008). Ambient intelligence—the next step for artificial intelligence. *IEEE Intelligent Systems*, *23*(2), 15–18.
Rathmell, J.M. (1966). What is meant by services? *Journal of marketing*, *30*(4), 32–36.
Romaniuk, J., Wight, S. and Faulkner, M. (2017). Brand awareness: revisiting an old metric for a new world. *Journal of Product & Brand Management,* 26(5): 469–476.
Russell, R.S., and Taylor, B.W. (2006). *Operation Management: Quality and Competitiveness in a Global Environment* (5th ed.). New Jersey: John Wiley & Sons, Inc.
Schmitt, B.H. and Rogers, D.L. (2008). *Handbook on Brand and Experience Management,* Cheltenham, UK: Edward Elgar.
Schmitt, B.H., Brakus, J. and Zarantonello, L. (2014). The current state and future of brand experience. *Journal of Brand Management,* 21(9): 727–733.
Schmitt, C. and Munn, A. (1999). Published. *Against the nominal mapping parameter: Bare nouns in Brazilian Portuguese*. Proceedings-Nels, Michigan State University, 339–354.
Tarafdar, M., Beath, C.M., and Ross, J.W. (2019). Using AI to enhance business operations. *MIT Sloan Management Review*, *60*(4).
Valavi, P. (2014). Factors influencing mobile services adoption: A brandequity perspective. *International Journal of Research in Social Sciences,* 4(3): 1–18.
Varsha, P.S., Akter, S., Kumar, A., Gochhait, S., and Patagundi, B. (2021). The impact of artificial intelligence on branding: a bibliometric analysis (1982–2019). *Journal of Global Information Management (JGIM)*, *29*(4), 221–246.
Verma, S., Sharma, R., Deb, S., and Maitra, D. (2021). Artificial intelligence in marketing: Systematic review and future research direction. *International Journal of Information Management Data Insights*, *1*(1), 100002.
von Zahn, M., Feuerriegel, S., and Kuehl, N. (2021). The cost of fairness in AI: Evidence from e-commerce. *Business & information systems engineering*, 1–14.
White, K., Habib, R., and Hardisty, D.J. (2019). How to SHIFT consumer behaviors to be more sustainable: A literature review and guiding framework. *Journal of Marketing*, *83*(3), 22–49.
Yang, C., Feng, Y., and Whinston, A. (2022). Dynamic pricing and information disclosure for fresh produce: An artificial intelligence approach. *Production and Operations Management*, *31*(1), 155–171.
Yoon, N., and Lee, H.K. (2021). AI recommendation service acceptance: Assessing the effects of perceived empathy and need for cognition. *Journal of Theoretical and Applied Electronic Commerce Research*, *16*(5), 1912–1928.

Author index

Aïmeur, E. 234
Abad, J.M. 242
Abbood, S.K. 297
Abraham, SA 88
Adediran, O.A. 175
Ajia, A.Y. 121
AL Abri, Z. 189
Al Akhir 218
Al Kindi, S. 189
Alshareef, A.G. 152
Amen, U. 169

Bakhtiyorov, A. 202
Banerjee, A. 49
Banerjee, S. 49
Belen, M.L. 251
Belušić, N. 112
Bhuram, S.K. 315, 323

Candaza, J.C. 251
Ceballos, G.E. 242
Cheng, J. 273
Constantine Metallinos, Vasilios (Billy) 61

Dee, C.N.F. 266
Dela Cruz, R.A. 251
Dela Paz, J.L.B. 266
Dimaano, F.N.R.A. 266
Dwivedula 54

Esdelle, DE 88

Fahad, O. 181
Faisal, G.M. 297
Flores, J. 251

Galit, S.M.L. 266
Gebhardt, R. 289
Goodermote, J. 278
Goodermote, L. 278
Gopinathan, S.A.P. 338
Gottimukkala, S.R. 315, 323

Hasan, K.M. 218
Hasan, M.A. 209
Hernandez, P. 251
Hosein, IH 88
Hossen, Md S. 218

Idrizi, O. 97
Islam, A. 218
Islam, N. 181

Jaquias, A.A.P. 242
Jerin, I. 338

Kamran, T. 189
Kamruzzaman, A. 30, 104
Kazo, M. 97
Khan, M.L. 189
Khan, M.N. 38
Khee Pek, P.C. 338
Khumalo, N. 8, 144
Komilov, S. 227

Landicho, M.T. 251
Loutis, M. 234

Mapuko, A. 144
Maquilan, D.A.S. 266
Mazumder, M.T.R. 209
Mehrabani, S.E. 307
Melchor, B.T. 242
Mendes, L.L. 104
Muniraju, Y 126, 161

Nashid, S. 209
Navarro, M. 251
Nawaz, S. 169
Nurse, D. 30

Ogbodo, E.U. 104
Olaleye, B.R. 8, 144
Opurum, C.N. 68

Padullon, J.A. 251
Paramashivaiah, P 126, 136
Pham, J. 278
Phan, T. 278

QUAYE, E.S. 331

Rajendran, J. 46
Ramdhan, J. 88
Riaz, T. 1

Samdrup, N. 30
Santiago, J.A.A. 242
Sekhampu, T.J. 8
Shahnazarian, V. 273

Shajari, M. 307
Shang, D. 15
Sharfuddin, Md 181
Shourov, M.S.H. 209
Singh, MS 88
Sumayya, U. 169
Suresh, B K 126, 161

Tabasa, N.L. 251
Tenerife, J. 251
Tenerife, J.T. 242, 266

Untalan, E.T. 242
Uzir, M.U.H 338

Vatti, R.R. 286
Venkateshwarlu, M 126
Vidović, M. 112
Vragov, R. 15

Wahab, S.N. 338
Williams, TW 88
Winterhalter, J. 289

For Product Safety Concerns and Information please contact our EU representative GPSR@taylorandfrancis.com
Taylor & Francis Verlag GmbH, Kaufingerstraße 24, 80331 München, Germany

www.ingramcontent.com/pod-product-compliance
Ingram Content Group UK Ltd.
Pitfield, Milton Keynes, MK11 3LW, UK
UKHW062200220926
475880UK00006B/649
* 9 7 8 1 0 4 1 0 8 8 7 5 2 *